Regulating Strikes in Essential Services

Studies in Employment and Social Policy

VOLUME 52

Editors

Professor Alan Neal (founding editor of the *International Journal of Labour Law and Industrial Relations*, and Convenor of the European Association of Labour Law Judges); Professor Manfred Weiss (past president of the International Industrial Relations Association); and Professor Birgitta Nyström (professor of private law at the Law Faculty, University of Lund, Sweden, and member of the European Committee of Social Rights).

Objective

Studies in Employment and Social Policy series seeks to provide a forum for highlighting international and comparative research on contemporary areas of significance for evaluation and regulation of the world of work.

Introduction

Launched in 1997, the Studies in Employment and Social Policy Series now boasts over fifty titles, addressing key policy and development issues in the fields of industrial relations, labour law, social security, and international labour regulation.

Content

With contributions from leading figures in the field, the series brings together key policymakers, academics, and regulators, providing a unique context in which to analyse and evaluate the rapid and dramatic work and social policy developments taking place around the globe.

The titles published in this series are listed at the end of this volume.

Regulating Strikes in Essential Services

A Comparative 'Law in Action' Perspective

Edited by

Moti (Mordehai) Mironi

Monika Schlachter

Wolters Kluwer

Published by:
Kluwer Law International B.V.
PO Box 316
2400 AH Alphen aan den Rijn
The Netherlands
E-mail: international-sales@wolterskluwer.com
Website: lrus.wolterskluwer.com

Sold and distributed in North, Central and South America by:
Wolters Kluwer Legal & Regulatory U.S.
7201 McKinney Circle
Frederick, MD 21704
United States of America
Email: customer.service@wolterskluwer.com

Sold and distributed in all other countries by:
Air Business Subscriptions
Rockwood House
Haywards Heath
West Sussex
RH16 3DH
United Kingdom
Email: international-customerservice@wolterskluwer.com

ISBN 978-90-411-8997-4

e-Book: ISBN 978-90-411-9018-5
web-PDF: ISBN 978-90-411-9019-2

Editors

Moti (Mordehai) Mironi, Professor of Law (Emeritus), Haifa University Faculty of Law, specializes in labour and employment law, ADR, negotiation, mediation and arbitration. His research interests include ADR and labour employment law, in general, and strikes and labour dispute resolution, in particular. Professor Mironi practices as a mediator in labour, commercial, sport and political disputes. In this capacity he has mediated and arbitrated several nationwide mega disputes in essential services.

Monika Schlachter, Professor, Trier University; Director, Institute for Labour Law and Industrial Relations in the EU, Trier; since 2010 vice president of the Council of Europe's European Committee of Social Rights; specializes in German, European and International labour and employment law, human rights and anti-discrimination.

Contributors

Darcy Du Toit, Emeritus Professor, Faculty of Law, University of the Western Cape. Apart from collective bargaining and strike law, areas of special interest are the regulation of non-standard forms of work in general and platform work in particular, responsive regulation (including self-governance) as means of promoting social justice in work relationships, and discrimination law.

Roberto Fragale Filho, Labour Judge in Rio de Janeiro (Brazil) and Socio-Legal Professor at Universidade Federal Fluminense. He holds a PhD in Political Science from the Université de Montpellier I, and has been a fellow at the Institut d'Études Avancées de Nantes in a long and fruitful collaboration with French academia. As a visiting professor, he has taught in Angola, Macao and Portugal as well as in France and the United States. His main research interests are related to labour law, legal professions and education, and judicial training.

Christina Hießl, Senior Research Associate, Trier University Institute for Labour Law and Industrial Relations in the European Union; Invited Professor, Seoul Yonsei Graduate School of Social Welfare; Lecturer, Seoul Ehwa University. Focuses on international-comparative aspects of labour and social security law and policy.

Mario Jacobs, Researcher, Labour and Enterprise Policy Research Group, Faculty of Law, University of Cape Town. Current research interest includes Global Value Chains (GVC), Trade Union organization and Collective Bargaining.

Yumiko Kuwamura, Associate Professor at School of Law, Tohoku University, Sendai. She was a visiting scholar at Goethe University of Frankfurt am Main from 2010 to 2012. Her main research interest is legal framework of collective autonomy.

Sylvaine Laulom, Professor of Labour Law at University Lumière Lyon 2. Her research interests include labour law, comparative labour law and International and European labour law.

Olivier Leclerc, CNRS Research Professor at the Center for Critical Legal Research (CERCRID), University of Lyon and University Jean Monnet (Saint-Etienne, France). His research interests include comparative labour law, scientific work and 'science and society' issues.

Nikita L. Lyutov, Professor; heads the Department of Labour and Social Law at the Kutafin Moscow State Law University (MSAL). His main academic activity includes the international labour law and the interaction of globalization and trans-national corporations' activity with the international labour standards. The full list of publications is available at: https://www.hse.ru/org/persons/66956091#sci.

Richard Naughton, Senior Fellow, Faculty of Law, Monash University. Richard's research interests include the background to Australia's conciliation and arbitration system and the operation of Australia's present bargaining laws.

Tonia Novitz, Professor of Labour Law at the University of Bristol. Her research interests focus predominantly on labour law, international and EU trade and the protection of human rights. A graduate of the University of Canterbury (Christchurch, New Zealand) and Balliol College, Oxford, Tonia Novitz has held fellowships at the International Institute for Labour Studies (Geneva), the European University Institute (Florence), as well as the universities of Auckland and Melbourne. She has been a professor of Labour Law at Bristol since 2008.

Birgitta Nyström, Professor of Private Law, Faculty of Law, University of Lund, Sweden. Her main research field is labour law, especially European labour law and its influences on the Swedish and Nordic labour law systems. She is a member of the European Committee of Social Rights.

Marilyn Pittard, Professor of Law and Associate Dean Academic Resourcing, Faculty of Law, Monash University and President of the Australian Labour Law Association. Her recent books include *Australian Labour and Employment Law*, LexisNexis, 2015, co-edited books on labour perspectives on business innovation (Edward Elgar) and Asia-Pacific Judiciaries (Cambridge University Press, 2018). Her labour law interests include collective and individual labour relationships, electronic workplace law, and employment aspects of criminal records.

Roger Ronnie, Researcher, Social Law Project, Faculty of Law, University of the Western Cape. Areas of interest are regulation of non-standard work and forms of worker organizations.

Joseph Slater, Eugene N. Balk Professor of Law and Values and a Distinguished University Professor at the University of Toledo College of Law, where he has taught since 1999. He specializes in labour and employment law, with many of his writings focusing on the public sector. Prior to teaching, he practiced labour and employment law in Washington, DC, for twelve years. He has a BA from Oberlin College (1983), a

JD from the University of Michigan Law School (1986), and a PhD in History from Georgetown University (1998).

Andrzej Marian Świątkowski, Jean Monnet Professor of European Labour Law and Social Policy. Ordinary Professor at Jesuit University Ignatianum in Krakow, Poland.

Adriana Topo, Full Professor of Labour Law, Law School, Università degli Studi di Padova, and PhD School in International Law, Private Law, and Labour Law of the University of Padova. On 2017 she was Visiting Fellow at IALS London, and Founder (with prof. Gian Guido Balandi) of the Summer School on International Labour and Business Law. She has written extensively on strike, dismissal and redundancies, public sector employment, protection of privacy in the workplace, apprenticeship.

Eric Tucker, Professor, Osgoode Hall Law School, York University, Toronto and Distinguished Scholar in Residence, Cleveland Marshall College of Law, Cleveland State University, has written extensively on labour and employment issues, including books on the history of health and safety regulation and collective bargaining law in Canada.

Ryuichi Yamakawa, Chairman of the Central Labour Relations Commission of Japan, currently on leave from the University of Tokyo. His main research interests are resolution of labour disputes and implementation of labour law.

Summary of Contents

Preface

Regulating strikes in essential services or by essential employees has always posed a challenge to democratic societies. It stems from the inherent conflict of the population's interest in continuously provided essential services, on the one hand, and workers' right to promote and protect their economic and social interests if need be by withdrawing their labour, on the other hand. It is, however, also quite a timely a topic due to several recent worldwide developments and given the political pressure on states seemingly losing influence on labour market conditions driven by globalization, while citizens as consumers continue to rely on services labelled 'essential' for their indispensability. Hence, while the problem has become more acute, the search of legal orders and societies around the globe for seek an effective and well-balanced public policy is more challenging and complex. No wonder that as a subject for research it has attracted much discussion and produced voluminous literature including several comparative law books.

In embarking on this research project we hoped to make a contribution to the public policy debate and academic discourse in two ways. First, by constructing a theoretically grounded comprehensive conceptual framework which would capture the various aspects that together produce the landscape of regulating strikes in essential services. Such a framework is likely to offer more accurate conceptualization for describing, analysing and evaluating the wide variety of models that can be observed around the world. It has also a clear potential advantage for public policy discourse and for researchers who may use it to refine their studies to determine which model and which tool perform best in different political, sociological, economic, ideological, cultural and institutional contexts. Second, by conducting a systematic comparative 'law in action' research. This was achieved through highly structured, systematically construed national reports written by experts from around the world. The 'law in action' aspect was secured by instructing the national reporters not to limit their investigation to studying written rules and published materials. By and large, these sources are of limited value if one wants to gain insights and deep appreciation of the models in context, to understand how they work in practice and to assess their actual efficacy, advantages, shortcomings and necessary conditions for success.

Fourteen countries are included in the study: Australia, Brazil, Canada, France, Germany, Japan, Israel, Italy, Poland, Russia, South Africa, Sweden, the UK and the US. The selection of countries included in this study follows an inclusive approach, bringing in as many diverse legal and industrial relations systems as possible without reaching an unmanageable number of countries. Other than Germany and Israel represented by the principal investigators and editors, the selection was based on securing the inclusion of states with relatively high numbers of working days lost as well as others with relatively low such numbers. Countries preferring statutory regulation of collective actions are represented as well as others using executive powers, referring conflicts to the judicial system or relying on self-regulation by the labour market parties. Some countries follow international law developments whereas others neglect them or do not recognize them altogether.

In retrospect, a cross-country comparison on strikes in essential services including not only legal aspects but also the 'law in action' component has proven to be quite a challenge given the diversity of participating legal systems and the need to view the contemporary legal regimes as systems with multiple and distinct but interacting models of regulation. Obviously, the one model solution seeking to balance the interests of employers, workers and consumers cannot be extracted from the reports assembled here. All legal systems follow their country-specific approach, the 'transplantability' of which into other legal and social environments may be questionable, to say the least. What may be provided, though, is a set of models for regulating and intervening in such strikes applicable elsewhere and a toolbox comprising an impressive number of different aspects as well as insights regarding their efficacy and workability.

Different approaches may produce comparably effective results in terms of reducing the frequency and intensity as well as the numbers of working days lost by strike actions. This is, however, effective primarily in furthering the interests of consumers and employers of the respective services. Balancing the interests of workers in parallel too is not automatically ensured by applying effective restrictions or other means guaranteeing uninterrupted essential services, even though some instruments may be specifically successful in reaching also this goal. Whenever this is not possible, the best way to cope with strikes in essential services is probably to provide robust collective-bargaining rights accompanied by an acceptable, effective and fair alternative mechanisms for resolving bargaining impasses that will act as strike substitutes.

Readers will have to choose their specific angle from which to read this book and assess its contribution. For alleviating this procedure, the first part of the book portrays the theoretical infrastructure. It includes a discussion of the inherent normative policy dilemma and the conceptual and evaluative framework developed for this study. The second part of the book is devoted to regulating strikes in essential services from an international law perspective. The third part of the book is the heart of the study, it includes the contextually rich country reports in alphabetical order. The fourth and concluding part of the book presents a comparative overview and analysis of the insights gained.

We are grateful to GIF – German-Israeli Foundation for Scientific Research and Development – for providing financial support for this research. Mounting a large-scale comparative research project requires the support and cooperation of a large number of individuals. First, we wish to express our deep gratitude to the national reporters for their valuable contributions, including the insightful refinement of a common approach to the drafting procedure during the workshops. Second, we thank Christina Hießl who, in addition to collaborating closely with Monika Schlachter, was responsible for much of the organizational implications of the editing process. Moti Mironi wishes to thank Myriam Feinberg for her valuable assistance and Minerva Centre for the Study of the Rule of Law under Extreme Conditions at Haifa University for the seed money which enabled the initiation of this project. Last but not least, our thanks for flawless organization of the workshops in Trier and Haifa, respectively, are attributed to Ulrike Kuhn and Lily Faibish-Schor.

Moti (Mordehai) Mironi and Monika Schlachter
Haifa/Trier July 2018

Acknowledgement

This research was supported by a Grant from GIF (German-Israeli Foundation for Scientific Research and Development).

PART I Theoretical Infrastructure

CHAPTER 1

Introduction: Theory, Conceptualization and Methodology

Moti (Mordehai) Mironi

1 THE NORMATIVE DILEMMA OF REGULATING STRIKES IN ESSENTIAL SERVICES

Strikes in essential services or by essential employees have always posed a challenge to democratic societies. This challenge stems from the built-in tension between two basic rights that are expected to be secured by the state and through the legal system, and by the need to find an optimal balance between these rights: (a) the fundamental human right of workers to strike, embedded in the power-based collective labour relations model.[1] This right includes the right to organize, bargain collectively and to exert pressure by directly inflicting pain and cost on the employer and quite often on the public and the government through strike or a threat of strike; and (b) the right of the public at large to security, safety, health and to an uninterrupted flow of what that particular society regards as essential services.

It has been argued that, in addition to posing a challenge to democratic societies, such strikes may challenge the very democratic order of states. The pressure to urgently resolve strikes in essential services bestows upon unions undue political and economic power. It may constitute a threat to democracy and interfere with the democratic process. Giving such power to the workers and their union as an interest group may collide with the increasingly perceived need for accountability and responsible management of public finance and public expenditures.[2]

Therefore, the more essential the service provided by the workers, the less acceptable and tolerable is the power-based discourse – which is the basic premise of collective bargaining as a mode of autonomous regulation – and the less relevant are the collective bargaining model's underlying assumptions.

The fundamental premise underlying the paradigm of industrial and labour relations has always been that the right to call a strike is a *condition sine qua non* for the efficacy of the collective labour relations model to promote and protect workers' economic and social interests.

The model rests on two further assumptions. First, the damage caused by the strike or the cost borne by the employer in direct and indirect losses is somewhat related to the cost incurred by the workers in lost wages and benefits, in the short term, and to the potential damage to the survival and success of their place of work, in the long term. Second, the power struggle takes place primarily at the labour relations level and between the employer on one side and the

1. *Adell*, 1989, 31 et seqq.
2. *Kochan/Mironi/Ehrenberg/Baderschneider/Jick*, 1979, ix–xi.

workers and their union on the other side. They are the pivotal actors and stakeholders.

The essential nature of the service inherently changes these two assumptions. In addition, the degree to which these assumptions become obsolete depends on how essential the service or the product is, on its public and monopolistic character and on the intensity and length of the strike. First, the relationship between the damage caused by the strike and the cost to the workers and their union is severely weakening and may disappear altogether. Second, and more importantly, the conflict migrates from the private labour relations level or field into the public sphere, impacting and engaging different actors and stakeholders. Instead of the employer, the non-involved, innocent public bears the lion's share of the damage and cost of the strike. At the same time, the public at large and state authorities that are responsible for securing an uninterrupted flow of essential services, move to the front stage and become the pivotal actors and stakeholders.

Therefore, designing a fair, effective and acceptable regime that will reconcile public interest and the public's need for an uninterrupted flow of essential services on the one hand, while maintaining the basic premise and important properties of 'free' collective bargaining on the other, has drawn much attention and has been perceived as a tough challenge for labour law, industrial and labour relations and strike law.[3]

The above inherent social and normative dilemma is reflected in the five international conventions that are considered the sources of employees' basic human rights to organize and bargain collectively in international law. The International Labour Organization (ILO)'s Conventions No. 87 of 1948 and No. 98 of 1949, the United Nations International Covenant on Economic, Social and Cultural Rights of 1966 as well as the European Convention of Human Rights and the European Social Charter all bestow upon the state wide, albeit bounded, discretion to impose particular restrictions on one or more of the three collective labour law rights of employees in essential services, namely the right to organize, the right to bargain collectively and the corollary right to strike.

In practice, all democratic legal systems that secure the right to form unions, to organize and to bargain collectively, are engaged in an ongoing search for an appropriate and well-balanced public policy and for new and innovative ways to cope with the challenge of regulating[4] strikes in essential services.

2 THE INCREASING RELEVANCE OF STRIKES IN ESSENTIAL SERVICES

It appears as though several recent worldwide developments have exacerbated the problems associated with regulating strikes in essential services. Phenomena

3. *Weiler*, 1990, 183; *Haiven*, 1995, 237.
4. *Novitz*, 2003, 310 et seqq.

such as globalization and the advances in technology, that have increased interdependence,[5] have transformed strikes in essential services from a domestic issue to an international concern.[6] Similarly, organizational, sociological and psychological trends such as privatization, outsourcing, and the decline of unions and workers' solidarity, have intensified and enhanced the significance of strikes in essential services and the need to re-design the modes of regulating and intervening in such strikes.

First, with the sharp worldwide decline of union density in the private sector and the declining utility of strikes,[7] the collective labour relations model in general, and more specifically the use of strikes has become a public sector phenomenon.[8] Since a large segment of public sector employees perform services that are essential to the population as a whole and are placed at the most strategic or critical junctions of economic and social life, strikes in essential services dominate the public policy discourse regarding strikes and strike law.

Second, traditionally, many essential services had been provided by state and local government employees who often were denied the right to strike by virtue of being Civil Service, public sector or Crown employees. Many of these essential services have been privatized in recent years and are now operated by private firms. Moreover, an increasing number of functions that are considered essential have been outsourced to private contractors. In both cases, the employees who now perform these essential services or functions are regular private sector employees and, legally speaking, they are not subject to the no-strike regime. They are para-public employees.[9]

Third, the decline of collectivism and solidarity have caused groups of highly skilled employees (elite functionaries) or employees who perform essential services, like pilots, air traffic controllers or train drivers in Germany, to form their own niche unions, also referred to as splinter or guerrilla unions, and marshal their striking power as bargaining leverage.[10]

Fourth, modern life has increased people's intolerance towards strikes in essential services, in general, and enlarged the scope of services and products that are perceived by the public as essential. Such a trend has been reported also

5. For example, a few hours long strike by baggage handlers and other airport staff in Frankfurt international airport on 27 March 2014 grounded about 30 % of all domestic and international flights operated by Lufthansa; a five-day long strike by air traffic controller in the same airport in February 2012 grounded more than 1700 flights (see: *Handelsblatt*, 2012). A strike by telecommunication and cellular company employees may have a similar devastating impact due to our total dependency on such services following advances in technology.
6. *Franzen/Thüsing/Waldhoff*, 2012, 6.
7. *Stern*, 1964, 60.
8. *Novitz*, 2010, 173 et seq.; *Laulom*, 2010, 31 et seq.; *Adell*, 2013, 413 et seq.; *Cohen/Haberfeld/Kristal/Mundlak*, 2007, 255, 268.
9. *Adell*, 2013, 414.
10. *Olaf*, 2010, 73.

in a country like Israel,[11] where collective labour relations and unions are held in high esteem.

Fifth, recent court decisions of the European Court of Human Rights and national courts in Europe and North America pointed out the supremacy of the basic human right to organize. The courts criticized the sweeping ban imposed by legislation on the corollary rights to bargain collectively and strike, which leave large groups of workers, such as civil servants,[12] church employees who provide a broad array of health, education and welfare services in Germany[13] and the Royal Canadian Mounted Police in Canada,[14] with no alternative means to promote and protect their economic and social interests.

In sum, the subject of regulating strikes in essential services has become more timely and acute for legal orders and societies around the globe, while the search for an effective and well-balanced public policy is more challenging and complex.

3 THE STUDY: ITS OBJECTIVES AND STRUCTURE

3.1 Objectives

The subject of strikes in essential services has attracted much discussion and produced voluminous research. While a large portion of the discussion and the literature is informative and insightful, previous research tended to focus on one country[15] or one type of intervention[16] and tended to be normative and descriptive. Such research has neither provided a systematic and comprehensive analysis as to how strikes in essential services have been dealt with around the world in practice, nor has it attempted to assess the relative success of the various models that have been used. Similarly, bearing in mind that collective labour relations are intimately intertwined with political, economic, historical and sociological structures of a given society and that each model of intervention or regulation is embedded in a particular cultural, institutional and legal infrastructure, the literature has failed to flesh out the conditions that must complement such models.

On this basis, the goal of this book is to develop principles, insights, ideas and models for the effective, fair and acceptable treatment and regulation of strikes in essential services that is grounded in a comprehensive and multidisciplinary 'law in action' comparative study. The project aims to provide a rich

11. In a poll conducted in Israel, 50% were in favour of prohibiting all public sector strikes and 70% would like to deny the right to strike to employees in health services and electricity and water supply. *Itzchaki*, 2003.
12. *Turkey Dilek and others v. Turkey; Tum Haber Sen v. Turkey.*
13. *BAG 20 November 2012 – 1 AZR 179/11 and 1 AZR 611/11.*
14. *Mounted Police Ass'n of Ontario v. Canada* (A.G.) 2015 SCC 1.
15. *Adell/Grant/Ponak*, 2001; *Morris*, 1986.
16. *Cullen*, 1968; *Marcus*, 1977; *Mironi*, 1986, 350; *Ibid.*, 1988; *Mironi*, 2008.

account, a systematic analysis and a theoretically grounded performance assessment of the broad array of approaches, regulating regimes and models that have been employed around the world to balance the right to organize and take collective action, as a human right, and strikes in essential services. Furthermore, it seeks to explore the political, sociological, cultural, economic, legal, and institutional contexts that give rise to diverging solutions to common problems and germinate for each country a particular legal regime, approach or model of regulation.

The study is designed to serve the following four objectives:

(1) To construct a theoretically grounded conceptual framework for analysing and designing models of regulating strikes in essential services
(2) To develop a set of criteria that might be used in the present study and future research for assessing the performance and efficacy of different legal regimes and types of interventions in strikes in essential services.
(3) To provide an analytical account of the international law framework and to examine how particular states' interventions in the right to strikes in essential services are treated in public international law jurisprudence.
(4) To canvass, compare, examine and conceptualize different models that are employed around the world to cope with strikes in essential services both in the public and private sectors of the economy, and to assess their efficacy and workability.

Although one may expect to find some common denominators between different legal regimes since all are designed to deal with similar problems, searching for these common denominators is not the primary purpose of this study. Its main purpose is twofold. First, to unearth the rich and diverse plethora of models and to assess their performance and the underlying reasons for their success or failure. Second, to shed light on the complementary conditions – sociological, cultural, political, organizational and institutional – in order to ensure the success and sustainability of the different models.

The expected significance of this research project is threefold: theoretical, empirical and practical. Theoretically, the project is likely to make a distinctive contribution to the existing body of literature. Despite numerous studies of the subject, a broad and systematic analysis grounded in 'law in action' type comparative research is still missing. Moreover, the discourse regarding the normative and labour relations dilemmas, the conceptual framework and the analysis of the comparative data are expected to produce theoretical insights into the unique challenges and inherent tensions faced by different countries in dealing with strikes in essential services and into the large and multifaceted arsenal of tools and processes that have been invented and tested around the world.

Empirically, the study is designed to systematically survey and analyse the particular strategic and tactical choices made in approaching or reacting to the challenge of strikes in essential services by different countries as well as their efficacy or success.

Practically, the result of the study may enrich the legal and public policy discourse in countries that decide to revisit or revise their regimes for regulating or dealing with strikes in essential services. Several key questions that might come up in such discourse may benefit from the information and insights learned through this study. Among them: what is the optimal division of responsibility between autonomous arrangements and exogenous regulation of strikes in essential services and why? What are the reasons to explain the perceived success or failure of a particular type of intervention? What are the essential conditions that must exist and the likely obstacles that must be overcome for the regulation or the intervention to be effective? Regarding the latter, the key factors to examine are the sources of regulation and division of labour among branches of government, institutional features, the type and character of the restrictions on the right to strike and their coverage, enforcement models and dispute resolution process design.

One caveat: with all this accumulated knowledge on worldwide practical experience with various regimes of regulation, suggesting an optimal complete model is neither desirable nor feasible. Instead, the ultimate goal here is to highlight several models and principles that may streamline the debate among the different stakeholders and guide policy makers and legislatures in developing and improving their own regime.

3.2 Structure

The next section of this part will lay out the research methodology. The two sections devoted to the conceptual framework and the assessment criteria will conclude the theoretical infrastructure and the first part of the book.

The second part of the book is entitled International Law Perspective. Aside from constitutional law, international treaties at the global and European levels are also relevant when it comes to restricting or even abolishing strike action for economic reasons. Furthermore, international law has produced the largest and most detailed jurisprudence as to the legitimate boundaries for restricting collective action in essential services.

The third part of the book, entitled Comparative and Law in Action Perspective, is the heart of the study. It explores and analyses in depth the treatment of strikes in essential services over a substantial period of time in fourteen countries: Australia, Brazil, Canada, France, Germany, Japan, Israel, Italy, Poland, Russia, South Africa, Sweden, the UK and the US.

The fourth and concluding part of the book provides a comparative analysis and discussion. This analysis is both theoretical and empirical, building upon the insights gained from the actual experience of the fourteen jurisdictions as expressed in the systematically crafted national reports.

4 RESEARCH METHODOLOGY

The study is based on an integrative research approach. It crosses and operates between disciplinary lines and employs two methodologies. Disciplinarily, it combines labour law, industrial and labour relations, and alternative dispute resolution (ADR). Methodologically, it applies thematic and theoretical, along with 'law in action' comparative research.

The central pillar of the research project and this book is the comparative 'law in action' perspective. The research required a careful design and implementation. It included selecting a sample of countries and national experts, constructing the research instruments and assembling the national experts to constitute a collaborating working group or an international taskforce through a 'partnering' approach.

4.1 Selecting the Participating Countries

The selection of countries included in the study depended on the built-in tension between inclusivity and manageability. Other than Germany and Israel as the countries represented by the editors and principal investigators, the countries were selected with the aim of including as many countries as possible, emanating from different regions of the world that represent diverse industrial relations and labour law traditions and cultures.

In addition to Germany, five European countries were selected: one representative of the Nordic model of collective labour relations, with its strong unions and little state interference into the collective bargaining process (Sweden); one country representing the strike-prone southern European countries with low union density but highly developed political influence (France); one representative of countries strongly affected by the economic crisis (Italy); and two participants representing former members of the Eastern Bloc – Russia and Poland.

The Anglo-Saxon approach heralding free enterprise and rebutting state interference in economic activities is represented by three countries: the US, the UK and Australia. Another Anglo-Saxon country, Canada, was selected due to its tendency to experiment with variegated and quite innovative models of regulating strikes in essential services.[17] Other relevant legal regions are represented by Japan, Brazil and South Africa.

4.2 Constructing the Research Instruments

The aim was to conduct a systematic comparative research; one which will enable a robust analysis of different aspects of regulating strikes in essential services across the fourteen legal systems. This could be secured by collecting

17. *Adell/Grant/Ponak*, 2001.

data through highly structured, systematically construed and contextually rich national reports written by experts from each country. Following a thorough literature survey, four documents were constructed: the conceptual framework, the criteria for evaluation, a questionnaire and an outline for national reports. These documents were designed to serve as infrastructure and common basis for all national reports.

Being a 'law in action' research, the experts were directed not to limit their investigation for the national reports by studying written rules and published materials. By and large, these sources are of limited value if one wants to gain insights and deep appreciation of the models in context, to understand how they work in practice and to assess their actual efficacy, advantages, shortcomings and necessary condition for success.

4.3 The National Experts as a Collaborating Working Group

A major instrument for assuring high quality national reports were two workshops conducted at the beginning and toward the end of the project.

The first two-day workshop was held in Trier in the first year of the project. For most of the experts, it was the first opportunity to meet and work together. During the workshop, the national reporters discussed and refined the four research instruments that were designed to serve as infrastructure for the national reports. The goal of the workshop was not only to benefit from the national reporters' input and discourse, but also to come up with a common terminology and agreed-upon framework, which have both proven to be crucial for systematic comparative research.

The second workshop, which turned into a colloquium, was held in Haifa in January 2018. During the course of the workshop, drafts of all national reports was presented, critiqued and discussed by the national reporters and invited experts. The goal of the second workshop was to benefit from the national reporters' comments and accumulative expertise in writing the final report.

In retrospect, the contribution of these two workshops that brought together a group of scholars who specialize in strikes in essential services from different countries and traditions was not limited to enhancing the systematic quality of the comparative research. It also stirred up an international dialogue and created a network aimed at facilitating future spin-off research.

5 REGULATING STRIKES IN ESSENTIAL SERVICES: A CONCEPTUAL FRAMEWORK

A survey of the rich and diverse plethora of regimes that are employed around the world to regulate or intervene in strikes in essential services yields the following general observations:

First, the various regimes of regulation are made up of several intertwined components and tend to be multifaceted. Quite often, the legal regime in a particular jurisdiction is not monolithic and contains within itself multiple types or different models of regulation that operate side by side. Each model or regime applies on a particular level of government e.g., federal, state or municipality, and on a specific sector (public vs. private) or on a cluster of employees, e.g., police, civil service, hospital workers.

Second, and generally speaking, in analysing or profiling different models of regulating strikes in essential services, it is suggested to look at the following four basic components and the variety of options that exist under each of them: (1) the source of regulation; (2) the definition of essential services, including who is defining, when and how, i.e., by which criteria and procedures; (3) the restrictions that are imposed on one or more of the three collective labour relations rights, due to the essential nature of the service; (4) the alternative means for promoting and protecting economic and social interests of those workers who, due to the essential nature of the service, are denied one or more of the three collective labour relations rights.

5.1 The Source of Regulation

Generally speaking, there are four distinctive sources or modes of regulation: external or exogenous; bilateral autonomous; unilateral autonomous; and hybrid or mixed mode, i.e., a combination of external and autonomous regulation.

These four sources of regulation tend to operate like communicating vessels, rotating lead positions in dealing with strikes in essential services.

5.1.1 External or Exogenous Regulation

The basic tenet of industrial and labour relations as well as the modern dispute resolution discourse conveys a strong preference for voluntary, autonomous and consent-based regulation over mandatory, exogenous and decree-based regulation. In practice however, save for few notable exceptions, the latter, i.e., exogenous and externally imposed regulation of one sort or another, dominate the field. Namely, the state, through its organs, dictates and enforces special rules applicable only to strikes in essential services or may intervene in other way or form to prevent or stop a strike in essential service. The three branches of government – the legislature, the executive and the judiciary – separately or in rare cases jointly,[18] are involved in regulating strikes in essential services. In some cases, the three branches of government may rotate in the lead position or in who bears the lion's share of responsibility for dealing with such strikes.

18. A good example is the miners' strike in the UK. The court's declaration as to the illegality of the strike provided the needed legitimacy and support for the executive branch's demand for a special budget of three billion pound in order to defeat the strike. See *Novitz*, 2003, 14.

5.1.2 Bilateral Autonomous Regulation

This mode of regulation is actually the core of collective labour relations. The restrictions on the right to strike due to the essential nature of the service are the product of an agreement between the parties or the social partners. A good example is the no-strike arbitration agreement signed in 2000 between the Israeli state and other employers in public health care and the medical doctors' union, in which the union waived the right to strike, including for contract renewal negotiation, for ten years.[19] Another example is collective agreements regarding minimum service such as the agreement signed in Denmark where the union undertook that all computer services would operate during the strike.[20]

5.1.3 Unilateral Autonomous Regulation

This mode of regulation refers to self-imposed restrictions on the right to strike adopted by a union in order to minimize the damage caused by a strike in essential services. Such restrictions may be announced either ex-ante in the union's constitution or bylaws or on an ad-hoc basis before a particular strike. A good example of the former was reported in Italy, where unions in essential services such as public transportation, health care and education, have adopted a special code which includes a ten-day prior notice, an obligation not to strike before and during holiday seasons, rush hours and examination period as well as an assurance of minimum service.[21] An example of the latter are the exceptions committees commonly used in Israel. They are an ad-hoc and informal internal forum authorized to decide, on a case by case basis, whether in spite of the strike, service will be provided fully or partially in acute or exceptional circumstances.[22]

5.1.4 Hybrid or Mixed Mode Regulation

Under this type of regulation, the restrictions on the right to strike due to the essential nature of the service are determined through a two-tier process. The first is an autonomous bilateral or unilateral regulation. The second, which comes into play only in case the union or the social partners fail to secure an adequate level of essential services during the strike, is exogenous or externally imposed. Here, the external regulation is only a substitute or a fall-back for an autonomous regulation. A good example is the German model of minimum

---

19. *Mironi*, 2008, 56 et seqq.
20. *ILO*, 1988.
21. *Ales*, 2003, 159.
22. 51092-01-12 *National Insurance Institute v. The Histadrut* (2012); 8299-06-12 *Mikud Security v. The National Workers Union* (2012).

service[23] and the way designated services that must be maintained in the event of a strike are determined in the federal public service and in several provinces in Canada.[24]

5.2 The Definition of Essential Service

As a legal construct, the term 'essential service' has been the subject of voluminous literature and jurisprudence that has tried to produce an operative and comprehensive definition. The most advanced and frequently cited one is the distinction between essential and non-essential in the strict sense of the term, originated from the ILO Freedom of Organization Committee's jurisprudence.[25] Nonetheless, adding on another construct, namely 'in the strict sense of the term' does not help to operationally define the concept of essential service. Furthermore, the casuistic interpretation of the construct of essentiality in the strict sense of the term does not capture the diversity of the models of regulation observed around the world.

What is needed, therefore, is a richer, more nuanced model for conceptualizing, understanding and evaluating the range of forms or approaches of defining essential service. The definition of essential service is not an end but a means in itself. Its function is to identify the population of workers whose collective labour rights are restricted due to the essential nature of their work. Therefore, it is suggested to abandon the traditionally used dichotomous essential versus non-essential paradigm and adopting instead, a multidimensional and continuum-based typology of approaches. A typology that is functional, process-oriented and more varied, nuanced and dynamic. It highlights the interface between the definition of essential service and the restrictions imposed, while capturing the underlying strategic approach of various models of regulation in terms of scope and timing.

The new conceptual framework proposed here characterizes the strategic approaches along two dimensions. The first dimension refers to scope. Namely, the way by which a particular model of regulation defines the population to which the restrictions, whatever they are, may apply. It differentiates between general and fixed versus selective approaches. The second dimension refers to timing. Namely, the point of time at which the determination regarding essentiality for the sake of imposing restrictions is taken. It differentiates between ex-ante/pre-dispute versus ad-hoc/post-dispute. Combined, the two dimensions can accurately portray not only the diversity of existing models of regulation observed around the world, but also the different options that exist between and alongside them.

23. *Weiss*, 1994, 64, 79.
24. *Adell/Grant/Ponak*, 2001, 30.
25. *Servais*, 2009–2010, 153.

5.2.1 The Scope Dimension: General and Fixed Versus Selective

Under the general/fixed approach, once a particular service is considered essential, the restrictions apply to all the employees engaged by the provider of the essential service and stay constant for unspecified period. Under a selective approach, the restrictions apply only to specified workers who hold positions or perform duties that are deemed essential. The selective definition approach may take two forms. It can either be fixed or dynamic. Under the latter, the makeup of the group whose right to strike is restricted is dynamic and can be changed by adding or subtracting services, functions or employees during the strike in response to actual needs.

5.2.2 The Timing Dimension: Ex-Ante Versus Ad-Hoc

Essential services or essential employees may be defined for the purpose of regulation either in advance (ex-ante) or ad-hoc. Under an ex-ante or pre-dispute approach, the regulator determines ex-ante and long before the strike or the dispute that gave rise to the strike that a particular service or group of workers is essential, thereby subjecting them to the restrictions. In contrast, under the ad-hoc post-dispute approach, the regulator is called upon to act only in the presence of a strike or a threat of strike and the regulation is dispute-specific only. Namely, the service or the group of workers are defined as essential only on the eve of a strike or during the strike, and the restrictions apply only to the particular strike or dispute. This type was named the 'consequence-based approach'[26] and the 'unfettered strike model'.[27]

5.2.3 The Matrix

The explanatory power of the two dimensions and their implications can better be appreciated by viewing the 2 × 2 matrix shown in Figure 1.1.

26. *Morris*, 1986, 189 et seq.
27. *Adell/Grant/Ponak*, 2001, 14.

Figure 1.1 The Typology of Regulating Strikes in Essential Services

		Scope: General-Fixed	Scope: Selective
Timing	Ex-ante	1	2
	Ad hoc	3	4

Cell 1 (Ex-Ante & General – Fixed) is the most frequent type. The service is defined in advance as essential and the restrictions apply to all those employed, including workers who do not perform functions that can be considered essential. This type of regulation has been referred to as the 'enumeration approach'[28] and the 'no-strike regime' or model.[29] The common example is when essential employees (e.g., policemen and fire-fighters in many states in the US and Canada) are given the right to form unions, organize and bargain collectively, but are denied the right to strike. In its more extreme version, the law identifies a particular service as essential (e.g., policemen, secret service employees and prison guards in Israel) and denies all workers the three collective labour rights, including the right to organize.[30] A middle of the road approach, albeit no less encroaching on the right to strike, is the German model regarding civil service employees. They are allowed to organize, but denied the right to bargain collectively and hence also to strike.[31]

Cell 2 (Ex-Ante & Selective) refers to a situation or model under which, long before a dispute arises and unrelatedly to any particular strike or a strike threat, specific functions or employees are defined as essential and, consequently, will not be part of a strike if and when it takes place. Probably the most sophisticated and nuanced example of such ex-ante or pre-dispute regulation is the 'designation model' which has been primarily practiced in Canada. Under this regime, the right to strike is granted, provided that there is an ex-ante agreement or an adjudicative decision as to a list of designated services, i.e., services which will

28. *Morris*, 1986, 189.
29. *Adell/Grant/Ponak*, 2001, 50 et seqq.
30. Section 93 (b) of the Police Ordinance [New version] 1971; Section 129 (a) of the Prisons Ordinance [New version] 1971; Section 20 of the General Secret Service Law 2002.
31. *Weiss/Schmidt*, 1994, 67, 77 et seq.

be provided during the strike.[32] Another example is air traffic controllers, public transportation and public education employees in France.

Cell 3 (Ad-Hoc & General – Fixed) refers to cases in which, during a strike, the regulator acts to bring an end to a strike in essential services through ad-hoc back-to-work regulation. Notable examples are the use of an ad-hoc legislation in Canada, where pro-dispute restrictions of the right to strike have regularly been imposed during a strike through ad-hoc legislation.[33] Other examples exist in some Scandinavian countries like Denmark[34] which used ad-hoc legislation to end a strike by computer employees. Examples of ad-hoc interventions by the executive branch include the National Emergency Procedure[35] and Presidential Seizure in the US[36] and the use of the US army's air traffic controllers as strike replacements in 1981.[37] In most case, injunctions issued by the judiciary against a particular strike in essential services follow the same pattern. They are issued on an ad-hoc basis and apply to the workforce involved in the strike as a whole.

Cell 4 (Ad-Hoc & Selective) relates to regimes under which, during a strike or when facing a clear threat of a strike, selected employees or functions are declared as essential and disallowed to be part of the strike. Following such declaration or determination, the strike will go on, provided that these essential functions are performed without interruption. A common example can be found in minimum service arrangements in Germany, Spain and many other European countries. The judiciary is usually involved in such an ad-hoc selective definition through adjudicating disputes between employers and unions over designation or minimum service.

As alluded previously, the ad-hoc selective approach may be employed in a dynamic form. When this approach is adopted, the makeup of the group whose right to strike is restricted can be altered during the strike by adding or subtracting services, functions or employees in response to actual needs. An illuminating example of the use of ad-hoc selective dynamic approach for regulating strikes in essential services are the back-to-work emergency orders under the Emergency Ordinance in Israel.[38] These back-to-work orders are personally issued to employees according to changing circumstantial needs.

Generally speaking, in deciding which service or employee is essential, the three branches of government and the social partners tend to employ different

32. *Adell/Grant/Ponak*, 2001, 30 et seqq.
33. *Swimmer/Bartikiw*, 2003, 581, 585; *Adell*, 2013, 415.
34. The legislation was used in order to stop a strike by computer employees.
35. *Cullen*, 1968.
36. *Marcus*, 1977. In the US, the President was authorized to temporarily seize a plant or business in order to secure the continuous flow of essential services. Once seized, the plant or business was managed by the federal government and work resumed since federal sector employees were not allowed to strike. The US Supreme Court struck down the use of such presidential powers in the 'steel seizure' case, *Youngstown Sheet & Tube Co. v. Sawyer*, 343 US 579 (1952).
37. *Sunstein/Meltzer*, 1983, 761.
38. *Mironi*, 1986, 350.

cells of the proposed matrix. The legislator concentrates on Cells 1 and 3; the executive branch on Cells 3 and 4; the judiciary on Cells 2, 3 and 4; and the social partners or the disputing parties on Cells 3 and 4.

5.3 The Menu of Restrictions

The menu of special restrictions commonly used around the world for regulating and intervening in strikes in essential services is broad and rich. These direct restrictions encroach on workers' collective labour relations rights for one reason – the essential nature of the service provided by these workers.[39] In addition to the direct restrictions, most legal regimes also include indirect restrictions applicable to strikes in essential services that are part of criminal and civil law, e.g., tort law.[40] The direct restrictions can be divided into two groups – substantive restrictions and procedural restrictions.

5.3.1 Substantive Restrictions

The most extreme type of substantive restriction is the exclusion, full prohibition or sweeping ban. Under this model of regulation, workers are excluded from or denied all three collective labour law rights, including the right to organize, e.g., police, prison guards and secret service in Israel. Somewhat less intruding is the model under which workers enjoy the right to organize, but are denied the right to take any form of collective action, including collective bargaining, e.g., all employees having the status of Beamte (civil servants with a specific public law status) in Germany. A third and relatively less questionable restriction in terms of the basic human right to organize is the full prohibition or sweeping exclusion model, applicable to police, prison guards and fire-fighters in countries like Japan, France and many states in the US and provinces in Canada. These employees enjoy the right to organize and the right to collective bargaining, but have no right to strike.

A second and less extreme type of substantive restriction includes various forms of partial prohibition and special limitation that are imposed, most often externally, on the right to strike of essential service employees. These limitations may take an abstract form, such as the requirement of proportionality,[41] or a more concrete limitation, such as a requirement of minimum service or indispensable performances, imposing a maximum length of a strike or authorizing the regulator to suspend the strike due to the essential nature of the service.

39. Note however that sometimes the most far-going restrictions, such as a sweeping ban on the right to bargain collectively and to strike have different reasons, e.g., general public service exclusion.
40. *Morris*, 1991, 68 et seq.
41. *Weiss/Schmidt*, 2000, 180 et seq., 203; *Davidov*, 2008, 5, 16 et seqq.

A third and more innovating as well as promising type of restriction is the no-stoppage strike, known also as synthetic or virtual strike. A synthetic or virtual strike is a model of striking aimed at producing the effect of strike in essential service without hurting the public. Even though a strike is called, the employees involved continue to work as normal, securing the continuous flow of essential services. In order to simulate the impact of a strike while inflicting pain exclusively on the conflicting parties, all of the employer's income and the employees' salaries for the duration of the strike are channelled into a trust fund. At the end of the strike, part of the money accumulated in the trust fund is paid to the employer and to the employees in inverse relation to the length of the strike. This type of ad-hoc restriction may be agreed upon by the disputing parties or externally imposed.

5.3.2 Procedural Restrictions

Subjecting employees in essential services to special procedural restrictions enables the regulator to ensure that collective labour rights stay intact while reducing the incidents of strikes, shortening their duration and mitigating their negative impact on the public. The list of procedural restrictions includes, among others, prior notice, employee balloting, and exhausting consent-based dispute processing procedures, such as mediation and various types of non-binding recommendations.

The requirement of a prior notice, where such measure is not part of regular strike law, or the requirement of an extended notice before a strike in essential services, serves two objectives. First, it enables the employer and the public to prepare or make the necessary arrangements for the strike. Second, much like employee balloting, a prior notice requirement, especially when it is an extended notice which has been commonly referred to as a cooling-off period, is intended to reduce the incidents of strikes and ensure that they are used only as a last resort.

Cooling-off periods avail the parties of a last minute opportunity to reach an agreement on the unresolved issues underlying the strike, either directly or assisted by a third party, under the shadow of a clear and present threat of a strike.

Requiring the disputing parties to exhaust third party consent-based impasse procedures as a prerequisite for striking serves similar purpose. It aims at reducing the number of strikes or shortening their duration and it ensures that all other means to avoid the strike have actually been attempted and failed. Calling a strike in essential service is not different from other strikes. It is a sign that the parties reached an impasse or a deadlock in their negotiation. Forcing the disputing parties to try mediation and non-binding recommendations, such as advisory arbitration, fact-finding or 'Schlichtung', may bring about a settlement rendering the strike unnecessary altogether.

5.4 Alternative Means to Promote and Protect Employees' Interests

According to ILO jurisprudence, whenever the right to organize and its corollary rights are denied or substantially curtailed, compensating measures or alternative means for promoting and protecting economic and social interests should be provided for. A survey of the literature demonstrates that, as a subject, this aspect has received very limited attention in the public policy debate regarding models of regulating strikes in essential services.

There are two types of compensating measures or alternative means for promoting and protecting economic and social interests that can be distilled from the literature. They vary by their function. The first relates to those workers who, due to the essential nature of their service, are not allowed by law to organize and bargain collectively. The second to those who are allowed to organize and bargain collectively but do not have the right to strike. In some instances, alternative means for promoting and protecting employees' economic and social interests are accompanied by special benefits or privileges bestowed upon the workers and their union, compensating them for the denial of collective labour law rights.[42]

The compensating or alternative means that are the *quid pro quo* for the right to organize and bargain collectively serve as a substitute for the effective voice and added power, which otherwise could be enjoyed by the individual employees under the collective labour relations model of employment. These alternative means include automatic parity or indexing and public review boards.

The compensating or alternative means that are the *quid pro quo* for the right to strike serve different function. They serve as a strike substitute in the otherwise power-based collective labour relations model and as a means to assure finality in collective bargaining negotiations. The underlying idea is to avoid a situation under which, in the absence of a strike leverage, the employer may act unilaterally in case the parties reach an impasse in the negotiations.

Therefore, the two alternative means that are the *quid pro quo* for the right to strike are special dispute resolution procedures culminating in binding and final arbitration on the one hand, and legislative determination on the other. Both can be unilaterally invoked and they ensure that, in case of a failure to reach agreement through negotiation, the ultimate decision-making power will not return to the hands of the employer. In the former, the ultimate decision-making power is taken from the employer and entrusted in the hands of the

42. For example, in Israel the statute which imposed restrictions on strikes in the public service bestowed upon unions a privilege akin to punitive damages. A union in the public service is entitled to receive compensation for any breach of a collective agreement by an employer without proof that such breach caused any damage to the union or the employees. See Section 37d of The Settlement of Labour Dispute Law 1957 as amended. Frequently, general 'privileges' of public servants, such as employment security and legislative wage determination, are considered sufficient to justify their exclusion.

arbitration body leaving the balancing of interests in its hands; in the latter – in the hands of the politically elected legislative body.

A closing note: the conceptual framework presented here attempts to capture the rich landscape of models by which legal regimes around the world regulate and cope with strikes in essential services. Naturally, it concentrated on the restrictions. It overlooked the important role played by the broad array of special measures employed by the state and which can be justified by the necessity to cope with exceptionally difficult strikes in essential service. These special measures are completely divorced from and go beyond the various direct and indirect restrictions on the right to strike. The literature provides a non-exhaustive list of examples that can be clustered into two groups. The first include measures that enable the employer, quite often the state itself, to operate the essential service in spite of the strike. Among them: using soldiers as strike replacements, drafting the strikers to the army or national service, replacing the workers on strike by employees from excluded groups (e.g., civil service employees having the status of *Beamte* in Germany)[43] or by volunteers. The second refers to different administrative measures that might be employed by the executive branch in order to secure an alternative service. These measures may include using army installations as an alternative to struck services and providing alternative service through ad-hoc licensing of contractors[44] and removal of authorization requirements.

6 EVALUATIVE FRAMEWORK

With a few exceptions,[45] the literature does not offer criteria for assessing the performance of different models of regulating or intervening in strikes in essential services. The last section of the theoretical infrastructure attempts to fill this gap. It suggests a set of objective and subjective criteria, some of which are process-driven, and some outcome-driven. Since the criteria are designed to assess both the restrictions and the special measures, on one hand, and the alternative means provided to workers and their unions to promote and protect economic and social interests, on the other hand, they are not mutually exclusive. For instance, as research findings demonstrate,[46] the availability of acceptable means to promote and protect workers' interests is likely to affect the level of workers' tolerance towards the restrictions and to enhance voluntary compliance. Save for the overreaching criterion of acceptability, all other criteria

43. See the Federal Constitutional Court's ruling in Germany regarding the postal service strike BVerfG 2 March 1993 – 1 BvR 1213/85.
44. In the midst of a long strike by a local bus company's drivers in Israel, the minister of transportation brought the strike to an end by issuing temporary licenses to other bus companies. 57/05 *The Histadrut v. The State of Israel and Metrodan*, 40 P.D.A 481 (2005).
45. *Adell/Grant/Ponak*, 2001, 193 et seqq; *Kochan/Lipsky/Newhart/Benson*, 2010, 565, 569 et seqq; *Mironi*, 2011, 223 et seqq.
46. *Kochan/Mironi/Ehrenberg/Baderschneider/Jick*, 1979, 146.

are largely self-explanatory as they derive from the normative dilemma and the conceptual framework. They are:

(1) Proper level of service
(2) Level of compliance
(3) The impact on negotiations and collective bargaining relationships
(4) Compliance with international standards
(5) Preference for autonomous regulation (self-imposed or agreed-upon) over external regulation
(6) The model's internal consistency
(7) Acceptability – as to process and outcomes.

The first three criteria relate to the regulating model's components and often, to more than one. For instance, the level of compliance may relate to compliance with the restrictions or compliance with an arbitration award, whenever the model calls for special impasse procedures culminating in compulsory binding arbitration. Similarly, the impact on effective collective bargaining may relate to the degree to which the restrictions interfered with effective negotiations, or were exploited by the employer which resorted to unilateral action knowing that the workers were stripped of their collective action power. It can also relate to the question of whether the availability of arbitration as a post negotiations step created a 'chilling effect' (Kochan, Lipsky, Newhart & Benson, 2010, 4): instead of negotiating, the parties were rushing to arbitration; and instead of conceding and moving during the negotiations, the parties adopted extreme positions and stuck to them in preparation for arbitration.

The fourth criterion may be applicable to the regulating model as a whole, as well as to a particular component thereof. For instance, in assessing the model as a whole, one needs to inquire whether it adheres to ILO jurisprudence, which requires that the infringement on the workers' right to strike should be compensated by an alternative means to protect the workers' interests. In contrast, in assessing the specific profile of the compulsory arbitration procedures provided for by the regulating model, one needs to examine to what extent it complies with the 'protocol' which was promulgated by the ILO Freedom of Association Committee's jurisprudence. Criteria No. 5 and No. 6 assess the regulating model as a whole – namely, its overall design and performance.

Criterion No. 7 is a multilevel and dual faceted criterion. Multilevel, in that it may be used to assess not only the regulating model as a whole or the regulating model's particular components, but also the performance of different elements or aspects that make up or characterize a regulating model's particular components. For instance, in assessing an alternative means to protect employees' interests, the criterion of acceptability may be applied for evaluating the level of neutrality and integrity of the decision-making body or the quality of its decisions.[47]

The criterion of acceptability is dual-faceted as it may be used to assess the model or a particular component or an element in terms of process and outcomes separately, each leading to different results. For instance, the acceptability of determining a minimum service or designated employees may be assessed as low in terms of outcomes, and high in terms of the process by which such outcomes were reached.

Bibliography

-----, Tarifkonflikt: Unternehmen prüft Einsatz externer Piloten, Handelsblatt, 2012. Available at http://www.handelsblatt.com/unternehmen/handel-dienstleister/tarifkonflikt-unternehmen-prueft-einsatz-externer-piloten/10778058-2.html

Adell, Bernard, Perspectives of Power and Perspectives of Principle in Canadian Labour Law Scholarship, in Ian B. McKenna, (ed.) Labour Relations into the 1990s, 1989, 27 et seqq.

Adell, Bernard, Regulating Strikes in Essential (and other) Services after the 'New Trilogy' 17 Canada Labour and Employment Law Journal, 2013, 17, 413 et seqq.

Ales, Edoardo, Strike in public - essential services in Italy, in Rigaux/Dorssemont (eds), Vitale Behoeften, Essentiële Diensten, Minimumprestaties en Stakingrecht, 2003, 159 et seqq.

Cohen, Yinon/Haberfeld, Yitchak/Kristal Tali/Mundlak, Guy, The State of Organized Labour in Israel, Journal of Labour Research, 28/2007, 255 et seqq.

Cullen, Donald, National Emergency Strikes, 1968

Davidov, Guy, The Proportionality Principle in Labour Law, Tel Aviv University Law Review, 31/2008, 5 et seqq.

Deinert, Olaf, Collective Action in Germany: A Union-Based System, in Ales/Novitz (eds), Collective Action and Fundamental Freedoms in Europe, 2010, 55 et seqq.

Franzen, Martin/Thüsing Gregor/Waldhoff, Christian, Arbeitskampf in der Daseinsvorsorge, 2012

Haiven, Larry, Industrial Relations in Health Care: Regulation, Conflicts and Transition to the 'Wellness Model', in Swimmer/Thompson (eds), Public Sector Collective Bargaining in Canada, 1995, 236 et seqq.

ILO, Definitive Report - Report No 259, November 1988, Case No 1443 (Denmark) - Complaint date: 10 March 1988, - Closed. Available at http://www.ilo.org/dyn/normlex/en/f?p = NORMLEXPUB:50002:0::NO::P50002_COMPLAINT_TEXT_ID:2901703

47. *Ibid.*, 146 et seqq.

Itzchaki, Shlomo, Workers' Attitude towards Labor Relation Issues: 2003 Survey, 2003

Kochan, Thomas A/Lipsky, David B/Newhart, Mary/Benson, Alan, The Long-Haul Effects of Interest Arbitration: The Case of New York State's Taylor Law, Industrial and Labor Relations Review, 63/2010, 565 et seqq.

Kochan, Thomas A/Mironi, Mordehai/Ehrenberg, Ronald G/Baderschneider, Jean/Jick, Todd, Dispute Resolution under Fact-finding and Arbitration, 1979

Laulom, Sylvaine, Collective Action in France: towards a Restriction of the Right to Strike?, in Ales/Novitz (eds), Collective Action and Fundamental Freedoms in Europe - Striking The Balance, 2010, 31 et seqq.

Marcus, Maeva, Truman and the Steel Seizure Case: The Limits of Presidential Power, 1994

Mironi, Mordehai, Back-to-Work Emergency Orders: Government Intervention in Labour Disputes in Essential Services, Hebrew University Law Review, 1986, 15, 350 et seqq.

Mironi, Mordehai, Experimenting with ADR as a Means for Peaceful Resolution of Interest Labour Disputes in Public Health Care - A Case Study, Law and Contemporary Problems, 2011, 71, 201 et seqq.

Mironi, Mordehai, Mediation and Strategic Change, 2008

Mironi, Mordehai, The Arbitration of Labour Disputes - A Critical Study of the Institute of Voluntary Arbitration in the Public Service, 1988

Morris, Gillian S, Industrial Action in Essential Services: Restriction through the Backdoor, Human Resource Management, 2/1991, 63 et seqq.

Morris, Gillian S, Industrial Action in Essential Services: the new law, Industrial Law Journal, 20/1991, 89 et seqq.

Morris, Gillian S, Strikes in Essential Services, 1986

Novitz, Tonia, Collective Action in the United Kingdom, in *Edoardo/Novitz* (eds), Collective Action and Fundamental Freedoms in Europe, 2010, 173 et seqq.

Novitz, Tonia, International and European Protection of the Right to Strike, 2003

Servais, JM, ILO Law and the Right to Strike, Canadian Labour & Employment Law, 15/2009-2010, 147 et seqq.

Stern, James L, The Declining Utility of the Strike, Industrial and Labour Review, 18/1964, 60 et seqq.

Sunstein, Cass R/Meltzer, Bernard D, Public Employee Strikes, Executive Discretion, and the Air Traffic Controllers, University of Chicago Law Review, 50/1983, 731 et seqq.

Swimmer, Gene/Bartkiw, Tim, The Future of Public Sector Collective bargaining in Canada, Journal of Labour Research, 24/2003, 579 et seqq.

Weiler, Paul C., The Charter at Work: Reflections on the Constitutionalizing of Labour and Employment Law, University of Toronto Law Journal, 40/1990, 117 et seqq.

Weiss, Manfred, Strikes and Lock-outs in Germany, in *Blanpain/Ben Israel* (eds), Strikes and Lock-outs in Industrialized Market Economies, Bulletin of Comparative Labour Relations, 29/1994 79, et seqq.

Weiss, Manfred/Schmidt, Marlene, Labour Law and Industrial Relations in Germany, 2000

PART II International Law on Strikes in Essential Services

CHAPTER 2

Regulating Strikes in Essential Services from an International Law Perspective*

Monika Schlachter

* This chapter elaborates on my article 'Strikes in essential services under international law', published in the Bulletin of Comparative Labour Relations Vol. 100 (2018) Chapter 7.

1 INTRODUCTION

Collective action is acknowledged under international law as being the most fundamental means available to workers and their organizations for promoting their economic and social interests. As a social right, bargaining collectively and eventually taking collective action is part of human rights guarantees and an emanation of core international labour rights at the international level. Strike action is the most visible and controversial form of a labour dispute and mostly seen as the last resort of workers' organizations in pursuit of their demands for improving employment conditions.[1] For specific sectors of the economy, frequently labelled *essential services*, it is, however, not only (and at times not even primarily) the other party to the employment contract that is negatively affected by strikes. Much rather, they concern the public as consumers of the services provisionally denied during a labour dispute. Where the steady supply of specific services is part of a state's social policy, the interruption of the delivery process becomes problematic also for the state. A conflict originating in the employee's demand for better employment conditions stretches beyond the employment relationship, and the state may assume responsibility for solving the conflict to avoid negatively affecting the public interest.

It must be underlined, however, that the dilemma of solving such conflict for the benefit of consumers evolved in many states from the governments' own decisions made in the context of economic globalization.[2] Where essential services used to be part of a public service guaranteeing 'essential' features to the whole of the population, it seems comparably easy for the state as employer to bargain for working conditions and settle conflicts arising from collective disputes. Where privatization of public functions became dominant, also services considered to be the responsibility of the state became an issue of private supply and demand.[3] Workers in privatized essential services then work under market conditions of an essentially fragmented private sector, the state lost much influence on the process and outcome of bargaining for terms and conditions of employment.[4] However, the state's responsibility for setting policy goals remained, and consumers continued to depend on the constant flow of such services because there are rarely sufficient and affordable alternative

1. *Servais*, 2008, 148.
2. *Schlachter*, 2018.
3. *Hänsle*, 2016, 189 et seq.
4. *Cohen/Le Roux*, 2015, 129 et seq.

supplies to turn to.[5] Therefore, states maintain specific rules governing the possibility to withhold essential services for improving working conditions.[6]

To define whether a right to strike may be restricted and replaced by other forms of determining working conditions, and which services are to be considered *essential,* is a delicate matter. As collective labour relations in general developed under the conditions of the industrial relations system historically evolved in a specific country, they essentially depend on the social and economic model followed. Given the substantial differences between legal systems it might be expected that any comparison between them might provide few promising results. Collective labour law therefore has been traditionally considered a specifically challenging field for conducting comparative studies. However, the right to strike and its limitations might be slightly more apt for comparison as it benefits from the existence of a common frame of reference in international law. Even though not considered binding by all jurisdictions, international law at least establishes a widely accepted general framework, functioning as a suitable comparator for national legal systems built on rather different legal, social and economic traditions.

For establishing such a frame of reference, the present chapter on international law is not presenting all international labour standards in the context of strikes in essential services. Specifically, it neither deals with Article 22 of the International Covenant on Civil and Political Rights nor with Article 8 of the International Covenant on Economic, Social or Cultural Rights, as both refer to the more specific guarantees provided for in the International Labour Organization (ILO) Convention No. 87. This reference clearly indicates that ILO standards are perceived as the most important global source of international law on the right to strike, also accepted by the major part of United Nations (UN) member states. In addition, these guarantees are provided with the most detailed interpretation developed so far at international level, given by the ILO supervisory bodies.[7] This chapter therefore focuses on presenting ILO Convention No. 87 and its interpretation by the relevant monitoring bodies as the legal basis of a right to strike and of limitations accepted in case of essential services. For highlighting the on-going process of developing a coordinated approach in applying international social rights, a regional European instrument explicitly prescribing a right to strike – the European Social Charter – is referred to where appropriate.[8]

2 THE LEGAL BASIS AND ITS INTERPRETATION

The right to strike is recognized by the International Labour Organization (ILO) supervisory bodies as *an intrinsic corollary of the right to organize protected by*

5. *Morris*, 1986, 1.
6. *Cohen/Le Roux*, 2015, 129 et seq.
7. *Novitz*, 2014, 364.
8. *Sädevirta*, 2016, 451; Schlachter, 2016, 25.

Convention No. 87 (Freedom of Association and Protection of the Right to Organize Convention, 1948).[9] Its connection to the right to bargain collectively is strong, even though a situation of collective bargaining is as such not conditional for collective action. However, the potential recourse to collective action in a concrete bargaining situation is an effective means for rendering bargaining a 'meaningful' process.[10] Under Convention No. 87, the right to strike is derived from the right of workers' organizations to formulate their programmes of activities to further and defend the economic and social interests of their members.[11]

The Convention in general has been interpreted by the ILO supervisory bodies,[12] namely the Committee on Freedom of Association (CFA), a tripartite congregation of workers', employers' and government representatives, and the Committee of Experts on the Application of Conventions and Recommendation (CEACR), a body of independent legal experts. The interpretation by these supervisory bodies has evolved into a body of principles on the right to strike broadly shared by the international community.[13] Besides the two ILO Committees having a different composition and different mandates, the principles regarding the right to strike laid down by them coincide on practically all essential points. The principles are provided within a framework which simultaneously takes account of the diversity of national legal systems, seeks to establish sufficient levels of protection for the exercise of the right to strike, and to balance the rights of trade unions, employers, users of essential services or public utility services, and the State.[14] The pertinent principles of the ILO are summarized in its publication 'ILO Principles Concerning the Right to Strike',[15] as well as by the Digest of decisions and principles of the Freedom of Association Committee of the Governing Body of the ILO.[16]

From these sources it can be derived that the right to strike should principally be guaranteed to all workers irrespective of the sector they work in or the type of contract governing their contractual relationship. This broad personal scope of application is accompanied by the understanding that this right is not considered absolute; it much rather can be subject to legal conditions and restrictions, and under exceptional circumstances even be denied completely. Applying it in the field of essential services therefore demands balancing a

9. *ILO*, 2006, 523.
10. *Weiss*, 2013, 29; *Smit*, 2017, 400.
11. ILC, 1994a, 151.
12. The Committee on Freedom of Association is a tripartite body of the ILO Governing Body which examines complaints submitted in regard to breaches of trade unions rights, including the right to strike; while the Committee of Experts (composed of independent legal experts) carries out regular monitoring of compliance with ratified Conventions, ie Convention 87.
13. *Novitz*, 2017.
14. *Gernigon* et al., 1998, 57 et seqq.
15. *Ibid.*
16. *ILO*, 2006, 581 et seqq.

principally broadly defined human rights guarantee with legitimate expectations of third parties towards an uninterrupted flow of certain services. While taking on a responsibility for the continuing offer of essential services even if not literally providing the services, the state interferes in the process of bargaining for terms and conditions of employment by restricting the means of workers to promote their economic interests.

3 MEANS OF IDENTIFYING 'ESSENTIAL' SERVICES

The case law of the ILO supervisory bodies applies a functional approach to the notion of essential services. Therefore, at ILO level no complete list of services accepted as 'essential' was developed that would include all sectors that legitimately could be excluded from a right to strike. Much rather, to determine whether a specific service might be exempted from the right to strike depends on the function a job holder is fulfilling. This function could either concern the functioning of the state, described as 'public service' under ILO standards (see *infra*) or the functioning of services the receipt of which is protected by fundamental rights of the customer to have access to 'essential services'. Both terms imply that in services accepted as being 'public' or 'essential' the right to strike may be severely limited or even prohibited. It follows from there that it could not be the states' own definition of what is domestically considered public or essential that could justify restrictions applied in such state also at international level. Much rather, the ILO supervisory bodies accept limitations to the right to strike once they are proportionate to the importance of the function fulfilled, and the threat to rights protected by such limitation. This is assessed on a case-by case basis: Specific sectors and professions are identified (see *infra*) for which it deems generally likely that the interruption of their services might severely damage the functioning of the state or the life, health or personal security of the population, while others generally don't. As a next step, however, the concrete circumstances of a strike must be considered. Therefore, even services not generally considered to be essential might become so, or jobs belonging to a sector generally considered essential might not be included in the limitations.

The ILO Conventions do, however, not aim at creating unified legal expressions at domestic level, they are not understood as requiring states to use the term 'public' or 'essential' services in the same sense as the autonomous concept developed at ILO level. It remains in the competence of each state to determine what is considered 'essential' or which functions should qualify as exclusive prerogative to public services organized by the state. Yet, when applying restrictions to the right to strike for such personnel, states must ensure to limit them to those persons who would also come under the ILO's definition.

4 RESTRICTIONS TO THE RIGHT TO STRIKE IN ESSENTIAL SERVICES

The fundamental right to strike must not be restricted any further than necessary and appropriate for the protection of the functioning of the state or interests of consumers of essential services. Whereas the following sections enlist areas and situations in which even a full prohibition of strikes has been acknowledged as being in line with the international labour standards, it should be stressed that the justification of a restricting measure depends on assessing also the conditions set up under the criterion, the circumstances of each individual case. Consequently, where the detrimental consequences of the strike for the state or consumers might be accommodated by measures less severe than a total ban – especially by delaying the onset of a strike, limiting its scope to a part of the workforce and/or limiting its duration, a prohibition would be disproportionate as the restrictions chosen must be the least intrusive.

4.1 Full or Partial Prohibition to Strike

4.1.1 Restrictions Applicable to Specific Groups of Employees or Specific Situations

As far as explicit exceptions are concerned, Article 9 of ILO Convention No. 87 states that 'the extent to which the guarantees provided for in this Convention shall apply to the armed forces and the police shall be determined by national laws or regulations'. As a result, the Committee on Freedom of Association found no objection to legislation which denies the right to strike to such groups of workers.[17] Essentially this means that for the professions explicitly mentioned in the Convention, the margin of discretion for states is wide. Whenever persons are to be considered members of these specific categories, states are entitled to decide whether and to what extent they are entitled to collective action.

By comparison, under Article 6 § 4 of the European Social Charter even restrictions imposed on members of those specifically pronounced categories of civil servants need to satisfy the conditions of proportionality: the total prohibition of conducting a strike by members of the police force was held to violate Article 6 § 4 of the Charter,[18] as such prohibition would need compelling reasons justifying it. Otherwise, merely restrictions as to the mode and form of such strike action can be in conformity to the Charter.

Under ILO instruments, the CFA has considered a general prohibition of strikes to be also justified 'in the event of an acute national crisis and for a limited period of time'.[19] Establishing the existence of an 'acute national crisis', however, is dependent on extremely severe circumstances such as a *coup d'état*

17. *Gernigon et al.*, 1998, 17.
18. *ECSR*, *EuroCOP v. Ireland*, Complaint No. 83/2012, §§ 201-214.
19. *ILO*, 2006, 570 et seq.

against a constitutional government leading to the declaration of a state of emergency in accordance with the national constitution.[20] Such national emergency may even be of an economic nature, once the severity of the situation is comparably harsh. The CEACR has emphasized that the acknowledgement of a crisis situation depends on severe circumstances such as serious conflicts, insurrections, natural, sanitary or humanitarian disasters, in which normal conditions for the functioning of societies are lacking.[21] Also for this category, if established in a convincing manner, a general prohibition of strikes may be acceptable. Given the far-reaching restrictions that could be imposed to specific categories of employees and for specific situations, it is obvious that both categories are construed narrowly and unable to cover the regular inconvenience caused by a lack of 'essential services'.

4.1.2 Restrictions Based on the Essential Nature of the Service

Other cases for which limitations to the right to strike are considered adequate allow only a more limited margin of discretion for states. Possible exceptions from the generally guaranteed strike right are based on the nature of the services provided, i.e., the specific function employees are tasked with. The Committee on Freedom of Association has recognized possible exceptions from the wide personal scope of the right to strike which may be imposed for (1) public servants exercising authority in the name of the State and for (2) workers in essential services in the strict sense of the term.[22] However, for employees falling under these categories, states are not free to deliberately limit their rights. Much rather, they need an objective justification for restrictions, given that strike action is one of the crucial means for rendering effective a fundamental right. The justification depends on acting in accordance with the principle of proportionality, i.e., limitations must serve a legitimate aim (such as protecting rights and freedoms of others), and the ways and means of applying the restriction may not go beyond what is strictly necessary to achieve that legitimate goal.

In comparison, also according to Article 6 § 4 of the European Social Charter the right to strike may be restricted provided that any restriction satisfies the conditions laid down in Article G, i.e., that restrictions on the rights guaranteed by the Charter be prescribed by law, serve a legitimate purpose and be necessary in a democratic society for the protection of the rights and freedoms of others or for the protection of public interest, national security, public health or morals.[23] Prohibiting strikes in sectors which are essential to the community therefore may serve a legitimate purpose, if such strikes indeed pose a threat to

20. *CFA*, Report No. 284, Case No. 1626, para. 91.
21. *ILC*, 2012, 140.
22. *ILO*, 2006, 576; and CFA, Report No. 337, Case No. 2244, para. 1268.
23. *ECSR*, Conclusions 1987, Norway (regarding Article 31 of the Charter).

public interest, national security and/or public health.[24] However, simply banning strikes even in essential sectors – particularly when these are extensively defined, e.g., 'energy' or 'health' – is not deemed proportionate to the specific requirements of each sector. At most, the introduction of a minimum service requirement in these sectors might be considered in conformity with Article 6 § 4.[25]

– Public Service

It follows from what has just been stated that the mere categorization of certain workers as public servants under national law will, as such, not be sufficient for restricting their right to strike.[26] The same applies to categories of workers obliged to engage in a specific duty of loyalty to the state. Much rather, the ILO supervisory bodies assess the concrete function the categories of workers are tasked with, and the relevance of such function for assuring the proper functioning of the state authority.

It may be deduced from the statements of both the CEACR and of the CFA that in principle the right to strike may be restricted or prohibited only for those public servants who exercise authority in the name of the State.[27] The nature of the function that public servants actually undertake is conditional for determining who may be excluded; having a specific status under national law would therefore generally not be sufficient.[28] For example, in its case law, the CFA has held that officials working in the administration of justice and the judiciary are officials who exercise authority in the name of the State;[29] the same applies to customs officers.[30] Other categories of public servants, however, do not exercise authority in the name of the State, such as employees in state-owned commercial or industrial enterprises,[31] in oil, banking and metropolitan transport undertakings or those employed in the education sector.

One of the main difficulties in assessing the existence of an objective justification to restricting strike rights is the considerable variation of the concept of *public servant* from one national legal system to another. For example, the terms *civil servant*, *fonctionnaire* and *funcionario* are far from implying the same meaning in the respective languages; furthermore, an identical term used in the same language does not always mean the same thing in different countries; lastly, some systems classify public servants in different categories, with different status, obligations and rights, while such distinctions

24. *ECSR*, Conclusions 1969, Statement of Interpretation on Article 6§4. *ECSR*, CITUB, *Podkrepa and ETUC v. Bulgaria*, Complaint No. 32/2005.
25. *ECSR*, Conclusions 2004, Czech Republic.
26. *Novitz*, 2003, 305.
27. *ILO*, 2006, 574; CFA, Report No. 338, Case No. 2363 para. 731 and Case No. 2364 para. 975.
28. *ILC*, 1994: C 87 Germany.
29. *ILO*, 2006, 578; CFA, Report No. 336, Case No. 2383, para. 763.
30. *ILO*, 2006, 579; CFA, Report No. 304, Case No. 1719, para. 413.
31. *ILO*, 2006, 577; *CFA*, Report No. 338, Case No. 2348, para. 997.

do not exist in other systems or do not have the same consequences.[32] Thus, the CEACR has held that despite the special characteristics and legal and social traditions of each country, fairly uniform criteria must be established for examining the compatibility of national legislation with the provisions of Convention No. 87. This cannot be achieved by drawing up an exhaustive and universally applicable list of categories of public servants who should enjoy the right to strike or may be denied such a right. For this reason, the CEACR has suggested in general to not impose a total prohibition on strikes, but rather to provide for a defined and limited category of staff maintaining a negotiated minimum service when a total and prolonged stoppage might result in serious consequences for the public.[33]

Among the categories of public servants who do not exercise authority in the name of the State, those who carry out an essential service in the strict sense of the term may nevertheless be limited in their recourse to strike action. The two concepts, public service and essential services, both of which are in principle able to justify restrictions to the right to strike, are therefore considered as having a partly overlapping scope.

In comparison, public officials also enjoy the right to strike under Article 6 § 4 of the European Social Charter. They must be entitled to withdraw their labour;[34] allowing them to merely declare symbolic strikes is not sufficient.[35] Restrictions to this right are acceptable only where limited to public officials whose duties and functions, given their nature or level of responsibility, are directly related to national security or general interest.[36]

– Essential services in the strict sense of the term

The ILO's supervisory bodies have held it admissible to restrict substantially the right to strike once the concept of essential services applied includes merely essential services in the strict sense of the term.[37] This category is defined as services '*the interruption of which would endanger the life, personal safety or health of the whole or part of the population*'.[38]

The CFA has established that what is meant by essential services in the strict sense of the term depends to a large extent on the particular circumstances of the concrete case. Specific services that may not regularly be labelled 'essential' *in abstracto*, i.e., in absolute terms, may become essential if strikes affecting it exceed a certain time or extend beyond a certain scope, and thereby finally do endanger the life, personal safety or health of the whole or part of the population. For example, the CFA has considered that the refuse collection

32. *Gernigon et al.*, 1998, 19.
33. *CFA*, Report 1994a, para. 158.
34. *ECSR*, Conclusions 1969, §§ 38 et seq.
35. *Ibid.*, CITUB, *Podkrepa and ETUC v. Bulgaria*, Complaint No. 32/2005, §§ 44 et seqq.
36. *Ibid.*, Conclusions 1969, §§ 38 et seq.
37. *Servais*, 2008, 153.
38. *ILO*, 2006, 581; *CFA*, Report 1983b, para. 214; *Ibid.*, Report No. 338, Case No. 2326, para. 446 and Case No. 2329, para. 1275.

service, while not being considered essential immediately and in all cases, might become so if the strike affecting it exceeds a certain duration or extent with potentially dangerous consequences for the health of the population.[39]

The CEACR has agreed that account must be taken of specific circumstances existing in the various contracting States, since the interruption of certain services which in some countries might at worst cause economic hardship could prove disastrous in other countries and rapidly lead to conditions endangering the life, personal safety and health of the population. For example, a strike in the port or maritime transport services might more rapidly cause serious disruptions for an island which is heavily dependent on such services to provide basic supplies to its population than it would for a country on a continent.[40]

Examples

For illustrative purposes, the CFA has given its opinion on the essential or non-essential nature of a series of specific sectors. The CFA has listed as essential in the strict sense the following service sectors:[41]

- the hospital and ambulance services;
- electricity services;
- water supply services;
- the telephone service;
- the police and the armed forces;
- the fire-fighting services;
- public or private prison services;
- the provision of food to pupils of school age;
- air traffic control.[42]

Changes related to the basic needs of the population or the evolution of technology might cause a service which has hitherto not been considered essential in the strict sense of the term to become so in the future (for example internet services have meanwhile become more important than the telephone service).

Other sectors have been considered non-essential in the strict sense of the term: radio and television; the petroleum sector; ports (loading and unloading); banking; computer services for the collection of excise duties and taxes; department stores and pleasure parks; the metal sector; the mining sector; transport generally; airline pilots; production and distribution of fuel; railway services;[43] postal services; refuse collection services; refrigeration enterprises; hotel services; construction; automobile manufacturing; aircraft repairs; agricultural

39. *ILO*, 2006, 582, 591; *CFA*, Report No. 309 Case No. 1916, para.100.
40. *CFA*, Report 1994a, paras 159 and 160.
41. *ILO*, 2006, 585.
42. *Ibid.*, 586.
43. *CFA*, Report No. 372, Case No. 3022, para. 614.

activities; the supply and distribution of foodstuffs; the Mint; the government printing service; the state alcohol, salt and tobacco monopolies; the education sector; mineral water bottling services.[44]

Categorizing a complete sector, however, represents only the first step of assessing the legitimacy of restrictions to the right to strike. Following this, the specific functions of the profession concerned need to be considered: a substantive restriction to a human right must not go any further than necessary for securing the legitimate goal it is intended to achieve. This approach may be illustrated by the hospital service, which in general is perceived to be essential. Nevertheless, this categorization is not automatically exempting everyone working for hospitals from the right to strike; whether or not persons employed by a hospital would be included depends on their services' necessity for protecting the health and safety of parts of the population. Consequentially, certain categories of employees, such as hospital labourers and gardeners, should not be deprived of the right to strike.[45]

By comparison, under Article 6 § 4 of the European Social Charter, defining categories of essential services for exempting them from the right to strike is considered generally disproportionate, as assessing whole sectors or professions would be too broad for restricting the right to strike.[46] Therefore, the concrete function of employees must be assessed also when working in sectors generally considered 'essential', such as energy supply services;[47] the communication sector, railway services;[48] electricity and water supply services, telecommunication;[49] customs authorities;[50] healthcare or social care facilities; nuclear power plants, judges, prosecutors; air traffic controllers; members of the fire brigade, emergency and rescue services, underground undertakings, and transport.[51]

Under the ILO instruments, also possible serious long-term consequences of a strike for the national economy were unable to justify a total prohibition.[52]

44. *ILO*, 2006, 587 et seqq.
45. *Ibid.*, 593; *CFA*, Report No. 333, Case No. 2277, para. 274; *CFA*, Report No. 338, Case No. 2403, para. 601; *CFA*, Report No. 374, Case No. 3057, para. 215.
46. *ECSR*, Conclusions 2014, Serbia, Article 6§4. The Committee asked the Government '*to state, in relation to every service subject to restrictions with regard to the right to strike, if and to what extent work stoppages may undermine respect for the rights and freedoms of others or threaten the public interest, national security, public health, or morals. In this context, it also asks whether such restrictions are in all cases proportionate in a democratic society to achieve the aim of ensuring respect for the rights and freedoms of others or preventing threats to the public interest, national security, public health, or morals.*'
47. *ECSR*, Conclusions 2014, Armenia, Article 6§4.
48. *Ibid.*, Bulgaria, Article 6§4.
49. *Ibid.*, Slovak Republic, Article 6§4.
50. *Ibid.*, Republic of Moldova, Article 6§4.
51. *Ibid.*, Ukraine, Article 6§4.
52. *CFA*, Report No. 234, para. 190; ILO, 2006, 592.

Much rather, states should prohibit only strikes in the essential services in the strict sense of the term (the interruption of which would endanger the life, personal safety or health of the whole or part of the population),[53] and should not impose compulsory arbitration for ending strike actions.[54]

Much along the same line, also under Article 6 § 4 of the European Social Charter an intervention by national authorities for terminating collective action for economic reasons was criticized.[55] Even though a strike may have a negative impact on the economy, state intervention terminating an on-going collective action may not be necessary for the protection of (economic) rights and freedoms of others or of (economic) public interest: while the implications of an on-going industrial action may become serious in terms of provisional loss of revenue, this loss would not necessarily have been of a permanent nature.[56]

4.2 Procedural Requirements

4.2.1 Cooling Off Periods

As far as national systems require the parties to a future conflict to undergo a mediation or conciliation process *prior* to calling a strike, this is considered equivalent to 'cooling off' periods (periods foreseen for mediation and conciliation). The CFA has also considered that the legal requirement of a cooling-off period of 40 days before a strike is declared in an essential service, in so far as it is designed to provide the parties with a period of reflection, may be not automatically contrary to the principles of freedom of association. Any clause deferring action for a certain period may enable both parties to go back to bargaining and possibly reach an agreement without having recourse to a strike.[57] However, time constraints are proportionate only insofar as they do not render a collective action at a later time virtually ineffective.

Also under Article 6 of the European Social Charter the exhaustion of a conciliation/mediation procedures requirement before conducting a strike is acceptable as long as such machinery is not so slow that the effect of a strike is severely affected.[58]

53. *Ibid.*, Report No. 233, paras 668 and 669.
54. *Ibid.*, Report No. 378, Case No. 3147, paras 561 et seqq.; *CFA*, Report No. 373, Case No. 3084, para. 871.
55. *ECSR*, Conclusions 2014, Norway, Article 6§4 – e.g., the Government intervened to end disputes in the health sector, oil sector and in security guard sector; Conclusions (2014, Iceland, Article 6§4 – e.g., the Icelandic Parliament adopted legislation to terminate a strike in the aviation sector.
56. *ECSR*, Conclusions 2014, Norway, Article 6§4.
57. *ILO*, 2006, 554.
58. *ECSR*, Conclusions 2004, Czech Republic, Article 6§4.

4.2.2 *Prior Notice*

Where the law requires workers and their organizations to give a prior notice of their intention to strike, again the required notice period should not be so long as to unduly restrict the right to strike. Significantly shorter periods of notice should be required where a preceding period of conciliation and mediation is already lengthy and has enabled the remaining matters in dispute to be clearly identified.[59]

Notice periods that are applicable in general to all types of establishment should be short, whereas those applying specifically in essential services or services of social or public interest may reasonably be longer. The CFA has found that an obligation to give prior notice to the employer before calling a strike may be considered acceptable,[60] and a 20-day notice period in the case of services of social or public interest does not undermine the principles of freedom of association.[61] However, the ILO CEACR has considered an advance notice of 60 days to be excessive.[62]

Periods of notice or cooling-off periods prescribed in connection with pre-strike conciliation procedures are also in conformity with Article 6 § 4 of the European Social Charter if they are of a reasonable duration.[63] By contrast, the requirement to notify the duration of the strike to the employer prior to strike action is contrary to article 6 § 4 of the Social Charter, even for essential public services.[64]

4.2.3 *Arbitration Requirements*

The CFA and the CEACR both agree that when employees are legitimately excluded from exercising the right to strike, they must enjoy sufficient options to protect their interests, i.e., replacement means including appropriate, impartial and prompt conciliation and arbitration procedures. Such replacement must ensure that workers can participate at all stages of the process determining wages and working conditions, and that arbitrated working conditions are binding on the employer and are fully and promptly applied.[65] The CFA has generally accepted that provision may be made for recourse to conciliation, mediation and voluntary arbitration procedures in industrial disputes *before* a strike may be called, provided that the guarantees just mentioned are in place.[66] This aims at creating additional options for a voluntary agreement between both

59. *ILC*, 2012, 145.
60. *ILO*, 2006, 552; *CFA*, Report No. 333, Case No. 2251, para. 996.
61. *ILO*, 2006, 553; *CFA*, Report No. 309, Case No. 1912, para. 365.
62. *CEACR* Observations 2011 (United Republic of Tanzania).
63. *ECSR*, Conclusions 1998, Cyprus, Article 6§4.
64. *Ibid.*, Conclusions 2006, Italy, Article 6§4.
65. *ILO*, 2006, Chapter 10, para. 596; *CFA*, Report No. 336, Case No. 2340, para. 649.
66. *CFA*, Report, 1994a, para. 171.

parties with external help. Compulsory arbitration, however, is regularly acceptable only if provided for in the collective agreement as a means of settling disputes, or if approved by the parties during bargaining carried out regarding the problems which gave rise to the industrial dispute in question.

4.3 Requirement of Retaining a Minimum Service

The retention of a '*minimum service*' – i.e., the continued provision of service by a part of the workforce – may be required in situations in which a substantive restriction or total prohibition of strike action would not be justified but where, without calling into question the right to strike of the majority of workers, it is necessary to ensure that users' basic needs are met and that facilities operate safely.[67] For avoiding damages which are irreversible or out of all proportion to the occupational interests of the parties to the dispute, as well as damages to third parties, namely the users or consumers who suffer the economic effects of collective disputes, authorities can impose a system of determining minimum service in services of public utility (*services d'utilité publique*) rather than impose an outright ban on strikes.[68]

4.3.1 Minimum Safety Service

The CFA has considered that a '*minimum safety service*' may be imposed in all cases of strike action for ensuring the safety of persons, the prevention of accidents and the maintenance of machinery and equipment. It further stated that restrictions on the right to strike in certain sectors to the extent necessary to comply with statutory safety requirements are acceptable.[69]

4.3.2 Minimum Operational Service

The CFA has defined '*minimum operational services*' as being those intended to maintain a certain level of production or services of the company or institution in which the strike takes place. The Committee has stated that the establishment of minimum services during a strike should only be possible in (1) services the interruption of which would endanger the life, personal safety or health of the whole or part of the population (essential services in the strict sense of the term); (2) services which are not essential in the strict sense of the term but where the extent and duration of a strike might be such as to result in an acute national crisis endangering the normal living conditions of the population; and (3) public services of fundamental importance while strikes may not be banned.[70]

67. *Ibid.*, para. 162.
68. *Ibid.*, 1994a, paras 159 and 160.
69. *ILO*, 2006, 604 et seq.; *CFA*, Report No. 310, Case No. 1931, para. 496.
70. *ILO*, 2006, 606.

Regularly the CFA has considered that the conditions were met for requiring that minimum operational services be maintained in the event of a strike in sectors like the ferry services on islands;[71] the services provided by the National Ports Enterprise;[72] the underground transport service;[73] rail transport service;[74] postal services;[75] refuse collection services;[76] education sector;[77] the Mint, banking services and the petroleum sector.[78]

For determining minimum services to be maintained and the minimum number of workers providing them, the CFA has stated that this should involve not only the public authorities, but also the relevant employers' and workers' organizations. This not only allows a careful exchange of views on what should be considered the minimum services that are strictly necessary, but also contributes to guaranteeing that the scope of the minimum service does not result in the strike becoming ineffective in practice because of its limited impact, and to dissipating possible impressions on the trade union organizations that the strike has come to nothing because of over-generous and unilaterally fixed minimum services.[79] Furthermore, it is important for provisions regarding the minimum service to be established clearly, to be applied strictly and made known to those concerned in due time.[80] If there is any disagreement between the parties as to the number and duties of the workers concerned by a minimum service, legislation should provide for any such disagreement to be settled by an independent body and not by the ministry of labour, or the public enterprise concerned.[81]

The CFA also found that a definitive ruling on whether the level of minimum services was indispensable or not – made in full knowledge of the facts – can be pronounced only by the judicial authorities, in so far as it depends on a thorough knowledge of the structure and functioning of the enterprises and establishments concerned and of the real impact of the strike action.[82]

The CEACR adopted a similar approach regarding minimum operational services (which it accepts in essential services in the strict sense when legislation

71. *Ibid.*, 615; CFA, Report No. 336, Case No. 2324, para.282.
72. *ILO*, 2006, 616; *CFA*, Report No. 321, Case No. 2066, para. 340.
73. *ILO*, 2006, 617 et seq.; *CFA*, Report No. 320, Case No. 2057, para. 780.
74. *ILO*, 2006, 619 et seq.; *CFA*, Report No. 308, Case No. 1923, para. 221.
75. *ILO*, 2006, 622; *CFA*, Report No. 316, Case No. 1985, para. 324.
76. *ILO*, 2006, 623.
77. *Ibid.*, 625; *CFA*, Report No. 330, Case No. 2173, para. 297.
78. *ILO*, 2006, 624; *CFA*, Report No. 309, Case No. 1865 para. 149; CFA, Report No. 337, Case No. 2355, para. 630.
79. *ILO*, 2006, 612; *CFA*, Report No. 338, Case No. 2373 para. 381.
80. *ILO*, 2006, 611; *CFA*, Report No. 330, Case No. 2212, para. 751.
81. *ILO*, 2006, 613; *CFA*, Report No. 320, Case No. 2044, para. 753; *Ibid.*, Report No. 376, Case No. 3096, para. 890.
82. *ILO*, 2006, 614; *CFA*, Report No. 304, Case No. 1866, para. 114; *Ibid.*, Report No. 376, Case No. 3096, para. 891.

does not ban strike action, and in companies and institutions which provide 'services of public utility'). The Committee noted, however, that in practice governments frequently determine unilaterally, without consultation, the level of minimum services required, by demanding a specific percentage of services to be provided during strikes.[83] In the view of the CEACR, a minimum service 'should meet at least two requirements. First, it must genuinely and exclusively be a *minimum service*, that is, one which is limited to the operations which are strictly necessary to meet the basic needs of the population or the minimum requirements of the service, while maintaining the effectiveness of the pressure brought to bear. Second, since this system restricts one of the essential means of pressure available to workers to defend their economic and social interests, their organizations should be able, if they so wish, to participate in defining such a service, along with employers and the public authorities. It would be highly desirable for negotiations on the definition of the organization of the minimum service not to be held during a labour dispute, so that all parties can examine the matter with the necessary objectivity and detachment. The parties might also envisage the establishment of a joint or independent body responsible for examining rapidly and without formalities the difficulties raised by the definition and application of such a minimum service and empowered to issue enforceable decisions'.[84]

The main principles developed by the ILO supervisory bodies in respect of the minimum service requirements can be summarized as follows: (i) the organizations of workers should be able to participate along with the employers and the public authorities in defining the minimum service; (ii) in case of disagreement among the parties, the minimum service should be defined by a joint or independent body; and (iii) the minimum service must genuinely and exclusively be a minimum service.[85]

Also under Article 6 § 4 of the European Social Charter the establishment of a minimum service requirement is conditional on specific guarantees: workers or their representatives must be involved in determining, on an equal footing with employers,[86] the nature of the 'minimum service'[87] required, i.e., in determining what a reasonable minimum service would be and how and by how many workers it has to be provided.[88] In case there is no agreement on the establishment of such minimum service, adequate means for replacing it must be available.

83. *ILC*, 2012, 138; *CEACR*, Observations 2011 (Bulgaria; Romania).
84. *CFA*, Report, 1994a, para. 161.
85. *ILC*, 2012, 136 et seqq.
86. *ECSR*, Conclusions 2014, Article 6§4, Serbia.
87. *Ibid.*, Czech Republic, Estonia, Bosnia and Herzegovina, Lithuania, Russian Federation, Serbia.
88. *Novitz*, 2003, 312.

4.4 Requisitioning or Back-to-Work Orders

The requisitioning of workers of a company or institution in which a strike is taking place, that is, a *back-to-work order*, has been brought on different occasions before the CFA, which has laid down the following principles in its case law:

> Where a total and prolonged strike in a vital sector of the economy might cause a situation in which the life, health or personal safety of the population might be endangered, a back-to-work order might be lawful, if applied to a specific category of staff in the event of a strike whose scope and duration could cause such a situation. However, back-to-work requirements outside such cases must be refrained from.[89] The use of the military, and requisitioning orders to break a strike over occupational claims, unless these actions aim at maintaining essential services in circumstances of the utmost gravity, constitutes a serious violation of the freedom of association.[90]

Although it is recognized that a stoppage in services or undertakings such as transport companies, railways and the oil sector might disturb the normal life of the community, it can hardly be claimed that this incidence could cause a state of acute national emergency. The Committee has therefore considered that measures taken to mobilize workers in services of this kind are restricting workers' right to strike.[91] Also the requisitioning of railway workers during a strike, the threat of dismissal of strike pickets, the recruitment of underpaid workers and a ban on joining a trade union in order to break up lawful and peaceful strikes in services which are not essential in the strict sense of the term are not in accordance with freedom of association.[92]

The CEACR also restricted requisitioning to circumstances of utmost gravity or to ensure the operation of essential services in the strict sense of the term; otherwise, it considered that requisitioning could be abused as a means of terminating labour disputes and therefore should be avoided.[93]

4.5 The Hiring of Workers During a Strike

The CFA has considered the replacement of strikers to be justified only (a) in the event of a strike in an essential service in which strikes are forbidden by law, and (b) when a situation of acute national crisis arises.[94]

Where an essential public service, such as the telephone service, is interrupted by an unlawful strike, a government may have to assume the responsibility of assuring its functioning in the interest of the community and,

89. *ILO*, 2006, 634; *CFA*, Report No. 333, Case No. 2281, para. 634.
90. *ILO*, 2006, 635; *CFA*, Report No. 333, Case No. 2288, para. 831.
91. *ILO*, 2006, 637; *CFA*, Report No. 337, Case No. 2249, para. 1478.
92. *ILO*, 2006, 638.
93. *Ibid.*, 163.
94. *CFA*, Report, 1996d, paras 570 and 574.

for this purpose, may consider it expedient to call in other persons to perform the duties which have been suspended and take the necessary steps to enable such persons to be installed in the premises where such duties are performed.[95] By contrast, the CFA has emphasized that the hiring of workers to break a strike in a sector which cannot be regarded as essential in the strict sense of the term constitutes a serious violation of freedom of association.[96]

The CEACR has considered that a special problem arises when legislation or practice allows enterprises to recruit workers to replace their own employees on *legal* strike. The difficulty is even more serious if, under legislative provisions or case-law, strikers do not, as of right, find their job waiting for them at the end of the dispute. The Committee considered that this type of provision or practice seriously impairs the right to strike and affects the free exercise of trade union rights, so that legislation should provide for genuine protection in this respect.[97] In principle, the CEACR recalled that the maintenance of the employment relationship is a normal legal consequence of recognition of the right to strike.[98] Similarly, the CFA has also considered that if a strike is legal, recourse to the use of labour drawn from outside the undertaking to replace strikers for an indeterminate period entails a risk of derogation from the right to strike, which may affect the free exercise of trade union rights.[99]

5 COMPENSATORY MEASURES

The CFA has stated that where the right to strike is restricted or denied in essential services or in the public service, adequate protection should be provided to the workers to compensate for these restrictions.[100] This should include a corresponding denial of the right to lock out.

Replacing strike action by unilaterally imposed compulsory arbitration, however, is rarely acceptable. This is due to the fact that the right to strike as an intrinsic corollary to collective bargaining is not coinciding with a right to a fair remuneration or a general right to fair and just working conditions. It additionally represents a form of worker self-determination, the right to have a say in establishing one's own working conditions. Such right is for employment contracts not automatically guaranteed by reaching an agreement to establish the contractual relationship as such. In contracts of employment, bargaining terms and conditions individually is rarely an option; they are much rather set by the employer on a unilateral basis. An applicant would usually have the choice between rejecting the employment relationship and accepting the conditions

95. *ILO*, 2006, 639.
96. *Ibid.*, 632; *CFA*, Report No. 335, Case No. 1865, para. 826; *Ibid.*, Report No. 376, Case No. 3096, para. 893.
97. *CFA* Report, 1994a, para. 175.
98. *ILC*, 2012, 151 et seq.
99. *ILO*, 2006, 633; *CFA*, Report No. 333, Case No. 2251, para. 998.
100. *ILO*, 2006, 595; *CFA*, Report No. 337, Case No. 2244, para. 1269.

presented. Workers' opportunity of influencing the employment conditions is regularly provided only by collective bargaining, and therefore closely connected also to the option of conducting collective action.

Where important third party rights are endangered by the withdrawal of services, the state's responsibility for guaranteeing essential services to the population may tip the balance in favour of restricting the right to collective action or even replacing it by compulsory arbitration. This could, however, only be a means of last resort, if all other options for establishing a necessary level of services to the general population fail. Should collective action be compulsorily replaced by arbitration, it would therefore not suffice that the outcome in terms of improved working conditions is fair and adequate, but worker involvement in the process of establishing the conditions would also have to be secured.

According to CFA case law, *compulsory arbitration to end a strike* is usually not adequate, the exception being strikes in essential services in the strict sense of the term, an acute national crisis, or in the public service.[101]

Where governments hold specific services interrupted by a strike as being essential, this is not always supported by the facts of the case; inconveniences to some part of the population, such as the interruption of services of metropolitan transport, could rather be balanced by the establishment of a minimum service.[102] The CFA has thus established[103] that legislation cannot impose compulsory binding arbitration as a replacement for strike action, neither at the outset nor during the course of an industrial dispute, except in the case of an essential service, or when a regularly non-essential service is interrupted for so long that it endangers the life, safety or health of the whole or part of the population (and thereby becomes essential), or when, after protracted and fruitless negotiations, it is obvious that the deadlock in bargaining will not be broken without some initiative on the part of the authorities.[104] Government-imposed compulsory arbitration is not acceptable once a minimum service could have been established for guaranteeing that basic needs of the population are met.[105]

Regarding the mediation and arbitration proceedings, the CFA has further stated that it is essential that 'all the members of the bodies entrusted with such functions should not only be strictly impartial but, if the confidence of both sides, on which the successful outcome even of compulsory arbitration really depends, is to be gained and maintained, they should also appear to be impartial both to the employers and to the workers concerned'.[106] For example, the CFA considered[107] that the appointment by a minister of all five members of the

101. *ILO*, 2006, 564 et seq.; *CFA*, Report No. 338, Case no. 2329, para. 1275; *Ibid.*, Report No. 380 Case No. 3126, para. 722.
102. *CFA*, Report No. 377, Case No. 3107, paras 340 et seqq.
103. *Ibid.*, Report No. 236, para. 144.
104. *Ibid.*, Report, 1994a, paras 256 et seqq.
105. *CFA*, Report No. 378, Case No. 3147 paras 561 et seqq.; *Ibid.*, Report No. 372, Case No. 3038, paras 468 et seqq.
106. *ILO*, 2006, 598.
107. *Ibid.*, 599; *CFA*, Report No. 328, Case No. 2114, para. 406.

Essential Services Arbitration Tribunal calls into question the independence and impartiality of such a tribunal, as well as the confidence of the parties in such a system. The representative organizations of workers and employers should, respectively, be able to select the members of such arbitration tribunal who represent them.

6 CONCLUSION

The exercise of the right to strike in essential services is a complex matter also under international law. It implies that the right balance must be struck between the fundamental right to strike (which is a necessary element of a labour relations system based on collective agreements) and legitimate interests of the general public, whose dependency on the service interrupted by strikes defines the notion of 'essential services'. In determining possible restrictions to strike action for preserving a basic level of such services, the state is considering the consumers' dependency on their continuous availability. However, the restrictions must not be more intrusive than necessary for protecting consumers' legitimate interests. To decide otherwise by accepting as a justification for imposing restrictions also the prevention of economic loss for undertakings (which represents an inherent consequence of any collective action) or the consumers' wish for receiving full services at any time would affect the right to strike in a disproportionate manner. Substantive limitations to the right to strike must remain strictly proportionate in scope and be open to judicial review. Any negative consequences for the effectiveness of collective bargaining must be compensated as far as possible.

Bibliography

Cohen, Tamara/Le Roux, Rochelle, Limitations of the Right to Strike in the Public Sector and Essential Services, 2015

Gernigon, Bernard/Odero, Alberto/Guido, Horacio, ILO Principles Concerning the Right to Strike, International Labour Review 1998 Vol. 137 No. 4, 57 et seqq.

Hänsle, Walter, Streik und Daseinsvorsorge, 2016

Sädevirta, Markus, Freedom of Association and the Right to Strike, Europäische Zeitschrift für Arbeitsrecht 2016, 445 et seq.

Morris, Gillian, Strikes in Essential Services, 1986

Novitz, Tonia, International and European Protection of the Right to Strike, 2003

Novitz, Tonia, The Internationally Recognized Right to Strike, International Journal of Comparative Labour Law & Industrial Relations 2014, 357 et seq.

Novitz, Tonia, The Restricted Freedom to Strike, Comparative Labor Law & Policy Journal 2017

Schlachter, Monika, The Right to Strike: a need to align different interpretations, in Appiah/Van der Heijden, Ensuring Coherence in Fundamental Labor Rights Case Law: Challenges and Opportunities, 2016

Schlachter, Monika, Strikes in Essential Services under International Law, Bulletin of Comparative Labour Relations 2018 Vol. 100, 7 et seq.

Servais, Jean-Michel, ILO Law and the Right to Strike, Canadian Labour & Employment Law Journal 2008, 148 et seq.

Smit, Nicola, International Developments Regarding the Implementation of the Right to Strike, Comparative Labor Law & Policy Journal 2017 vol. 38, 395 et seq.

Weiss, Manfred, International Standards: A Complex Public-Private Mix, International Journal of Comparative Labour Law & Industrial Relations 2013, 7 et seq.

ILO publications and case law

CEACR (Committee of Experts on the Application of Conventions and Recommendations), Observations 2011 (Bulgaria; Romania; United Republic of Tanzania)

CFA (Committee on Freedom of Association), Report No. 304, Case No. 1719 and No. 1866

CFA (Committee on Freedom of Association), Report No. 308, Case No. 1923

CFA (Committee on Freedom of Association), Report No. 309, Case No. 1865, No. 1916 and No. 1912

CFA (Committee on Freedom of Association), Report No. 310, Case No. 1931

CFA (Committee on Freedom of Association), Report No. 316, Case No. 1985

CFA (Committee on Freedom of Association), Report No. 320, Case No. 2044 and No. 2057

CFA (Committee on Freedom of Association), Report No. 321, Case No. 2066

CFA (Committee on Freedom of Association), Report No. 328, Case No. 2114

CFA (Committee on Freedom of Association), Report No. 330, Case No. 2173 and No. 2212

CFA (Committee on Freedom of Association), Report No. 333, Case No. 2251, No. 2277, No. 2281 and No. 2288

CFA (Committee on Freedom of Association), Report No. 335, Case No. 1865

CFA (Committee on Freedom of Association), Report No. 336, Case No. 2329, No. 2340 and No. 2383

CFA (Committee on Freedom of Association), Report No. 337, Case No. 2244, No. 2249 and No. 2355

CFA (Committee on Freedom of Association), Report No. 338, Case No. 2348, No. 2363, No. 2364, No. 2373 and No. 2403

CFA (Committee on Freedom of Association), Report No. 372, Case No. 3022 and No. 3038

CFA (Committee on Freedom of Association), Report No. 373, Case No. 3084

CFA (Committee on Freedom of Association), Report No. 374, Case No. 3057

CFA (Committee on Freedom of Association), Report No. 376, Case No. 3096

CFA (Committee on Freedom of Association), Report No. 377, Case No. 3107
CFA (Committee on Freedom of Association), Report No. 378, Case No. 3147 No. 372,
CFA (Committee on Freedom of Association), Report No. 380 Case No. 3126
CFA (Committee on Freedom of Association), Report No. 284 Case no. 1626
ILC (International Labour Conference), 81st Session (1994) Report of the Committee on the Application of Standards, at 25/91: C 87 Germany
ILC (International Labour Conference), General Survey on Freedom of Association and Collective Bargaining, 1994, para. 151 (ILC 1994a)
ILC (International Labour Conference), General Survey on the Fundamental Conventions Concerning Rights at Work in Light of the ILO Declaration on Social Justice for a Fair Globalization, 2012
ILO (International Labour Organisation, Freedom of Association: Digest of Decisions and Principles of the Freedom of Association Committee of the Governing Body of the ILO, 2006
ECSR publications and case law
ECSR (European Committee of Social Rights), Conclusions I (1969), Statement of Interpretation on Article 6§4
ECSR (European Committee of Social Rights), Conclusions X-1 (1987), Norway (regarding Article 31 of the Charter)
ECSR (European Committee of Social Rights), Conclusions XIV-1 (1998)
ECSR (European Committee of Social Rights), Conclusions XVII-1 (2004), Czech Republic
ECSR (European Committee of Social Rights), Conclusions XIX-1 (2006)
ECSR (European Committee of Social Rights), Conclusions XX-3 (2014), Article 6§4 in respect of: Czech Republic, Estonia, Bosnia and Herzegovina, Lithuania, Russian Federation, and Serbia___
ECSR (European Committee of Social Rights), Confederation of Independent Trade Unions in Bulgaria (CITUB), Confederation of Labour 'Podkrepa' and European Trade Union Confederation (ETUC) v. Bulgaria, Complaint No. 32/2005, Decision on the merits of 16 October 2006, §24
ECSR (European Committee of Social Rights), European Confederation of Police (EuroCOP) v. Ireland, Complaint No. 83/2012, Decision on the admissibility and merits of 2 December 2013, §§71–72; §§ 201–214

PART III Country Report

CHAPTER 3

Australia

Richard B. Naughton & Marilyn J. Pittard

1 GENERAL BACKGROUND: COUNTRY PROFILE

A snapshot of Australia's current workforce and employment data[1] shows that over 12.3 million workers are employed; unemployment is steady at 5.5% of the workforce; and the participation rate is 65.2%. Fifty-four per cent of the workforce is male; whilst casual workers comprise 25% of the workforce, with a slightly higher percentage of women causal workers (nearly 27%) than men casual workers (23%). Unionization in the private sector is 13.3% for men and 15.4% for women, with the percentage of public sector workers in a union reflecting higher rates of unionization at 39% in 2016, though there has been a decrease since 2011. Industrial action has also declined significantly, especially in the period 2013 to 2018 (see chart in the Annex). The total number of disputes in the year ending March 2018 was only 153, with 137,700 working days lost, representing the low figure of less than 0.11 days per worker in the Australian workforce.

Australia's labour law regulation under the *Fair Work Act 2009* (Cth) (*FW Act 2009*) provides for a national system of collective bargaining for enterprise level agreements, underpinned by a safety net. This safety net comprises two sources – legislated minimum labour standards (called National Employment Standards) and modern awards, which are statutory instruments providing for minimum pay and conditions in a range of employment matters.[2] Whilst collective agreements are at enterprise level, modern awards are usually industry based and sometimes occupationally based. This system under the *FW Act 2009* evolved from the system of conciliation and arbitration introduced by the *Conciliation and Arbitration Act 1904* (Cth), which had been in existence for about nine decades.

2 COLLECTIVE LABOUR RELATIONS

The conciliation and arbitration system had enabled collective agreements negotiated by unions and employers to be binding and enforceable; and

1. The data is derived from *Australian Bureau of Statistics*, 2017.
2. *Pittard/Naughton*, 2015, ch. 11, esp. 543 et seqq. for discussion of the safety net; and ch. 12 for discussion of making enterprise agreements. *See also McCallum*, 2011.

empowered an independent tribunal to arbitrate industrial awards to prescribe minimum terms and conditions, where the parties themselves could not settle the industrial disputes by conciliation. Awards then were comprehensive documents covering a broad range of employment matters and reached a peak number of approximately 4,500 awards.[3] They were the forerunners to today's modern awards which are, after a rationalization process, only 123 in number. There were originally no legislated conditions in the federal system due to constitutional limitations on the parliament's ability to legislate directly, and the tribunal could not set general conditions applying to all Australian workers.[4] Though the system had changed since 1904 – and very dramatically for the period 2005 to 2009 when a less regulated system with significantly diminished protections for employees existed – there were some constant features of the system that endured through these changes, namely an independent tribunal; emphasis on protection of weaker groups and the 'public interest'; and unions.[5]

Whilst the states of Australia historically and over many decades had their own separate systems of industrial relations, since the *FW Act 2009* the federal system is national – as all states, except Western Australia, have referred their industrial relations law-making powers to the Commonwealth. This chapter focuses on the national federal law, but refers to relevant state law from time to time.

The Constitution of Australia, unlike some countries' constitutions, does not enshrine any labour rights. However it confers on the Commonwealth Parliament the power to make laws with respect to conciliation and arbitration to prevent and settle industrial disputes, which are interstate in nature.[6] Since the mid-2000s the constitutional power to make laws with respect to corporations[7] has been used by Parliament as the main the source of power to legislate for labour law and relations.[8]

3. *Pittard/Naughton*, 2015, 543.
4. The industrial tribunal was, in fact, able to provide award coverage to whole industries (up to the introduction of modern awards). However, the language of section 51(35) of the Constitution meant that the tribunal's powers were limited to assuming jurisdiction over industrial disputes that were *interstate* in nature. In these circumstances, the High Court endorsed the practice of creating interstate industrial disputes on paper – unions served demands (logs of claims) on all interstate employers in the industry, and the dispute was created when the interstate employers served did not agree to the demands. This process gave rise to the traditional awards (that existed prior to modern awards) having broad industry coverage (see below, note 6).
5. *Naughton*, 2017. For features of the system, see *Pittard*, 2013.
6. Section 51(xxxv) of the Constitution.
7. Section 51(xx) of the Constitution. *See Pittard/Naughton*, 2015, ch 10.
8. For sources of labour law, *see* generally, *Pittard/Butterworth*, 2015.

3 THE RIGHT TO STRIKE

3.1 Collective Labour Rights

The three fundamental labour rights – the right to organize, the right to bargain collectively and the right to strike – are recognized in the *FW Act 2009*, although with qualifications and sometimes not fully in accord with the International Labour Organization (ILO) conventions that theoretically underpin these rights.

Collective bargaining co-existed with compulsory arbitration in the period for 90 years from 1904.[9] The right to form and organize trade unions was an essential part of the new conciliation and arbitration system as it was thought that unions were necessary to represent employees in arbitration, rather than the then Commonwealth Court of Conciliation and Arbitration dealing with many individual employees.[10] Hence the system conferred trade union recognition and legal status on registered unions in the first Act regulating conciliation and arbitration. It also provided protections against victimization of unionists. The early concept of federal regulation of industrial disputes, however, did not envisage a right to strike: industrial action, both strikes and lockouts, were prohibited under the legislation until the late 1920s under pain of monetary penalty. The underlying philosophy was that the formal system of dispute resolution replaced the need for industrial action. The prohibition on strikes was linked then to the arbitration system – if industrial action took place in the course of negotiations for collective agreements that strike action might breach the *Conciliation and Arbitration Act*. It would expose the unions and the striking workers to monetary penalty for contravening the prohibition on strikes, to litigation in the industrial torts under the common law, and to the risk of awards of damages and restraining orders (injunctions) by the courts. The idea was that instead of taking direct industrial action, the parties could refer the dispute to the tribunal for settlement by means of conciliation, and, if that failed, by arbitration.

Whilst the prohibition against strikes was repealed fully by the early 1930s, various controls on strikes existed under the federal legislation and, as will be further discussed below, it was not until 1993 that a limited right to strike was conferred whilst collective bargaining was taking place.[11] For the first time the ILO conventions and other international laws were recognized to provide the basis for a right to strike.[12] The nature of the right to bargain collectively nevertheless had changed under 1993 reform legislation.[13] The form of collective

9. *Macintyre/Mitchell*, 1989.
10. The High Court of Australia confirmed the constitutional validity of provisions conferring trade union registration in the case of *Jumbunna Coal Mine NL v Victorian Coal Miners' Association* [1908] HCA 95, (1908) 6 CLR 309. *See Pittard/Naughton*, 2015, ch 9
11. *Pittard/Naughton*, 2014, 96; Industrial Relations Reform Act 1993 (Cth).
12. *Pittard/Naughton*, 2015, ch 17.
13. Industrial Relations Reform Act 1993 (Cth).

bargaining was enterprise level bargaining, with industry bargaining permitted in restricted circumstances only. That concept persisted under the *FW Act 2009* and it remains the feature of bargaining under Australian law.

3.2 General Background: The Right to Strike

3.2.1 Lawful and Unlawful Strikes and Australia's Industrial Relations System

It is frequently postulated that the *right to strike* is available so that workers are able to exercise some countervailing power to the authority of capital.[14] There is an on-going argument whether the right to strike exists merely as a subset of the principles of freedom of association, or is a fundamental human right.[15]

The various relevant international labour standards promoting collective bargaining[16] indicate that, in order for any system of collective bargaining to be effective, it must take place within a framework that respects the independence and autonomy of the parties.[17] Institutional bodies within the ILO (for example the Committee of Freedom of Association and the Committee of Experts) have long recognized that the right to strike exists as an unusual means available to workers for the protection of their interests. What the international conventions envisage is some form of 'voluntary and free bargaining',[18] whereby restrictions on the right to strike can be justified in only the most limited of circumstances.

In spite of this, it has been acknowledged that some restrictions must be placed on the right to strike, in acknowledgment of the fact that it is not an absolute right. It is assumed, for example, that there may be some areas of work, such as the public sector, the armed forces, or the police, where the outcome of any strike activity is likely to so adversely affect and inconvenience members of the public, that it should be the subject of significant limitation.[19] These areas can be described as 'essential services' industries, where on-going strike action is likely to cause more harm to the *community at large* than any individual employer or employers. Well-established ILO standards indicate that the right to strike should not necessarily apply to essential services, 'whose interruption would threaten the life, personal safety, or health of all or part of the population'.[20] It is possible that the workers in these industries may have access to the possibility of engaging in forms of industrial action so long as they have access

14. *Pittard/Naughton*, 2015. *McCrystal*, 2010, *1; Kahn-Freund/Hepple*, 1989, *1; Ewing*, 1991.
15. *McCrystal*, 2010, 1; *Ewing*, 2004, 41; *Novitz*, 2003, Pt 1; *Novitz/Fenwick*, 2010; *Fudge*, 2007, 38 et seqq.
16. ILO Right to Organise and Collective Bargaining Convention 1949 (ILO Convention No 98); ILO Convention concerning Freedom of Association and Protection of the Right to Organise (ILO Convention No 87).
17. *Carabetta*, 2014, 276.
18. *Gerignon/Odero/Guido*, 2000, 27.
19. See, e.g., discussion of these matters by *Carabetta*, 2014, 293-4.
20. *ILO*, 2006.

to alternative safeguards such as the availability of forms of mediation, conciliation and arbitration.[21]

It is evident that what constitutes an 'essential service' is extremely limited under the ILO framework definition, but it is evident that the armed forces, the police, and other emergency services would satisfy the requirements of an 'essential service' (as services whose interruption would 'threaten the life, personal safety or health of all or part of the population').[22] In addition, it appears that other services, such as a nation's water supply, could conceivably become an essential service, depending on the length and context of the industrial action.[23]

In many ways these *international principles* are somewhat difficult to impose directly upon the Australian system that has always proved a little idiosyncratic within the international system. It is necessary to consider the historical antecedents of the present Australian system as a 'conciliation and arbitration' system where the principal function conducted by the independent tribunal was that of *dispute settlement*. In such a system all strikes were, strictly speaking, unlawful.[24] The original founders of the conciliation and arbitration system wrote that this system established at the outset of the twentieth century would substitute 'for the rude and barbarous processes of the strike and lockout',[25] and the result of its adoption would be that *reason would displace force*.

Thus, under the traditional conciliation and arbitration system operating in Australia from 1904 until 1994, there was *no legal right to strike*. The tribunal-based system functioned according to the premise that the industrial parties resolved their differences in accordance with more civilized strategies. In reality, of course, there were many illegal (or unlawful) strikes during the conciliation and arbitration phase.[26]

There may, however, have been a problem in a system that simply outlawed all strikes, in the way it dealt with the issue of strikes in *essential services*. Niland possibly was making this point when he wrote that because all strikes were outlawed, it was not possible 'to effectively prohibit those types of strikes which are seen as *especially* detrimental'.[27]

As noted above, the general prohibition on strikes was removed in the late 1920s by amendment to the *Conciliation and Arbitration Act*. After that strikes remained unlawful in a number of ways – through potential liability under the industrial torts at common law for damage inflicted by striking workers; and, for

21. See *infra* Section 5.
22. *Carabetta*, 2014, 297.
23. *Ibid.*
24. *Pittard/Naughton*, 2015, ch. 10; *Peetz*, 2012, 162.
25. *Higgins*, 1915, 14.
26. See, for example, figures concerning strike density in Australia for periods between 1967-1982; 1983-990; 1991-996; and under various enterprise bargaining legislation: *Peetz*, 2012, 166 et seqq.; see also *Creighton/Ford/Mitchell*, 1993, 1137 et seq.
27. *Niland*, 2008, 52 (Here the emphasis is added).

contravening bans clauses (or 'no strike' clauses in awards), injunctions could be granted and fines imposed. Later on, in 1977, when the *Trade Practices Act 1974* (Cth) was extended to apply to unions, liability could be imposed for secondary boycott conduct in industrial disputes.[28] In 1993, the passage of the *Industrial Relations Reform Act* established the form of enterprise bargaining legislation that continues in similar form today in the *FW Act 2009*. This allows for a *limited right to strike* (or the ability to take 'protected industrial action') in those circumstances where parties are negotiating fresh enterprise agreements at a workplace.

No industrial action is permitted prior to the enterprise agreement's nominal expiry date. This rule does not distinguish between essential or non-essential services – it applies across the board. Protected industrial action is however permissible after that expiry date while parties are engaged in bargaining towards a new enterprise agreement. The provisions dealing with protected action are now consolidated in Part 3-3 of the *FW Act 2009*.[29] These provisions allow forms of 'employee claim action' or 'employer response action' to be undertaken when parties are negotiating a *single enterprise agreement*.[30] Notwithstanding these arrangements, under the bargaining provisions that have been in place since 1993 the statutory tribunal has always had power to step in to either suspend or terminate these forms of industrial action (and it may be in this context that the tribunal is called upon to take action in the event of a 'essential services' dispute).[31]

It is notable that this ability to engage in protected action (or strike action) during the negotiation process extends to public sector workers, and it is now reasonably common for Federal public sector workers to take industrial action or vote against proposed public sector agreements that seek to impose cost cutting measures.[32] Indeed there has been a remarkable stand-off between the Federal government and public sector unions and agencies during the current bargaining round, in the period since 2014, which demonstrates a willingness on the part of public sector workers to pursue industrial action in support of improved conditions.

---

28. This prohibition on secondary boycotts is now contained in the *Competition and Consumer Act 2010* (Cth). See further *Pittard/Naughton*, 2015, 1034 et seqq.
29. For discussion, *see McCrystal*, 2012, 114.
30. They do not apply in the case of a multiple employer agreement or a greenfields agreement (*see* section 413(2), *FW Act 2009*). As they stand the provisions require that the forms of protected action for 'employee claim action' are supported by a ballot of workers, and this protection (or immunity) from legal claims (*see* section 415 of the *FW Act 2009*) may be lost if the industrial action that is subsequently taken is not strictly in accordance with the terms of the action that had been the subject of the ballot notice: For further discussion, *see Esso Australia Pty Ltd v The Australian Workers Union; The Australian Workers' Union v Esso Australia Pty Ltd* [2017] HCA 54.
31. See e.g., sections 424 and 431, FW Act 2009.
32. *Bailey/Peetz*, 2015, 405.

An on-going dispute between the public sector bodies and the Federal government gathered pace during 2016 when a number of major agencies including the Department of Human Services, Defence, Immigration and Border Protection (DIBP), and the Australian Tax Office all repeatedly voted down offers made by the Federal government in relation to various public sector agreements.[33] During the course of the year the Community and Public Sector Union (CPSU) had engaged in a campaign of protected industrial action in an effort to progress negotiations with the different agencies. In October 2016 the Fair Work Commission (FWC) *terminated* protected industrial action by employees of DIBP at airports, cruise ship terminals, and major airports around Australia according to the requirements of section 424 of the *FW Act 2009*.[34] In such circumstances once the industrial action is terminated there is initially an onus on the parties themselves to resolve the dispute, but when this fails the tribunal is called upon to *arbitrate* the matter.

It should also be noted that protected action and therefore 'lawful action' is circumscribed with detailed processes. For industrial action to be 'protected', and therefore lawful, it must not only take place during negotiations for an enterprise agreement *after* the nominal expiry date of the existing enterprise agreement, but it also must be authorized by the employees. To be lawfully authorized industrial action, the bargaining representative (usually the union) must first apply for and obtain a 'protected action ballot order' from the FWC approving the form of strike ballot to be put to employees to be covered by the agreement. A 'protected action ballot order' will be made by the FWC only after it is satisfied of certain requirements under the statute, including for example that the bargaining representatives have been genuinely trying to reach agreement. The ballot must be conducted officially (usually by the Commonwealth Electoral Commission) and can only support proposed industrial action where at least 50% of employees to be covered by the agreement have participated in the vote, and a majority (more than 50%) of those employees who voted in support of taking the proposed action. Even where the ballot supports the taking of industrial action, strike notice of three days must be given prior to taking that authorized industrial action.[35] Hence the path to taking lawful industrial action - exercising the right to strike - involves strict compliance with process under the statute, and the involvement of the independent tribunal. The days of going on strike spontaneously by a simple show of hands are long gone - and, should that occur, the *FW Act 2009* would be contravened and the union and employees exposed to the imposition of large fines.

33. *Nicholson/Pekarek/Gahan*, 2017, 315.
34. For further discussion, see *infra*, latter part of Section 5.
35. *See Pittard/Naughton*, 2015, [14.62]-[14.77]. See also *Pittard/Naughton*, 2014, 95-120. A further point is that any protection (or immunity) from legal claims (see section 415 of the *FW Act*) *2009* may be lost if the industrial action that is subsequently taken is not strictly in accordance with the terms of the action as described in or the subject of the ballot notice: For further discussion, *see Esso Australia Pty Ltd v The Australian Workers Union; The Australian Workers' Union v Esso Australia Pty Ltd* [2017] HCA 54.

3.2.2 *Common Law in Action in Industrial Disputes*

The High Court of Australia recently summarized the unlawful nature of all strikes at common law, whether in essential services or other non-essential industries, as follows:

At common law, industrial action in the form of strikes and lock-outs was and is, generally speaking, unlawful. In the scheme of things, it is likely to involve a breach of contract and one or more of the industrial torts of nuisance, besetting or inducing breach of contract, or other forms of tortious interference with economic relations.[36]

Since 1993 and now under the *FW Act 2009*, statute has conferred immunity from civil litigation on unions and participants in industrial action, for example in contract or the industrial torts, where the industrial action has met the requirements for 'protected action' under the statute.[37] Prior to 1993, there was no immunity from civil proceedings under statute to unions, union officials or employees. Thus industrial action, whether it be work stoppages, go slows, work bans and so on that inflicted economic loss on an employer's business or was likely to inflict that damage, could be litigated by employers in court and stopped by a court order of restraining injunctions; and sometimes employers would proceed to seek recovery of the economic harm suffered by pursuing awards of damages in the courts. It was more usual for the dispute to be settled after the grant of an injunction, and employers would not proceed to full hearing for a damages claim

One such case that did go beyond merely seeking injunctive relief involved airline pilots, engaged by four Australian airline companies, who adopted industrial action in the form of working 9.00am to 5.00pm, which considerably disrupted airline schedules, and, ultimately, in a move aimed at minimizing any responsibility for economic loss inflicted on the airlines, the pilots took the dramatic step of resigning their jobs. In these circumstances, without their vital resource, the airlines were unable to fly their planes. The pilots were seeking very large wage increases outside tribunal set guidelines for pay rises. As a matter of past practice, when the pilots had sought pay rises the airline companies had agreed to the demands, as labour costs were not significant compared to capital costs in the industry. However, a changed attitude prevailed

36. *Esso Australia Pty Ltd v The Australian Workers' Union; The Australian Workers' Union v Esso Australia Pty Ltd* [2017] HCA 54, at [30] per Kiefel CJ, Keane, Nettle and Edelman JJ.
37. See FW Act 2009 section 415 which provides:

(1) No action lies under any law (whether written or unwritten) in force in a State or Territory in relation to any industrial action that is protected industrial action unless the industrial action has involved or is likely to involve:
   (a) personal injury; or
   (b) wilful or reckless destruction of, or damage to, property; or
   (c) the unlawful taking, keeping or use of property.

(2) However, subsection (1) does not prevent an action for defamation being brought in relation to anything that occurred in the course of industrial action.

with this dispute – and interestingly, a Labor government supported the airlines in their dispute with the pilots. The four airline companies sued the union, the Australian Federation of Airline Pilots, as well as several union officials as individual defendants, in the industrial torts.[38] The torts claimed were: 'the torts of interference with contractual relations, interference with trade or business by unlawful means, conspiracy, the 'action on the case' and intimidation, in respect of the directive to work 9 am to 5 pm; conspiracy in respect of the resignations; and intimidation in respect of 'strike breakers' warning'.[39] Ultimately the plaintiffs were awarded damages of AUD 6.48 million.

This industrial dispute, referred to in this chapter as the 'Airline pilots dispute 1991', stands out in the history of common law litigation in industrial disputes –first, for the award of considerable damages against the pilots' federation and union officials; and, secondly, because of the direct involvement of the federal government in the strike: by providing RAAF aircraft to fly passengers and also by changing regulations to make it easier for foreign pilots to obtain visas to enter and work for airlines in Australia.[40] The airline industry was changed significantly – as a result, the bulk of Australian pilots could never obtain work in Australia and had to seek work overseas with foreign airline companies.[41] The case also decided that, in this instance of pilots going on strike and employers yielding to the demands, there was no *right to strike* implied in the employment contracts, such that industrial action could not breach the pilots' contracts of employment.[42] As there was then no measure of a right to strike conferred by statute and no such right at common law, the pilots and their union suffered the full force of litigation in the industrial torts.[43]

The issue of common law proceedings and their implications in the case of industrial action arose more recently in December 2017 when the stevedoring company Victoria International Container Terminal (VICT) refused to allocate shifts to a Maritime Union of Australia (MUA) delegate, when he did not have appropriate security documentation. As a consequence union parties engaged in a picket-line, although this was characterized as a 'community protest', but the outcome was that the business of VICT was shut down during the three-week period of the picket, and in the run-up to Christmas. According to VICT, the economic damages it suffered as a result of the 'community protest' were beyond AUD 100 million based on loss of earnings and reputational damages.

38. *Ansett Transport Industries (Operations) Pty Ltd v. Australian Federation of Airline Pilots* (1989) 95 ALR 211; *Ansett Transport Industries (Operations) Pty Ltd v. Australian Federation of Airline Pilots (No 2)* [1991] 2 VR 636.
39. *Pittard/Naughton*, 2015, 1021.
40. See further discussion this chapter at Section 6.
41. *Fox/Howard/Pittard*, 1995, ch. 4.
42. *Ansett Transport Industries (Operations) Pty Ltd v. Australian Federation of Airline Pilots* (1989) 95 ALR 211 at 230-231. See also *Smith*, 1990; *Burgess/Sappey*, 1992.
43. It seems, however, that the plaintiff airline companies never enforced the award of damages so the sum remained unpaid. For further discussion of the pilots' dispute, see also: *McEvoy/Owens*, 1990; *Smith*, 1990; *Burgess/Sappey*, 1992.

During the course of the picket-line, what was termed a 'representative order' was made against the Victorian Trades Hall Council secretary, and injunctions were granted against two unions, the MUA, and the Construction, Forestry, Mining and Energy Union (CFMEU), preventing their officials from attending or organizing the picket or else being within a particular exclusion zone.[44] The alleged causes of action which gave rise to the serious issue to be tried were conspiracy to injure by unlawful means of the picket, which was a tort of nuisance, and conspiracy by unlawful means of trespass to VICT's premises, both intentionally injuring VICT; inducing breaches of VICT's stevedoring contracts or unlawful interference in those contracts; and the tort of nuisance.[45] Ultimately the matter was 'resolved', when it was agreed that VICT would temporarily reinstate the MUA delegate and the picket line was consequently dismantled. Notwithstanding this, however, in January 2018 VICT launched a damages claim for AUD 8 million against the MUA and the CFMEU, arguing the company had suffered loss as a result of their involvement in the picket-line activity.[46]

Had the industrial action in this case been true industrial action and not a community protest *and* taken as 'protected action' (albeit in the limited circumstances that generate 'protected' action), there would have been immunity conferred by section 415 of the *FW Act 2009* in respect of litigation at common law, except in respect of any defamation and injury to persons and property.[47]

Whilst this *FW Act 2009* provision confers a degree of 'right' to strike by protecting participants from common law litigation, the High Court of Australia has recently ruled in *Esso Australia Pty Ltd v. The Australian Workers' Union* that if employees do not strictly adhere to the requirements for protected action in the statute, that action loses its protected status.[48] In this instance the union had contravened an earlier order made by the industrial tribunal to stop industrial action, thereby, held the court, depriving the subsequent industrial action of protected status, because a pre-condition in the statute laid down a requirement that a bargaining representative not contravene orders in relation to the industrial action. Thus, by this interpretation of the statute to include past contraventions, the majority of the High Court narrowed the scope for protected action, thereby exposing the participants in the strike to litigation at common law. In his spirited dissenting judgment, Gageler J was acutely aware of the impact of the majority's interpretation on the lawfulness of industrial action in

44. *Victoria International Container Terminal Ltd t/a VICT v Maritime Union of Australia and Construction, Forestry, Mining and Energy Union; VICT v Hilakari* [2017] VSC 762 (12 December 2017).
45. *Ibid.*, 35.
46. *Workplace Express*, 12 and 19 December 2017, 15 and 22 January 2018.
47. See *supra* note Subsection 3.2 for full text of section 415 *FW Act 2009*.
48. *Esso Australia Pty Ltd v The Australian Workers' Union; The Australian Workers' Union v Esso Australia Pty Ltd* [2017] HCA 54.

the context of a bargaining system.[49] The president of the peak union organization, the Australian Council of Trade Unions (ACTU), was also critical of the impact of the decision on the right to strike saying that: 'The judgment puts in place even higher hurdles working people must face before being able to take so-called 'legal' or 'protected'' industrial action'.[50] Moreover, '[t]here are currently a myriad of complex and onerous rules restricting industrial action to a very limited window with severe penalties should not all these rules and red tape be complied with.'[51]

Thus there are not insignificant hurdles to surmount to render industrial action 'protected industrial action' to attract the immunity in section 415 and to be lawful. This applies to strikes in either essential services or those not categorized as essential – in other words there is no relevant distinction between essential and non-essential services strikes.

4 THE EXPERIENCE WITH STRIKES IN ESSENTIAL SERVICES

Australia has not seen significant strike action in essential services. This is due in large part to the previous prohibitions on strikes under the *Conciliation and Arbitration Act* and the controls by statute on strike action since 1993 where a limited right to strike has been available whilst negotiating an agreement. It is also no doubt because the culture is that employees providing key services are reluctant to strike and indeed may have no strike clauses in their union rules.[52] A notable historical exception was the nurses' strike of the 1986 where nurses went on strike for 50 days and even withdrew their labour from critical care units, in what was quite unprecedented action for workers who were involved in day to day care of patients.[53] The Victorian government threatened the use of essential services legislation to force the nurses to return to work.

Federal government intervention was notable and highly unusual in the airline pilots dispute 1991 discussed above – where over 350 airline pilots undertook industrial action in pursuit of wages claims outside the national wage guidelines – at first working between 9am to 5pm only (with consequent disruption to airline schedules) and then, in a move designed to limit damages from industrial torts litigation, resigned their positions as airline pilots – in what was an en masse resignation. In that matter the federal government retaliated by changing the visa regulations to permit foreign pilots to enter and work in Australia to fly the planes that would otherwise be idle, thus using its powers in terms of regulation-making to assist the airlines by providing them with the ability to obtain a new or substitute workforce of pilots. Importantly, and most

49. *Ibid.*, 104.
50. *Workplace Express*, 2017.
51. *Ibid.*
52. The Australian Nurses Federation had such a clause in its union rules, but this was altered in 1984.
53. See *Fox/Howard/Pittard*, 1995, ch 4.

unusually, the government also directly assisted in easing the impact of the industrial action by providing transport, in the form of RAAF Hercules jets, to ensure essential travel nationally.[54] Whilst arguably there was a degree of *essential* travel interfered with, many businesses utilized alternatives to meeting in person, for example. The government had, for reasons not altogether motivated by the need to ensure essential travel, succeeded in using its not inconsiderable powers to directly intervene in the dispute.[55]

The dockworkers strike of 1990s, which significantly affected the public and businesses generally, arose when a restructuring of the employing companies took place – without the knowledge of the union and employees – with the effect that termination of employment could be triggered where labour was not supplied due to industrial action. In the events that ensued, additional staff were trained by the maritime companies and brought in on individual agreements to unload the ships, picket lines were set up and litigation commenced: this included the Maritime Union of Australia being sued in the industrial torts, though the case was resolved by the labour being reinstated before final proceedings.[56]

It is important to note that these instances of significant industrial action in key industries took place prior to the *FW Act* 2009. As we will discuss, there are now formal mechanisms for intervention in strikes that are otherwise lawful to reduce or diminish the impact on the public and its welfare, and the provision of essential services. Strikes or industrial action in essential services that have been the subject of proceedings to halt or suspend that action by the FWC are discussed *infra* at Subsection 5.2.

Often the parties themselves are aware of avoiding the impact on essential services. The Australian Bureau of Meteorology (BOM), for example, saw authorized strike action in the context of bargaining for a new agreement; the aim was to target the BOM internally and not to disrupt its performance of essential services, with the BOM stating: 'The bureau has robust procedures and practices in place to ensure services essential for the safety and security of the Australian public will continue.'[57] The employer, BOM, was mindful too of the essential service it was providing.

54. *Ansett Transport Industries (Operations) Pty Ltd v. Australian Federation of Airline Pilots* (1989) 95 ALR 211; *Ansett Transport Industries (Operations) Pty Ltd v. Australian Federation of Airline Pilots (No 2)* [1991] 2 VR 636.
55. The government was determined to uphold the principles of the national wage fixing system which the pilots were not adhering to in seeking large wage increases: *see* interviews with the then Prime Minister the Hon Robert Hawke, *Hawke*, Transcript of Interview – Bob Maumill – Radio 2KY – 25 August 1989, 1989, 2; and *Hawke*, Transcript of News Conference – 13 September 1989, 1989, 3 and 12.
56. See *Maritime Union of Australia v. Patrick Stevedores Operations Pty Ltd* [1998] 4 VR 143; and *Patrick Stevedores Operations No 2 Pty Ltd v. Maritime Union of Australia* (1998) 195 CLR 1. See also *Orr*, 1998, 159.
57. *Timms*, 2017.

5 RESTRICTIONS OF THE RIGHT TO STRIKE IN ESSENTIAL SERVICES

5.1 Securing Essential Services by Exclusion from Collective Labour Relations Rights

In Australia legislation that limits the ability of parties to engage in industrial action in the case of *essential services* has arisen most obviously in the various *State* jurisdictions. For example, the New South Wales *Essential Services Act 1988* permits prohibitions on industrial action in essential services which are stated to include, amongst other things, energy services; transport of persons or freight; fire-fighting; health, ambulance and pharmaceutical services; sanitation; water supply and the conduct of welfare institutions and prisons.[58] The legislation also allows for the deregistration of trade unions that engage in activities contrary to the public interest while an essential services *proclamation* is in force.[59] On its face this legislation is far more expansive than the various standards and regulations that apply to emergency services under the ILO provisions.

The State of Victoria has legislation entitled the *Essential Services Act* 1958 (Vic). Under that legislation penalties apply in the event of a strike in an essential service unless the strike action is first approved in a ballot by a majority of eligible union members conducted by the Victorian Electoral Commission.[60] The legislation refers to 'essential services' as services provided by *State government instrumentalities* in the areas of transport, fuel, light, power, water, and sewerage, or other service specified from time to time by order of the Governor in Council.[61]

This type of 'essential services' legislation has continuing application in the different States, even though it is little relied on in practice, and if used would be more likely to exacerbate than resolve any on-going industrial dispute.[62] However, the regulation of industrial relations in Australia principally takes place under federal law, most particularly the *FW Act 2009*. Indeed, it will be recalled that all States, with the exception of Western Australia, have now referred their powers with respect to industrial relations to the Federal Government.[63]

58. One description of this legislation indicated that it broke new ground in treating services provided by persons other than Governments as 'essential services': *Russell QC*, 1998.
59. See s 17, Essential Services Act 1988 (NSW); *McCrystal*, 2010, 92.
60. See s 11, Essential Services Act 1958 (Vic); *McCrystal*, 2010, 92.
61. Section 3, Essential Services Act *1958* (Vic). Similar legislation is the *Vital State Industries (Work and Services) Act 1992* (Vic) that enables the Governor-in-Council to declare virtually any industry to be a 'vital industry'. Note also the Essential Services Act 1979 (Qld) which on its face permitted the Governor-in-Council to declare a state of emergency in an 'essential service', with such a declaration giving the relevant Minister the right to prohibit strike action in the relevant industry. This legislation was repealed in 1990.
62. *Stewart/Forsyth/Irving/Johnstone/McCrystal*, 2016, [26.47].
63. Note the significance of the *Fair Work Amendment (State Referrals and Other Measures) Act 2009*.

At Federal level, section 30J of the *Crimes Act 1914* (Cth) empowers the Governor General, who is bound by convention to act on the advice of the government of the day, to make a proclamation as to the existence of a 'serious industrial disturbance prejudicing or threatening' interstate or overseas trade. Whilst such a proclamation remains in force it is an offence to participate in or encourage a strike in connection with overseas or interstate transport of goods or transport of passengers, or with the provision of any public service by the Commonwealth, or an authority of the Commonwealth. The stated penalty for a breach of section 30J is imprisonment for a period of up to one year.[64] These *Crimes Act* penalties are rarely used, but they remain on the statute books notwithstanding they are regularly adjudged as being in breach of Australia's obligations under international law.[65]

5.2 Securing Essential Services by Imposing Limitations on the Right to Strike (Controlled Strike Model)

5.2.1 The FW Act's Regulation of Essential Services Strikes

As discussed earlier, there is a limited right to strike under Australian Federal law. The *FW Act 2009* permits parties to engage in what is termed 'protected industrial action' while negotiating an enterprise agreement,[66] and this action must be in accordance with a range of procedural requirements specified in the legislation.[67] The relevance of these requirements to 'essential services' arises in the context of the FWC's power to *suspend or terminate* protected industrial action. According to section 424(1) of the *FW Act 2009* the FWC has this power if satisfied that the protected industrial action 'has threatened, is threatening, or would threaten' ...

> (c) to endanger the life, the personal safety or health, or the welfare, of the population or a part of it; or
> (d) to cause significant damage to the Australian economy or an important part of it.

In circumstances where the industrial action is terminated or suspended in this way, there are related provisions under the *FW Act 2009* that enable the

64. Section 30K of the *Crimes Act* (Cth) is a similar provision with a similar penalty. That provision refers to the obstruction or hindrance of interstate or overseas trade or different public services by violence, or spoken or written threats or intimidation of any kind.
65. *Stewart/Forsyth/Irving/Johnstone/McCrystal*, 2016, [26.45]; see also *ILO*, 2014; *McCrystal*, 2010, ch. 10.
66. Section 408, *FW Act 2009*.
67. See *supra* Section 2. *See*, e.g., sections 409, and 413-414, and requirements concerning the giving of 'notice', and the conduct of a 'protected action ballot' (Part 3.3, Division 8, *FW Act 2009*).

FWC to make an arbitrated determination to resolve the matter (an industrial action-related workplace determination).[68] What is significant about the language of section 424 of the *FW Act 2009* is the apparent similarity between that provision and restrictions on the right to strike that may be allowable under ILO standards. However, it should be explained that section 424 appears in the context of Australia's bargaining framework under the legislation. It has been interpreted broadly and provides a more extensive limit on the right to take protected industrial action in this 'essential services' area than may have been anticipated.

5.2.2 Economic Damage: Meaning?

The drafting of section 424 has also been the subject of some criticism because of the reference to 'economic damage' in section 424 (1) (d), as one area that may allow for suspension or termination of industrial action. The difficulty is that the requirement of economic damage is not necessarily relevant to the designation of essential services under ILO standards 'unless the damage itself constitutes a threat to public safety'.[69] According to section 424, however, economic damage alone is sufficient to limit the protected industrial action. The emphasis on economic damage has appeared in a number of precursor provisions to section 424, and has been the subject of considerable criticism by international bodies.[70] Generally, the view of international bodies has been that economic damage should be treated as a *consequence* of strike action, and allowing for the suspension or termination on economic grounds has the potential to undermine the right to strike. It is arguably a violation of Convention No 87.

5.2.3 Intervention of Government Minister

Another difficulty with the relevant statutory provisions under the *FW Act 2009* is section 431, which allows the relevant government Minister to declare they are satisfied that industrial action is likely to endanger the life or health of the population or cause damage to the economy. Strictly speaking, the provision is not necessary given that the tribunal maintains responsibility for managing essential services disputes, and the provision has actually not been used. This type of provision, which appeared in predecessor Australian legislation, has been criticized as being in violation of ILO standards. Those standards suggest

68. See section 266 (1) and (2), FW Act 2009.
69. *McCrystal*, 2010, 253.
70. *ILO*, 1999, 2005-6. *See also*: *ILO*, 2000, 229.

that the responsibility for making declarations on industrial action should rest with an independent and impartial body.[71]

According to ILO jurisprudence there may then be an issue whether there are adequate 'compensatory guarantees', such as 'conciliation and mediation procedures leading, in the event of a deadlock, to arbitration machinery seen to be reliable by the parties concerned'.[72] For example, the parties must be able to participate in determining and implementing the procedures that 'provide sufficient guarantees of impartiality and rapidity'.[73] There have been consistent criticisms that the provisions in the Federal legislation do not necessarily satisfy these ILO requirements.

The scheme concerning 'protected industrial action' under the *FW Act* 2009 is similar to its predecessor provisions,[74] and permitted or 'protected' industrial action is limited to action in support of 'enterprise-level' bargaining.[75] As explained, under the 'essential services' provision in section 424 of the *FW Act 2009*, the FWC *must* make an order terminating or suspending protected industrial action where the action is taking place, or is threatened, impending or probable, and the tribunal is satisfied that the protected industrial action *causes damages to or will threaten* 'to endanger the life, the personal safety or health, or the welfare of the population or of part of it'; or 'to cause damage to the Australian economy or an important part of it'.[76]

Such an order may be made at the initiative of the FWC,[77] or on the application of a bargaining representative for the agreement, or the government Minister.[78] Statutory regulations have now extended just who is able to make an application under the provision. For example, Fair Work Regulation 3.10 provides that the person able to bring such an application under section

71. The predecessor provision appeared in s 498 of the *Workplace Relations (Work Choices) Act 2005* (Cth). That provision was criticized by the CEACR in 2007 and 2008. In 2007 the committee noted that strikes can only be prohibited under Convention No 87 art 3 in essential services, and that prohibitions regarding subjects such as danger to the economy went beyond the permissible restrictions of the Convention: *ILO*, 2007, 43. In 2008, the committee again noted that s 498 (amongst others) required amendment to conform with Convention No 87: *ILO*, 2008, 46. Section 424 was also criticised by the Committee on Freedom of Association in 2010: *ILO*, 2010, 52 et seqq. See *McCrystal*, 2010, 255.
72. *ILO*, 1994 para. 164; *Creighton/Stewart*, 1994, para. 1122; *Creighton/Stewart*, 2000, 162.
73. *Ibid.* See further, *Stewart/Forsyth/Irving/McCrystal*, 2016, with references to the Committee of Experts referring to the management of these issues through 'negotiation (not imposition) of minimum service arrangements' (at para. 18.44). See also, *ILO*, 1996.
74. See Part 3-3, FW Act 2009.
75. *Pittard/Naughton*, 2015, ch 14, esp. 723. As noted above, this means that protected industrial action is not available in the case of multiple employer bargaining, or greenfields agreements.
76. Section 424(2), *FW Act 2009*.
77. *National Tertiary Education Union v University of South Australia* [2010] FWAFB 1014, at [11] - [13]; *McCrystal*, 2010, at 189.
78. Section 424(2), *FW Act 2009*. Where such an application is made the FWC is required, so far as possible to determine the matter within 5 days, or else make an order suspending the industrial action until the application is determined: *see* section 424(4).

424(2)(b)(ii) may be 'an organisation or other person directly affected, or who would be directly affected by the industrial action other than the employee who will be covered by the agreement.' This extension of the provision and the type of applications that may be bought under it can presumably only result in an expansion of what is meant by 'essential services'.

5.2.4 Powers of FWC to Make Workplace Determination

The consequences of an order of the FWC or a Ministerial declaration terminating protected industrial action are to enliven those provisions of the *FW Act 2009* dealing with *Workplace Determinations* under Part 2-5 of the legislation. Where an order is made terminating protected industrial action, or a Ministerial declaration is given, the parties enter a 21-day 'post-industrial action negotiating period'.[79] In circumstances when they are unable to resolve the matters in dispute within that time, a Full Bench of the FWC is called upon to make an *industrial action-related workplace determination* 'as quickly as possible'.[80] This determination must include certain core terms,[81] terms that may have been agreed between the parties at the end of the 21-day period,[82] plus those terms the Full Bench considers remain unresolved between the parties at the end of that period (and it proceeds to determine by arbitration).

When exercising its *arbitral powers* in these circumstances the FWC must take into account:

(a) the merits of the case;
(b) ...
(c) ... the interests of the employers and the employees who will be covered by the determination;
(d) *the public interest* [emphasis added];
(e) how productivity might be improved in the enterprise or enterprises concerned;[83]
(f) the extent to which the conduct of the bargaining representatives for the proposed enterprise agreement concerned was reasonable during bargaining for the agreement;

79. Section 266(3), although this period may be extended for a further 21 days. The legislation refers to a 'termination action instrument' triggering a 21-day post-industrial action negotiation period (s 266(2)).
80. Section 266(1). See also section 616(4) which refers to matters that must be performed by a Full Bench.
81. These core terms include the Nominal Expiry Date, safety net requirements, and a guarantee the determination meets the 'better off overall' test: section 272, FW Act 2009. A further mandatory provision is that the determination includes a dispute settling provision (section 273, FW Act 2009).
82. Section 274(2), FW Act 2009.
83. The reference to 'enterprises' is presumably only applicable to a Workplace Determination in the event of the Low-Paid Workplace Determination Provisions: See Part 2.5, Division 2, *FW Act 2009.*

(g) the extent to which the bargaining representatives for the proposed enterprise agreement concerned have complied with the good faith bargaining requirements;
(h) incentives to continue to bargaining at a later time.[84]

A *workplace determination* covers those employers, employees or employee organizations that it is specified to cover,[85] and it applies until an enterprise agreement covering the employee's employment may subsequently come into operation.[86]

5.2.5 Cases Interpreting Section 424 of FW Act 2009: The 'Essential Services' Provision

What we are now able to say is that there has been an apparent willingness on the part of the FWC to read the terms of section 424 broadly. One would have assumed that a statutory provision tantamount to an 'essential services' limitation on the right to strike would have been interpreted more cautiously.

Short-term effects

An early interpretation of the 'essential services' provision under the *FW Act 2009* arose in the *Toyota Motor Corporation Australia Ltd* case[87] where the employer's application involved an attempt to *suspend* industrial action being taken by two unions in the motor vehicle industry over a period of two months. The company's argument was based on evidence of (i) possible harm to Toyota; (ii) possible harm to Toyota's suppliers; and (ii) possible harm to the automotive sector.

Ultimately, however, the tribunal member hearing the application indicated that that any evidence of there being a threat to *personal safety or health*, or upon *collective welfare* 'could only be described ... as temporary and confined'.[88] The industrial action in the *Toyota* matter was in the nature of short-term bans, and in the view of the tribunal member, the action failed to constitute 'significant damage to the automotive industry'.[89] The nature and degree of the threatened harm was not considered to be exceptional, and did not go 'sufficiently beyond the common inconvenience and common consequence of industrial action'.[90]

84. Section 275.
85. Section 277(1).
86. Section 278(1).
87. *Toyota Motor Corporation Australia Ltd v Australian Manufacturing Workers' Union (AMWU); Communications, Electrical, Electronic, Energy, Information, Postal, Plumbing and Allied Services Union of Australia (CEPU)* [2011] FWA 6268 (12 September 2011).
88. *Ibid.*, at para. [36].
89. [2011] FWA 6268, at para. 42.
90. *Ibid.*

Airline dispute and application of essential services power to employer lockouts

The *Qantas* dispute was a major industrial dispute arising under the bargaining provisions of the *FW Act 2009*, and it was the first case *where orders were made* under section 424. The case proved to be interesting because ultimately the FWC was required to reach a decision about terminating industrial action (and whether this was in the *public interest*) when the particular industrial action at the centre of the proceedings was taken by the *employer party*. Prior to this time there had been various instances of employee claim action taken by various unions in respective bargaining disputes against the airline, but they were not considered sufficiently serious to activate section 424. In the *Qantas* decision[91] a Full Bench of Fair Work Australia (now the FWC) granted an order terminating the protected industrial action (or employer response action).[92] The application to the tribunal made by *the Minister* under section 424 was for termination of the protected industrial action, or alternatively a suspension for a period of 90 days. This proved to be the first Ministerial resort to section 424(2).

The employer response action taken by the company on the weekend on 29–30 October, 2011 involved a lock-out of pilots, ramp, baggage handling and catering employees, and licensed aircraft engineers to be covered by the proposed enterprise agreements that were the subject of negotiations. The proposed lockout was to take effect from 8.00 p.m. on Monday 31 October. On making its lockout announcement, Qantas grounded its fleet worldwide. It was a lockout instigated in response to the on-going industrial action of the three unions, and it complied with the requirements concerning notice in section 414(5)(a), that is, that there was *reasonable notice* to bargaining representatives, in that the company took all *reasonable steps* to notify employees who were to be covered by the proposed agreements.[93]

One difficulty with the company's response was that it prevented (or threatened to prevent) *all Qantas employees* from being able to work, not just those involved in the bargaining disputes.[94] It therefore raised questions whether the response was 'proportionate' to the types of action the company had been subjected to – particularly the minor forms of industrial action undertaken by the long haul pilots (such as wearing red ties and making in-flight

91. *Minister for Tertiary Education, Skills, Jobs and Workplace Relations* [2011] FWAFB 7444 (31 October 2011). This was the decision to terminate industrial action which triggered those provisions of the legislation that enabled FWA to subsequently make workplace determinations between Qantas and the three unions. For chronology of events in the dispute, *see O'Neill, Steve,* 2012.
92. See section 411, FW Act 2009.
93. The Explanatory Memorandum accompanying the Fair Work Bill 2008 had indicated that emails to individual employees or bulletins on notice boards in the enterprise may constitute 'reasonable steps': Explanatory Memorandum, Fair Work Bill 2008, at para. 1671. This differs from employee claim action that must be supported by a protected action ballot, and requires a minimum of 3 days' notice to be given of the proposed action (see sections 409(2) and 414, FW Act 2009).
94. *Forsyth/Stewart,* Submission to Review of the Fair Work Act 2009, 2012, 22.

announcements), and whether this issue of 'proportionality' should be borne in mind in any decision to terminate protected industrial action under the relevant provisions.

The Full Bench found that it was unlikely that the original protected industrial action taken by *the three unions* had threatened to cause significant damage 'to the tourism and air transport industries'.[95] However *the employer response action* did threaten 'to cause significant damage to the tourism and air transport industries and indirectly to industry generally because of the effect on consumers of air passenger and cargo services'.[96] Therefore as noted, this was a remarkable situation where it was action taken *by the employer* that shut down negotiations, and forced parties towards *an arbitrated solution* under the relevant provisions, which, on their face, exist to resolve *essential services disputes*. Union parties suggested that the *Qantas* case represented a 'loophole' in the legislation 'which allowed a multi-national employer to obtain arbitration by locking out its workforce – while the tests for *employees* or *unions* were too difficult to meet'.[97] Rather than agreeing to *a suspension* of the protected industrial action for a period of either 90 or 120 days (the outcome desired by the union parties),[98] the Full Bench ordered *a termination* of protected industrial action.[99]

Under the legislation, the issue then became whether the tribunal was called upon the make a *workplace determination*. As noted, where the parties remain in dispute at the end of a 21-day post industrial action negotiating period, those matters proceed to the FWC for arbitration, 'as soon as possible'.[100] There was eventually a *consent* workplace determination settling the matters in dispute between Qantas and the Australian Licensed Aircraft Engineers' Association, based on an agreement reached between the parties,[101] and a Full Bench determination of matters remaining in dispute between Qantas and the Transport Workers' Union,[102] and the Australian and International Pilots' Association

95. [2011] FWAFB 7444 at [10].
96. *Ibid.*
97. *Forsyth/Stewart,* Kamaikazes and Mad Men: The Fall Out from the Qantas Industrial Dispute, 2012, 821.
98. [2011] FWAFB 7444 at [11].
99. The Australian and International Pilots' Association (AIPA) sought to appeal the order terminating the industrial action in proceedings before the Federal Court. The AIPA's appeal was dismissed by a Full Court of the Federal Court: *Australian and International Pilots' Association v Fair Work Australia* [2012] FCAFC 65 (10 May 2012). The AIPA's argument in the appeal was that the FWA had erred by terminating employee action in its order, when the focus of the inquiry was on the employer lockout. However the Full Court indicated this did not matter. The determination under section 413(7)(a) had the effect of precluding any industrial action in relation to the same proposed agreement.
100. See e.g. sections 266, 272 and 275, FW Act 2009.
101. *The Australian Licensed Aircraft Engineers Association v Qantas Airways Ltd* [2012] FWAFB 236.
102. *Transport Workers' Union of Australia v Qantas Airlines Ltd re Qantas Airways Limited and QCatering Limited – Transport Workers Workplace Determination 2012 [2012]*

(the long haul pilots).[103] In both cases the eventual *workplace determination* was not handed down until over 12 months from the time the order terminating industrial action was made.

Academic commentators have indicated that the decision to terminate rather than suspend the industrial action could be construed as a 'win' for Qantas. Arbitration of matters in dispute was 'more in the interests of Qantas than the unions'.[104] According to McCallum, any arbitrated decision meant there was probably little chance that specific union claims pertaining to job security would be successful. He suggests, for example, that it was unlikely the tribunal would actually tell a company how to run its business.[105] A workplace determination of this nature nevertheless saw the statutory tribunal, in what was very much its traditional role, being called upon to impose a binding determination on the parties in dispute. It did this having regard to what was in *the public interest*, alongside the rights of the parties. It may remain open to question whether it meets the necessary ILO requirements concerning voluntariness, and the compensatory guarantees of 'impartiality and rapidity'.[106]

Nurses' Industrial Action Endangering Health and Safety of Patients

Shortly after the *Qantas* dispute another application for termination of industrial action was made by the Victorian Hospital Industrial Association (VHIA) on behalf of employers in the Victorian hospital sector faced by industrial action taken by nurses.[107] The argument made by the VHIA was that the action being undertaken was 'designed to reduce the volume of services provided by employers in the Victorian public health system'.[108] This had resulted in less people receiving treatment, or treatment being delayed or administered less efficiently. The employers claimed that the consequences of the protected industrial action threatened to endanger 'the personal health, and potentially the safety, or the welfare, of those who may be in need of public health care services',[109] and the employer's submission was supported by the State Government of Victoria. In response, the Australian Nursing Federation (ANF) contended that the industrial

---

FWAFB 6612 (8 August 2012). In that decision the Full Bench rejected the Transport Workers' Union's claims for a site rates clause, and a more restrictive clause concerning the use of contract labour.

103. *Australian and International Pilots' Association v Qantas Airways Ltd* [2013] FWCFB 317 (17 January 2013).
104. *The Australian Financial Review*, Qantas in the recovery room, 1 November 2011.
105. *Ibid.*; see also *The Australian Financial Review*, Pilots Challenge FAW's Qantas' Ruling, 10 November 2011.
106. See, for example, requirements discussed above.
107. *Victorian Hospitals' Industrial Association v Australian Nursing Federation* [2011] FWAFB 8165 (15 December 2011).
108. *Ibid.*, 43.
109. *Ibid.*

action being taken was especially crafted to ensure that there was 'no *endangerment* in the relevant sense to anyone'.[110]

In that matter the Full Bench of the Fair Work Australia tribunal (FWC's predecessor) stated that it was necessary for there to be a sufficient evidential basis to satisfy the requirements of section 424. Here the Full Bench indicated that issues such as the 'welfare of the population' and 'endangerment' were widely understood concepts in the community, and they were to be given their ordinary meaning.[111] According to the Full Bench, while conduct or activities engaged in by the ANF might not be likely to endanger 'life', it could be such 'as to constitute a significant risk to 'personal safety or health''.[112]

The Full Bench found that the protected industrial action had adversely affected 'the quality and timeliness of the treatment that can be provided to patients, especially those in Emergency Departments and those requiring surgical procedures',[113] and this endangered the safety or health of patients or their welfare. It was 'more than just inconvenience.'[114] In the circumstances, however, it was a case where *suspending* the protected industrial action for a period of 90 days was considered more appropriate than *termination*. This was partly because negotiations towards a new agreement between the parties had only recently begun (which made the circumstances different from *Qantas*).

5.2.6 Do Decisions Conform to ILO Principles in Relation to Strikes in Emergency or Essential Services?

Cases such as *Qantas* and the *VHIA* Case have to some extent emphasized the ways in which section 424 has been given an extremely liberal reading, and one that is somewhat detached from ILO principles. The *Qantas* decision was triggered by *employer response action* and strongly emphasized the element of 'economic damage' in section 424(1)(d). In the *VHIA Case* the FWC has given an extremely broad interpretation to the concepts of endangering health and welfare in section 424(1), that are also likely to limit the application of strike

110. *Ibid.*, 45. Emphasis added.
111. *Ibid.*, 51. Here the Full Bench referred to previous decisions of the tribunal: For example, in relation to 'welfare of the population': see *Coal & Allied Operations v Coal & Allied Operations v Construction, Forestry, Mining and Energy Union* (1998) 80 IR 14 (1998) 80 IR 14; and *State of Victoria v Health Services Union Australia* AIRC Print L9810. Alternatively, in relation to 'endanger': see *Metropolitan Ambulance Service v Liquor, Hospitality and Miscellaneous Union* PR950276, *St. John Ambulance (NT) Inc. v United Voice* [2011] FWA 4782, and *Tyco Australia Pty Limited T/A Wormald v Communications, Electrical, Electronic, Energy, Information, Postal, Plumbing and Allied Services Union of Australia – Electrical, Energy and Services Division – Queensland Divisional Branch* [2011] FWAFB 1598.
112. [2011] FWAFB 8101, at para. [51].
113. *Ibid.*, 56.
114. *Ibid.*

action in many circumstances, and this approach has been followed in subsequent decisions.

In *National Tertiary Employees' Union v. Monash University*[115] an order under section 424(1)(c) was made, suspending University staff from engaging in industrial action in the form of an examination results' ban on the basis of a perceived threat to the mental health of students whose results were withheld. The action that was taken was presumed to endanger 'the health' or 'welfare' of the 'population or part of it', in accordance with section 424(1)(c). It nevertheless appears to be an excessively broad interpretation of the provision and again bears little similarity to the meaning of ILO standards.

Another unusual interpretation of section 424 arose in *Commissioner for Public Employment v. Australian Education Union Northern Territory Branch*[116] where teachers in the Northern Territory proposed engaging in industrial action by taking attendance rolls manually, rather than electronically, and thereby not providing relevant information to school administrators. This was found to constitute an 'endangerment to personal health and safety or welfare' and was *suspended* by the FWC. The tribunal member's decision was based on the fact that schools apparently relied on class roll information in order to exercise their duties of care, and they needed regular and timely access to this information. Again, the question is whether the proposed or threatened action can legitimately be said to have:

(1) met the test of 'endangerment'; or
(2) amounted to action which itself was likely to affect the personal safety or health, or the welfare, or the population, or a part of it.

Arguably, however, much of the Australian case law on these issues seems to be oddly in favour of those seeking to shut down industrial action, and those threatening industrial action cannot necessarily be said to have engaged in *essential or emergency services* as understood according to ILO standards.

5.2.7 Suspension Vversus Termination of Industrial Action and Processes of the Commission

During 2016 the FWC relied upon section 424 to terminate protected industrial action at the New South Wales electricity distributor, Essential Energy.[117] In that matter Senior Deputy President Hamberger found that a planned 80-hour strike was likely to endanger the life, the personal safety, or health of the population.

115. [2013] FWCFB 5982.
116. [2013] FWC 9479.
117. Order made under s 424, PR580630 (23 May 2016); *Essential Energy v Communications, Electrical, Electronic, Energy, Information, Postal, Plumbing and Allied Services Union of Australia* [2016] FWC 3338.

In this decision it was assumed that this particular issue was uncontested.[118] In the proceedings the principal contest was whether the interests of the parties were best served by either *suspending* or *terminating* the industrial action. According to the tribunal member this raised questions about the length of time the negotiations had been going on; the progress made in negotiations; whether there had been prior industrial action; the views of the parties; and the potential for any further industrial action that was likely to endanger the public. Matters of this nature supported a decision to *terminate*, rather than *suspend*. Following the termination of industrial action a Full Bench of the FWC proceeded to make an industrial action-related workplace determination in November 2016.[119] This enabled the employer to proceed with a large number of forced redundancies that eventually comprised part of the arbitrated determination. The determination was ultimately advantageous to the employer as it had been prohibited from imposing redundancies under the existing agreement. However in making its *determination*, the Full Bench was persuaded by evidence concerning the financial and commercial position of Essential Energy, and the need to adjust the size of its work force.

As noted above,[120] during 2016 there was an upsurge of bargaining disputes involving Australian public sector workers. The dispute involving the DIBP workers was important in the present context, as these workers might be most closely analogous to 'essential service' employees, with their border force responsibilities undertaken at national airports and ports. At the time of writing this particular dispute now awaits the outcome of a workplace determination hearing.[121] Initially in this matter the FWC made a finding that rolling strikes and work bans at airports presented a threat to the lives and safety of travellers and the community. This was sufficient for the tribunal to grant what was initially an interim order.[122]

On-going protected industrial action took place in the form of strikes following this interim order, and ultimately the FWC *terminated* the industrial action under section 424 of the *FW Act 2009* in October 2016.[123] Arguably this was regarded as a victory for the union as it has forced the matter towards

118. [2016] FWC 3338, at para. [27].
119. *Essential Energy Workplace Determination* [2016] FWCFB 7641 (23 November 2016).
120. *Supra*, notes on Section 3.
121. The Full Bench proceedings to hear submissions in relation to this matter commenced in October 2017, and the proceedings are on-going: see eg [2018] FWCFB 3415 (8 June 2018).
122. *Commonwealth of Australian (represented by the Department of Immigration and Border Protection)* [2016] FWC 2090 (5 April 2016). The CPSU had argued that the terms of s 424 did not allow for the making of an *interim* order. A further interim suspension order was made in September 2016.
123. *Commonwealth of Australia represented by the Department of Immigration and Border Protection v CPSU, the Community and Public Sector Union* [2016] FWC 7184 (6 October 2016).

arbitration, when the preferred position of the Department was that the industrial action be suspended, as this would have enabled negotiations to continue and for employees to vote on a new agreement offer.

In its decision in the *Border Force* decision the FWC noted that bargaining was at a standstill, and that suspending the action was 'unlikely to do more than put a further hiatus' in the bargaining process[124] between the CPSU and the department. The tribunal member Commissioner Wilson indicated that it was evident that negotiations had been 'unproductive' for a considerable time. It was the Commissioner's view that the impact of the strike action, particularly in the Australian Border Force, had been extensive and he pointed to periods of rolling strikes, coinciding with school holidays and periods of high travel, which endangered the welfare of the community.

After a year of post-industrial action negotiations the FWC Full Bench commenced a hearing for a workplace determination in late 2017. It appears that no matters have been agreed between the parties in these DIBP proceedings,[125] and the FWC will effectively have full authority to determine all matters in dispute.

An order granting the *suspension* of industrial action was granted in the Sydney rail dispute in January 2018. This was a remarkable set of circumstances as there had not been a major rail strike in Australia since the mid-1990s, but in the context of a bargaining dispute, the Rail Tram and Bus Union (RTBU) indicated that it was determined to shut down all train services in metropolitan Sydney on Monday 29 January 2018. Its bargaining demand was for a 24% wage increase over the period of a 4-year agreement.

Ultimately the case was decided on a somewhat similar basis to the *Qantas* decision, whereby section 424 of the *FW Act 2009* was utilized to argue that the proposed industrial action should be suspended or terminated on the basis of 'endangering life, the personal safety or health, or the welfare of the population', or else causing 'significant damage to the economy'. The matter for termination or suspension of the industrial action was ultimately an application jointly made by the New South Wales Minister for Industrial Relations, and the relevant employer party.[126] In his decision Senior Deputy President Hamberger of the FWC suspended the proposed strike, finding that it would 'endanger the welfare' of a large number of those persons who lived in Sydney and surrounding areas and relied on train travel to get to work, or otherwise go about their business.[127] In the tribunal's view the action also threatened 'to cause significant damage to the economy of Sydney – the largest and most economically important city in Australia'.[128] Both the issues of 'economic hardship' and questions about threats

124. [2016] FWC 7184, at [66].
125. Section 274(2), *FW Act 2009*.
126. *Sydney Trains; NSW Trains; The Hon Dominic Perrottett, Minister for Industrial Relations (New South Wales)* [2018] FWC 519 (25 January 2018).
127. *Ibid.*, para. 3.
128. *Ibid.*, para. 4.

to the 'health and welfare of members of the population' were emphasized in arguments to the tribunal. The response of union leaders to the decision, considering that the proposed industrial action was to be taken as 'protected action' in accordance with the terms of the legislation, is that the right to strike is effectively dead.[129]

6 COMPENSATORY MEASURES FOR RESTRICTIONS

See last section for the arbitration mechanisms envisaged for situations where strike is restricted.

7 SECURING ESSENTIAL SERVICES BY FURTHER MEANS

In *supra* Section 5 we discussed provisions outside the industrial relations legislation that provide governments with strong powers in respect of essential services. These have not been widely used. Rather in some instances governments have directly intervened to alter visa regulations to permit entry of workers in the case of foreign pilots; or provided government services such as RAAF jets in that same dispute, the airline pilots dispute 1991. Government intervention has tended to utilize the provisions of the *FW Act 2009*, as in the case of the Qantas dispute where the Minister intervened in relation to the lockout of the employees. Certainly the Minister has that power of intervention under the statute so that course is always open to the government.

8 EVALUATION AND CONCLUSION

8.1 Performance Evaluation: Review of the Statutory Provisions

In its commentary on the provisions allowing for termination or suspension of industrial action, the *Review of the Fair Work Act 2009* (conducted in 2012)[130] was reluctant to recommend changes to the provisions that might be called 'essential services' provisions, such as section 424. It was persuaded in part by the fact that similar provisions had existed under earlier legislative regimes.[131] As foreshadowed earlier, the Review Panel did recommend that section 431, which presently confers power on *the Minister* to terminate industrial action should be deleted from the legislation. In its view this provision arguably enables political interference in matters including serious industrial disputes, and any exercise of the power could be the subject of legal challenge.[132]

129. *The Australian*, 2018.
130. *Edwards/McCallum/Moore*, 2012.
131. *Ibid.*, 186.
132. *Ibid.*, 187. See *supra* Section 5.

The Productivity Commission, an independent authority established by Commonwealth statute,[133] was asked to undertake a review and assessment of the operation of the Australian workplace relations system. Its report, the *Productivity Commission Inquiry Report* of 2015,[134] made a number of observations and recommendations concerning the practical operation of the powers in the *FW Act 2009* for dealing with the suspension and termination of protected industrial action. The Productivity Commission noted some of the problems that have arisen in the application of *a related provision*, section 423. That provision allows for the termination of protected industrial action in circumstances where the tribunal (in cases of 'employee claim action') is satisfied that the action is causing or threatening to cause 'significant economic harm', both to the employer or any of the employers that will be covered by the agreement, and any of the employees who will be covered by the agreement.[135] However, interestingly, this provision is treated quite separately from the 'essential services' provision in section 424, and the requirement of significant economic harm has been interpreted quite differently and more rigorously from the cases arising under the 'essential services' provision.[136] There has in fact been only one occasion on which a section 423 order has been made.[137]

The Productivity Commission notes that the FWC appears to intervene more frequently in cases arising under section 424 (or what might be termed, the 'essential services' provision), being those cases where the industrial action is threatening or would threaten to endanger the life, personal safety or health or the welfare, of the population or of part of it; or to cause significant damage to the Australian economy or an important part of it. According to the Report, almost half the section 424 applications that have been made since 2009 have been successful.[138] In its view this is partly due to the fact that there is a relatively low bar for workers in certain public sector work – who are focussed on delivering health services or maintaining public safety – in taking industrial

133. Productivity Commission Act 1998 (Cth).
134. *Productivity Commission*, 2015.
135. Section 423(2)(a) and (b).
136. *Construction, Forestry, Mining and Energy Union v Woodside Burrup Pty Ltd* (2010) 198 IR 360.
137. *Fair Work Australia v Schweppes Australia Pty Ltd v United Voice – Victoria Branch* [2012] FWAFB 8599 (8 October 2012). This matter was essentially an interim order, and effectively obtained by consent.
138. In the period since the Productivity Commission Report, there have been the following applications under section 424 to suspend or terminate protected industrial action:

> December 2015–June 2016 – 5 applications; July 2016–June 2017 – 5 applications; July 2017–March 2018 – 2 applications. See Fair Work Commission website: https://www.fwc.gov.au/search/document/decision-order?items_per_page=100&search_api_views_fulltext=%22s.424%22&display_switcher=/search/document/decision-order&print_signed_date%5Bdate%5D=&print_signed_date_1%5Bdate%5D=&matter_title=&matter_number=&member_title=All&reference=&sort_bef_combine=field_fwc_doc_print_EVT_PRINT_SIGNED_DATE%20DESC (accessed 24 March 2018).

action.[139] It is arguably relatively easy in these circumstances for the statutory requirements in section 424 (the threatened endangerment of life or significant damage to the economy or an important part of it) to be triggered. This raises on-going issues about just how well the relevant Australian provisions may address the right to strike, or how any necessary limits on that right to strike may comply with relevant international requirements.

8.2 Summary and Conclusions

The *FW Act 2009* limits the scope for taking lawful industrial action. The ILO expert committees have been critical of Australia's strike laws for not being in accord with the ILO Conventions. Even where industrial action meets the many and detailed steps for being 'protected' industrial action and therefore lawful, that action can still be the subject of orders by the industrial tribunal, to suspend or terminate that industrial action it if it has or may have an adverse effect on the population (or even part of the population) or their health and safety. The overall result of the limited right to strike and its legal regulation is that the number of industrial disputes, has fallen significantly over the year.[140] Strikes in essential services, broadly defined, can be terminated or suspended quite easily due to the current interpretation of the legislative provisions.

Bibliography

Books/Articles/Reports

Bailey, Janis/Peetz, David, Australian Unions and Collective Bargaining in 2014, Journal of Industrial Relations, 2015 (57(3)), 401 et seqq.

Burgess, John/Sappey, Richard, The Australian Domestic Pilots' Dispute of 1989 and Its Implications: An Interpretation, New Zealand Journal of Industrial Relations 1992 (17(3)), 283 et seqq.

Carabetta, Giuseppe, International Labour Law Standards Concerning Collective Bargaining in Public Essential Services, Deakin Law Review, 2014 (19(2)), 275 et seqq.

Creighton, Breen/Stewart, Andrew, Labour Law - An Introduction, 2nd ed., 1994

Creighton, Breen/Stewart, Andrew, Labour Law - An Introduction, 3rd ed., 2000

Creighton, WB/Ford, WJ/Mitchell, RJ, Labour Law - Text and Materials, 2nd ed., 1993

139. Productivity Commission, 2015, at 889.

140. The Australian Bureau of Statistics notes: 'During the year ended March 2018, there were 153 disputes, 61 fewer than in the year ended March 2017. Over the same period, there were 137,700 working days lost, 13% more than in the year ended March 2017 (122,200).' *Australian Bureau of Statistics*, 2018.

Edwards, J/McCallum, R/Moore, M, Review of the Fair Work Legislation - 'Towards Productive and Equitable Workplaces' - An Evaluation of the Fair Work Legislation, Australian Government Publishing Service, 2012

Ewing, Keith, The Right to Strike, 1991

Ewing, Keith, Laws against Strikes Revisited, in Barnard/Deakin/Morris (eds), The Future of Labour Law, 2004, Hart Publishing, 41 et seqq.

Forsyth, Anthony/Stewart, Andrew, Of 'Kamaikazes' and 'Mad Men': The Fallout from the Qantas Industrial Dispute, Melbourne University Law Review, 2012 (36(3)), 785 et seqq.

Forsyth, Anthony/Stewart, Andrew, Submission to Review of the Fair Work Act 2009, 2012. Available at https://docs.jobs.gov.au/sites/docs_employment/files/submissions/43021/forsyth_anthonyandstewart_andrew.pdf

Fox, Carol/Howard, William/Pittard, Marilyn, Industrial Relations in Australia: Development, Law and Operation, 1995, Longman Australia

Fudge, Judy, The New Discourse of Labor Rights: from Social to Fundamental Rights?, Comparative Labor Law and Policy Journal, 2007 (29(1)), 29 et seqq.

Gernignon, Bernard/Odero, Alberto/Guido, Horacio, Collective Bargaining: ILO Standards and the Principles of the Supervisory Bodies International Labour Organisation, 2000. Available at http://www.ilo.org/wcmsp5/groups/public/@ed_norm/@normes/documents/publication/wcms_087931.pdf

Hawke, Robert, Prime Minister, Transcript of Interview - Bob Maumill - Radio 2KY - 25 August 1989, PM Transcripts, 1989. Available at http://pmtranscripts.pmc.gov.au/sites/default/files/original/00007728.pdf

Hawke, Robert, Prime Minister, Transcript of News Conference - 13 September 1989, PM Transcripts, 1989. Available at http://pmtranscripts.pmc.gov.au/sites/default/files/original/00007739.pdf

Higgins, Henry Bournes, A New Province for Law and Order: Industrial Peace through Minimum Wage and Arbitration, Part 1, Harvard Law Review, 1915 (29(1)), 13 et seqq.

Kahn-Freund, Otto/Hepple, Bob, Laws Against Strikes, 1972

Macintyre, Stuart/Mitchell, Richard (eds), Foundations of Arbitration, 1989

McCallum, Ron, Legislated Standards: The Australian Approach, in *Baird/Hancock/Isaac* (eds), Work and Employment Relations: An Era of Change, 2011, The Federation Press, 6 et seqq.

McCrystal, Shae, Protected Industrial Action, Recognition and Bargaining, in B Creighton and A Forsyth (eds), Rediscovering Collective Bargaining - Australia's Fair Work Act in International Perspective, 2012, Routledge, 114 et seqq.

McCrystal, Shae, The Right to Strike in Australia, 2010, The Federation Press

McEvoy, Kathleen/Owens, Rosemary, The Flight of Icarus: Legal Aspects of the Pilots' Dispute, Australian Journal of Labour Law, 1990 (3(2)), 87 et seqq.

Naughton Richard, The Shaping of Labour Law Legislation - Underlying Elements of Australia's Workplace Relations System, 2017, LexisNexis

Nicholson, Daniel/Pekarek, Andreas/Gahan, Peter, Unions and Collective Bargaining in Australia in 2016, Journal of Industrial Relations, 2017 (59(3)), 305 et seqq.

Niland, John R, Collective Bargaining and Collective Agreements in Australia, 2008, New South Wales University Press

Novitz, Tonia/Fenwick, Colin, The Application of Human Rights Discourse to Labour Relations: Translation of Theory into Practice, in *Fenwick/Novitz* (eds), Human Rights at Work: Perspectives on Law and Regulation, 2010

Novitz, Tonia, International and European Protection of the Right to Strike, 2003

O'Neill, Steve, The Gods Must Be Crazy: Chronology of and Issues in the Qantas Industrial Dispute 2011, 2012. Available at https://www.aph.gov.au/About_Parliament/Parliamentary_Departments/Parliamentary_Library/pubs/BN/2011-2012/ChronQantas

Orr, Graeme, Conspiracy of the Waterfront, Australian Journal of Labour Law, 1998 (11(3)), 159 et seqq.

Peetz, David, Industrial Conflict with Awards, Choices and Fairness, in *Creighton/Forsyth* (eds), Rediscovering Collective Bargaining, Australia's Fair Work Act in International Perspective, 2012, 159 et seqq.

Pittard, Marilyn, Australian Employment Regulation, in *Teicher/Holland/Gough* (eds), Australian Workplace Relations, 2013, 81 et seqq.

Pittard, Marilyn/Butterworth, Stewart, The Rich Panoply of Sources of Labor Law: National, Regional and International, in *Finkin/Mandlak* (eds), Comparative Labor Law, 2015, 21 et seqq.

Pittard, Marilyn/Naughton, Richard, Australian Labour and Employment Law, 2015

Pittard, Marilyn/Naughton, Richard, The Right to Strike - Australia, in *Waas* (ed.), The Right to Strike - A Comparative View, 2014, 95 et seqq.

Productivity Commission, Productivity Commission Inquiry Report of 2015: Workplace Relations Framework, Report number 76, volumes 1 and 2, Commonwealth of Australia, 2015

Russell QC, David, In Search of the Magic Pudding: Essential Services Legislation - Magic Pudding or Boarding School Blancmange, 1988

Smith, Graham, From Consensus to Coercion, the Australian Air Pilots Dispute, Journal of Industrial Relations 1990 (32(2)), 238 et seqq.

Stewart, Andrew/Forsyth, Anthony/Irving, Mark/Johnstone, Richard/McCrystal, Shae, Creighton and Stewart's Labour Law, 6th edition, 2016

The Australian, We've Lost the Right to Strike, ACTU declares, 26 January 2018

The Australian Financial Review, Qantas in the Recovery Room, 1 November 2011

The Australian Financial Review, Pilots Challenge FWA's Qantas Ruling, 10 November 2011

Timms, Penny, BOM Strike: Bureau of Meteorology staff to take industrial action for next three weeks, ABC News, 2017. Available at http://www.abc.net.au/news/2017-07-19/bom-are-going-on-strike-for-the-next-three-weeks/8725062

Wedderburn, Lord, Freedom of Association and Philosophies of Labour Law, Industrial Law Journal, 1989 (18(1)), 1 et seqq.

Workplace Express, 12 and 19 December 2017, 15 and 22 January 2018

Workplace Express, High Court Raises Bar for Industrial Action: ACTU, 7 December 2017

Statutes

Australian Constitution
Competition and Consumer Act 2010 (Cth)
Crimes Act 1914 (Cth)
Essential Services Act 1958 (Vic)
Essential Services Act 1979 (Qld)
Essential Services Act 1988 (NSW)
Fair Work Act 2009 (Cth)
Fair Work Amendment (State Referrals and Other Measures) Act 2009 (Cth)
Industrial Relations Reform Act 1993 (Cth)
Vital State Industries (Work and Services) Act 1992 (Vic)
Workplace Relations (Work Choices) Act 2005 (Cth)

Cases

Australian Licensed Aircraft Engineers Association, The v. Qantas Airways Ltd [2012] FWAFB 236

Ansett Transport Industries (Operations) Pty Ltd v. Australian Federation of Airline Pilots (1989) 95 ALR 211

Ansett Transport Industries (Operations) Pty Ltd v. Australian Federation of Airline Pilots (No 2) [1991] 2 VR 636

Australian and International Pilots' Association v. Fair Work Australia [2012] FCAFC 65

Australian and International Pilots' Association v. Qantas Airways Ltd [2013] FWCFB 317

Construction, Forestry, Mining and Energy Union v. Woodside Burrup Pty Ltd (2010) 198 IR 360

Coal & Allied Operations v. Construction, Forestry, Mining and Energy Union (1998) 80 IR 14

Commissioner for Public Employment v. Australian Education Union Northern Territory Branch [2013] FWC 9479

Commonwealth of Australian (represented by the Department of Immigration and Border Protection) [2016] FWC 2090

Essential Energy v. Communications, Electrical, Electronic, Energy, Information, Postal, Plumbing and Allied Services Union of Australia [2016] FWC 3338

Essential Energy Workplace Determination [2016] FWCFB 7641

Esso Australia Pty Ltd v. The Australian Workers Union; The Australian Workers' Union v. Esso Australia Pty Ltd [2017] HCA 54
Fair Work Australia v. Schweppes Australia Pty Ltd v. United Voice – Victoria Branch [2012] FWAFB 8599
Jumbunna Coal Mine NL v. Victorian Coal Miners' Association [1908] HCA 95, (1908) 6 CLR 309
Maritime Union of Australia v. Patrick Stevedores Operations Pty Ltd [1998] 4 VR 143
Metropolitan Ambulance Service v. Liquor, Hospitality and Miscellaneous Union PR950276
Minister for Tertiary Education, Skills, Jobs and Workplace Relations [2011] FWAFB 7444
National Tertiary Employees' Union v. Monash University [2013] FWCFB 5982
National Tertiary Education Union v. University of South Australia [2010] FWAFB 1014
Order made under s 424, PR580630
Patrick Stevedores Operations No 2 Pty Ltd v. Maritime Union of Australia (1998) 195 CLR
St. John Ambulance (NT) Inc. v. United Voice [2011] FWA 4782
State of Victoria v. Health Services Union Australia AIRC Print L9810
Sydney Trains; NSW Trains; The Hon Dominic Perrottett, Minister for Industrial Relations (New South Wales) [2018] FWC 519
Toyota Motor Corporation Australia Ltd v. Australian Manufacturing Workers' Union (AMWU); Communications, Electrical, Electronic, Energy, Information, Postal, Plumbing and Allied Services Union of Australia (CEPU) [2011] FWA 6268
Transport Workers' Union of Australia v. Qantas Airlines Ltd re Qantas Airways Limited and QCatering Limited – Transport Workers Workplace Determination 2012 [2012] FWAFB 6612 (8 August 2012)
Tyco Australia Pty Limited T/A Wormald v. Communications, Electrical, Electronic, Energy, Information, Postal, Plumbing and Allied Services Union of Australia – Electrical, Energy and Services Division – Queensland Divisional Branch [2011] FWAFB 1598
Victoria International Container Terminal Ltd t/a VICT v. Maritime Union of Australia and Construction, Forestry, Mining and Energy Union; VICT v. Hilakari [2017] VSC 762
Victorian Hospitals' Industrial Association v. Australian Nursing Federation [2011] FWAFB 8165 (15 December 2011)

Other

Australian Bureau of Statistics, 6202.0 Labour Force, 2017
Australian Bureau of Statistics, 6321.0.55.001 Industrial Disputes, March 2018
Explanatory Memorandum, Fair Work Bill 2008 (Cth)

Id. – *Committee of Experts on the Application of Conventions and Recommendations*, Freedom of Association and Collective Bargaining: General Survey, International Labour Conference, 81st Session, Report III (Part 4B), 1994

Id., 320th Report of the Committee on Freedom of Association, Case No. 1963 (Australia) Report in which the Committee requests to be kept informed of developments, GB.277/9/1, 308th Session, 2000

Id., 357th Report of the Committee on Freedom of Association, Case No. 2698 (Australia) Report in which the Committee requests to be kept informed of developments, GB.308/3, 308th Session, 2010

Id., Convention concerning Freedom of Association and Protection of the Right to Organise (ILO Convention No 87)

Id., Freedom of Association: Digest of decisions and Principles of Freedom of Association Committee of the Governing Body of the ILO, 4th rev ed., 1996

Id., Freedom of Association: Digest of decisions and Principles of Freedom of Association Committee of the Governing Body of the ILO, 5th rev ed., 2006

Id., Report of the Committee of Experts on the Application of Conventions and Recommendations, International Labour Conference, 87th Session, Report III (Part IA), 1999

Id., Report of the Committee of Experts on the Application of Conventions and Recommendations, International Labour Conference, 96th Session, Report III (Part IA), 2007

Id., Report of the Committee of Experts on the Application of Conventions and Recommendations, International Labour Conference, 97th Session, Report III (Part IA), 2008

Id., Report of the Committee of Experts on the Application of Conventions and Recommendations, International Labour Conference, 103rd Session, Report III (Part IA), 2014

Id., Right to Organise and Collective Bargaining Convention 1949 (ILO Convention No 98)

ANNEX

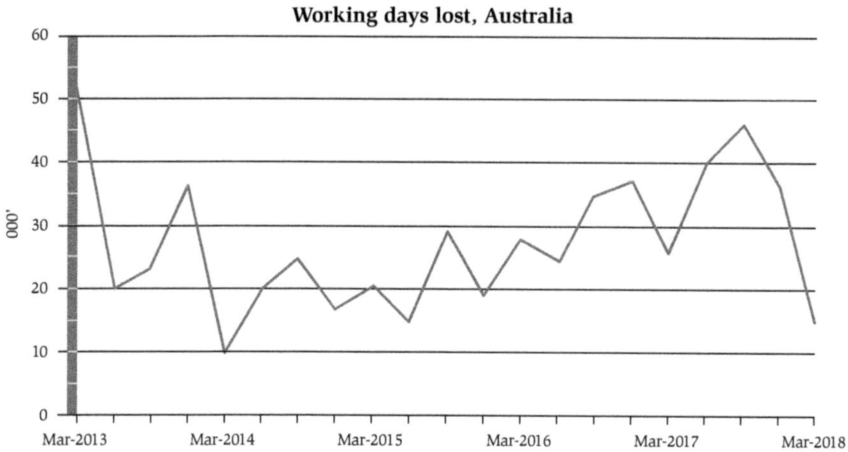

Source: Australian Bureau of Statistics, 6321.0.55.001 – Industrial Disputes, Australia, March 2018.

CHAPTER 4

Brazil

Roberto Fragale Filho[*]

1 GENERAL BACKGROUND: COUNTRY PROFILE

The right to strike has always been a major issue in Brazilian labour legal academia and three different phases can be clearly identified when examining its recent production. First, after authoritarian rule, during the democratic transition and the writing of the 1988 Federal Constitution, focus was on strikes as a legal right.[1] Then, right after the 1988 Federal Constitution promulgation, the need to regulate the right to strike as engraved in the new constitutional text

* This chapter has benefited from a critical reading from José Francisco Siqueira Neto, Sayonara Grillo Coutinho Leonardo da Silva, and Sergio Torres Teixeira, whose comments helped to improve its contents. Of course, the remaining problems are to be credited only to its author.

1. *Moraes Filho*, 1986, 775; *Costa*, 1986, 1289; *Tavares*, 1987, 10; *Gottschalk*, 1987, 1302.

became the main issue.[2] While preparing the 1988 Federal Constitution's first anniversary, the right to strike was finally regulated by Federal Statute 7,783 (28 June 1989) and criticism about limitations imposed on it became the new emphasis of legal debate.[3] Yet, as time went by, interest on the right to strike faded away and it was only occasionally revisited,[4] especially to discuss its use by public employees, which was not necessarily related to the debate about strikes in essential services. As a matter of fact, although some legal doctrine and judicial opinions may be found in legal journals, academic databases[5] show a very limited production of four master's dissertations[6] and one PhD thesis[7] examining strikes in essential services over the last decades. Most of them limit their investigation to legal text, sometimes incorporating a description of foreign legislation, and do not present any empirical evidence to corroborate their analysis. This paper relies on these previous academic efforts but also tries to integrate quantitative data as well as some empirical description in order to facilitate comparison with other countries participating in this collection.

Brazil is a federation, comprising twenty-six States, its Municipalities and the Federal District (Brasília). It is a complex political structure, which concentrates power on the federal level. Such political structure may be credited to historical reasons as the country after its independence in 1822 was originally organized as a centralized Empire. Federal importance as a trend has thus survived the proclamation of the Republic in 1889 and the seven constitutions[8] the country has known since its independence.

The Brazilian system of government is presidential and elections are held every four years. The President is directly elected by the people and the electoral body is actually composed of 146,988,142 voters.[9] As for the National Congress, the electoral system is purely proportional for a scenario of thirty-five political parties, the oldest ones dating back to 1981 and the latest being created in

2. *Barros*, 1988, 1336; *Prado*, 1988, 1388; *Sussekind*, 1989, 28; *Leite*, 1989, 163; *Silva*, 1989, 266.
3. *Guimarães*, 1989, 1318; *Coelho*, 1989, 1341; *Martins*, 1990, 160.
4. *Academia Nacional de Direito do Trabalho*, 1993; *Melo*, 2017.
5. For this research, I mainly used the *Biblioteca Digital Brasileira de Teses e Dissertações* (BDTD) [Brazilian Digital Library of Thesis and Dissertations], a public database that publishes online thesis and dissertations from the Brazilian graduate studies system. Although some other databases mainly related to journals and books are also available, BDTD is the one that can better portray new academic contributions to the theme. Cf. http://bdtd.ibict.br/vufind/ (accessed 28 March 2018).
6. *Frediani*, 2001; *Pinto*, 2007; *Cardoso*, 2009; *Oliveira*, 2012.
7. *Momezzo*, 2007.
8. Brazil became independent from Portugal in 1822 and its first constitution dates from 1824. The country became a Republic in 1891 and a novel constitution was promulgated two years later in 1893. Different political circumstances throughout the 20th century resulted in new constitutions in 1934, 1937, 1946, 1967 and 1988.
9. As of the 2016 elections, there were 144,088,912 voters (http://www.tse.jus.br/eleitor-e-eleicoes/estatisticas/eleicoes/eleicoes-anteriores/estatisticas-eleitorais-2016/eleicoes-2016). For the actual figures, see http://www.tse.jus.br/eleitor-e-eleicoes/estatisticas/estatisticas-de-eleitorado/consulta-quantitativo (both accessed 29 March 2018).

September 2015.[10] No party has been able to obtain a Congressional majority which has to be negotiated in the beginning of every legislature term. Hence there is a clear separation between the legislature and the executive.

The National Congress is a bicameral parliament entitled to a wide array of exclusive legislative competence, which may be delegated to the States through the approval of a specific statute by a higher quorum and includes labour law. The Union, the States and Federal District also have a concurrent legislative competence, though if any of their statutes are inconsistent with a valid federal law, the federal law will prevail. Accordingly, States and Federal District may legislate on any matter which is not an exclusive prerogative of the Union or the Municipalities as the latter also have exclusive legislative competences. Each State has its own Constitution, parliament and court system.

Brazil promulgated in 1988 its seventh written constitution. It establishes a system of federal courts, which has four different branches: federal (which exams cases that have a State agency as one of the litigants), electoral, labour and military (which exam, respectively, electoral, labour and military matters). Brazil's legal system is clearly civil based although a complex system of judicial precedents has been developed by the Higher Courts over the years.

Labour regulation and courts are currently facing a major reform which has strongly blurred the hegemonic legal interpretation and national jurisprudence on individual and collective labour relations.[11] As a matter of fact, Federal Statute 13,467 (13 July 2017) which became effective after a *vacatio legis* of 120 days, clearly jumbles up legal sources as statute prevalence over collective agreement or convention whenever the latter disregarded the minimum legal standards is no longer a general rule.

By 2015, Brazil had 94.4 million occupied workers aged 16 or over of which 18.4 million (19.5%) were unionized. As shown in table 1, union density has been declining over the years, although this trend may be changing as an increase can be verified in the last data available.[12] Once only formal employment is used as reference, unionization rate has been increasing over the years reaching up to 32.9% in 2013. While data suggests that occupation and formal employment do have an impact over unionization, their trends do not follow the same pace.

10. For a Brazilian political parties' complete list, see http://www.tse.jus.br/partidos/partidos-politicos/registrados-no-tse (accessed 29 March 2018).
11. *Fragale Filho/Siqueira Neto*, 2018, 48.
12. An interesting analysis suggests that this trend may be related to domestic work formalization; see *Instituto Brasileiro de Geografia e Estatística (IBGE)*, 2017.

Table 4.1 Brazilian Union Density

Year	*Union Density*
2004	18.5%
2005	18.9%
2006	19.1%
2007	18.2%
2008	18.6%
2009	18.1%
2011	17.5%
2012	16.9%
2013	16.2%
2014	16.9%
2015	19.5%

Source: *IBGE*, 2017.

Brazil has an astounding figure of 16,491 organizations representing economic and professional interests. 15,892 of them are unions. There are 549 federations, each one regrouping a minimum of five unions which represent the majority of a given economic activity. A minimum of three federations is required to form each one of the 43 existing confederations in the country. Finally, there are six trade union centrals which meet the legal requirements for recognition and whose representation is not directly related to an economic activity.[13] They are eligible to public funds and do play a strong role in the political life of the country. They reunite at least 100 unions from the five different Brazilian regions with a minimum of 20 unions in three different Brazilian regions; cover five different economic sectors; and represent at least 7% of all unionized workers in the country. Employers and workers are represented respectively by 5,705 and 10,817 unions. 1,882 (17.4%) of the latter regroup a little bit over one-third (36.8%) of unionized workers who are public employees.[14]

An analysis over the last three decades assuming the different Brazilian presidencies as a parameter indicates that strikes have decreased since Fernando Cardoso's presidency (1994-2002) and have stabilized during Lula's presidency (2003-2010). This trend was though modified during Dilma Rousseff's presidency (2011-2016), when they recovered similar numbers as in the beginning of

13. The six trade union centrals and their respectively index of representativeness are: Central Única dos Trabalhadores - CUT (30.40 %), União Geral dos Trabalhadores - UGT (11.29%), Central dos Trabalhadores e Trabalhadoras do Brasil - CTB (10.08%), Força Sindical - FS (10.08%), Central dos Sindicatos Brasileiros - CSB (8.15%), and Nova Central Sindical de Trabalhadores - NCST (7.45%), see *Diário Oficial da União* (Brazilian Official Journal), 1ª Seção, n. 62, 1 April 2016.
14. *Campos*, 2016.

the 1990s.[15] Coincidentally both periods were of strong economic recession in the country. Although strikes in the private sector prevail, the amount of strike hours averages 34% more in the public sector. Recent figures (table 2) show that Brazil has reached its peak in 2016 when 2,093 strikes were registered.

Table 4.2 Strikes

Year	*Public*	*Private*	*Both*	*Total*
2004	185 (61.3%)	114 (37.7%)	03 (1%)	302
2005	162 (54.2%)	135 (45.2%)	02 (0.7%)	299
2007	161 (50.9%)	149 (47.2%)	06 (1.9%)	316
2008	184 (44.8%)	224 (54.5%)	03 (0.7%)	411
2009	251 (48.5%)	266 (51.4%)	01 (0.2%)	518
2010	269 (60.3%)	176 (39.5%)	01 (0.2%)	446
2011	325 (58.7%)	227 (41%)	02 (0.4%)	554
2012	410 (46.8%)	464 (52.9%)	03 (0.3%)	877
2013	933 (45.5%)	1,106 (54%)	11 (0.5%)	2,050
2016	1,100 (52.6%)	986 (47.1%)	07 (0.3%)	2,093

Source: *Dieese*, 2005, 2006, 2008, 2009, 2012a, 2012b, 2013, 2015 and 2016.

As only about one-third of Brazilian occupied workers is on the formal market and therefore eligible to labour legal protection, informality is a major problem. Labour market biggest challenge is thus about how to incorporate informal workers and grant them formal coverage.[16]

2 COLLECTIVE LABOUR RELATIONS

The right to organize is recognized by the 1988 Federal Constitution which no longer requires State approval for the creation of a union, although registration at the Labour and Employment Ministry is still necessary. Registration is important in order to assure the 'unicity' principle which allows the sole existence of one single union for each economical or professional category in a given territorial basis which cannot be inferior to a Municipality. Workers are free to join a union and until recently regardless of being unionized, every employee was required to pay an annual union tax equivalent to one day of work. This compulsory payment was made optional by Federal Statute 13,467/

15. *Couto/Vasconcellos*, 2017.
16. For the most recent data, see https://g1.globo.com/economia/noticia/trabalho-sem-carteira-assinada-e-por-conta-propria-supera-pela-1-vez-emprego-formal-em-2017-aponta-ibge.ghtml (accessed 29 March 2018).

2017, whose impact is still too early to assess. This peculiar scenario has allowed unions to exist despite of their legitimacy.[17]

Employers and Employees unions are respectively established based on an economical or professional basis. Collective bargaining, as established by 1988 Federal Constitution, requires mandatory union participation. Unions do not depend on workers' active engagement to bargain (or to exist) and its outcome applies to all labour contracts in the economic category in the territorial base. Once again, this circumstance has been modified by Federal Statute 13,467/2017, which now allows for individual bargaining on certain labour issues. Yet, doubts about the constitutionality of this new arrangement remain as different parts of the new legislation have already been challenged at the *Supremo Tribunal Federal* (Brazilian Supreme Court, hereinafter STF).[18] Collective agreements and conventions are supposed to be registered at the Labour and Employment Ministry to ensure validity. Once parties do engage in a bargaining process, they are required to act in good faith even though they are under no obligation to reach a final result.

The right to strike is also ensured by the 1988 Federal Constitution and it is up to workers to decide on its convenience and which interests they wish to defend through it. Federal Statute 7,783/1989 regulates the right to strike in the private sector, also defining essential services and how community's urgent needs are to be secured. As strike in the public service has not yet been regulated, STF approved a Legislative Injunction in October 2007 extending such legislation to the public sector due to Congress inaction.[19]

The rights to organize, to bargain collectively and to strike mainly rely on constitutional and federal statutes and labour jurisprudence scarcely refers to international law, even though International Labour Organization (ILO) Conventions 98, 151 and 154 have been respectively ratified in 18 November 1952, 15 June 2010 and 12 May 1992. While Brazil has ratified the International Covenant on Civil and Political Rights and the International Covenant on Economic Social and Cultural Rights both in 6 July 1992, ILO Convention 87 has never been ratified as it would undoubtedly challenge the 'unicity' principle.

17. *Gomes/Prado*, 2010, 843.
18. As of December 2017, ten *ações diretas de inconstitucionalidade* (direct unconstitutionality action) had already been filed at STF arguing the unconstitutionality of specific items of the labour reform. For a complete list, see https://www.conjur.com.br/2017-dez-11/reforma-trabalhista-questionada-10-processos-supremo (accessed 15 March 2018).
19. Mandado de Injunção (Legislative Injunction) n. 712, Ministro [Justice] Eros Grau, http://redir.stf.jus.br/paginadorpub/paginador.jsp?docTP=AC&docID=558553 and http://redir.stf.jus.br/paginadorpub/paginador.jsp?docTP=AC&docID=495484 (both accessed 29 March 2018). Previously an attempt to provide a new regulation to unions and labour relations including the right to strike for public employees was done by the *Fórum Nacional do Trabalho* (Labour National Forum), a tripartite organization created during Lula's first presidency, but its propositions were never endorsed by the Brazilian Legislative. For a good description of its work, see *Almeida*, 2007, 54; *Ostrowski/Meneguin/Assis*, 2004.

3 THE RIGHT TO STRIKE

While the constitution recognizes the right to strike, it also forbids its exercise by the armed forces, including military police and fire-fighters.[20] This interdiction has been extended to all public services that are directly involved in public safety, including all police forces, by a STF decision.[21] Although strike is clearly illegal for such categories, Brazil has experienced a few cases where military police and/or fire-fighters have gone on strike. The leading episode was the military police strike at Minas Gerais State in June 1997 which led to the exclusion of 185 police officers, including its leader, *Cabo* Júlio, under allegation of carrying out a mutiny. *Cabo* Júlio was later elected to the National Congress in 1998, re-elected in 2002. He was amnestied in 1999 by Minas Gerais Governor Itamar Franco and reintegrated in the military force as a fire-fighter.[22]

More recently, in 3 February 2017 family members from the military police force of Espírito Santo State camped before their headquarters preventing policeman from leaving it. They asked for better salaries as they did not get any increase on their payments for the last seven years as well as better working conditions. Although a State Court decision declared the strike illegal and imposed a one hundred thousand *reais* (≈ USD 30,000.00) daily fine if the military police did not get immediately back to work, the situation worsened generating an enormous crisis on public security and a total of 199 people suffered a violent death. As of 25 February 2017 the strike ended without any gain and the indictment of more than 700 policemen for mutiny.[23] As unlikely as it may seem, this was not an isolated episode as comparable events previously occurred in the States of Tocantins (May 2011), Rio de Janeiro (February 2012), Mato Grosso do Sul (May 2013), Bahia (April 2014) and Pernambuco (May 2014).

A similar narrative can be found on the fire-fighters' strike of 2011 in Rio de Janeiro State. Indeed, as of 14 April 2011 demands for salaries' raise and better working conditions were unsuccessfully forwarded to the government originating a series of public manifestations and an informal negotiation mediated by the State Assembly. On 3 June 2011 as negotiations failed, fire-fighters and their family members marched from the State Assembly to the corporation headquarters and occupied it for thirteen hours until they were evacuated by the military police. The occupation resulted in the incarceration of 429 fire-fighters and two military policemen. Due to the governmental vigorous reaction, the fire-fighters' movement gained the population's sympathy and on 10 June 2011 a collective

20. Article 142, § 3°, IV, Federal Constitution.
21. *Recurso Extraordinário com Agravo (*Extraordinary Appeal) n. 654,432, Ministro (Justice) Alexandre de Moraes, http://www.stf.jus.br/portal/cms/verNoticiaDetalhe.asp?idConteudo=340096 (accessed 30 March 2018).
22. *Santos*, 1998; *Almeida*, 2004 and 2010.
23. *Rocha*, 2017.

habeas corpus was granted to all of them. Released, the fire-fighters still faced an indictment for mutiny.[24]

Workers are free to decide on a strike's convenience and interests which have to be deliberated in a general assembly duly and specifically designated for it. As demands and means are to be considered in such general assembly, workers are free to decide if a strike is to be total or partial and no distinctions are to be made on the basis of its objective or goal. Yet, previous, direct and pacific negotiation is a requirement for any strike, as indicated at the Jurisprudential Orientation 11 from the *Seção de Dissídios Individuais* (Collective Bargaining Section, hereinafter SDC) of the *Tribunal Superior do Trabalho* (Labour Superior Tribunal, hereinafter TST). Once frustrated the negotiation and decided the strike in essential services, employers' unions or employers directly affected by it are to be notified 72 hours previously to the strike's beginning, differently from the general rule of 48 hours for any other strike.

4 THE EXPERIENCE WITH STRIKES IN ESSENTIAL SERVICES

Strikes in essential services are quite important as they directly affect the general population. This is clearly observed in the case of public transportation, which has repeatedly been examined by labour courts. As a matter of fact, almost every year, labour courts are asked to decide on the abusive character of strikes on public transportation based on the claim that essential services were not assured by the parties involved. Basically, the same scenario reproduces year after year: the parties do not agree on the workers' demands for salaries' raise and are unable to decide what percentage of services is to be secured during the strike. As the strike becomes imminent, labour courts are called up by the *Ministério Público do Trabalho* (Labour Prosecution Office, hereinafter MPT) to decide about the service's continuity and, once the strike is over, to decide on the payment of imposed fines. Even for other areas considered as essential services, workers' demands are almost exclusively related to salaries' raises and better working conditions, hardly dealing with circumstances related to privatization, outsourcing, technological advancements and/or structural changes.

The normative policy dilemma is clearly framed around the question of how essential services are to be guaranteed without jeopardizing the right to strike. Legislation does not provide a clear answer as Federal Statute 7,783/1989 basically limits itself to exhaustively indicate what is to be considered an essential service or activity. Yet, legislation indicates that in essential services or activities, unions, employers and workers are bound by common agreement to ensure, during the strike, the provision of services necessary to meet the urgent needs of the community, which are defined as those that, if unmet, would

24. *Silva/Gondim*, 2017, 28.

endanger the life, personal safety or health of the whole or part of the population. Although reproducing ILO discourse,[25] this broad definition does not forward any parameters for securing the right to strike in essential services.

5 RESTRICTIONS OF THE RIGHT TO STRIKE IN ESSENTIAL SERVICES

As indicated above, armed forces members including military police and fire-fighters are fully prohibited on exercising their right to strike and public employees benefit from a STF Legislative Injunction extending the private sector regulation to the public sector. Therefore, Federal Statute 7,783/1989 applies either to public and private sectors and previously lists what is to be considered essential services. As the eleven references contained in such list encompasses broad definitions that may amplify what is to be considered essential services and as a consequence severely restrict the right to strike, legal interpretation has been extremely rigid on the list's exhaustiveness which includes the following references: water treatment and supply, electric energy, gas and oil production and distribution, medical and hospital assistance, food and medicine distribution and commercialization, funerary, public transportation, sewage and waste collection and treatment, telecommunications, guarding, use and control of radioactive substances, nuclear equipment and materials, air traffic control, bank clearing, and data processing related to essential services.

Once one examines the legislation, it becomes clear that essential services are so broadly defined that Brazilian legislation can hardly entirely be placed in one of the four types conceived in a typology based on timing and character. On one hand, it is an ex-ante and general fixed system for armed forces members including military police and fire-fighters and, on other hand, it is an ex-ante and selective dynamic system for the broadly defined essential services. Yet, as parties do not agree on how to secure essential services, the system moves to an ad-hoc and selective dynamic type in which labour courts are called upon to decide on a strike's legality.

Federal Statute 7,783/1989 does not distinguish essential services in the strict sense and just essential. It also does not forward any clear criteria as to how what is to be considered essential services is to be decided. It just lists eleven entries and clearly establishes procedures to be followed for strikes in essential services: proof of bargaining attempts have to be given indicating that negotiations are deadlocked; a general assembly duly and specifically designated has to deliberate on the strike's pertinence drawing its claims; and previous communication has to be made to employers and community at least 72 hours in advance. Whereas parties are supposed to come to an understanding as to establish the minimum amount of service to be guaranteed, this is very seldom the case and it has been up to labour courts to fix this minima while exercising their legal competence to exam cases dealing with the right to strike.

25. *Gernigon/Odero/Guido*, 1998, 441.

However a glance at labour jurisprudence shows that no pattern can be obtained from previous decisions. Indeed, judicial decisions from TST and regional labour tribunals concerning public transportation order service maintenance during rush and non-rush hours varying respectively from 50% to 80% and from 20% to 50%. It is important to notice that difference between rush and non-rush hours never exceeds 30%. A different logic is to be detected in other essential services as judicial decisions have established that a strike on electric energy facilities had to assure maintenance of 50% of all employees working while the same circumstance in a data processing service required only 40%. As for health services, judicial decisions have imposed the maintenance of all services related to urgencies (especially intensive care unit) and of 70% of the remaining hospital services. As one can see, a clear pattern to establish what is to be considered a minimum required amount of service is hardly perceived.

Compliance with labour courts orders for assuring a minimum service during a strike in essential services is basically obtained through severe fines that usually oscillate from fifty thousand (≈ USD 15,000.00) to one hundred thousand (≈ USD 30,000.00) *reais* on a daily basis. Once established by lower labour courts, judicial review can be obtained at TST which may re-examine its suitability and reasonableness. Fines do work as a very discouraging mechanism for strikes, although non-compliance is quite common. A case that has gone classic is the oil workers' strike that has lasted 32 days from 3 May to 4 June 1995. Although most of its demands were related to wages, the strike was inserted in a national movement of resistance against the President Cardoso's neoliberal agenda. On 6 May TST ordered the maintenance of 30% of services and imposed a daily fine of one hundred thousand *reais* for non-compliance. On 9 May the strike was judged illegal and a return to work was ordered for the following day subject to the same previous fine. As the strike was upheld by the oil workers, some employees including union leaders were dismissed for cause and an attempt to hire temporary workers failed due to the activity's specialized character. On 17 May an appeal was filed on TST to review its previous decision considering the strike abusive. On 26 May, under the impact of the army's occupation of some oil plants that took place two days before, the appeal was rejected. Resistance went on for a few more days until 4 June when the strike was finally called off. As a result, 73 oil workers were terminated for cause, more than a thousand were suspended for up to 29 days and unions' fines reached up to two million and a hundred thousand *reais* (≈ USD 630,000.00). Later, Federal Stature 9,689 (14 July 1998) granted amnesty to these fines without authorizing the reimbursement of previous payments or money seizures related to them and Federal Statute 10,790 (28 November 2003) while granting amnesty to all workers punished for their involvement in the 1995 strike, ordered their employment reintegration.

6 COMPENSATORY MEASURES FOR RESTRICTIONS

The 1988 Federal Constitution establishes that public employees' salaries are to be stipulated by law observing the right to an annual general review, always on the same date and without distinction of indexes. This basically means a linear increase for all public employees recomposing purchasing power diminished by previous inflation, still limited to the maximum salary allowed in the public sector, which corresponds to the amount paid to STF Justices and is also to be annually reviewed. Thus, public employees who are not allowed to strike (and also unionize and collectively bargain) – armed forces members including military police and fire-fighters – were to benefit from this salary indexation. Nevertheless the constitutional provision, different Brazilian governments regardless of their ideological affinity have deliberately ignored this normative command either delaying legislation approval or proposing pre-determined increases (which do not necessarily will correspond to the future inflation). Accordingly, the last salary cap review was done by Federal Statute 13,091 (12 January 2015) while Federal Statute 12,771 (28 December 2012) previously established the maximum salary for 2013, 2014 and 2015. Other public employees (who do not necessarily overlap with essential services) also benefit from this constitutional salary indexation, a system that has undoubtedly not functioned well over the years as the constitution predicts and is far from a change as a presidential veto was imposed on a legislative proposition to outspread the right to collectively bargain to public employees.[26]

Employees on essential services, although enjoying a limited right to strike, do not benefit from any particular measure assuring their right to collective bargain and/or settle labour disputes. Both circumstances are actually dealt with in the same way the Brazilian legal system generally treats all collective bargaining and labour disputes: if parties did not reach an agreement, they could appeal to the judicial system. Indeed, for decades labour courts have played a major role on both aspects due to its *Poder Normativo* [Normative Powers], a jurisdictional competence to decide collective labour conflicts and to establish new working conditions whenever demanded by one of the parties of a deadlocked collective bargaining situation. Due to this competence, labour courts were able to produce normative decisions that were to be treated as a legal source for many workplace circumstances. The 1988 Federal Constitution reviewed this judicial competence indicating that, on one hand, once frustrated the negotiation, the bargaining parties could choose an arbitrator or, on other hand, one of the parties could appeal to labour courts who were entitled to establish work conditions, as long as conventional and legal minimum work protection dispositions were respected. A last change was introduced by

26. *Projeto de Lei* (Bill Proposition) n. 3,831/2015 was approved by Congress in 27 November 2017 after three years of legislative debate and vetoed by President Michel Temer in 18 December 2017; see http://www.camara.gov.br/proposicoesWeb/fichadetramitacao?idProposicao=2057818 (accessed 2 April 2018).

Emenda Constitucional [Constitutional Amendment, hereinafter EC] 45 (31 December 2004) indicating that appealing to labour courts was to be done under mutual agreement and not by just one of the negotiating parties. Furthermore, it gave MPT authority to act as a third interested partner and start a judicial procedure to decide about the bargaining process in case of a strike in essential services.

As TST embraced the mutual agreement requirement, labour courts were emptied out of their normative powers, giving rise to a judicial debate about this prerequisite's unconstitutionality for supposedly limiting access to justice, an unachieved legal controversy still under scrutiny at STF. Meanwhile, different interpretations suggest that EC 45/2004 has made arbitration the preferred means to unlock collective bargaining giving the parties the option to use either private arbitrators or labour courts as a public judicial arbitrator. Insofar as the debate remains open, the only certitude has been the impact of these constitutional changes in the labour courts' normative powers which have clearly weakened.

7 SECURING ESSENTIAL SERVICES BY FURTHER MEANS

Strikes in essential services are not only about work relations but do affect public services and community interests. They usually go beyond the specific employer/employees' relation and as a result, they witness an unusual involvement of the three government branches. Yet, as the Brazilian labour arrangement strongly relies on labour courts as the main locus for labour dispute resolution,[27] executive and legislative branches have a more peripheral involvement. As a general trend, the former is usually one of the directly interested parties of the strike while the latter ordinarily presents itself as an outsider negotiator. Accordingly, the executive branch has often declared a state of emergency whenever a strike affects public security mainly because is conducted by those not entitled to such right (armed forces, including military police and fire-fighters). This circumstance increases pressure on strikers as to remind them of the illegality of their actions. In very few occasions, the armed forces have been mobilized to guarantee services' continuity as described above for the 1995 oil workers' strike. As for the legislative branch, quite often it just echoes the debate over strikers' demands and very rarely it works as a space for negotiating after strike consequences such as the above mentioned amnesty also for the 1995 oil workers' strike.

Back to work orders, declaring a strike illegal and/or abusive, establishing minimum percentages of service to be upheld during a strike, imposing fines, and working as conciliators or just simply adjudicators for a collective labour

27. Due to the Legislative Injunction extending the right to strike to public employees (see *supra* Section 2) and labour courts' lack of jurisdiction over the latter, State and Federal courts are being seized to discuss such kind of labour dispute. Nevertheless caseload is still very scarce to provide a general trend of their behaviour.

relation are measures reserved to the judiciary branch, more specifically to its labour courts. Criminal and tort procedures are an exception. As for public employees, a recent STF decision has decided that salaries are to be retained and discounted for each and every day of strike.[28] As social partners rely on labour courts as an important locus to decide on a strike development, joint and/or self-regulation is almost unknown to the Brazilian legal system.

8 EVALUATION AND CONCLUSION

8.1 Evaluation

Statute's preponderance, workers representation organized under the 'unicity' principle and compulsorily financed, and labour courts as a locus for negotiation: this has been the fundamental pillars for the Brazilian labour scenario over the last decades. The problem of strikes in essential services has not been perceived as something unique and entitled to a different treatment but rather as one more aspect of the general regulatory system. Yet, mostly due to Federal Statute 13,467/2017, this unique labour relation system is witnessing a probable change whose impact is still too early to assess. As a matter of fact, an important modification might be on the way due to the new legislation that has recently modified all of the three elements according prevalence to collective bargaining, extinguishing unions' compulsory funding, and introducing restrictions on labour courts access and intervention. As new problems related to collective bargaining will most likely quickly appear, general questions dealing with the right to strike probably will be rephrased, including the one related to strikes in essential services (as well as the right to strike for public employees). In an extremely fuzzy scenario it is hard to imagine what the outcome might as well be.

As a general trend, three aspects draw immediately one's attention. First of all, the enormous gap between regulation and ordinary practice. Indeed, strikes' ban for military police and fire-fighters is persistently disrespected as well as a broad and vague list of activities considered to be essential services minimizes any regulatory predictability. Second, this conceptual latitude amplifies the already enormous role of labour courts, which have undeniably strongly intervened not only on strike issues but generally speaking in all Brazilian labour relations. Finally, this continuous labour courts' intervention has over the years weakened collective bargaining efforts, which are also debilitated by the gap between labour representatives and represented employees and employers.

This general trend can also be found in the issue of strikes in essential services. Basically, autonomous, self-imposed or agreed-upon regulation is

28. Recurso Extraordinário (Extraordinary Appeal) n. 693,456, Ministro (Justice) Dias Toffoli, http://redir.stf.jus.br/paginadorpub/paginador.jsp?docTP=TP&docID=13866341 (accessed 29 March 2018).

almost unknown and as the parties never agree on what is to be a proper level of service, this decision is set by labour courts whose metrics are hard to seize. The system is so self-centred and consistent with its long trajectory that international standards do not play a major role. All parties involved have internalized its procedural rules and have frequently played accordingly although the outcome has not necessarily been the one they desired for. Definitely, strikes in essential services do not come to an end because parties have reached an agreement, but mainly because labour courts usually make them unfeasible as they impose a substantial level of service and strong fines. Essentially, it is not a system to guarantee the right to strike but rather to control its impact.

8.2 Summary and Conclusions

Strikes in essential services have fundamentally been regulated by Federal Statute 7,783/1989, which establishes which economic activities are to be alike considered and defines some procedural aspects as to how dispose of the right to strike: a deadlock collective bargaining procedure, a general assembly deliberating over the strike's realization and its demand agenda, and a 72 hours warning to either general public and employers. Legislation also requires parties to jointly establish the amount of services to be assured during the strike and provides for labour courts intrusion once the parties fail to define for themselves the amount of services to be provided for. Nonetheless it is a legal system that has failed to empower social partners and has amplified the role of labour courts. A change may be actually happening due to a complete new regulation of workers' representation but it is still too soon to predict what the future framing of legal regulation will be. Definitely, like many other social arrangements, labour regulation is also awaiting on fundamental societal options as the choice seems to lie between reinforcing its previous labour structure or reinventing itself. Maybe time has come to get hold of our destinies and to decide for once and for all what is to be our labour regulation including strikes in essential services.

Bibliography

Academia Nacional de Direito do Trabalho, Revista da Academia Nacional de Direito do Trabalho, 1993

Almeida, Gelsom Rozentino de, O governo Lula, o Fórum Nacional do Trabalho e reforma sindical, Katálysis 2007, 54 et seqq. Available at http://www.scielo.br/pdf/rk/v10n1/v10n1a07.pdf (accessed 30 March 2018)

Almeida, Juniele Rabêlo de, Um Novo Repertório da Ação Coletiva: Movimento Reivindicatório dos Praças da Polícia Militar em Belo Horizonte no ano de 1997 (dissertação de mestrado [master's dissertation]). Departamento de História, Faculdade de Filosofia e Ciências Humanas, Universidade Federal de Minas Gerais (UFMG), 2004

Almeida, Juniele Rabêlo de, Tropas em Protesto: o Ciclo de Movimentos Reivindicatórios dos Policiais Militares Brasileiros no Ano de 1997 (tese de doutorado [PhD's thesis]), Faculdade de Filosofia, Letras e Ciências Humanas, Programa de Pós-Graduação em História Social, Universidade de São Paulo (USP), 2010. Available at http://www.teses.usp.br/teses/disponiveis/8/8138/tde-12112010-150942/publico/2010_JunieleRabelodeAlmeida.pdf (accessed 4 April 2018)

Barros, Cássio Mesquita, O direito de greve na Constituição de 5 de outubro de 1988, Revista LTr 1988, 1336 et seqq.

Campos, André Gambier, Sindicatos no Brasil: O que esperar no futuro próximo? (Texto para discussão [Working Paper] 2262), Instituto de Pesquisa Econômica Aplicada (IPEA), 2016. Available at http://www.ipea.gov.br/portal/images/stories/PDFs/TDs/td_2262.pdf (accessed 15 November 2017)

Cardoso, José Claudemir Bezerra, O exercício da greve nas atividades essenciais do serviço público e a inexecução da prestação dos serviços básicos à população (dissertação de mestrado [master's dissertation]). Faculdade de Direito, Programa de Pós-Graduação em Direito, Universidade Federal de Alagoas (UFAL), 2009. Available at http://www.repositorio.ufal.br/bitstream/riufal/1287/1/O%20EXERC%c3%8dCIO%20DA%20GREVE%20NAS%20ATIVIDADES%20ESSENCIAIS%20DO%20SERVI%c3%87O.pdf (accessed 20 December 2017)

Coelho, Rogério, A greve, os grevistas e os não-grevistas, Revista LTr 1989, 1341 et seqq.

Costa, Orlando Teixeira da, O direito à greve na futura Constituição, Revista LTr 1986, 1289 et seqq.

Couto, Marlen/Vasconcellos, Fábio, Total de greves caiu após FHC e depois retomou aumento no fim do 2° governo Lula, Blog Na Base dos Dados, O Globo, 28 April 2017. Available at https://blogs.oglobo.globo.com/na-base-dos-dados/post/total-de-greves-apresenta-queda-e-depois-retomada-apos-segundo-governo-lula.html (accessed 30 March 2018)

Departamento Intersindical de Estatística e Estudos Socioeconômicos (Dieese), O movimento grevista em 2004 [Estudos e Pesquisas n. 12], 2005. Available at https://www.dieese.org.br/balancodasgreves/2004/estpesq12102005_greve2004.pdf (accessed 15 November 2017)

Departamento Intersindical de Estatística e Estudos Socioeconômicos (Dieese), As greves em 2005 [Estudos e Pesquisas n. 20], 2006. Available at https://www.dieese.org.br/balancodasgreves/2005/estpesq20_greves2005.pdf (accessed 15 November 2017)

Departamento Intersindical de Estatística e Estudos Socioeconômicos (Dieese), Balanço das greves em 2007 [Estudos e Pesquisas n. 41], 2008. Available at https://www.dieese.org.br/balancodasgreves/2007/estPesq41Greves2007.pdf (accessed 15 November 2017)

Departamento Intersindical de Estatística e Estudos Socioeconômicos (Dieese), Balanço das greves em 2008 [Estudos e Pesquisas n. 45], 2009. Available at https://www.dieese.org.br/balancodasgreves/2008/estPesq45balancoGreves2008.pdf (accessed 15 November 2017)

Departamento Intersindical de Estatística e Estudos Socioeconômicos (Dieese), Balanço das greves em 2009 e 2010 [Estudos e Pesquisas n. 60], 2012a. Available at https://www.dieese.org.br/balancodasgreves/2010/estPesq60balGreves20092010.pdf (accessed 15 November 2017)

Departamento Intersindical de Estatística e Estudos Socioeconômicos (Dieese), Balanço das greves em 2010-2011 [Estudos e Pesquisas n. 63], 2012b. Available at https://www.dieese.org.br/balancodasgreves/2011/estPesq63balGreves2010_2011.pdf (accessed 15 November 2017)

Departamento Intersindical de Estatística e Estudos Socioeconômicos (Dieese), Balanço das greves em 2012 [Estudos e Pesquisas n. 66], 2013. Available at https://www.dieese.org.br/balancodasgreves/2012/estPesq66balancogreves2012.pdf (accessed 15 November 2017)

Departamento Intersindical de Estatística e Estudos Socioeconômicos (Dieese), Balanço das greves em 2013 [Estudos e Pesquisas n. 79], 2015. Available at https://www.dieese.org.br/balancodasgreves/2013/estPesq79balancogreves2013.pdf (accessed 15 November 2017)

Departamento Intersindical de Estatística e Estudos Socioeconômicos (Dieese), Balanço das greves de 2016 [Estudos e Pesquisas n. 84], 2016. Available at https://www.dieese.org.br/balancodasgreves/2016/estPesq84balancogreves2016.pdf (accessed 15 November 2017)

Fragale Filho, Roberto/Siqueira Neto, José Francisco, Reforma trabalhista: uma cartografia das discussões equivocadas, esquecidas e frustrantes, Fevereiro 2018, 48 et seqq. Available at http://www.revistafevereiro.com/pdf/10/1.pdf (accessed 29 March 2018)

Frediani, Yone, Greve nos serviços essenciais à luz da Constituição Federal de 1988 (dissertação de mestrado [master's dissertation]). Faculdade de Direito, Programa de Pós-Graduação em Direito, Centro Universitário Fundação Instituto de Ensino para Osasco (UNIFIEO), 2001. Available at http://www.unifieo.br/pdfs/marketing/dissertacoes_mestrado_2005/yone%20frediani.pdf (accessed 20 December 2017)

Gernigon, Bernard/Odero, Alberto/Guido, Horacio, ILO Principles Concerning the Right to Strike, International Labour Review 1998, 441 et seqq. Available at http://www.ilo.org/wcmsp5/groups/public/---ed_norm/---normes/documents/publication/wcms_087987.pdf (accessed 20 December 2017)

Gomes, Ana Virginia/Prado, Mariana Mota, Flawed Freedom of Association in Brazil: How Unions Can Become an Obstacle to Meaningful Reforms in the Labor Law System, Comparative Labor Law & Policy Journal 2010, 843 et seqq.

Gottschalk, Elson, Greve, Conceito, Titulares (e) Modalidades, Revista LTr 1987, 1302 et seqq.

Guimarães, Carlos Alfredo Cruz, Direito de greve, Revista LTr 1989, 1318 et seqq.

Instituto Brasileiro de Geografia e Estatística (IBGE), Diretoria de Pesquisas, Coordenação de Trabalho e Rendimento, Pesquisa Nacional por Amostra de Domicílios. Aspectos das relações de trabalho e sindicalização, IBGE, 2017. Available at https://biblioteca.ibge.gov.br/visualizacao/livros/liv100322.pdf (accessed 15 November 2017)

Leite, Celso Barroso, Greve de servidores públicos, Revista LTr 1989, 163 et seqq.

Martins, Ildélio, Dimensões atuais do direito de greve, Revista LTr 1990, 160 et seqq.

Melo, Raimundo Simão de, A greve no direito brasileiro (4th edition), Editora LTr, 2017

Momezzo, Marta Casadei, A greve em serviços essenciais e a atuação do Ministério Público do Trabalho (tese de doutorado [PhD's thesis]), Faculdade de Direito, Programa de Pós-Graduação em Direito, Pontifícia Universidade Católica de São Paulo (PUC-SP), 2007. Available at https://tede2.pucsp.br/bitstream/handle/7686/1/Marta%20Casadei%20Momezzo.pdf (accessed 20 December 2017)

Moraes Filho, Evaristo de, Direito de greve, Revista LTr 1986, 775 et seqq.

Oliveira, Carlos Roberto de, A greve nos serviços essenciais no Brasil e na Itália (dissertação de mestrado [master's dissertation]). Faculdade de Direito, Programa de Pós-Graduação em Direito, Universidade de São Paulo (USP), 2012. Available at http://www.teses.usp.br/teses/disponiveis/2/2138/tde-02102012-164015/publico/Dissertacao_Carlos_Roberto_de_Oliveira.pdf (accessed 20 December 2017)

Ostrowski, Antonio/Meneguin, Fernando Boarato/Assis, Roberta Maria Corrêa de, Reforma sindical – Reflexões sobre o relatório final do Fórum Nacional do Trabalho (Texto para discussão [Working paper] 10), Coordenadoria Legislativa do Senado Federal (Conleg), 2004. Available at https://www12.senado.leg.br/publicacoes/estudos-legislativos/tipos-de-estudos/textos-para-discussao/td-10-reforma-sindical-reflexoes-sobre-o-relatorio-final-do-forum-nacional-do-trabalho (accessed 30 March 2018)

Pinto, Graciene Ferreira, Limites ao direito de greve no Brasil após a constituição de 1988 (dissertação de mestrado [master's dissertation]). Faculdade de Direito, Programa de Pós-Graduação em Direito, Pontifícia Universidade Católica de São Paulo (PUC-SP), 2007. Available at https://tede2.pucsp.br/bitstream/handle/7722/1/Graciene%20Ferreira%20Pinto.pdf (accessed 20 December 2017)

Prado, Roberto Barreto, O direito de greve em face da Constituição de 5-10-1988, Revista LTr 1988, 1388 et seqq.

Rocha, Guilherme Dall'Orto, 'Quis custodiet ipsos custodes?' Quando entram em greve aqueles que as devem coibir: linhas introdutórias sobre a 'greve branca' da polícia militar do Espírito Santo, Anais do Seminário de Ciências Sociais PGCS-UFES, 2017. Available at. Available at http://www.publicacoes.ufes.br/scs/article/view/18404/12359 (accessed 20 December 2017)

Santos, Júlio César Gomes dos, O Dia em que a Polícia Parou: a Verdadeira História da Greve da Polícia Mineira que Parou o Brasil, Júlio César Gomes dos Santos, 1998

Silva, José Ajuricaba da Costa e, A greve na nova Constituição, Revista LTr 1989, 266 et seqq.

Silva, Sayonara Grillo Coutinho Leonardo da/Gondim, Thiago Patrício, Conflitos coletivos de trabalho: implicações institucionais e evidências empíricas sobre a greve dos bombeiros militares do Estado do Rio de Janeiro, Revista da Faculdade Mineira de Direito 2017, 28 et seqq. Available at http://periodicos.pucminas.br/index.php/Direito/article/view/P.2318-7999.2017v20n39p28 (accessed 20 December 2017)

Sussekind, Arnaldo, Limitações ao direito de greve, Revista LTr 1989, 28 et seqq.

Tavares, Telma Núbia, Um enfoque sociológico acerca da greve, Revista LTr 1987, 10 et seqq.

Chapter 5

Canada

*Eric Tucker**

* I would like to thank Tyler Fram and Andrew Link for their outstanding research assistance and Christopher Rootham for his insightful comments on an earlier draft. Of course, I am responsible for any remaining errors.

1 GENERAL BACKGROUND: COUNTRY PROFILE

Canada is a federal state in which, as a general matter, labour relations come under provincial or territorial jurisdiction with a residual federal jurisdiction covering labour relations in federally regulated areas, including the federal public service, inter-provincial transportation and communications, and the postal service. Although it is estimated federal labour law covers about 10% of the Canadian workforce, because its jurisdiction extends to matters of national importance the federal government plays a disproportionately large role in regulating essential service strikes. Because there are ten provinces and three territories in Canada, each with their own labour relations laws, it is impossible to provide a comprehensive account of Canadian essential service strikes regulation. Therefore, the focus of this report is on federal and Ontario laws, with occasional forays into other jurisdictions where warranted.

Canada is best described as a liberal market economy with some social democratic tendencies. Historically, it has generally preferred to give capitalist enterprises a large measure of market freedom, but it has, to different degrees at different times and places, established public enterprises and created regulatory structures that limit market freedom in the name of securing the public welfare. In part, this can be explained by the fact that it is a large territory with a relatively small population, but more importantly since the turn of the twentieth century there have been various populist and labourist political formations that pressed for such arrangements. The New Democratic Party, founded in 1961, is the current heir to this tradition and it has formed the government at one time or another in seven provinces and one territory, although it has never formed the federal government. Its influence has fluctuated; at the end of 2017 it formed two provincial governments and was the official opposition in two others. Two other parties have dominated Canadian politics: the Liberals (centre-left) and Conservatives (centre-right).

In broad political terms, it is important to recognize that, like most advanced capitalist countries, since the 1970s its policy orientation shifted away from the Keynesian welfare state model that dominated in the decades after World War II toward neoliberalism.[1] The neoliberal turn has had a significant impact on the legal regulation of essential services, which this chapter explores in detail.

Canada is a parliamentary democracy based on the English model it inherited. Its legal system is rooted in the common law, with the exception of Quebec, which is a civil law jurisdiction. Prior to 1982, the principle of

1. *Harvey*, 2005; *Cahill/Konings*, 2017.

parliamentary sovereignty within jurisdictional boundaries was near absolute. This changed dramatically in 1982 with the adoption of the *Charter of Rights and Freedoms*.[2] Charter rights now limit executive and legislative powers and, in the last fifteen years, the Charter has become an important source of labour rights with significant consequences for the regulation of essential service strikes.

The legal status of trade unions was ambiguous in Canada prior to 1872 when the government enacted the *Trade Union Act*.[3] As a result, workers became formally free to join a union, bargain collectively and, under certain conditions, collectively withdraw their labour, without fear of prosecution. But none of these freedoms was legally protected by rights. Employers could fire workers for joining unions or acting collectively.

It was not until the Second World War and its immediate aftermath that Canadian jurisdictions adopted the Wagner Act model (WAM) of labour relations, which provided a legally protected right to organize and engage in lawful trade union activities, including striking, in exchange for severe limitations on legal freedoms, most importantly the freedom to strike.[4] Statutory collective bargaining schemes, however, did not extend to most public sector workers until the late 1960s. The public sector collective bargaining laws of the 1960s often departed from the private sector model in significant ways, including the freedom to strike which was more tightly controlled, in part because of concerns about the disruption of essential services. Again, these limits will be explored in more detail.

Under the WAM, private sector union density increased, peaking at around 30% in the late-1950s to early 1960s. So too did collective bargaining coverage.[5] Since that time density has steadily declined and is now estimated to be about 16%. Public sector union density grew rapidly in the late 1960s, reaching around 70%, where it has hovered ever since.

Since enterprise bargaining is built into the DNA of the WAM, there is little incentive for employers' associations to form for the purposes of collective bargaining. While there are exceptions, such as large-scale construction where sectoral bargaining is the norm, employer associations do not play a direct role in Canadian collective bargaining, although they actively seek to advance employer interests, including by intervening in legal cases where permitted.

Strike activity in Canada, like in most of the advanced capitalist countries, has declined precipitously in recent decades.[6] Figure 1[7] illustrates the downward trend for both private and public sector strikes in Canada from 1979 to 2007. In the past decade the number of person days lost to strikes in the private and

2. Canadian Charter of Rights and Freedoms, Part I of the Constitution Act, 1982, being Schedule B to the Canada Act 1982 (UK), 1982, c 11.
3. *Tucker*, 1991.
4. *Fudge/Tucker*, 2001 and 2010, 15.
5. The discrepancy arises because bargaining unit members are not always required to be union members.
6. *Tucker*, 2014.
7. *Ibid.*

public sectors has fluctuated widely but the overall downward trend has not changed.[8]

Figure 5.1 Public and Private Sector Strike Rates per 1000 Workers, 1979 to 2007

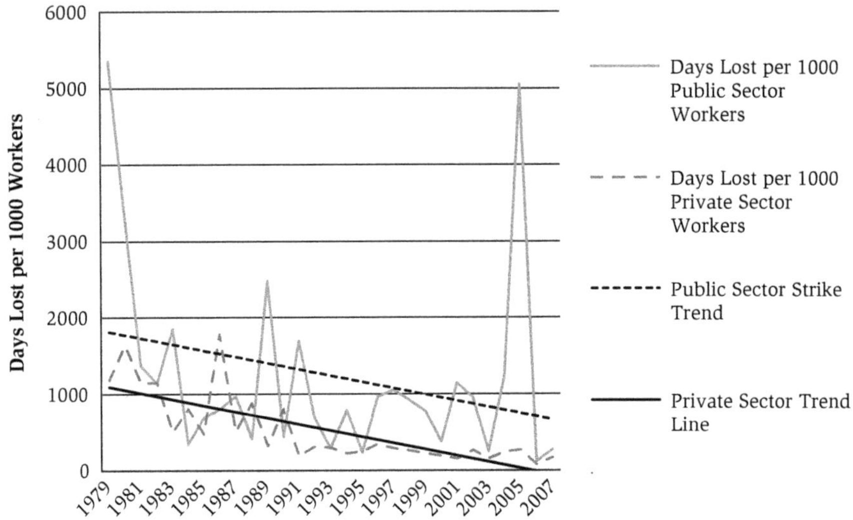

2 COLLECTIVE LABOUR RELATIONS

As mentioned above, the Canadian collective bargaining regime is based on the WAM, but before clarifying its principal features regarding organizing, bargaining, and striking, it is important to highlight the distinction between freedoms and rights already averted to. Using the Hohfeldian conceptual framework, we think of freedoms and rights as jural relations between people.[9] You are free to do something when no one else can call upon the state to stop you. This is different from a legal right, which entails a legal duty on others not to interfere with your action. The distinction is crucial in labour law.

Beginning with organizing, as noted above, Canadians were legally free to organize unions from at least the late-nineteenth century, but it was only in the late-1930s that organizing became a legally protected right. Labour statutes prohibited employers from interfering with or threatening union organizing activity, although the law preserved their freedom to express their opposition to

8. *Government of Canada*, 2018.
9. *Hohfeld*, 1919.

unions. This produced a grey zone about the boundary between fair and unfair employer labour practices.[10]

The law also formally decriminalized collective bargaining in the late-nineteenth century but collective agreements were not legally enforceable since the common law viewed them as contracts in restraint of trade. Moreover, employees had no protected right to bargain collectively until post-war labour legislation imposed a duty on employers to bargain in good faith with certified trade unions that demonstrated majority support within a bargaining unit. As well, those laws made agreements enforceable through grievance arbitration.

The issue of strikes is a bit more complex. Workers also were generally free to strike but, under common law, the withdrawal of labour was a breach of contract that allowed the employer to summarily dismiss the striking workers. Statutory collective bargaining laws gave workers a legal right to strike in that it protected their employment status while on strike and provided a legal right to return to their jobs after the strike ended. However, these laws also placed severe restrictions on the freedom to strike, discussed below.

As already mentioned, public sector workers were frequently subject to a different legal regime regarding strikes. Some statutes denied public sector workers any freedom to strike, while others permitted limited strikes but required the maintenance of essential services. Often interest arbitration was a substitute to resolve bargaining disputes. We will return to these issues, *infra*.

Prior to the *Charter*, labour rights and freedoms were rooted in common law and statute. This has now changed. The *Charter* explicitly protects freedom of association, but the scope of that protection is undefined and requires judicial interpretation. From the outset courts accepted that freedom of association protected the freedom to organize, but that freedom was not under threat in Canada since it was rarely restricted by government. The more important issue for workers excluded from statutory collective bargaining schemes was whether the *Charter* required the government to protect the right to organize. The general answer was no, except in limited cases where it could be demonstrated that workers are incapable of exercising their freedom without rights protection.[11]

The question of whether the *Charter* protects the freedom or right to bargain and strike is much more important in the context of essential services where governments frequently restrict these freedoms. The Supreme Court of Canada (SCC) initially rejected the proposition that freedom of association protected either, but in 2007 the court unexpectedly reversed itself. It held that freedom of association protected the freedom to bargain collectively and that it entailed a duty to bargain in good faith. This made collective bargaining both a

10. *Slinn*, 2008, 53.
11. *Dunmore v Ontario (Attorney General)*, 2001 SCC 94 (2001).

constitutionally protected freedom and right.[12] Eight years later, the SCC also held that freedom of association protects the freedom to strike.[13]

There are, however, two important caveats. The first is that the *Charter* only applies to government action. This is less of an issue in the essential services context where government is normally the actor, either as legislator or as employer. The second caveat is that the *Charter* permits violations of protected rights where the restriction can be demonstrably justified in a free and democratic society. This is very significant since the SCC stated that interference with associational rights may be permitted in situations involving essential services.[14] This issue will be examined in more detail, *infra*.

Until recently, international labour rights played an insignificant role in Canadian labour law. There were several reasons for this. One is that since Canada is a dualist country, international treaty obligations entered into by the federal government does not become domestic law unless implemented by domestic legislation, and provincial legislatures are under no constitutional obligation to pass implementing legislation.[15]

A second reason is Canadian governments' limited embrace of International Labour Organization (ILO) norms. This was evidenced by the fact that prior to 14 June 2017, Canada had only ratified one of the two foundational conventions supporting freedom of association (Convention 87, but not Convention 98). Of course, the lack of ratifications did not immunize Canada from complaints that it violated freedom of association, since the ILO considers that all members are bound to respect freedom of association regardless of whether they have ratified its underlying conventions. In fact, Canadian unions frequently complained to the ILO and its supervisory bodies often upheld those complaints and made recommendations to the offending government. However, those recommendations had no legal force and no political impact either. As a result, governments felt free to ignore the ILO and the violations continued.[16]

In recent years, however, international law has come to play a much more significant role through its influence on the development of constitutional law. The turning point came when the SCC determined that the meaning of freedom of association under the *Charter* should be as generous as it is in international law and thought. The SCC translated the soft law of the ILO and various UN declarations into hard constitutional law in Canada and, as we shall see, that has had a significant influence on the development of constitutional labour rights in Canada.[17]

12. *Health Services and Support – Facilities Subsector Bargaining Assn v British Columbia*, 2007 SCC 27 (2007).
13. *Saskatchewan Federation of Labour v Saskatchewan*, 2015 SCC 4 (2015).
14. *Health Services*, para. 108.
15. *Macklem*, 2012.
16. *Adams*, 2006
17. *Health Services*; *Bogg/Ewing*, 2012, 379; *Langille*, 2007, 363.

3 THE RIGHT TO STRIKE

As mentioned, the WAM imposes significant restrictions on the freedom to strike. In particular, recognition strikes and strikes during the life of a collective agreement are prohibited. There are also procedural requirements that must be satisfied for a strike or lockout to be legal. These vary from jurisdiction to jurisdiction, but typically include the following. First, the union must have won a strike vote among the members of the bargaining unit. Second, the union and the employer must have bargained to impasse and undergone mediation or conciliation without success. Third, they must wait a prescribed number of days after mediation/conciliation has failed before taking industrial action. Fourth, some jurisdictions, including the federal jurisdiction but not Ontario, require the union provide the employer with advance notice of the strike.[18]

In general, the law only permits economic strikes to support collective bargaining demands. Sympathy or political strikes are almost always unlawful since unions can only legally strike during the narrow window of opportunity that opens when no collective agreement is in force and the procedural hurdles have been cleared. Political and sympathy strikes are not exempt from these general rules and so are illegal if they are untimely. Canadian unions have so deeply absorbed these norms that no case has ever posed the question of whether a union in a legal strike position could engage in a sympathy or a political strike.

The definition of a strike is quite broad and in addition to a complete work stoppage includes any concerted action undertaken with a common understanding designed to restrict or limit output. Thus, a partial work stoppage, a slowdown, or a work-to-rule campaign are all considered strikes.[19]

It is important to emphasize that while the general restrictions described here apply to both private and public sector workers, public sectors workers and particularly essential service workers are subject to additional restrictions, described *infra*.

4 THE EXPERIENCE WITH STRIKES IN ESSENTIAL SERVICES

There are no recent studies of the prevalence of strikes in essential services, if only because in Canada essential services strikes are heavily regulated and,

18. *Fudge/Tucker*, 2001 and 2010; *Slinn/Tucker*, 2016, 171; *Adams*, 1993, 11.7 et seq.
19. Labour Relations Act, 1995, SO 1995, c 1, s 1(1) 'strike' includes a cessation of work, a refusal to work or to continue to work by employees in combination or in concert or in accordance with a common understanding, or a slow-down or other concerted activity on the part of employees designed to restrict or limit output; Canada Labour Code, RSC, 1985, c L-2, s 3(1) 'strike' includes a cessation of work or a refusal to work or to continue to work by employees, in combination, in concert or in accordance with a common understanding, and a slowdown of work or other concerted activity on the part of employees in relation to their work that is designed to restrict or limit output; *Adams*, 1993, 11.1(i).

because of that fact, likely infrequent. This was not always the case. As statutory collective bargaining laws were extended to public sector workers in the 1960s, much attention was paid to the issue of essential service strikes. For example, in 1968 Professor Harry Arthurs conducted a major study of strikes in essential services and reported that from 1946 to 1966 strikes in essential industries had become more frequent and that person days lost in total and per strike were increasing. [20]

If we consider the Canadian experience with essential service strike regulation from a qualitative perspective, it has revolved around two fundamental questions: what are essential services and how should essential service disputes be resolved? We address the former question here and the latter in Section 5 of this chapter.

Historically, the concept of essentiality in Canada has been a political one. What activities are so important to the public welfare such that stoppages pose unacceptable risk and hardship to the broader public? The answer to that question has changed over time and place. For example, one of Canada's earliest collective bargaining laws, the *Industrial Disputes Investigation Act* of 1907 (IDIA) required the parties to undergo a process of conciliation prior to a labour stoppage in mining, transportation, communications and public utilities. These services were understood at the time to be so essential as to warrant restrictions on actions that the parties were otherwise free to undertake.[21] During war time the IDIA was extended to war production industries, expanding the scope of essential services. The post-World War II collective bargaining statutes retained compulsory conciliation as a general requirement, not because governments considered the economy as a whole an essential service, but rather because compulsory conciliation had come to be seen as a good industrial relations strategy for avoiding unnecessary conflict. However, these laws only applied to the private sector and so there was not a great need to be concerned over the definition essential services.

The exception was with respect to municipal police and fire-fighters. Although these workers were generally excluded from the normative private sector schemes, they were soon given access to collective bargaining through sector specific statutes.[22] While some statutes permitted police strikes, in practice *ad hoc* legislation usually prevented police from exercising this freedom.[23] However, most statutory schemes applicable to police and fire-fighters expressly prohibited strikes and substituted binding interest arbitration by

20. *Arthurs*, 1971, 1 et seqq.
21. Industrial Disputes Investigation Act, 6-7 Edward VII, ch. 20 (1907); *Fudge/Tucker*, 2001 and 2010, 52 et seqq.
22. For example, see the Fire Departments Act, SO 1947, c 37; the Police Amendment Act, SO 1947, c 77.
23. In October 1969 Montreal police and fire-fighters went on a legal strike. During the sixteen hours that the strikes were permitted bank robberies increased and a riot occurred during which one police officer was fatally wounded. The army was called out and back to work legislation was quickly passed. Online at http://archives.cbc.ca/on_this_day/10/07/.

neutral third parties. This interference with free collective bargaining was justified because of the overriding public safety interest in maintaining these services and that judgment has never been seriously challenged.[24]

Outside of police and fire-fighters, the issue of determining which services were essential only became pressing when government extended collective bargaining to the public and para-public sectors more broadly, beginning in the mid to late 1960s. One contemporary commentator, Paul Phillips, described the scope of essential services to be 'whatever the responsible public authority believes it to be at any point in time.' Reflecting the ambiguities of the time, Harry Arthurs described essentiality as lying 'mid-way along the progression from very limited cases where a labour dispute actually does create (or threatens to create) a danger, to that very broad class of cases where the dispute touches the public interest in a very incidental way.'[25]

We will look more closely *infra* at the ways in which Canadian governments have defined essential services in the context of the strike regulation laws of Ontario and the federal jurisdiction. However, the freedom of governments to define essential services (and to regulate essential service strikes) is now limited by the SCC's interpretation of the *Charter*'s protection of freedom of association. Here we deal only with constitutional limits on the government's freedom to define essential services.

The basic question asked by the court in the *Saskatchewan Federation of Labour* (*SFL*) case is 'whether the legislative interference with the right to strike in a particular case amounts to a substantial interference with collective bargaining.'[26] If a law substantially interferes, then the burden shifts to the government to demonstrate that the restriction is demonstrably justified in a free and democratic society. Here is where the scope of essentiality comes into play. The first step in a section 1 defence under the *Charter* is to establish that the law aims to achieve a pressing and substantial objective. In the *SFL* case, the court accepted that maintaining essential services is such an objective, but before the argument can succeed, the court has to be convinced that the services the government is protecting are sufficiently essential so that their protection is a pressing and substantial objective. This raises the need to demarcate what services are essential or when the consequences of a labour disruption are sufficiently serious to justify interference with the constitutional freedom to strike.[27]

The court begins its discussion with the definition of essential services in international law. For this purpose, they accept a summary of that law presented in an affidavit filed by Professor Patrick Macklem, who identifies three situations

24. *Jackson*, 1995, 313 et seqq.; *Haney*, 1974; *Downie/Jackson*, 1980.
25. *Phillips*, 1975, 39 (italics in original); *Arthurs*, 1971.
26. *Saskatchewan*, at para. 78.
27. *Ibid.*, para. 86.

in which the ILO's supervisory bodies have justified strike restrictions on essential service grounds:

(1) in the public service only for public servants exercising authority in the name of the state;
(2) in essential services in the strict sense of the term (that is, services the interruption of which would endanger the life, personal safety or health of the whole or part of the population); or
(3) in the event of an acute national emergency and for a limited period of time.[28]

Without getting into the details of the contested Saskatchewan legislation, the SCC found that it was overly broad because 'the categories of workers whose right to strike may be abrogated because they provide essential services is subject to the employer's unilateral discretion.'[29] While the court does not provide a bright-line definition of essential services, its reference to international law is significant because in the past the court has expressed the opinion that freedom of association in Canada should be interpreted as generously as it is in international law. The court was also disturbed by the absence of a collaborative process for categorizing services as essential and determining the number of employees necessary to maintain them.[30]

Since the *SFL* decision, there has been one lower court judgment that dealt directly with the question of whether the government had a pressing and substantial interest that justified an infringement of the right to strike. The case arose out of continuing conflicts between the teachers' unions and the Ontario provincial government, which the government resolved by passing legislation that imposed terms and conditions on unions that did not reach an agreement by a set date. One effect of measure was that it deprived workers of the freedom to strike that they otherwise would have enjoyed. The unions successfully challenged the legislation as a violation of their *Charter* rights. The court accepted that the legislation substantially interfered with their freedom to strike and held that the interference was not justified. Central to the court's holding was its conclusion that the government's purpose was fiscal restraint rather than maintaining or restoring essential services. It then stated: 'It is only in exceptional circumstances that a breach of rights under the *Charter* will be justified based on economic concerns.'[31]

It will take further litigation to clarify where and how courts will draw the line demarcating services as essential, but it is clear that governments no longer have the absolute right unilaterally to make that determination.

28. *Ibid.*
29. *Ibid.*, para. 87.
30. *Ibid.*, at para. 89.
31. *OPSEU v Ontario*, 2016 ONSC 2197, at para. 238 (2016).

5 RESTRICTIONS ON THE RIGHT TO STRIKE IN ESSENTIAL SERVICES

5.1 The Constitutional Framework

It is clear that any discussion of statutory restrictions on the right to strike of employees in essential services must begin with a consideration of Canada's newly constitutionalized labour rights, including the right to unionize, the right to bargain collectively, and the right to strike. We have previously discussed how this body of law affects the definition of essentiality. Here we discuss the impact of constitutional labour rights on the government's power to regulate essential service strikes by excluding workers from the right to organize, bargain, or strike, or imposing substantial limits on their exercise.

Canada historically rarely deprived workers of their freedom to form associations, even for police and other public security workers. As well, it rarely denied workers the freedom to bargain collectively. Instead, Canada has generally secured essential services related to public security by denying workers the freedom to strike - the no-strike model - or limiting the strike to maintain essential services - the designation model. There are exceptions,[32] however, including members of the armed forces, who are not covered by any collective bargaining legislation.[33]

Another exception was the he Royal Canadian Mounted Police (RCMP) whose situation merits closer examination because of their recent successful constitutional challenge to their exclusion from collective labour rights. The RCMP provides police service at the federal level and for many of Canada's provinces and territories. As such, it is the closest thing Canada has to a national police force. In part because of its long history of involvement in internal security and strikebreaking, the government was concerned about RCMP officers having connections to the labour movement. Indeed, from 1918 to 1974 they were prohibited by an order-in-council from engaging in union-related activity on pain of instant dismissal.[34] When the order-in-council was lifted in 1974, the head of the RCMP recognized there was a high level of discontent among officers and instituted the Division Staff Relations Representation Program (DSRRP) to

32. An interesting recent exception was 2003 legislation passed in Quebec, which declared certain home care and child-care workers not to be employees. The effect of the law was to remove them from any statutory collective bargaining scheme so that any attempt to bargain collectively was potentially a violation of competition law. The legislation was declared unconstitutional in 2008, a year after the SCC recognized that freedom of association protected collective bargaining. See *Confédération des syndicats nationaux c Québec (Procureur General)*, 2008 QCCS 5076 (2008).
33. The Public Service Alliance of Canada (PSAC) unsuccessfully petitioned the Canadian government in 1971 to create statutory collective bargaining schemes for the military. See PSAC, *Collective Bargaining Rights for Members of the Armed Forces* (Presented to the Committee on Legislation Review April 1971).
34. *Fudge/Tucker*, 2001 and 2010, 100 et seqq. For a history of the restrictions on freedom of association of RCMP members, see *Mounted Police Association of Ontario v. Canada (Attorney General)*, 2009 CanLII 15149 (ON SC), <http://canlii.ca/t/2315w>, retrieved

provide for a weak form of consultation. The program was formalized in regulation in 1989 and renamed the Staff Relations Representation Program (SSRP). Then, in 1996, a Pay Council was created to provide officers with a mechanism for being consulted on compensation issues. RCMP officers chose representatives to participate in both these bodies, which were the only bodies the RCMP recognized for the purposes of discussing workplace and wage issues. Neither body was independent of government nor was there a role for collective bargaining. Both bodies were limited to consultation.

RCMP officers first challenged their exclusion from any statutory collective bargaining law in early years of *Charter* litigation but were unsuccessful. The SCC embraced a thin interpretation of freedom of association as only protecting the freedom to form associations. Since the law did not prohibit RCMP officers from forming associations their *Charter* rights were not violated.[35]

In 2006, an independent association of RCMP officers, the Mounted Police Association of Ontario (MPAO), launched a fresh challenge to the constitutionality of the RCMP's representation scheme. Their case was bolstered in 2007 when the SCC adopted a broader view that freedom of association that protected collective bargaining and this time the challenge succeeded. The SCC held that the SRRP substantially failed to provide RCMP officers with a meaningful process of collective bargaining by denying them representation by an association independent of government and by depriving officers of a sufficient degree of choice in the selection of their representatives. The SCC also rejected the government's defence that the infringement was justified because unionization would compromise the force's neutrality.[36] The effect of the judgment is to limit severely the power of government to protect essential services by depriving workers of the right to form independent unions or bargain collectively.

This leaves governments with the option of regulating strikes, but their power is constitutionally limited. In order to determine whether restrictions on strikes are constitutional, the court must answer two key questions. The first is whether the restrictions on the freedom to strike substantially interfere with a process of collective bargaining. A complete ban on strikes, or even broadly drawn restrictions, will constitute substantial interference, so this is unlikely to be the difficult point in litigation. Rather, the key question will be whether the government can satisfy the court that the interference is demonstrably justified. The starting point for the justification will be that the freedom to strike is limited to maintain essential services, which, as discussed in section 4, involves the court in patrolling the boundaries of what constitute essential services. Assuming the government satisfies the court that it has a pressing and substantial objective, it must then demonstrate minimum impairment. That inquiry will

on 2018-03-08. Even today, statutes prohibit police from being members of unions that are affiliated with the labour movement. For example, see Police Services Act, RSO 1990, c P-15, s 117.

35. *Delisle v Canada (Deputy Attorney General)*, [1999] 2 SCR 989 (1999).
36. *Mounted Police Association of Ontario v Canada (Attorney General)*, 2015 SCC 1 (2015).

lead the court to examine the scope of the restrictions, the process by which they were developed, and the alternative provided to the strike.

Where the government adopts the no-strike model, the court will want to be satisfied that a less restrictive approach that preserved a limited right to strike could not have met its legitimate interest in preserving essential services. As well, it will require that the strike alternative provides the affected workers with an acceptable substitute, such as binding interest arbitration by a neutral third party. Where the government has selected a designation model, as in the *SFL* case, the court will examine whether the processes for determining which services are essential and how those essential services will be provided are minimally impairing.

In the *SFL* case, the trial judge found that the restrictions went far beyond what was necessary to maintain essential services. The SCC agreed:

> The *unilateral* authority of public employers to determine whether and how essential services are to be maintained during a work stoppage with no adequate review mechanism, and the absence of a meaningful dispute resolution mechanism to resolve bargaining impasses, justify the trial judge's conclusion that the *PSESA* impairs the s. 2 (*d*) rights more than is necessary.[37]

5.2 Securing Essential Services by Exclusion from Collective Labour Relations Rights (No Right to Bargain Collectively and/or No Right to Strike)

In general, few Canadian workers are *ex ante* deprived of the right to bargain collectively. One such group is employees of the Canadian Security and Intelligence Service. Except for clerical and secretarial employees, they have no right to bargain or strike. As discussed earlier, RCMP officers were in a similar situation until the SCC found their exclusion was unconstitutional in 2015. In response, the government enacted legislation in 2017 that provides RCMP officers with a process to unionize and bargain collectively.[38]

It is far more common for governments to deprive essential service workers *ex ante* of the right to strike. As mentioned earlier, this is the common approach to public security workers, such as police, fire-fighters and prison guards. Not surprisingly, when the federal government provided RCMP officers with a statutory collective bargaining scheme, they adopted the no-strike model, providing them with arbitration instead.

Ontario, hospital workers are the other major group subject to the no-strike model. In 1965 following a strike at a public hospital, the Ontario government enacted the *Hospital Labour Disputes Arbitration Act* (HLDAA), which provides that in the event of an impasse the parties are obliged to submit their dispute to

37. *Saskatchewan*, 81.
38. *Federal Public Sector Labour Relations Act*, SC 2017, c 9.

arbitration.[39] Another group of workers recently deprived of the right to strike are employees of the Toronto Transit Commission (TTC).[40] The government enacted the exclusion in 2011 at the request of the City of Toronto. Prior to the enactment, the government had ended a number of TTC strikes through back-to-work legislation.

Workers and unions who strike unlawfully potentially face very serious penalties regardless of the circumstances. Some no-strike laws specify the consequences of violations of the law, but many incorporate the laws that govern unlawful strikes generally. For example, the recent TTC strike law expressly incorporates by reference the provisions of the *Labour Relations Act* (LRA) regarding unlawful strikes.[41] All contraventions of the LRA, including untimely strikes, are regulatory offences for which individuals are liable to fines of up to $2,000 and unions up to $25,000 for each day they are in violation. However, prosecutions can only be instituted with the written consent of the Labour Board. Labour boards also have the power to issue unlawful strike declarations, which have the same legal effect as a court order. Striking workers and union leaders who defy court orders could face civil or criminal contempt proceedings that could result in fines or jail.[42]

Apart from statute, employers can discipline individual workers who strike illegally, including termination. Employees can challenge disciplinary action through the grievance procedure, but arbitrators accept that unlawful striking is a disciplinary matter, the only issue being whether the severity of the penalty is justified in the circumstances of the case. As well, employers can bring grievances against the union, which is under a strict obligation not to participate in or facilitate unlawful strikes and to use its influence to end them when they occur. Arbitrators have the power to award damages against the union should they breach the peace obligation.

Unlawful strikes may give rise to tort liability. While there is no nominal tort of breach of statute (unless it was the intent of the legislature to create such liability), unlawful strikes by essential service workers will likely be tortious on other grounds. For example, an action for civil conspiracy using unlawful means could succeed on the basis that the strike violated a statutory prohibition on strikes.

In addition to the sanctions discussed above, in some circumstances essential service workers could be prosecuted for criminal breach of contract. Under the law, which dates back to 1878, it is a crime to wilfully breach a contract if you have reasonable cause to believe that the probable consequences

39. For the background and early experience, see *White*, 1995, 82 et seqq; *Arthurs*, 1971, 82 et seqq. The current statute is RSO 1990, c H-14.
40. *Toronto Transit Commission Labour Disputes Resolution Act*, 2011, SO 2011, c 2.
41. *Ibid.*, s 17.
42. *Fudge/Glasbeek*, 1992. In another famous incident, the leader of the postal workers' union, Jean-Claude Parrot was convicted of criminal contempt for refusing to order his members back to work after Parliament enacted back-to-work legislation. See *R v Parrot*, 106 DLR (3d) 296 (ONCA) (1979) and *Mandel/Glasbeek*, 1979, 10.

of doing so will be to endanger human life, cause serious bodily injury, expose valuable property to serious injury or destruction, deprive the residents of a municipality of their supply of light, power or gas, or delay or prevent the running of trains.[43] However, the likelihood of prosecution is remote. Indeed, we have not located a single reported case.[44]

Strikes in defiance of the no-strike model are uncommon. The authors of a study of public sector bargaining between 1978 and 2008 found that of the 791 contracts negotiated under this regime, unions struck just 4 times.[45] The most significant strike undertaken by Ontario workers under the no-strike regime was in 1981 when approximately 10,000 health care workers covered by the HLDAA walked off the job. The Ontario government obtained a court injunction ordering the nurses back to work. The leader of the union, Grace Hartman, refused to order her members back to work and the Attorney General threatened mass prosecution of union leaders and even possibly of members. The strike collapsed soon thereafter. Seventeen union leaders were subsequently charged with contempt. Pursuant to a plea deal, Hartman was sentenced to 45 days of imprisonment, two other leaders received 15 day sentences, and the remainder received suspended sentences and were fined $300 each. Striking workers faced disciplinary action by their employers. Thirty-four local leaders were dismissed but arbitrators reinstated most, subject to lengthy disciplinary suspensions without pay. Striking workers were meted out 5,500 letters of reprimand and 3,442 disciplinary suspensions.[46] Later that year acute care nurses implemented a work-to-rule campaign and an overtime ban to show their displeasure over the lack of progress in negotiations. While these actions are strikes under Ontario law, no disciplinary action followed.[47]

To date, unions have not challenged the constitutionality of the no-strike model, but it only became possible to do so in 2015 after the *SFL* decision.[48] Prior to that time, unions would have brought their complaints to the ILO. There were two early complaints by unions in Ontario and Alberta objecting to older legislation that barred government employees from striking, the *Public Service Employee Relations Act* (Alberta) and the *Crown Employees Collective Bargaining Act* (Ontario).[49] In its reports, the Committee on Freedom of Association (CFA) found that both statutes were overly broad because they covered employees of

43. *Criminal Code of Canada*, RSC 1985, c C-46, s 422. Craven, 1999, 142 et seqq.
44. But, see *Johnston et al v Mackey et al.*, (1937) 67 CCC 196 (NSSC), where the court held that a strike involving wilful breaches of contract, where the probable consequence of the strike would have resulted in serious property damage in violation of the Code, was tortious.
45. *Campolieti/Hebdon/Dachis*, 2016, 201.
46. *Deverell*, 1982, 179; *White*, 1990, 73 et seqq.
47. *Haiven/Haiven*, 2002, 5 et seqq.
48. At the time of writing, the Amalgamated Transit Workers Union, Local 113 filed an application challenging the no-strike legislation, but as of the time of writing there is no report of the case's progress. See *Kalinowski/Ferguson*, 2015.
49. SA 1977, c 40; SO 1972, c 67, s 25.

crown agencies such as liquor control boards whose work was not essential. Apart from over-breadth, the Committee found the restrictions were otherwise justified and that the statutes provided adequate safeguards to protect the interests of those workers deprived of the right to strike, including adequate, impartial and binding conciliation, and arbitration procedures.[50]

The most recent ILO complaint arose out of the 2011 legislation prohibiting strikes by TTC workers. The Committee did not consider metropolitan transportation to be an essential service in the strict sense of the term, but it recognized urban transit as a public service of primary importance where the requirement of a minimum service might be justified.[51] Both Ontario and Alberta subsequently replaced the no-strike model for public sector workers with a controlled strike model, but in neither case was the action taken as a response to the CFA's findings. Rather, in both provinces, their first elected New Democratic Party government made the change.[52]

5.3 Securing Essential Services by Imposing Limitations on the Right to Strike (Controlled Strike Model)

The controlled strike model is the predominant approach to regulating essential service strikes in Canada that do not involve public security service workers. The approach was first adopted by the Federal government when it created a statutory collective bargaining scheme for the federal public service in the *Public Service Staff Relations Act* in 1967 (PSSRA)(now the *Federal Public Service Labour Relations Act* (FPSLRA).[53] The PSSRA was unusual in that it offered unions the choice between the no-strike model, leading to binding arbitration, and the controlled strike model. Many governments subsequently adopted the controlled-strike model when they created public sector statutory collective bargaining schemes, although most did not offer unions the choice of opting for the no-strike/binding interest arbitration model, except under limited circumstances.

Three Canadian jurisdictions also integrated the controlled strike model into their private sector collective bargaining statutes where the unfettered strike model is the norm. One justification for imposing *ex ante* restrictions on private sector strikes is that private sector workers are increasingly performing work

50. Interim Report - Report No 187, Nov. 1978, Case No 893 (Canada) - Complaint date: 04-NOV-77 - Closed; Definitive Report - Report No 214, March 1982, Case No 1071 (Canada) - Complaint date: 06-JUL-81 - Closed.
51. Report in which the committee requests to be kept informed of development - Report No 377, March, 2016, Case No 3107 (Canada) - Complaint date: 05-DEC-14 - Follow-up.
52. For Ontario, SO 1993, c 38, for Alberta, SA 2016, c 10.
53. SC 1967, c 72. In 2003, the statute was renamed the *Public Service Labour Relations Act*, SC 2003, c 22 and in 2017 it was renamed again as the *Federal Public Sector Labour Relations Act*, S.C. 2017, c. 9. Unless I am making specific reference to an earlier version of the legislation, I will use FPSLRA acronym. On the origins and background of the act, see *Arthurs*, 1971, ch. 3, and *Rootham*, 2007, 27 et seqq.

that is vital to public health and safety. For example, a 1995 Task Force Report recommended there be a designation process in the *Canada Labour Code* (CLC), in part because privatization of certain crucial functions, like air traffic control, shifted their labour relations from the FPSLRA to the CLC.[54]

As well, in British Columbia and Quebec, the use of replacement workers during strikes is highly restricted. As a result, the risk increases that a work stoppage could significantly disrupt the production of goods and services necessary for the public's health and safety or result in substantial property damage or deterioration, thus providing a justification for *ex ante* strike restrictions.[55]

It is not possible to provide an account of the many variations on the controlled strike model in Canada and so we will focus on two, the FPSLRA and the CLC.

5.3.1 Federal Public Service Labour Relations Act

The designation process under the FPSLRA has been quite controversial and has undergone at least three major changes. At the time of writing, it is likely to revert to the model that was in place prior to the most recent changes in 2013.

In its first iteration, the act defined essential services narrowly as 'a service, facility or activity of the Government of Canada that is or will be, at any time, necessary for the safety or security of the public or a segment of the public.' This definition closely tracked the ILO's definition. The government initiated the designation process by proposing a list of designated positions and then the parties bargained in an attempt to reach an agreement. If the parties could not agree, the Public Service Staff Relations Board had jurisdiction to resolve the matter. A 1982 SCC judgment, *CATCA*, narrowly interpreted the scope of the board's powers, so that it could only determine which services were essential, but could not interfere with the government's determination of the level of service required.[56] The effect of the SCC's judgment was to expand the government's power to designate and, in the following years, the percentage of public service positions designated as essential jumped sharply.[57] However, because unions had the option of electing arbitration, they could opt out of the controlled strike model if designation levels made the strike option ineffective.

54. For a discussion of the background to the adoption of the designation model and its rationale, see *Adell*, 2001, 28 et seqq.
55. For a discussion and strong expression of judicial support for limiting the freedom to strike to protect essential services, see *Canadian Union of Public Employees, Local 301 v Montreal (City)*, [1997] 1 SCR 793 (1997).
56. *Canadian Air Traffic Control Association v Canada (Treasury Board)*, [1982] 1 SCR 696 (1982).
57. *Adell*, 2001, 30 et seqq.; *Swimmer*, 1995, 377 et seqq.; *Panitch/Swartz*, 2003, 93 et seqq.; *Finkelman*, 1986, 691 (limited use of designations prior to CATCA; effect of SCC judgment severely limits capability of union to mount an effective strike).

The government tweaked the model in 2003 after a lengthy review process by an Advisory Committee and a Task Force. The government repealed and replaced the PSSRA with the *Public Service Labour Relations Act* (PSLRA). With regard to essential services, the new law aimed to strengthen the role of negotiation in creating essential service agreements. It required the government to notify the union within 20 days after the union gave notice to bargain that it considered employees in the bargaining unit occupied essential service positions. The parties were then required to begin good faith bargaining to enter into an essential services agreement. This involved a three step process. First, it was necessary to determine which services are necessary to insure public safety or security in the vent of a strike. If the parties cannot agree, the PSLRB (now the Federal Public Service Labour and Employment Relations Board (FPSLREB) will decide the issue. The next step is to determine the level of service to be performed during a strike. This question is determined exclusively by the employer, subject to very limited review. Once these two matters are settled, the third step is to determine the types, number and specific positions necessary to provide the essential services at the designated level of service. If the parties cannot agree, the FPSLREB will decide the issue.[58]

The third iteration was enacted in 2013 by a Conservative government that was quite hostile toward organized labour. Bill C-4, *Economic Action Plan Act 2013 No. 2*, greatly expanded the power of the government to act unilaterally in almost every phase of the designation process. The amended act provides:

> Section 119(1): The employer has the exclusive right to determine whether any service, facility or activity of the Government of Canada is essential because it is or will be necessary for the safety or security of the public or a segment of the public.

While the statute preserved a narrow definition of essential service, it granted the government near total discretion to determine what activities fit within it. The statute also gave the government the exclusive right to designate which positions perform essential services. While the law requires the government to consult with the union after it has made its decision, the union has no power to challenge the decision and submit the disagreement to the FPSLREB for a determination. Furthermore, the option of selecting arbitration rather than the controlled strike model is sharply limited so that unions can only demand arbitration if 80% or more of the bargaining unit is designated as essential. Given the power of the government, this creates an incentive to designate just under 80% of the bargaining unit leaving the union with an ineffective strike weapon and little or no bargaining power. Moreover, even in those circumstances when a union can opt for arbitration, the government changed the rules to tilt

58. See *PSLRA*, S.C. 2003, c. 22; Rootham, 2007, 195 et seqq. for a lengthy description. Subsequent cases further clarified the process. For a summary, see *Professional Institute of the Public Service of Canada v. Canada (Attorney General)*, 2011 FCA 143 (CanLII). The change in the name of the labour board was made in 2017. See S.C. 2017, c. 9.

arbitration outcomes in its direction. It lists two factors to which the arbitrator must give preponderant weight. While one of these factors existed in the previous model, the necessity of attracting and retaining public servants, the second is new. It requires the arbitrator to give preponderant weight to 'Canada's fiscal circumstances relative to its stated budgetary policies.' This sharply steers arbitrations toward outcomes favourable to the government, compared to prior language requiring consideration of ability to pay, which arbitrators treated cautiously because of the power of government to increase taxes.[59]

The 2013 version of the law remains on the books but the current Liberal government introduced legislation in 2016 to repeal the 2013 amendments.[60] The more labour friendly orientation of the Liberals is one motivation for the change, but the more important story is the constitutional one. In order to determine whether the *Charter* right to strike has been violated, the court asks 'whether the legislative interference with the right to strike in a particular case amounts to substantial interference with collective bargaining.'[61] In the *SFL* case, the court was considering Saskatchewan's *Public Service Essential Services Act* (PSESA), passed in 2008, which introduced a designation model for regulating essential service strikes.[62] The SCC found that the PSESA violated the right to strike 'because it prevents designated employees from engaging in *any* work stoppage as part of the bargaining process.'[63] Of course, this is true for all designation models, so the constitutionality of the law will depend on whether the violation can be justified under s. 1.

The SCC accepted that the 'maintenance of essential public services is self-evidently a pressing and substantial objective' and that the prohibition on strikes including the sanctions imposed on violators of the essential service restrictions are rationally connected to the goal of maintaining essential public services. 'The determinative issue here, in my view, is whether the means chosen by the government are minimally impairing…'[64]

The SCC found the government went well beyond what was reasonably required to protect its legitimate interest in the maintenance of public services. First, the legislation provided the government with unilateral discretion to identify by regulation which services are essential without any opportunity for discussion or access to an impartial and effective process to dispute the government's determination. Second, the law also provided that in the event an essential services agreement is not reached, the employer had the unilateral power to determine how essential services would be maintained, including the classifications of employees who must continue to work and the number and

59. S.C. 2013, c. 40; *Rootham et al.*, 2013; *Goldman/Scott*, 2013.
60. Bill C-34, An Act to amend the Public Service Labour Relations Act and other Acts, 42nd Parliament, 1st Session (2016).
61. *Saskatchewan*, para. 78.
62. Public Service Essential Services Act, SS 2008, c P-42.2.
63. *Saskatchewan*, at para. 78.
64. *Ibid.*, paras. 79 et seq.

names of employees within each classification. Finally, the SCC also found the act failed to provide access to a meaningful alternative mechanism for resolving bargaining disputes, such as arbitration. The court summed up its findings:

> Given the breadth of essential services that the employer is entitled to designate unilaterally without an independent review process, and the absence of an adequate, impartial and effective alternative mechanism for resolving collective bargaining impasses, there can be little doubt that the trial judge was right to conclude that the scheme was not minimally impairing.[65]

The *FPSLRA* clearly violates the right to strike. The only question is whether the violation is minimally impairing. Based on the *SFL* judgment, it is almost certain the current law could not be justified under s. 1. It allows the government unilaterally designate which services are essential without access to an effective and impartial process to dispute the government's determination, and it severely limits access to arbitration when extensive designations deprive bargaining units of the effective ability to strike.

Interestingly, the Canadian Labour Congress filed a complaint with the ILO regarding the 2013 legislation after the *SFL* judgment, perhaps in the belief it would provide it with additional leverage in lobbying the federal government to amend the FPSLRA.[66] Although at the time of writing the amending legislation has not moved beyond first reading, which occurred on 28 November 2016, in the most recent round of bargaining the government offered all affected unions the option of selecting interest arbitration as a dispute resolution mechanism, essentially putting them back in the pre-2013 regime.

5.3.2 Canada Labour Code

As noted earlier, the CLC is one of the few private sector collective bargaining statutes that deals with essential service strikes *ex ante* and does so through the designation model. The CLC provides:

> 87.4 (1) During a strike or lockout not prohibited by this Part, the employer, the trade union and the employees in the bargaining unit must continue the supply of services, operation of facilities or production of goods to the extent necessary to prevent an immediate and serious danger to the safety or health of the public.

The law provides that within fifteen days after notice to bargain has been given either the employer or the union may give notice of the services that must be provided in the event of a strike or lockout and the number of employees in the bargaining unit that would be required for that purpose. If the parties are

65. *Ibid.*, at para. 96.
66. By the time the Committee issued its definitive report in March, 2017, the Canadian government had introduced a measure to repeal Bill C-4. See ILO Case No. 3143 – Complaint Date 13-May-2015; Report of the Committee on Freedom of Association, 381st Report of the Committee on Freedom of Association, GB.329/INS/17, at paras. 173–219.

unable to reach an essential services agreement, either may refer outstanding differences to the labour board. The Minister of Labour may intervene in the labour board's hearing to provide her views on what is required to maintain essential services. The law gives the board broad powers to determine what services are essential and to specify the manner and extent to which those services are to be provided. The board also has the power to review and modify its orders during a strike or lockout. Finally, if the board is satisfied the provision of essential services will render the strike or lockout ineffective, it may direct that binding arbitration be available to resolve the dispute (s. 87.4 (2) – (8)).[67]

In addition to the formal designation process, the law grants the Minister extraordinarily wide discretionary power:

> 107. The Minister, where the Minister deems it expedient, may do such things as to the Minister seem likely to maintain or secure industrial peace and to promote conditions favourable to the settlement of industrial disputes or differences and to those ends the Minister may refer any question to the Board or direct the Board to do such things as the Minister deems necessary.

As we shall see in Section 7 of this chapter, the Minister has used this section to bypass the designation process.

5.4 General Observations on the Controlled or Designated Strike Model

Strikes in violation of the designation provision are rare in Canada. Indeed, strikes under the designation model are uncommon. A study of public sector strikes between 1978 and 2008 found that among the 422 contracts negotiated under this regime, unions struck 34 times or in about 8.0% of all negotiations.[68] This study did not identify which strikes, if any, were illegal. However, it seems illegal strikes under the designation model are exceedingly rare. For example, Haiven & Haiven's examination of strikes in the Canadian health care sector between 1999 and 2002, identified only one unlawful strike among those governed by the designation model, and that dispute was resolved within a few days with no record of disciplinary action being taken.[69] The penalties against a union or a designated essential service worker who strikes unlawfully are much the same as those available against workers and unions who strike unlawfully under the no-strike model.

As mentioned earlier, the designation model violates the right to strike, so to pass constitutional muster it must be justified on the basis that it was enacted to achieve a pressing and substantial objective and that the means used minimally impaired the right to strike. Depending on how the courts interpret

67. For a brief overview, see *Adell*, 2001, 32 et seqq.

68. *Campolieti/Hebdon/Dachis*, 2016, 201. It is interesting to note that the frequency of strikes under this model is nearly double the frequency under the right-to-strike model (4.6%).

69. *Haiven/Haiven*, 2002, 8 et seq.

these requirements, they impose a counterweight to the propensity of governments to extend its control over the designation process in order to increase designations, while restricting or barring access to arbitration when the result is to render strikes ineffective.

6 COMPENSATORY MEASURES FOR RESTRICTIONS

It bears repeating that the constitutional right to strike recognized in the 2015 *SFL* case constrains the government in its choice of alternatives when strikes are prohibited or controlled. The SCC considers the quid quo pro in the context of the s. 1 defence, where it asks whether the violation was minimally impairing. In the *SFL* case, the SCC did not really have to consider the suitability of substitutes because the legislation failed at an earlier step in the analysis. However, the court did point to the failure of the law to provide 'any access to a meaningful alternative mechanism for resolving impasses, such as arbitration.'[70] The court then cited former Chief Justice Dickson's dissenting opinion in the *Alberta Reference* case, which it has now embraced, on the need for a fair and effective substitute:

> Clearly, if the freedom to strike were denied and no effective and fair means for resolving bargaining disputes were put in its place, employees would be denied any input at all in ensuring fair and decent working conditions, and labour relations law would be skewed entirely to the advantage of the employer. It is for this reason that legislative prohibition of freedom to strike must be accompanied by a mechanism for dispute resolution by a third party...The purpose of such a mechanism is to ensure that the loss in bargaining power through legislative prohibition of strikes is balanced by access to a system which is capable of resolving in a fair, effective and expeditious manner disputes which arise between employees and employers.[71]

In the *SFL* case, the law provided no alternative dispute resolution mechanism for bargaining units that lost an effective right to strike. As a result, the SCC did not need to elaborate on what would be a fair and effective substitute.

The approach taken in the Saskatchewan legislation was highly unusual. The common practice in most essential service schemes is to provide impartial binding interest arbitration as the alternative to the right to strike. This is certainly true when the no-strike model is adopted, such as is the case for police, firefighters, hospital workers and, most recently in Ontario, Toronto transit workers. In the context of the designation or controlled strike model, the usual practice is to provide access to arbitration either by election of the union, or when the percentage of bargaining unit members prohibited from striking exceeds a certain percentage, rendering the right to strike ineffective. The PSLRA originally adopted the former approach, while the 2013 amendment introduced

70. *Saskatchewan*, para. 93.
71. *Ibid.*, para. 94.

the latter, with 80% being the magic number. If passed, Bill C-34 will restore the election model. If not, it is arguable that the law will fail to pass constitutional muster because of the very restrictive access it provides to arbitration as an alternative dispute resolution mechanism.

The arbitration model used in Canada generally complies with the ILO's protocol, which requires access, independence, and binding-ness. The largest conflict has arisen around various attempts by government to tilt the proceedings in the employer's favour by requiring arbitrators to take into account the government's ability to pay. For example, the TTC legislation requires the arbitrator to consider the following factors:[72]

(1) The employer's ability to pay in light of its fiscal situation.
(2) The extent to which services may have to be reduced, in light of the decision or award, if current funding and taxation levels are not increased.
(3) The economic situation in Ontario and the City of Toronto.
(4) A comparison, as between the employees and other comparable employees in the public and private sectors, of the terms and conditions of employment and the nature of the work performed.
(5) The employer's ability to attract and retain qualified employees.

While the last three considerations would likely be viewed as neutral and widely accepted in arbitral jurisprudence, the first two are part of a more recent trend to bend arbitral awards in the direction of employer interests. Nevertheless, the ILO's Committee of Freedom of Association found the prescribed considerations to be acceptable because they 'would appear to allow for sufficient discretion and flexibility.'[73]

It should also be noted that Canadian interest arbitrators have traditionally resisted giving great weight to employer ability to pay arguments, if only because the government's ability to pay is, to a significantly degree, a function of its own fiscal policies. As one prominent arbitrator stated:

> Interest arbitrators in the Canadian public sector have, apparently, universally rejected the legitimacy of an 'ability to pay' argument. They have not allowed governments as employers to hide behind their own skirts in their role as the source of funds, to escape pay increases indicated by the other criteria.[74]

This attitude, and the belief that strengthening the ability to pay criteria would reduce wage premiums associated with arbitration (see below), has recently led governments to require arbitrators to take into account the government's fiscal situation and policies in making their awards. Indeed, the same

72. *Toronto Transit Commission, supra* Section 5.1.
73. Case No. 3107, para. 242.
74. *University of Toronto* (13 Feb 1981) (Christie) at 8, cited in *Atlantic Pilotage Authority v Canadian Merchant Service Guild*, [2006] CLAD No 457 (Christie), at para. 37.

arbitrator quoted above returned to the issue 25 years later and expressed a more nuanced view:

> In a 2004 interest arbitration between The Saint John Board of Police Commissioners and the Saint John Police Protective Association, CUPE, Local 61 (June 9, 2004, unreported) the I stated:
>
> > I continue to adhere to the views of interest arbitrators as I saw them in the University of Toronto Award with respect to a 'pure' ability to pay argument by an employer in an interest arbitration. By this I mean the argument that a public employer lacks 'ability to pay' because there is no money allocated in its budget, or in the budget of the employer's governmental funding body. On the other hand, I accept that what constitutes an appropriate wage settlement may well be affected by the economic circumstances in which a public employer finds itself. I also recognize that these two concepts may be very closely related.
>
> Thus, while a public sector employer's budget, whether self-imposed or struck by another government funding agency, cannot be accepted as a simple proxy for economic circumstances, what constitutes an appropriate wage settlement may well be affected by economic circumstances.[75]

The other way some governments have attempted to influence the outcome of interest arbitration is by intervening in the appointment process. Although statutes vary, the common practice is that only individuals mutually agreeable to the parties are appointed. However, in an effort to influence the process, in 1995, a newly elected Conservative government abandoned the practice of appointing experienced arbitrators and instead appointed retired judges, without consulting with the unions involved. The first four judges approached by the government refused the appointment but it found other retired judges who agreed to take the position. The Canadian Union of Public Employees (CUPE) challenged the government's action on administrative law grounds since at the time courts had not recognized constitutional labour rights. The case went to the SCC, which held that the minister's exercise of authority was patently unreasonable:

> The Minister, as a matter of law, was required to exercise his power of appointment in a manner consistent with the purpose and objects of the statute that conferred the power. A fundamental purpose and object of the ...HLDAA... was to provide an adequate substitute for strikes and lockouts. To achieve the statutory purpose, as the Minister himself wrote on February 2, 1998, 'the parties must perceive the system as neutral and credible'. ... I would ... affirm the fundamental principle ... that the HLDAA required the Minister to select arbitrators from candidates who were qualified not only by their impartiality, but by their expertise and general acceptance in the labour relations community.[76]

There is a large literature examining the impact of different dispute resolution mechanisms on collective bargaining outcomes. For example, interest arbitration has often been criticized because of its so-called chilling and narcotic

75. *Ibid.*, at paras. 39 et seq.
76. *CUPE v Ontario (Minister of Labour)*, 2003 SCC 29 at para. 49.

effects: the parties become dependent on arbitration to resolve their difference and hence become less able to achieve mutually acceptable bargaining outcomes. Joseph Rose reviewed the Canadian research and found that it strongly supported the conclusion that arbitration is associated with low settlement rates.[77] Rose also found that arbitration results in protracted delays in achieving settlement.[78]

The greatest concern, however, is on the model's impact on wage settlements. Initial studies focused on the no-strike model versus the right-to-strike model. One of the earliest Canadian studies found that while the switch to the no-strike model reduced dispute costs, the trade-off was higher wage costs. The study also found that ability to pay did not influence arbitrated outcomes.[79] A much more recent study by Campolieti, Hebdon, and Dachis compared the impact of the three models on wage outcomes over the period from 1978 to 2008. The authors found that the no-strike model with compulsory arbitration produced a higher wage premium compared to the right-to-strike model. As well, they found that legislative strengthening of the ability to pay criterion did not reduce the wage premium. They also found that the designation or controlled strike model was associated with a statistically significant decrease in wages relative to the right-to-strike model, making it the least favourable for unionized public sector workers. The reasons for this are not hard to fathom. Essential service designation reduces the effectiveness of the strike threat, especially in a context in which the percentage of bargaining unit members designated as essential has been increasing and access to arbitration as an alternative to limited strikes has been decreasing.[80]

7 SECURING ESSENTIAL SERVICES BY FURTHER MEANS

In addition to the three models for regulating essential service strikes discussed so far (right to strike; no-right to strike; and controlled strike), governments in Canada have invoked other powers in an ad hoc manner to end or postpone otherwise legal strikes. Indeed, the frequent use of such measures led Leo Panitch and Don Swartz to claim that we are living in a state of 'permanent exceptionalism', while Bernie Adell has suggested the emergence of a fourth model of regulation, the 'instant back-to-work model.'[81] The principal tool here is back-to-work (BTW) legislation, where governments terminate lawful strikes by ad hoc, post-dispute statutory enactments, although a few statutes grant the

---

77. Rose, 2008, 552. Earlier studies include: *Anderson/Thomas*, 1977; *Rose*, 1996; *Hebdon/Mazerolle*, 2003. A more recent study reached similar conclusions. See *Campolieti/Hebdon/Dachis*, 2016, 202 et seqq.
78. *Rose*, 2008, 551.
79. *Currie/McConnell*, 1991, 693.
80. *Campolieti/Hebdon/Dachis*, 2016. Also, see *Dachis*, 2008
81. *Panitch/Swartz*, 2003, 423.

executive extraordinary power to intervene on an ad hoc basis to end or postpone strikes. Collectively, these will be referred to as BTW measures.

A good example of this kind of ad hoc intervention occurred at the time I was writing this chapter. College teachers in Ontario went on a lawful strike that affected 500,000 students. Negotiations were bogged down and after five weeks the Ontario government enacted BTW legislation.[82] While post-secondary education is clearly not an essential service and college teachers enjoy the right to strike, the government ended the strike when it became convinced that an end was not in sight and the strike's continuation threatened to put the students' terms in jeopardy. In its view, the substantial harm to the public justified this ad hoc intervention. The act provides for mediation/arbitration to resolve the dispute. The union has promised to challenge the measure's constitutionality, but I suspect it will face an uphill battle.[83]

BTW legislation ending strikes at post-secondary institutions is rare, but BTW measures are not. Since 1950, governments in Canada resorted to back to work measures 169 times.[84] A comprehensive analysis of trends in the usage of these measures is beyond the scope of this paper, however, it should be noted that they were used quite infrequently prior to the 1970s. Not surprising, the frequency of their use increased with the retreat from Keynesianism and the beginnings of the neo-liberal turn in the mid-1970s. Interestingly, the use of BTW measures has declined recently. Since 2003, Canadian governments deployed BTW measures fifteen times. However, this decline should be viewed in the context of the decline in strike frequency in both the public and private sectors noted earlier.

BTW measures are used most frequently to end strikes in the education (primary and secondary), health care, and transportation and communication sectors. For jurisdictional reasons, provincial governments are responsible for BTW measures in education, health care and local transport, while the federal government is largely responsible for BTW measures in inter-provincial transport and communications.

When governments use BTW measures, they must decide how the dispute should be resolved. Again, a detailed study of the dispute resolution mechanisms invoked is beyond the scope of this study, but the Canadian Foundation of Labour Rights (CFLR) maintains a database of BTW measures from 1982 to the present, which records whether the dispute was resolved by arbitration or by a government imposed settlement. According to their calculation, binding arbitration was used in 40 of the 90 recorded cases. However, a perusal of the 'settlement imposed' cases reveals that they include a diversity of settlement procedures, including instances where particular terms were imposed but others were sent to arbitration, or where final offer selection was ordered rather than

82. *Colleges of Applied Arts and Technology Labour Dispute Resolution Act, 2017*, SO 2017, c 21.
83. *Breen*, 2017.
84. *Panitch/Swartz*, 2003, 184; *Canadian Foundation for Labour Rights*, 2018.

interest arbitration. Therefore, while it is certainly the case that governments do impose settlements, the CFLR's database likely overstates its frequency.[85]

One additional factor that influences the use of BTW measures is the political orientation of the government in power. Broadly speaking, conservative governments are more likely to invoke BTW measures than more liberal ones. I have intentionally not attached party labels to these descriptors, however, because in the current context in which parties of all stripes have embraced or at least accepted the austerity agenda, the use of BTW measures cannot be neatly mapped onto the political label of the party in power.[86]

That said, it will be helpful to provide an illustration of the way BTW measures were used by the last Conservative federal government in 2011.[87] The first strike in which this government directly intervened was by the Canadian Union of Postal Workers. The union adopted the tactic of short, local rotating strikes. It did this because there is a history of the federal government ending their strikes through BTW work legislation on the basis that the disruption endangered the safety and security of the public, even though governments have not declared Canada Post to be an essential service. The union aimed to avoid this outcome because brief rotating local strikes did not realistically pose any threat to the public. The rotating strikes started on 2 June 2011 and continued until 15 June when Canada Post declared a national lockout. On the same day, the Minister of Labour, Lisa Raitt, announced the government would be introducing BTW legislation. Minister Raitt justified the government's action by referring to the impact of the dispute 'on Canadians and on the Canadian economy.'[88] There was no suggestion that the rotating strikes endangered the safety or security of the public.

The bill was introduced on 20 June and passed and received Royal Assent on 26 June, after a 58-hour filibuster by the opposition. Rather than send the entire dispute to arbitration, the government imposed a wage settlement that was less generous than the employer's last offer and left other outstanding matters to be resolved by final offer selection.[89]

On 14 June, in the midst of the postal workers strike, the Canadian Autoworkers (CAW) announced that its 3,800 members employed by Air Canada in sales and services were going on strike following 10 weeks of negotiation. Although Air Canada is a private carrier, on 16 June, the Minister announced she was tabling BTW legislation. When questioned, the Minister responded that the strike would cause economic difficulty for Canadians, even though reports suggested that the economic effects of the strike were minimal and her own department advised against using BTW legislation because the

85. *Canadian Foundation for Labour Rights*, 2018.
86. *Evans/Smith*, 2015.
87. Generally, see *Stevens/Nesbitt*, 2014, 118.
88. Quoted in *Lee*, 2012, 216.
89. Restoring Mail Delivery for Canadians Act, SC 2011, c 17.

walkout was little more than a nuisance.[90] The union and the employer reached an agreement later that day.

That was not the end of Air Canada's troubles. Its unionized flight attendants rejected tentative deals negotiated by the union in August and October 2011. Following the second rejection, the union gave notice that it was going to strike on 13 October. The Minister stated that the government would intervene. 'We will be clear that a work stoppage is unacceptable in this time of fragile economy.'[91] The House was not sitting and so it would have been necessary to call it back into session to pass BTW legislation. Minister Raitt discovered a way around this and invoked her power under the little-used s. 107 of the CLC, referred to earlier, that empowers the Minister to 'do such things as to the Minister seem likely to maintain or secure industrial peace...' She referred the dispute to the Canadian Industrial Relations Board asking it to determine whether the rejection of the two tentative agreements by the bargaining unit 'created conditions that are unfavourable to the settlement of the industrial dispute at hand.'[92] This was, of course, a nonsensical question, but it had the effect of precluding a strike until the Board addressed the matter. The parties subsequently agreed to refer their dispute to binding arbitration.

Air Canada still had to settle with its baggage handlers, represented by the IAMAW, and pilots, represented by Air Canada Pilots Association. The baggage handlers rejected a tentative deal and on 6 March 2012, the union gave strike notice. Within 24 hours Air Canada notified the pilots that they would be locked out. Before a strike or lockout materialized, on 12 March Minister Raitt introduced Bill C-33, which prohibited strikes and lockouts and substituted final offer selection for the resolution of any outstanding matters. The bill sped through the legislative process and received royal assent on 15 March.[93]

The baggage handlers responded with wildcat strikes, the first occurring in Toronto when Minister Raitt landed there. Air Canada disciplined three participating workers, but an arbitrator subsequently substituted a three-day suspension. Air Canada later disciplined eight organizers of the protest. Of these eight, four resigned and two were later reinstated. Wildcat strikes spread to Montreal and Air Canada fired 37 baggage handlers, although arbitrators subsequently reinstated most. Union officials stepped in and called for the wildcat actions to end, as required by law. Some Air Canada pilots subsequently conducted a 'sick-out' in protest, but the CIRB ruled that the action was an unlawful strike in violation of the BTW legislation and ordered it to end. The pilots' union was also under and obligation to counsel its members to end the job action, which it did, and the protest ended.[94]

90. *Stevens/Nesbitt*, 2014, 127.
91. Quoted in *Lee*, 2012, 217 et seq.
92. *Ibid.*, at 218.
93. Protecting Air Services Act, SC 2012, c 2.
94. *Stevens/Nesbitt*, 2014, 127 et seq.

Of course, these BTW measures were undertaken prior to the SCC's recognition of a constitutional right to strike. Nevertheless, the Canadian Union of Postal Workers (CUPW) launched a Charter challenge, and the court delivered its judgment in 2016, after the *SFL* decision.[95] Justice Firestone found that the legislation clearly abrogated the union members' right to strike. The only question was whether the violation was demonstrably justified. The judge found that the government had a pressing and substantial objective in preventing a postal disruption but that the legislation was not minimally impairing. In particular, he found that the imposition of a wage settlement by the government violated the requirement to provide an impartial substitute for the strike. He also found that the process for appointing the arbitrator was flawed because the parties were not consulted. Notably, even before the *Charter* challenge, the Federal court quashed the first two appointments, the second on the ground of a reasonable apprehension of bias.[96]

As with other areas of strike regulation, governments will now have to defend the constitutionality of BTW measures and this may discourage their promiscuous use. However, the level of constitutional protection will depend on the future development of the case law.

Before leaving this section, it is also necessary to advert to an additional mechanism for securing essential services, informal agreements or unilateral undertakings by the union. Haiven and Haiven's research demonstrates that health care unions covered by the unfettered strike model maintained essential health care services during strikes. They did this both because of their commitment to professional responsibility and because they understood that unless these services were provided critical public support would be lost and governments would likely step in with BTW measures. In these situations, nurses tended to go beyond what was necessary and undermined their own bargaining leverage.[97]

8 EVALUATION AND CONCLUSION

Because of the jurisdictional and legislative diversity that characterizes Canadian labour law, this study has focused on Ontario and the Federal jurisdiction and has not attempted to provide a comprehensive overview of the practice of essential service strike regulation.[98] Nevertheless, our discussion has ranged over the principal models currently used and has touched on important cases that have arisen in other Canadian jurisdictions. Therefore, the picture presented

95. *Canadian Union of Postal Workers v Her Majesty in Right of Canada*, 2016 ONSC 418. (Disclosure: I provided an expert witness affidavit in support of the union's claim).
96. *Ibid.*, paras 194 et seqq. Unions representing workers various groups of Air Canada employees also challenged the BTW measures. These cases have now been settled.
97. *Haiven/Haiven*, 2002, 44 et seqq.
98. See *Adell*, 2015, for a broader although by no means comprehensive study of Canadian essential service strike regulation.

is a fair representation of the 'Canadian' approach to the regulation of strikes in essential services.

As this study has demonstrated, Canada uses three models to regulate essential service strikes: 1) the unfettered strike model (backstopped by BTW measures); 2) the no-strike model; and 3) the designation model. I assess each model according to the following criteria: its effectiveness at maintaining a proper level of service; supporting effective collective bargaining; and its compliance with constitutional and international standards.

8.1 The Unfettered Strike Model (Including BTW Measures)

As we have seen, the unfettered strike model does not generally operate in sectors where services are essential in the strict sense, such as in police and fire-fighting. However, it does apply to some groups of workers who provide services that, if withdrawn for an extended period, could cause significant harm to the public. Teachers are a good example.

Intuitively, one might think the unfettered strike model is ineffective at maintaining essential services. After all, it cannot guarantee the maintenance of essential services during a strike. However, defenders of the unfettered strike model argue that notwithstanding this possibility, the reality is quite different. As we have seen, Haiven and Haiven present evidence that health care workers under the unfettered-strike model voluntarily maintained essential services during their work stoppages. Indeed, they argued that the level of service exceeded what was necessary and thereby undermined the efficacy of their strike.[99] There are no examples of health care workers taking industrial action that endangered patient safety.

On the other hand, there have been rare instances where police and fire-fighters took advantage of their right to strike and failed to provide essential services, with serious consequences.[100] As well, there have also been instances where lengthy teachers' strikes, if allowed to continue, might have caused serious harm to the public, either because students were at risk of losing a term or because of the challenges parents faced in providing childcare, and there was no prospect that voluntary arrangements would avoid the harm.

On balance, it would be fair to conclude that the unfettered strike model is only moderately effective at securing essential services and for this reason never applies to workers providing essential services in the strict sense of the term, such as police, fire-fighters and prison guards. As well, it rarely applies to public service workers generally. Rather, the model tends to be applied to workers who provide services where a withdrawal poses no immediate threat to the public.

However, as we have noted, the unfettered strike model actually does not exist in Canada for workers when an extended withdrawal of services could

99. *Haiven/Haiven*, 2002, 44 et seqq.
100. *Adams*, 1993.

result in serious harm to the public, since governments enjoy – and exercise – the power to end lawful strikes through back to work measures. From a purely functional perspective, this feature significantly reduces the risk that the Canadian right to strike model fails to protect essential services. Indeed, given the frequent use of BTW measures, their use against strikes that did not threaten essential services, and the hasty resort to these measures, sometimes even before workers have gone on strike, it is arguable governments are using BTW measures in a manner that goes beyond what is needed to maintain a proper level of service.

This observation has important implications for the efficiency of collective bargaining under the right-to-strike/BTW measures model because if the parties believe that the government's tolerance for strikes or lockouts is limited they may be disinclined to agree to concessions or compromises. This can be especially true for employers if they believe the BTW measures will tilt the outcome in their favour. The most glaring example of this was in the Canada Post negotiations where the employer locked out its workers out, presumably knowing this would provide the government with an excuse to pass BTW legislation favourable to its position. Even where the government does not act quickly, the knowledge that the government will terminate the strike sooner or later may discourage the employer from making concessions on novel bargaining demands that challenge traditional management rights, knowing that arbitrators are unlikely to alter the status quo. Moreover, it is also important to keep in mind that during public sector strikes, the employer will often be saving money so that it can afford to wait until the government steps in. This was arguably management's strategy in the recent Ontario college teachers' strike, discussed previously.

Finally, the unfettered strike model obviously does not violate the constitutional right to strike or international labour standards. So the real question is whether the use of BTW measures complies with these rights and standards. As we have seen, this may or may not be the case, depending on the circumstances in which these measures are used and the alternative provided. For example, the intervention of the Canadian government to end Canada Post's lockout of its workers was found to both violate the ILO's principles of freedom of association and Canada's *Charter*.[101]

8.2 The No-Strike Model

The no-strike model is generally effective at ensuring that essential services are maintained without interruption, but not perfect. Strikes by workers subject to this model are rare, but there certainly have been instances when Canadian workers defied the law by engaging in various job actions, including full strikes, despite the risk they and their union will suffer significant penalties as a result.

101. *Canadian Union of Postal Workers; ILO*, Case No 2894 (2011).

This model is most frequently applied to workers providing essential services in the strict sense. Its domain, however, has been shrinking as in recent years governments that previously applied the no-strike model to their public service (e.g., Ontario and Alberta) have shifted it into the controlled-strike model.

It is a very different story when we turn to the question of the model's impact on collective bargaining efficacy. As discussed earlier, binding compulsory interest arbitration is the normal alternative to strikes. Canadian research confirms that the substitution of interest arbitration for strikes results in a significant decrease in the likelihood of bargained settlements. This finding is consistent with the narcotic effect of arbitration discussed in the literature.[102]

On the other hand, many workers subject to the no-strike model do not seem to object to it, arguably because the model provides them with a wage premium.[103] For example, police, fire-fighters, prions guards, and nurses in Ontario have neither lobbied the government to shift them to the unfettered or designated strike model nor launched *Charter* challenges alleging that the arrangement violates their right to strike. By contrast, nurses in Alberta, who have a longer tradition of militancy, defied the no-strike model and challenged its constitutionality when applied to them.[104]

This leads to the question of whether the no-strike model violates the constitutional right to strike or is in violation of ILO principles of freedom of association. As we have seen, this will depend on the ambit of the model and whether a suitable substitute, like binding interest arbitration by a neutral third party, is provided. Because the SCC has only recently recognized the constitutional right to strike, and because many workers subject to the no strike model do not object, there are no judicial decisions in this area. The key question will be whether the no-strike model is minimally impairing and presumably that will depend on the court's view of whether the government has shown that neither the controlled nor the right to strike models could achieve the same pressing and substantial objective and that the alternative is fair. With regard to ILO principles, the CFA has criticized Canada for imposing the model on groups of workers who are neither civil servants nor essential service workers.[105]

8.3 The Controlled Strike Model

The controlled strike model has also proven itself to be effective at maintaining essential services during a strike. Indeed, Adell et al. found that 'maintenance of essential services is most likely to be assured by what we would call a true designation system – one where the parties themselves play a real part in working out essential service levels and where disagreements in that respect are

102. *Campolieti/Hebdon/Dachis*, 2016, 202 et seqq.
103. See *supra* Section 6.
104. *Kauffman*, 2017.
105. See *supra* Sections 5.1 et seqq.

resolved by an independent adjudicative tribunal.'[106] However, actual designation models in Canada do not always fully fit this description and tend to decrease the role of unions in negotiating designations and unilaterally increase the level of service that must be provided and the number of positions that must be filled. There can be little doubt that these deviations insure that essential services (and more) are provided.[107] Moreover, at least in the federal jurisdiction, the process of negotiating essential service agreements (under the pre-2013 model, which is now being restored) has been a lengthy and time consuming one. This limits the freedom to strike, since a pre-requisite to a lawful strike is the existence of an essential service agreement.

But, like the no-strike model, its underside is that it undermines unions' ability to engage in effective collective bargaining. As we saw, the loss of bargaining leverage that unions suffer, particularly as designations become more expansive, results in lower wage increases relative to the other models. Giving workers the option to choose the no-strike model partly offsets this effect because of the wage premium from interest arbitration, but then the narcotic effect kicks in to reduce the likelihood of a negotiated resolution.

The controlled strike model may or may not pass constitutional muster or comply with ILO standards, depending on how it is constructed. As we saw, in the *SFL* case, a draconian version of the model that gives the employer the unilateral right to designate without adequate independent supervision, and that does not provide workers with a strike alternative where the level of designation renders strikes ineffective clearly crosses the line. More recently a Quebec labour tribunal applied the *SFL* decision to a provision in the Quebec Labour Code that required a set minimum percentage of employees to remain on the job during a strike in health and social service institutions. The tribunal found that the system of mandatory minima without a right of review by an independent tribunal went beyond what was necessary to ensure the uninterrupted delivery of essential services during a strike. The infringement of the right to strike was not minimally impairing and the tribunal found the provision was unconstitutional.[108] It is unlikely, however, that a scheme that more closely fit the ideal of the 'true designation system' would meet a similar fate.

8.4 Final Observations

From a purely functionalist perspective, it is arguable that Canada's pluralist approach to regulating essential service strikes achieves a reasonable balance between the goal of maintaining required essential services while providing workers with minimally impairing alternatives. Workers providing essential

106. *Adell*, 2015, 195.
107. *Campolieti/Hebdon/Dachis*, 2016, 210.
108. *Syndicat des travailleuses et travailleurs du CIUSSS du Centre-Ouest-de-l'Île-de-Montréal – CSN et Centre intégré universitaire de santé et des services sociaux du Centre-Ouest-de-l'Île-de-Montréal*, 2017 QCAT 4004.

services in the strict sense are deprived of the right to strike, but are provided with binding interest arbitration by a neutral third party. Workers who provide services not all of which are essential in the strict sense are required to negotiate essential service agreements before striking, with disputes to be resolved by neutral labour boards and may opt for arbitration if the level of designation renders strikes ineffective. And finally, there are workers who provide services that are not immediately essential but whose extended interruption may cause serious harm to the public, enjoy a right to strike that may be ended by ad hoc BTW measures with the dispute to be resolved by interest arbitration.

However, there is a discrepancy between Canadian pluralism in theory and practice. In particular, the recent turn to neo-liberal austerity has frequently prompted governments to manipulate the models to reduce unionized public sector workers' bargaining power. The behaviour of the Conservative federal government in 2011 and 2012 is the clearest example of this tendency, but certainly not the only one. While in the past, unions lacking political clout and grassroots militancy took their cases to the ILO where they often won moral victories, since 2015 they can challenge the constitutionality of these laws and Canadian courts have shown some willingness to rein in government to preserve the 'Canadian' pluralist model. It remains to be seen how governments will respond and whether judicial oversight will be strict and sustained.

Bibliography

Legislation

An Act to Implement a Supreme Court Ruling Governing Essential Services, SA 2016, c 10 (2016).

Bill C-34, An Act to amend the Public Service Labour Relations Act and other Acts, 42nd Parliament, 1st Session (2016).

Canada Labour Code, RSC, 1985, c L-2 (1985).

Canadian Charter of Rights and Freedoms, Part I of the Constitution Act, 1982, being Schedule B to the Canada Act 1982 (UK), 1982, c 11 (1982).

Colleges of Applied Arts and Technology Labour Dispute Resolution Act, 2017, SO 2017, c 21 (2017).

Criminal Code of Canada, RSC 1985, c C-46 (1985).

Crown Employees Collective Bargaining Act, 1993, SO 1993, c 38 (1993).

Crown Employees Collective Bargaining Act, SO 1972, c 67 (1972).

Economic Action Plan Act 2013 No. 2, SC 2013, c 40 (2013).

Federal Public Sector Labour Relations Act, SC 2017, c 9 (2017).

Fire Departments Act, SO 1947, c 37 (1947).

Hospital Labour Disputes Arbitration Act, RSO 1990, c H-14 (1990).

Industrial Disputes Investigation Act, 6-7 Edward VII, ch 20 (1907).

Labour Relations Act, 1995, SO 1995, c 1 (1995).

Police Amendment Act, SO 1947, c 77 (1947).

Police Services Act, RSO 1990, c P-15 (1990).

Protecting Air Services Act, SC 2012, c 2 (2012).
Public Service Employee Relations Act, SA 1977, c 40 (1977).
Public Service Essential Services Act, SS 2008, c P-42.2 (2008).
Public Service Labour Relations Act, SC 2003, c 22 (2003).
Public Service Staff Relations Act, SC 1967, c 72 (1967).
Restoring Mail Delivery for Canadians Act, SC 2011, c 17 (2011).
Toronto Transit Commission Labour Disputes Resolution Act, 2011, SO 2011, c 2 (2011).
Trade Union Act, SC 1872, c 30 (1872).

Case Law

Atlantic Pilotage Authority v. Canadian Merchant Service Guild, [2006] CLAD No 457 (Christie) (2006).
Canadian Air Traffic Control Association v. Canada (Treasury Board), [1982] 1 SCR 696 (1982).
Canadian Union of Postal Workers v. Her Majesty in Right of Canada, 2016 ONSC 418 (2016).
Canadian Union of Public Employees, Local 301 v. Montreal (City), [1997] 1 SCR 793 (1997).
Confédération des syndicats nationaux c Québec (Procureur General), 2008 QCCS 5076 (2008).
CUPE v. Ontario (Minister of Labour), 2003 SCC 29 (2003).
Delisle v. Canada (Deputy Attorney General), [1999] 2 SCR 989 (1999).
Dunmore v. Ontario (Attorney General), 2001 SCC 94 (2001).
Health Services and Support – Facilities Subsector Bargaining Assn. v. British Columbia, 2007 SCC 27 (2007).
Johnston et al v. Mackey et al., (1937) 67 CCC 196 (NSSC) (1937).
Mounted Police Association of Ontario v. Canada (Attorney General), 2009 CanLII 15149 (ON SC).
Mounted Police Association of Ontario v. Canada (Attorney General), 2015 SCC 1 (2015).
OPSEU v. Ontario, 2016 ONSC 2197 (2016).
Professional Institute of the Public Service of Canada v. Canada (Attorney General), 2011 FCA 143 (CanLII).
R v. Parrot, 106 DLR (3d) 296 (ONCA) (1979).
Saskatchewan Federation of Labour v. Saskatchewan, 2015 SCC 4 (2015).
Syndicat des travailleuses et travailleurs du CIUSSS du Centre-Ouest-de-l'Île-de-Montréal – CSN et Centre intégré universitaire de santé et des services sociaux du Centre-Ouest-de-l'Île-de-Montréal, 2017 QCAT 4004 (2017).
United Nurses of Alberta v. Attorney General (Alta), [1992] 1 SCR 901 (1992).

Monographs

Adams, George, Canadian Labour Law, 1993
Adams, Roy J, Labour Left Out: Canada's Failure to Protect and Promote Collective Bargaining as a Human Right, 2006

Adell, Bernard, Grant, Michel/Ponak, Allen, Strikes in Essential Services, 2001
Arthurs, Harry W, Collective Bargaining by Public Employees in Canada: Five Models, 1971
Cahill, Damien/Konings, Martijn, Neoliberalism, 2017
Canadian Foundation for Labour Rights, Restrictive Labour Laws Directory (2003 to the present), 2018. Available at https://labourrights.ca/restrictive-labour-laws
Craven, Paul, 'The Modern Spirit of the Law': Blake, Mowat, and the Breaches of Contract Act, 1877, in Baker/Phillips (eds,), Essays in the History of Canadian Law: In Honour of R.C.B. Risk, 1999
Dachis, Benjamin, No Free Ride: The Cost of Essential Service Designation, 2008
Downie, Bryan M/Jackson, Richard L, Conflict and Cooperation in Police Labour Relations, 1980
Evans, Bryan M/Smith, Charles W, Transforming Provincial Politics: The Political Economy of Canada's Provinces and Territories in the Neoliberal Era, 2015
Fudge, Judy/Tucker, Eric, Labour before the Law: The Regulation of Workers' Collective Action in Canada, 1900–1948, 2001
Goldman, Barry J/Scott, Matthew G, Changing the Rules: Reforms to the Public Service Labour Relations Act, 2013. Available at https://www.shibleyrighton.com/ModuleFile/13 + 10 + 25 + - + changing + the + rules + - + reforms + to + the + public + servants + labour + relations + act.pdf?id = 335
Government of Canada, Work Stoppages, 2018. Available at https://www.canada.ca/en/employment-social-development/services/collective-bargaining-data/work-stoppages.html#wb-cont
Haiven, Larry/Haiven, Judy, The Right to Strike and the Provision of Emergency Services in Canadian Health Care, 2002
Haney, Reginald A, Police Labour Relations in Ontario under the Police Act (1946–1973), 1974
Harvey, David, A Brief History of Neoliberalism, 2005
Hohfeld, Wesley Newcomb, Fundamental Legal Conceptions as Applied in Judicial Reasoning, 1919
International Labour Organization (ILO), Case No 2894, 2011
International Labour Organization (ILO), Case No 3143 – Complaint Date 13 May 2015, 2015
International Labour Organization (ILO), Definitive Report – Report No 214, March 1982, Case No 1071 (Canada) – Complaint date: 06 July 1981 – Closed, 1982
International Labour Organization (ILO), Interim Report – Report No 187, Nov. 1978, Case No 893 (Canada) – Complaint date: 04 November 77 – Closed, 1978
International Labour Organization (ILO), Report No 377, March, 2016, Case No 3107 (Canada) – Complaint date: 05 December 14 – Follow-up, 2016

International Labour Organization (ILO), Report of the Committee on Freedom of Association, 381st Report of the Committee on Freedom of Association, GB.329/INS/17, 2017

Jackson, Richard L, Police and Firefighter Labour Relations in Canada in Public Sector Collective Bargaining in Canada, 1995

Macklem, Patrick, The International Constitution in Constitutional Labour Rights, in Faraday/Fudge/Tucker (eds), Canada: Farm Workers and the Fraser Case, 2012

Panitch, Leo/Swartz, Donald, From Consent to Coercion, 2003

Phillips, Paul, Collective Dynamics and the Public Interest Sectors: The Market and Politics in Collective Bargaining in the Essential and Public Service Sectors, 1975

Public Service Alliance of Canada, Collective Bargaining Rights for Members of the Armed Forces, 1971

Rootham, Christopher C/McEwen, Alison/McGee, Sean T, Bill C-4: A Series of Retrograde Changes to Labour Relations in the Federal Public Service, 2013. Available at https://nelligan.ca/article/bill-c-4-a-series-of-retrograde-changes-to-labour-relations-in-the-federal-public-service/

Rootham, Christopher C, Labour and Employment Law in the Federal Public Service, 2007

Swimmer, Gene, Collective Bargaining in the Federal Public Service of Canada: The Last Twenty Years in Public Sector Collective Bargaining in Canada, 1995

Tucker, Eric, Can Worker Voice Strike Back? Law and the Decline and Uncertain Future of Strikes, in Voices at Work: Continuity and Change in the Common Law World, 2014

White, Jerry, Hospital Strike: Women, Unions, and Public Sector Conflict, 1990

Periodicals

-----, Settlement Rates and Settlement Stages in Compulsory Interest Arbitration, 51:4 Relations Industrielles 1996, 643 et seqq.

Adell, Bernard, Regulating Strikes in Essential (and Other) Services after the 'New Trilogy', 17 Canadian Labour and Employment Law Journal 2015, 413 et seqq.

Anderson, John C/Kochan, Thomas A, Impasse Procedures in the Canadian Federal Service: Effects on the Bargaining Process, 30:3 Industrial and Labor Relations Review 1977, 283 et seqq.

Bogg, Alan L/Ewing, KD, A (Muted) Voice at Work? Collective Bargaining in the Supreme Court of Canada, 33(3) Comparative Labor Law and Policy Journal 2012, 379 et seqq.

Breen, Kerri, Ontario College Strike: OPSEU Promises to Challenge Back-To-Work Legislation, Global News, 2017. Available at https://globalnews.ca/news/3877238/ontario-college-strike-opseu-challege/

Campolieti, Michele/Hebdon, Robert/Dachis, Benjamin, Collective Bargaining in the Canadian Public Sector, 1978–2008: The Consequences of Restraint and

Structural Change, 54:1 British Journal of Industrial Relations 2016, 192 et seqq.

Currie, Janet/McConnell, Sheena, Collective Bargaining in the Public Sector: The Effect of Legal Structure on Dispute Costs and Wages, 81:4 American Economic Review 1991, 693 et seqq.

Deverell, John, The Ontario Hospital Dispute, 1980–1981, 9 Studies in Political Economy 1982, 179 et seqq.

Finkelman, Jacob, Public Sector Collective Bargaining, 41:4 Relations Industrielles 1986, 691 et seqq.

Fudge, Judy/Tucker, Eric, The Freedom to Strike in Canada: A Brief Legal History, 15 Can Lab & Emp LJ 2010, 333 et seqq.

Fudge, Judy/Glasbeek, Harry, Alberta Nurses v. A Contemptuous Supreme Court of Canada, 4:1 Constitutional Forum 1, 1992

Hebdon, Robert/Mazerolle, Maurice, Regulating Conflict in Public Sector Labour Relations: The Ontario Experience (1984–1993), 58:4 Relations Industrielles 2003, 667 et seqq.

Kalinowski, Tess/Ferguson, Rob, TTC workers' union fights for a return of the right to strike, Toronto Star 26 October 2015

Kauffman, Bill, Alberta nurses, AHS negotiating a possible end to strike prohibition, Calgary Herald 1 June 2017

Langille, Brian A, Can We Rely on the ILO?, 13 Canadian Labour and Employment Law Journal 2007, 363 et seqq.

Lee, Ian, Striking Out: The New Normal in Canadian Labour Relations?, 6 Journal of Parliamentary and Political Law 2012, 213 et seqq.

Mandel, Michael/Glasbeek, Harry, The Crime and Punishment of Jean-Claude Parrot, 69 Canadian Forum 1979, 10 et seqq.

Rose, Joseph, Regulating and Resolving Public Sector Disputes in Canada, 50:4 Journal of Industrial Relations 2008, 545 et seqq.

Id., Settlement Rates and Settlement Stages in Compulsory Interest Arbitration, 51:4 Relations Industrielles 1996, 643 et seqq.

Slinn, Sara/Tucker, Eric, Canadian Strike Ballot and Notice Law: Barely a Tempest in a Teapot, 29 Australian Journal of Labour Law 2016, 171 et seqq.

Slinn, Sara, No Right (To Organize) Without a Remedy: Evidence and Consequences of Failure to Provide Compensatory Remedies for Unfair Labour Practices in British Columbia, 53 McGill LJ 2008, 687 et seqq.

Stevens, Andrew/Nesbitt, Doug, An Era of Wildcats and Sick-outs in Canada? The Continued Decline of Industrial Pluralism and the Case of Air Canada, 39:2 Labor Studies Journal 2014, 118 et seqq.

Tucker, Eric, 'That Indefinite Area of Toleration': Criminal Conspiracy and Trade Unions in Ontario, 1837–1877, 27 Labour/Le Travail 1991, 15 et seqq.

CHAPTER 6

France

Sylvaine Laulom & Olivier Leclerc

1 GENERAL BACKGROUND: COUNTRY PROFILE

1.1 Trade Union Representation of Workers

The vast majority of trade unions in France are organised into confederal structures, in other words sectoral or local trade unions are legally permitted to adhere to national confederations. These confederations have long played a major role in union representativeness and, hence, in the capacity to negotiate and sign collective agreements. In 1966, a governmental decree[1] recognised five confederations - and hence their constituents - as being representative, namely the *Confédération Générale du Travail* (CGT), the *Confédération Française Démocratique du Travail* (CFDT), the *Confédération Française des Travailleurs Chrétiens* (CFTC), *Force Ouvrière* (FO) and the *Confédération Française de l'Encadrement- Confédération Générale des Cadres* (CFE-CGC) (the latter with only sectoral representativeness). In 2008, the way in which representative trade unions were recognised changed. All trade unions are now required to demonstrate that they are representative in line with a set of conditions, including a sufficient electoral result when workers' representatives are elected. These changes have had an impact on the relative influence of the five union confederations, although they all continue to be key players.

The changes that have occurred over time are much more visible as regards the rate of unionisation. In 1949, just over 30% of all workers were members of a trade union. This figure fell throughout the twentieth century to 11% in 2013. The rate of unionisation is far from homogeneous throughout the private sector. First of all, the rate of unionisation decreases in proportion to the size of the company. For example, in private companies with fewer than 50 employees, the rate of unionisation rarely exceeds 5%. Unsurprisingly, differences also exist between professional sectors. The sectors with higher rates of unionisation are those in which large public companies formerly existed and have been privatised (e.g., transportation, with a union membership rate of 18%) and those where

1. Arrêté du 31 mars 1966 relatif à la détermination des organisations appelées à la discussion et à la négociation des conventions collectives de travail.

unionisation was traditionally higher for cultural reasons (e.g., industry, 12%, banking and financial activities, 13%, education, 10%). Conversely, unionisation is below average in sectors such as hotels and catering (4%), construction (4%), and car repair (6%). Similarly, in the private sector, the rate of unionisation declines with the employee's level of qualification: lower qualified workers are more likely to be unionised than white collar workers (on average, executive managers are 1.7 times less likely to join a trade union than manual labourers). Among many other factors (age, gender, seniority), the stability of the employment also influences unionisation rates. Employees are more likely to be unionised when working full-time and when holding a permanent employment contract.

On the employers' side, a few large associations exist. The scope of the membership of employers' associations was reshaped in 2014 and 2016.[2] The conditions under which associations can be granted the title of representative association at sectoral or national level are now identical for both trade unions and employers' associations (French Labour Code, Article L 2151-1 *et seq.)*. Nevertheless, when it comes to employers' associations, there is a distinction between the scope of membership within companies (the percentage of the company that joins the association) and among employees (the percentage of employees employed by companies who are members of the association). Therefore, the measure of the scope of employers' associations distinguishes between the companies and the workers.[3] At the national and inter-branch levels, company membership is split between three main organisations: the MEDEF (29.41%), the CPME (34.54%) and the U2P (35.89%). The MEDEF covers companies with a broad range of activities while the other two respectively organise SMEs (the CPME) and the craft and independent professions (the U2P). These figures give an interesting insight into the structure of companies in France. Of the 3,144,065 undertakings registered in France in 2011, 3.13 million were SMEs or individual undertakings, and 243 companies employed 30% of all employees.[4] It therefore is no surprise that 70.72% of employees are employed in companies affiliated to the MEDEF (25% to the CPME and 4.22% to the U2P).

Significant differences also exist between the private and public sector.[5] The rate of unionisation is twice as high in the public sector (20%) as in the private sector (9%). This difference can be explained by the situation of workers in the public sector. The vast majority of civil servants have greater job security than privately employed workers, which makes unionisation easier. That said, rates of unionisation differ in the three branches that make up the public sector, namely the national civil service (24%), local civil service (16%), and public

2. Loi n° 2014-288 du 5 mars 2014 relative à la formation professionnelle, à l'emploi et à la démocratie sociale and Loi n° 2016-1088 du 8 août 2016 relative au travail, à la modernisation du dialogue social et à la sécurisation des parcours professionnels.
3. Portail d'information de la Représentativité Patronale, 2018.
4. *Lemasson*, 2014, 1.
5. *DARES*, 2016, 1.

hospitals (17%). Within the national civil service, higher rates of unionisation can be seen in sectors such as the police (49%), public finances (37.6%), and education, training and research (24%). The stark contrast in the unionisation rates in the public and private sectors is also due to the fact that in the public sector, the role of trade unions in managing the careers of civil servants is significantly greater than in the private sector, as illustrated by their participation in a range of representative bodies alongside government representatives.

1.2 Representation and Collective Bargaining

In France, the rules that regulate representation and collective bargaining in the public sector are highly centralised. These rules were recently reshaped with the Act on Renewing Social Dialogue in the Public Sector, which was adopted in July 2010.[6] The Act follows an agreement known as the 'Bercy Agreement', which was signed on 2 June 2008 between the Minister for the Budget and the Civil Service, the Secretary of State for the Public Sector and six out of eight representative trade unions in the public sector. The law sets out new rules on the validity of collective agreements, strengthens the role of collective bargaining in public services, and widens the scope of the subjects that are open to discussion between the social partners.

In France, civil servants are recruited in hierarchically categorised groups known as '*corps*', which are themselves divided into grades. The various levels comprising each '*corps*' are agreed in joint administrative committees (*Commissions administratives paritaires*, CAP) which include trade unions and representatives of the State. A joint administrative committee is established for each category of public servants. Though purely advisory in nature, these committees are the basic institution of public sector employment relations where workers, speaking through their elected representatives, make their views known to their supervisors. These committees are consulted on a wide range of individual elements of employment relations (recruitment, assessment, assignment, promotion, disciplinary action, etc.).

The scope of collective bargaining has long been extremely limited in the public sector. Although some scope for negotiations was recognized in 1983, the government has never been obliged to open negotiations, much less to reach an agreement. Regarding wages, the wage-setting system remains highly centralised. The government can even set or freeze wage rates unilaterally. Public servants in each grade are classified according to a wage grid: depending on their position, they are assigned a number of 'index points'. The base wage is calculated by multiplying the number of index point by the value of the index point. Traditionally, the value of the index point is subject to an annual wage bargaining procedure on the national level. The 2010 law extended the scope of

6. Loi n° 2010-751 du 5 juillet 2010 relative à la rénovation du dialogue social et comportant diverses dispositions relatives à la fonction publique.

the bargaining procedure but it did not change the wage bargaining system. In the event that an agreement is reached, it cannot be implemented directly. Because of its impact on public budgets, it must be confirmed by the Parliament before entering into force.

Beside CAPs, public servants are also represented in Technical Committees (*Comités techniques*, CT) on an inter-categorial basis. These committees are consulted on organisational changes and working conditions. The most significant changes arising from the 2010 Act relate to CTs. The 2010 Act extended the prerogatives granted to CTs and makes them the central forum for employee representation. It is notable that, while employee representatives used to be appointed by trade unions, they are now elected.

2 COLLECTIVE LABOUR RELATIONS

France is a unitary state and the regulation of strikes in essential services therefore applies to the entire country, including metropolitan France and overseas departments. Although the specific situation of the French overseas territories occasionally gives rise to adaptations of the Labour Code, this is not the case as regards the right to strike.

Collective labour relations rights, i.e., the right to organise, the right to bargain collectively and the right to strike, are constitutional rights. According to the Preamble to the French Constitution of 27 October 1946:

> 6. *All men may defend their rights and interests through union action and may belong to the union of their choice.*
> 7. *The right to strike shall be exercised within the framework of the laws governing it.*
> 8. *All workers shall, through the intermediary of their representatives, participate in the collective determination of their conditions of work and in the management of the work place.*

These constitutional provisions survived the adoption of a new Constitution in 1958: the current Constitution of the Fifth Republic refers to the Preamble of the Constitution of 1946 and thus integrates its provisions.

Such constitutional recognition of the right to strike limits the restrictions that can be placed by law on the exercise of this right. In controlling these limits, the Constitutional Court plays an important role in laying down the general principles that Parliament must follow when regulating the right to strike.[7]

The principle defined in §7 of the Preamble of the Constitution of 1946 seemed to require a regulation.[8] However, in the private sector no general legislative intervention exists on the right to strike.

The situation differs in the public sector, as the legislature has intervened, at various points, often in response to a specific and political context, to regulate

7. *Gahdoun*, 2014, 349.
8. Conseil constitutionnel, 16 August 2007, DC n°2007-556.

the right to strike. However, even in the public sector (or for essential services), there is no general, coherent and comprehensive regulation of the right to strike, but rather a patchwork of legislation.[9]

Due to the lack of legislation or because the legislation is incomplete, case law plays a fundamental role in France in terms of interpretation of the sparse set of rules concerning the right to strike. The right to strike, its scope and the conditions governing its exercise are mainly defined by case law and the Courts take into account the constitutional nature of the right to strike. Besides the aforementioned role of the Constitutional Court, the two supreme Courts, the *Cour de cassation* for private law and the *Conseil d'Etat* for public law, also play an important role in regulating the right to strike.

France has ratified the two fundamental ILO conventions on freedom of association and collective bargaining (Convention No. 87 on Freedom of Association and Protection of the Right to Organise and Convention No. 98 on the Right to Organize and Collective Bargaining), the European Social Charter and the European Convention of Human Rights.

International regulation could have a strong impact on French Labour Law in general, in that international regulation takes precedence over national regulations. Nevertheless, the influence of international regulation on the right to strike has long been limited. Unlike in other areas, judges have not used the various international instruments recognising the right to strike to shape the general principles applying to collective action. However, changes can be observed. French law has not always complied with international standards on the right to strike and trade unions tend to rely on these international standards to claim, occasionally successfully, for changes to the law (see *infra*).

3 THE RIGHT TO STRIKE

3.1 The Right to Strike in the Private Sector

One immediate result of the French Revolution was the prohibition on workers associating in corporations. Corporations had played a central role for centuries in organising the professions and had been strongly criticised for limiting access to work and imposing unbearable working conditions. The promotion of the individual entailed the reduction in professional associations. The prohibition of corporations became effective in 1791.[10] Therefore, as in other European countries, the right to take collective action was prohibited during the nineteenth century and was considered as a criminal offence punishable by a penal sanction. It was not until 1864 that the law abolished criminal sanctions against industrial actions, except in the case of violence or picketing, and legalised coalitions, *i.e.*, making it possible for workers to form a temporary association in

9. *Petit*, 2017, 503.
10. *Le Crom*, 1998, 17.

support of a claim. This first recognition of collective action was introduced before trade unions were legalised in 1884 by the 'Loi Waldeck-Rousseau' which stated that trade unions are 'created freely without governmental approval'. However, although the right to strike was recognised under certain conditions, protection of the workers remained weak, as a strike was regarded under civil law as a breach of the employment contract. For public servants, strikes were regarded as being contrary to the principle of the continuity of public services and were, therefore, prohibited.

Immediately after World War II, the enactment of the Constitution of the Fourth Republic in 1946, was an illustration of the compromise which was reached between the social actors engaged in the Resistance against both the Nazis and the French collaborationist government. The common platform of the Resistance (*Programme commun de la Résistance*) accommodated the views of Gaullists as well as the French communist party and gave a constitutional basis to the right to strike in the private and public sectors. Since then, the right to strike has been recognised and protected in both the public and private sectors.

Although the private and public sectors have some features in common (constitutional status of the right to strike and the definition of a strike), the regulation of the right to strike differs in the two sectors.

In the private sector, the right to strike is seen as an individual right which is exercised collectively. As we will see, this conception has important consequences in terms of defining, for example, who has the right to strike, the limits to this right and the consequences of illegal strikes.

As the right to strike is conceived as an individual right which is exercised collectively, the holder of the right is the worker, and it is not a union prerogative. As a consequence, while collective agreements in France can provide for a peace obligation this provision cannot be imposed upon the workers. Likewise, there is no need to follow a procedure before a strike. Specifically, there is no need to give notice (except in the public sector or in essential services, see *infra*), as a collective agreement cannot provide for prior notice of a strike. This is also a somewhat paradoxical consequence of the constitutional status of the right to strike. Collective agreements cannot regulate the exercise of the right to strike unless an Act of Parliament so allows. They can provide for prior notice of a strike with an obligation to negotiate during this period, but this obligation will be mandatory only for those trade unions which signed the collective agreement – not for the workers.[11]

Lightning strikes without advance notice are lawful in France. The only obligation on workers is to inform the employer of the strike. The employer must be informed of the employees' demands when the strike commences.[12] The term 'strike' is defined by case law. This definition is critical, as collective action that falls outside the scope of the definition is not protected. For example, a worker

11. Cass. Soc. 7 June 1995, n° 93-46448.
12. See for example Cass. Soc. 7 February 1990, Bull. civ. V, n°42.

participating in collective action that is not a strike, as defined by the Courts, risks dismissal.

A strike is defined by case law as a concerted cessation of work in support of employment-related claims. The strike must be called to support work-related demands, such as wages and working conditions. This means that a 'purely' political strike is unlawful. Nevertheless, the complex nature of the organisation of a political strike is not altogether clear. The *Cour de cassation* and the *Conseil d'Etat* give an extensive interpretation of industrial claims and are consequently reluctant to endow a collective action with a solely political nature: a strike only has to be *connected* to occupation and employment issues. Thus, it is acceptable that strikes may have mixed objectives and be simultaneously work-related and political. Whenever the governmental action being denounced by strikers has an impact on the position of employees (nationalisation or privatisation, social security, retirement etc.), the courts recognise such actions as lawful.[13] The same interpretation prevails concerning sympathy or solidarity strikes. 'Internal' sympathy strikes are allowed if they relate to a collective work-related demand concerning all the employees of the company or companies involved.

The definition of a strike implies a complete cessation of work. A collective action without such stoppage of work is not a legal strike. For example, work-to-rule action (in other words, scrupulous observance of all working rules with the aim of delaying or disrupting production) is not covered by protection of the right to strike, because it does not involve a stoppage of work. Slowing down the pace of work, when it does not involve a total cessation of the activity is, therefore, held by the courts to constitute defective performance of obligations under the contract of employment, and is not a lawful exercise of the right to strike. Such a finding renders employees liable to cuts in pay and disciplinary sanctions. Selective or rotating strikes involving work stoppages successively affecting different areas of activity are legal, at least in the private sector. However, the courts have occasionally applied a principle of 'proportionate' damage and have interpreted these collective actions as an abuse of the right to strike.[14]

Article L2511-1 of the Labour Code, which was enacted in 1950, establishes the basic protection granted to workers on strike. Strikers' jobs are protected, as the exercise of the right to strike suspends but does not breach the contract of employment. Strikes suspend the worker's obligation to work and, as a counterpoint, suspend the employer's obligation to pay wages. Interruption of the performance of a contract of employment has no effect on its existence. Moreover, it is strictly forbidden to dismiss a worker who is on strike except in the case of gross misconduct. A specific sanction is attached to the right to strike and to the prohibition of dismissal. A dismissal on the ground of strike will be

13. Cass. Soc. 15 February 2006, Bull. civ. N°65. Cass. Soc. 22 October 2014, n° 13-19.858 à n° 13-19.860.
14. Cass. Soc. 16 October 1991, Bull. civ. V n° 319.

regarded as null and void because, as of right, the employee retains all previously held rights, and has a right to reinstatement.

3.2 The Right to Strike in (Essential) Public Services

3.2.1 Overview

Before enactment of the Constitution of 1946 and the enshrining of the right to strike, the continuity of public service was raised as a barrier to the right to strike in public services. Civil servants or privately employed workers in public services were not granted the right to strike and the administration was entitled to revoke and replace them immediately. As the *Conseil d'Etat* stated it in *Winkell* (1909), 'by accepting his position, a civil servant thereby accepts to fulfil all the obligations that derive from the necessity of the public service and renounces all rights that are not compatible with the continuity which is essential to national life.'[15] The national life, the court implicitly states, shall not be interrupted by whatever means, including by the exercise of the right to strike. Therefore, the continuity of public service and the exercise of the right to strike are not compatible: the cessation of work by any person contributing to a public service is a breach of the obligations that derive from the law.

The changes that came with the end of World War II left scope for conciliation between the right to strike and the continuity in public services. The Constitution of 1946 not only admits the right to strike but also encourages the exercise of new economic and social rights 'as being especially necessary to our times'.

Shortly after enactment of the Constitution of 1946, the highest administrative court, the *Conseil d'Etat*, ruled on the *Dehaene* case. Indeed, the court could hardly continue to adhere to *Winkell*. Yet, it was nonetheless not eager to open up the right to strike without restrictions to workers in the public services. In 1950, the *Dehaene*[16] ruling illustrated a prudent compromise. In its ruling, the *Conseil d'Etat* decided that civil servants do have the right to strike. At the same time, the court limited the exercise of this right in order to 'avoid use of the right to strike which is abusive or against the necessities of public order'. In addition, the *Conseil d'Etat* gives the administration the responsibility of balancing the right to strike with the continuity of public service, under the control of the administrative courts. As the *Conseil d'Etat* has stated in many later sentences: '[the constitutional assembly in 1946] urged the legislator to handle the necessary conciliation between defence of professional interests, of which the right to strike is one modality, and safeguarding the general interest, which the former can adversely affect'.[17] Administrative case law illustrates what counts as the

15. C.E. Ass. 7 August 1909, *Winkell*, n°373317, Rec. Leb. 826 and 1296.
16. C.E. Ass. 7 July 1950, *Dehaene*, n° 01645, Rec. Leb. 426.
17. C. E. Ass. 23 October, 1964, *Fédération des syndicats chrétiens de cheminots*, n° 56194, Rec. 484.

necessities of public order that authorises the administration to restrict the right to strike in public services and where the balance between the right to strike and the continuity of public services lies.[18]

This trend was reinforced in 1979 when the constitutional court declared that even though the continuity of public services was not mentioned in the constitutional text it must be considered as a principle of constitutional value.[19] The *Conseil constitutionnel* ruled that 'as regards public services, recognition of the right to strike does not prevent the legislator from limiting this right when necessary in order to guarantee the continuity of public service, which is a principle of constitutional value, as is also the case of the right to strike'. In this sentence, the *Conseil constitutionnel* considers that these limitations can go as far as to deprive certain workers from the right to strike when their presence is indispensable to the realisation of a public service that, if interrupted, would damage the essential needs of the country (public radio and TV broadcasting).[20] The *Conseil constitutionnel* has adopted a broad understanding of the continuity of public services. For example, the *Conseil* had to decide on the Constitutional conformity of the law limiting strikes in primary schools. The law intended to create a childcare service in schools in the event of the teachers striking. Although childcare is not the same as teaching and therefore this service was not, strictly speaking, permitting the continuity of public service, the *Conseil constitutionnel* considered that the provision of childcare 'is directly related [to the public service of teaching] and [hence] contributes to its continuity'.[21] The *Conseil* also decided that the right to strike could be restricted because of other aspects of public interest, including 'protection of the health and safety of people and goods'.[22]

As this development reveals, French law relies on a conciliation of the right to strike with the continuity of public services *in general*, as well as with the protection of the health and safety of people and goods. Hence, no public services have been defined as 'essential' in nature. Although some recently argued for an integration of the concept of essential services in French law,[23] this has never been used neither in the legislation nor in case law. Instead, the French regulation of the right to strike in the public sector has been built on the notion of public service,[24] which is at the core of the construction of French public law at large. Therefore, the legal construction of striking in domains where the public interest is at stake has been and remains conceptualised in

18. Courrège, 2015.
19. Conseil Constitutionnel, 25 July 1979, n° 79-105 DC, *Loi modifiant les dispositions de la loi n° 74-696 du 7 août 1974 relatives à la continuité du service public de la radio et de la télévision en cas de cessation concertée du travail*, Rec. Cons. Const. 33.
20. *Ibid.*, § 1.
21. Conseil constitutionnel, 7 August 2008, n° 2008-569 DC, § 7.
22. Conseil constitutionnel, 22 July. 1980, n° 80-117 DC; Conseil constitutionnel, 15 March 2012, n° 2012-650 DC, § 7.
23. *Courrège*, 2015, 371.
24. *Gugliemi/Koubi/Long*, 2016; *Braconnier*, 2007.

terms of public services rather than of essential services. The regulation of strikes in public services stems from acts of Parliament and administrative decisions. In both cases, the right to strike has to be reconciled with the principle of the continuity of public services.

3.2.2 *Legislative Regulation of the Right to Strike*

While the Preamble of the Constitution of the French Fourth Republic referred to the possibility for Parliament to regulate the right to strike, few laws have been passed on this subject since 1946. These have been either general in scope or sectoral. In this section, we will explain the context of these pieces of legislation and their main objectives. The regulations will be described in more detail in Part V.

3.2.2.1 *General Limitation of the Right to Strike*

After World War II, the State played a major role in the reconstruction of France.[25] While several activities had already been nationalised in 1936 and 1937 (armament factories, rail transportation, aircraft construction), an even broader range of activities were nationalised between 1944 and 1948, including coal mines, car manufacturing (Renault), air transportation, banks, gas and electricity. As a result, employees of national companies together with civil servants represented a significant part of the workforce in France: 1.2 million in 1947, i.e., 9.9% of the employed workforce. Their number increased to 1.9 million in 1984 shortly after the nationalisations that followed the election of President Mitterrand in 1982. Even after the privatisations that took place in France in 1986 and 1993, public sector employees continued to amount to 7.7% of the workforce. In 2016, the public sector employed 5.4 million people, including civil servants (3.8 million in state and regional public sectors and the public hospitals), the military (303,400), and privately employed workers (1.3 million).[26] The public sector currently represents 20% of the total workforce in France.

Given the importance of the public sector in the economy, and in a context where strikes in the public sector were fairly frequent, the law of 31 July 1963[27] aimed at regulating strike in all public services. The 1963 Act also represented a response to a very important strike which took place that year in the mines.

In public services, exercise of the right to strike is conditional upon the existence of a provisional notice of strike issued by a nationally representative trade union. Furthermore, the law also prohibits rotating strikes in the public sector.

25. *Chabanas/Vergeau*, 1996.
26. *Portail de la Fonction publique*, 2016.
27. Loi n° 63-777 du 31 juillet 1963 relative à certaines modalités de la grève dans les services publics, JORF, 2 août 1963, 7156.

The law of 1963 applies not only to civil servants, but also to privately employed workers in private or public companies which are 'in charge of a public service', provided that these workers participate in the provision of the public service.[28] These workers are hence in an intermediary situation, where they fall neither under the civil service regulations nor are they treated like privately employed workers. For example, the law of 1963 not only limits the right for privately employed workers participating in a public service to go on strike unless a strike notice has been issued by a nationally representative trade union (Article 3), it also extends to these application by these trade unions of the rule that applies to civil servants according to which their salary will not be reduced in proportion to the duration of the cessation of work but rather for one entire day of work, even if they stop working for a shorter period (Article 6 of the Law of 1963, now Article L. 2512-5 of the Labour Code).[29] Conversely, employees who do not take part in the provision of a public service within a private company are not covered by the Law of 31 July 1963.

This piece of legislation was introduced into the Labour Code and remains to this day the only *general* regulation on striking in public services (Labour Code, Article L. 2512-1 *et seq.)*.

3.2.2.2 Sectoral Regulation of the Right to Strike

Besides the aforementioned general limitation to the right to strike in all public services, a few pieces of legislation have been passed with the effect of tightening the regulation of the right to strike in some specific public services. Unlike the law of 1963, these regulations were not issued as a reaction to industrial action but were part of a broader effort to regulate specific sectors of activity.

Between 1947 and 1984, the principle of continuity in some specific public services prevailed over the right to strike, so that civil servants in those sectors are expressly excluded from the ambit of the right to strike. This was justified by

28. Cass. Soc. 8 October 2014, JCP ed S, 2014, 1449, note E. Jeansen.
29. Trade unions have challenged this rule, without success to date. The European Committee of Social Rights (ECSR) has repeatedly declared that the provision according to which a full day of work should be deducted from the wages of civil servants on strike, even if they stop working for a shorter period, is a disproportionate penalty that violates Article 6 of the European Social Charter (*ECSR*, Conclusions (France) 2006 and 2010). According to the French government, this rule is simply a consequence of an accounting rule and does not intend to impose any financial penalty on civil servants on strike. On the contrary, for the ECSR, any deduction from strikers' wages should not exceed the proportion of their wage that would be attributable to the duration of their strike participation. Recently, the French trade union CGT decided to present a claim on this issue. The complaint *Confédération Générale du Travail (CGT) v. France*, 155/2017 was registered on 28 July 2017. It relates to Article 6§4 (the right to bargain collectively – collective action). The trade union alleges that the so-called rule of 'indivisible thirtieth', which applies to strikes in the public service, entails an unjustified violation of the right to strike of public officials.

the fact that their presence is needed to maintain an element of service which, if it were interrupted, would disrupt the essential needs of the country.[30] As will be explained in further detail in Part V, the legislator banned the police forces, prison staff, judges, military personnel and some categories of employees in air navigation from exercising their right to strike.

Between 2007 and 2012, a new wave of limitations to the exercise of the right to strike occurred. In 2007, 2008 and 2012, three laws were passed regulating the right to strike in the domains of the land transportation of persons,[31] public primary schools[32] and air transport.[33] This new regulation came with a completely new set of objectives.[34] To this point, the legislation had intended to *avoid strikes* through prohibiting strikes, imposing a minimum level of service, or through collective bargaining. In 2007, the right-wing party won the legislative and presidential elections. During his campaign, future President Sarkozy announced that he would reform the right to strike in sectors where the cessation of work was deemed particularly harmful for the population. The sector of transportation epitomised the changes to come. Strikes in this sector in recent years had caused huge delays for workers as well as for holidaymakers. The same was true for public primary schools where strikes forced parents to take time off to care for their children. Hence, regulation of the right to strike in those sectors was closely related to the idea that the economic activity of the country should not suffer from strikes in public services. From 2007 onwards, the objective of the legislation switched from the avoidance of strikes to *the limitation (and possibly the disappearance) of their effects* on the users of public service. In these sectors, there is no prohibition of strikes, nor an obligation to provide minimum services. Should all employees go on strike, there would be no service at all. Nevertheless, some limitations apply that will give the users of the service the opportunity to avoid suffering from the inconvenience of any strike. As former President Nicolas Sarkozy, the promoter of this legislation, said in July 2008: 'now when there is a strike no-one notices'. It does not come as a surprise that the sectors where these changes occurred are those where strikes are particularly unpopular because they affect family life as well as work/private mobility.

30. Decision No. 89-230 DC.
31. Loi n° 2007-1224 du 21 août 2007 sur le dialogue social et la continuité du service public dans les transports terrestres réguliers de voyageurs (Codified in the French Transport Code, Art. L. 1324-1 et seq.).
32. Loi n° 2008-790 du 20 août 2008 instituant un droit d'accueil pour les élèves des écoles maternelles et élémentaires pendant le temps scolaire (Codified in Code de l'éducation, art. L. 133-1 et seq.).
33. Loi n° 2012-375 du 19 mars 2012 relative à l'organisation du service et à l'information des passagers dans les entreprises de transport aérien de passagers et à diverses dispositions dans le domaine des transports, (Codified in Code des transports, art. L. 1114-1 et seq.).
34. *Leclerc*, 2012, 570.

3.2.2.3 *Administrative Regulation of the Right to Strike*

While the Preamble of the Constitution of 1946 explicitly affirmed the right to strike and admitted that the law (i.e., an Act of Parliament) can restrict its exercise, the question arose as to whether any restrictions can be put on the right to strike in cases where no legislation has been passed. In *Dehaene* (1950), the *Conseil d'Etat* responded positively to this question, while imposing conditions upon it. Later rulings gave a range of clarifications regarding the *Dehaene* ruling.

In *Dehaene*, the *Conseil d'Etat* ruled that workers in public services (in that case prefectural office managers) had the right to go on strike provided that this is neither abusive nor in conflict with the requirements of public order. The notion that a strike in public services should not infringe upon public order was obviously very open-ended. Later cases led to the precision that a strike should not 'compromise essential governmental action'[35] nor threaten the security of people or goods.[36]

In *Dehaene*, the *Conseil d'Etat* also ruled that, in the absence of legislative provisions on the exercise of the right to strike, the administration can decide, under the control of the administrative courts, what the limitations to the right to strike in public services should be.[37] Despite the criticisms that were raised and despite the fact that the *Cour de Cassation* (the superior court in private law matters) has decided otherwise, the *Conseil d'Etat* has repeatedly affirmed this ruling.[38] The *Conseil d'Etat* even recognised in a later ruling the validity of administrative restrictions on the right to strike in a sector where statutory law regulates the right to strike (rail transportation), insofar as the latter cannot be considered to be 'complete legislation'.[39] Consequently, limitations on the right to strike for specific categories of workers in public services have been enacted by Ministries in various sectors including radio broadcasting, weather forecasting, rail transportation, postal services and air transportation.

Moreover, while in *Dehaene* 'the government' was entitled to regulate the right to strike, the *Conseil d'Etat* enlarged this prerogative in later cases to any 'head of department'[40] in public services, 'governing bodies of public institutions'[41] and even 'governing bodies of private institutions in charge of a public service'.[42] The extension of those entitled to regulate the right to strike in public

35. C.E. 28 November 1958, *Lepouse*, Rec. 1958, n° 596.
36. C.E. 16 December 1966, Rec. 1966, n° 662
37. *Merley*, 2017, 59.
38. Cass. Soc. 7 June 1995, n°93-45448, Bull. 1995, V, N°180, p.132.
39. C.E. 11 June 2010, *Syndicat sud RATP*, n° 333262. Comp. CE 6 déc. 1996, RJS 1/97, n° 106.
40. C.E. Section 19 January 1962 *Bernardet*, Rec. Leb. 49.
41. C.E. 14 October 1977 *Syndicat général CGT du personnel des affaires sociales et de l'union syndicale CFDT des affaires sociales*, n°98807, Rec. Leb. 383; C.E. 1 December 2004, RJS 2005, n° 307 ; C.E. 8 March 2006 *Onesto et autres c/RATP*, n°278 999, RJS 7/06, n° 882 ; RDT 4/2006, 259, obs. O. *Leclerc*.
42. C.E. Ass. 12 April 2013 *Fédération Force Ouvrière Energie Mines et autres*, n°s 329570, 329683, 330539, 30847.

services has been challenged.[43] First, the limits of this extension, if any, remain unclear (the notions of 'head of department' and 'governing bodies' are far from clear-cut). Second, the nature of the restrictions on the right to strike have not been defined, leaving scope for a very broad range of limitations, including the obligation to give strike notice, the prohibition on certain categories of employees to cease working,[44] the possibility to oblige certain categories of workers to resume work,[45] and even to replace workers on strike with temporary workers.[46]

Nevertheless, it is incumbent upon the administrative courts to check that the limitation to the right to strike is necessary and proportionate[47] and that the number of persons suffering from these restrictions on the right to strike does not exceed what is needed.[48]

Taking a closer look at the objectives of the legislative measures adopted since 1950 and the case law of the Constitutional Court and the *Conseil d'Etat*, it appears that there has been a shift in the frame of the normative policy dilemma and discourse around the right to strike. Indeed, a retrospective review of case law reveals that the continuity of public services has increasingly predominated over the right to strike. Over the same period, the continuity of public services has been conceived less as being inherent to the public order and more as a subjective right for users or clients of the public services.

4 THE EXPERIENCE WITH STRIKES IN ESSENTIAL SERVICES

Immediately after World War II and during the early 1970s, the number of days not worked in the private sector reached a peak (approximately 3.5 million days not worked per year). Since the mid-1970s, when an economic crisis hit France, the number of days not worked dramatically decreased to fewer than 300,000 days per year in the 2000s (193,000 in 2004). In 2014, strikes occurred in 1.4% of the companies with more than 10 employees in the private sector.[49] Approximately 57% of these strikes related to national and inter-sectoral actions. In cases where strikes were purely motivated by internal professional motives, wage increases were the main demand made by striking employees. In addition, in the private sector not only has the number of strikes decreased, but their intensity also has: the duration of industrial action has been shorter and fewer

43. *Dupré de Boulois*, 2013, 15.
44. C.E. 13 November 1992, n° 83177 83702; RJS 2/93, n° 173 ; C.E. 17 March 1997, Dr. soc. 1997, 533, obs. Ray (n° 123912, publié au Rec. et n° 160684, inédit) ; C.E. 15 March 2006, n° 270171, JCP S 2006, 1699, note Vatinet.
45. C.E. 25 September 1996, RJS 12/96, n° 1313.
46. C.E. Ass. 18 January 1980, *Syndicat CFDT des postes et télécommunications du Haut-Rhin*, n° 076636, Rec. Leb, 31.
47. C.E. Ass., 4 February 1966, n° 63050 63181, Publié au recueil Lebon ; D. 1966, 720 ; C.E. 21 October 1970, Rec. n° 596 ; C.E. 27 July 2005, JCP S 2005, 1266, X. Prétot. See Vannes, 2014.
48. C.E. 7 January 1976, Rec. 10.
49. *Rosankis*, 2016, 6.

employees have stopped working. On average, the number of days not worked in 2014 amounted to 81 days for every 1,000 employees (22 days in the service sector, 147 days in the commerce sector), as compared to 164 days in 2005.[50]

While the *number* of strikes has decreased dramatically over the past 70 years, the *proportion* of strikes in the public sector has increased. While fewer than 10% of strikes took place in the public sector in the early 1980s, this percentage increased continuously since then, rising to 62% in 2001.[51] This is all the more noteworthy in that these statistics do not take into account strikes in hospital settings and the regional public sector. Hence, the number of days not worked is higher in the public sector than in the private sector (e.g., in 2004, 491,650 days in the national public sector[52] as compared to 193,000 in the private sector). As wages and working conditions are mainly agreed within the CAPs and CTs, these are not often the reason for strikes. In the public sector, most strikes are designed to influence national policies, as illustrated by the following example. Although the annual number of days not worked in the public sector has remained below 500,000 in recent years (345,387 in 2014[53]), this figure has been very sensitive to national and inter-sectoral disputes, notably in relation to the age of retirement (over 3.5 million days not worked in 1995 and over 4 million in 2003 when the age of retirement increased by law).

5 RESTRICTIONS OF THE RIGHT TO STRIKE IN ESSENTIAL SERVICES

The restrictions imposed by French law on the right to strike of employees in public services either involve a complete exclusion from the right to strike or the imposition of a set of specific conditions that do not prohibit the right to strike but rather limit its exercise. There is no general, coherent and comprehensive regulation of the right to strike but instead a patchwork of legislation which is supplemented as required by case law. The prohibitions on the right to strike and the limitations on it have sometimes been challenged but the ways of challenging these limits have also depended on the ways the right to strike is regulated.

5.1 Securing Essential Services Through Exclusion from Collective Labour Relations Rights

The French legal system completely excludes certain groups of employees from the right to strike. There are also some partial exclusions from the right to strike. Except in cases of requisition, where penal sanctions are possible (striking workers who are requisitioned and refuse to return to work are committing a criminal offence and are liable to six months' imprisonment and a €10,000 fine)

50. *DARES*, 2016a, 1.
51. *Merlier*, 2003, 7.
52. Rapport annuel de la fonction publique, 2004, 239.
53. Rapport annuel sur l'état de la fonction publique, 2016, 626.

the sanctions are those applicable in French labour law (for employees working under private law) and in public law. In *Dehaene*, the *Conseil d'Etat* stated that the irregular exercise of the right to strike constitutes misconduct justifying a disciplinary sanction (from one of the following four categories: 1. disciplinary warning, reprimand, temporary suspension of a maximum of five days; 2. disbarment or delay in advancement, relegation in step, temporary suspension for a maximum of 15 days, reassignment; 3. downgrading, temporary suspension from six months to two years; 4. compulsory retirement, revocation). For some categories of workers who are totally excluded from the right to strike (riot police, prison staff) the sanction may be issued without following the disciplinary procedure. It has been questioned whether this exclusion from the disciplinary procedure is constitutional.[54]

5.1.1 *Complete Exclusion from the Right to Strike*

For some public services, the principle of continuity has prevailed over the right to strike so that civil servants in those sectors are expressly excluded from the ambit of the right to strike. This is justified by the fact that their presence is necessary to maintain an element of service which, if it were to be interrupted, would disrupt the essential needs of the country.[55] The legislator has successively banned the following categories of workers from exercising their right to strike: the CRS (riot police) with the Act of 27 December 1947,[56] the police with the Act of 28 September 1948,[57] prison staff with the Decree of 6 August 1958,[58] judges with the Decree of 22 December 1958,[59] military personnel with the Act of 13 July 1972[60], and some categories of employees in air navigation with the Act of 31 December 1984.[61]

Only one group (the military) has also been excluded from the right to unionize. French soldiers (the military and gendarmerie) are not allowed to join military trade unions or associations with trade union goals. This exclusion has been successfully challenged. It is certainly the clearest example of the influence of international (and here European) standards on the French right to strike. The

54. *Terneyre*, 2016-2017. See Décision du Conseil constitutionnel no 88-248 DC, 17 January 1989.
55. Decision No 89-230 DC.
56. Loi n° 47-2384 du 27 décembre 1947, portant réorganisation des CRS (art. 6).
57. Loi n° 48-1504 du 28 septembre 1948 relative au statut spécial des personnels de police (art. 2).
58. Ordonnance n° 58-696 du 6 août 1958 relative au statut spécial des services extérieurs de l'administration pénitentiaire (art. 3).
59. Ordonnance n° 58-1270 du 22 décembre 1958 portant loi organique relative au statut de la magistrature (art. 10).
60. Loi n° 72-662 du 13 juillet 1972 portant statut général des militaires (art. 11).
61. Loi n° 84-1286 du 31 décembre 1984 relative à l'exercice du droit de grève dans les services de la navigation aérienne.

two decisions of the European Court of Human Rights delivered on 2 October 2014[62] have not been without consequence.

In the case of *Mattely*, an officer in the French gendarmerie, which in France forms part of the military, was forced to resign from an association named *Forum gendarmes et citoyens*. The forum was considered by the Director General of the National Gendarmerie to be a trade-union-like occupational group, which was prohibited under Article L. 4121-4 of the Defence Code. In the ADEFDROMIL case, the *Association de Défense des Droits des Militaires (ADEFDROMIL)*, a professional organisation for service personnel, complained about its denial of access to justice, as it was considered to be in breach of the same provisions of Article L. 4121-4 of the Defence Code. This article states that the existence of occupational organisations for military personnel as well as membership of such organisations is incompatible with the prescriptions of the military discipline.

The ECtHR emphasised that the right to freedom of association, of which trade union freedom was one aspect, did not exclude any occupation or office from its scope. Despite the fact that Article 11 provided, particularly in respect of members of the armed forces, that States could impose 'lawful restrictions', the Court reiterated that those 'lawful restrictions' were to be construed strictly and to be confined to the 'exercise' of the rights in question, and must not impair the very essence of the right to organise.

In both cases, the interference had been prescribed by law, since the Defence Code specifically distinguished between membership of ordinary associations, which was authorised, and membership of occupational groups, which was forbidden. Given that this prohibition pursued a legitimate aim, namely preservation of the order and discipline necessary in the armed forces, of which the gendarmerie formed a part, the Court then examined whether this interference was necessary in a democratic society. It noted at the outset that the relevant provisions of the Defence Code prohibited military personnel, purely and simply, from joining any trade-union-like group. While the Court noted that the French state had established special bodies and procedures to take into account the concerns of military personnel, it nonetheless considered that those institutions did not replace the granting of freedom of association to military personnel, a freedom which included the right to form and join trade unions.

The Court was aware that the special nature of the armed forces' mission required that trade union activity – which, in fulfilling its purpose, could bring to light critical views regarding certain decisions affecting the non-pecuniary and pecuniary situation of military personnel – be adapted to those particular circumstances. It therefore emphasised that, under Article 11, restrictions, even significant ones, could be imposed on the forms of action and expression of an occupational association and of the military personnel who joined it, provided that such restrictions did not deprive them of the general right of association in

62. ECtHR, Matelly c. France, Req. n° 10609/10, 2 October 2014 and ECtHR, Adefdromil c. France Req. n° 32131/09, 2 October 2014.

defence of their occupational and non-pecuniary interests. However, in *Mattely*, the Court noted that the order to resign from the association had been taken solely on the basis of its memorandum of association and the possible existence, in a relatively wide interpretation of its purpose, of a trade union dimension. Moreover, the authorities had not considered the applicant's attitude and his willingness to comply with his obligations by amending the association's memorandum. With regard to *ADEFDROMIL*, the Court found out that the applicant was deprived of every right to take legal action only because of its occupational interests, while the concrete restrictions on the right to take legal action must be justified by the specific missions of the military.

The Court concluded that the grounds put forward by the authorities to justify the interference in both the applicants' rights had been neither relevant nor sufficient, given that their decision amounted to an absolute prohibition on military personnel joining a trade-union-like occupational group which had been set up to defend their occupational and non-pecuniary interests. This blanket ban on forming or joining a trade union encroached on the very essence of freedom of association and could not be considered proportionate and necessary in a democratic society. Consequently, there had been a violation of Article 11.

Following the judgements of the ECtHR, the Law of 28 July 2015 was adopted. According to the new legislation, French soldiers could henceforth create and join professional military associations, also known under the French acronym APNM. [63]

In the other sectors where it is prohibited to strike, the right to unionise is recognised and, usually, the ban on striking is respected. However, there are a few recorded instances of non-compliance of prison staff. In 1989, a major strike by prison staff took place. 297 prison guards were threatened with revocation and letters advising them of these sanctions were issued. The prison guards had 12 hours after receiving the letter to go back to work. The threat was sufficient, the prison staff decided to return to work and the sanctions were lifted.[64] A significant national social movement involving prison guards developed in January 2018, following an attack on guards in a high security facility, on 11 January. Two of the biggest trade unions in this sector called for a 'general blockade' of the prisons. Their grievances were about dangerous working conditions and pay. According to the unions, between 120 and 130 of France's 188 prisons were affected by this action. In some prisons, the police were called in to fill in for the guards who were on strike. Negotiations quickly began with the Ministry of Justice and following two weeks of strikes, a favourable agreement was reached with a pay increase and the decision to create new jobs. This was not the first time that the prohibition of the right to strike was not respected in this sector. Officially, strikers can be sanctioned and could even lose

63. *Moniolle*, 2017, 509.
64. *Terneyre*, 2016-2017.

their jobs. During the last dispute, the director of the national prison administration recalled the prohibition of the right to strike. However, once the dispute is over, sanctions are rarely implemented.

5.1.2 Partial Exclusion from the Right to Strike

Apart from the sectors where the right to strike is excluded, partial exclusions are also possible. In such cases, there is no outright ban on striking, but it is stated that if a strike should take place, the activity must not fall below a certain level. In other words, a minimum service must be provided to ensure the continuity of certain essential services or activities of vital importance. Hence, the continuation of a minimal level of service effectively denies certain workers the right to strike.

In France, this minimum service obligation is recognised in very few sectors by the law. It is the case in public broadcasting and aviation safety services. In other cases, it is the administrative authority that organises the minimum service, when necessary through regulatory circulars.

5.1.2.1 Legislative Regulation of the Right to Strike in a Few Sectors

Between 1945 and 1982, the French State had a complete monopoly over the broadcasting sector and the first law providing for continuation of a minimum service was adopted in 1972.[65] Since then, various laws have been adopted in relation to the broadcasting sector, including the 1979 Act which gave the *Conseil Constitutionnel* the capacity to rule on the right to strike.[66] The actual regulation is based on the Law on Freedom of Communication of 1986, as modified in 2003,[67] which recognises the right of employees to go on strike by setting out the formal conditions that strikers must respect, including giving five days' prior notice. It also states that, in the event of a strike, continuity of service must be ensured, although the decree specifying the details of this requirement (particularly which programmes must be provided on strike days, at what time, and by whom) has thus far not been issued. In practice, broadcast programming on strike days depends to a large extent on the agreements that the station's management reaches with employees and trade unions. Generally, public broadcasters provide a minimum schedule, including the 8pm news bulletin and a film on television stations, and a music programme on radio stations with a news broadcast at 1pm and 7pm.

65. Loi n°72-553 du 3 juillet 1972.
66. Décision n° 79-105 DC, 25 July 1979, Loi modifiant les dispositions de la loi n° 74-696 du 7 août 1974 relatives à la continuité du service public de la radio et de la télévision en cas de cessation concertée du travail. See also Décision n° 80-117 DC, 22 July 1980, Loi sur la protection et le contrôle des matières nucléaires.
67. *Leclerc*, 2012, 570.

Similar principles apply to aviation safety services (Act No. 84-1286 of 31 December 1984 and Decree of 17 December 1985). In the event of a strike, the vital interests or needs of France must be safeguarded, and its international commitments must be respected, particularly the right of overflight of the territory.

5.1.2.2 Administrative Regulation of Strikes in Essential Services

Under specific circumstances, the government is allowed to implement requisitions. This is possible for the purposes of national defence in times of war, but also for the needs of the State (Article L. 2141-3 and Article L. 2211-1 et seq. of the Defence Code). The Internal Security Act of 18 March 2003 also clarified and strengthened the administrative policing powers currently devolved to the Prefect and reformulated the power of requisition which can apply when a strike occurs. The 2003 Act was not specifically intended to apply to strikes and its main objectives had more to do with combating criminality and delinquency, but the power of requisition which it redefines could also apply in the context of a strike.

Under the terms of the General Code of Territorial Units, striking workers can be requisitioned under the following conditions: '*in an emergency, when required by a real or foreseeable breach of the peace, public health, public order or public safety and when the means at the prefect's disposal no longer allow him to pursue the objectives for which he has powers of enforcement, he may, by means of an order setting out the grounds for the decision, and for all, several or only one of the communes in the department, requisition any good or service, requisition any persons needed for that service to function or that good to be of use and prescribe all appropriate action until the breach of the peace has come to an end or the conditions to maintain public order are in place. The order setting out the grounds for the decision establishes the nature of the requisitioned services, the duration of the requisition and how it will be carried out*' (Article L. 2215-1, paragraph 4).

Penal sanctions are possible in this case. Striking workers who are requisitioned and who refuse to return to work are committing a criminal offence and are liable to six months' imprisonment and a €10,000 fine.

This power to order workers to return to work is controlled by the administrative tribunals and some disputes have highlighted how judges control this power. In 2003, a Prefect requisitioned 100% of midwifes in a private clinic. This decision was contested and the judge ruled that the decision was illegal.[68] For the Court, the Prefect could not require all the midwives of the hospital to work in order to maintain the clinic's entire obstetrical activity. The Prefect should have considered redeploying activities to other hospitals or a reduced functioning of the service. It should have been analysed whether the basic needs

68. C.E. 9 December 2003, 262186, Aguillon et al., Rec. *Lebon*.

of the population could have been met otherwise, given the general capacities of the other hospitals in the Department.

In another case, staff in the oil sector were requisitioned during a collective action in October 2010. The workers on strike took part in a national collective action against pension reform. Large demonstrations were also organised. Following several orders of 22 October 2010 (prefectural back-to-work orders Nos. 183/DSCS/SIDPC and SIDPC 2010-303), the Prefects of regions such as Yvelines and Seine-et-Marne requisitioned the majority of the striking workers at the Gargenville oil storage facility and the Grandpuits refinery. The aim of the requisitions was to restore the fuel supply to the Île-de-France region, particularly at the Roissy-Charles de Gaulle airport. The workers and the trade union organisations tried to have the back-to-work orders suspended. French law includes a provision for an emergency procedure that enables administrative judges to halt serious and manifestly illegal violations of fundamental freedoms. The *Conseil d'Etat* found the requisition to be legal.[69] It recognised that '*Prefects may requisition the striking employees of a private company if its work is particularly important to maintaining economic activity, meeting the basic needs of the population or operating public services when the disturbances caused by the strike threaten public order, and the Prefects may only take the necessary measures, as required by the emergency and proportionate to the requirements of public order*'. The CGT alleged that the requisitions violated the right of freedom of association and, in particular, the right to strike. The trade union then lodged a complaint with the ILO's Committee on Freedom of Association. The Committee requested that the French Government '*ensure that, in the future, in cases where a non-essential service is paralysed, but there is justification for taking measures to ensure a minimum operational service, the workers' and employers' organizations concerned are involved in the decision-making process, and that measures are not implemented unilaterally*'.[70]

5.2 Securing Essential Services by Imposing Limitations on the Right to Strike (Controlled Strike Model)

The French labour Code not only excludes certain categories of employees from the right to strike; on occasion it also limits the *exercise* of the right to strike. In this case, employees are not deprived of the right to go on strike, but the exercise of this right is subject to special conditions. These conditions either refer to the validity of the strike (should they not be fulfilled, the cessation of work would not count as a strike, hence the employee would not receive the benefits related to it), or will expose employees to disciplinary sanctions (although the cessation

69. C.E. 27 October 2010, n° 343966, *Fédération nationale des industries chimiques CGT et autres TA Melun*, 22 October 2010, n° 1007329/6, CGT et autres.
70. Rapport No. 362, Novembre 2011, Case n° 2841. http://www.ilo.org/dyn/normlex/fr/f?p=NORMLEXPUB:50002:0::NO::P50002_COMPLAINT_TEXT_ID,P50002_LANG_CODE:2912582,en.

of work is acknowledged as a strike, employees or the employer may be prosecuted for their behaviour). These limitations on the exercise of the right to strike encompass a large range of measures, from trade union giving notice of a strike, individuals giving notice of their intention to go on strike, and internal procedures, to public information.

Two important caveats should be mentioned. First, as will be illustrated below, it is clear that some of these measures apply to a wide array of situations while others are of narrower application, either because they apply only to specific sectors or because they have been used on few occasions. In some cases, it is extremely difficult to think of a single example where certain conditions have applied. Therefore, while describing the variety of limitations to the right to strike in public services in France, we will give a sense of the scope with which they apply. Second, it is important to maintain a dynamic view of the situation at hand, as the conditions on the exercise of the right to strike in public services have changed over time.

5.2.1 Representative Trade Union Strike Notice

5.2.1.1 Strike Notice in Public Services

The Law of 31 July 1963 states that the validity of a strike in public services is conditional upon prior receipt of a strike notice. This requirement is justified by the need to ensure the continuity of public service.[71] This notice must be issued by at least one nationally representative trade union. The European Committee of Social Rights considered that restricting the right to initiate a strike in the public sector to the representative national trade unions restricts the right to strike and violates Article 6 of the European Social Charter 1961.[72] In practice, however, in a context of multiple trade unions, the condition does not appear to significantly restrict the right to strike.

Hence, it is unlawful for the workers covered by this legislation to go on strike without prior notice being given by a nationally representative trade union. In the event of infringement, disciplinary sanctions may be issued by the employer.[73] Nevertheless, these workers need not be members of the trade union that issued the strike notice, nor even be unionised at all: the very existence of a strike notice suffices, regardless of the nationally representative trade union which issued the notice. The strike notice must have been received by the administration or by the management of the company at least five clear days before the strike begins. The strike notice must state the reasons for the strike, the geographical perimeter of the strike as well as the duration of the cessation of work. The strike notice may be limited or unlimited. In the latter

71. TGI Nancy, 9e ch. 10 janv 2007, JCP ed S, 2007, 1208, note L. Drai.
72. *ECSR*, Conclusions (France) 2010, Article 6, 20.
73. Cass. Soc. 11 January 2007, n° 04-17116.

case, only the trade union that issued the notice can determine when that notice has lapsed. The fact that all employees have returned to work does not by itself render the notice obsolete.[74]

The main purpose of the strike notice is to organise a cooling-off period during which the parties are compelled to negotiate on the workers' claims. Therefore, '*for the duration of the period of notice, the parties shall be obliged to negotiate*' (Labour Code, Article L. 2512-2 *in fine*). It is expected that negotiations will culminate in an agreement and will ultimately put an end to the intended strike. This provision is all the more remarkable that it is one of the few occasions where French labour law connects the right to strike and the right to bargain (on this, see *supra* Section 2). Furthermore, this occurs even when trade unions are not granted the right to conclude collective agreements in the public sector because of budgetary implications. Therefore, only limited arrangements are likely to result from this negotiation.

In practice, trade unions have mostly used strike notice as a pressure tactic. Indeed, trade unions often issue several provisional notices of strike action, each starting when the other ends.[75] If trade unions agree to coordinate their action, they can also issue one strike notice after another.[76] When this occurs, workers are virtually permanently covered by a trade union notice. The existence of a strike notice issued by a trade union by no means obliges workers to go on strike, even if they happen to be members of this trade union: 'only employees hold the right to strike' and they can, therefore, decide either not to go on strike, or to go on strike at any time as long as the strike notice holds,[77] and resume working at any time as long as the notice still holds.[78] Similarly, workers are not compelled to give *individual* notice of their intention to go on strike.[79] The authority has no means of knowing in advance how many workers will go on strike, nor even if the strike that has been notified will ever take place at all. This situation opened the door to sectoral reforms where individual strike notices were made compulsory (see *infra*).

5.2.1.2 Preliminary Negotiations in Specific Sectors

The most recent legislation on strikes in the sectors of the land transportation of passengers (2007), primary schools (2008) and air transportation of passengers (2012) expanded on the five clear days' notice period established by the Law of

74. Cass. Soc. 4 July 2012, JCP ed S, 2012, 1412, note Duquesne; Cass. Soc. 8 December 2016, n° 15-16078, JCP ed. S, 2017, 1024, note F. *Duquesne*.
75. Cass. Soc. 7 June 2006, JCP ed S, 2006, 1734, note R. Vatinet; Cass. Soc. 30 June 2008, 06-21781; Cass. Soc. 25 January 2012, 10-26237, Dr soc 2012, 433, note *Chaumette*.
76. Cass. Soc. 4 February 2004, n° 01-15.709.
77. Cass. Soc. 12 January 1999 bull civ V, 6.
78. Cass. Soc. 11 February 2015, JCP ed S, 2015, 1116, not *Jeansen*; Cass. Soc. 8 December 2016, n° 15-16.078.
79. Cass. Ass. plén., 23 June 2006, n° 04-40.289.

1963, by imposing an obligation on trade unions which intend to issue a strike warning to engage into a preliminary bargaining procedure. For example, the Law of 21 August 2007 stipulates that in companies that fall within the scope of the law, '*no strike notice can be issued unless preliminary negotiations have taken place between the employer and the representative trade union(s) which intends to issue a strike notice*' (Article 2).[80] The Law of 2008 on public primary schools (Code of Education, Article L. 133-2)[81] and the Law of 2012 (Code of Transport, Article L. 1114-2)[82] on the air transportation of passenger include similar provisions.

This bargaining period prior to issuing a strike notice is termed by the law as a 'dispute prevention procedure'. It aims at giving the parties the opportunity to agree on measures and, ultimately, to have the trade unions renounce the issuance of a strike notice. It should be recalled that should a strike notice be issued under the provisions of the law of 1963 (Labour Code, Article L. 2512-2), negotiations must begin. Therefore, rather than enlarging the negotiation period under Article L. 2512-2, the recent legislation combines this negotiation with a 'preliminary' bargaining process. Preference was given to negotiations clearly aimed at avoiding the cessation of work over longer negotiations under the threat of an already pending strike notice. It has, therefore, been judged that the absence of preliminary negotiation renders any ensuing strike notice unlawful, and ultimately the cessation of work is illegal and can be sanctioned.[83]

The features of the preliminary negotiations differ from one sector to another. In the sectors of land and air transportation of passengers, the duration of these negotiations and their conditions can be agreed by employers and representative trade unions in a company framework agreement or in a branch agreement. In the absence of such an agreement, the conditions of the negotiations are determined by the law and by implementing decrees as is the case in the sector of primary schools. According to these regulations, in the three aforementioned sectors, the employer must meet the trade unions which have notified their intention to call a strike, within three days. The ensuing negotiations may not exceed eight clear days. In the largest companies,[84] as well as in some sectors, agreements have been signed.[85] The other cases are regulated by

80. *Leclerc*, 2008, 251.
81. *Ibid.*, 674.
82. *Leclerc*, 2012, 570.
83. Cass. Soc. 30 January 2013, JCP ed. S, 2013, 1173, note L *Péru-Pirotte*.
84. For example, train: Avenant du 13 déc. 2007 au protocole d'accord du 28 oct. 2004 sur l'amélioration du dialogue social et la prévention des conflits à la SNCF (*Liaisons soc.*, Conv., C3/440, n° 316, 8 nov. 2004) ; Paris tube : Avenant au protocole d'accord relatif au droit syndical et l'amélioration du dialogue social à la RATP (*Liaisons soc.*, Conv., C3/410, n° 203, 26 mars 2002).
85. For example, Accord de branche du 3 déc. 2007 sur le développement du dialogue social, la prévention des conflits et la continuité du service public dans les transports urbains de voyageurs, *Liaisons soc.*, bref soc., n° 15024, 28 déc. 2007.

legal provisions and their implementing decrees.[86] In practice, the agreements don't differ greatly from legal provisions. In these domains, a total of 13 days must be devoted to negotiations before the strike can begin: eight days before the notification of strike action and five days while the notification is pending.

5.2.2 Work Planning in the Event of Strikes

One important aspect of the legislation enacted in 2007, 2008 and 2012 was to impose an obligation on employers to draft several documents in advance, aiming at anticipating a new organisation of work according to how many workers stop working. Employers are expected to follow the procedures which have been decided in advance. This obligation reveals a change in the regulation of strikes in public services: rather than imposing a minimal level of service, the law requires that various levels of service are anticipated, together with the organisation of people's work and allocation of machines in each of these situations.

In the domain of land transportation of passengers, the Law of 21 August 2007 first requires the public authorities or private bodies responsible for these services (or the Prefect, should they fail to do so) to identify the stations that will be called at in the event of a strike, taking into consideration various hypotheses depending on the number of employees on strike (e.g., the plan adopted by the national train company specifies levels of service according to a three-tiered scale). Determining whether and how frequently each train station will be called at, is obviously a delicate matter. The law only stipulates that this plan 'must meet the essential needs of the population' and must guarantee access to the public service of education during national exam days and give full consideration to the situation of disabled people. Other instructions stem from an administrative circular that stresses the need to serve public health institutions, social and administrative centres and access points to other transportation networks. It furthermore insists on the need to concentrate the available resources on mornings and evenings, to facilitate the journeys of passengers travelling to and from work.

According to each planned level of service, the employer must then draft a document assigning the workers (i.e., any workers who didn't stop working) and the machines to identified tasks. The employer must discuss this reallocation of workers with the representative trade unions. If they fail to reach an agreement, the employer can make a unilateral decision. This plan identifies the categories of workers and the material resources needed to implement each level of service (as will be seen below, those workers whose activity is essential to the continuation of the planned level of service must provide notice of their intention to stop working. See *infra* Subsection 5.2).

86. Décret n° 2008-82 du 24 janvier 2008 ; Décret n° 2008-1246 du 1er décembre 2008.

The purpose of these documents (identification of levels of service in the event of cessation of work, redistribution of workers and material resources) is to achieve the most appropriate organisation and, hence, to minimize the damages created by the cessation of work. If the company fails to meet the level of service it committed to provide, it must refund passengers accordingly.

In primary schools, the law does not order that pupils be redistributed among the teachers remaining at work. The law imposes that the State (or the Mayor in situations where more than 25% of the teachers of a given school stop working) organises a reception service for those pupils whose teachers are on strike (Code de l'Education, Article L. 133-1). The service provided is not, therefore, teaching but childcare and entertainment. The Ministry of Education and the mayors – who are responsible for primary schools within the French education system – then have to identify, in advance, a list of persons able to care for the children during the strike and to provide appropriate facilities.

5.2.3 Individual Notice of the Intention to Strike

Implementation of the plans should a strike occur is possible only if the employer knows in advance how many employees will go on strike. As explained in Section 5.2.2), the notification of a strike in public services by nationally representative trade unions does not in itself help, as it says nothing about what employees will decide for themselves: they can join the strike or continue working without any warning. This is even more the case, given that the *Cour de Cassation* has ruled that workers are not obliged to give *individual* notice of their intention to go on strike.[87] Recent legislation has broken with this rule and imposes upon certain categories of employees the obligation to individually declare their intention to go on strike.

In land transportation services, workers whose presence is deemed 'indispensable' for the anticipated reorganisation of work must give 48 hours' individual notice of their intention to go on strike before they stop working (Code des Transports, Article L. 1324-7). The same applies in public primary schools to the workers responsible for teaching children (Code de l'Education, Article L. 133-4: 48 hours, including at least one working day) and in the sector of air transportation of passengers to 'employees whose absence might directly affect the flights' (Code des Transports, Article L. 1114-3). Failure by an individual to provide notice of their intention to go on strike is liable to disciplinary sanctions. Nevertheless, the law does not impose formal conditions on the individual notification.[88] Some sectoral collective agreements have opened a large range of channels to employees wishing to notify their intention to go on strike (e.g., in the sector of urban land transportation this may take the

87. C. Cass., Ass. plén., 23 June 2006, op. cit.
88. Cass. Soc. 8 December. 2016, n° 15-16999, JCP ed S, 2017, 1124, note F. *Duquesne*.

form of an oral statement, an email or a registered letter).[89] It has been ruled that the notification is lawful when done collectively, provided that the document is signed by each employee on strike and that it gives an indication of the time when each of them will stop work.[90]

On a more practical level, could the obligation for employees to give notice of their intention to go on strike infringe their constitutional right to strike? The company that runs the Paris underground system obliged employees to declare their intention '48 hours *before the strike begins*'. On the request of a trade union, this provision was overturned by the administrative court on the grounds that this provision would force the employees who want to join the strike to do so from the start. This provision was considered to be against the law that stipulates a 48 hours delay *before the cessation of work,* not before the start of the strike.[91] Indeed, as the *Conseil Constitutionnel* stated, '*the individual notice does not prevent an employee from joining an ongoing strike that they did not initially intend to take part in, or from leaving a strike in which they had participated, as long as they inform their employer at the latest 48 hours in advance*'.[92] Empirical data shows that these legal discussions on the moment when the individual notification should take place has modified trade union practices. Trade unions play a major role in providing guidance to employees on the notification procedure, and the 48 hours delay creates a need to mobilise employees earlier.[93]

After the enactment of the law of 21 August 2007, the practice developed in public rail transportation of providing the individual notice of the intention to go strike and subsequently not stop working. Employees must give notice of their *intention* to go on strike and may ultimately very well decide not to join the strike. In such cases, the individual notice does not enable the employer to effectively reorganise the work according to the plan decided in advance. During debates around the law of 2012 on the air transportation of passengers, this practice was criticised in Parliament as a misuse of the law of 2007.[94] As a result, the 2012 law now imposes an obligation on employees in the sector of air transportation, when they have provided notice of their intention to go on strike, also to notify the employer 24 hours in advance of their intention to resume working or their decision not to go on strike. This does not apply in the event that the employee resumes working because the strike has come to an end (Code des Transports, Article L. 1114-3). The 2012 law also modified the 2007 law and extended this provision to the land transportation of passengers (Code des Transports, Article L. 1324-7). However, this does not apply to workers in the public primary school sector, where, if an employee fails to declare their

89. See Cass. Soc. 23 March 2017, JCP ed S, 2017, 1154, note E. Jeansen.
90. Cass. Soc. 8 December 2016, n° 15-16.999.
91. C.E., 2e et 7e s.-sect. réun., 19 May 2008, n° 312329 ; Cass. Soc. 18 May 2016, n° 1426700, JCP ed S, 2016, 1244, note F. *Duquesne*.
92. Conseil constitutionnel, 16 August 2007, n° 2007-556 DC, *JO* 22 August, 13971, consid. 29.
93. *Béroud/Giraud*, 2010, 9 et seqq.
94. Rapport d'information de MM. Kossowski et Bono sur la mise en application de la loi n° 2007-1224 du 21 août 2007 (Ass. nat., n° 1502, 4 mars 2009).

intention to resume working or fails to go on strike, the employer may take sanctions. Nevertheless, the law introduces a distinction between workers who fail to provide notice of their intention to go on strike (48 hours in advance) and those who fail to provide notice of their intention to go to work (24 hours in advance). While the former *may* face sanctions, it is only in case of *repeated failures* that it is possible for the latter to be sanctioned.

5.2.4 Public Information

Generally speaking, the law does not impose an obligation to provide any specific information to users or clients in the event of a strike. Most of the time, this information is simply not available on a timely basis, because public authorities and companies have no idea how many employees will go on strike before they do not go to work and declare a strike.

However, in the sectors of land and air transportation, obliging the employers to anticipate the organisation of work in the event of a strike and requiring employees to provide individual notice of their intention to stop working, is meant to enable companies to have a clear view of the level of service they will be able to provide. As a result, the law stipulates that this information must be communicated to their users or clients. In relation to land transportation, the law stipulates that '*in the event of disruption to traffic, users are entitled to free, accurate and reliable information on the service that will be provided*' (Code des Transports, Article L. 1222-8). If a disruption to traffic is foreseeable – which is the case when a strike has been notified – the company must make this information available to the public at least 24 hours before the strike begins. The same conditions has applied to air transportation since 2012 (Code des Transports, Article L. 1114-7).

6 COMPENSATORY MEASURES FOR RESTRICTIONS

Some provisions of the French Labour Code regulate the procedures to be followed to resolve collective conflicts. These procedures are designed mainly for the private sector, but also apply to industrial and commercial public establishments (when their activity is purely commercial or industrial or if they provide a public service of a mixed administrative and commercial nature). In the event of collective action, the Labour Code sets out a three-tiered procedure.

First the representative of the state in the region (the Prefect) or the Ministry of Labour can decide to submit the conflict to a national or regional conciliation body (Labour Code, Article L. 2522-1). A collective agreement can also requires the parties to submit any disputes related to its implementation to an *ad hoc* committee. The conciliation bodies are organised by the labour administration and are tripartite in nature: their members represent the employers, the employees, and the administration and are appointed for three years. If the parties reach an agreement, this applies in just the same way as any other collective agreement. If they cannot reach an agreement, the commission records the disagreement and the conflict is submitted either to a mediation procedure or to arbitration. This conciliation procedure applies to collective action in both the private and public sectors. Nevertheless, because of the budgetary impact of the agreement in the public sector, the Labour Code provides for a specific conciliation framework for the public sector (Labour Code, Article L. 2522-8). In every public company or public establishment, the executive board, the representative trade unions and the State must agree on a protocol providing for conciliation in the event of a strike. This scheme must be followed and it is only when no agreement has been reached through this process that the parties can engage in the aforementioned ordinary conciliation procedure.

Second, the president of the conciliation commission or the administration can ask the conflicting parties to ask a mediator to settle their dispute (Labour Code, Article L. 2523-1). If they do not reach a consensus on the name of the mediator, it can be drawn from a list of mediators held by the Ministry of Labour. Within a month, the mediator must propose measures to resolve the dispute. If the parties accept the measures proposed by the mediator, they are bound by the agreement.

Third, the parties can decide either in advance (in a collective agreement) or when a conflict arises to appoint an arbitrator (Labour Code, Article L.2524-1). The arbitrator's decision has the same effect as a collective agreement.

Although the Labour Code provides a detailed regulation of dispute resolution in the event of collective action, there is no duty to exhaust the dispute resolution procedure. In practice, these procedures are rarely used. On the few occasions where a mediator has been appointed, the efficiency of the measures has been questioned.[95] The fact that in most cases the parties do go to court leaves little room for the dispute resolution procedure. It is when a collective agreement imposes conciliation or mediation as a first step that the procedures have the best chance of success. Nevertheless, in these cases mediation would only be compulsory for the trade unions that have signed the agreement.

7 SECURING ESSENTIAL SERVICES BY FURTHER MEANS

7.1 Interlocutory Procedure

The measures adopted by the legislature or by the executive branch are controlled by the judiciary (the Constitutional Court or administrative or private courts), as explained above. In practice, the interlocutory procedure is widely used, as it is designed to avoid the onset of a strike or, at the very least, to limit its effects.

95. *Sinay*, 1966, 421; *Lyon-Caen*, 1977, 445 ; *Ramin*, 1989, 839 ; *Encinas de Munagorri*, 2001, 163.

The French Code of Civil Procedure allows employers, employees, trade unions and every individual involved in an industrial action to go to court using the fastest interlocutory procedure. As a strike does not relate to the execution of the contract of employment (which is suspended during the cessation of work), the appropriate jurisdiction is usually the president of a civil court (*tribunal de grande instance*) and, more rarely, labour courts (*conseils de prud'hommes*) when an employer sanctions an employee on strike. In civil matters, a party can introduce an interlocutory procedure in the event of an emergency, when it is necessary to prevent immediate damage or to stop an illegal situation (Code de Procedure Civile, Articles 808 *et seq.*). The administrative courts are also competent to adjudicate on cases of strikes in public services, where the party may use the interlocutory procedure. As the *Conseil d'Etat* has recognised the right to strike as a 'fundamental freedom',[96] the specific interlocutory procedure in the event of violation of a fundamental freedom (*référé-liberté*) may also be used under Article L. 521-2 of the Code of Administrative Justice.

The interlocutory procedure is, therefore, widely used in relation to strikes. The parties' intention is to oppose the strike before it starts or during the cessation of work as illustrated the following examples.

In one case, a public service employer asked the interim relief judge to suspend the effects of a strike notice because meeting the professional claims of the employees was beyond his capacity. The interim judge rejected his request, stating that it is not for the judge to express an opinion on these professional claims.[97]

The interim judge may order the forced eviction of striking workers in the event of illegal occupation,[98] when the workers on strike prevent other employees from going to work[99], or when they are causing a risk to human health or the environment.[100] The judge can impose a penalty payment upon a trade union if the court can justify the trade union's involvement in the illegal industrial action.[101]

In all these situations, the president of the tribunal must rule on whether an illegal situation exists. The onus of proof is on the employer. In some cases, employers have engaged a court bailiff to witness the existence of illegal behaviour. The judicial officer is only allowed to report factual findings.[102]

Although it is hard to determine the prevalence of this practice, litigation shows that in some cases the president of the tribunal has appointed an expert

96. C.E. Ord. Réf. 9 December 2003 *Mme Aiguillon*, n°262186, Rec. 497.
97. TGI Paris, référé, 13 July 2001, Droit ouvrier, 2001, 486.
98. Cass. Soc. 21 June 1984, GADT, n° 4, 212; Cass. Soc. 23 June 2004, RJS 2004.835, n° 1187.
99. Cass. Soc. 17 May 1977, D. 1977, 645, note A. *Jeammaud*.
100. Cass. Soc. 26 February 1992, Bull. Civ. V, n° 125.
101. Cass. Soc. 22 June 2004, Bull civ. V, n° 174.
102. Cass. Soc. 28 April 2006, Bull. Civ. V, n° 153.

to determine the cause of the industrial action and to suggest possible solutions to end the strike.[103]

The interlocutory procedure has also been used to oppose a prefectural order requisitioning employees on strike.[104] In a case where the employer had dismissed an employee on strike for gross misconduct, the *conseil de prud'hommes* (competent in matters related to the termination of the employment contract) decided, following an interlocutory procedure, that the dismissal was void and that the employee should be reintegrated.[105]

7.2 Ballot

In France, the decision to go on strike falls to each employee individually. Nevertheless, this right is exercised collectively: one employee cannot stop working alone (unless the company employs a single worker). Therefore, employees must agree on the decision to go on strike, whether or not this is organised in the form of a trade union. The law does not regulate the decision to stop work. Most of the time, this decision is taken during a general assembly of the workers, by means of a vote. The employees in attendance decide to stop working or to return to work. In any case, the result of this ballot has no formal consequences and it is left to every worker to decide to go on strike or not. Although this voting process is informal (and therefore no statistics are available), it plays a major role in the mobilisation of workers both in terms of its organisation and in its consequences. It provides an opportunity for workers to discuss their claims of a professional nature and to decide whether they should stop working or not. The voting process appears to be a crucial mechanism of expression in a social democracy. Therefore, it has long been considered that although voting is of tantamount importance for the fate of strikes, it must be left solely to the self-organisation of workers.

Nevertheless, in the rail transportation sector, the law of 21 August 2007 (Code des Transports, Article L. 1324-10) changed this perspective by ruling that the decision to organise a ballot may be taken by the employer, a representative trade union (not necessarily a trade union that supported the strike) or the designated mediator, if any exists.[106] This ballot can be organised by the employer only if the strike lasts more than eight days. The question submitted to vote is whether the strike should continue. The reason for the ballot has thus changed: it is not intended to let the striking employees decide the fate of the strike, but enables opponents of the strike to call a vote. Furthermore, striking employees are not the only voters: every employee concerned by the professional claims must have a say. The vote must be secret. The law stipulates that

103. Cass. Soc. 26 July 1984, Droit social, 1985, 118, note *Savatier*.
104. Tribunal administratif de Lyon, référé, 1er June 2008, Droit ouvrier, 2008, 613.
105. Cass. Soc. 28 April 1994, Droit ouvrier, 1994, 442, note *Benamara-Bouaziz*; Cour d'appel de Versailles, 9 September 2008, Droit ouvrier, 2009, 139
106. *Peskine/Borenfreund/Leclerc*, 2007, 664.

'the result [of the ballot] does not affect the exercise of the right to strike'. This is easily explained by the fact that the right to strike is individual and that an employee's decision whether to strike is not determined by a trade union's decision nor by a vote. With no obvious use, such a ballot is meant to put pressure on striking employees and to undermine the legitimacy of the strike in the event that a small minority decides to continue the strike. It may also shed light on diverging strategies among representative trade unions (e.g., in 2009, during industrial action in urban transportation in Lyon, one trade union organised a vote on its strategy and, in so doing, set itself apart from other trade unions).[107]

Although the Law of 2007 illustrates a major shift in the conception of the role of ballots in industrial relations,[108] its practical consequences must not be overestimated. First, this voting process only applies to the rail transportation of passengers sector. Second, when such a vote is initiated by the employer, this can only take place if the strike lasts more than eight days, which rarely occurs. This procedure has rarely been used since its enactment.

8 EVALUATION AND CONCLUSION

Evaluating the French regulations on strikes in essential services is a complex, and perhaps impossible task for various reasons. First of all, it is difficult to agree on the criteria used to define what effective regulation is. The fact, for example, that few strikes are reported in a country may be a sign of a very good system of collective bargaining, where the social partners manage to negotiate before any strike takes place, but it could also be the consequence of a limited recognition of the right to strike. Indeed, recent studies have questioned the reliability of a measure of strikes relying on an 'individual days not worked' indicator. This indicator implies that every cessation of work has the same nature (pressuring the employer to support professional claims) and therefore can be added together. Researchers have argued that disputes are multi-faceted.[109] Hence, a decreased number of days not worked does not necessarily mean that fewer conflicts have arisen. A reduction in the number of strikes may very well mean that professional action has taken other forms: protests, rallies, occupations, boycotts, petitions, refusals to work overtime, etc. In 2014, 2.2% of companies in the French private sector faced at least one of these kinds of disputes.[110] These actions also took place in addition to strikes in 26.5% of the companies where a strike took place in 2014.

Second, as explained in this article, the right to strike in essential services in France is remarkably lacking in unity. First, as regards the scope of the regulation: whereas some provisions apply to all public services and private

107. *Béroud/Giraud*, 2010, 16.
108. *Leclerc/Lyon-Caen*, 2010.
109. *Carlier, Tenret*, 2007, 1; *Beroud/Denis/Desage/Giraud*, 2008.
110. *Rosankis*, 2016, 6.

companies 'in charge of a public service' (such as the trade union strike notice), others are highly sectoral (e.g., specific to land and air transportation or primary schools). Second, French labour law encompasses a broad range of measures regulating the right to strike in essential services, extending from outright denying this right in certain sectors, imposing minimum levels of service to negotiation periods in other sectors, to the individual notice of the intention to go on strike. Third, numerous actors are involved in regulating strikes in essential services. For constitutional reasons, statutory laws play a major role in imposing limitations on the right to strike, however, the government and the authorities in charge of a public service are also entitled to do so. Because there is no general regulation of the right to strike in essential services in place in France, no overarching evaluation can be made.

In most cases, the various existing mechanisms have enabled a proper level of services in essential services to be maintained. For example, in public transport, an assessment made of the implementation of the 2007 Act was positive.[111] The new obligations have been respected and it has been possible to schedule transportation plans and to inform the clients of these plans. In term of compliance and performance evaluation, this report made a distinction between 'institutional strikes' (or national strikes) and 'professional strikes' (or local strikes). The report also proposed some modifications in order to improve the preparation of the transportation plan, such as limiting the practice of sequential strike notices. The report evaluated the correct level of service but not the effect of the Act on collective bargaining. However, it can be argued that compliance by individual and collective actors with the obligations defined in the 2007 Act, also depends on a proper level of collective bargaining in the transportation sector. In 2008, Nicolas Sarkozy stated that 'now when there is a strike, no-one notices'. This personal evaluation of the effects of the 2007 Act is debatable. The 2007 Act has certainly reduced the harmfulness of strikes in this sector and perhaps reduced the bargaining power of trade unions. However, strikes in transportation always generate great controversy and all transport users notice them.

All in all, the various aspects of regulation in France must be understood as successive layers, shaped not only by legal concerns but to at least the same extent by economic reasons. Most of the provisions denying the right to strike and imposing minimum levels of service were enacted at a time when many economic sectors were nationalised (between 1945 and 1986). The situation changed dramatically from the mid-eighties onwards when most economic activities returned to the private sector. The majority of regulations passed since then have tended only to limit the consequences for the public of the exercise of the right to strike. The regulations passed during these very different economic periods remains in force to this day. Hence, the study of the regulation of the right to strike in essential services offers an ideal vantage point for observing the

111. See *Mariton*, 2009.

changes that occurred over time in managing public services and the workers involved in essential services.

Bibliography

Beroud, Sophie/Denis, Jean-Michel/Desage, Guillaume/Giraud, Baptiste, Entre grèves et conflits : les luttes quotidiennes au travail, Centre d'études de l'emploi, 2008

Béroud, Sophie/Giraud, Baptiste, Restriction du droit de grève et stratégies syndicales dans les transports publics. L'exemple du mouvement des TCL à l'automne 2009, 2010

Braconnier, Stéphane, Droit des services publics, 2[d] éd., 2007

Carlier, Alexandre/Tenret, Elise, Des conflits du travail plus nombreux et plus diversifiés, DARES Premières Synthèses, 2007, 1 et seqq.

Chabanas, Nicole/Vergeau, Eric, Nationalisations et privatisation depuis 50 ans, INSEE Première, 1996, 1 et seqq.

Courrège, Marie, Le principe de continuité du service public confronté au droit de grève, 2015

DARES, La syndicalisation en France. Des salariés deux fois plus syndiqués dans la fonction publique, DARES Analyses, 2016, 1 et seqq.

DARES, Les journées individuelles non travaillées (JINT), *DARES Données annuelles,* 2016, 1 et seqq. (DARES, 2016a)

Dupré de Boulois, Xavier, Retour sur la jurisprudence Dehaene. Réflexions autour de l'arrêt d'assemblée du 12 avril 2013, Fédération Force ouvrière Energie et Mines, Revue des droits et libertés fondamentaux, 2013, 15 et seqq.

Encinas de Munagorri, Rafael, Les techniques juridiques de règlement des conflits collectifs du travail, in *Fortunet* (ed.), Un siècle de régulation pacifique des conflits du travail, Publications du Centre Georges Chevrier, 2001, 163 et seqq.

Gahdoun, Pierre-Yves, Les aléas du droit de grève dans la Constitution, Droit Social 2014, 349 et seqq.

Gugliemi, Gilles/Koubi, Geneviève/Long, Martine, Droit du service public, Montchrestien, 4th ed., 2016

Le Crom, Jean-Pierre, Deux siècles de droit du travail. L'histoire par les lois, Ed. de l'Atelier, 1998.

Leclerc, Olivier, Actualité de la mise en œuvre de la loi du 21 août 2007: la procédure de prévention des conflits, Revue de droit du travail 2008, 251 et seqq.

Leclerc, Olivier, L'encadrement législatif de l'exercice du droit de grève. Observations à partir de la loi n° 2008-790 du 20 août 2008 instituant un droit d'accueil pour les élèves des écoles pendant le temps scolaire, Revue de droit du travail 2008, 674 et seqq.

Leclerc, Olivier, Où va le droit spécial de la grève?, Revue de droit du travail 2012, 570 et seqq.

Leclerc, Olivier/Lyon-Caen, Antoine, L'essor du vote dans les relations professionnelles, 2010

Lemasson, Julien Les catégories d'entreprise en France : de la microentreprise à la grande entreprise, INSEE Focus, 2014, 1 et seqq.

Lyon-Caen, Gérard, Le conflit du Parisien Libéré et le système français de règlement des conflits du travail, Droit social, 1977, 438 et seqq.

Mariton, MP, Parliamentary report on the evaluation of the implementation of the Act, Rapport d'information sur l'évaluation économique et financière des récents mouvements sociaux à la SNCF et l'impact du service minimum, 2009, http://www.assemblee-nationale.fr/13/rap-info/i1436.asp#P182_19580

Merley, Nathalie, La jurisprudence administrative facteur de fragilisation du droit de grève dans les services publics, in *Crouzatier-Durand/Kada* (eds), Grève et droit public. 70 ans de reconnaissance, 2017, 59 et seqq.

Merlier, Jocelyne, Les conflits en 2001 : une légère baisse, Premières Synthèses, 2003, 7 et seqq.

Moniolle, Carole, La Liberté d'association dans l'armée, Droit Social 2017, 509 et seqq.

Peskine, Elsa/Borenfreund, Georges/Leclerc, Olivier, Le droit de grève dans les services publics de transport: regards sur la loi du 21 août 2007, Revue de droit du travail 2007, 664 et seqq.

Petit, Franck, Le droit de grève dans les services publics: un puzzle à recomposer, Droit Social 2017, 503 et seqq.

Portail d'information de la Représentativité Patronale, Accueil, 2018. Available at https://www.representativite-patronale.travail.gouv.fr/PortailUberwar/Accueil.action;jsessionid=7FB22EF85EF34E56D85DD49BD0021112

Portail de la Fonction publique, Les chiffres clés de la fonction publique, 2016. Available at https://www.fonction-publique.gouv.fr/chiffres-cles

Ramin, Alain, Du rôle et de l'utilité du médiateur au travers d'une grève significative : le conflit SNECMA, Droit social, 1989, 839 et seqq.

Rosankis, Elodie, Les grèves en 2014, DARES Résultats, 2016, 6 et seqq.

Sinay, Hélène, Traité de droit du travail : la grève, 1966

Terneyre, Philippe, Grève dans les services publics, Répertoire de droit du travail, 2016-2017

Vannes, Vivianne, Le droit de grève. Concilier le droit de grève et les autres droits fondamentaux : recours au principe de proportionnalité ?, 2e éd. 2014

CHAPTER 7

Germany

Monika Schlachter & Christina Hießl

1 GENERAL BACKGROUND: COUNTRY PROFILE

Germany is a federal state comprised of 16 single states where legislative power is attributed to the federal or state level, jointly or exclusively, by the Constitution. Article 74 (1) No. 12 of the Constitution (Basic Law) establishes a joint competency of the federation and the states for regulating matters of labour law. States may use their power, however, only insofar as the federal level had not already taken the lead. There exist plenty of statues on labour law at federal level, including rules on collective labour relations deduced from the general provision on the right to organize in Article 9 (3), and the Act on Collective Agreements (TVG). However, no explicit statute on trade unions rights or collective action was ever created, existing rules are judge-made law based on interpreting the general provision in Article 9 (3) of the Constitution.

The German legal order has traditionally been characterized by a lack of statutory regulation on industrial action. Despite continuous political attempts to overcome the stalemate situation pre-eminent for decades, it is left to the courts to deduce most of the applicable rules on preconditions and consequences of legal strikes from constitutional principles. Against this backdrop, an increase of the number of strikes in essential services, which has been much in the centre of attention in the recent past, had been taken as an indicator by several legal scholars for their doubts on the capability of judge-made law to deliver solutions appropriately balancing the interests at stake. Unions, however, express their acceptance of the status quo, primarily for judge-made law's heightened adaptability to changing economic or social developments. The ensuing sections will provide an insight into the pertinence of the issue in legal as well as practical terms, remaining uncertainties and the debate on the way forward.

2 COLLECTIVE LABOUR RELATIONS

Collective labour relations have traditionally played a crucial role in the socio-economic and political development in Germany and are considered a key ingredient of the concept of its 'social market economy'. Yet, this role is confronted with various pressures and challenges these days, much of which relates to the significant decline of the social partners' coverage rates among workers and employers in the present-day labour market. Membership in trade unions declined to 27% in 1994 and further to 21% in 2012 and 15% until 2014;[1]

1. *Anders/Biebeler/Lesch*, 2015; IWD, 2016.

the national trade union federation DGB (*Deutscher Gewerkschaftsbund*)'s member count[2] shows a decline to barely above 6 million members in 2016. Coverage by collective bargaining agreements remains higher but still fell significantly. Until 2015, coverage decreased to 31 % of undertakings (59 % of employees) in the West and 21 % of undertakings (49 % of employees) in the East.[3]

With the system no longer functioning undisputedly, labour relations are becoming more controversial. Germany for decades remained the No. 3 European country with the lowest number of days lost per worker for strike activities, short only to Austria and Switzerland with their significant corporatist features. For strike activity, official statistics drawn up by the federal employment office (*Streikstatistik der Bundesagentur für Arbeit*) are based on information by employers; an alternative statistic is based on information by unions and media coverage[4]. Both show, additionally to the 'normal' rather low numbers, some specifically strike-intensive years in all decades, culminating in the singularly high number of over 2 million working days lost to strike action in 2015. It can be stated that, while the incident of strikes in Germany is still low in international comparison,[5] it has been on the rise in specific sectors recently,[6] and – as will be set out *infra* – this has received much attention in the general society for its increasing likelihood to occur in branches intensely affecting the interests of consumers.

In collective labour relations, all employees, whether working in the public or private sector, enjoy a right to form and join trade unions. However, the rights to bargain collectively to conclude collective agreements and to strike are restricted for two broad categories of employees: firstly, such public servants whose terms and conditions of employment are established by statute. Employees concerned may be represented by their trade unions in a consultative process prior to the enactment of conditions but the final say will rest on (federal and state level) governments, so no meaningful bargaining procedure may take place and no collective agreements may be pursued. Secondly, the collective rights of persons employed by church-related employers are substantially restricted for their perceived incompatibility with religious values (for details, see *infra*). Both types of restrictions are principally independent from any essentiality of the work undertaken.

2. Accessible at http://www.dgb.de/uber-uns/dgb-heute/mitgliederzahlen.
3. *Ellguth/Kohaut/Möller*, 2016.
4. *WSI*, 2017, 6 et seq.
5. *Ibid.*, 7. Especially Southern European and Scandinavian countries show much higher values for the average annual loss of working days due to strike since 2006 (FR: 123; DK: 122) than Germany (7 according to the official, 20 according to the 'alternative' statistic). Austria and Switzerland come last with 2 days each.
6. *Fischer*, 2008, 2; *Seeling/Probst*, 2014, 2421.

3 THE RIGHT TO STRIKE

3.1 A Constitutional Right

Although German statutory law does not stipulate a right to collective action explicitly, it is settled case law that the right to strike is an inherent part of the constitutional guarantee of the freedom of association in Article 9(3) (1) of the Basic Law.[7] Basically, the wording of that provision guarantees the right to organize for everyone and all trades for furthering and defending their social and economic interests. Additionally, s.3 prohibits measures by the state directed against peaceful collective action, thereby implicitly acknowledging the conduct of collective actions. Starting with a landmark decision of the Federal Labour Court back in 1955,[8] jurisdiction has referred to this general provision for determining the conditions under which a measure of collective action is considered legal, and the consequences of that assessment also for contractual relations and liability for damages.[9]

Article 9 (3) of the Basic Law is understood, in parallel to international law, as providing a collective as well as an individual component. As for the former, its beneficiaries are so-called *coalitions*, i.e., notably trade unions and employers' organizations, which have both the purpose and the ability to play an independent role in collective labour relations.[10] In their individual dimension, the rights established by Article 9 (3) are granted to every worker in dependent employment, including trainees and apprentices;[11] whether it applies also to the self-employed is disputed, but nevertheless indicated by the wording of the constitution.[12] All workers, independent from an existing affiliation with a union, are entitled to participate in collective activities, including strikes. Case law has held constantly that participation in a legal strike must not be considered a violation of the employment contract. Much rather, participating in legal collective action (by both employees or employers) has the effect of rendering the main mutual contractual obligations transitionally ineffective, so that an employee's failure to perform their work does not entitle an employer to terminate the contract, claim damages or apply other sanctions. Vice versa, the transitional suspension concerns also the employer's main contractual duties,

7. BVerfG 26 June 1991 – 1 BvR 779/85. Cf. *Linsenmaier*, 2017, 102; *Klein*, 2017, 238; *Däubler*, 2017, § 9, 1 et seqq.; *Kissel*, 2002, § 17, 1 et seqq.
8. BAG 28 January 1955 – GS 1/54.
9. Cf. also BGH 31 January 1978 – VI ZR 32/77; *Hänsle*, 2015, 442 et seq.
10. *Scholz*, 2016, 216 et seq.
11. BAG 12 September 1984 – 1 AZR 342/83; *Bepler*, 2016a, 14.
12. *Schlachter*, 2010, 634. However, panel doctors working under a collective contractual framework between the Medical board and social security institutions are not protected when engaging in strike-like actions to put insurance institutions under pressure, Federal Social Court, BSG 30 November 2016 – B 6 KA 38/15 R. The court referred to the relevant contractual framework according to which all parties must resort to arbitration should no agreement be reached.

specifically the duty to pay the agreed wage.[13] For the state, Article 9(3) of the Basic Law contains an obligation of neutrality (*Neutralitätspflicht*), which excludes paying unemployment benefits to workers affected by collective action and notably also forbids the resolution of collective disputes by compulsory arbitration.[14]

Importantly, the right to initiate a strike is traditionally interpreted as being reserved to unions, so that 'wildcat strikes' by non-unionized workers do not enjoy the protection of Article 9(3). Case law has permitted a subsequent 'legitimization' of such strikes by a supporting trade union, though.[15] Provided the strike has been called by a trade union, the individual dimension of the guarantee entitles all workers of an affected establishment to take part in it, irrespective of their membership in that union.[16] By the same token, freedom of association is held to include the protection of the right *not* to take part in a strike. For employees deciding not to participate, there is no suspension of mutual contractual duties, so that they remain entitled to their wage and obliged to perform their ordinary work tasks. While employers are neither entitled to require them to replace their striking colleagues nor entitled to hire temporary workers for replacing striking workers,[17] they are free to uphold their business by convincing their own employees to not participate in the strike and take on additional work abandoned by strikers, or to provisionally outsource some tasks to affiliated companies. If ordinary work performance by own employees becomes outright impossible due to the strike, they lose their wage entitlement if they can be expected to benefit from the strike results.[18]

3.2 General Restrictions

As a constitutional right, the right to strike enjoys special protection without explicit limitations; limitations nevertheless do apply where other constitutional guarantees are at stake. The principal guideline used by German constitutional jurisdiction in this regard is the so-called principle of 'practical concordance'

13. *Scholz*, 2016, 244; *Gamillscheg*, 1997, 1188 et seq.; *Otto*, 2006, § 14, 2; *Treber*, 2017, § 194, 6.
14. BVerfG 4 July 1995 – 1 BvF 2/86; BAG 19 June 2007 – 1 AZR 396/06; *Scholz*, 2016, 216; *Löwisch/Rieble*, 1997, 14.
15. BAG 5 September 1955 – 1 AZR480/04. Cf. also ArbG Berlin 29 April 2008 – 58 Ga 6014/08; *Kissel*, 2002, § 25, 15 et seqq. and *Fischer*, 2008, 2.
16. BAG 30 August 1984 – 1 AZR 765/93; *Scholz*, 2016, 153 et seq.; *Bepler*, 2016a, 14.
17. Cf. the recent amendment of the German law on temporary employment (*Arbeitnehmerüberlassungsgesetz*, AÜG), which now contains a clear prohibition for temporary work agencies to provide employers with 'strike replacements'. See *Klein/Leist*, AuR 2017, 100 et seqq. Furthermore they do not need to uphold their business by convincing their own employees to not participate in the strike and take on additional work abandoned by strikers, or provisionally outsource some tasks to affiliated companies.
18. BAG 25 July 1957 – 1 AZR 194/56; BAG 22 December 1980 – 1 ABR 2/79; *Linsenmaier*, 2017, 143 et seq.; *Giesen*, 2016, 266; *Scholz*, 2016, 138 et seq.

(*praktische Konkordanz*) according to which colliding fundamental rights need to be balanced against each other so that in their interplay the effectiveness of opposing rights may become limited but none of them be totally excluded. Much rather, a balance must be struck, keeping all rights concerned at the best available level. One distinct feature of this balancing process concerns the structural differences between private parties' ability to realize their respective rights.[19]

Accordingly, relevant fundamental rights of the employer such as their own right to conduct collective action, their freedom to conduct a business (protected under Article 12 of the Basic Law on the free choice and exercise of occupations), and the right to personal property (Article 14 of the Basic Law) need to be taken into account, but with due regard to the typical structural imbalance of power between management and labour. This has led to the stipulation of a 'parity' requirement,[20] which indicates that the functioning of collective labour relations is conditional, among others, on the availability of effective collective means for workers in their structurally weaker position to pursue their interests.[21] In accordance with this principle, the most prominent employer-sided measure of collective action, a lockout, is permissible under strict preconditions; in practice, due to associated costs for businesses lockouts have been virtually absent in German collective relations for decades.[22] An otherwise legal strike crosses the line of tolerable action when it risks to be 'ruinous' for the employer's business.[23] As will be set out in more detail below, its acceptability frequently depends on the unions' provision of a minimum service agreement guaranteeing the maintenance of employer property and machinery and the continued delivery of specific minimum services to the general public. Needless to say, the balancing of rights becomes substantially more complex once the constitutional rights of third parties are involved, as it will regularly be the case at times of strike in essential services (see *infra* Section 4).[24]

19. BVerfG 19 October 1993 – 1 BvR 567/89; BVerfG 27 April 1999 – 1 BvR 2203/93; *Scholz*, 2016, 255 et seq.; *Hänsle*, 2015, 448 et seq.
20. Developed by the Federal Labour Court and confirmed by the Constitutional Court: BAG 21 April 1971 – GS 1/68; BVerfG 2 March 1993 – 1 BvR 1213/85; BVerfG 4 July 1995 – 1 BvF 1/87; *Scholz*, 2016, 133 et seq.
21. *Blanpain's* famous formulation that collective bargaining without a right to strike amounts essentially to 'collective begging' is used also by German jurisdiction: cf. BAG 10 June 1980 – 1 AZR 822/79; BAG 12 March 1985 – 1 AZR 636/82; BVerfG 4 July 1995 – 1 BvF 2/86; *Scholz*, 2016, 219.
22. BAG 10 June 1980 – 1 AZR 822/79; *Rieble*, 2005, 218 et seqq.; *Id.*, 2008, 1506 et seqq.; *Rödl*, § 21, 5 et seqq.
23. *Scholz*, 2016, 222, 240. See, however, the *ultima ratio* requirement set out *infra* (Subsection c). The correction of structural imbalances must not call into question the principle of state neutrality.
24. *Scholz*, 2016, 132 et seq.

Basically, the doctrine (*Wesentlichkeitslehre*) developed by the Constitutional Court states that, when it comes to permissible restrictions of constitutional rights, all 'essential' decisions need to be made by the legislature.[25] Yet, despite several judgments of the Court explicitly calling upon the legislator to regulate crucial areas of law concerning industrial action,[26] virtually no such regulation has been passed until today. This compels the judiciary to assert a quasi-legislative function, which sits uneasily with the role judges are expected to play in the German legal system. However, concretizing the right to collective action via court decisions has ultimately been justified both by constitutional doctrine[27] and the Constitutional Court.[28] Courts must ensure the greatest possible realization of the constitutional rights enshrined in Article 9(3) of the Basic Law, subject only to the limitations necessary to ensure other constitutional guarantees.[29]

3.3 Concretization by Case Law

For a strike to be legal, it needs to concern issues that could be settled by an agreement with the employer or employers' organization against which it is directed – i.e., essentially issues of working conditions.[30] This follows from the concept of an ancillary function of the right to strike for the collective bargaining process. Due to this conditionality, a strike can only be legitimate if it aims at the conclusion of a collective agreement.[31] This principle excludes strikes for other reasons, even if workers' interests are clearly affected. Notably, decisions on relocation, outsourcing and other forms of restructuring remain subject to the managerial prerogative.[32] Once the parties are bound by an existing collective agreement, a *relative peace obligation* makes strikes aiming at issues already settled therein illegal. Even where only one among several demands of the union violates the peace obligation, this makes a strike as such illegal, irrespective of

25. BVerfG 8 August 1978 – 2 BvL 8/77; BVerfG 2 March 1993 – 1 BvR 1213/85.
26. BVerfG 26 June 1991 – 1 BvR 779/85; BVerfG 4 July 1995 – 1 BvF 1/87. Cf. *Hänsle*, 2015, 595 et seq.
27. *Lassahn*, 2017.
28. BVerfG 26 June 1991 – 1 BvR 779/85.
29. BVerfG 26 June 1991 – 1 BvR 779/85; references to the countless critical remarks by academics can be found, e.g., in *Fischer*, 2009, 287 et seq.; *Scholz*, 2016, 132 et seq.
30. *Scholz*, 2016, 235, 261; *Otto*, 2006, § 5, 2 et seqq.; *Kissel*, 2002, § 24, 1 et seqq.; *Treber*, 2017, § 192, 2.
31. BAG 24 April 2007 – 1 AZR 252/06; *Treber*, 2017, § 192, 2. Cf. the critical remarks by *Däubler*, 2017, § 13, 5.
32. Yet, as strikes in favour of collective agreement regulating, e.g., the consequences of a relocation for workers must be admissible, courts will be cautious when asked to declare strikes in this context illegal, as it will usually be impossible to establish that the trade union's only aim was to prevent the restructuring altogether: cf. LAG Hamm 31 May 2000 – 18a Sa 858/00; LAG Schleswig-Holstein 27 March 2003 – 5 Sa 137/03; BAG 24 April 2007 – 1 AZR 252/06; *Kerwer* 2008, 338 with further references.

its (claimed) importance in relation to the permissible aims.[33] Beyond this automatic consequence of concluding a collective agreement, an *absolute peace obligation* (in the sense that, until expiry of a collective agreement, industrial action between the parties to this agreement is generally ruled out irrespective of its aim) would need to be expressly stated in that agreement.

Apart from this requirement of a legitimate aim, the key aspect of assessing the legality of a strike is the proportionality test, which is a necessary tool for balancing the conflicting (fundamental) rights of the parties (*Übermaßverbot*, 'excess ban'). As reiterated numerous times in settled case law,[34] any measure announced or already taken by parties to a collective action must be assessed with a view to the maintenance of a reasonable relation between its aims and the damage caused; a measure as drastic as calling a strike can be permitted only as a means of last resort, once there is no realistic expectation of reaching the stated aims (amelioration of working conditions) by peaceful means.

Whether or not industrial action complies with the excess ban is assessed according to the facts of the individual case. As the right to strike is generally not regulated by statute, there are also no universally prescribed rules as to the kind, intensity and duration of attempts to settle a dispute peacefully before a trade union may call a strike. Also, jurisprudence has rejected to stipulate specific formal preconditions for exercising the constitutional right to strike, such as a strike ballot ensuring that a certain majority of the workers concerned support the action, a formal declaration of failure of negotiations, or an arbitration procedure between the conflicting parties. However, most of those instruments are effectively applied, based on self-regulation by the labour market parties. In practice, the by-laws of all relevant German trade unions do contain prescriptions on strike ballots and/or formal procedures involving higher-level bodies within the union;[35] voluntary arbitration is very common and frequently agreed upon in framework agreements between unions and employers' organizations.[36] However, voluntary arbitration would only be binding on the parties if explicitly foreseen in the respective agreement; otherwise, both parties are free to decide after the arbiter's proposal was made, potentially rejecting it and continue with collective action to assert their demands.[37]

This illustrates the general approach of the courts: rather than stipulating binding formal preconditions to the legality of collective action, parties in principle enjoy the freedom of opting for means they think necessary for achieving their goals. That includes not only established forms of collective action such as strikes and lockouts, but allows inventing new ones better

33. BAG 26 Juli 2016 – 1 AZR 160/14; LAG Hessen 9 September 2015 – 9 SaGa 1082/15; *Dieterich*, 2009, 125. Cf. the critical remarks by *Reinfelder*, 2017, § 15, 27.
34. Starting with BAG 21 April 1971 – GS 1/68. Cf. *Dieterich*, 2009, 130; *Scholz*, 2016, 238, 244.
35. *Absenger*, 2016, 35 et seq.
36. *Ibid.*, 38 et seq.
37. Cf. BAG 17 December 1976 – 1 AZR 605/75; BAG 12 September 1984 – 1 AZR 342/83; BAG 21 June 1988 – 1 AZR 653/86 and 651/86; *Scholz*, 2016, 216; *Otto*, 2006, § 21, 21 et seqq.

equipped to conditions of a globalized economy, and employ them at a moment the respective party considers adequate. This far-reaching freedom is restricted by the necessity of operating within the principle of proportionality, considering a variety of aspects in each individual case, and by respecting the rules of criminal law, prohibiting damage to property etc.[38]

This case-to-case approach is illustrated by the developments of rules concerning secondary action. This notion includes collective action conducted with the aim of supporting another (the principal) strike through targeting additional employers. Strikes against such employers not in the position to become a party to the collective agreement desired by the union, after a landmark decision rendered in 2007[39] by the Federal Labour Court, were declared not to be excluded from constitutional protection. This had earlier been a generally accepted line of reasoning as a secondary action would not have aimed at concluding a collective agreement between the disputing parties. The employer concerned by such action therefore was seen as lacking any means to influence the disputed working conditions, thereby becoming a helpless victim of a dispute originating elsewhere. The Court meanwhile reasons, that the question of the employers' affectedness by a foreign conflict is but one aspect that needs to be considered in the overall assessment of proportionality. Hence, solidarity strikes may be permissible especially in cases of existing ties between employers, which allow for the assumption that the employer affected by the secondary strike could indeed influence the conclusion of a collective agreement with this other employer.

Another prominent (but singular) example relates to the use of a flash mob to obstruct the employer's business in the retail sector: the Federal Labour Court in 2009 rejected an absolute ban for this means of collective action supported by consumers, largely considered as generally illegitimate by legal doctrine, and was subsequently confirmed by the Constitutional Court in 2014.[40] Also here, whether or not the means of action chosen by the trade union complies with the proportionality requirement needs to be decided for each case individually. Courts have also refrained from assessing short 'warning strikes' differently from 'regular strikes': the *ultima ratio* requirement is applicable to every collective action, which may only be taken as a means of last resort after other attempts of reaching an agreement have failed. This implies that the union has presented its demands, bargaining actually has taken place and preconditions potentially enshrined in the collective agreement such as voluntary arbitration

38. *Giesen*, 2016, 272; *Buchner*, 2008, 106 et seqq.; *Rieble*, 2008, 1506 et seqq.; *Scholz*, 2016, 231 et seq.
39. BAG 19 June 2007 – 1 AZR 396/06. On the mixed academic reception cf. e.g., *Klein*, 2017, 336 et seqq.; *Kerwer*, 2008, 337; *Buchner*, 2008, 106; *Giesen*, 2016, 268; *Rieble*, 2008, 1506 et seqq.; *Scholz*, 2016, 239 et seq.; *Fütterer*, 2013; *Bertke*, 2014; *Rödl*, 2017, § 17, 85 et seqq.
40. BAG 22 September 2009 – 1 AZR 972/08; BVerfG 26 March 2014 – 1 BvR 3185/09; *Klein*, 2017, 240 et seq. Needless to say, the mentioned decisions were subject to much academic criticism. See, e.g., *Rieble*, 2008, 796 et seq.; *Giesen*, 2016, 269; *Scholz*, 2016, 234 et seqq, 262.

have been applied without success. However, there is no need for any explicit declaration that, for the union, negotiations have failed. Once a union deems it reasonable that no agreement can be reached, the calling of a strike will represent the indicator for finishing the negotiation phase.[41]

The probably most controversial development in relation to the right to strike in recent years concerned the question of how to deal with situations characterized by the presence of more than one union competing for representing workers in the same establishment or bargaining unit, and the risk of an 'abuse' of the right to strike by unions representing a small group of workers in strategic positions. For decades, this type of conflict was almost unheard of as the courts had stipulated a principle of 'unity' of collective agreements (*Tarifeinheit*), indicating that a more specific collective agreement concluded with one trade union would prevail over a concurring more general agreement with another union, rendering the latter one effectively inapplicable.[42] As a consequence, also the peace obligation enshrined in the most specific collective agreement would cover everyone to whom the agreement was applied. That principle was subject to continuous debate in the light of its conflict with the freedom to bargain collectively as well as the considerable uncertainties in determining this prevalence of collective agreements.[43] It was finally given up in a landmark decision of the Federal Labour Court in 2010.[44] In the aftermath of this newly developed case law, unions representing specialist workers such as doctors, pilots or engine drivers (specifically in the privatized former public sector, compare *infra* Subsection 4) started to use their power for furthering their interests despite the existence of applicable collective agreements for general workers in the respective establishment. Companies were facing consecutive collective disputes with different unions, so that concerns were raised about the aggravation of the risk of strikes with major economic impact: even in the presence of a valid collective agreement that, at least in principle, could have covered also the specialists, these groups of employees could legally associate with another union and consequently go on strike for better terms and conditions than those envisaged by the general agreement.

3.4 Legislative Abstinence and Its Implications

In the light of the jurisdictional U-turn described in the last paragraph, the German legislator took the exceptional step of codifying a form of the unity

41. BAG 21 June 1988 – 1 AZR 653/86 and 651/86; *Rieble*, 2008, 1510; *Scholz*, 2016, 238 et seq.; *Kocher*, 2015, 151.
42. BAG 14 June 1989 – 4 AZR 200/89; BAG 5 September 1990 – 4 AZR 59/90; BAG 4 December 2002 – 10 AZR 113/02; BAG 18 October 2006 – 10 AZR 576/05; BAG 15 November 2006 – 10 AZR 665/05; *Lehmann*, 2014, 634; *Bepler*, 2016b, 15 et seqq.
43. *Kerwer*, 2008, 336; *Greiner*, 2012, 529 et seqq.; *Schliemann*, 2012, 515 et seqq.
44. BAG 7 July 2010 – 4 AZR 549/08.

principle by means of a law passed in May 2015.[45] According to this statute, in case of competing collective agreements, only the one agreement concluded by the union representing the most workers in a specific enterprise will prevail and become applicable there. So instead of applying the most specialized of concurring agreements, this variety of unity principle will favour the agreement concluded by the most representative union. Typically, but not automatically, this will be advantageous for the general unions who, in absolute terms, have many more members than the specialists' organizations. At any rate, the major issue of concern, a potentially increasing number of strikes in the sectors with active specialists' unions, is not addressed by this law. The legislator in the accompanying explanatory statements again left it to the courts to decide whether the proportionality principle might eventually forbid collective action for obtaining an agreement which would anyhow become inapplicable due to the lack of representativeness of the union demanding it. The Federal Constitutional Court in pronouncing the constitutionality of most parts of the new law, explicitly declared that the law would not justify denying minority unions the right to strike for their collective agreements.[46]

It should not go unmentioned that a side effect of the far-reaching competence for courts to establish and develop the rules for collective action might be the connected power to also incorporate international standards.[47] Basically, German courts depart from a principle according to which the interpretation of national norms should take applicable rules of international law into account as far as possible. This principle (known as *völkerrechtsfreundliche Auslegung*) urges courts to avoid contradictions between national law (including constitutional law) and international standards, unless this seems irreconcilable with established methods of legal interpretation. Concerning the right to strike, this would indicate that it could be interpreted in the light of international standards as described *supra* in Part II, particularly Article 11 ECHR.[48] Also the interpretation of the European Social Charter, in matters of industrial action partly conflicting with national case law, could become more relevant for developing national law in such case.[49] However, the Constitutional Court holds firmly to its ultimate power to control all domestically applicable norms, including

45. Tarifeinheitsgesetz, 3 July 2015, BGBl. I, 1130.
46. BVerfG, 11 July 2017 - 1 BVR 1571/15.
47. *Schlachter*, 2017, 10 et seqq.
48. BVerfG 14 October 2004 - 2 BvR 1481/04; BVerwG 27 February 2014 - 2 C 1/13; cf. *Lörcher*, 2017, § 10, 11 et seqq. The ECHR itself has the status of ordinary law in Germany and could thus not alter Art. 9(3) of the Basic Law as a provision of constitutional law: cf. *Schlachter*, 2015, 218.
49. Cf. the criticism of German case law by the Committee of Ministers of the Council of Europe in 1998 and repeatedly in the literature: e.g., *Seifert*, 2013, 214 et seqq, *Waltermann*, 2015, 19; *Kerwer*, 2008, 351.

international norms, against the national constitution.[50] In essence, the potential for applying international standards specifically to the right to strike is seldom used in practice.[51] Much rather, courts tend to refer to international law in passing, for enforcing a result they already arrived at upon applying national standards.

Of more practical relevance for the conduct of a strike than international standards are preliminary injunctions, which are frequently sought by employers to achieve an immediate judicial prohibition of strike action, possibly before it has even begun. The role of this procedural instrument is to provide a fast remedy against actions that are probably illegal and likely to cause irreversible damage to the party seeking the injunction. An early identification and stoppage of illegal strikes can prevent economic losses, and the ensuing claims for damages which unions would be confronted with. Also, at this early stage there is still room for intermediate solutions if both a comprehensive permission of the proposed strike action and a complete prohibition are found to be disproportionate. The court can thus reject the employer's quest for prohibition while stipulating conditions for the union, such as a limitation in scope or the maintenance of a minimum service.[52] However, as urgent summary decisions injunctions need to be rendered quickly, sometimes within a matter of hours,[53] so they are not subject to appeal in third instance. While, in principle, an in-depth review of the case (including regular appeal) is always possible in the subsequent main procedure that the injunction was intended to secure (i.e., the claim for a judicial prohibition of the strike and/or the payment of damages), in practice these main procedures are regularly discontinued for lack of interest in a judicial solution once collective action has in fact been terminated.[54] Consequently, in the absence of highest-instance precedents providing uniform guidance, diverging practices by different courts are almost unavoidable.[55]

In the end, the judge-made rules on collective action are accused by some of not being precise enough, lacking necessary legal certainty and foreseeability

50. BVerfG 15 December 2015 – 2 BvL 1/12.
51. *Buchholtz*, 2014, 199.
52. The German Civil Procedural Code (§ 940 ZPO) prescribes the necessity of 'preventing significant disadvantage' as the basis for granting an injunction. Despite the time pressure characterizing this type of procedure, this amounts to a comprehensive proportionality test in which the judge has to decide whether the action proposed by the union would amount to an inacceptable disruption of the legal order. It may include questions of a violation of peace obligations or whether the union's aims could actually be a valid content of a collective agreement. Cf. *Buchner*, 2003, 2130. Actually, jurisdiction has found the application for an injunction to be an inherent part of the employer's obligation to contribute to damage limitation: if the employer waits for the illegal strike to go ahead and seeks compensation afterwards, it risks to be found partially responsible and thereby forego a part of the compensation entitlement: LAG Hessen 5 December 2013 – Sa 592/13.
53. *von Steinau-Steinrück*, 2012, 26.
54. *Rieble*, 2008, 1514 et seq.
55. *Fischer*, 2015, 1 et seq.; *Id.*, 2009, 293 et seqq.

especially when precedence is changing (*infra* 5.4) In a legal system like Germany's, generally defined by statutes, many academic writers regularly attribute this outcome to the lack of legislative decisions. Yet, even if, in the light of the constitutional principle, legislation should accept responsibility for the development of the law on collective action, the desired outcome of legal certainty might not be achieved even by statutes, which would almost necessarily also consist of rather general formulations.

While judge made law represents the primary source of authoritative regulation governing the right to strike, in practice social partners have frequently created their own rules in collective agreements. Specifically, the potential of collective action to cause economic harm has given rise to substantial as well as procedural rules in agreements, created with the goal of avoiding direct action as far as possible. These rules include means for establishing minimum services during a collective conflict, dispute resolution methods or the obligation to provide notice. It is the understanding of both parties that collective action should be used as '*ultima ratio*' only, i.e., if all other options for reaching an agreement fail, which has for a long time contributed to the comparatively peaceful labour relations dominating in Germany. The fact that especially privatized formerly state-run essential services have lately become more strike-prone is no contradiction to this approach. This does, however, not translate into accepting state-imposed forms of conflict resolution: due to the devastating effect of state-imposed mandatory arbitration during the Weimar Republic (which according to social scientists has contributed to social unrest and the division of society), state-set wage scales or obligatory dispute resolution mechanisms are met with utmost suspicion. Self-regulation, on the other hand, is not only widely accepted but also regularly applied in practice.

Parties agree on forms of dispute resolution by a neutral arbitrator or a committee comprised of representatives of the parties plus a neutral chairperson. The agreement may establish the dispute resolution procedure as a precondition for starting collective measures or a means to be invoked again for provisionally interrupting already ongoing actions. The arbitrator/members of the arbitration committee are selected and agreed upon by the parties themselves; as the neutral arbitrator, high-ranking ex-politicians or respected public figures tend to be chosen. Implementing the conflict resolution procedure is regularly mandatory, conflicting parties are contractually disallowed from starting or continuing collective measures until after the procedure is completed. Arbitrators deliver a recommendation to be put before both parties for acceptance. If both sides agree, the recommendation is turned into a collective agreement. If it is not accepted, collective action may legitimately start or continue. Alternatively, also a state-run arbitration procedure is available, also depending on the agreement of both parties to submit their conflict; it is, however, rarely used in practice.

4 THE EXPERIENCE WITH STRIKES IN ESSENTIAL SERVICES

4.1 Identifying 'Essential Services'

In the recent past, there has been a major shift towards strikes in parts of the economy that might be counted among 'essential services'.[56] Given the lack of any legal or otherwise standardized definition of that term, measuring the amplitude of collective action relating to this field remains complicated. Although a rough equivalent to 'essential services' may be found in the German expression *Daseinsvorsorge*, relating to the state's duty to care for citizens' basic needs, also this term lacks precise definition or application.[57] It can occasionally be found in legislative provisions (e.g., relating to local traffic service) but the concept's interpretation may differ depending on the context and purpose of the respective provision, so that effectively not much can be gained from their consideration for the assessment of strikes.[58] In practice, the term is used for services the non-performance of which affects not only the employer's interest in business continuity and financial gain, but also affects the general public as users of the service, for lack of reasonable alternatives. This latter feature is prevalent specifically in sectors formerly exclusively provided by the state, such as health care, education, transportation, water and heating, IT infrastructure etc., which were privatized with the aim of minimizing tax money spent on the public service. Not only is such competition-orientated environment more likely to produce cost-cutting tendencies by employers and ensuing collective disputes; it also removes the boundaries to collective action applicable to civil servants, as will be described *infra*.[59] While the State as a consequence of privatization de facto lost its ability to actuality determine the availability of such services for the general public, the principal duty to provide at least basic social standards remained. Now economists argue for legislature on limiting strike rights for guaranteeing continuous provision of services independent from the level of working conditions of the workers providing such services.

4.2 Examples

In fact, the strike incidents described (*supra* Section 2) were mostly caused by the cumulative strikes in sectors with links to public interest. This can be illustrated by a closer look at the two most turbulent years in this regard since the turn of the millennium. First, the year 2006 (when over 1600 working days were lost) was characterized by strikes around a major collective dispute in the railway sector, followed by long strikes in services such as local traffic, hospitals,

56. Cf. *Franzen*, 2015, 1 et seq.
57. *Schlachter*, 2017, 10 et seqq.
58. *Büttner/Richter/Zimmermann*, 2016, 441. For a detailed analysis of the term and its use in relation to strike see *Hänsle*, 2015, 211 et seq.
59. *Wissenschaftlicher Beirat beim BMVI*, 2016, 118; *Franzen*, 2015, 1.

childcare, public administration and municipal cleaning.[60] Similarly, the year 2015 saw a wave of strikes in the railway sector, the postal services, hospitals and educational institutions, particularly prolonged in child day-care. Significantly, much of the lost working days were essentially due to the strike of employees in social and educational services plus postal services (1.5 million lost working days).[61] Additionally, though usually shorter in duration and therefore less significant for the total number of lost working days, strikes in the transport services (especially airline and railway staff) have caused heavily debated disturbances over the last few years.[62]

To motivate their own constituency to conduct strikes, wage claims by trade unions representing 'functional elites', e.g.in the transport sector, were frequently grossly exaggerated. Illustrative examples can be found for the pilots' union *Vereinigung Cockpit (VC)*, which in 2002 initiated collective action to support a historical demand of a 35% wage increase,[63] or the engine drivers' union *Gewerkschaft Deutscher Lokführer (GDL)*, which followed in 2007 demanding a 31% increase.[64] The air traffic controllers' strike in 2012 was accompanied by wage increase claims of up to 70%.[65] Such conflicts finally had to settle at substantially lower margins, but gains were still much higher than what ordinary workers were able to achieve, and public opinion reacted shocked and upset. While strikes in sectors such as pre-school education and care, where workers are notoriously underpaid despite their large degree of responsibilities, can usually count on public support for their wage claims, the specialized unions' approach was met with wide-spread anger.

These developments became also challenging for general unions not in the position to achieve impressive increases for their remaining constituencies, notably after their negotiating power decreased following the exodus of some of the more powerful groups of workers to the specialist unions. In some cases, general unions tried to overcome this problem by interacting with the specialist unions, but with relatively poor results: This can be illustrated by the tactical cooperation between the flight attendant union *Ufo (Unabhängige Flugbegleiterorganisation)* and the general service sector union *Ver.di (Vereinte Dienstleistungsgewerkschaft)* in a negotiation community in December 2011, which was subsequently terminated by Ufo only weeks after its conclusion in order to aim at a separate agreement with more favourable conditions for its own members.[66] A similarly problematic relationship characterized the collective disputes in the railway sector, where the GDL co-exists with the general railway personnel union EVG (*Eisenbahn- und Verkehrsgewerkschaft*), but for a long time no

60. *Kerwer*, 2008, 335; *Kolbe*, 2009, 1414.
61. *Absenger*, 2016, 9 et seq.; *Blattner*, 2015, 2037.
62. *Henssler*, 2014, 1 et seqq. A comprehensive overview can be found in *Lesch*, 2016, 155 et seqq.
63. *Bayreuther*, 2005, 2640; *Buchner*, 2003, 2128 et seqq.
64. Cf. *Buchner*, 2008, 106 et seqq.
65. *von Steinau-Steinrück*, 2012, 1 et seqq. For further examples, see *Lesch*, 2012, 8 et seq.
66. *Seeling/Probst*, 2014, 2423

agreement of cooperation was achieved. Finally, after escalating collective conflicts in the railway sector, an arbitration agreement was concluded in 2015, in which GDL has subjected itself to arbitration that can be initiated by either of the parties to the collective agreement for all collective disputes emerging until 2020.[67] All in all, an empirical assessment of 123 collective disputes including specialists unions found that, compared to conflicts in other areas, they are characterized by significantly longer negotiations and an elevated probability of escalation.[68]

4.3 Legal Implications

One of the key elements of the debate concerning the described strike actions is the appropriate way of coping with the specialized 'sectoral unions'. Their increasing relevance marks a point of departure from the traditional German culture of collective relations basing itself on the so-called industry union principle (*Industrieverbandsprinzip*), according to which one single trade union would represent and accept as their members all workers employed in establishments belonging to a specific industry, e.g., in the metal branch, and therefore be competent to conclude collective agreements applicable to all unionized workers in the respective establishment, independent of their profession. Non-unionized workers' terms and conditions would regularly also be regulated according to the terms of these collective agreements, as the employer would insert reference clauses relating to that agreement (*Bezugnahmeklauseln*) in their individual labour contracts.[69]

The 'sectoral unions', however, organize and represent primarily workers of a specific profession, notably specialists who are difficult to replace, resulting in their substantial bargaining power.[70] With collective action, they would aim not at relatively better working conditions in the whole establishment, but at much better conditions for their specific group. Employers' representatives and academic commentators have argued that such form of collective action is less worthy of protection, especially considering that the costs of the privileges of the few would likely be borne also by colleagues, so that industrial action is actually not in the interest of the majority of the staff.[71] It furthermore undermines the public interest in uninterrupted services, which in the former single union system resulted as a side effect of the fact that the peace obligation covered everyone, so that a strike-free period until the expiry of the applicable agreement was guaranteed.[72] This argumentation was supported by the fact that courts had

67. *Lehmann*, 2015, 2232; *Absenger*, 2016, 9.
68. *von Steinau-Steinrück/Reiter*, 2015, 38 et seqq.
69. Cf. *Lehmann*, 2014, 636
70. *Schlachter*, 2015, 217 et seqq.
71. E.g., *Giesen*, 2016, 270; *Bayreuther*, 2005, 2641.
72. *Lehmann*, 2014, 635; *Seeling/Probst*, 2014, 2423 et seq., with further references to authors predicting a 'paralyzation of the economy' if strike measures must constantly be expected.

declared engine drivers' strike actions in 2003 and 2007 illegal basically by reliance on the above-mentioned unity principle,[73] whereas a similar strike in 2014 was allowed with explicit reference to its abolishment by the Federal Labour Court.[74]

The legislator's reaction to the phenomenon of specialized unions was (as described above, Subsection 3.4) not targeted at strikes, but merely constrained the applicability of collective agreements concluded by minority unions once a collective agreement with a majority union is in place. Even with this restricted scope of application, the draft bill was challenged before the Constitutional Court for its alleged infringement of freedom of association, but was eventually principally upheld[75]. For the purpose of the current study, however, this development does not represent a solution, as a regulation of strike in essential services is not provided (see next section).[76]

5 RESTRICTIONS OF THE RIGHT TO STRIKE IN ESSENTIAL SERVICES

5.1 Consideration of the 'Essential' Nature of a Service

As indicated above, statutory law does not address the question of strike in essential services, nor give a definition of the latter. Basically, the only difference between these strikes and 'ordinary' strikes is that an additional element is considered by the courts when deciding whether a strike might violate the proportionality principle: the strike might be illegal also due to an unacceptable detriment to the rights of third persons or public interest.[77]

Provided that rights of an essential nature are at stake, the prohibition of a strike may in principle also be sought by third parties who can establish that their legal position would be disproportionately affected by that strike, and an injunction against it may be granted by a court upon their application. These persons might be individuals like travellers, parents or patients, or also undertakings whose own economic activity is dependent on the service in question.[78] However, to be able to claim an own entitlement vis-à-vis the union, the claimants must establish that the strike violated an obligation that was meant to protect (also) their rights. In practice, this will usually not be the case for typical constellations of strike in essential services, as notably peace obligations flowing from a collective agreement with the employer are regularly not intended to

73. LAG Hessen 2 May 2003 – 7 SaGa 19/07; LAG Chemnitz 2 November 2007 – 7 Sa Ga 19/07; LAG Rheinland-Pfalz 14 June 2007 – 11 Sa 208/07; *Buchner*, 2003, 2121; *Id.*, 2008, 106 et seq.; *von Steinau-Steinrück*, 2012, 1 et seq.; *Wilhelm*, 2013, 122 et seqq.
74. LAG Hessen 7 November 2014 – 9 SaGa 1496/14.
75. BVerfG, 11 July 2017 – 1 BvR 1571/15.
76. *Schlachter*, 2015, 222; *Greiner*, 2012, 529 et seqq.; *Henssler*, 2014, 1 et seq.
77. BAG 21 April 1971 – GS 1/68; BAG 12 March 1985 – 1 AZR 636/82; LAG Sachsen 2 November 2007 – 7 SaGa 19/07; *Greiner*, 2007, 1028; *Dieterich* 2014, 134; *Scholz*, 2016, 254; *Hänsle*, 2015, 495 et seq., 709 et seq.
78. *Scharff*, 2015, 1845; *Kolbe*, 2009, 1415.

protect third persons (see *infra* Subsection 7.2). Rather, the latter would have to establish that their own constitutional rights are affected in a way that would force the striking workers to put them above the pursuit of their right enshrined in Article 9(3). Reference can be had to a 2009 Court of Appeals decision[79] concerning parents seeking an injunction against a union organizing a strike in a child day-care institution. This was one of the very rare occasions of a claim brought by users relying on essential services, claiming that the absence of reasonable alternative services confronted them with almost unresolvable problems of reconciling work and childcare necessities.[80] The Court, though, denied both reliance on the union's peace obligation vis-à-vis the employer and found the affectedness of the claimants' constitutional position (parents' rights, psychological health of children) insufficient for declaring the strike (which did provide for a minimum service) disproportional.

Irrespective of whether the 'essential' nature of a service is claimed in court by third persons or by the employer itself, there is no definitive list of criteria that courts use to assess whether detriments to third parties go beyond what needs to be tolerated in the interest of protecting the effectiveness of collective action. Judgments rendered in the transport sector, an area frequently affected by strikes with large-scale impact on third parties, referred to criteria such as the duration and timing of the strike, the number of persons concerned, the existence of realistic alternative means of transport for cases of genuine necessity, including the question whether, e.g., railway strikes coincide with airline strikes, and the precautions taken by the union to reduce the impact on third parties.[81] As will be set out subsequently, the most important such precautions are an early announcement of the strike and the maintenance of a minimum service.

5.2 Restrictions Based on the Essential Nature

The finding that a service is essential for third persons or the public will most likely not lead the courts to prohibit strikes altogether, but rather to stipulate conditions for the proportionality of collective action, which take this fact into account. The number of activities in which each and any deviation from ordinary full delivery would amount to an unacceptable detriment to public interest will be extremely limited. It may be illustrative that the Berlin Labour Court of Appeals found that ruling out strike activity completely is not warranted even for undertakings entrusted with security surveillance in a nuclear power plant.[82]

79. LAG Hamm 29 Oktober 2009 – 8 SaGa 22/09.
80. Cf. *Giesen*, 2016, 270.
81. *Fischer*, 2015, 1 et seq.
82. LAG Berlin-Brandenburg 14 August 2012 – 22 SaGa 1131/12.

Among the conditions for proportionality, timely prior announcement (*Vorankündigung*) may play a crucial role. Again, there is not statutory requirement in this perspective, only collective agreements may contain such obligation. Otherwise, the courts will evaluate the proportionality of a collective action taken place with (very) short notice against the legitimate interests of the employer or (for essential services) the general public. However, no absolute rule can be distilled from case law: neither is a prior announcement necessary in all cases to make a strike in essential services legal, nor can other aspects rendering strikes disproportionate necessarily be compensated for by a sufficiently early announcement. To illustrate this, in 2008, an injunction against an entirely unannounced strike in the Berlin local traffic service was denied despite significant temporary disturbances due to the halt of tramway traffic;[83] 24 hours were considered sufficient for announcing a pilot strike in 2014.[84]

Next, the installation of mechanisms ensuring the maintenance of a basic level of minimum services (*Notdienst*) is particularly crucial where not only the employer's interests are at stake. For a number of activities, there is broad agreement about the fact that the fundamental public interest in their maintenance makes strike action illegal in the absence of prior arrangements for upholding a minimum level of delivery.[85] This is specifically prevalent for health care, fire-fighting, water- and electricity supply, the maintenance of public order and security or the delivery of social security payments. The necessity to offer continued services also in public transport or schooling, however, which are not considered to be essential in the strict sense of the term, is highly controversial. Conversely, where a well-designed minimum service mechanism is established, this may justify large-scale strikes, e.g., in the railway sector.[86]

Thereby, certain workers basically participating in the strike might continue working even in full, so that the services remain available in lower intensity, and particularly crucial services (such as specific hospital sections or public water supply) are not interrupted. The practical necessity of employer-employee cooperation in order to enable such a service indicates a mutual

83. ArbG Berlin 29 April 2008 – 58 Ga 6014/08.
84. LAG Hessen 20 October 2014 – Az 9 Ta 573/14. Cf. also BAG 21 June 1988 – 1 AZR 653/86 and 651/86; BAG 18 February 2003 – 1 AZR 142/02; BAG 19 June 2012 – 1 AZR 775/10, on the importance of the surprise moment for the effect of a strike.
85. Cf. BAG 30 March 1982 – 1 AZR 265/07 and 1 AZR 265/80; BAG 31 January 1995 – 1 AZR 142/94; LAG Sachsen 2 November 2007 – 7 SaGa 19/07; LAG Berlin-Brandenburg 24 October 2007 – 7 SaGa 2044/07; *Dieterich*, 2014, 128; *Greiner*, 2007, 1028; *Rudkowski*, 2010, 114 et seq.; *Giesen*, 2016, 267; *Scholz*, 2016, 240; *Linsenmaier*, 2017 189 et seq.
86. LAG Sachsen 2 November 2007 – 7 SaGa 19/07; LAG Hessen 7 November 2014 – 9 SaGa 1496/14. For an overview of court decisions in recent years permitting strike in essential services (hospitals, air traffic control, railway, local traffic, security in nuclear power plants) with a view to sufficient minimum service arrangements see *Hänsle*, 2015, 573, who also stresses the fragmentation of case law (with individual courts significantly more willing to prohibit strikes affecting public interest).

obligation of both parties.[87] In some areas, main elements of minimum services in case of strike are pre-defined in trade union statutes or framework agreements with employers' organizations.[88] Representatives of both sides would then bargain during the preparatory phase of a concrete labour dispute, which proportion of the work force would continue to deliver which concrete services during the strike. Where no agreement can be reached between the parties, the details may be decided directly by the court called to rule on an injunction request against a strike. This practice ensures that, while priority is given to an autonomous design by agreement, employers cannot use a failure to agree for postponing a strike substantially. Ultimately, the well-functioning of this mechanism may thus be considered an essential precondition for extending the right to strike to most employees.[89]

5.3 Restrictions Applicable to Particular Groups of Employees

Only two groups of employees, both of which may perform services that partly can be considered essential also by international law standards, are subject to specific restrictions regarding their right to strike: both civil servants and employees of religious institutions are subject to a general ex-ante exclusion from the right to strike, and also to significant limitations of the right to collective bargaining. The following paragraphs will briefly outline the legal framework applicable to these groups, whereby it should be stressed beforehand that for neither of them the reasons for the described restrictions are related to the 'essential' nature of their work.

5.3.1 Employees of Religious Institutions

Religious institutions are given special protection by the German constitution. Historically, the personal scope of these entitlements includes the Catholic Church and the Lutheran churches; whether it could be applicable to other religious communities per analogy has not been decided. Articles 4(1), 4(2) and 140 of the Basic Law combined with Article 137(3) of the Weimar Constitution grant the churches a fundamental right to self-determination. Beneficiaries of this guarantee include all establishments affiliated to a religious organization, whose purpose is in some way related to the implementation of the religious mission.[90] As this notion includes all emanations of social care provided by

87. LAG Mainz 14 June 2007 - 11 Sa 208/07 Rn 88; LAG Hannover 1 February 1980 - 10 Sa 110/79; BAG 31 January 1995 - 1 AZR 142/94; *Bepler* 2016a, 15.
88. *Absenger*, 2016, 42; *Reinfelder*, 2017, § 15, 48.
89. *Seeling/Probst*, 2014, 2425; *Hänsle*, 2015, 724.
90. This must be established in the individual case, especially in complex constructions involving outsourcing of tasks to legally independent service agencies: BAG 20 November 2012 - 1 AZR 179/11 and 1 AZR 611/11; *Reichold*, 2013, 587 et seq.; *Id.*, 2009, 1382; *von Tiling*, 2013, 162.

church-related institutions, the churches and their affiliated institutions have become one of the largest employers in health care, child care, elderly care or disability care institutions in the country. Whereas the Catholic Church and its affiliated service organization (Caritas) employed in 2017 about 797,000 persons,[91] the Lutheran churches and their service organization (Diakonie) employed about 525,700.[92] The employment relationship bases itself on a civil law contract of employment which, in principle, is regulated by labour law. The churches' right to self-determination in relation to their employees does not totally exempt them from labour law, but includes the entitlement to determine the working conditions of the establishments' employees via restricted form of employee participation.[93]

Relying on this constitutional entitlement, churches have developed practices of determining working conditions in ways that differ significantly from the general model envisaged for worldly employers. Specifically, both Catholic and Lutheran religious institutions have adopted a model known as the 'Third way', in which no collective bargaining takes place between unions and representatives of the churches. Rather, working conditions are determined by joint commissions in which employers and workers are represented.[94] Alternatively, the 'modified Second way' as practiced in parts of the Lutheran church envisages collective bargaining and the conclusion of collective agreements with a union, which however involve both an absolute peace obligation and binding arbitration in case of disputes. Both models strictly exclude the right to strike.[95]

It was only recently that the question of the compatibility of these arrangements with the Basic Law has been brought before the highest courts for scrutiny. This was triggered by strike calls of service union *Ver.di* and doctors' union *Marburger Bund* as a reaction to the refusal of the representatives of various religious institutions to engage into collective bargaining with them on their employees' working conditions. In one case, a strike actually took place, albeit with limited impact. Among the lawsuits brought by the institutions concerned to prohibit the strikes, two were eventually brought before the Federal Labour Court. In its judgments rendered in late 2012,[96] the Court confirmed the necessity to strike a balance between two fundamental rights protected by the constitution, with due regard to the principle of 'practical concordance' mentioned above. In essence, this amounted to an assessment whether the severe restrictions of the right to collective bargaining and collective action, which for other employers would constitute a violation of Article 9(3) of the Basic Law, could be considered appropriate and necessary for the realization

91. *Deutsche Bischofskonferenz*, 2018, 4.
92. *Diakonie Deutschland*, 2018.
93. BVerfG, 4 June 1985 – 2 BvR 1703/83, 2 BvR 1718/83 and 2 BvR 856/84; *Reichold*, 2013, 585.
94. *Strake*, 2017, 247; *Schmidt*, 2017, 52.
95. *Reichold*, 2013, 586 et seq.; *Schmidt*, 2017, 54.
96. BAG 20 November 2012 – 1 AZR 179/11 and 1 AZR 611/11.

of the constitutional right to self-determination of religious institutions. As far as relevant in the present context, the Court confirmed that both mentioned models practiced by the churches were in principle compatible with the constitution, as far as certain guarantees of employee involvement prevented the rights enshrined in Article 9(3) from becoming meaningless.[97] Section VI will deal with these requirements in more detail.

The reception of this decision by academic observers has been mixed, with some fiercely criticizing the far-reaching restriction of fundamental workers' rights.[98] In favour of compliance of this approach with the ECHR, it has been argued that also the ECtHR's Grand Chamber found the self-determination of churches (as protected also by Article 9(1) ECHR) as establishing sufficient grounds to justify the prohibition of a priests' trade union in *Sindicatul Păstorul cel Bun*.[99] However, doubts remain with a view to the wide scope of the German protection of religious self-determination, which deems conceptualized broader than in Article. 9(1) ECHR.[100] A constitutional complaint against the Federal Labour Court's judgment by the unions was rejected as inadmissible by the Constitutional Court in 2015[101] for lack of individual affectedness of the union, thereby leaving the substantive question unanswered.

5.3.2 Civil Servants, Soldiers and Judges

The considerations concerning the restrictions of the right to strike not necessarily going beyond what is admissible under international law are not applicable to the second group of employees facing restrictions: civil servants. For those, restrictions considered compatible with Article 11(2) ECHR and the ILO's conventions have been defined quite clearly by the competent international bodies as depending on the concrete function exercised by the servant. In contrast to that, Article 33(5) of the German Basic Law, as interpreted by the courts,[102] stipulates a sweeping exclusion of all employees having the status of *Beamte* (civil servants under a specific public law contract) from the right to take

97. *Reichold*, 2013, 588 et seq.; *Klein*, 2017, 241.
98. *Schubert*, 2014, 176 et seqq.; *Schubert/Wolter*, 2013, 285 et seqq.; *Strake*, 2016, 227 et seqq.; *Strake*, 2017, 248; *Bepler*, 2016a, 15; *von Tiling*, 2013, 180; *Grzeszick*, 2013, 1378 et seq.
99. ECtHR 31 January 2012, followed by Grand Chamber decision on 9 July 2013 – 2330/09 – Romania. Cf. *Reichold*, 2014, 390 et seqq.; *Waltermann*, 2015, 21 et seq.; *Greiner*, 2013, 263 et seqq.; *Reichold*, 2013, 588 et seq.
100. Employees addressed by the strike call in Germany, were no priests, but a.o. medical staff of hospitals. Cf. *Grzeszick*, 2013, 1382 et seq.; *Schlachter*, 2017 b, 117 et seqq.
101. BVerfG 15 July 2015 – 2 BvR 2292/13; cf. *Giesen*, 2015, 290 et seqq.; *Groeger*, 2015, 179 et seqq.
102. Notably also case law of the Constitutional Court – cf. BverfG, 12 June 2018 – 2 BvR 1738/12 et al;. BVerfG, 19 September 2007 – 2 BvF 3/02; BVerfG, 11 June 1958 – 1 BvL 149/52; BVerwG 27 February 2014 – 2 C 1/13.

collective action[103]. The same restriction applies to soldiers and judges.[104] All such groups taken together include 1,836,470 personnel[105] compared to 2,808,190 regular employees in the public sector.

The most recent occasion at which this unconditional exclusion was confirmed by last-instance jurisdiction emerged in the context of strikes organized in the education sector in 2010. Basically, as the working conditions of civil servants are regulated by legislation, the collective dispute at issue concerned negotiations on a collective agreement that would be applicable only to the few teachers employed by regional governments under a contract of private law. Yet, as the union aimed to achieve a commitment by the governments to reproduce the agreed conditions in the laws applicable to teachers with civil servant status, the latter had a concrete interest in the outcome of those negotiations. Against this backdrop, civil servants who had participated in the strike and cancelled their lectures on the strike days were confronted with disciplinary sanctions, which they sought to invalidate in court by reliance on their claimed right to strike. After a series of contradictory judgments by lower-instance courts, partly considering a deviation from prior established case law justified in the light of the ECtHR-decisions,[106] a 2014 ruling by the Federal Administrative Court[107] held that such a deviation would be unconstitutional. In line with previous case law, it found that 'the traditional principles of civil servant status' guaranteed by Article 33(5) Basic Law are unequivocally providing for an exemption of all servants having the status of *Beamte* (and thus not regarded as employees) from the right to strike. Its reasoning was broadly reflecting the opinion developed in academia, according to which neither the stipulation of working conditions by agreement[108] nor industrial action could be reconciled with the status accorded to a person appointed as a civil servant. This status obliges the persons to unconditional loyalty to the state and the exercise of their function in its administration, which categorically forbids a refusal of this performance for the self-interested pursuit of better working conditions. Whereas Article 9(3) of the Basic Law is not considered totally inapplicable to

103. *Seifert*, KritV 2009, 357–376; *Lörcher*, AuR 2009, 229–242; *Schlachter*, RdA 2011, 341–348; *Lindner*, DÖV2011, 305 et seqq.; *Hebeler*, ZBR 2012, 325 et seqq.; *Di Fabio*, 2012; *Battis*, 2013; *Pollin*, 2015, 34 et seqq.; *Schulz*, 2016, 16 et seqq.; *Klein*, 2017, 242 et seqq.
104. *Scholz*, 2016, 263; *Hänsle*, 2015, 487 et seq.; *Junker*, 2015, 220.
105. *Statistisches Bundesamt*, 2016.
106. OVG Münster 7 March 2012 – 3 d A 317/11O; VG Düsseldorf 15 December 2010 – 31 K 3904/10 O; VG Kassel 27 July 2011 – 28 K 1208/10 KSD and 28 K 574/10 KSD; cf. *Polakiewicz/Kessler*, 2012, 841 et seq.
107. BVerwG 27 February 2014 – 2 C 1/13; confirmed by BVerwG 26 February 2015 – 2 B 6/15.
108. Cf. the legal stipulation (§ 2 BBesG) on civil servants' wages to be determined by law.

these public employees,[109] the rights it conveys are strictly limited by the necessary integrity of the status of civil servant.[110]

A justification for this conclusion is notably seen in the specific privileges granted to civil servants, to be described (*infra* Section 6). The argument in the sense that the fundamentally restricted applicability of constitutional rights might not be warranted for persons whose function is not the exercise of authority in the name of the state is confronted with the doctrine that civil servant status is based on an all-or-nothing principle: as it deems not possible to endow a person only partly with the powers and privileges of a civil servant, it was hold to be equally impossible to apply the restrictions that go with it selectively only to some types of civil servants.[111] Regarding the inconsistence with international standards, the Federal Administrative Court admitted the non-conformity with the ECHR but nevertheless invoked the principle that the constitution establishes an absolute limit for the consideration of international standards by interpretation. Consequently, it considered a resolution by regular courts impossible. The judgment expressly found the legislator obliged to resolve the contradiction between the status-based differentiation of the German constitution and the function-based differentiation of the ECHR.[112]

The described view of administrative courts, which was by no means universally shared by academic commenters,[113] was challenged before the Federal Constitutional Court by several teachers with civil servant status, referring notably to international law developments.[114] The final decision rendered by the Constitutional Court in June 2018 upheld the total ban on strikes for all categories of civil servants. Contrary to the Administrative Court's understanding, the Constitutional Court is of the opinion that there is no contradiction to international law, whereas the supporting trade union is considering bringing the issue to the scrutiny of the ECtHR.[115]

Notwithstanding the controversies evolving around the subject,[116] eventually this non-compliance with the ECHR is expected by some commentators to gradually lose its relevance as a consequence of present-day practices of according the status of civil servant more restrictively due to financial considerations. Consequently, the number of persons possessing that status without

109. Cf. also BVerfG 30 November 1965 – 2 BvR 54/62; *Linsenmaier*, 2017, 27, with further references.
110. *Kutscha*, 2014, 206 et seqq.; *Rothballer*, 2016, 1119 et seq.
111. *Rothballer*, 2016, 1120.
112. *Linsenmaier*, 2017, 189 et seqq.
113. Cf. e.g., *Schlachter*, 2011, 341 et seqq.; *Schubert*, 2014, 176 et seqq.; *Neuhäuser/Otto*, 2016, 393 et seqq.; *Hensche*, 2017, § 18a, 15 et seqq.
114. BVerfG, 12 June 2018, 2 BvR 1738/12, 2 BvR 1395/13, 2 BvR 1068/14 and 2 BvR 646/15.
115. Cf. *GEW*, 2018.
116. Including dissenting voices considering the German regulation justifiable under Art. 11(2) ECHR (*Rothballer*, 2016, 1122), calls for the legislator to eliminate a fundamentally outdated concept of a civil service status of unconditional loyalty; (*Schubert*, 2014, 183; *Kutscha*, 2014, 206 et seq.) and precautions that this would require a major amendment of constitutional principles (*Rothballer*, 2016, 1122; *Junker*, 2015, 221).

performing functions that justify restrictions also under international (case) law might be declining.[117] This tendency is, however, not universally applied by all public sector employers, specifically not by those finding it difficult to attract employees in much sought after specializations. However, for the time being, the tendencies of down-sizing the public service through privatization of formerly public functions has led to the incongruous situation that civil servants excluded from the right to strike are not only employed by the state but also by privatized, formerly state-owned companies providing postal services or rail transport. For this group of persons, not even the theoretical justification for exempting them from a right to strike mentioned above could properly be established.[118]

5.4 The Debate about Regulating Strike in Essential Services

The argument for a legislative regulation of collective action is specifically pronounced in relation to essential services, as situations in which the scope of persons affected by strike action goes beyond the employer have brought about very opinionated debates.[119] Over the last couple of years, numerous proposals on possible contents of such regulation have been put forward in the academic literature. Proposals are essentially procedural, i.e., not questioning the principal possibility of engaging in strike action also in essential services.[120] The most well-known of these is the so-called 'professors' draft' developed by three labour law professors in 2012.[121] It contains notably a very wide, but still non-exhaustive enumeration of sectors considered to provide essential services (health and personal care; energy and water supply; fire, disaster and waste management; funeral services; public security and defence; traffic; education and childcare; communication infrastructure; monetary services) and a number of requirements for the legality of strike measures in these sectors. Several of the

117. Among the 4.6 million persons employed by the state in 2015, only 1.8 million had the status of civil servant. Cf. *Statistisches Bundesamt*, 2016.
118. *Schlachter*, 2011, 341 et seqq.; *Klein*, 2017, 274 et seqq. and 290 et seqq.
119. *Franzen*, 2015, 1 et seqq.; *Fischer*, 2009, 287; *Giesen*, 2016, 266 et seqq.
120. A notable exception is the proposal by *Ziebarth* (2015, 122 et seqq) to replace any real strike action with major 'collateral damage' to the interests of third persons by merely symbolic action, which could be initiated unilaterally by a trade union and would 'hurt' the employer in the same way a strike would. Essentially, workers would continue to perform all services also on strike days, but the employer would be obliged to donate any economic gain generated on these days to a common fund administered by the social partners. Equally, employees would be obliged to donate the wage received in respect of those days, so that also for them the economic outcome is equal to a strike day on which they are not entitled to wage payment. That would create pressure on the parties to resolve the conflict without detriment to third parties. The funds thereby created could be used for aims stipulated by the responsible parties in advance.
121. *Franzen/Thüsing/Waldhoff*, 2012 – also referred to as the 'second professors' draft', as an earlier initiative (*Birk/Konzen/Löwisch/Raiser*, 1988) had already proposed a model for the regulation of strike law in general.

sectors considered essential there go beyond what is considered 'essential' under international law. The drafts fundamentally restrict the right to strike for all sectors connected to needs of the general public which would allow for reaching limitations to collective action in large parts of the economy. Notably, strikes may be called exclusively for a collective agreement that would cover minimum 15% of employment contracts in the establishment(s) concerned, upon a strike vote within the initiating trade union with minimum 50% turnout and minimum 50% approval among the voters. Arbitration by a public body is to be initiated upon the request of either of the parties, whereby the arbiter's proposal needs to be delivered within a prescribed period of six to eight weeks. Strike measures are permissible only after that proposal has been renounced by either of the parties. They must be announced four days in advance, indicating their concrete ambit and duration, and ensure this information is available to the public. There are no exceptions for warning strikes in this regard. Finally, minimum services for safeguarding 'basic personal, social and public needs' must be maintained. If an agreement on these arrangements is not reached with the employer(s), their scope is determined by arbitration.

Given the total lack of political intention to regulate collective action, the 'professors' draft' has since become a standard point of reference in the discussion, generally welcomed by employers' representatives, but also widely criticized, mainly for leaving out important aspects and for containing too far-reaching restrictions.[122] Several publications contain similar or diverging proposals for a legislative regulation of strike in essential services.[123] Clearly, any restriction of the right to strike by (ordinary) legislation will need to make sure to be in line with Article 9 of the Basic Law, especially the requirements of state neutrality and proportionality, i.e., be necessary and appropriate for reaching aims of crucial public interest.[124] Yet, to date no clear picture has emerged where such border lies.

6 COMPENSATORY MEASURES FOR RESTRICTIONS

For both groups of employees who at present are denied a right to strike, compensatory measures in a broader sense play an important role for justifying their exclusion.

122. E.g., *Bayreuther*, 2013, 704 et seqq.; *Rudkowski*, 2012, 467 et seqq.; Berg, 2013, 278 et seqq.; *Uhl*, 2012, 310 et seqq.; *Hänsle*, 2015, 584 et seq.
123. *Rudkowski*, 2015, 93 et seqq.; *Seeling/Probst*, 2014, 2423 et seq.; *Stegmüller*, 2015, 723 et seqq.; *Freistaat Bayern*, 2015; *Franzen*, 2015, 1 et seq.; *Kranz*, 2015, 1 et seqq., and many more.
124. ArbG Berlin 29 April 2008 – 58 Ga 6014/08; cf. *Lehmann*, 2015, 2229; *Scholz*, 2016, 224 et seq., 251.

6.1 Civil Servants, Soldiers and Judges

As for civil servants, they are basically in a secure position in relation to their employment rights due to the principle of care and 'alimentation' by the public employer (*Fürsorge- und Alimentationsprinzip*). The state is thus constitutionally obliged to ensure its servants an income in conformity with their status (*standesgemäß*) and can withdraw that status only in case of very serious misconduct. These privileges are granted irrespective of the performance of the servant's function, and accordingly maintained also at times of temporary or durable incapacity to work and after retirement. This absence of typical risks related to income and dismissal is considered the *quid pro quo* in relation to the requirement of unrestricted loyalty: if 'good working conditions' are a legal entitlement, the individual is not considered in need of a tool of industrial action to achieve it.[125]

However, some aspects concerning the determination of 'good working conditions' in civil service changed over time. While it used to be the custom for state entities to transfer the main results of public sector collective bargaining also into the statutes regulating working conditions for civil servants, thereby accepting that working conditions should at least increase at a level similar to the general public sector, this practice was abandoned in consonance with the political goal to reduce public spending. As civil servants' pay and working condition are established by law, the easiest way of cost-cutting is simply to not adapt them to the general increases of wages and conditions. Many public employers have opted for not transferring collective bargaining results at all, or transferring merely parts of it or transferring with substantial time delay. Additionally, working hours have been extended, allowances abandoned and alleviations for the elderly cut. So it became more and more questionable whether the civil service status remains indeed secured even without the collective tools available to employees, notwithstanding judgements by the Constitutional Court aiming at securing a decent level of conditions.

6.2 Employees of Religious Institutions

For employees of establishments with a religious background, comparable privileges do not exist. Rather, one of the cornerstones of the justification of their exemption from the right to strike is the availability of alternative mechanisms of employee involvement. These mechanisms, though undeniably weaker than the right to 'ordinary' collective bargaining and collective action, are to safeguard the constitutional guarantee of the right to bargain collectively at the minimum level necessary for ensuring that the concessions to religious institutions'

125. *Rothballer*, 2016, 1120. This justification has been doubted by several authors (cf. *Schubert*, 2014, 176 et seqq., and the references there); some are also proposing a solution in analogy to the church institutions as described *infra* (with an only conditional exclusion: cf. *Greiner*, 2013, 623 et seqq., with further references).

self-determination rights remain basically proportionate. The above-mentioned decision of the Federal Labour Court in 2012[126] has stated clearly that the 'Third way' of employee involvement practiced in this sector must comply with strict conditions to ensure that it is genuine and effective. This requires notably the establishment of an autonomous bipartite body within the institution for determining working conditions, in which the representation of the employees' side is granted and which provides for an impartial arbitration procedure in case of disputes. Trade unions, too, cannot be totally left out but must be given a voice in these bodies. The decisions taken in this framework must be binding for the employer as minimum standards.[127] Equally, the modified 'Second way' was found permissible on the condition of genuine collective bargaining procedures underlying the collective agreements applied. The Court made it clear that failure to ensure such genuine involvement of the workers' side entitles the latter to engage into measures of collective action.[128] Thus, other than for civil servants, the ex-ante prohibition of strike in religious institutions is actually a conditional one.

In practice, church institutions, also within the Catholic Church, which was only very recently faced by one strike call yet,[129] have taken the judgment as a starting point for a number of reforms in order to bring their internal organization in line with the criteria set up by the Court.[130] Over the last few years, various institutions have been equipped with bipartite bodies, whereby a certain number of employee representatives' seats are reserved for union representatives, and procedures for independent and impartial arbitration adopted. These endeavours to design 'Third way' labour relations in a way compatible with the prerequisites stipulated by the Federal Labour Court illustrate just how precious the preservation of their specific prerogatives – or the avoidance of having to accept the general model of collective bargaining – is to the institutions at issue.

7 SECURING ESSENTIAL SERVICES BY FURTHER MEANS

7.1 Replacement of Striking Workers

Basically, securing essential services also in times of collective action limits itself to the conditionality of the strike's legality upon the installation of a minimum service where required by public interest (see *supra* Subsection 4.2). Mechanisms safeguarding the service by anyone else than a part of the striking workers

126. BAG 20 November 2012 – 1 AZR 179/11 and 1 AZR 611/11.
127. This last requirement was not fulfilled in the cases brought before the Federal Labour Court, as church institutions had the possibility to reject the proposals of the bipartite commission.
128. *Grzeszick*, 2013, 1382 et seq.; *Reichold*, 2013, 588 et seq.; *von Tiling*, 2013, 162 et seq.
129. Die Zeit, 2017; *von Tiling*, 2013, 163.
130. *Klumpp*, 2015, 181 et seqq.; *von Tiling*, 2015, 227 et seq., who finds that the new internal regulation of the Catholic Church is 'strike proof beyond doubt'.

themselves are not envisaged by regulations concerning collective action;[131] particularly, as mentioned above, their replacement by temporary workers was recently explicitly prohibited. Their temporary replacement by newly hired external workers would face no legal restrictions; however, as the striking worker's contract remains legally valid, they are entitled to continue working after the strikes end. So for practical reasons, replacement hiring is not an option for employers.

A question that emerges specifically in areas where parts of the workforce have civil servant status is whether an employer can use such civil servants (who, as described, may not participate in a strike) to replace striking workers. Up to now, the courts have been confronted with this question mainly in relation to the formerly public postal services, where a significant number of employees[132] are still civil servants. The first such incident was the postal strike of 1980, in which civil servants were ordered to take over activities to fill the gaps left by striking workers. While the Federal Labour Court[133] was willing to accept this as a mere redistribution (the employer was still under economic pressure, as now the civil servants' normal work tasks remained undone), the Constitutional Court[134] found it to constitute a severe restriction of Article 9(3) of the Basic Law, which, in the absence of a legal basis, was not permissible.[135] The question was reopened at the occasion of the large-scale strike in 2015, when civil servants were again used as strike replacements, but without an order by decree and not if they expressed their objection to perform such work. Under these circumstances, the labour court invoked by the trade union found no violation of Article 9(3), as voluntary strike work is possible also in private employment relationships.[136] The reception of that decision in the literature was mixed;[137] a review in higher instance was not sought by the parties.[138]

7.2 Monetary Compensation

It might also be asked whether, in the absence of possibilities to secure the provision of an essential service, those affected could claim compensation from

131. *Hänsle*, 2015, 561, 727 et seq.
132. More recent figures are provided by *Klein*, 2017, 94 et seq.
133. BAG, 10 September 1985 - 1 AZR 262/84.
134. BVerfG 2 March 1993 - 1 BvR 1213/85.
135. *Scholz*, 2016, 136; *Klein*, 2017, 250 et seq.
136. ArbG Bonn 26 May 2015 - 3 Ga 18/15 and 2 July 2015 - 3 Ga 20/15.
137. *Blattner*, 2015, 2037 et seqq.; *Linsenmaier*, 2017, 189 et seqq.; *Klein*, 2017, 253 (footnote 914).
138. In practice, the employer's possibility to re-distribute civil servants in case of a strike might even enable a wider participation by the 'private personnel' in essential services, as the necessary minimum services are maintained by the civil servants. Cf. a decision in 2013 (ArbG Berlin 22 April 2013 - 59 Ga 5770/13) finding that teaching staff could legitimately strike even on the day of secondary school leaving examinations, based on the reasoning that schools could replace them by teachers with civil servant status.

the conflicting parties. In this respect, few affected parties may be able to rely on a concrete violation of a contract by the undertaking which does not deliver due to a strike of its staff. Compensation, however, would only be available once the violation of the contract would be based on a fault on the part of the undertaking, which usually is lacking in case of a strike. Furthermore, the damage incurred by third parties is due simply to the reliance on being able to purchase or use the service at issue, and the fact that alternatives are not available or significantly more costly.

This has given rise to the question whether a trade union might be liable for damages vis-à-vis third persons in case of an illegal strike. Case law tends to answer this in the affirmative, but only in the rare case of businesses whose immediate obstruction by the strike action is targeted and specifically obvious.[139] In 2015, the Federal Labour Court denied a compensation claim of airline companies against a trade union representing air traffic controllers striking against an airport (their employer). The union's strike announcement had led to substantial losses for airlines dependent on that service. It flows from the Court's reasoning that third persons cannot usually rely on a peace obligation that the union might have violated as they are not protected by the collective contract creating such obligation. Reliance on a violation of own constitutional rights such as protection of property or the freedom to conduct a business would require a serious and targeted obstruction by the union, which was not found to be the case. [140] These rulings were of key importance in respect of the guarantee of the strike right also in essential services, as the risk of being held responsible for hardly predictable and potentially very significant damage incurred by third persons would amount to a substantial obstacle for trade unions. Also individual workers would, in principle, not be liable for damages even when participating in an illegal strike, as long as such strike has been called by a union.[141] This follows from a lack of fault on the workers' part when trusting in the unions' assessment of the legality of a strike.

In conclusion, there is essentially no basis for ensuring public interests in essential services by any 'other means' apart from the maintenance of a minimum service, which may, as described, ultimately be imposed by means of injunction.

---

139. Cf. BGH 16 June 1977 – III ZR 179/75, on (the then still public) airlines deprived of air traffic control services, BAG 21 June 1988 – 1 AZR 653/86 and 651/86, on newspaper publishers affected by a strike in the printing centre, BGH 9 December 1958 – VI ZR 199/57, on a strike involving the targeted obstruction of electric power provision to a discotheque; OLG Dresden 16 November 2010 – 9 U 765/10 on undertakings sharing their business premises, which were inaccessible due to a strike against one of them. Cf. *Scharff*, 2015, 1845 et seqq.
140. BAG 25 August 2015 – 1 AZR 754/13 and 1 AZR 875/13; later confirmed by BAG 26 Juli 2016 – 1 AZR 160/14. For the mixed reception in literature see *Zimmer*, 2016, 207 et seq.; *Gräf*, 2016, 3; but also *Löwisch*, 2015, 182. Cf. also the similar approach of the Constitutional Court in BVerfG 26 March 2014 – 1 BvR 3185/09.
141. BAG 29 November 1983 – 1 AZR 469/82.

8 EVALUATION AND CONCLUSION

All in all, the German situation concerning strikes in essential services is characterized by reliance on judge-made law. In an essentially civil-law-based legal order resting upon statutory regulation, this represents an anomaly, frequently deplored by academic commentators and employers' organizations. Their main concern in this perspective relates to the resulting lack of legal certainty in such economically important fields as collective action. It can, however, be stated that the existing protection of the right to strike is mostly (not considering the controversies on the two totally excluded groups, *supra* Section 5.3) equivalent to international standards, even if more by coincidence than through conscious methods of taking international law into consideration. Whether or not a statutory rule could provide the sought-after legal certainty is not clear, either, given that it most likely would have to rely on general clauses and provisions open to much interpretation. This is all the more likely as debates evolving around concrete suggestions of regulation such as the mentioned 'professors' draft' show the utmost conflict potential of virtually each and every aspect – including the definition of essential services, announcement periods, strike ballot and arbitration requirements, maximum strike durations, thresholds for 'minority unions' and possible coordination duties of several unions. However, the State's real lack of influence on an uninterrupted flow of services the general public depends on is becoming a matter of increasing concern and public debate. Whether cutting back on the personal scope of the right to strike for counterbalancing this lack of influence is an appropriate tool, remains also intensely disputed, with the unions arguing strongly against.

They refer to the fact that, as described, public interests are taken into account also under the judge-made proportionality test, while additional legal certainty would hardly be guaranteed by statutory provisions. If explicit rules should be created, they don't necessarily have to be provided by statute regulating the necessary details itself. Alternatively, a regulation might compel collective agreements to establish formal preconditions, e.g., for calling a strike in essential services. Agreements could require 'reasonable' early announcement of a strike, or combine this with concrete waiting periods for particularly sensitive sectors, possibly dependent on the duration of the announced strike. Also, the instalment of a general arbitration procedure could be considered, initiation of which could be sought by either of the parties and the outcome of which, to be delivered in a pre-defined short time period, must at least be awaited before a strike can be called. Finally, the perceived risk of 'egoistic' strikes by minority unions representing functional elites might also be better addressed by focusing on their competence to call a strike, rather than stipulating the primacy of one collective agreement over another. For instance, it might be worth considering a strike vote requirement that must reach a certain quorum among the total workforce of the establishment(s) concerned. Given the described utter controversy among the viewpoints of relevant stakeholders, such regulation may, however, not likely be enacted in the foreseeable future.

Bibliography

-----, Erstmals Streik in katholischer Einrichtung in Deutschland, Die Zeit 11/11/2017. Available at https://www.zeit.de/wirtschaft/2017-10/marienhaus-klinik-streik-katholische-kirche

Absenger, Nadine, Auswirkungen der Streikbegrenzungen auf Bereiche Außerhalb der Daseinsvorsorge?, FES/DGB-Tagung Streikrecht (Conference presentation, Kassel 2016)

Anders, Carsten/Biebeler, Hendrik/Lesch, Hagen, Gewerkschaftsmitglieder. Mitgliederentwicklung und politische Einflussnahme: Die deutschen Gewerkschaften im Aufbruch? 2015

Battis, Ulrich, Streikverbot für Beamte, 2013

Bayreuther, Frank, Gewerkschaftspluralismus im Spiegel der aktuellen Rechtsprechung – Abschied vom 'Einheitstarifvertrag'? Betriebs-Berater 2005, 2633 et seqq.

Bayreuther, Frank, Gesetzliche Regelungen kollektiver Arbeitskonflikte in der Daseinsvorsorge, Neue Zeitschrift für Arbeitsrecht 2013, 704 et seqq.

Bepler, Klaus, Vorbemerkung vor § 160 SGB III, in Gagel (ed.), Sozialgesetzbuch II / III (Commentary), 64th edition 2016 (2016a), 15 et seqq.

Bepler, Klaus, in: Däubler/Bepler, Das neue Tarifeinheitsrecht, 2016 (2016b)

Berg, Peter, Streikverbot durch Verfahren – „Tariffrieden' statt Tarifautonomie in der Daseinsvorsorge? in Schubert (ed.) Anforderungen an ein modernes kollektives Arbeitsrecht, 2013, 278 et seqq.

Bertke, Anne-Kathrin, Zur Zulässigkeit von Sympathiestreiks, 2014

Birk, Rolf/Konzen, Horst/Löwisch, Manfred/Raiser, Thomas, Entwurf eines Gesetzes zur Regelung kollektiver Arbeitskonflikte, 1988

Blattner, Jessica, Die Zulässigkeit von Streikarbeit durch Beamte, Betriebs-Berater 2015, 2037 et seqq.

Buchholtz, Gabriele, Streiken im europäischen Grundrechtsgefüge, 2014

Buchner, Herbert, Der 'Funktionseliten'-Streik – Zu den Grenzen der Durchsetzbarkeit von Spartentarifverträgen, Betriebs-Berater 2003, 2121 et seqq.

Buchner, Herbert, Turbulenzen im Arbeitskampfrecht, Betriebs-Berater 2008, 106 et seqq.

Büttner, Thiess/Richter, Wolfram/Zimmermann, Horst, Plädoyer zur gesetzlichen Regelung des Streikrechts – eine Replik, Wirtschaftsdienst 2016 | 6440 et seqq.

Däubler, Wolfgang, in: Däubler (ed.) Arbeitskampfrecht – Handbuch für die Praxis, 4th edition 2017

Deutsche Bischofskonferenz, Zahlen und Fakten 2016/17, 2018. Available at www.dbk.de

Dieterich, Thomas, Art. 9 GG, in: Erfurter Kommentar zum Arbeitsrecht, 14th edition 2014

Di Fabio, Udo, Das beamtenrechtliche Streikverbot, 2012

Ellguth, Peter/Kohaut, Susanne/Möller, Iris, Das IAB-Betriebspanel: (Analyse-)Potenzial und Datenzugang, in: Liebig/Matiaske/Rosenbohm (eds), Handbuch empirische Organisationsforschung, 2016

Fischer, Ulrich, Anmerkung zu LAG Frankfurt – 9 SaGa 1496/14, Juris-PraxisReport Arbeitsrecht 4/2015, 1 et seqq.

Fischer, Ulrich, Anmerkung zu: ArbG Berlin – 58 Ga 6014/08, Juris-PraxisReport Arbeitsrecht 51/2008, 2 et seqq.

Fischer, Ulrich, Der blinde Fleck in der Wesentlichkeitslehre des Bundesverfassungsgerichts beim Arbeitskampfrecht – Ein arbeitsrechtlicher Zwischenruf aus der Praxis – Erfahrungen aus dem Bahnstreik 2007, Recht der Arbeit 2009, 287 et seqq.

Franzen, Martin, Plädoyer für die gesetzliche Regelung von Arbeitskämpfen in der Daseinsvorsorge, Betriebs-Berater 45/2015, 1 et seqq.

Franzen, Martin/Thüsing, Gregor/Waldhoff, Christian, Arbeitskampf in der Daseinsvorsorge: Vorschläge zur Gesetzlichen Regelung von Streik und Aussperrung in Unternehmen der Daseinsvorsorge, 2012

Freistaat Bayern, Antrag an den Bundesrat „Entschließung des Bundesrates zur Regelung des Streikrechts in Bereichen der Daseinsvorsorge', BR-Drs. 294/15, 2015

Fütterer, Patrick, Die Reichweite des Solidaritätsstreikrechts, 2013

Gamillscheg, Franz, Kollektives Arbeitsrecht Band II, 1997

GEW (Gewerkschaft Erziehung und Wissenschaft), Beamtenstreik, 2018. Available at https://www.gew.de/tarif/streik/beamtenstreik

Giesen, Richard, Arbeitskämpfe und Drittbetroffenheit: Regelungsbedarf für den Gesetzgeber, Sozialer Fortschritt 2016, 266 et seqq.

Giesen, Richard, Der 'Dritte Weg' vor dem Bundesverfassungsgericht, Fachanwalt Arbeitsrecht 2015, 290 et seqq.

Gräf, Stephan, Schadensersatzanspruch Drittbetroffener beim Streik, Juris-PraxisReport Arbeitsrecht 9/2016, 3 et seqq.

Greiner, Stefan, Die Ausgestaltung eines 'Tarifeinheitsgesetzes' und der Streik am Frankfurter Flughafen, Neue Zeitschrift für Arbeitsrecht 2012, 529 et seqq.

Greiner, Stefan, EMRK, Beamtenstreik und Daseinsvorsorge oder: Was der öffentliche Dienst vom kirchlichen Arbeitsrecht lernen kann, Die Öffentliche Verwaltung 2013, 623 et seqq.

Groeger, Axel, Der Dritte Weg vor dem Bundesverfassungsgericht – blinder Spiegel oder der Vorhang zu und alle Fragen offen? KuR 2015, 179 et seqq.

Grzeszick, Bernd, Das Urteil des BAG zum Streikverbot in Kirchen auf dem Prüfstand des Verfassungs- und Europarechts, Neue Zeitschrift für Arbeitsrecht 2013, 1377 et seqq.

Hänsle, Walter, Streik und Daseinsvorsorge, 2016

Henne, Michael, Keine Schadensersatzansprüche drittbetroffener Fluglinien bei Unterstützungsstreik der Fluglotsen gegen Betreiber der Flugsicherung, Gesellschafts-und Wirtschaftsrecht 2013, 503 et seqq.

Hensche, Martin, in: Däubler (ed.), Arbeitskampfrecht – Handbuch für die Rechtspraxis, 4th edition 2017

Henssler, Martin, Die Wiedereinführung der Tarifeinheit: Keine Rechtssicherheit ohne flankierende Regelung des Streikrechts, Betriebs-Berater 40/2014, 1 et seqq.

IWD (Institut der deutschen Wirtschaft), Organisationsgrad: Gewerkschaften verlieren europaweit an Rückhalt, 2016

Joussen, Jacob, Arbeitskampf in kirchlichen Einrichtungen – Dritter Weg, Arbeitsrechtliche Praxis Nr 179 zu Art 9 GG Arbeitskampf

Junker, Abbo, Koalitionsfreiheit und Streikrecht im öffentlichen Dienst nach der Rechtsprechung des EGMR – Eine Skizze, in Henssler et al. (eds), Festschrift Wank, 2015, 219 et seqq.

Kerwer, Christof, Von Lokführern, solidarischen Druckern und Nürnberger Haushaltsgeräten: Neue Tendenzen im Arbeitskampfrecht, Europäische Zeitschrift für Arbeitsrecht 2008, 335 et seqq.

Kissel, Otto Rudolf, Arbeitskampfrecht, 2002

Klein, Thomas, Das Kollektivvertrags- und Streikrecht für Beamte in privatisierten Unternehmen – Am Beispiel der Postnachfolgeunternehmen, 2017

Klein, Thomas/Leist, Dominik, Kein Einsatz von Leiharbeitnehmern als Streikbrecher – Die Neuregelung in § 11 Abs. 5 AÜG n.F. im Hinblick auf Auslegung, Schutzlücken, Rechtsfolgen und Durchsetzung, Arbeit und Recht 2017, 100 et seqq.

Klumpp, Steffen, Zum Stand der Reform des Dritten Weges in der katholischen Kirche, Zeitschrift für Arbeitsrecht und Tarifpolitik in Kirche und Caritas 2015, 181 et seqq.

Kocher, Eva, in: Berg/Kocher/Schumann (eds), Tarifvertragsgesetz und Arbeitskampfrecht (Commentary), Teil 3, 5th edition 2015

Kolbe, Sebastian, Kindergartenstreik und Konsequenzen, Betriebs-Berater 2009, 1414 et seqq.

Kranz, Ines, Landesarbeitskampfgesetze? Schriften zum Arbeitsrecht und Wirtschaftsrecht Bd 88, 2015

Kutscha, Martin, Beamtenstreikrecht – Leipziger Verbeugung vor Straßburg, Recht und Politik 2014, 206 et seqq.

Lassahn, Philipp, Rechtsprechung und Parlamentsgesetz, 2017

Lehmann, Friedrich-Wilhelm, Koalitionsbeschluss über die Schaffung eines Gesetzes über die Tarifeinheit – ein Fall für das Bundesverfassungsgericht? Betriebs-Berater 2014, 634 et seqq.

Lehmann, Friedrich-Wilhelm, Tarifeinheitsgesetz: Die neue Unordnung in der gewillkürten Ordnung (Teil 1) Interimslösungen für die Betriebspraxis bis zur Entscheidung des Bundesverfassungsgerichtes, Betriebs-Berater 2015, 2229 et seqq.

Lesch, Hagen, Ökonomik des Arbeitskampfrechts, 2013

Lesch, Hagen, Spartengewerkschaften: Abspaltungsmotive, Lohnpolitik und Konfliktverhalten, Zeitschrift für Politikwissenschaft 26/2016, 155 et seqq.

Linsenmaier, Wolfgang, Art. 9 GG, in: Erfurter Kommentar zum Arbeitsrecht (Commentary), 17th edition 2017, 189 et seqq.

Lörcher, Klaus, in: Däubler (ed.), Arbeitskampfrecht - Handbuch für die Rechtspraxis, 4th edition 2017

Löwisch, Manfred, Streik - Schadensersatzanspruch Drittbetroffener, Arbeitsrechtliche Praxis Nr 182, 2015

Löwisch, Manfred/Rieble, Volker, in: Löwisch (ed.), Arbeitskampf- und Schlichtungsrecht, 1997

Markus Sprenger, Haftung der Gewerkschaft für Gegner- und Drittschäden aus rechtswidrigen Streiks, Betriebs-Berater 2013, 1146 et seqq.

Neuhäuser, Gert/Otto, Patrick, Kein generelles Streikverbot für Beamte! DVBl 2016, 393 et seqq.

Otto, Hansjörg, Arbeitskampf- und Schlichtungsrecht, 2006

Polakiewicz, Jörg/Kessler, Adriana, Das Streikverbot für deutsche BeamtInnen: Die Bedeutung der Rechtsprechung des EGMR für deutsche Gerichte, NVwZ 2012, 841 et seqq.

Pollin, Ulrike, Das Streikverbot für verbeamtete Lehrer, 2015

Reichold, Hermann, Europäische Zeitschrift für Arbeitsrecht 7 (2014), 386 et seqq.

Reichold, Hermann, Ein „Ja, aber' zum Streikverbot in den Kirchen und ihren Einrichtungen, Neue Zeitschrift für Arbeitsrecht 2013, 587 et seqq.

Reichold, Hermann, Neues zum Arbeitsrecht der Kirchen: Konsolidierung oder Irritation durch das BAG? Neue Zeitschrift für Arbeitsrecht 2009, 1377 et seqq.

Reinfelder, Waldemar, in: Däubler (ed.), Arbeitskampfrecht - Handbuch für die Rechtspraxis, 4th edition 2017

Rieble, Volker, Das neue Arbeitskampfrecht des BAG, Betriebs-Berater 2008, 1506 et seqq.

Rödl, Florian, in: Däubler (ed.), Arbeitskampfrecht - Handbuch für die Rechtspraxis, 4th edition 2017

Rothballer, Thomas, Zulässigkeit des Beamtenstreiks? Neue Zeitschrift für Arbeitsrecht 2016, 1119 et seqq.

Rudkowski, Lena, Der Streik in der Daseinsvorsorge - ausgewählte Probleme einer gesetzlichen Regelung, Arbeitsrecht - für wen und wofür? 2015, 93 et seqq.

Rudkowski, Lena, Eine »scharfe Waffe« wohl gebrauchen: Der Professorenentwurf zur Regelung des Arbeitskampfs in der Daseinsvorsorge, Zeitschrift für Arbeitswissenschaft 2012, 467 et seqq.

Scharff, Bettina, Rechtsschutzmöglichkeiten Dritter bei Arbeitskampfmaßnahmen, Betriebs-Berater 2015, 1845 et seqq.

Schlachter, Monika, Streikrecht außerhalb des Arbeitsverhältnisses, Gedächtnisschrift für U. Zachert, 2010, 634 et seqq.

Schlachter, Monika, Beamtenstreikrecht im Mehrebenensystem, Recht der Arbeit 2011, 341 et seqq.

Schlachter, Monika, Die Vereinbarkeit gesetzlich vorgeschriebener Tarifeinheit mit Art. 11 EMRK und den ILO-Übereinkommen, Arbeit und Recht 63/2015, 217 et seqq.

Schlachter, Monika, Streiks in der Daseinsvorsorge aus völkerrechtlicher Sicht, Arbeit und Recht 2017, 10 et seqq.

Schlachter, Monika, Der Einfluss des Arbeitsvölkerrechts auf das nationale Recht, Soziales Recht 2017, 111 et seqq.

Schliemann, Harald, Handlungsbedarf für die gesetzliche Tarifeinheit? Arbeitsgerichtsbarkeit und Wissenschaft 2012, 515 et seqq.

Schmidt, Ingrid, Art. 4 GG, in: Erfurter Kommentar zum Arbeitsrecht (Commentary), 17th edition 2017.

Scholz, Rupert, Art. 9 GG, in: Maunz, Theodor/Dürig, Günter, Grundgesetz (Commentary), 78th edition 2016

Schubert, Jens, Beamte, Kirchen und Daseinsvorsorge – arbeitskampffreie Zonen? Eine Thesenschrift, Arbeit und Recht 2014, 176 et seqq.

Schubert, Jens/Wolter, Henner, Fremdbestimmung des gewerkschaftlichen Streikrechts durch Kirchen – verfassungswidrig? Arbeit und Recht 2013, 285 et seqq.

Schulz, Matthias, Zum Streikrecht von Beamten, 2016

Seeling, Rolf/Probst, Ulrich, Tarifpluralität – Auswirkungen auf die Gewerkschaftslandschaft und das Arbeitskampfrecht, Betriebs-Berater 2014, 2421 et seqq.

Seifert, Achim, Die Bedeutung von EMRK und GRCh für das deutsche kollektive Arbeitsrecht, Europäische Zeitschrift für Arbeitsrecht 6 (2013), 205 et seqq.

Seiler, Christoph, Der Rechtsweg gegen den Streikeinsatz von Beamten, Neue Juristische Wochenschrift 1986, 413 et seqq.

Statistisches Bundesamt, Personal des öffentlichen Dienstes – Fachserie 14 Reihe 6, 2016. Available at https://www.destatis.de/DE/Publikationen/Thematisch/FinanzenSteuern/OeffentlicherDienst/PersonaloeffentlicherDienst.html

Stegmüller, Martin, Einschränkungen des Streikrechts in Betrieben der Daseinsvorsorge: Varianten einer denkbaren gesetzlichen Normierung, Neue Zeitschrift für Arbeitsrecht 2015, 723 et seqq.

Strake, Martin, Streikausschluss in karitativ kirchlichen Einrichtungen durch den Zweiten Weg? Arbeit und Recht 2016, 227 et seqq.

Strake, Martin, Ausschluss des Streikrechts in karitativen Einrichtungen der evangelischen Kirche durch den Dritten Weg, Recht der Arbeit 2017, 245 et seqq.

von Steinau-Steinrück, Robert, Kommt ein Gesetz zur Regelung von Arbeitskämpfen in der Daseinsvorsorge? Betriebs-Berater 26/2012, 1 et seqq.

von Steinau-Steinrück, Robert/Reiter, Elin, Die Zukunft der Spartengewerkschaften, Personalführung 2015/2, 38 et seqq.

von Tiling, Christian, Blick ins Kirchenarbeitsrecht: Was bedeuten die 'Streik-Urteile' des BAG für die Praxis? Zeitschrift für das öffentliche Arbeits- und Tarifrecht 2013, 160 et seqq.

von Tiling, Christian, Blick ins Kirchenarbeitsrecht: Die neue Grundordnung für das Arbeitsrecht der katholischen Kirche Zeitschrift für das öffentliche Arbeits- und Tarifrecht 2015, 227 et seqq.

Treber, Jürgen, in: Schaub, Arbeitsrechts-Handbuch, 17th edition 2017

Uhl, Nikolaus/Raif, Alexander, Streikrecht nur für Große? Der Professoren-Entwurf zu Streiks in der Daseinsvorsorge, Arbeitsrecht Aktuell 2012, 310 et seqq.

Waltermann, Raimund, Auslegung von Art. 9 Abs. 3 GG im Licht der europarechtlichen Gewährleistung der Tarifautonomie, Europäische Zeitschrift für Arbeitsrecht 2015, 15 et seqq.

Wilhelm, Christoph, Tarifpluralität und Arbeitskampf – die besondere Problematik von Arbeitskonflikten in Unternehmen der infrastrukturellen Daseinsvorsorge, in Lehmann (ed.), Deutsche und europäische Tariflandschaft im Wandel, 2013, 122 et seqq.

Wissenschaftlicher Beirat beim Bundesminister für Verkehr und digitale Infrastruktur (BMVI), Streiks und die Zuverlässigkeit der Verkehrsbedienung, Wirtschaftsdienst 2016 | 2, 114 et seqq.

WSI (Wirtschafts- und Sozialwissenschaftliches Institut der Hans-Böckler-Stiftung), WSI-Arbeitskampfbilanz 2016: Deutlicher Rückgang der Ausfalltage bei hoher Streikbeteiligung, 2017

Ziebarth, Wolfgang, Ein Plädoyer für rein 'monetäre Arbeitskämpfe' im Bereich der Daseinsvorsorge, Arbeitsrecht Aktuell 2015, 122 et seqq.

Zimmer, Reingard, Streik – Schadensersatzanspruch Drittbetroffener, Arbeit und Recht 2016, 207 et seqq.

Case List

Constitutional Court

- BVerfG, 11 June 1958 – 1 BvL 149/52
- BVerfG 6 May 1964 – 1 BvR 79/62
- BVerfG 30 November 1965 – 2 BvR 54/62
- BVerfG 8 August 1978 – 2 BvL 8/77
- BVerfG, 4 June 1985 – 2 BvR 1703/83, 2 BvR 1718/83 and 2 BvR 856/84
- BVerfG 26 June 1991 – 1 BvR 779/85
- BVerfG 2 March 1993 – 1 BvR 1213/85
- BVerfG 19 October 1993 – 1 BvR 567/89
- BVerfG 4 July 1995 – 1 BvF 1/87
- BVerfG 4 July 1995 – 1 BvF 2/86
- BVerfG 4 July 1995 – 1 BvF 2/86
- BVerfG 14 November 1995 – 1 BvR 601/92
- BVerfG 27 April 1999 – 1 BvR 2203/93
- BVerfG 14 October 2004 – 2 BvR 1481/04
- BVerfG, 19 September 2007 – 2 BvF 3/02
- BVerfG 4 May 2011 – 2 BvR 2333/08

- BVerfG 26 March 2014 – 1 BvR 3185/09
- BVerfG 15 July 2015 – 2 BvR 2292/13
- [pending; judgment expected 2018] BvR 1738/12, 2 BvR 1395/13, 2 BvR 1068/14 and 2 BvR 646/15

Federal Labour Court

- BAG 26 Juli 2016 – 1 AZR 160/14
- BAG 14 Dezember 2004 – 1 ABR 51/03
- BAG 28 January 1955 – GS 1/54
- BAG 5 September 1955 – 1 AZR480/04
- BAG 25 July 1957 – 1 AZR 194/56
- BAG 21 April 1971 – GS 1/68
- BAG 17 December 1976 – 1 AZR 605/75
- BAG 10 June 1980 – 1 AZR 822/79
- BAG 22 December 1980 – 1 ABR 2/79
- BAG 30 March 1982 – 1 AZR 265/07 and 1 AZR 265/80
- BAG 30 August 1984 – 1 AZR 765/93
- BAG 12 September 1984 – 1 AZR 342/83
- BAG 12 March 1985 – 1 AZR 636/82
- BAG, 10 September 1985 – 1 AZR 262/84
- BAG 21 June 1988 – 1 AZR 653/86 and 651/86
- BAG 14 June 1989 – 4 AZR 200/89
- BAG 5 September 1990 – 4 AZR 59/90
- BAG 31 January 1995 – 1 AZR 142/94
- BAG 4 December 2002 – 10 AZR 113/02
- BAG 10 December 2002 – 1 AZR 96/02
- BAG 18 February 2003 – 1 AZR 142/02
- BAG 18 October 2006 – 10 AZR 576/05
- BAG 15 November 2006 – 10 AZR 665/05
- BAG 24 April 2007 – 1 AZR 252/06
- BAG 19 June 2007 – 1 AZR 396/06
- BAG 22 September 2009 – 1 AZR 972/08
- BAG 7 July 2010 – 4 AZR 549/08
- BAG 19 June 2012 – 1 AZR 775/10
- BAG 20 November 2012 – 1 AZR 179/11 and 1 AZR 611/11
- BAG 25 August 2015 – 1 AZR 754/13 and 1 AZR 875/13

Second instance labour courts

- LAG Hannover 1 February 1980 – 10 Sa 110/79
- LAG Hamm 31 May 2000 – 18a Sa 858/00
- LAG Schleswig-Holstein 27 March 2003 – 5 Sa 137/03
- LAG Hessen 2 May 2003 – 7 SaGa 19/07
- LAG Mainz 14 June 2007 – 11 Sa 208/07 Rn 88
- LAG Rheinland-Pfalz 14 June 2007 – 11 Sa 208/07
- LAG Berlin-Brandenburg 24 October 2007 – 7 SaGa 2044/07

- LAG Chemnitz 2 November 2007 - 7 SaGa 19/07
- LAG Sachsen 2 November 2007 - 7 SaGa 19/07
- LAG Hamm 29 October 2009 - 8 SaGa 22/09
- LAG Berlin-Brandenburg 14 August 2012 - 22 SaGa 1131/12
- LAG Hessen 25 April 2013 - 9 Sa 561/12
- LAG Hessen 5 December 2013 - Sa 592/13
- LAG Hessen 20 October 2014 - Az 9 Ta 573/14
- LAG Hessen 7 November 2014 - 9 SaGa 1496/14
- LAG Hessen 9 September 2015 - 9 SaGa 1082/15

First instance labour courts

- ArbG Berlin 29 April 2008 - 58 Ga 6014/08
- ArbG Berlin 22 April 2013 - 59 Ga 5770/13
- ArbG Bonn 26 May 2015 - 3 Ga 18/15
- ArbG Bonn 2 July 2015 - 3 Ga 20/15

Federal Administrative Court

- BVerwG 27 February 2014 - 2 C 1/13
- BVerwG 26 February 2015 - 2 B 6/15

Second instance administrative courts

- OVG Münster 7 March 2012 - 3 d A 317/11O

First instance administrative courts

- VG Düsseldorf 15 December 2010 - 31 K 3904/10 O
- VG Kassel 27 July 2011 - 28 K 1208/10 KSD and 28 K 574/10 KSD

Federal Civil Court

- BGH 9 December 1958 - VI ZR 199/57
- BGH 16 June 1977 - III ZR 179/75
- BGH 31 January 1978 - VI ZR 32/77

Second instance civil courts

- OLG Dresden 16 November 2010 - 9 U 765/10

Federal Social Court

- BSG 30 November 2016 - B 6 KA 38/15 R

European Court of Human Rights

- ECtHR 31 January 2012 - 2330/09 - Romania
- ECtHR Grand Chamber 9 July 2013 - 2330/09 - Romania

CHAPTER 8

Japan

Ryuichi Yamakawa & Yumiko Kuwamura

1 GENERAL BACKGROUND: COUNTRY PROFILE

This chapter is intended to introduce and analyse Japan's situation regarding strike regulations and 'essential services' under collective labour relations law. First, this paper introduces Japan's political regime, its population economy, and industrial relations as a background of legal situation. Next, this paper briefly describes basic contents of collective labour relations law in Japan, including special regulations in the public sector. Then, this paper explains the details of Japanese law regarding the right to strike. After referring to the situation of strikes in 'essential services', this paper analyses strike regulation in 'essential services', including situations in the public sector. Also in order are brief notes on the compensatory measures for restrictions on strikes and other measures for securing 'essential services.' In conclusion, this paper points out the feature of

Japan's situation regarding the strike regulation in view of the comparison of situation regarding 'essential services' and the public sector.

1.1 Political Regime

Japan's political regime is based on constitutional democracy. The preface of the Constitution of Japan (hereinafter 'Constitution') promulgated in 1946 declares that 'sovereign power resides with the people.' The Constitution also states that 'The Diet shall be the highest organ of state power, and shall be the sole law-making organ of the State' (Article 41). The Diet consists of the House of Representative, the lower house, and the House of Councillors, the upper house (Article 42). 'Both Houses shall consist of elected members, representative of all the people' (Article 43).

Other than the legislative branch, the Constitution establishes executive branch as well as judicial branch. Regarding executive branch, the Constitution states that 'Executive power shall be vested in the Cabinet' (Article 65). With respect to judicial branch, the Constitution provides that 'The whole judicial power is vested in the Supreme Court and in such inferior courts as are established by law' (Article 76). Thus, regarding government structure, Japan has a political regime that is based on the notion of separation of powers like many other major democratic countries.

1.2 Population, Economy, and Industrial Relations

1.2.1 Population

Japan's population was about 127 million in 2015.[1] Its population has begun decreasing since 2011 mainly due to declining birth rate. In addition, since average lifespan of Japanese people has become longer, Japan has become an aging society. Currently 26.3% of the population is 65 years of age or older.[2] Japan's working-age population (15–64) in 2015 is 77 million,[3] about 61 % of the total population. Among them, 56 million are employed workers.[4] While the unemployment rate in Japan had been about 4% or more since 2000, the labour market situation has been improved since 2014.[5] As of June 2018, the unemployment rate was 2.4%.[6]

Employed workers are largely divided into employees in the private sector and employees in the public sector. Public sector employees employed by the

1. *Japan Institute of Labour Policy and Training*, 2017a, 14.
2. *Ibid.*, 18.
3. *Id.*, 2017, 58.
4. *Id.*, 2017a, 20.
5. *Ibid.*
6. *Id.*, 2018, 15.

national government are called 'national public employees', while public employees employed by local governments are called 'local public employees.' In 2017, Japan had about 58,400 national public employees and about 2,739,000 local public employees.[7] Also, there are employees who work for government enterprises. Although they are not 'public employees' in the strict sense, they are often called 'industrial public employees.' In the past, Japan had several large government enterprises and institutions such as national railroads, telephone and telegraph, and postal services. However, most of such government enterprises have been privatized and their employees are private employees now. Thus, a large part of Japan's public employees are non-industrial public employees. 'Non-industrial public employees' are public employees who are employed by executive branches of national and local governments such as the Ministry of Health, Labour and Welfare. Still, some government enterprises still remain as 'incorporated administrative enforcement agencies' such as the Mint Bureau. Although the term 'enforcement agency' is somewhat misleading, the 'incorporated administrative enforcement agencies' are doing their businesses as enterprises, except that they are run by the government. The employees of such agencies are characterized as 'industrial public employees' as they have similar status to typical public employees (non-industrial public employees).

1.2.2 Economy

Japan's GDP in 2015 stood at 4,124 billion US dollars, which is ranked third in the world, second to the United States and China.[8] The per capita GDP of Japan was $32,479. Japan's real economic growth rate in 2015 was 0.5%. In 2008, the economic growth rate fell down to –5.5% due to the 'Lehman Shock' that originated from the United States. Also, in 2011, the huge earthquake and tsunami followed by the accident at the Fukushima atomic power plant hit Japan's economy, and its economic growth rate went down to –0.1%. Since then, however, Japan's economy is in the process of recovery.[9]

As regards industrial structure, Japan is one of the most industrialized countries in the world. When we look at Japan's GDP by economic activities,[10] manufacturing occupies 20.5%. Industries of retail, transportation, communication etc. occupy 26.7%. Moreover, finance, banking, real estate etc. occupy 23.3%. On the other hand, agriculture occupies only 1.1%.

7. *National Personnel Agency*, 2017, 3.
8. Regarding Japan's GDP, see *Japan Institute of Labour Policy and Training, 2017a*, 10.
9. *Id., 2012*, 27; Id, 2017, 27.
10. *Ibid.*, 29.

1.2.3 *Industrial Relations*

Japan's union density in 2017 was 17.1%.[11] In 1949 it was 55.8%, the record highest. After that, the union density fell, but continued to be more than 30 %. Since 1983, however, it has almost consistently been declining. In the public sector, however, the union density is relatively high. In 2017, it was 37.2%.

One of the most notable features regarding industrial relations in Japan is enterprise-based unionism. The usual way of union organization is that workers organize their unions on an enterprise basis. Here, the term 'enterprise' may mean entities that employ workers (such as A corporation) or factories or branch offices of such entities (such as B branch of A corporation). These unions ('basic-unit unions') often are affiliated with larger industry-based unions. Such industry-based unions, in turn, are often affiliated with nationwide federations called 'national centres'. Still, collective bargaining usually takes place at the enterprise level.

2 COLLECTIVE LABOUR RELATIONS

Collective labour relations are mainly regulated by the Constitution, the Trade Union Act of 1949 and the Labour Relations Adjustment Act of 1946.

2.1 Article 28 of the Constitution

2.1.1 *Overview*

The Constitution of Japan guarantees workers' fundamental rights. Article 28 of the Constitution reads, 'the right of workers to organize and to bargain and act collectively is guaranteed.' It means, workers have the right to organize trade unions, and these trade unions have the right to bargain collectively with employers and to act collectively. The important content of the right to act collectively is industrial actions, which are often referred to as 'dispute acts' of workers under Japanese labour legislation. The term 'industrial action' is broader than the term 'strike', since the 'industrial action' includes picketing, boycott and other collective means than strike. In any event, the right to strike is constitutionally secured as the most representative means of industrial actions. Therefore, this paper sometime uses the term 'strike' in a manner that generally refers to 'industrial action' and 'dispute act.'

Any legislative or administrative act that infringes on the rights guaranteed by Article 28 of the Constitution without reasonable justification is unconstitutional and void. Workers are immune from any criminal or civil liability for their engagement in proper union activities. In the opinion of most, Article 28 is understood as regulating not only relations between the state and private

11. Kosei-Rodo Sho (Ministry of Health, Labour and Welfare), 2017, 8.

citizens, but also relations between employers and workers. Consequently, a disadvantageous treatment of a worker, such as dismissal or disciplinary action, by reason of his/her proper union activities is deemed to be null and void.

Furthermore, Article 28 obliges the nation to adjust its legislative system of collective labour relations so that it matches Article 28's policy objectives of encouraging collective bargaining. Enacted legislation that conforms to this political obligation includes the Trade Union Act and the Labour Relations Adjustment Act. At the same time, this declaration of a political obligation impliedly authorizes legislation aimed at implementing the policy objectives.

2.1.2 The Main Purpose of Article 28

In the legal theory, the main purpose of Article 28 of the Constitution has been discussed. Does the major significance of Article 28 lie in the guarantee of the right to bargain collectively?

Some theorists say 'no'. They argue that, as a part of the basic right to a livelihood,[12] Article 28 broadly guarantees the right of workers to engage in activities aimed at improving their lives,[13] or that, the labour union rights guaranteed by Article 28 contain the protection of union action to pressure the government and the legislature to represent their interests, since workers can secure their lives only by improving their general status in the society.[14]

However, others insist that, because collective bargaining rights severely conflicted with the principles of the civil law, Article 28 had to revise those principles; Article 28 should thus be understood – both historically and from its fundamental purpose of guaranteeing a right to a livelihood – as having the main aim of establishing equality in decision making over terms and conditions of employment through collective bargaining. More precisely, that article's primary objective is to provide the legal basis for industrial autonomy through the pivotal collective bargaining device.[15] This position is generally accepted in Japan, and therefore, strikes are permitted only in relation to a collective bargaining (see *infra* Subsection 3.2).

2.2 Trade Union Act

In Japan, the Trade Union Act (TUA) of 1949 is the main statute which realizes the concept of Article 28 of the Constitution. The TUA sets requirement for a

12. The right to a livelihood, i.e. the right of all citizens to lead a healthful and cultural life, is provided as a fundamental right in Article 25 of the Constitution.
13. *Hokao*, 1975, 9.
14. *Kataoka*, 1998, 91.
15. *Sugeno*, 2017, 30.

'trade union',[16] establishes the unfair labour practice system prohibiting employers' anti-union actions,[17] gives collective bargaining agreements normative effect,[18] and establishes the Prefectural and Central Labour Relations Commissions.[19] From a comparative perspective, it is noteworthy that Japanese law not only gives civil and criminal immunity to proper acts of trade unions, but also encourages collective bargaining by administrative intervention through the unfair labour practice system.

Regarding labour disputes, the TUA provides explicitly the three protections to 'proper' industrial actions which result from the guarantee of Article 28 of the Constitution: (1) exemption from criminal liability,[20] (2) exemption from civil liability or liability for damages caused by industrial actions,[21] and (3) prohibition of disadvantageous treatment.[22]

2.3 Special Legislation Regarding Public Sector

2.3.1 Non-industrial Public Employees

As noted above, Article 28 of the Constitution guarantees workers' rights to organize and to bargain and act collectively. Since public employees are 'workers', Article 28 applies to public employees in principle. Indeed, most public employees have a right to organize unions, except for limited category of public employees such as police officers and firefighters. However, collective rights of non-industrial public employees are governed by the National Civil Service Act and the Local Civil Service Act, not the Trade Union Act. To begin with, most of their working conditions are regulated not by employment contract but by statutes such as the National Civil Service Act or related regulations in the case of national public employees or local ordinances or related norms in the case of local public employees.

Although public employee unions have a right to collective bargaining in principle, they do not, however, have the right to conclude collective bargaining agreements.[23] As a result, an agreement between a public employee union and a government entity does not have a normative power that regulates working conditions of union members. Furthermore, public employees in Japan do not

16. Art. 2 of the TUA.
17. Art. 7 of the TUA.
18. Art. 16 of the TUA.
19. Arts. 19 ff. of the TUA. The Labour Relations Commission is an independent administrative committee comprising an equal number of commissioners representing employers, workers and the public interests. The Prefectural Labour Relations Commissions in each of the 47 prefectures and the Central Labour Relations Commission at the national level deal with collective labour disputes.
20. Art. 1 (2) of the TUA and Art. 35 of the Penal Code.
21. Art. 8 of the TUA.
22. Art. 7, no.1 of the TUA.
23. Art. 108-5 of the National Civil Service Act; Art. 55 of the Local Civil Service Act.

have a right to strike or engage in industrial actions as a means to solve industrial disputes.[24] Theoretical basis of such restriction will be explored later in relation to the debate whether such restriction is permissible under Article 28 of the Constitution (see Subsection 5.1).

2.3.2 Industrial Public Employees

On the other hand, 'industrial public employees' employed by certain government enterprises called 'incorporated administrative enforcement agencies' are not subject to the National Civil Service Act or the Local Civil Service Act. Unlike non-industrial public employees, their working conditions are determined by contract or work rules[25] rather than laws and related regulations. Also, many provisions of the TUA apply to their collective labour relations. However, there are a number of exceptions to this principle under the Act on the Labour Relations of Incorporated Administrative Enforcement Agencies or the Act on the Labour Relations of Local Public Enterprises. For example, with respect to local government enterprises, expenditures based on collective agreement that are permissible under government budget are prohibited until local legislature takes measures to make such expenditure permissible.[26] Also, like non-industrial government employees, statutes regarding 'industrial public employees' and their unions have provisions that explicitly prohibit them from conducting strikes and all other industrial actions.[27] However, as mentioned above, many government enterprises have been privatized and their employees are entitled to the right to strike now, since they are no longer 'industrial public employees.'

3 THE RIGHT TO STRIKE[28]

3.1 Legal Definition of Strikes

In Japan, there is no official definition of strikes. Some legislative provisions[29] mention 'industrial actions' including strikes, but there is no legal definition of

24. Art. 98 (2) of the National Civil Service Act; Art. 37(1) of the Local Civil Service Act.
25. Work rules are documents that contain working conditions as well as orders of workplaces. Although work rules are usually provided by employers, they have a legal effect to bind their employees if the employers disseminate them and their contents are reasonable (Arts. 7 and 10 of the Labour Contract Act).
26. Art. 10 of the Act on the Labour Relations of Local Public Enterprises.
27. Art. 17 of the Act on the Labour Relations of Incorporated Administrative Enforcement Agencies; Art. 11 of the Act on the Labour Relations of Local Public Enterprises.
28. For details, see *Kuwamura*, 2014, 351.
29. For example Art. 7 of the Labour Relations Adjustment Act.

a 'strike' itself. In judicial doctrine, a 'strike' is generally defined as a complete cessation of work simultaneously conducted by a group of workers.[30]

3.2 Propriety of Strikes

Since only proper acts of dispute are entitled to the three legal protections (see *supra* Subsection 2.2), the main legal issue concerning industrial actions is the determination of their propriety. The TUA remains silent on the criteria for determining propriety, and thus judicial interpretation controls it. According to the established interpretation, the following four elements are examined in a determination of propriety: (1) the parties to the industrial actions, (2) their purposes, (3) procedures used to initiate the acts and (4) their means or manners. Strikes are the most representative means of industrial actions and thus, their propriety is examined according to these four elements.

3.2.1 Parties

The right to industrial actions is understood as ensuring equality between employers and workers in collective bargaining and as a means of overcoming deadlocked negotiations. Therefore, for a strike to be recognized as proper, it must be conducted by an organization that can be a party to collective bargaining.

A party to a strike, namely a party to a collective bargaining must be a union in the meaning of Article 28 of the Constitution (a so-called *constitutional union*). The basic definition of a constitutional union is written in the main text of Article 2 of the TUA. According to this, the labour organization must be (1) primarily formed by workers, (2) independent of the employer, and (3) its main purpose must be to maintain and improve the working conditions and to raise the economic status of the workers. A union or a coalition of unions meeting all these requirements enjoys the protection of the right to collective bargaining and strikes. Majority support of the workers is not required in Japan.

According to most academics, individual workers are not entitled to the right to strike independent from their unions. Wildcat strikes or strikes conducted by factions within a union without the approval of the union's competent organs are improper in Japan. However, where an unorganized group of workers (dispute group) selects a person as its representative and prepares a bargaining structure, it has the right to strike protected by Article 28 of the Constitution.

In Japan, a basic-unit union is a basic party to collective bargaining and strikes. The parent organizations (federations) of basic-unit unions also have their own right to collective bargaining and strikes over their independent organizational concerns, as long as they come within the basic definition of a

30. *Nishitani*, 2012, 428.

union in Article 2 of the TUA and have power of control over their member unions.

Labour organizations which lack the essentials of a union, i.e., independent charter and finances and an independent bargaining structure can only engage in collective bargaining with respect to specific matters that have been entrusted to them for that purpose by the basic-unit union. In this case, they are not the parties to the collective bargaining, but can just conduct the negotiations on behalf of the basic-unit union.

In Japan, persons who belong to another trade union than the union which is the party to the strike or persons who do not belong to any trade union are not entitled to participate in the strike.

3.2.2 Purposes of Strike

The main purpose of Article 28 of the Constitution is to provide the principal foundation for labour-management autonomy and to guarantee the dispute right as a way of making the collective bargaining process function. Therefore, the strike must be aimed at achieving an object of collective bargaining. Strikes relating to issues that cannot be settled by the parties to collective bargaining are improper. From this view, political strikes,[31] sympathy strikes, secondary strikes and strikes to announce certain concerns to the public lack propriety and warrant no legal protection.

The propriety of strikes concerned about so-called management prerogatives depends on to what extent the demands are related to working conditions and other treatment of workers. For example, even though a demand for the removal of the chief officer of a mine appears at first glance to interfere with management's personnel sphere, a strike to achieve such demand is considered proper if their true intention is recognized as a demand for the improvement of working conditions.[32]

3.2.3 Procedures for Strike

Notice

Except in the 'public-welfare undertakings' provided in the Labour Relations Adjustment Act (see *infra* Subsection 5.2.1), there is no legal obligation for a union to provide prior notice to employers, and sudden attacks of strikes in the course of bargaining are not *per se* improper in their procedure. In one case, a court held that a strike without prior warning by members of an airplane crew

31. The *Tokyo Chuo Yubin-kyoku* case, Supr. Ct., Grand Bench, October 26 1966, 20 *Keishu* 901.
32. The *Ohama Tanko* case, Supr. Ct., 2nd Petty Bench, April 23 1949, 3 *Keishu* 592.

union was proper because the company could have foreseen its occurrence and it was not the type of action that caused general paralysis of the business.[33]

Once negotiations have started, it is up to the union to decide at what stage it will resort to strikes even while negotiations are still in progress. There is no principle of *ultima ratio* in Japan. However, strikes without previous collective bargaining are understood to be improper. In Japan, an unjustified refusal of an employer to bargain collectively constitutes an unfair labour practice (see Subsection 2.2) and is legally forbidden.[34] Therefore, strikes to make the employer negotiate are not necessary.

Peace obligations

Parties to a collective agreement have the duty not to resort to industrial actions during the period of validity of the agreement in order to change matters that have been fixed by it. This *relative peace obligation* is understood to be inherent in all collective agreements. In contrast, the duty not to resort to strike as to all matters (*absolute peace obligation*) does not arise without a special provision in a collective agreement.

It is much debated whether a strike which violates the peace obligation is proper. Some legal theorists[35] regard the basic character of a collective agreement as a contract and contend that violations of that duty are only contract violations which should not be regarded as improper for that reason alone. However, others[36] insist that the propriety of a strike against the peace obligation should be negatively evaluated in its procedures because of the important function of the peace obligation that stabilizes the rules which have been fixed in the collective agreement.

Ballot

In Japan, the approval of the strike by the workers' rank and file is not necessary to get the propriety of the strike. Article 5 Para. 2 No. 8 of the TUA provides that a trade union charter should include a direct secret ballot vote of the members or their delegates to approve the start of a strike. However, this provision is only a requirement for a union to get the TUA's special remedies for unfair labour practices. It does not determine the criteria of the propriety of strikes guaranteed by the Constitution.

On the other hand, in practice, most trade union statutes require a direct secret vote before starting a strike, and the propriety of the strike in violation of such union procedures has been discussed much. Most courts[37] say that they are no more than defects in internal union formalities for launching strikes which

33. The *Nihon Koku* case, Tokyo Dist. Ct., February 26 1966, 17 *Rominshu* 102.
34. Art. 7 no. 2 of the TUA.
35. For example see *Nishitani*, 2012, 369; *Id.*, 2003, 138.
36. For example, *Sugeno*, 2017, 915; *Id.* (Leo Kanowitz Trans.), 2002, 630.
37. For example the *Seishin Tetorapakku* case, Kobe Dist. Ct., June 5 1998, 747 *Rohan* 64.

should have no effect on the question of propriety in connection with external responsibility.

3.2.4 Means of Strike

The last aspect of the propriety of a strike concerns the means of its exercise.

First, acts that are either partial or complete withholdings of work are broadly recognized to be proper. There are various types of strikes that represent a complete cessation of work, such as an all-out strike, a partial strike,[38] a nomination strike,[39] a rolling strike, a limited-duration strike. All of these will be proper.

Second, there is the principle of fair-play resulting from the faithfulness principle in union-management relations. Since employer-union relations are premised to continue after a collective bargaining agreement is reached, a fair fight is required in the parties' exercise of economic pressures.

Third, a strike must be reconciled with the employer's freedom and rights. During a strike, an employer is free to mobilize supervisors or workers who are not members of the union to continue its operations. For enterprise unions in Japan, picketing is effective or might be even necessary to make the effect of the strike last. However, according to the Supreme Court, picketing is permitted only within the confines of peaceful verbal persuasion.[40]

Fourth, where the nature of the business is such that its cessation would create hazards to the lives, physical condition, and health of related persons in the workplace, strikes are restricted. This rule is especially provided for in the text of laws concerning such things as factory safety equipment,[41] enterprises that supply electricity, and mining-industry security measures.[42] The same reason has been pointed out where strikes occur at hospital. According to the Supreme Court, strikes by workers in a hospital will be proper only after the measures not to endanger the lives and physical conditions of the patients have been taken.[43]

3.3 Legal Consequences of Strike

3.3.1 Proper Strikes

When a strike is proper, an employer is not permitted to seek the liability for non-performance of contract obligations. As for the pay claims of workers, the

38. This is a strike by only a portion of the members of a union.
39. This is a strike by a few members or sometimes even only one member nominated by a union.
40. The *Asahi Shinbunsha* case, Supr. Ct., Grand Bench, October 22 1952, 6 *Minshu* 857.
41. Art. 36 of the Labour Relations Adjustment Act. See *infra* Subsection 5.2.1.
42. Arts. 2 and 3 of the Strike Regulation Act of 1953. See *infra* Subsection 5.2.2.
43. The *Niigata Seishin Byoin* case, Supr. Ct., 3rd Petty Bench, August 4 1964, 18 *Minshu* 1263.

employer can deduct wages during the strike based on the principle of 'no work, no pay.' [44] However, the 'no work, no pay'-principle is a mere guideline for an interpretation of contractual rights and duties. If there is an agreement provision that, for instance, no wage deduction is to be made for certain days of non-performance, wage should be paid according to the contractual agreement.

The question is how the wage claims of non-participants in the strike should be treated with regard to the work that cannot be performed because of the strike. According to the Supreme Court, if the employer has to interrupt the business due to the strike and the work of the non-strikers no longer exists, they are not entitled to wages, since strikes are phenomena beyond the employer's control.[45]

However, non-strikers can be entitled to a special allocation under the Labour Standards Act (LSA). According to Article 26 of the LSA, if an interruption of business is attributable to the employer, he is required to pay an allowance equal to at least 60% of the worker's average wage to each worker concerned during the period of business-interruption. The term 'business interruption attributable to the employer' is interpreted to be broader than the 'cause for which the obligee (i.e., employer) is responsible',[46] which gives rise to the obligor's (i.e., worker's) right to wages. A judicial decision took the same position in the case of a strike conducted by the union to which the non-strikers concerned do *not* belong; it held that such a strike could not be said to be the cause for which the employer was responsible for purposes of the Civil Code, but did hold that it fell under LSA's 'attributable to the employer' wording.[47] On the other hand, the Supreme Court has held that the inability to work by a shutdown resulting from the strike of one's own union at a separate workplace cannot be said to be attributable to the employer for the purpose of a business-interruption allowance.[48]

3.3.2 *Improper Strikes*

When a strike is improper, the workers involved do not enjoy the legal protections resulting from Art. 28 of the Constitution, i.e., exemption from civil and criminal liability and prohibition of disadvantageous treatment.

As for civil liability, improper industrial actions constitute the torts of intentionally infringing upon the employer's right to demand to accomplish the work and to operate a business, and in some cases employer's property rights as well. It is broadly accepted that the union itself is liable for damages because of this tort responsibility. The question is whether individual participants in

44. Art. 624 (1) of the Civil Code.
45. The *Northwest Koku* case, Supr. Ct., 2nd Petty Bench, July 17 1987, 41 *Minshu* 1283 [in case of a strike conducted by the union which the non-strikers belong to].
46. Art. 536 (2) of the Civil Code.
47. The *Meisei Denki* case, Maebashi Dist. Ct., Nov 14 1963, 14 *Rominshu* 1419.
48. The *Northwest Koku* case, *supra* note 45.

improper strikes also bear tort responsibility. Theories of professors are divided on this point, but the courts have affirmed the tort responsibility of individual members for illegal industrial actions.[49]

Since dismissals are strictly limited in Japan, disciplinary measures are a more customary method for punishing workers for their misconduct. When the employer has institutionalized disciplinary acts like disciplinary discharges, participants in improper strikes can be subject to it. However, there are also strict rules for disciplinary measures, and it is not necessarily easy for an employer to punish improper strikers legally with disciplinary measures.

4 THE EXPERIENCE WITH STRIKES IN ESSENTIAL SERVICES

4.1 Strikes in General

In Japan, strike has become quite rare in recent years.[50] Since 2009, the number of collective labour disputes in which industrial actions took place has been less than one hundred per year. In 2016, the number of such disputes was only 78. [51] Forty years ago, however, a large number of industrial actions took place. In 1973, for example, there were 12,040 collective labour disputes in which industrial actions took place.[52]

4.2 Strikes in Essential Services

No statistics are available to show how many industrial actions actually took place in essential services. As explained below, parties in 'public-welfare undertakings' must notify the Labour Relations Commission and the Health, Labour and Welfare Minister or the prefectural governor at least 10 days prior to the day on which the dispute act is to be commenced. According to the annual report of the Central Labour Relations Commission, about one hundred notices of industrial actions are filed in recent years.[53] In view of the fact that the number of collective labour disputes in which industrial actions took place has been less than one hundred in all industries, it is estimated that in many of the cases where prior notices of industrial actions were filed, industrial action did not take place after all.

More than 40 years ago, as stated above, strikes were not as rare in Japan as they are today. This must have been the case with strikes in essential services

49. The *Shosen* case, Tokyo Dist. Ct., May 6 1992, 625 *Rohan* 44; The *Okaso* case, Tokyo High Ct., November 8 2001, 815 *Rohan* 14.
50. Regarding the historical trend of industrial actions in labour disputes, see Ministry of Health, Labour and Welfare, 2013, Annex Table.
51. Kosei Rodo Sho, 2016, Table 2.
52. See Ministry of Health, Labour and Welfare, 2013, Annex Table.
53. See *Chuo Rodo Iinkai Jimukyoku* (Secretarial Office of the Central Labour Relations Commission), 2016, 119.

and the public sector, although no statistics can be found regarding their number. However, since strikes in the public sector is prohibited in Japan, employers in the public sector claimed civil or criminal liability against union leaders who directed such strikes. As stated below, the Supreme Court of Japan held that statutory restrictions on public employees' strikes did not violate the provision in the Constitution that guarantees workers the right to strike. Since then, public sector unions in the public sector have become hesitant to carry out strikes. Although the strike regulation regarding essential services in the private sector is mostly limited to the requirement of prior notice, strikes in essential service have become rare like strikes in non-essential services, in the course of the stabilization of industrial relations in Japan as well as its economic development.

5 RESTRICTIONS OF THE RIGHT TO STRIKE IN ESSENTIAL SERVICES

5.1 Public Employees

5.1.1 Non-industrial Public Employees

As stated above, public employees in Japan are not entitled to the right to strike and other industrial actions. With respect to non-industrial national and local employees, such industrial actions are specifically prohibited.[54] This prohibition does not depend on the nature of work performed by public employees or the nature of government organization to which they belong.

It has long been debated whether such prohibition on strike or other industrial actions are permissible under Article 28 of the Constitution that guarantees workers the right to industrial actions. The Supreme Court of Japan has consistently held that such prohibition is not unconstitutional. In the latter half of 1960's, however, the Court restricted the scope of the prohibition as a condition of its constitutionality since the Tokyo Chuo Yubin-kyoku case decided in 1966.[55] For example, the limitation on union rights should be minimal and reasonably necessary for the protection and promotion of the common interests of public as a whole. Also, a limitation on union rights is permissible only with respect to work or duties the cessation of which would disturb the common interests of public as a whole due to the strongly public nature of such work and duties. Here, the influence on the citizens' life played an important role in determining the possibility of the restriction on industrial actions in the public sector.

However, the Supreme Court took a dramatic turn in 1973, introducing a new theory to uphold the constitutionality of statutes that restrict public

54. Art. 98 (2) of the National Civil Service Act; Art. 37(1) of the Local Civil Service Act.
55. The *Tokyo Chuo Yubin-kyoku* case, Supr. Ct., Grand Bench, October 26 1966, 20 *Keishu* 901.

employee union rights. In the Zen-norin case,[56] the Court stated that, since wages of public employees are paid from tax revenues, the determination of wages should be made by the legislature in accordance with rules of democratic states, and there is no leeway to compel decisions in this regard through strikes and other industrial actions. The Court also stated that, while industrial actions of unions in the private sector, if they become excessive, may endanger the existence of the enterprises and may be deterred by market forces, industrial actions of public employees are not subject to such deterrent power of market. According to the Court's view, industrial actions by public employees would distort the democratic process of determination of their working conditions. Since the Court' theory relied on the notion of democracy under the Constitution that the determination of working conditions of public employees should be made by the legislature, the influence on the citizens' life played little role in determining the possibility of the restriction on industrial actions.[57] This theory is called 'the principle of determination of public employees' working condition through legislation'. Although there has been much criticism of this theory, the Supreme Court has maintained this case law since then.

5.1.2 Industrial Public Employees

Like non-industrial government employees, 'industrial public employees' of their unions are prohibited from strikes and all other industrial actions. It has also been debated whether such prohibition of industrial action violates Article 28 of the Constitution. In a case regarding post office employees' union when the Japan Post was one of government enterprises, the Supreme Court held that such prohibition was constitutional, relying on the similar theory relied on post-1973 cases involving non-industrial public employees.[58] Since industrial public employees' working conditions are not determined by law, the Court did not refer to the principle that determination of wages should be made by the legislature. Still, the Court reasoned that, since working conditions of industrial government employees are based on the expenditure from the national budget, they are subject to the democratic principle that the expenditure from the national budget must be determined by legislature rather than collective bargaining agreements. This theory is called 'the principle of financial democracy' regarding working conditions of industrial public employees. Since this theory is grounded on the mechanism of financial expenditure for industrial public employees, restrictions on their industrial actions may apply regardless of the nature of government enterprises and the influence of their industrial actions on citizen's life.

56. The Zen-norin case, Supr. Ct., Grand Bench, April 25 1973, 27 *Keishu* 541.
57. For details, see *Yamakawa*, 2013, 349 et seqq.
58. The *Nagoya Chuo Yubin-kyoku* case, Supr. Ct. Grand Bench, May 4 1977, 31 Keishu 182.

5.1.3 Recent Development

In 2011, a bill to amend the National Civil Service Act was submitted to the Diet.[59] As one of the bills for the reform of civil service, the bill contained a provision that would restore, at least partially, the non-industrial public employees' right to conclude collective bargaining agreements. Regarding local non-industrial public employees, a similar bill was submitted to the Diet. These bills did not have a provision that would restore their right to strike. However, in the course of the preparation of the bill, the Cabinet Office of the Japanese government established a study group regarding the issue of the restoration of their right to strike. The report of the study group did not reach a conclusion that the restoration of the right to strike should be included in the bill, but merely pointed out matters to be examined if such restoration is to be achieved.[60] The above-mentioned bills were prepared when the Democratic Party took the government. In 2012, however, the Liberal Democratic Party returned to power, and the bills did not pass the Diet. At present there is little likelihood that the bills will be revived.

5.2 Private Sector

5.2.1 Labour Relations Adjustment Act

Overview

In the private sector, several restrictions to the industrial actions including strikes are stipulated in the Labour Relations Adjustment Act (LRAA). The aim of the LRAA is - in conjunction with the TUA - to promote the fair adjustment of labour relations and to prevent or settle collective labour disputes and thereby to contribute to the maintenance of industrial peace and to economic development. Under this Act, the Labour Relations Commissions are entrusted with the conciliation, mediation and arbitration of labour disputes.

Prohibition of industrial actions which endanger human life

According to the LRAA, industrial actions which hamper or cause the stoppage of normal maintenance or operation of safety equipment in a factory or establishment are prohibited.[61] This is interpreted as meaning that the Act prohibits any act which endangers human life in the workplace. Negative acts which may eventually cause the destruction of the property of the company such as refusing to do maintenance work are not necessarily illegal because in such

59. See *Yamakawa*, 2013, 363 et seqq.
60. See Kokka Komuin no Rodo Kihon-ken (Sogi-ken) ni Kansuru Kondankai Hokoku (Report of the Study Group on the Basic Labour Right (Right to Industrial Actions) of National Public Employees), 2010.
61. Art. 36 of the LRAA.

cases the employer can and may take the steps required to avoid destruction as long as the unions do not obstruct him.[62]

Special regulation in public-welfare undertakings: prior notice of strike

Parties in 'public-welfare undertakings' must notify the Labour Relations Commission and the Health, Labour and Welfare Minister or the prefectural governor at least 10 days prior to the day on which the dispute act is to be commenced.[63] Upon receipt of this notice, the Minister or prefectural governor must immediately announce it in a way that will alert the public. This duty to provide notice is designed to prevent loss to the public as a result of an unexpected dispute act, and to enable the Labour Relations Commission to engage in adjustment activities that could prevent the dispute act from occurring. Although the violation of this notification requirement is subject to criminal punishment, i.e., fine, strikes that are carried out without prior notification are not prohibited under the LRAA.[64]

'Public-welfare undertakings' is defined as undertakings which provide services essential to the daily life of the general public: transportation, post and telecommunications, the supply of water, electricity or gas, medical treatment or public health.[65] In addition, with the approval of the Diet, the Prime Minister may designate as a public-welfare undertaking for a period not to exceed one year any other undertaking, the stoppage of which will seriously affect the national economy or seriously endanger the daily life of the general public.[66] When the Prime Minister has designated any other undertaking as a public-welfare undertaking, he must immediately announce it to the public.[67]

Emergency adjustment

Public-welfare undertakings can also be subject to 'emergency adjustments' provided in the LRAA. Where the Prime Minister believes, because the case (1) is related to a public-welfare undertaking, (2) is of large scope or (3) is related to work of a special nature, that suspensions of operations by a dispute act would gravely imperil the normal operation of the national economy or the daily lives of people, he may decide on emergency adjustment, but only when such a threat actually exists. When the Prime Minister has decided on emergency adjustment, he/she must immediately publish the decision with the reasons, and notify the Central Labour Relations Commission and the parties concerned. For 50 days after the publication of this decision, the parties may not resort to any dispute

62. *Hanami et al.*, 2015, 203.
63. Art. 37 of the LRAA. A fine not exceeding JPY 100,000 is prescribed for a violation of this duty, Art. 39.
64. Lower courts view are divided regarding whether industrial actions in violation of the notice requirement automatically lose the protection of the Trade Union Act as 'improper' actions.
65. Art. 8 Par.1 of the LRAA.
66. Art. 8 Par.2 of the LRAA.
67. Art. 8 Par.3 of the LRAA.

act.[68] When the Central Labour Relations Commission has received notice of the Prime Minister's decision, it must exert its utmost efforts to settle the dispute.

The emergency adjustment is based on the idea that large strikes with a serious impact on the daily life should be eliminated even if they meet all the requirements for their propriety. This ban of strikes applies to the parties, regardless of the propriety of the dispute act, and therefore, it must be really exceptional. In fact, the emergency adjustment procedure was utilized only once in our history: In October 1952, the Japan Coal Mine Union started unlimited-duration strikes demanding higher wages. In early December in that year, the Central Labour Relations Commission tried to settle the dispute through a conciliation procedure, but its settlement plan was refused by the Union. After that, the strikes of the Union became harder and harder and led to the lack of the supply of coal. Then, the use of gas was largely restricted and the national economy and the daily lives of people were imperilled. However, the Union ordered its members who secured the operation of safety equipment in coal industry to prepare strikes on the 17th and 18th of December. In this extraordinary situation, the Prime Minister published on the 17th of December 1952 the emergency adjustment forbidding strikes in coal industry for 50 days. Soon after the publication of the emergency adjustment, the Union called off the strikes and accepted the proposal to settle the labour dispute by the Central Labour Relations Commission. Thus, the long-term strikes came to end in 63 days.

5.2.2 Strike Regulation Act

In the industries of electricity and coal mining, a special legislation called Strike Regulation Act (SRA) [69] of 1953 prohibits industrial actions that hamper the normal supply of electricity and normal operation of security and safety measures in coal mines.[70] However, this Act has not set any special requirement for industrial actions in electricity and coal mines industry, but just made it clear that industrial actions which seriously impact on the daily life of the people are not proper in their means (see *supra* Subsection 3.2.4).

After the nuclear disaster in Fukushima in 2011, the Japanese Government was forced to change the policy promoting nuclear energy. In order to secure the steady supply of electricity, the Government deregulated electricity undertakings and the SRA was correspondingly revised in 2014. While the contents of strike regulations remain unchanged, the framework of the SRA was modified as follows. The electricity undertakings regulated by the SRA are divided into undertakings for power generation, transmission or distribution. While the electricity undertakings where strikes were restricted had been all pre-determined by legislation before the amendment, it is the Health, Labour and

68. Art. 38 of the LRAA. Violation of this regulation subjects to a fine. Art. 40 of the LRAA.
69. The official name is Act concerning Regulation of the Ways and Means of Conducting Labour Strikes in the Electric Utilities and Coal Mining Industries.
70. Arts. 2 and 3 of the SRA.

Welfare Minister that under the new framework of the SRA designates the undertakings which hamper the steady supply of electricity to which the strike regulation applies.

With the background of this new framework of the designation, it has been discussed whether the regulation of the SRA for electricity industry should be reconsidered. In 2015, the Council consisting of three parties (representatives of workers, employers and the public interests) in the Ministry of Health, Labour and Welfare published a report[71] that the supply of electricity is not stable yet and the restrictions of the SRA are still necessary to eliminate the disorder in electricity industry. After the publication of this report, the administration made a guideline[72] to exclude an abusive use of the strike restriction of the SRA. According to this, 'Industrial actions that hamper the normal supply of electricity' forbidden by the SRA should be interpreted in an objective way and strikes may be restricted not generally but on an *ad hoc* basis.

6 COMPENSATORY MEASURES FOR RESTRICTIONS

6.1 Public Employees

6.1.1 Non-industrial Public Employees: Recommendation by National Personnel Agency

In the absence of a system to determine working conditions through collective bargaining and strikes, what is the guiding principle for the legislature to determine the working conditions of public employees? Article 28, Paragraph 1 of the National Civil Service Act provides that the fundamental matters concerning remuneration, hours of work and other working conditions to be established pursuant to this Act may at any time be changed by the Diet to bring them into accord with general conditions of society. It shall be the duty of the National Personnel Authority, an independent national administrative agency, to recommend such changes.[73]

Thus, in the case of national public employees, the guiding principle for the determination of their working conditions is the 'general conditions of society.' Although this standard is quite vague as statutory language, the most important

71. The report on 7 February 2015 (http://www.mhlw.go.jp/file/06-Seisakujouhou-12600000-Seisakutoukatsukan/0000090781.pdf).
72. Kosei Rodo Sho (Ministry of Health, Labour and Welfare), Circular no. 0703-1, July 3, 2015, Denki Jigyo oyobi Sekitan Kogyo no Sogi Koi no Hoho no Kisei ni kansuru Horitsu (Denki Jigyo Kankei) no Kaishaku ni Tsuite (Interpretation of the Act concerning Regulation of the Ways and Means of Conducting Labour Strikes in the Electric Utilities and Coal Mining Industries (Electric utilities)) (http://www.mhlw.go.jp/file/06-Seisakujouhou-12600000-Seisakutoukatsukan/0000119861.pdf).
73. As regards local public employees, the Local Civil Service Act provides for the Personnel Committee.

factor is the comparison with the private sector.[74] The National Personnel Agency conducts detailed research annually on the wages and other working conditions in the private sector. Based on this research, the National Personnel Agency makes a recommendation to the government regarding the change of the working conditions of national public employees. Since the introduction of this recommendation system, the Cabinet has in most cases respected the annual recommendation of the National Personnel Agency and submitted bills to change national public employee working conditions accordingly. This recommendation system has been regarded as a substitute for the restriction of union rights of national public employees.[75]

6.1.2 Industrial Public Employees: Mandatory Arbitration

Since industrial public employees do not have the right to engage in industrial actions, the Act for the Labour Relations of Incorporated Administrative Enforcement Agencies provides for a mandatory arbitration procedure to resolve collective interest disputes.[76] Since the process of ordinary arbitration begins based on the agreement of parties to the dispute, ordinary arbitration has a nature of voluntary measures of dispute resolution. On the other hand, in the case of arbitration regarding industrial public employees, the arbitration procedure may begin unilaterally by one of the parties to a collective dispute when the dispute is not resolved for two months after conciliation or mediation by the Labour Relations Commission started. Since strike is one of the major means for resolving collective labour disputes, this mandatory arbitration procedure is a compensatory measure that can substitute for strike with respect to industrial public employees who cannot conduct strike.

6.2 Private Sector

As mentioned above (Subsection 5.2), strikes in essential services are restricted not only by the propriety-principle, but also by the special regulations of the LRAA. They can be procedurally restricted by the regulation for prior notice and forbidden when they endanger human life in a workplace or the Prime Minister has decided on emergency adjustment. The prohibition of strikes in emergency adjustment is strong because it can prohibit strikes that would be proper under the TUA. In addition, the SRA prohibits strikes that hamper the normal supply of electricity and normal operation of security and safety measures in coal mines.

74. See, e.g., *Kagoshima* et al. (eds) 1988, 268.
75. The *Zen-norin* case, *supra* Subsection 5.1.
76. Art. 33-3 of the Act. As regards the employees of local public enterprises, Arts. 15 and 16 of the Act on the Labour Relations of Local Public Enterprises provide for mandatory arbitration procedure.

There is no compensatory measure for these restrictions in private sector and this system has never been questioned.

7 SECURING ESSENTIAL SERVICES BY FURTHER MEANS

7.1 Self-Regulation by Collective Agreements

Aside from the regulations by legislation and case law, unions and employers sometimes conclude clauses restricting industrial actions in collective agreements. There are two types of such clauses. One is 'dispute-act clauses' which require prior notice or determine the scope of non-strikers to secure the operation of safety equipment in a factory. The other is 'peace clauses' according to which industrial actions may not be resorted to before certain procedures, such as consultation, conciliation and mediation, have been exhausted. In a 2011 survey[77], unions concluded prior notice (62.2%), the scope of non-strikers (48.6%) and 'dispute-acts adjustment' (58.2%) in any collective agreement. It is possible for the parties in essential services to restrict strikes voluntarily by these clauses, but there is no statistic on how often they do this.

7.2 Effects of a Violation

When a union has violated peace or dispute-acts clauses, the employer can sue for damage resulting from the violation. In the case of a violation of peace clauses, it is logical that the other party can also demand performance of the contract (collective agreement) by petitioning to stop or suspend acts that violate duties it imposes.[78]

The question is whether the violation of such clauses can lead to the impropriety of the dispute act. Some courts say, dispute-act clauses don't restrict the exercise of the dispute right itself und therefore, the dispute act which violates such a clause are not improper.[79] Much debated is the propriety of industrial actions violating peace clauses. Like in the case of a violation of peace obligation (see *supra* Subsection 3.2.3), scholarly opinions are divided on this point. Today, more legal theorists insist that, in light of the important role of peace clauses that govern union-employer relations, industrial actions violating those clauses can be improper. According to them, this propriety evaluation is an individualized, concrete question, however: the form of the collective agreement, the content of peace clauses, the parties' expectations, the form of the

77. Kosei Rodo Sho, 2012, Figure 1 (http://www.mhlw.go.jp/stf/houdou/2r9852000002dlia-att/2r9852000002dlqq.pdf (accessed March 2018)).
78. *Sugeno*, 2017, 887.
79. For example, The *Sanden* case, Yamaguchi-Shimonoseki Dist. Ct., March 28 1994, 657 *Rohan* 71.

dispute act, the type of liability and the like should all be individually taken into account.[80]

8 EVALUATION AND CONCLUSION

8.1 Relationship with Strike Regulation Regarding Public Employees

In analysing Japan's situation on the restriction of the right to strike in essential services, it is helpful to understand the situation in the public sector, since some of the function of essential services are conducted in the public sector. In Japan, both non-industrial public employees and industrial public employees are prohibited under statutory law from engaging in strikes and other industrial actions without regard to the nature of their work or activities. This is the prohibition imposed ex-ante by legislature. The Supreme Court has held that such restriction is permissible under Article 28 of the Constitution that provides for workers' right to industrial actions, relying on the democratic principle under the Constitution that expenditure for public employees' wages and other working conditions must be determined by legislature, not by parties to collective bargaining. As a result, employees in services such public enterprises as the Mint, the government printing office and public schools, which are not regarded as essential services under the International Labour Organization (ILO) principles, are prohibited from engaging in strikes.

8.2 Prohibition of Strikes in the Private Sector

In the private sector, the prohibition of strikes and other industrial actions applies to (1) industrial actions which hamper or cause the stoppage of normal maintenance or operation of safety equipment in a factory or establishment (safety equipment prohibition), (2) industrial actions which hamper the normal supply of electricity and normal operation of security and safety measures in coal mines (Strike Regulation Act prohibition), and (3) industrial actions regarding which the Prime Minister has made the Emergency Adjustment determination to avoid grave imperilment of the normal operation of the national economy or the daily lives of people (Emergency Adjustment prohibition).

Among these three types of prohibitions, the safety equipment prohibition can be classified as the prohibition that is imposed ex-ante by legislature, focusing selectively on specific safety equipment rather than the nature of service. As regards the Strike Regulation Act prohibition, the prohibition is also imposed ex-ante by legislature, but only with respect to services of electricity and coal mines. On the other hand, Emergency Adjustment prohibition is available only when the Prime Minister makes a determination of Emergency Adjustment on an ad hoc basis. The statutory requirement regarding the nature

80. *Sugeno*, 2017, 916.

of service under Emergency Adjustment prohibition is quite general, in that the case (1) is related to a public-welfare undertaking, (2) is of large scope or (3) is related to work of a special nature.

8.3 The Scope of 'Essential Services' and Regulation of Strikes

The 'pubic welfare undertakings' to which the strike regulations under the Labour Relations Act apply are broader than the 'essential services' defined by the ILO principle, since the notion of 'pubic welfare undertakings' includes transportation and postal services which are not regarded as 'essential services' by the ILO. However, the main measure of strike regulations is merely a requirement of prior notice rather than prohibition of strikes. Although the violation of this notification requirement is subject to criminal punishment, i.e., fine, strikes that are carried out without prior notification are not prohibited under the LRAA.

On the other hand, employees of hospitals and air traffic control, which are regarded as 'essential services' under the ILO principle are not generally prohibited from engaging in strikes, unless their conduct is subject to prohibition regarding safety equipment.

The scope of prohibition of strikes in Japan is determined ex-ante by legislature, although in some cases the scope of prohibition is focused on the nature of service or employers' activity, while in other cases the focus is on the nature of the work done by employees. The only exception is the Emergency Adjustment in which the Prime Minister determines whether specific strikes shall be prohibited in individual cases, although this procedure has rarely been utilized.

8.4 The Feature of Theoretical Situation on 'Essential Services' in Japan

While the restriction of collective labour rights in the public sector has been fiercely discussed and litigated, discussion regarding strike regulation of 'essential services' in the private sector has not been very active in Japan at least in the last few decades. Although the background of such situation needs further analysis, one of the reasons may be that strikes and other industrial actions have been quite rare in recent industrial relations in Japan. It may also be because the strike regulations regarding 'public welfare undertakings' are less restrictive than the total strike prohibition in the public sector, in that trade unions in 'public welfare undertakings' are merely required to provide a prior notice of strike in most cases. Such large difference in the regulation of strikes between public sector and 'public welfare undertakings' is one of the notable characteristics of Japan's regulation of strikes involving 'Essential Services.'

Bibliography

Chuo Rodo Iinkai Jimukyoku (Secretarial Office of the Central Labour Relations Commission), Heisei 27 Nen Rodo Iinkai Nenpo (Annual Report on Labour Relations Commission 2015), 2016

Hanami, Tadashi/Komiya, Fumito/Yamakawa, Ryuichi, Labour Law in Japan, 2nd edition, 2015

Hokao, Kenichi, Rodo-Dantai-ho (Collective Labour Law), 1975

Japan Institute of Labour Policy and Training, Databook of International Labour Statistics 2012, 2012

Japan Institute of Labour Policy and Training, Databook of International Labour Statistics 2017, 2017

Japan Institute of Labour Policy and Training, Japanese Working Life Profile 2016/2017, 2017 (*Japan Institute of Labour Policy and Training* 2017a)

Japan Institute of Labour Policy and Training, Main Labour Economic Indicators, August 2018 (*Japan Institute of Labour Policy and Training* 2018)

Kagoshima, Juji/Morizono, Yukio/Kitamura, Isamu (eds)), Chikujo Kokka Komuin Ho (Commentary on the National Civil Service Act), 1988

Kataoka, Noboru, Rodo-ho (Labour Law) I, 3rd edition with supplements, 1998

Kosei Rodo Sho (Ministry of Health, Labour and Welfare), 2013 Survey on Labour Disputes, 2013

Kosei Rodo Sho (Ministry of Health, Labour and Welfare), Heisei 23 Nen Rodo Kyoyaku tou Jittai Chosa (Statistic on Collective Agreements in 2011), 2012

Kosei Rodo Sho (Ministry of Health, Labour and Welfare), Rodo Sogi Tokei Chosa (Survey on Labour Disputes), 2016

Kosei Rodo Sho (Ministry of Health, Labour and Welfare), Heisei 29 Nen Rodo Kumiai Kiso Chosa (Basic Survey on Labour Unions 2017), 2017

Kuwamura, Yumiko, The Right to Strike: Japan, in Waas (ed.), The Right to Strike – A Comparative View, 2014

Naikaku Kanbo Jimukyoku (Office of Cabinet Secretariat), Kokka Komuin no Rodo Kihon-ken (Sogi-ken) ni Kansuru Kondankai Hokoku (Report of the Study Group on the Basic Labour Right (Right to Industrial Actions) of National Public Employees), 2010

National Personnel Agency, 2016 Profile of National Public Employees in Japan, 2016

Nishitani, Satoshi, Rodo-kumiai-ho (Trade Union Law), 3rd edition, 2012

Nishitani, Satoshi, Vergleichende Einführung in das japanische Arbeitsrecht, 2003

Sugeno, Kazuo (Leo Kanowitz Trans.), Japanese Employment and Labour Law, 2002

Sugeno, Kazuo, Rodo-ho (Employment and Labour Law), 11th edition with supplements, 2017

Yamakawa, Ryuichi, Japan's Collective Labour Relations Law in the Public Sector: Constitutional Conflict between Union Rights and Democracy, Comparative Labour Law and Policy Journal vol. 34, 2013, 349 et seqq.

CHAPTER 9

Israel

Moti (Mordehai) Mironi

1 GENERAL BACKGROUND: COUNTRY PROFILE

1.1 Economic, Political and Historical Background

The state of Israel gained independence in 1948 after years of British Mandate. Israel is a highly developed, technologically advanced, country with a population of 8,000,000. Historically speaking, Israel is a unique state, especially in the context of a study that deals with labour law, labour relations and strikes, as it was once described as a 'labour state' – a state run by a labour movement.[1] The expression 'labour state' reflected the unique role of its largest labour union, the Histadrut (General Federation of Labour), in the history of the new nation.

The Histadrut was founded in 1920, twenty-eight years before the state was established. It functioned as a government in anticipation of a government, and amassed enormous economic and political power and influence.[2] Since statehood, the Histadrut has historically been party to all economic and social welfare initiatives of national concern. The Histadrut was governed from the outset by the same political parties that later formed the unicameral parliament, and the first prime minister of the state had formerly served as the Secretary General (chairman) of the Histadrut.

1. *Safran*, 1963, 127 et seqq.
2. For many years the Histadrut provided a broad array of social services which are commonly provided by the state, such as education, culture, welfare and health care. It also built the economic infrastructure through its labour owned economic institutions in various areas such as banking, commerce, industry and insurance, making it the second largest employer.

For close to 30 years Israel was led by a very dominant Labour Party which formed coalitions with other centre-to-left political parties. Labour's hegemony came to an end in 1977. Since then, right-wing parties have been in power, promoting capitalistic, conservative and nationalistic policies.

1.2 Legal Framework

In conjunction with the British Mandate tradition, Israel is a common law country with no written constitution. There are however several constitution-like basic laws, such as The Basic Law of Human Dignity and Freedom and The Basic Law of Freedom of Occupation. The head of state is the prime minister, who is elected in personal elections but in order to lead, the executive branch must rely on a broadly based coalition government.

The legislative branch is composed of a unicameral parliament consisting of 120 members who are elected in proportional state-wide elections in which multiple political parties take part. The judicial branch has been held in highest esteem among the three branches of government and other public institutions throughout the history of the state. It has a three tier general court system headed by the Supreme Court which, while serving as the highest appellate court for civil and criminal cases, acts also as the High Court of Justice. In the latter capacity, it hears cases of public importance and oversees the work of the executive and legislative branches in a manner similar to a constitutional court, albeit as a court of first instance.

Israel has a two tier specialized labour court system – regional and national. Like other specialized tribunals, the decisions of the National Labour Court are subject to limited judicial review by the High Court of Justice.[3]

1.3 The Status and Role of Collective Labour Relations

As a state which was founded by a labour movement, the model of collective labour relations has been well received and supported in Israeli society. Nevertheless, as elsewhere, the status of collective bargaining and the density of trade union membership have declined over the years. When the Histadrut was the main provider of medical care, the unionization rate was 85% and it represented practically every unionized worker in Israel. Recent studies show overall union density of 33% with only 15% in the private sector.[4] The collective bargaining coverage is much higher, at 56%.[5] This is due to the prevalence of industry-wide collective agreements and the frequent use of extension orders.[6]

3. *Goldberg*, 1982, 137 et seqq.
4. *Cohen/Haberfeld/Kristal/Mundlak*, 2007, 255, 259.
5. *Ibid.* and *Cohen/Haberfeld/Mundak/Saporta*, 2003, 702.
6. *Goldberg*, 1982, 79 et seqq.

Alongside the Histadrut, which is by far the largest union, there are two general unions – the National Federation of Labour which was established in 1934 and a small but fast growing grass root general union – Power for Labour. In addition there are several non-affiliated independent sectoral unions such as the Israel Medical Association (IMA) which represents 90% of the medical doctors, [7] the two teachers' unions representing high school and primary school teachers, the Association of Academic Staff, and the Journalists Association. Interestingly, in recent years Israel has witnessed a substantial growth of unionization among young employees in high-tech enterprises and services such as banking, finance and insurance.

With the exception of one employers' association representing small cities and town, public sector employers are not organized. In sharp contrast, beginning in 1970, employers in the private sector felt the need to organize, primarily in order to counter the power of the Histadrut. There are 13 large employers' associations that act either separately or together under a loosely federated roof organization – The Presidium of Business Organizations.

2 COLLECTIVE LABOUR RELATIONS

Collective labour law in Israel tends to follow the European model, blended with several North American paradigms or concepts such as exclusive representation, appropriate bargaining units, and duty of fair representation. The three collective labour relations rights, i.e., the right to organize, the right to bargain collectively and the right to strike, are an enshrined part of labour law. In the absence of a written constitution, these rights are secured either by statute (the right to organize) or by case-law (the right to bargain collectively and the right to strike).

Israel signed and ratified the ILO Conventions 87 of 1948 and 98 of 1949. The National Labour Court frequently refers in passing to these two ILO conventions in support of its somewhat controversial decisions regarding employers' legal obligations towards employees and unions during organization campaigns and with regard to the right to bargain collectively. In contrast, it appears as though the courts have rarely mentioned, let alone relied upon, international law conventions and jurisprudence in its discourse regarding domestic strike law.

3 THE RIGHT TO STRIKE

Israel is a world super-power as far as number of strikes and days lost due to strikes are concerned. The vast majority of strikes (90%–95%) are in the public sector. Traditionally, strikes tend to be of short duration and partial strikes

7. *Mironi*, 2008, 1 et seq.

(sanctions), rather than full strikes. Legally speaking, there is no difference between a partial strike and a full strike.[8]

With the exception of three groups of employees, i.e., the police force, prison guards and secret service employees, all employees in Israel have the freedom to strike. Statutory law requires a prior notice of 15 days before any strike or lockout.[9] Case law requires honouring the industrial peace obligation embedded in the idea of collective agreement. The court declared that even in the absence of specific wording, any collective agreement has an implied term prohibiting strikes regarding subjects covered by the collective agreement during its term.[10]

The National Labour Court emphasizes that employees and unions have the 'freedom' to strike rather than the 'right' to strike. According to the courts, the right to strike may be restricted by law or contract and practically speaking this freedom bestows upon employees and their union certain legal immunities.[11] The concept of illegal strike does not exist in Israeli labour law. Consequently, unless provided otherwise, the immunities also apply to strikes without notice and to those in breach of the industrial peace obligation. The only legal remedy available to the employers in case of a strike or a threat of strike is a petition for injunction.

In its voluminous strike law jurisprudence, the labour court has declared that, in exercising its discretion as to whether or not to grant an injunction against a strike, it may take into account three considerations. First, the distinction between strikes on the basis of their underling objective or goal. Here the court distinguishes between a purely economic strike and a political strike, and it further recognizes a middle of the road quasi-political strike;[12] second, the means employed. The court uses the concept of proportionality in examining the relationship between the goals and the means of the strike;[13] and third, the behaviour of the parties in trying to resolve the dispute underlying the strike. Here the court examines whether the petitioning party bargained in good faith and whether it has availed itself of mediation. In instances where the labour court assesses the parties' behaviour, it may take into account the degree to which each party participated and cooperated in the mediation proceedings.[14]

For many years the private and public sector employees were under the same regime of strike law. In 1972 the legal framework of strikes in the public sector was slightly changed by amending the Settlement of Labour Dispute Law

8. 36/4-5 *Ginstler v. The State of Israel* 8 P.D.A. 3 (1976).
9. The Settlement of Labour Disputes Law, 5717-1957 Sec. 5a 11 Laws of the State of Israel No. 28 (1957)
10. 33/4-4 *Jerusalem University v. Teachers of the Jerusalem University* 5 P.D.A. 115,130 (1973).
11. Regarding alleged breach of contract and inducing a breach of contract.
12. 1013/04 *Discount Bank Ltd. v. The Histadrut* (2004). See also HCJ 1074/93 *The Attorney General v. The National Labour Court* 49 (2) P.D. 485, 490, 452 (1995).
13. *Davidov*, 2008, 16 et seqq.
14. *Ben Israel/Mironi*, 1989, 356, 361.

of 1957.[15] The amendment changed the legal ramification of a strike without a proper notice or during the term of the agreement, provided that the enterprise under strike was part of the public service. Under the amended law, such a strike is considered an 'unprotected strike' and the employees involved and their unions may lose the legal immunities accorded to a strike under the law.[16]

4 THE EXPERIENCE WITH STRIKES IN ESSENTIAL SERVICES

Since most of the strikes take place in the public sector, it is no wonder that strikes in essential services are a prevalent problem in Israel. In recent years the subject of strikes in essential services has increased in relevance and has ceased to be only a public sector phenomenon. This is attributed to initiatives taken by the government at the national and local level to introduce major structural changes as well as to promote privatization and outsourcing.

For reasons alluded to below, the normative policy dilemma and public discourse regarding strikes in essential services in Israel have always been multifaceted and complex. First and most important, the issue goes back in history to 1907 when the leader of the right-wing party declared that strikes, all strikes, should be banned for the period of building the state and all unresolved labour disputes should be brought to compulsory arbitration. The left-wing parties vehemently resisted the idea. It was perceived and labelled as fascist, anti-democratic and motivated by anti-union ideology.

Once labelled as such, the no-strike compulsory arbitration regime turned into a flag or a symbol in the bitter political fighting between the right and the left, colouring and tainting the public policy debate ever since. As a result, discourse regarding limiting the right to strike with or without compulsory arbitration has been extremely emotional, confrontational and politically charged.[17] Second, in the absence of a consensus as to which services are truly essential, the debate has lacked focus and the distinction between public services and essential services has often been blurred. Third, since many of the strikes have taken place in essential services operated by powerful monopolies, the discourse has not been framed as a search for the right balance between the human right to strike and the public right for continued flow of essential services. Instead, it has been framed as a debate about enhancing competition, and the pros and cons of privatization as well as about more general or basic democratic principles. These include governability and the need to make public policy decisions and control public expenditures not under a threat of painful strikes in critical junctions of the economy but through an orderly political process which assures transparency and accountability.

15. The Settlement of Labour Disputes (Amendment No. 2) Law, 5732-1970, 26 Laws of the State of Israel No. 37 (1972).
16. *Raday*, 1977; *Goldberg*, 1982, 130 et seq.
17. *Mironi*, 1990, 122 et seqq, 142.

5 RESTRICTIONS OF THE RIGHT TO STRIKE IN ESSENTIAL SERVICES

Generally speaking, Israeli law does not contain statutory restrictions on the right to strike of employees in essential services. The only exception is the full prohibition imposed on police force, prison guards and general secret service employees.

5.1 Securing Essential Services by Exclusion from Collective Labour Relations Rights

Employees who belong to the police force, prison guards and general secret service employees are denied ab-initio the right to form and join unions and are thus excluded completely and ex-ante from basic collective labour relations rights, including the right to strike. This is due to the presumed essential nature of their service and the military-like organizational culture within which they perform their work. It is noteworthy that initially, the government tried to deny policemen the right to unionize by police regulations (secondary legislation). The Policemen's Association challenged this, alleging, amongst others, that a basic human right secured under ILO convention may not be denied through secondary legislation. The High Court of Justice accepted this argument and declared the regulations invalid.[18] Shortly thereafter, the same prohibition was re-enacted.[19]

The relevant statutes do not provide special legal sanctions, other than the ordinary disciplinary measures, against policemen, prison guards and secret service employees who form or join a union or go on strike, in spite of the prohibition.[20] Actually, there has been no recorded instance of non-compliance by employees who belong to these excluded groups. There have however been several instances in which the policemen tried to exert pressure as a collectivity in order to promote or protect their work-related interests. This was done through public demonstrations conducted by an interesting body - The Association of Policemen's Wives.

The three statutes that exclude the police force, prison guards and general secret service employees from collective bargaining rights do not provide for genuine complementary or compensatory measures in order to advance employees' interests. Section 93c of the Police Ordinance calls for the appointment of a public welfare board. Shortly after the law was enacted, a public welfare board for the police was appointed. It has never been made clear whether the board was supposed to act as a substitute for collective bargaining, i.e., as a means for improving wages and/or working conditions, or to act as a non-union voice

18. HCJ 789 /78 *David Ofek v. Interior Minister*, P.D. 33 (3) 480 (1979).
19. Police Ordinance [New Version] 5731-1971 Sec. 93b. 26 Laws of the State of Israel No. 10 (1972).
20. Prisons Ordinance [New Version] 5732-1971 Sec.129a. 26 Laws of the State of Israel N. 11 (1972): General Security Service Law, 5762-2002 Sec. 20. Laws of the State of Israel (2002).

system. In practice, this has proven to be a theoretical question. As a matter of fact, the public welfare board has existed only on paper as it has never been operative.

A second and much more effective, albeit non-formal, measure for advancing employees' interests is the principle of parity. Over the years, a formula linking wages and working condition of secret service employees, the police force and prison guards to those of army officers and personnel has been adopted.[21] Although far from being a real substitute for collective bargaining and collective voice, given the importance and high status of the army in Israel, such parity or linking formula has proven to be a very important measure for securing adequate wage and working conditions for the three populations of employees who are excluded from collective bargaining rights.

In recent years, there have been repeated attempts by the government to include fire-fighters as a fourth group of employees who are excluded from all three basic collective bargaining rights. These attempts, including a softer model under which the fire-fighters may join unions and bargain collectively but will not be allowed to strike, have been in vain.

5.2 Securing Essential Services by Imposing Statutory Limitations on the Right to Strike

Other than the three aforementioned excluded groups of employees, Israel does not have a specific statute which imposes ex-ante special restrictions on the right to strike of employees in essential services.

Nonetheless, as alluded briefly above,[22] under an amendment to the Settlement of Labour Dispute Law of 1957, enacted in 1972,[23] strikes in essential services are treated differently from other strikes.

The amendment was a result of mounting criticism voiced against the government for its failure to cope with strike waves in the public sector, and repeated attempts led by the opposition parties to enact a no-strike compulsory arbitration law for the public sector. The legislator, which at that time was led by the left-wing parties, was hesitant to act. Imposing restrictions on the ideologically cherished right to strike was out of the question and the idea of compulsory arbitration has always been a politically charged issue. This led to a compromise solution. As many of the strikes were wildcat strikes and in breach of the peace

21. Although the armed forces are not excluded by law from collective bargaining rights, the army has never been unionized.
22. See *supra* Section 3.
23. *Ibid.* This was the second time that the Settlement of Labour Dispute Law was amended since its enactment in 1957. The first time was three years earlier – in 1969 – when the duty to give 15-days prior notice before any strike or lockout was enacted. The Settlement of Labour Disputes (Amendment No.1) Law, 5729-1969 23 Laws of the State of Israel No. 69 (1969).

obligation,[24] the law was amended to strengthen the deterrence against such strikes while leaving the right to strike intact. The underlying idea was that adding employment and tort law based sanctions would reduce the number of strikes in essential services and assure that those which do take place would be conducted according to the statutory rules and internal union bylaws.

With regard to strikes, the amendment changed the legal landscape of strike law in somewhat novel ways by introducing two new concepts: 'public service' and 'unprotected strike'. In terms of definition, the amendment employed the *ex-ante general* approach.

Under the heading 'public service', the legislator attempted to compose a comprehensive list of essential services which included almost all of the public sector and a substantial number of privately owned and run activities or services that were deemed essential. Among them: the whole civil service, all statutory bodies, municipalities and local governments, healthcare services, the whole education system including higher education, air transportation and cargo, and production and supply of fuel, electricity, water and telephone services, both line and cellular.

Being a political compromise, one can assume that the list contains services that may not be regarded by all standards as essential, such as universities and colleges, whereas others which are deemed more essential, such as seaports, trains and public transportation, are missing.

The second new concept – 'unprotected strike' – referred to a strike characterized by one or more of three problematic features: an unauthorized strike which was not called by the union and according to its by-laws (a wildcat strike); a strike in breach of the statutory duty to give a 15-day prior notice; a strike during the time when an applicable collective agreement was in force. According to the amendment, an 'unprotected strike' was not recognized legally as a strike. As a result, the employees involved would lose their immunity and might be subject to legal action for breach of their employment contract as well as for inducing breach of contract in tort. The union involved might also be subject to a tort claim filed by the employer for inducing breach of contract.

6 COMPENSATORY MEASURES FOR RESTRICTIONS

Section 37e of the amended law introduced and externally imposed quasi-mandatory dispute resolution procedures culminating in arbitration. In the appendix to the law, a two-tier dispute resolution process is provided. It includes proceedings before a bi-partite committee[25] and binding arbitration. Its quasi-mandatory character stems from the fact that the dispute resolution procedures

24. *Zamir*, 1974, 555.
25. *Ben Israel/Mironi*, 1989, 368. A bi-partite committee is a very popular and effective consent-based dispute resolution process in collective labour relations in Israel. A bi-partite committee always has an equal number of members who are non-neutral partisan, but are not the disputing parties. Usually they come from one level above the

come into force only if the particular dispute between the parties is not subject to a contractual dispute resolution procedure that assures a final and binding resolution.

Section 3 of the appendix is devoted to the arbitration body. Although the section is brief and does not state much, it appears as if the arbitration model is in tune with the 'protocol' developed by the ILO Committee on Freedom of Association which includes a list of expected safeguards that need to be assured whenever an externally imposed or compulsory arbitration model is introduced as a form of a strike substitute:

(1) Each side has equal power to invoke arbitration and keep the arbitration process going in spite of the other side's opposition;
(2) Both sides have equal opportunity and authority to choose and appoint the single arbitrator or the arbitration body. In the case of three arbitrators, each side appoints one arbitrator and the two arbitrators select the third by mutual consent. These appointment procedures assure that the arbitration body is objective, neutral, and independent of the state or the employer;
(3) Being part of the Settlement of Labour Dispute Law of 1957, the arbitration body has full and independent discretion as well as authority to decide on every issue which might be subject to a collective agreement;
(4) Finally, the arbitrator's or the arbitration body's decision is final and binding.

Section 37d of the law introduced an innovative compensatory measure. It bestowed upon unions in the public services a privilege akin to punitive damages. A union in the public service is entitled to receive compensation for any breach of a collective agreement by an employer in the public service without needing proof that such breach caused any damage to the union or the employees who are subject to the collective agreement.

6.1 Evaluation

The 1972 amendment failed to achieve its underlying objectives, i.e., to reduce the frequency and length of strikes in essential services as well as the damage caused by such strikes. Since the 1972 amendment neither added statutory restrictions nor provided new means for coping with strikes in essential services, it hardly left a mark, both normatively and practically, on strike law and strike activity in Israel. The well-intended and crafted amendment has become a dead letter law.

---

disputants. A by-partite committee can be used to resolve a legal/right dispute or an economic/interest dispute and its decision is final and binding.

Over the following 46 years there have been many strikes in public services, as defined by the law, including wildcat strikes, but only one recorded incidence of disciplinary procedures against three employees who took part in an unprotected strike.[26]

The fate of the innovative compensatory measures was no better. First, the special quasi-mandatory dispute resolution procedures were activated only a few times, primarily by the public service employers.[27] The second compensatory measure, punitive damages, has remained on the books for 46 years and has not seen the light of day. For unknown reasons, unions in the public services have hardly tried, let alone succeeded, in making use of their special privilege to collect punitive type damages in claim for breach of collective agreement by employers in the public services.[28] Consequently, it is impossible to evaluate whether the two compensatory measures were workable, effective and acceptable.

7 SECURING ESSENTIAL SERVICES BY FURTHER MEANS

This part is the heart of the report. It discusses and analyses how the three branches of government and the collective autonomy, i.e., the conflicting or social partners, unions, employers and employers' associations, have dealt with the challenges associated with strikes in essential services. As will be demonstrated, the three branches of government, each in its turn as communicating vessels, have been very active and innovative when it came to intervening in strikes in essential services. The unions have similarly been active and effective in innovating and adopting autonomous measures either unilaterally or jointly with employers. Hence, it is safe to say that save for the exclusion of secret service employees, the police force and prison guards, which is an *ex-ante general* approach (Cell 1 in the matrix), the dominant approaches in Israel have always been *ad-hoc general* (Cell 3 in the matrix) and *ad-hoc selective & dynamic* (Cell 4 in the matrix).

7.1 The Legislative Branch

As alluded in the preceding sections, there were only four instances in which the legislature used its legislative power in order to intervene in the right to strike in essential services. In these instances, it chose to adopt the extreme poles of the

26. BDM 31/75 Case 384 (1976).
27. In the first notable case the government forced the two teachers' unions to submit a protracted dispute to arbitration 4-45 *The State of Israel v. The High School Teachers Union* (1998). In the second the National Labour Court rejected the government's petition for injunctive relief compelling arbitration as a means to bring a nationwide medical doctors strike to an end. 48472-06-11 *The State of Israel v. Israel Medical Association* (2011).
28. Over the period of 46 years there were only nine recorded cases in which a union tried to claim punitive damages. None were successful.

regulation continuum and tended to use its legislative power imprudently both procedurally and substantively.

When dealing with the police force, prison guards and general secret service employees, the legislature took a very extreme position, excluding the whole workforce from the three collective bargaining rights, including the right to organize. The statutory exclusion was passed without a public debate as to whether a sweeping ban was in fact necessary and whether a less extreme measure, such as allowing employees to organize and bargain collectively but not to strike, or imposing a strictly defined and enforced minimum service, would suffice. Additionally, the legislature disregarded the ILO Convention's requirement to provide an effective and workable alternative means to advance and protect employees' interests in lieu of the right to strike.

In contrast, the single time the legislator tried to deal with the broader phenomenon of strikes in essential services, rather than with particular occupational army-like employees, it went the other way, adopting a minimalistic approach towards restricting the right to strike. At the same time, it was generous and innovative in providing the newly defined public service employees with compensatory measures.

Apart from the four statutes mentioned, the legislative branch's action in the area of strikes in essential services and its contribution to the public policy discourse has been characterized by much noise, commotion and hot air with very little practical impact. This is unexpected, especially given the frequency of strikes in essential services and the extensive media coverage which echoes the public's outcry and low tolerance towards these strikes.

Throughout its history the Israeli parliament has been involved as an activist player in strikes in essential services through parliamentary committee hearings and deliberations as well as legislation initiatives. These two channels of activity are responsible for portraying the legislator as making much noise and very little practical impact.

Over the years the legislative branch has intensified its involvement in strikes in essential services through public hearings and deliberations in parliamentary committees, especially the Labour Committee and the Constitutional and Law Committee. According to parliament records, during the period 1999–2016, parliamentary committees initiated and conducted 30 hearings devoted to prolonged strikes in essential services. Such hearings usually draw a large number of participants. The list of invitees includes union leaders and management officials from the service under strike, the chairman of the Histadrut and the head of the industrial union involved, the Presidium of Economic Organization, relevant cabinet ministers and other stakeholders, especially those representing groups who have been affected by the strike.

The parliamentary committee protocols show that, in addition to eliciting information as to the underlying dispute and parties' positions, the committee often seized the opportunity to make suggestions and attempted to promote agreements that would end the strike. Legally speaking, parliamentary committees have no legislative or executive power, other than making public declaration and recommendations. As a result, these hearings and deliberations have become a ceremonial stage and a necessary part of the 'strikes in essential services' ritual. At most they serve as a platform for public debate and public relations propaganda, devoid of any practical meaning.

Over the years the Israeli parliament has dealt with no less than 100 bills which were put forward either by parliament members or by the government and aimed at restricting the right to strike in essential services. In the period 1987–2015, three bills were tabled and discussed yearly. Out of the 100 bills, four were initiated by the government, in 1977, 1978, 2003 and 2013. While the bills were somewhat different in terms of source, context and content, their fate or life-cycle was always the same. It followed a meteor-like pattern. Whenever such a bill was tabled, it immediately made its way to the headlines and gained extensive publicity and editorials. It aroused heated and confrontational political debate between the government and the Histadrut, as well as among and within all political parties. At times it even caused or threatened to cause a crisis within the coalition. Then it vanished; often without a parliamentary debate or only after a single one.

All the bills regarding strikes in essential services that were tabled in the parliament were designed to impose restrictions on the right to strike. In some cases, the bills provided for compensatory measures, such as arbitration as a quid-pro-quo for the right to strike. There was however one bill that went beyond. It was tabled after several short strikes at Tel Aviv International Airport which serves all flight to and outside Israel. It required the government to take the necessary steps to rebuild and upgrade the military airports' infrastructure and facilities in order to assure that, in a case of a strike, commercial flight could be rerouted to military airports.[29]

7.2 The Executive Branch

For many years and until 2000, the executive branch carried most of the burden of protecting the public interest in situations of strike or threat of strike in essential services. The primary means of intervention was back-to-work emergency orders.[30] Over the years and especially with the declining appeal of back-to-work emergency orders, the executive branch made use of three additional means, either tactical or more strategic. These have been: (a) replacing striking employees by soldiers; (b) adopting administrative measures aimed at reducing the essential nature of the struck service, on an ad-hoc basis; and (c) introducing structural and organizational changes aimed at curtailing the power of unions in essential services, especially those which rely on their monopolistic

29. This bill was in line with what the executive branch has done in order to curtail the power of unions in essential services that rely on their monopolistic position See *infra* Subsection 7.2.4.
30. *Mironi*, 1986.

position.[31] Below is a brief account of each means employed by the executive branch, followed by a short section devoted to performance evaluation.

7.2.1 Back-to-Work Emergency Orders

The use of back-to-work emergency orders has been possible since legally speaking, Israel has been in a 'state of emergency' which was declared in 1948 and has existed ever since. Section 9 of Law and Administration Ordinance of 1948[32] which was replaced by section 39 of the Basic Law: Government of 1968[33] authorizes each cabinet minister to issue special emergency regulations (secondary legislation) aimed at defending the security of the state and the public at large and securing the supply of essential services. This emergency power was meant to be used during real emergency situations and in times of war. In fact, 55% of the time it was used against strikes and always in time of peace.

The emergency regulations are issued with the approval of the government and are in force for a period of three months. This period may be extended only by the parliament. Issuing emergency regulations is the first stage in a two-tier process. The second and operative stage is issuing orders. When emergency regulations are used during a strike or in response to a threat of strike, they authorize the cabinet minister or the head of the relevant service, upon her or his full discretion, to issue orders forcing individual employees to resume work or to refrain from striking. Disobeying a back-to-work order entails criminal as well as employment law sanctions. Since the cabinet minister or the head of the relevant service may constantly change the employees who are subject to such orders, conceptually speaking, back-to-work emergency orders are an extreme example of an *ad-hoc selective and dynamic* approach (Cell 4 in the matrix).

Space constraints prevent the re-telling of the full story of Israel's experience with back-to-work emergency orders. As a 'law in action' report which aspires to provide insights and lessons, it is important to analyse the historical trends and accumulative experience of using back-to-work emergency orders as a unique means of coping with strikes in essential services.

(1) Despite the acute emergency-like times during the first twelve years of statehood, the government preferred to cope with strikes in essential services without using emergency regulations.
(2) Once the government put the emergency regulations to use successfully in 1960,[34] it quickly discovered the advantages of back-to-work

31. A fourth means – initiating general legislation aimed at restricting the right to strike in essential services – was already mentioned. See *supra*, end of section 6.1.
32. 5708-1948 1 Laws of the State of Israel 7 (1948).
33. 5728-1969 22 Laws of the State of Israel No. 54 (1969).
34. It was used to bring back El Al Israel Airline's aircrafts that had been left on the ground in airports abroad due to a strike by El Al's pilots.

emergency orders. As a means of unilateral intervention in strikes it proved to be easy to use and very effective and powerful.

(3) Since the executive branch became so accustomed to and dependent on the process, there were right-wing governments that issued emergency regulations as a means to intervene in strikes three times a month.

(4) With the increasing frequency, the government became less cautious and emergency regulations were issued against strikes that took place in enterprises that could not be considered by any standard essential and as a preventive measure, i.e., when there was no strike at all.

(5) During the blossoming years of emergency regulations and back-to-work orders, the executive branch felt no inhibition. Its power to act unilaterally was hardly challenged in courts. On the rare occasions when unions petitioned the Supreme Court sitting as the High Court of Justice, it refused to intervene in the cabinet ministers' discretion.[35]

(6) Since 2000 the executive branch has rarely used its power to issue emergency regulations as a means of intervention in strikes in essential services. The use of back-to-work emergency orders, which reached its peak in the period 1960–1983 with average of 5.9 times a year, declined drastically to an average of 0.4 times a year in the period 2000–2016.

Several reasons may account for the shift in government policy. First, in a celebrated decision by the Supreme Court sitting as the High Court of Justice,[36] Chief Justice Barak criticized the continuation of the state of emergency and admonished that the use of emergency regulations interferes with democratic values and violates the separation of power principle.

Second, because of the impact of an empirical study which attested to the misuse of back-to-work emergency orders[37] and under the threat of the aforementioned court decision,[38] the Attorney General, who needs to approve the use of emergency regulations, adopted a highly restrictive policy.[39] The Attorney General urged the executive branch to completely abandon the use of back-to-work emergency orders and opt instead for injunctions.

A third, conspiracy type explanation, is that the right-wing governments have chosen to refrain from using back-to-work emergency orders for strategic reasons. The idea was that relieving the public's suffering caused by strikes in

35. HCJ 188/79 *The National Insurance Workers Council v. The Minister of Labour* 33 P.D. (2) 449 (1979); HCJ 735/80 *Arye Nizan v. Shlomo Lahat – The Mayor of Tel Aviv* 35 P.D. (1) 555 (1980); HCJ 372/84 *Hana Kloper Nave v. The Minister of Education* 38 P.D. (3) 233 (1984).
36. HCJ 6971/98 *Paritzki v. Minister of Interior* 53 P.D. 763 (1999)
37. *Mironi*, 1986.
38. *Supra* note 36.
39. Recently the Attorney General refused to approve a demand for a highly selective use of back-to-work emergency orders in two relatively long strikes – one by Foreign Ministry employees and one by public prosecutors.

essential services went against the government's long run interests. It is preferable to capitalize on the public outcry in order to sway public opinion against unions and collective labour relations and in support of government initiatives to erode or better destroy the power base of unions in essential services through organizational and structural changes.

7.2.2 The Use of Army

Much like the threat of strike, which is often as effective as striking itself in changing perceptions and introducing momentum in times of deadlock, the threat of calling on the army to replace regular employees in strikes in essential services may be used. This tactic is relatively easy to implement in Israel, not only because the country maintains a large professional army. Indeed, after completing mandatory service of three years for men and two years for women, all released soldiers remain in reserve units for many years and can be drafted instantly.

The tactic of threatening to use the armed forces as strike replacements was used in the first big shipping industry strike, in the nationwide medical doctors' strikes and in a prolonged teachers strike. Furthermore, as part of the government's overall strategy to reduce the bargaining power of unions in essential and monopolistic services, it declared its initiative to build specially trained firefighters and dock workers units within the army that would be called upon in case of strikes.

In two instances the army officers and soldiers actually replaced striking employees. The first was in the 1960s, during the air-controllers strike.[40] The second was during the recent prolonged strike in the Foreign Ministry in 2013. As part of the strike, the union of Foreign Ministry employees refused to take part in preparing and managing two of the prime minister's visits – one to Greece and one to Poland. The prime minister, who was at that time also the foreign minister, directed the army and the secret service to replace the striking Foreign Ministry employees in Israel, Athens and Warsaw and assume full responsibility for arranging the two visits.

7.2.3 The Use of Administrative Measures to Offset Strike Impact

In two cases of strikes in essential services[41] the executive branch used its power as a regulator in order to introduce a change that would alleviate or altogether

40. This was the first strike regarding a separate bargaining unit. The air traffic controllers wanted to form a niche union. Since there are always ample highly qualified and trained air traffic controllers, both in the professional army and in the reserve units, who man the air traffic control towers in the military airfields, there was no problem in replacing the civilian air traffic controllers who were on strike.
41. Actually there was a third case in which administrative measures were taken but finally were not carried out. During a strike in the strike prone Ashdod seaport, the government

negate the strike's impact. In the two instances the regulatory changes or measures were challenged in court. Nevertheless, the steps taken by the government had a devastating effect on the strikes and brought them instantly to an end.

The first case was during a strike of Interior Ministry employees which took place just before the elections for local governments in 1999. The minister of interior's office is in charge of issuing, renewing and updating identity cards, which by law were the only means of identification that entitled its holder to vote. It was estimated that, as a result of the strike, 400,000 people would be unable to take part in the local government elections. One week before Election Day the minister of the interior issued an emergency regulation which also enabled the use of a passport or a driving license as a method of identification. One day later the strike ended.

The High Court of Justice[42] denied a motion to nullify the emergency regulation. The chief justice severely criticized the minister of the interior's use of emergency power. He said that issuing emergency regulations undermines the democratic principle of separation of powers by changing primary legislation through secondary legislation. According to Chief Justice Barak, the minister of interior sidestepped the jurisdiction of the legislator by using emergency powers that were bestowed upon the government only for times of a real emergency such as war or natural disaster. Nonetheless, the court upheld the emergency regulations. It reasoned that, in a democratic system, securing the right to vote is an essential service and the measure adopted by the minister of the interior was proportional given the short time left until Election Day.

The second time was during a long strike of a local bus company's drivers in a mid-sized town in 2005. The privately owned bus company provided local transportation services according to a license which had been granted after bidding against its competitors. The strike was part of a bitterly fought organization drive. The minister of transportation intervened in the strike by issuing temporary licenses to other bus companies, including those that had previously lost in the bid.

The union petitioned the National Labour Court for an injunction. The court granted the injunction and ordered a withdrawal of the licenses issued to the other bus companies. The court held that the minister of transportation's action was an unjustified intervention in the right to organize.[43] In fact, the court decision proved to be a Pyrrhic victory. The government petitioned the Supreme Court for a review of the National Labour Court's decision. It also asked for a stay, which was allowed. The Supreme Court's decision to maintain the status

---

ordered the Airports Authority – a statutory body in charge of all civilian airports and land ports – to take the necessary steps that would enable it to handle containers to be brought by trucks from ships rerouted during the strike from Ashdod to the sea port of Aqaba, Jordan.

42. *Paritzki* case, *supra* note 36.
43. 57/05 *The Histadrut v. The State of Israel and Metrodan*, 40 P.D.A 481 (2005).

quo and allow other bus companies to continue to operate the struck bus lines was the straw which broke the camel's back. It instantly brought the strike and the unionization drive to an end.

7.2.4 Restructuring and Reorganization of Essential Services

During the last twenty years the executive branch has invested enormous efforts and resources in promoting the restructuring and reorganization of the essential services. This policy has been carried out under the banner of promoting efficiency and free competition through de-monopolization. In fact, it has been motivated primarily as a strategic move to curtail the strike leverage of the unions in the strike-prone highly essential and monopolistic services, such as air transportation, telephone communication, bus transportation, train services, seaports and electric power.

So far, the actual restructuring and reorganization steps taken or threats thereof have proven to be a success story in services such as air transportation, telephone communication (line, mobile and internet), and local as well as inter-city bus transportation. These formerly known strike-prone services have become virtually strike-free. At the same time the bitter struggle over restructuring, de-monopolization, privatization and reorganization of train services, seaports and electricity is still going on. It has been a source of endless negotiations, bitter industrial strife, repeated legislative initiatives, many government resolutions and highly contested and costly court litigations.

7.2.5 Performance Evaluation

When it comes to evaluation, restructuring and reorganization is vastly different from the three ad-hoc measures that were employed by the executive branch, namely, back-to-work emergency orders, the use of the army to replace striking employees and reducing the strike's impact through administrative action. The latter ad-hoc measures operate at the tactical level. They are activated by the executive branch as a reaction to a strike or threat of a strike, and are aimed at reducing the negative consequences of a particular strike or threat of a strike in essential service in the short run. In contrast, restructuring and reorganization steps operate at the strategic systemic level. They are proactive and aimed at preventing strikes in essential services in the long run by encroaching on or eroding the power base of the unions and their ability to launch an effective strike in the future.

As a result, the ad-hoc measures need to be evaluated by their efficacy in securing an optimal level of essential services in a particular case with minimum interference in the process of collective bargaining and the underlying goals or functions of the right to strike. Since a strike is intended to enhance employees' power, ad-hoc measures should aspire to minimize their impact on union-management real power relationships or power balance. Restructuring and reorganization steps do quite the opposite. Such measures are intended to infringe upon what is perceived to be excessive power of employees and their unions. Hence, their success as a preventive means needs to be evaluated in the long run, while being cognizant of the fact that, in the short run, the very act of carrying out a restructuring and reorganization plan may cause interruptions in the continuing flow of essential services.

For many years, back-to-work emergency orders were the prominent measure of executive branch intervention in strikes in essential services. In fact, during a long period, the government had developed what is referred to in the literature as a 'narcotic effect'.[44] The cabinet ministers were expected to issue emergency regulations and back-to-work orders in every strike or threat of a strike in essential services, broadly defined.

The efficacy of back-to-work emergency orders in securing an appropriate level of essential services is dependent on obedience by employees and their unions. This, in turn, is influenced by the frequency and the way the government is exercising its authority and discretion in issuing emergency regulations and back-to-work orders in specific situations. As expected, there were inverse relationships between frequency and efficacy. In an empirical study which examined the peak period of back-to-work emergency orders, 1960–1983, it was found that the level of obedience was less than 70%. In spite of the severe criminal and employment law sanctions, employees who failed to obey the orders or interfered with the work of their fellow employees who were subject to an order, were rarely prosecuted. There were only two criminal proceedings that ended up with an acquittal for lack of evidence.[45]

From a collective labour relations and labour law perspective, the use of back-to-work emergency orders has been problematic. First, by definition, such orders compress the power of the strike and do not promote an amicable settlement of the underlying dispute; to the contrary, whenever an employer attempts to enforce an order, a new dispute is created. Second, while severely restricting the right to strike, back-to-work emergency orders are 'stand-alone' procedure, lacking any complementary or compensatory measures aimed at promoting employees' interests. Third, due to their individualistic nature, the orders tend to have a devastating effect on workers' solidarity and the ability of unions to exert pressure through strikes. It may come as a surprise, but the employees who continue to strike while their fellow employees resume work, experience inequity and humiliation. While the product of a strike is considered a collective or public good to be enjoyed by all,[46] the striking employees are the only ones who bear the cost by not being paid during the strike. More important, they feel that since they have not been called back, their work is not appreciated and valued as important.

44. *Subaroo*, 1978, 79.
45. *Mironi*, 1986, 377 et seqq.
46. *Mancur*, 1965, 14 et seqq.

It appears as if the additional two ad-hoc measures, i.e., the use of the army to replace striking employees and reducing the strike's impact through administrative action, have been more effective in securing essential services and equally destructive as far as free collective bargaining, collective labour relations and the right to strike are concerned. Their enhanced efficacy stems from the fact that these measures do not depend on striking employees and their union's compliance. They rely on exercising exclusive government power (e.g., issuing licenses or new regulations) or implementation by people who have no right to strike, e.g., army officers and secret service employees.

As expected, the long term actions undertaken by the government in restructuring, de-monopolization, privatization and reorganization have taken their toll in terms of industrial conflicts. They have been a source of many controversies, unrest and strikes in essential services. Nevertheless, these measures have proven to be very effective in the long run. In those cases where the process has been completed, the unions' power has substantially declined and strike prone enterprises have become largely strike-free.

7.3 The Judicial Branch

In recent years the judicial branch has emerged as a leading force in regulating and intervening in strikes in essential services. As in communicating vessels, in parallel to the declining use of emergency back-to-work orders as an ad-hoc measure, the hegemony has passed from the executive to the judicial branch, especially to the labour courts.

The judicial branch's work has been carried out in three avenues: (a) court decisions in civil tort claims emanating from strikes in essential services; (b) decisions by the Supreme Court sitting as the High Court of Justice in public petitions brought before the High Court of Justice as a first instance and when exercising its judicial review power over the National Labour Court's decisions; and (c) labour courts' decisions in petitions for injunction in strikes in essential services. A fourth avenue was discussed in the previous section – that of the High Court of Justice exercising its judicial review power over administrative actions by the executive branch.

7.3.1 The Civil Courts

There have been two celebrated court decisions that demonstrate the potential of tort claims as a means of regulating strikes in essential services.

The first was rendered by the Supreme Court in 1987.[47] As part of a seamen's strike, two ships remained docked in the port of Haifa. As a result, no container ship was able to enter the harbour and reach the docks. After a few days and with no sign that the strike was close to an end, several container ships

47. CA 593/81 *Mifaley Rechev Ashdod v. Tzizik* P.D. 41 (3) 169 (1987).

left the struck port in Haifa and downloaded their cargo in Cyprus. When the strike was over, the cargo was shipped back to Israel. The court ordered the union and its officers to pay full damages to the owners of the cargo based on negligence.

The second case involved a lifeguards strike.[48] According to a long held tradition, high school graduates from cities and towns along the Mediterranean celebrate their graduation by partying on the beach right after they finish the last class. When these thousands of high school students arrived at the beaches in the summer of 1999, there were no lifeguards on duty. As part of a prolonged labour dispute, the lifeguards had gone on strike. They had completed their regular working day of seven hours and left the beaches unguarded at 14:00. Since the union followed the rules and the strike adhered to the principle of proportionality, the National Labour Courts refused a petition filed by the Association of Local Governments to issue an injunction against the strike.

A high school student who went with his classmates to a municipal beach but could not swim, almost drowned. He was saved by an emergency crew but became a quadriplegic. His family brought a tort claim against the municipality, the union, and against the government for its failure to issue back-to-work emergency orders. Despite the fact that by labour law standards the strike was flawless, the district court found the union negligent and ordered it to pay 40% of the substantial amount of damages.[49]

7.3.2 The Supreme Court, Sitting as the High Court of Justice

The Supreme Court, sitting as the High Court of Justice, has been involved in strikes in essential services in two capacities. First, in dealing with public petitions that were brought before the High Court of Justice as a first instance.[50] When such a petition is filed during a strike in essential services, the petitioner asks the court to order the prime minister and the relevant cabinet minister to intervene in order to bring an end to the strike.[51] Second, in exercising its judicial review power over National Labour Court's decisions.

The Supreme Court, sitting as the High Court of Justice, has over the years built an impressive strike law jurisprudence. Nonetheless, it has never stated its normative position with regard to the subject of strikes in essential services. This has to do with the *modus operandi* adopted by the court. When a case involving strikes in essential services was brought before the High Court of Justice either

48. CC Haifa *000862/02 Ploni v. Rishon Lezion Municipality* (2008).
49. Together with the municipality which had to pay 50% and the state 10%.
50. According to case-law, any interested person is able to file a public petition with the Supreme Court siting as the High Court of Justice.
51. Public petitions are brought regularly before the High Court of Justice in mega disputes and nationwide strikes such as the strike of the medical doctors, the teachers, the state's attorneys etc.

as public petition or for judicial review,[52] it received a similar non-adjudicative treatment. The court neither heard legal arguments nor issued a well-reasoned judgement. Instead, it assumed a non-parochial role as facilitator[53] with clout.

The court sessions went on for many hours and late into the night.[54] During the long sessions, the court facilitated summit negotiations between parties' leaders and their attorneys in an attempt to reach a settlement regarding the underlying dispute that had led to the strike. Often, officials from the prime minister's office, the finance minister and relevant cabinet ministers, as well as the Histadrut chairman, union leaders and other stakeholders, were summoned in order to take part in the negotiations. In most cases the court was successful in bringing the parties to a procedural settlement agreement[55] under which the strike ended or was suspended and the underlying dispute would be brought to mediation or arbitration. The court's involvement tended to go beyond facilitating the agreement and into drafting the terms of references or the arbitration submissions as well as into personally appointing (hand-picking) the mediators and the arbitrators.[56]

7.3.3 The System of Labour Courts

The National Labour Court has repeatedly urged the legislature to enact a comprehensive law regulating the right to strike in essential services and providing for specially designed impasse procedures as a quid-pro-quo for the restrictions imposed on the right to strike.[57] According to the court, the subject of strike in essential services has always been politically sensitive and ideologically charged. It requires striking a delicate balance between competing societal values and interests, such as the human right to strike with the right of the citizenry to enjoy an uninterrupted flow of essential services. Consequently, it belongs to the political arena and the democratic process. It needs to be discussed and decided not in court through adjudication and case-law but in the

52. For instance, the case regarding the validity of the medical interns' collective resignation following the conclusion of a collective agreement signed by the medical doctor's union. See HCJ 7569/11 *Gadot v. The National Labour Court* (2011).
53. The term 'facilitation' was chosen since the High Court of Justice has rarely availed itself of caucusing and ex-parte communication which are commonly used in a full-fledged mediation.
54. The longest lasted for 22 hours and ended at 2:00 AM.
55. To distinguish from substantive settlement agreements in which the issues in dispute are resolved in the agreement.
56. For instance, in the public attorney's strike, HCJ 9531/10 *Herzelia Association v. The Prime Minister* (2010), the justices nominated the arbitrator and invested hours in drafting the submission. In the medical interns' case, *supra* note 52, the Chief Justice talked personally with the author offering him to mediate the dispute together with a former Justice.
57. 23/07 *Israel Electric Corporation v. The Histadrut* (2007); 19/99 *Mkorot Water Corporation v. The Histadrut* 36 P.D.A 560, 573 (2001).

parliament and through a political discourse and debate. As alluded previously, these calls have fallen on deaf ears.

In face of a prolonged failure to receive guidelines from the legislature and mounting petitions for injunctions that have been partly the result of the drastic decline in back-to-work emergency orders, the labour courts have had to undertake a leading role in fashioning public policy toward strikes in essential services. Led by an activist National Labour Court chamber, the labour court system has adopted a distinctive approach to dealing with injunction proceedings concerning strikes in essential services and has developed its own brand of strike law jurisprudence. The immense contribution of the labour courts to the regulation of strikes in essential services can be summarized under five categories.

(1) The labour courts have attempted to define essential services. According to the court, these include any service which, if interrupted, might substantially and instantly endanger the life, personal security and health of the public or parts thereof.[58]
(2) The labour courts, which long ago introduced the concept of proportionality as a leading paradigm in judging requests for injunctions against strikes, have developed a more nuanced version of a proportionality test for strikes in essential services.[59]
(3) By applying the duty of good faith and fair dealing to the right to strike, the labour court supplemented the statutory duty to give a general 15-day prior notice with a requirement to provide a special notice whenever the strike involves essential service. In addition, the union has to give a detailed notice including the exact type of strike action planned and its duration at least 2–3 days in advance.[60]
(4) The labour courts have promoted the idea of a virtual or synthetic strike[61] as a substitute for a regular strike in essential services. In some instances, the courts brought the parties to agree on a virtual strike;[62] in other instances it was by a court order.[63]
(5) The labour courts invented the idea, which was subsequently adopted by the High Court of Justice, to try and facilitate the negotiations over

58. 19/99 *Mekorot Water Co. v. The Histadrut* 36 P.D.A. 560, 576 (2001).
59. 23/07 *Israel's Electrity Co. v. The Histadrut* (Nevo, 2007).
60. 50556-09-11 *The Histadrut v. Israel Railways Co.* (Nevo 2011).
61. A synthetic or virtual strike is a model of striking aimed at producing the effect of strike in an essential service without hurting the public. Even though a strike is called, work continues as usual but in order to inflict pain on the conflicting parties, all employer's income and the employees' salaries for the duration go into a trust fund. At the end of the strike part of the money accumulated in the trust fund is paid to the employer and the employees in inverse relation to the length of the strike.
62. 41-8/98 *The National Parks and Nature Reserve Authority v. Itzhak Azulay* (1998); 13/03 *Federation of Chambers of Commerce v. The Histadrut* (2003).
63. 30/05 *Israel Electricity Corporation v. The Histadrut* (2005).

> the underlying (economic or interest) dispute rather than adjudicating the petition for injunction (legal or right dispute). It was further developed and reached its zenith when applied to strikes in essential services. In practice, the labour courts have employed three methods. First, the court offers the parties to closely accompany the negotiations through frequent follow-up and reporting.[64] Second, in order to promote settlement, the labour courts tend to schedule sessions at night, assuming that time matters, and it is much easier to summon high public officials and assure their presence on site for long marathon-like sessions.[65] Third, the court steps down into the negotiation arena, setting the stage and facilitating the summit negotiations, while rotating from the court halls to their more intimate chambers – a much more conducive environment for conducting sub-group meetings and cross-caucusing.[66]

With all the inhibitions and inherent ethical issues associated with courts exceeding their authority by delving into the non-legal dispute, deserting their traditional adjudicative role and changing hats, the labour courts have kept a very good record of either settling disputes or postponing and de-escalating strikes. Using these mixed mode processes,[67] the labour courts have gained public respect for their unique contribution in preventing, managing and settling strikes in essential services.[68]

7.4 Autonomous Regulation

Autonomous regulation has always played a major role in collective labour relations. The issue of strikes in essential services is not an exception. Autonomous regulation may take four forms: (a) a bilateral ex-ante regulation, such as a no-strike agreement; (b) a bilateral ad-hoc regulation, such as a minimum service agreement signed during or on the eve of a strike; (c) a unilateral ex-ante regulation by unions through union constitution bylaws; and (d) a unilateral ad-hoc regulation, for instance, when a union undertakes upon itself to provide minimum service or to establish an exceptions committee.

64. For instance, during the medical doctors' strike of 2011 the labour court accompanied the negotiations for a period of three consecutive weeks.
65. A major cause of strikes in the public sector in Israel has always been the absence of officials with decision making authority at the negotiation table.
66. Cross-caucusing refers to private meetings only with lawyers or with the parties alone.
67. Mixed mode processes are dispute resolution processes that combine adjudicative (e.g., court litigation and arbitration) and non-adjudicative (e.g., mediation and conciliation) processes.
68. 'Justice Zamir's report', The Committee for the Examination of the Labour Courts in Israel, 2006.

7.4.1 *Bilateral Autonomous Regulation*

The Israeli experience with autonomous bilateral ex-ante regulation of the right to strike in essential services has been quite limited. Three notable exceptions are discussed and analysed below.

7.4.1.1 *The Institute for Voluntary Arbitration in the Public Service*

In 1977 the government and the Histadrut signed a collective bargaining agreement which established the Institute for Voluntary Arbitration in the Public Service (IVAPS). The agreement came as response to a series of alarming developments in labour relations. Among them: continuing labour unrest and frequent strikes including wildcat strikes in public services, several arbitration awards that shook the wage structure in the public sector, and increasing public pressure to enact a no-strike compulsory arbitration law. The idea was to establish a neutral permanent and publicly accountable arbitration tribunal that would replace power-based discourse by a reason-based one, reduce the number of strikes of public sector and essential services employees and serve as a substitute for a no-strike compulsory arbitration statute.[69]

The agreement was signed initially for one year and covered only state employees. Since then it has been renewed several times and remains currently in force. Its coverage has also been extended to other groups of employees in the public and semi-public sectors. According to the agreement, both sides were supposed to share the cost of IVAPS. In fact, it has only been funded by the government. The agreement contains a no-strike clause. A breach of the no-strike clause bears the legal consequences of an 'unprotected strike'.[70] In addition, a party which engages in a strike after an arbitration award has been rendered may lose all the benefits awarded. The arbitration award is final and binding. Once rendered it becomes a collective agreement.

The IVAPS was launched with the hope that it would bring stability and peace to the turbulent and strike-prone labour relations. This was reflected by the appointment of a former Supreme Court justice as a leader and first chairman, as well as by selecting a large panel of distinguished professionals and public figures as arbitrators. In fact, after a relatively good start, the IVAPS's prestige and role quickly deteriorated and it became a broken dream. The numbers are telling. At its zenith, it dealt with 24 cases a year and gradually the number of cases submitted to arbitration with the IVAPS went down to a yearly average of less than two. Furthermore, throughout its history, no change has been observed in the tendency to strike in those undertakings covered by the

69. *Mironi*, 1988, 26 et seqq.
70. See *supra* Section 5.

agreement. Thus, is safe to conclude that although it still formally exists, in practice, the IVAPS has never fulfilled its mission to become an exclusive arbitration tribunal for public sector labour disputes and an acceptable and workable strike substitute.

In recent years, the Finance Ministry has rediscovered the IVAPS. It has tried to convince unions to sign no-strike arbitration agreements in which contract negotiation disputes will be arbitrated by the IVAPS. In addition, it has repeatedly stated a clear preference for IVAPS whenever arbitration is considered on an ad-hoc basis in public sector labour disputes. So far the government's efforts have failed since unions have lost faith in the IVAPS. There has been one notable exception however, relating to essential service employees. In 2009, the Histadrut signed a five-year collective agreement covering immigration and border control employees. The agreement includes a no-strike clause and refers unresolved contract negotiation (interest) disputes to be determined by the IVAPS.

7.4.1.2 The Medical Doctors No-Strike Arbitration Agreement

Medical care in Israel is predominantly public and semi-public. More than 90% of all medical doctors employed by hospitals and clinics in Israel are unionized in an old and well established union – the Israel Medical Association (IMA). In 2000 the IMA called a strike of doctors in all hospital and HMO-type clinics. Its collective agreement had expired in 1998 and two years of extensive negotiation had brought no progress. After the doctors had been on strike for more than ten weeks, the parties agreed to enter mediation upon the prime minister's request.

After 127 days of the strike and 42 days of marathon-style mediation the parties reached a revolutionary and innovative settlement.[71] An important part and the most daring component of the settlement was a no-strike arbitration agreement. Under the agreement, the IMA gave up its power to strike for ten years. In return, the state and other public health employers gave up their decision-making power. Unresolved issues regarding doctors' remuneration and working conditions were subjected to final and binding arbitration. This was the first time that a large and powerful union had given up its right to strike for an extended period of time in exchange for a final and binding arbitration. The agreement ran its course and was not extended. During its ten-year term there was one arbitration proceeding that was managed and conducted poorly and left all the participants badly bruised.

It is difficult to evaluate and analyse the no-strike arbitration model using one round of unsuccessful negotiations and a single incidence of arbitration. Nonetheless, similar to the experience elsewhere,[72] the no-strike arbitration

71. *Mironi*, 2008, 56 et seqq.
72. *Kochan/Lipsky/Newhart/Benson*, 2010, 569.

agreement's major success was in avoiding strikes. During the ten-year period, there were no reported instances of strikes and other job actions. The goal of uninterrupted medical care was fully achieved. From a labour relations standpoint, it was a major failure. The highly combative arbitration proceedings and the arbitration award left all the parties disappointed and the relationship between the union and the state and other public employers in deep crisis. No wonder the disenchanted union refused to extend the agreement and to give the experiment another chance.

On the basis of a detailed study,[73] it appears that the state and the public employers did not give the no-strike arbitration model a fair chance. As a result, it is difficult to answer the question of whether arbitration might serve as an acceptable quid-pro-quo for the right to strike in essential services. Certainly one may not draw conclusions on the basis of a single round of negotiations and arbitration that was conducted badly under unusual and negative exogenous events.

7.4.1.3 The Fire-Fighters Agreement

For many years fire-fighting services had been delivered in Israel at the municipal and regional levels. In 2012 the government took steps to establish a well-funded state-wide fire-fighting statutory authority. Part of the government's plan aimed at upgrading the level of fire-fighting services and securing that such an essential service would never be interrupted. Initially, the government drafted a bill which revoked the fire-fighters' right to unionize. Faced with the Histadrut's fierce opposition, the government retracted by proposing to only take away the right to strike.

Eventually, the government had to abandon this idea as well. In exchange, the Histadrut agreed to enter into a unique collective bargaining agreement imposing specific procedural restrictions on the right to strike for contract renewal (interest disputes) negotiation.[74] The agreement adds a contractual multi-stage procedure and cooling-off periods that the fire-fighters must follow and exhaust before they are allowed to serve a strike notice of 14 days as required by law.[75]

73. *Mironi*, 2010, 201.
74. In addition to the routine peace obligation which prohibits strikes during the term of the contact and with regard to subjects that are regulated therein.
75. The first and second stage consist of two preliminary cooling off periods of 14 days each, during which the issues in dispute are brought to summit-type direct or mediation-assisted negotiations with active participation of high government and Histadrut officials. The third stage requires the union to acquire approval from the Chairman of Trade Union Division of the Histadrut and from a special coordinating committee; the fourth, to secure Histadrut's Secretary General's permission to serve a strike notice.

7.4.2 Unilateral Autonomous Regulation

Israel has no experience with ex-ante unilateral regulation of strikes in essential services. Unions' constitutions and by-laws tend to lay out internal procedures for calling a strike but do not include special provisions regarding strikes in essential services. In contrast, an ad-hoc unilateral regulation by the union (ad-hoc selective dynamic – Cell 4) has been a common phenomenon in strikes in essential services. This practice usually takes two forms: first, a decision to call a partial strike or making a commitment to provide minimum service in spite of the strike; second, establishing an 'exceptions committee'.

7.4.2.1 Minimum Service

Strikes in essential services are rarely full strikes. In such cases, unions prefer to call a partial strike *ab-initio*. In other cases of strikes in essential services, on the eve of a strike or in a response to a petition for an injunction, unions announce that minimum service will be maintained during the strike. For instance, Israeli medical doctors have never taken the extreme step of a total walkout and have always preferred a partial strike.

As an example, during the 2000 strike, the doctors worked once a week with a skeleton crew on a rotating basis and in various locations. In addition, they performed only life-saving operations, and severely curtailed services in out-patient clinics. A similar approach was adopted recently by the union during a strike in the largest supplier of mobile and internet communications. The union maintained that the strike would not interfere with the regular work of the servers and that all service calls originated from and to hospitals army and security installations would be taken care of.[76]

7.4.2.2 Exceptions Committees

Often union's unilateral obligation to provide minimum service or to conduct only a partial strike due to the essential nature of the service under strike is accompanied by a union-run 'exceptions committee'. This ad-hoc and informal internal forum is authorized to decide, on a case by case basis, whether in spite of the strike, service will be provided fully or partially in acute or exceptional circumstances.

Every person or enterprise may petition the exceptions committee and ask to be exempted from the strike. The makeup of these committees, their *modus operandi*, decision making criteria and petitions' success rates have never made clear, let alone published or studied. Nonetheless, in the decision as to whether to issue an injunction in a strike in essential services, the labour courts have

76. 50253-02-17 *Pelephone Communication Ltd. v. The Histadrut* (2017).

traditionally accorded heavy weight to a union's obligation to avail the public with an exceptions committee.[77]

8 EVALUATION AND CONCLUSION

Throughout its history, Israel has suffered from recurrent strikes and threats of strike in public and essential services. In recent years, strikes have become a public and essential service phenomenon, accounting for more than 90% of all the strikes and 95% of the days lost due to strikes. The prevalence of strikes in public and essential services may be attributed to the power-based, highly adversarial and confrontational discourse as well as the low trust that has characterized collective bargaining relationships and the absence of a third party involvement tradition of either mediation or arbitration.

How to deal with strikes in essential services has always been a hotly debated and controversial political issue. The fact that in less than seventy years of statehood there have been 100 attempts to enact a no-strike compulsory arbitration statute for essential services and none was successful may attest to the constant threatening presence of the problem, on the one hand, and its complexity, on the other.

In the absence of a political consensus, save for the police force, prison guards and secret service employees, who are denied the right to unionize (the excluded groups), there are no special statutory ex-ante restrictions on the right to strike of essential services employees. Therefore, the three branches of government find themselves involved in such strikes or threats of strike, employing an ad-hoc, mostly selective dynamic approach. Naturally, an ad-hoc type intervention falls within the realm of the executive and judicial branches of government. These two bear most of the responsibility and, as in communicating vessels, rotate lead positions in dealing with strikes in essential services.

For many years the main vehicle for coping with strikes in essential services was back-to-work emergency orders issued by the executive branch. In 2000 the government changed course. With very rare exceptions, it stopped using back-to-work orders and opted instead for injunctions. In several notable instances, the executive branch made use or threatened to use the army and employees from the excluded groups as strike replacements. In other instances, cabinet ministers employed administrative measures, such as providing alternative service through ad-hoc licensing and removal of authorization requirements, to avert a strike in essential service. The experience with these measures reveals that they were very effective in securing a proper level of essential services to the public but failed to satisfy all other criteria. By their very nature,

77. 51092-01-12 *National Insurance Institute v. The Histadrut* (2012); 8299-06-12 *Mikud Security v. The National Workers Union* (2012).

all these measures interfere with effective and free collective bargaining, do not comply with international standards[78] and are procedurally unacceptable.

A more striking development has been the new approach or policy adopted by the executive branch towards strikes in essential services. Instead of reacting, the executive branch has identified a short list of strike-prone essential services and invested huge efforts and resources in a pro-active strategic move aimed at reducing the potential damage of strikes and bargaining power of unions in these services in the long run. In practice, this refers to the introduction of structural and organizational changes such as de-merger, privatization, breaking monopolies and creating alternatives to existing providers of essential services. In the short run, these governmental measures have not alleviated the hardships associated with strikes in essential services. Quite the contrary, these structural and organizational changes have been the source of industrial strife and unrest, resulting in strikes and extensive litigation. However, if and when these pro-active strategic changes are completed, there will be a completely new landscape where strikes in essential services will be reduced in number and impact or eliminated altogether.

Once the executive branch stopped using back-to-work orders and concentrated its efforts on long-run structural changes in strategic junctions of essential services, the judicial branch and autonomous regulation have taken control of regulating and coping with strikes in essential services. The judicial branch's involvement has not been limited to injunctions proceedings in the labour courts. Tort actions in civil courts and public petitions filed with the Supreme Court acting as the High Court of Justice have been as important.

As a mode of regulation and intervention, the judicial branch has been scoring relatively high on all criteria. Using the concepts of proportionality and good faith, it has promulgated new rules for strikes in essential services, given preference to autonomous regulation, issued injunctions with caution, and used court hearings as a platform to facilitated negotiation. The approach adopted by the judicial branch has secured a proper level of service while preserving the principles of free and effective collective bargaining, in compliance with international standards. Finally, it appears as if procedurally, the intervention by the judicial branch has achieved a high level of acceptability.

It is worth emphasizing that both the High Court of Justice and the labour courts have achieved these objectives by adopting a non-orthodox *modus operandi*. Instead of performing their traditional role as adjudicators, High Court of Justice and the labour courts have undertaken the role of mediators and conciliators with clout. Before exercising judgement, the justices and judges have invested substantial efforts and resources in trying to bring about a settlement. At times it has been adjudication by consent. But more often, the courts have actively facilitated negotiation not about the legal dispute which brought the parties to court, but about the strikes' underlying dispute.

78. For instance, they were not limited to essential services in the strict meaning and an alternative means to promote and protect employees' interests were not provided.

Bibliography

Ben Israel, Ruth/Mironi, Mordehai, The Role of Neutrals in the Resolution of Interest Disputes in Israel, Comparative Labor Law and Policy Journal, 1989, 10, 356 et seqq.

Cohen, Yinon/Haberfeld, Yitchak/Kristal Tali/Mundlak, Guy, The State of Organized Labour in Israel, Journal of Labour Research, 2007, 28, 255 et seqq.

Cohen, Yinon/Haberfeld, Yitchak/Mundlak, Guy/Saporta, Ishak, Unpacking Union Density: Membership and Coverage in the Transformation of the Israeli IR System, Industrial Relations, 2003, 42, 692 et seqq.

Davidov, Guy, The Proportionality Principle in Labour Law, Tel Aviv University Law Review, 2008, 31, 5 et seqq.

Goldberg, Menachem, Labour Law in Israel, 1982

Kochan, Thomas A./Lipsky, David B./Newhart, Mary/Benson, Alan, The Long-Haul Effects of Interest Arbitration: The Case of New York State's Taylor Law, Industrial and Labor Relations Review, 2010, 63, 565 et seqq.

Mancur, Olson, The Logic of Collective Action Public Goods and The Theory of Groups, 1965

Mironi, Mordehai, Back-to-Work Emergency Orders: Government Intervention in Labour Disputes in Essential Services, Hebrew University Law Review, 1986, 15, 350 et seqq.

Mironi, Mordehai, Compulsory Arbitration – 80 Years of Public Debate, Labour Law Yearbook, 1990, 1, 119 et seqq.

Mironi, Mordehai, Experimenting with ADR as a Means for Peaceful Resolution of Interest Labour Disputes in Public Health Care – A Case Study, Law and Contemporary Problems, 2011, 71, 201 et seqq.

Mironi, Mordehai, Mediation and Strategic Change, 2008

Mironi, Mordehai, The Arbitration of Labour Disputes – A Critical Study of The Institute of Voluntary Arbitration in The Public Service, 1988

Raday, Frances, The 'Unprotected' Strike: The Settlement of Labour Disputes (Amendment No. 2) Law, 1972 and its Application, Israel Law Review, 1977, 12, 86 et seqq.

Safran, Nadav, The United States and Israel, 1963.

Subaroo, A. V., The Impact of Binding Interest Arbitration on Negotiation Process and Outcome, Journal of Conflict Resolution, 1978, 22, 79 et seqq.

Zamir, Itzhak, The Law of Labour Disputes, Israel Law Review, 1974, 9, 548 et seqq.

CHAPTER 10

Italy

Adriana Topo

1 GENERAL BACKGROUND: COUNTRY PROFILE

1.1 The Legal Framework of Labour

1.1.1 Constitutional Background

The Constitution enacted in 1948 after a long dictatorship under Benito Mussolini, the Prime Minister who came to power in 1922,[1] is the foundation of the Italian legal system. The Constitution supports a republican form of government, in compliance with the rejection of the monarchic regime after a referendum held in 1948. The Constitution confers the sovereignty to Parliament. The President of the Republic has powers aimed at guaranteeing the balance between the constitutional bodies. Notably, the Italian Constitution does not only regulate civic and political liberties and political institutions but also economic and social rights. Labour is at the core of the constitutional chart.[2] Labour is mentioned in the opening of the Constitution, where Art. 1 states that 'Italy is a democratic republic founded on labour.'[3] Art. 4 recognises the right to work for all citizens. Interrelated with the right to work is the duty for citizens to cooperate to the material and moral progress of the society.[4] The right to work has therefore a fundamental value in the constitutional political project, which supports strategies aimed at protecting employees and workers whether under a subordinate or independent contract. The Titolo III of the Constitution details the basic protection for labour in few Articles. Courts have applied these Articles without the mediation of specific statutes in many occasions. One can find a very important example of the straight application by Courts of constitutional labour principles in the matter of remuneration. On the basis of Art. 36 of the Constitution, the remuneration ought to be proportional to the quantity and also to the quality of the work performed.[5] It is worth noting that Italy has not yet adopted a statute that details what is the minimum wage in every sector. As a consequence it had seemed problematic for an employee to sue an employer in Court in order to challenge a contractual agreement setting a wage apparently unfair. Civil Courts have nevertheless overcome the absence of legislation on minimum wage retrieving Art. 2099 of the Civil Code adopted in 1942 and clearly inspired by the fascist ideology on labour.[6]

1. *Lyttelton*, 2004.
2. *Mengoni*, 1998.
3. *Scognamiglio*, 2010, 113 et seq.
4. *Mancini*, 1975, 199.
5. *Gragnoli*, 2012, 1375 et seq.
6. *Martone*, 2010, 63 et seq.

1.1.2 *Remnant of Corporative Regulation*

1.1.2.1 Impact on Individual Cases

Article 2099 of the Civil Code allows Courts to settle an individual claim on the right to a fair pay simply by applying the sectorial national collective agreement. In order to understand the mechanics of the trial, it should be remembered that under the fascist regime every industrial conflict had to be settled through a collective agreement to be applied to the whole sector workforce or through a Court of Appeal's binding decision, if parts could not agree on the economic matter. The judge could then easily decide on a labourer's claim for a fair wage, because the solution of the case was in the necessary application of the existing, in the circumstances, collective agreement or the application of the Court of Appeal's award setting the dispute on interests. This regulation enabling Courts to decide on industrial disputes does not operate any more. Courts nevertheless still apply Article 2099 in claims about pay, even if the employer and the employee are not, in the circumstances, bound by to a collective agreement. The Italian regime based on the economic individual freedom to negotiate (Art. 41 Constitution) does not allow Courts to settle individual or collective disputes on interests. Notwithstanding these limits, Courts argue that the necessary application of the constitutional right to a sufficient and proportionate remuneration obliges judges to decide on what is, in the circumstances, a fair wage. How do judges decide what is fair? Courts actually take inspiration from tariffs provided for by collective agreements applied in the same sector or in similar sector, and this is exactly what Art. 2099 c.c. provides for in these cases.[7] Art. 2099, enacted in a totally different context, is fundamental in order to guarantee the right to a fair wage. The example on the fair pay is useful to understand the method of interpretation applied by Italian Courts to the industrial relations after the fall of the fascist regime. Courts have adapted, wherever possible, the corporative regulation of labour to the new constitutional principles.

1.1.2.2 Impact on Collective Cases

The contextualization of rules enacted during the corporative period has happened also in the matter of strike. As this essay will discuss in the following chapters, for a long time after the enactment of the new republican constitution, and notably since 1990, the regulation of strike was based on laws that had been adopted in 1930 and therefore clearly in a different political climate. This fact seems a paradox if one considers that strike was at that time a criminal offence. The Italian Criminal Code enacted in 1930, and still generally in effect, provided for with rules that punished strike and lock out as crimes against the national

7. Cass., 11 January 2012, no. 153, DL Rivista critica di diritto del lavoro, 2012, 200.

economy.[8] The Criminal Code punished strike and lock out distinguishing different situations on the basis of the strikers' typical aims. The list of crimes is not just historically interesting. In the legal jargon, operators still qualify an industrial action using the legal categories provided for by the Criminal Code. Courts specifically qualify a strike and lock out in respect of the aims of the agents interpreted on the basis of the criteria adopted by the Criminal Code. There are economic actions, solidarity actions, political strikes, The Constitutional Court from 1960 has produced a string of decisions assessing to what extent a strike aimed at a specific purpose is protected by the Constitution that guarantees the right to strike under Art. 40.[9] The clash between a perspective that considers industrial action as an individual fundamental right[10] and a perspective that qualifies a strike as a criminal offence is evident. The Constitutional Court had nonetheless to interpret criminal norms on strike in order to draw the limits of the right to strike,[11] which the Constitution does not regulate in detail. The Criminal Code also punished the 'desertion' of a public service or a service of public necessity on the basis of a provision that was interpreted as applicable to industrial actions.[12] In 1990, the provision relating to the desertion of a public service was abolished by statute when Parliament enacted the first regulation in the matter of strike in the public services on the basis of Legge no. 146/1990. This is the only criminal norm applicable on strike that has been abolished by statute. It is worth noting that the Parliament has adopted a statute only on the matter of strike in the essential services. The regulation of a normal strike is still based on the string of principles of law produced by the Corte constitutional in the assessment of the coherence between the Constitution and the criminal rules prohibiting strike.

2 COLLECTIVE LABOUR RELATIONS

2.1 Freedom of Association and Collective Bargaining: The Italian Paradox

One may find that many Italian statutes make reference to collective agreements as a way for regulating specific profiles of the employment relationship, in situations where by contrast the individual negotiation is forbidden.[13] Italy nonetheless still lacks a general regulation by statute on collective bargaining. In Italy does not exist a legal regulation of the private sector industrial relations, nor

8. *Santoni*, 2011, 3 et seq.
9. *Suppiej*, 1989, 25.
10. *Santoni*, 2011, 3 et seqq.
11. *Topo*, 1997, 203 et seqq.
12. Artt 330 and 333 Criminal Code.
13. A good example is the 'Testo Unico sulla Rappresentanza Confindustrial - CGIL, CISL, UIL' dated 10 January 2014, https://www.cisl.it/grandi-temi/rappresentanza/769-testo-unico-rappresentanza.html last visited on 24 March 2014.

a definition of collective agreement. As this essay pointed out above, the freedom of association and the freedom of collecting bargaining, which is theoretically associated with the freedom of association, are nevertheless fundamental principles of the Italian regulation on labour, because the Constitution provides for the freedom of association under Art. 39.[14] First paragraph of Art. 39, bestows freedom of unionization to individual subjects and collective agents. The second, third, and fourth paragraphs, of Art. 39, all regulate a procedure meant to extend the application of a national collective agreement on to a pool of employees under certain conditions. These Paragraphs are referred to as the 'second part' of Art. 39, and secondary legislation is necessary to make them applicable. The secondary legislation has not yet been adopted. The Second part of Art. 39 is nonetheless effective by not allowing the Parliament to regulate collective bargaining on the basis of principles other than the ones compliant with Art. 39 of the Constitution. There are few reasons explaining why Art. 39 of the Constitution was not regulated by secondary legislation. The second part of Art. 39 was detailed by secondary legislation, on the one side, because of the opposition of the most prominent national unions. These unions have opposed a detailed regulation of the process of collective bargaining, arguing that the constitutional process would have imposed an assessment of unions' membership in order to weight unions' right to participate in the decisional process. Only recently CGIL (Confederazione Generale Italiana del Lavoro) has changed its opinion on this issue but union representation has to be weighed, on the basis of the legal regulation, only in the public sector since collective bargaining has been introduced as the necessary method for regulating working conditions.[15] A theoretical argument was nevertheless also opposed to the enactment of the second part of Art. 39.[16] The second part imposes unions with duties that were similarly adopted by the fascist legislation, such as the unions' registration in a special register, the necessary assessment on the association's statute by the administrative authority in order to check the fairness of internal rules. Scholars[17] have therefore argued against the implementation of the registration rule on the basis of the incompatibility between this rule and the principle of freedom of unionization, which would not permit any interference with internal statutes and decisions adopted by trade unions.

2.1.1 The Regulation of Collective Bargaining

In the absence of a legal regulation, the discipline of collective bargaining can be found on the one side, in framework agreements negotiated by the most

14. *Giugni*, 1979, 257 et seq.; *Bellocchi*, 2014, 3 et seq.
15. See www.cgil.it/news/Default.aspx?ID = 21954, last visited on 1st December 2017. Proia, 2014, 608.
16. *Ghezzi*, 1963, 191 et seq.
17. *Bellocchi*, 2014, 95 et seq.

representative unions and employers' associations. These framework agreements regulate the very process of collective bargaining and industrial relations. Courts' decision on claims concerning the application of a collective agreement in specific circumstances set, on the other side, the precedents by the judiciary bodies that integrate the framework. The matter is eventually regulated by the combination of the regulation adopted by unions and employers' associations and the Courts' set of decisions on the same topic. However, one should point out that interestingly the regulation of few fundamental aspects of collective bargaining is still based on Civil Code's norms. The Code specifically regulates the corporative collective agreements. These agreements were substantially statutes. The application of corporative rules on collective bargaining is nevertheless still admitted by Courts today, whenever these rules can be interpreted in compliance with the principle of freedom of association, bestowed by the republican constitution, as explained above.[18]

2.1.2 Collective Bargaining and Collective Agreements

Collective relations are common practice at national level but also at local (regional or provincial) and plant level. As pointed out above the shared wide interpretation of the freedom of association means that industrial agents are free to decide at what level or levels regulating labour so that the regulation of the level or levels of negotiation is a typical content of framework agreements between employers' associations and unions. These are typical agreements involving more unions on the one side and more employers' associations on the other side. Normally these framework agreements regulating industrial relations apply to a wide range of businesses.[19] Besides, Italy has a long tradition, starting before the republican constitution, of national collective bargaining for most of the productive sectors. Lately since the start of the new millennium the law has provided incentives in order to enhance collective bargaining also at firm level so that businesses would possibly adapt the regulation of work to specific production models and strategies, for example on the matter of working time.[20] As we have already pointed out above, the hierarchy, between local or plant negotiations and national negotiation, is not regulated by statute. The link between agreements operating at different levels in practice is nevertheless frequently a matter for the framework agreements, described in the paragraph above. There may be sectors where a plant agreement is the only agreement applied to the workforce. This situation is not frequent and there is nonetheless an important example, which is the car maker FIAT's collective agreement. Fiat withdrew

18. *Proia/Gambacciani*, 2014, 595 et seqq.
19. *Maio*, 2014, 446 et seqq.
20. *Lassandari*, 2014, 717 et seqq.

from Confindustria (Italian associations of manufacturers) in 2009 and has since then started a process of collective bargaining on its own. The collective agreement, that has been agreed with unions but with Fiom-CGIL (the metal-workers' trade union linked to CGIL), is now applied to all of Fiat's workers in Italy and is considered by scholars both a plant agreement and also a national agreement given the presence of Fiat factories on different areas of the Italian territory.[21] The lacking of a general regulation by statute for collective bargaining and collective agreements means that collective agreements are interpreted as contracts not different from the commercial ones. Few specific norms on collective bargaining have been enacted and regulate very peculiar situations. One finds a good example of a peculiar regulation in Art. 8, Law no. 148 of 2011. This norm regulates the effectiveness of plant level agreements. The specific norm makes these agreements binding for all plant's employees once the plant agreement was submitted to a workforce referendum gaining the majority of votes in the poll.[22] This regulation that applies only to agreements regulating specific matters confirms nevertheless the prevailing approach to industrial relations based on the principle of no-interference and no-regulation by statute. An important exception to the principle of the limited efficacy of collective agreements is the collective agreement that sets the essential services to be performed by the workforce in case of strike. These agreements are in fact binding for all the workforce on the basis of their incorporation into the businesses' operational codes of practice adopted by employers in order to regulate organization of work in the undertaking.[23]

As the author pointed out above, Courts apply to collective bargaining also the rule on corporative collective agreements embedded in the Civil Code, if these norms are coherent with the Constitutional principles on labour. A good example to enlightening this method of interpretation is the application by Courts of Art. 2066. This Article provides for a fundamental rule in the perspective of safeguarding the effectiveness of collective bargaining. The Article says that individual contracts are not allowed to derogate terms set by collective agreements applicable to the workforce, unless the specific individual agreement is more favourable to employees. Courts have applied this Article to collective agreements even if this Article was adopted under the corporative regime that compared collective agreements to legal norms therefore regulating their legal efficacy.[24] Courts' decisions have also been fundamental in order to safeguard the effectiveness of a collective agreement to the whole workforce at

21. *De Luca*, 2010, 797 et seqq.
22. See *Lassandari*, 2014, 717 et seqq.
23. This point was made clear in 1996 by Corte costituzionale, 18 October 1996, no. 344, in http://www.giurcost.org/decisioni/1996/0344s-96.html, last visited on 26 March 2018.
24. *Proia/Gambacciani*, 2014, 612.

least on the matter of remuneration.[25] This is an issue, which the lack of regulation by statute on collective bargaining, imposes Courts to decide; an issue that has been approached through the interpretation of the Code civil and notably of Art. 2099 of the Civil Code, on the matter of wage, in connection with Art. 36 of the Constitution[26], as pointed out above.

2.2 Collective Bargaining in the Public Sector

2.2.1 Scope of Collective Bargaining: Public Servants

Besides the private sector, collective bargaining is a typical instrument for the regulation of labour relationships in the public sector. Not all public employees are subject to regulation by collective agreement. Members of the military force, police officers of the national body, members of the diplomatic body, members of the judiciary, university professors and university researchers, home office officers such as 'prefects' are not subject to collective bargaining. The fact that these categories do not have the right to collective bargaining does not mean, on the one side, that job terms and conditions of work are not regulated on the basis of negotiation between the public authority (the Government) and representatives of the bodies' members. In the circumstances terms of employment are incorporated into secondary legislation that, differently to collective bargaining, applies to all members of the bodies and not just the ones represented by the negotiator. Eventually it is worth noting that only a few categories, notably members of the military force and police officers, are expressly not allowed to strike, and only member of the armed forces were not allowed to join unions on the basis of Art. 1475 of Legislative Decree no. 66/2010. Considering the recent decisions by the ECtHR on Art. 11 of the ECHR,[27] in French cases, it seemed nevertheless unlawful the limit to join unions provided for by the law for the

25. *Ibid.*, 619.
26. See *supra* Section 1.1.
27. Cf. the observation by *Laulom/Leclerc* in the French report (*supra*) that in ECtHR, *Matelly v. France* (Req. n° 10609/10) 2 October 2014 and ECtHR, *Adefdromil v. France* (Req. n° 32131/09), 2 October 2014, related to the members of the armed forces freedom of association, 'The Court (ECtHR) concluded that, while the exercise by military personnel of freedom of association can be subject to legitimate restrictions, a blanket ban on forming or joining a trade union encroached on the very essence if this freedom, and was as such prohibited by the Convention (ECHR). The Court's judgment holds that an absolute prohibition may not be imposed on trade unions in the armed forces. However, it specifies that restrictions (even significant ones) may be placed on the exercise of freedom of association by military personnel, since the specific nature of the armed forces' mission requires that trade union activity be adapted in consequence. Nonetheless, those restrictions must not deprive service personnel of the general right of association'.

Italian armed forces, and in fact the Italian Constitutional Court has removed the unlawful limit in 2018 on the basis of decision no. 120.[28]

2.2.2 Public Employees

The largest section of public employees do not belong to the list of officers named above: for example the staff of governmental departments, the staff of local public authorities, teachers and administrative staff in state schools and state universities, doctors, nurses and administrative staff in the health service, fall under a different special legislation This legislation enacted in 1993 and amended many times[29] regulates on the basis of employment contractual rules and on the basis of collective bargaining the relationship between employers and employees. The most striking difference between the private and the public sector is the fact that the law regulates the process of collective bargaining and the efficacy of the collective agreement in the public sector. All employees are submitted to regulation by collective agreement. The application of the collective bargaining process into the public sector has been achieved as an important success by unions gradually starting in the late '60 of the last century, and has become the general rule in 1993.[30] Before the implementation of this method of regulation, secondary legislation was the legal instrument meant to regulate public employees' condition of work. Trade unions promoted industrial actions in order to negotiate first pay and subsequently other terms of work. It is worth remembering that one of the reasons behind the decision of the Government of the time to allow collective bargaining in the public sector, as a general rule for negotiating wages, was the issue of strikes.[31] The statute that initially regulated collective bargaining in the public sector excluded from the negotiation unions that had not yet adopted internal binding rules for member on how to behave in case of strikes in the essential services.[32] The public pressure on Government to reduce the impact of strikes in the essentials service was then a reason for overcoming the long-time approach by Government and trade unions on the matter and regulate the right to strike as prescribed by Art. 40 of the Constitution, which states that this right ought to be performed in compliance with legal norms regulating it. The Government, instead of adopting a statute with detailed rules on strikes in the essential services, decided to adopt a legal incentive for unions, so that unions had to take measures to regulate strikes through codes of conduct in order to participate in the collective bargaining process.

28. https://www.cortecostituzionale.it/actionSchedaPronuncia.do?anno = 2018&numero = 120, last visited on 9 September 2018.
29. Decree Legislative, 30 March 2001, no. 165 regulates today the employment relationship and collective bargaining in the public sector for all employees with the exception of the Public Servants as defined below.
30. *Carinci*, 2014, 981 et seq.
31. See Law 29 March 1983, no. 93, sub Art. 11.
32. *Romagnoli*, 1986.

3 THE RIGHT TO STRIKE

3.1 The Right to Strike in General

3.1.1 The Definition of Strike and the Right to Substitute Employees on Strike

The Italian constitution bestows the right to strike on the basis of Art. 40. The wording in Art. 40 is similar to the French Constitutional norm on strike.[33] Art. 40 of the Constitution is concise. It states that the right to strike shall be exercised in conformity with the legislation that governs the right. The Constitutional regulation of strikes does not define strike nor dictates principles, as the second part of Art. 39 of the Constitution does, to address the legislation to be adopted by the Parliament in order to detail how and in what circumstance one is allowed to strike.[34] The word strike was not new to the Italian legal language because strike and lock out were considered criminal offences during the fascist age. The definition of strike under the republican constitution was therefore influenced by the previous interpretation of strike. Courts agree that a strike is the act of abandoning work during working time in order to protect professional interests.[35] A strike itself is an individual action. Strike is nevertheless performed in order to protect interests that are shared by a group of workers. A large or a small group of workers can lawfully strike. It is not necessary that all of the group's members take on an industrial action in order to qualify the abandoning of work as strike. Under the Courts' interpretation not all industrial actions are strikes and the freedom to strike just refers to the abandoning of work by employees with the aim of protecting workers' interests. This interpretation was adopted by the Constitutional Court since 1962[36] and confirmed later in 1969[37] and again in 1974.[38] Also the Law no. 146 of 1990[39] regulating strike in the essential services gives the definition of a strike as the 'suspending of the act of performing'.[40] The employee does not have the right to partially suspend his work in order to perform only some tasks, because this behaviour would be an interference with the managing power of the employer, so that not performing certain tasks with the aim of protesting would be a breach of contract. Instead the employee has the right to strike for long or short periods of time and also only on overtime.

33. Constitution of the French Republic, 27 October 1946, Preamble Par. 7.
34. This situation is similar to the French situation regarding the regulation of strike. See *supra*, chapter by *Laulom/Leclerc*.
35. *Santini*, 2011, 83 et seqq.
36. Corte costituzionale, 28 December 1962, no. 123, Foro italiano, 1963, I, c.1.
37. Corte costituzionale, 17 March 1969, no. 31, Foro italiano, 1969, I, c. 795.
38. Corte costituzionale, 14 January 1974, no. 1, Foro italiano, 1974, I, c. 299.
39. Law 15 June 1990, no. 146.
40. Art. 2 bis, par. 1 and art. 8, par. 1, Law no. 146 of 1990.

Employees working on piece-work can lawfully relent production not nevertheless below the minimum standard.[41] A strike can be performed in various ways. Unions and workers are not required to give notice of the industrial action. Notice is a duty for unions only in the essential services, as this essay will analyse in the forthcoming chapters. As such, sudden strikes are lawful.[42] Hiccup strikes and chessboard strikes are also lawful. The only limitation for a strike is the effective damage suffered by people and by factory machineries, situation which happens, for example, when the suspension of production makes machineries and working tools no longer useable after the strike.[43] It's nevertheless worth noting that the employer might use employees that are not taking part in the industrial action in order to limit damages to the business activity during the suspension of work by part of the workforce.[44] In the essential services, the Constitutional Court[45] has therefore declared as compliant with the right to strike the specific rules[46] permitting the public administration to substitute courts' clerks and registrars on strike because the substitution prevents damages caused by the industrial actions. What is not permitted to the employers is the hiring of new staff in order to simply substitute employees on strike when the contract that the employer would apply is a short term contract, a temporary contract through agency, or an 'intermittente' contract, which is a sort of "zero hours" contract.

3.1.2 Classification of Strikes

For the absence of a statute on strike, the Constitutional Court has classified strikes according to the aim pursued in the circumstances by employees through the industrial action and on the basis of the definition adopted by the Criminal Code.[47] The typical aim pursued through the strike is the obtaining of better working conditions. This type of strike and the lock out meant to resist this claim were regulated as a crime by Art. 502 of the Criminal Code. The Constitutional Court declared since the early 1960s that Art. 502 is inconsistent with the Constitutional system and the Court of Cassazione[48] had already taken the same solution. A strike is legitimate when it pursues aims such as applying pressure on public authorities for the protection of employees' economic interests embedded

41. *Santini*, 2011, 130
42. Corte costituzionale, 28 December 1962, no. 124, Massimario di giurisprudenza del lavoro, 1962, 416.
43. Corte costituzionale, 28 December 1962, no. 124, quoted at nt. 31. Lately, Cass.17 December 2004, no. 23552, Foro italiano, 2005, I, c. 2774. Santini Fabrizia, Le forme di sciopero, quoted at not 24, at 119.
44. Cass., 13 March 1986, no. 1701, Massimario di giurisprudenza del lavoro, 1986, 336.
45. Corte costituzionale, 23 July 1980, no. 125, Foro italiano, 1980, I, c. 355.
46. Art. 34 D.P.R. 15 December 1959 no. 1229, and Art. 74, Law 23 October 1960 no. 1196.
47. *Santoni*, 2011, 52.
48. Cass., 7 June 1952, no. 1628, Foro italiano, 1953, I, c. 355.

in the principles of the part I, chapter III of the Constitution.[49] This situation is named "political economic strike" whereby the employer does not have the power to bargain with unions on the matter at stake, and public institutions, such as the Parliament, have the power to do so. A good example is a strike with the aim of ameliorating public pensions or increasing health and safety cover or public housing policies as well fiscal policies and the reduction of taxes. If a case like this occurs in the essential public services unions have nevertheless the duty to give notice to the employer[50] of the strike as they generally have, regardless the purpose of the action. The Constitutional Court has not declared Art. 505 of the Criminal Code, concerning strike in support of other categories of workers (sympathy strike), as contrary to the constitution and has referred lower Courts the competence to decide if in a given circumstance there is a significant link between the categories taking industrial actions, so that support by one category has a meaningful purpose in the circumstances.[51] Besides, the Criminal Code regulates also the purely political strike framed as a crime by Art. 503. The aim of a purely political strike is contesting the policy taken in given circumstances by the Government or other political institution, such the case when workers criticize foreign politics or the participation in a military action. Courts consider purely political strike as a situation differing from an economic-political strike, which happens when employees aim at promoting political reforms that impact on their economic or professional interests.[52] The Constitutional Court, reversing its original approach, has eventually declared Art. 503 of Criminal Code, on political strike, unconstitutional[53], because of the contrast between the freedom to take part in a national debate and the limit to political action. For the Courts political strike gives in fact 'voice' to citizens.[54] The freedom to strike for political reasons cannot be subject to interferences by the Government. It is nevertheless unclear on the basis of the constitutional rules if an employee taking part in a political strike has also a 'right' to strike in respect to the employer. Theoretically, it is in fact possible to distinguish between the freedom to strike and the right to strike, which is the immunity in respect to the possible reaction by the employer, when an employee does not work in order to strike. Italian Courts treat strike as a fundamental right through which workers convey their 'voice', in the Hirschman sense, on all the matters that they collectively consider as relevant. The wide application of the freedom to strike, which allows worker and employees to suspend work in order to express their opinion on professional and political issues, free from any interference from public powers, does not mean

49. Corte costituzionale, 14 January 1974, no. 1, quoted nt. 27.
50. Corte costituzionale, 10 June 1993, no. 276, Foro italiano, 1993, I, c. 2401.
51. Corte costituzionale, 28 December 1962, no. 123, Foro italiano, 1963, I. c. 1.
52. Corte costituzionale 14 January 1974, no. 1, Massimario di giurisprudenza del lavoro, 1974, p.11.
53. Corte costituzionale, 27 December 1974, no. 290, Massimario di giurisprudenza del lavoro, 1975, 1.
54. *Meny*, 2016, 621 links strike to the 'voice' function. On the voice function: *Hirschman*, 1970.

that strike has no impact on the employment contract. Could then an employer lawfully dismiss an employee for taking part in a merely political strike? For sure a political strike still falls under the Criminal code, if employees take industrial action in order to subvert the existing legitimate constitutional order (see *supra* note 51). It is worth noting that nevertheless a strike in the essential services without previous notice is lawful if the strike is meant to oppose a revolution against the existing constitutional order.[55] The revolutionary strike is anyway an uncommon situation, subjected to very specific if not exceptional rules. It's worth remembering that the Constitutional Court's arguments on strike could support the conclusion that the right to strike does not cover all industrial actions. It is nevertheless also undisputable that more recently the Court of Cassazione has adopted a perspective on the basis of which, independently from the strikers' aims in the circumstances, whatever the alleged purposes, workers have the freedom to strike and also the right not to be dismissed for their participation in industrial action,[56] on the ground of a wider interpretation of the freedom to strike. The Italian regulation therefore differs sensibly, for example, from the English regulation of strike where, 'at common law, the employer has entirely free discretion to dismiss an employee who has taken industrial action by reason of breach of a fundamental term of the contract of employment; although an employer may elect not to do so. Employees in England are therefore dependent on statutory intervention to provide for protection from dismissal (TULRCA 1992, ss 237, 238 and 238A)'.[57]

3.1.3 Balancing the Right to Strike with Other Fundamental Rights

As this essay has pointed out below the Constitutional Court has integrated with a body of decisions the basic regulation of strike adopted by the Constitution. Some of these decisions are based on the argument that the freedom to strike cannot overcome other freedoms and fundamental rights such as, for example, the right to be healthy and alive. Strikes that compromise other fundamental rights embedded in the Constitution are not lawful. Among the competing different interests Courts have acknowledged also the employer's freedom to continue the economic activity after the end of the industrial conflict, which means that a strike that compromises the economic resilience of the undertaking is unlawful.[58] As a consequence, in some circumstances or for some categories

55. Art. 2, par. 7, Law no. 146/1990. On the issue: Santoro Passarelli Giuseppe, Questioni aperte dello sciopero nei servizi pubblici essenziali: Sciopero politico-economico, sciopero politico, sciopero generale e preavviso, Diritto delle relazioni industriali, no.1, 2008.
56. Cass., 21 August 2004, no. 16515, www.iusexplorer, last visited on 24 March 2018. *Silvana*, 2017, 347; *Gino*, 1968, 220. For a comparative perspective on strike that enlights this difference: *Wedderburn*, 1991, 74 seq.
57. Cf. *Novitz* in the UK report, *infra*.
58. Among the recent decisions see Cass., 3 December 2015, no. 24653, www.iusexplorer last visited on 24 March 2018.

of workers, strike is forbidden o limited. The right to take action has to surrender in front of the duty of solidarity, recalled by Article 2 of the Constitution,[59] and therefore has to be balanced with other right of similar rank.

3.2 Actions Different from Strike

Types of industrial actions different from strike are not covered by the Constitutional protection. Behaviours meant at not collaborating with the employer and his/her staff, obstructionism, and behaviours meant to relent the business throughout the captious application of rules and procedures are not considered as strike.[60] Sabotage is not protected as an industrial action and the rule that punishes it as crime,[61] Art. 508, par. 2, of the Criminal Code is still applicable. Also the occupation of the plant by employees during the strike is a crime falling under Art. 8, par. 1, Criminal Code. The Constitutional Court has made it clear that for the purpose of striking employees do not have to necessarily occupy the workplace.[62] If they remain in the workplace during the strike, employees are not punished,[63] on the basis of their aim is not the interfering with the business. In the latter circumstance, where employees occupy the plant without the aim of interfering with production, they may be nevertheless punished for trespass to land on the basis of Art. 633 Criminal Code, except if their staying is very short. The right to strike does not cover the violent picketing[64] that happens when strikers embrace each other in a human chain with the purpose of stopping people from going to work, so that other employees have to break the chain to enter the workplace, or when strikers threaten with the menace of a violence other employees that do not want to strike. The blocking of goods from entering and exiting the plant is also a crime falling under Art. 610 Criminal Code, and is not covered by the right to strike. Other behaviours not covered by the right to strike is the boycotting of good produced by an employer with the intention of convincing other not to purchase them or persuading others not to accept job offers from the employer (Art. 507 Criminal Code). Blocking roads in order to protest and making excessive noise in a public space with the aim of protesting is not lawful. The employer and the public may react to these behaviours by calling police officers and asking the Court for an injunction to stop them depending of the size and length of the protest.

59. Corte costituzionale, 3 August 1976, no. 222, Foro italiano, 1976, I, c. 2297; Corte costituzionale, 12 January 1977 no. 4, Giurisprudenza costituzionale, 1977, I, 20; Corte costituzionale, 8 July 1992, no. 317, Foro italiano, 1992, I, c. 2904.
60. *Luciani*, 2011, 187.
61. Art. 508, par. 2, Criminal Code. Corte costituzionale, 17 July 1975, no. 220, Massimario di giurisprudenza del lavoro, 1975, 282.
62. Corte costituzionale, 17 July 1975, no. 220.
63. On the basis of Art. 508 Criminal Code.
64. *Luciani*, 2011, 190.

It's worth noting that employees have nevertheless the right to assembly[65] in the workplace whenever the workforce occupied in the factory is exceeds fifteen employees (or five employees in an agricultural business) and the purpose of the meeting is to debate labour issues. In practice employees' representatives typically call an assembly during strikes so as to 'occupy' part of the factory without incurring a potential crime. These assemblies may continue after working time or be held during the strike and in this case the employer cannot report any unlawful occupation of the property. Furthermore the employer has a duty to make the room available and fit for meeting during the assembly, providing for the utilities that may be required for the purpose.

3.3 The Right to Strike in the Essential Services

The difference between the regulation of strike in general and the regulation of strikes in the essential services is remarkable. Courts have developed rules on strike over a long time through a set of judgments, whereas the right to strike in the essential services is regulated by a statute enacted in 1990 (Law 15 Jun1990, no. 146/), when the practice of self-regulation by unions had already failed to produce a satisfactory protection for users of such services.[66] On the basis of the interpretation that qualifies a strike as a fundamental right,[67] strike is not permitted only in few exceptional situations that this essay will analyse below. Strikes therefore are also permitted in the essential services. Law no.146/1990 lists the constitutional rights that ought to be balanced with the right to strike. The fundamental rights enlisted in the statute are the right to life, the right to health and to personal freedom and security, the freedom to travel, the right to assistance and to social security, the right to education and the freedom to communication.[68] Subsequently the statute lists the essential services submitted to the application of special rules. These services are: the health service, the service of waste collection and disposal, the supplying of energy and primary goods, the service of justice, protection of the environment and surveillance on museums, transports, payment by banks of pensions and wages, education, the postal service, telecommunication services and public information on radio and television. The list is open to any other service that may be instrumental for the protection of the fundamental rights already listed in Art. 1, par.1. It does not matter if essential services are be provided for by enterprises or public agencies. Law no. 146/1990 regulates the industrial action regardless of the nature, public or private, of the employer. Law no. 146/1990 applies also to public agencies or

65. Law 15 May 1970 no. 300, Art. 20. Corso Fulvio, I diritti sindacali, in Proia Giampiero (ed.), Organizzazione sindacale e contrattazione collettiva, Trattato di diritto del lavoro, vol. II, 2014, 366.
66. *Pascucci*, 2011, 217 et seqq.; *Gaeta*, 2015, 161 et seqq.
67. *Santoni*, 2011, 17.
68. Law no. 146/1990, Art. 1, par.1.

private enterprises supplying goods or services to the employer that provide for essential services (Art. 13, lett. e).

3.3.1 Rules on Cooling Off and Arbitration Procedures

A very important issue in the regulation of strike in the essential service is the unions' duty to negotiate in order to prevent industrial conflicts. In order to prevent a strike the statute imposes a duty on employers and unions to regulate, in collective agreements, cooling off procedures and arbitration bodies meant to settle industrial conflicts.[69] Unions and employers ought to negotiate arbitration procedures on the basis of Art. 2, par. 2. If parts do not regulate arbitration procedures on the basis of collective agreements, the Commission that oversees industrial actions in the essential services,[70] now and thereafter the CGSSE, adopts a temporary regulation imposing the arbitration process. Employers and unions have a duty to activate and participate in the procedures before calling an industrial action. If they do not obey, they are submitted to sanctions by the CGSSE on the basis of Art. 4, par. 2. The arbitration process is not necessary when the strike is a political economic strike aimed at persuading the Government at adopting specific policies.

Generally speaking unions do not have any duty to give notice of a strike.[71] The duty to give notice is on the contrary one of the basic rules of the regulation of strike in the essential services. The written notice must be given at least ten days before the action and the communication must explain the reasons for the strike, the time length of the protest and also its operating methods (Art. 2, par 2). The duty falls on unions but workers do not lawfully strike if they take action in the absence of notice and information to the employer (Art. 4, par.1). Unions have to send the communication with the notice to the employer and to the public authority that has the power of issuing an injunction (*precettazione*) in case of strike. The public authority transmits the information to the CGSSE that starts monitoring the situation. The notice and the communication of the modalities of the industrial action is necessary for the employer in order to manage the situation and in order to organise the service during the industrial action. The employer also has the duty to alert and inform the public through the media, about the strike and the services that will be performed during the action, at least five days before the action. The workforce nevertheless does not have the duty to inform the employer whether or not they will take the action. The duty to give notice is excluded has an exception when the strike aims at protecting constitutional bodies or when the action is a reaction against situations of relevant damage to the security and health protection of workers. In these cases workers have to perform the essential services but they are not asked

69. *Topo*, 2004, no. 3, 351. *Pilati*, 2011, 277.
70. *Ferrari*, 2011, 419.
71. *Pilati*, 2011, 277.

to give notice of the protest (Art. 2, par. 7). Unions have to communicate the length of time during which the action will take place so that there cannot be strikes without a deadline. Also unions cannot give notice of more than one action at the same time because there must be an interval between the first strike and the second strike called by the same union.

3.3.2 *Cancellation of a Strike in the Essential Services*

The legislation enacted in 1990 was amended in 2000 and one of the aspects that the new legislation modified relates to the situation where a union, after having called a strike, cancel it. It is considered unfair practice to call a strike and then to cancel it without a reason (Art. 2, par. 6). The restriction to the right of calling an action is necessary in order to prevent strategies meant only at disrupting services with no consequences for the workforce that will continue to receive a wage for continuing to work. The cancellation of the action is fair when is communicated before the employer has already informed the public, and is always fair when, after the calling of a strike, unions and employers find an agreement that settles the dispute or the CGSSE or the authority with the power to issue an injunction invites the parties to suspend the strike (Art. 2, par. 6).

3.3.3 *The Definition by Collective Agreement of the Services That Have to Be Performed During a Strike in the Essential Services*

The wording 'essential services' does not only describe the rights that ought to be protected during an industrial conflict. Essential services also indicate that during an industrial action employees should be required to perform only what is strictly necessary in order not to jeopardize consumers' rights. Before the regulation by statute, the essential services were regulated in detail by an act of self-regulation adopted by trade unions or by collective agreements. Under the legislation adopted in 1990, the collective agreement between unions and employers is the most important legal instrument for the definition of the services that have to be performed during an industrial action (Art. 1, par. 2; Art. 2, paras 1 and 2). These collective agreements are agreements between public agencies or enterprises (or their associations) and trade unions (Art. 2, par. 2) at national level and also at local level. Typically agreements at national level demand to local agreements or plant agreements an even more specific regulation of the modality of the industrial actions in order to prevent very peculiar needs. The CGSSE evaluates if these agreements are adequate for the protection of fundamental rights listed by Law no. 146/1990. In case they are not adequate, CGSSE delivers a decision that details the activities that ought to be performed by employees and workers during the industrial action (Art. 13, lett. a). One might wonder if the regulation satisfies the constitutional principle embedded in Art. 40, of the Costituzione, that entrusts primary legislation the duty to limit the right to strike. The Constitutional Court has argued that the legal scheme is legitimate because regulation of strike on the basis of collective agreements fulfils the necessity of a very specific and detailed regulation for every specific sector.[72] Employers on the basis of the agreement may request employees to perform their job during a strike. Employers have to communicate to trade unions the name of employees required to work.[73]

Law no. 146/1990 nevertheless also specifies rules of behaviour that unions and employers have necessarily to agree on in order to negotiate an effective agreement on industrial actions, which means that the agreements must regulate some specific terms compliant with the legislation. One among the binding rules that relates to the agreements' content is the rule on the basis of which the workforce on duty during a strike should be on average no less than a third of the normal workforce. The service performed during a strike should be about the fifty per cent of a normal service. These rules aim at protecting the right to strike and nevertheless set only a theoretical balance because in many circumstances the situation may require a larger workforce and an almost complete service for not jeopardizing the safety of users of services (Art. 13, lett. a). Regarding the transport service to islands, for example, Law no. 146/1990 rules that transport of people and shipping of goods necessary for the people located on islands and all services instrumental to the latter have to be provided for during a strike (Art. 3), which means that the rule on the percentage of staff on duty cannot necessarily be a strict limit for the provider of services if the strict application of the percentage rule does not accommodate the population' needs. The fairness of the agreement is also conditional on the fact that parties accept that there must be an interval[74] between a strike and the call for the subsequent strike by the same union or even by a different union. It is not acceptable that a given essential service does not operate for a long time because of subsequent strikes, unless there is a valid alternative service for the users (Art. 13, lett. a). It is also evident that the call to strike by one union always limits another union's right to call a strike in the same sector for a given length of time. This rule seems to incentivise unions to compete through unfair practices meant at anticipating calls for strike that prevent other unions to promote an industrial actions. As the paper points out above, the Law no. 146/1990 forbids unions to give notice of a strike and then to cancel it after the employer has communicated the information to the public (Art. 2, par. 6) so that a specious use of the right to call an industrial action should be avoided.

3.3.4 *The Supervision on Strike by the CGSSE*

The CGSSE takes into consideration all relevant aspects in order to assess the lawfulness of the agreement on the essential services. Once an agreement has

72. Corte costituzionale, 18 October 1996, no. 344, Foro italiano, 1997, I, c. 381.
73. Cass., 23 June 2011, no. 13789, Giustizia civile, no. 11-12, 2012, 2698.
74. This is the 'rarefication' rule. See Art. 2, par. 2, Law no. 146/1990.

been negotiated, parties have to submit it to the CGSSE that assesses it through a complex process initially involving the relevant consumers' associations on whether the regulation is adequate to meet the needs of consumers. If the CGSSE approves the agreement, public administrations and private providers of essential services have the duty to apply the agreement to all the workforce independently of the fact that all employees are members of the unions that have agreed upon the regulation (Art. 2, par. 3). The general application of the agreement is the consequence of the participation of the CGSSE in the process meant at regulating strikes[75] so that the regulation of collective bargaining on strikes in the essential services does not violate the freedom of association. The statute also regulates the matter when parties do not reach an agreement. In this situation the CGSSE can promote a consultation in the work place in order to assess the opinion of the workforce on contentious terms. If parties do not reach an agreement or the CGSSE does not approve the possible agreement, the CGSSE indicates an alternative regulation and submits it to the unions and to the employer where both will have to decide whether to accept it within fifteen days (Art. 13, lett. A). If parties again do not accept the terms drawn up by the CGSSE, the latter enforces a temporary regulation, which is binding until parties do find an agreement on the regulation of strike (Art. 2, par. 2). Public administrations and private providers of services have the duty to affix the regulation in the workplace and the CGSSE may promote the publication of the regulation on the media. It is worth noting that the CGSSE' deliberations are also published on the Italian legal official journal, the 'Gazzetta Ufficiale' (Art. 13, let. l). Agreements and temporary regulations by the CGSSE can be modified and integrated if it is evident that it is reasonable to do it. The CGSSE also has the power to interpret its regulation and collective agreements when parties ask for it. The CGSSE is the body ruling in the field of strikes in the essential services through the exercise of its powers. The CGSSE has nine members selected by Parliament among experts in labour and constitutional law and industrial relations. Among CGSS's powers that have been described above, we find also other prerogatives. If the CGSS's opinion is that the industrial conflict could possibly be settled, the CGSSE, even after conciliation has been already been tried, is allowed to deliberate an adjournment of the strike in order to promote a new mediation between parties (Art. 13, lett. c). When conciliation fails, in the period of time between the communication of the strike and the suspension of work, the CGSSE assesses if cooling procedures have been applied by unions and employers and if not invites parties to postpone the strike in order to perform their duties relating to communication and arbitration. The CGSSE may also ask employer and public administrations providing directly for services to stop unlawful behaviours that are the ground for the industrial action (Art. 13, let. h). Finally the CGSSE has the power to communicate to the Prefect, who is the authority responsible for the '*precettazione*' (administrative injunction), that it is necessary to issue an

75. Corte costituzionale, 18 October 1996, no. 344, quoted at nt. 58.

injunction and detailing the injunction terms (Art. 13, let. h). The CGSSE monitors the industrial action and on the impulse of local authorities, or on the impulse of the users of services, or on its own, evaluates how unions, employers and workers, behave during the strike and if necessary, after a hearing with all parties involved, deliberate on sanctions to be applied in the circumstances (Art. 13, let. g, and Art. 4).

3.4.5 *The Fallback Option in Case of Strike in the Essential Services: the Administrative Authority Injunction*

The protection of fundamental rights during a strike in the essential services is not just in the hands of the CGSSE. The ultimate safety net is the administrative injunction (*precettazione*), which is the order by the administrative authority to end the industrial action.[76] Due to the lack of dedicated regulation on strike, the Constitutional Court had to assess if the regulation enacted during the fascist period and meant to regulate situations very different from strikes could be lawfully applied to strikes in the essential services in order to balance the right to take industrial action with the competing public rights.[77] The '*precettazione*' was at the time (and is now) the order by a public authority, such as the prefect and the city mayor, to make citizens take action without delay in order to protect health and safety and public order and security, whenever these goods and services are at risk in situations relating to housing, local security, and hygiene. The Court deciding about '*precettazione*' also made it clear that the contingent of people that is allowed to strike in an essential service depends on how many people are necessary in that service in order to guarantee not the full service and only the service which is necessary in order to protect fundamental rights. Thereafter authorities have used this legal tool in order to limit actions that are exceeding the bearable distress for consumers of services in the circumstances. Law no. 146/1990 has nevertheless regulated a peculiar 'precettazione', which applies only in the case of a strike in the essential services.

The authorities allowed to issue administrative injunctions in case of national conflicts are the Prime Minister (Presidente del Consiglio dei Ministri) and Ministers, and in case of local conflict the authority the Prefect (Central Government Agent at County level) (Art. 8, par 1). Whenever the interruption or the reduction of an essential service risks to damage fundamental rights enlisted in Art. 1 Law no. 146/1990, the authority has the duty to issue an injunction ordering to perform what is necessary in order to avoid any damage to constitutional rights. The injunction can be addressed to employees, self-employed workers and owners of small businesses and to unions and employers, or public authorities responsible for the providing of essential services. The

76. *Canavesi*, 2011, 542 et seqq.
77. Corte costituzionale, 12 January 1977, no. 4, in Massimario di giurisprudenza del lavoro, 1977, no. 1, 1, on Art. 20, Real Decree, 3 March 1934, no. 383.

process through which the authority issues the injunction is complex. The CGSSE takes the initiative to promote the issuing of the order but the authority is allowed to act independently in serious circumstances when there is an imminent risk of damage to users. In the latter situation the authority nevertheless has the duty to inform the CGSSE (Art. 8, par. 1). The authority has to invite parties to a hearing and has the duty to promote conciliation between them before the issuing of the order. Civil Courts have been very inflexible in interpreting these legal duties as all to be performed necessarily before the issuing of the injunction[78], so that the authority can issue the order only if the conciliation fails. The injunction dictates the activities that ought to be performed by staff and employers during the strike but can also suspend the strike or shorten the protest. The order is made public by the employer in the workplace through billposting and is also transmitted and published by media such as radio and television. The injunction is immediately self-executing but recipients are allowed to file a claim against it within seven days. The administrative tribunal suspend the injunction only if the claim is based upon reasonable arguments in order to allow the industrial action to continue. The tribunal has the power to also limit the suspension in regard only to the part of the injunction that exceeds what is necessary to protect fundamental rights (Art. 10, par. 2).

3.4.6 Sanctions for Unlawful Strike in the Essential Services

The application of sanctions in the case of an unlawful strike in the essential services is complex because the Law no. 146/1990 provides for different sanctions in relation to the specific agent accountable for the unlawful action. In short, the regulation provides for different sanctions to be applied to employees, self-employed, managers and unions involved in the unlawful strike.[79] The violation of the authority's injunction (*precettazione*) is also sanctioned through a specific process. Finally, a subject who has suffered damages because of the strike has the right to sue the party that caused it in front of the Civil Court. The Criminal Court may also be involved if a crime, for example manslaughter, has been committed in the circumstances. The specific sanctions linked to the violation of Law no. 146/1990 are disciplinary sanction for employees (Art. 4, par.1). It's worth noting that the employer is not allowed to terminate the employment relationship as a disciplinary sanction in the case of the violation of the rules on strikes in the essential services. The sanctions for unions are civil and administrative sanctions (Art. 4, par. 2 and par. 4 bis). The law provides for economic administrative sanctions against private and public managers (Art. 4, par. 4), and economic administrative sanctions for self-employed, and associations of self-employed (Art. 4, par. 4). Noncompliance with an administrative injunction is punished with administrative economic sanctions when the agent

78. Cass., 12 June 1999, no. 5797, Rivista Giuridica del Lavoro, 2000, II, 147.
79. *Pallini*, 355 et seqq.

is an employee, or a self-employed or a trade union (Art. 9, par. 2). If the agent is a manager the sanction is the suspension from the job position (Art. 9, par. 2). The economic sanctions are doubled when agents did not followed the request sent by the CGSSE to postpone the industrial action or the request to apply the specific strike regulation deliberated by the Commission itself. (Art. 4, par. 4 ter). The CGSSE is the key player in the process of applying sanctions, with an exception for the case of violations of the administrative injunction (*precettazione*). In the latter case the administrative authority itself applies directly the sanctions without hearing parties (Art. 9, paras 1 and 4).[80] Recalling sanctions for employees, it is worth remembering that on one side the employer has the duty to apply the sanction whenever employees violate legal and contractual rules, while, on the other hand, the CGSSE only has the duty to require the employer to apply disciplinary sanctions. This exception aside, the CGSSE decides on sanctions directly and takes its deliberation on sanctions after a hearing with the subjects involved, which have the right to present written and oral defences. After the hearing, the CGSSE deliberates on sanctions that the local employment authority (*Direzione provinciale del lavoro – sezione ispezione*) applies issuing an injunction of payment. Employers have the duty to communicate to the CGSSE the application of disciplinary sanctions to employees and the local employment authority has a duty to communicate the execution of the injunction to the CGSSE. The CGSSE has a duty to sanction employers that have not submitted employees to disciplinary sanctions. In the case of the latter the sanction for the employer must be multiplied for every day of delay in the application of the disciplinary sanction (Art. 4, par. 4 sexies). The CGSSE also has the power to deliberate on sanctions for unions after assessing if unions have behaved lawfully in the circumstances. The sanctions for unions applied by the employer are the suspension of trade union officials' right to working leaves for the performing of their functions in the workplace, the forfeiture of fees paid by employees through the deduction of salary, and finally a ban from the collective bargaining process for two months after the completion of the strike. The last sanction is however not effective if the union is powerful and the industrial action continues notwithstanding the banning from collective bargaining, because the sanction does not incentivise negotiation with the employer, and does not support the reaching of an agreement. The sanction for unions whose representatives do not have the right to working leaves is the duty to pay a sum of money (Art. 4, par. 2). The CGSSE deliberates on the amount of the economic sanction and on the amount of the penalty incurred if unions do not pay the sanction[81] on time. Public and private managers may also be subjected to sanctions if they omit the conciliation or information to the public and if essential services are not performed and they are responsible for the failure. The sanction for self-employed and for their unions is the payment of a

80. Cass., S.U., 30 March 2000, no. 11632, Foro italiano, 2000, I, c. 1792.
81. Corte costituzionale, 24 February1995, no. 57, Rivista italiana di diritto del lavoro, 1995, II, 738.

sum of money deliberated by the CGSSE. The CGSSE set the amount within a range regulated by Law no. 146/1990. Against the order of payment issued by the CGSSE all parts have the right to claim before the Rome Tribunal (Labour Section). Employees have the right to sue their employer for the application of disciplinary sanctions and unions have also the right to sue the employer for the application of civil sanctions such as the forfeiture of fees. The employer cannot retain fees but must instead deposit them into an account regulated by the collective agreement. If the collective agreement does not regulate the fund, the employer has to deposit the fees into an account managed by the public body in charge of managing social security for employees and self-employed (INPS).[82] The Administrative Tribunal has jurisdiction on claims against the administrative injunction (precettazione), which orders employers, employees, self-employed, to suspend the strike in order to perform specific duties during an industrial action.

4 THE EXPERIENCE WITH STRIKES IN ESSENTIAL SERVICES

4.1 The Earliest Approach to Strikes in the Essential Services

Industrial actions occur in many essential services as the normal consequence of the widely granted freedom to strike. It is worth remembering again that since 1960 public employees, especially in the health service, started taking industrial actions in order to obtain the right to collective bargaining. In order to limit the inconvenience for consumers, the law set a duty for the public administration to collective bargaining only with unions that had adopted the code of self-regulation on strikes.[83] Self-regulation is therefore one of the earliest strategies adopted by unions, contrary to a regulation by statute of the right to strike. The marginal regulation of strikes by statute in limited sectors[84] confirmed the support by all the political forces of the decision not to intervene in the matter. The Government itself supported as political guarantor an agreement meant to limit the recourse to disruptive strikes by unions impacting labourers and more generally users, especially in the transport sector (Accordo "Scotti"[85] 1983). Self-regulation was not effective enough in order to limit the distress and the damages to users caused by collective actions, mainly because unions did not sanction members that disregarded the code of self-conduct. Furthermore, when self-regulations was supported by the Government as the best strategy to limit strikes, some of the most radical members of unions founded new associations rejecting the self-regulating approach interpreted as a weakening strategy. These new agents started adopting the most disrupting industrial action in order to be admitted to the bargaining table. As pointed out earlier in this paper, the strategy

82. INPS is the public body that manages pensions and social security treatments.
83. *Pascucci*, 2011, 247.
84. See *infra* Section 5.
85. *Pascucci*, 2011, 251.

adopted by public powers in order to protect consumers' interests was to apply to the most disruptive situations the legislation enacted during the fascist period that gives to public authority, such as the prefect (the representative of the Government in counties) and the city mayor, the power to dictate emergency rules in order to contain disruption. These powers where not originally meant for the purpose of limiting industrial action, because strike and lock outs were crimes under the fascist government. These rules were therefore extended to strike under the new constitutional regime in order to limit risks in few services such as the health service, garbage collection and storage, or transport, in order to guarantee public order and safety jeopardised by industrial actions. The authority's order to stop the industrial action would be addressed to a group of recipients selected by way of indicating a professional category, or to individuals, and the order would nevertheless also reach the destination through billposting. Contravening to the order was a crime.

4.2 The Experience of Strike in the Essential Services under Law No. 146/1990

Eventually, in 1990, Law 146/1990, amended in 2000, was enacted with the aim of regulating strikes in the essential services.[86] The statute does not totally abandon the regulation by self-regulation and incentivises the regulation of strikes by collective agreements so that collective agreements and not detailed rules are the instrument for regulating the balance between industrial conflicts and consumers' rights. Also the public authorities' power to intervene in the last instance, whenever consumers' rights are at risk, is confirmed and supported by a special regulation of the injunction power. The Law has also regulated an independent agency of experts, the CGSSE, with the duty to assess the compliance of collective agreement's terms which regulate strikes in respect to the Law no. 146 principles. As this essay has pointed out above, the CGSSE intervenes when an industrial action, taken of the basis of an agreement that was assessed as an appropriate one, derails becoming problematic for consumers. The CGSSE dictates rules whenever parties do not find an agreement, addresses managers on the application of sanctions to employees, and deliberates on sanctions for unions that do not comply with the rules on strike set by the law or by the CGSSE. The body relates to the Parliament the evolution of industrial actions and strikes every year. Of most importance is the CGSSE's power to advise[87] unions on the observing full compliance to the regulations of an announced strike, so that unions may change the programme of the industrial action when it is derailing. The aim of the regulation is to prevent damages resulting from collective actions. The active presence and work of the CGSSE has made the judiciary's intervening an extremely rare occurrence for the regulation of strikes.

86. Law 11 April 2000, no. 83.
87. Art. 13, lett. d) Law no. 146/1990.

Intervention from the judiciary is also prevented by the power of public authorities to adopt an emergency order to perform work. The presence of an active board, which oversees the dynamics of strikes and operates to limit damages and disruptions does not exclude, on the one side, the direct regulation of some typical situations by the law, as for example the duty of unions to give notice in case of strike in the essential services. Besides, the power of institutions such as the CGSSE to reduce the impact of strikes in many situations is not totally decisive in order to prevent risk for users of services. Analysing the report that the CGSSE delivers every year on the state of industrial conflict in essential services provides a good perspective to understand critical situations relating to essential services that may affect the regulation of strikes. In order to proceed, this essay points again out that the qualification of a service as essential is provided by Law no. 146/1990. The statute lists constitutional rights that ought to be balanced with the freedom to strike. The list includes typical rights such as the right to health and safety, the right to freely travel and so on.[88] Essential services are then detailed in a longer list under Article 1, par. 2, that for example makes clear that the essential service of education means that the normal opening of nurseries should be guaranteed to users whereas universities should largely guarantee the right of students to be valuated at the end of a course of studies and therefore not necessarily the everyday lecturing.

4.2.1 The Issue of Defining as Essential a Service That Impacts on the Essential Service

Over the year the problem as to whether the list can be extensively interpreted has been faced many times, so that CGSSE has developed many decisions on this issue. One of the problems faced by interpreters relates to strikes in sectors that are not essential but that impact on essential services. This problem has become more important since public administrations have reduced internal operations relating to the services they have to provide. Cause for strikes is the fact local public authorities, in the perspective of reducing public expenditure, have over the years contracted public services, or elements of public services, out to private contractors. On the one side it means that local authorities lose control of employees that cooperate in the supply of services. Contractors are awarded contracts mainly because of their competitive prices so that when the contractor delays the payment of wages, as frequently happens due to narrow economic profit, employees start an industrial action and therefore do not collaborate with

88. Law no. 146/1990 Art. 1 'For the purposes of regulation essential services are services meant to protect the right to life, heath and safety, freedom and security, freedom of circulation, the right to social security, education and the freedom to communication. The rights have to be guaranteed by any type of worker, and also in the case the services contracted out by contract or licence' (statute translated by the author of this paper).

the body that provides essential services.[89] This has been the case for the catering services in state nurseries and schools which is not itself an essential service under Law no. 146/1990, but that has been qualified as an essential service for being instrumental to the functioning of schools. The CGSSE has pointed out that all the activities that are instrumental to the delivering of essential services fall under Law no. 146/1990.[90] The basic argument is that if the contractor has not agreed with unions on the activities that necessarily have to be performed during strikes, consumers should not pay the consequences of the defiance. In the situation relating to school catering, the CGSSE has therefore ordered the application of a collective agreement between unions of public sector teachers and the representatives of local public authorities regulating strikes in the essential services. What is worth noting is that the agreement was an agreement between totally different subjects from the ones involved in the catering service, given that catering was provided for by a private contractor. Another consequence is that in order to assess the accountability of the public bodies providing for essential services to consumers, as in the schools case, it is necessary to ascertain if public administrations, when contracting out, made clear in written contracts that contractors and subcontractors are required to respect the legislation on strikes in the essential services and related collective agreements.[91]

In relation to a different situation more recently the Parliament has added a new service into the list of the essential services amending Law no. 146/1990. This is the case of museums and places of cultural interests. Many such places are present in Italy and the possibility of visiting museums and sites of cultural and artistic interest is an incentive for tourists to travel the country. In 2015 the Parliament therefore added to the list of essential services embedded in Law no. 146/1990[92] artistic attractions such as museums and public art galleries. People working in (and for) museums and cultural and artistic sites are subject to the regulation of strikes in the essential services. The submission of museum's staff to essential services regulation is nevertheless controversial because museums and cultural sites do not provide for services necessary in order to protect the fundamental rights protected by Law no. 146/1990. In any case, collective agreements in the sector ought to guarantee not only accessibility for the public but also surveillance and security for art galleries, providing that during a strike museums ought to be accessible for at least for half the normal day opening, and that, during some periods over the year, strikes are not allowed at all. The enlarged definition of what is an essential service now also covers the digital centralized services for enrolling into courses provided to state universities by a

89. This is the issue at stake also in the private health sector, where contractors of services delay payment of wages due to the delays by public local administration to compensate contractors. See *CGSSE*, 2017, 53.
90. A good example is the refuelling of airplanes. See *CGSSE*, 2017, 79.
91. *CGSSE*, 2017, 50.
92. Law 12 November 2015, no. 182.

private subject 'Cineca' and the system of registration for appointments in the health and service units.[93] It seems nevertheless at least dubious that these rules enlarging the scope of the legislation on strike in essential services are compatible with the ILO definition of essential service as interpreted by the Committee of Experts on Freedom of Association. The Committee in fact clearly said that 'As an exception to the general principle of the right to strike, the essential services in which this principle may be entirely or partly waived should be defined restrictively: the Committee therefore considers that essential services are only those the interruption of which would endanger the life, personal safety or health of the whole or part of the population.[94]

4.2.2 The Fragmentation in Union Representation and Its Impact on Strikes in the Essential Services

An issue that is relevant in the education sector is the fragmentation of trade unions that are allowed to call a strike. As a matter of principle, under Italian law all trade unions have the right to call a strike regardless of the number of members, in general or in a specific sector. More precisely a temporary coalition of workers is also allowed to call a strike for the protection of professional interests. In the essential services, unions (or coalitions) nevertheless have the duty to give notice of the incoming actions and to give detailed information about the modality of strike to the provider of services, so that the provider informs clients. When representation is fragmented, strikes by different unions are frequently called, so that the public is on practically permanent alert of a probable reduced service and therefore looks for possible alternatives. Typically not so many employees join each industrial action but the percentage of workforce participation is not clear before the strike. The situation described above is recurrent in the education sector and especially in state schools, where strikes frequently do not involve more than the 1% of the staff possibly interested in the specific industrial conflict.[95] Notwithstanding a foreseen low participation, headmasters have to give notice of the strike as soon as called by unions and have to suspend the service if they believe that the strike will compromise it. The calling of strikes is lawful if and when at least one week runs between the first strike and the subsequent one (Law no. 146/1990, Art. 2, par. 2). Headmasters are not allowed to make inquires in advance in order to know if members of staff will effectively go on strike. The inquiry could be considered violation of Art. 8 Law no. 300/1970 prohibiting investigation by the employer on sensitive information. Employees are also free to decide at the very last moment if to go on strike. The consequence is the uncertainty about the full functioning of the service until the very strike should start. The problem has

93. *CGSSE*, 2017, 54 seq.
94. *ILO*, 2013, para. 669. On the matter of strike under the ILO regulation on Freedom of Association, see *Gernigon/Alberto/Horacio*, 2000.
95. *CGSSE*, 2017. See figures at 58 and 59.

been discussed in front of the CGSSE that has again invited parties to reach an agreement in order to overcome these issues, in consideration of the fact that it has been impossible until now the reaching of an agreement between Minister for Education (MIUR) and teachers unions aimed at defining what is the minimum service that would be provided during strikes. The fragmentation of work representatives is also one the most relevant problem in the transport sector, which is one of the most affected by strikes[96] especially at local level where unions compete with other unions by calling strikes in order to demonstrate which union is more representative of the workforce. Sometimes, on the contrary, unions do not compete against each other through strikes but join strikes called by different unions. This is a case that happened in the national rail transport service, when an action called by unions, that the CGSSE declared unlawful before the action was to start, continued under a different shape. The unions on the one hand withdrew the call and on the other hand invited workers through Facebook and other social media to join the strike already called by a different union. The CGSSE decided that this invitation was a new call by the first group of unions and declared the invitation unlawful for breaking the duty of notice in the circumstances.[97] These examples therefore demonstrate the disruptive impact that the absence of regulation about the entitlement to strike can cause in the essential services. Instead of making of strike a virtuous support for democracy, the subjective unlimited freedom to strike may transform industrial action into an 'unorganized social power'[98] that disrupts the rights and interests of the economically weakest part of the population that not always has resources to exercise the "exit" function, having limited access to the private market of services.

4.2.3 The Fragmentation of Business in Essential Services

On the other side, the fragmentation of business is a problem. This is the case in the rail transport sector. The rail service, once a monopoly, is now open to more competitors. A general agreement on strikes, which at once binds all providers and unions operating in the sector, does not yet exist. The CGSSE has therefore suggested with no result, to all parties to discuss the possibility of negotiating a general framework for strike regulation to be applied by all the suppliers of transport services.[99]

96. In 2016, Italian trade unions called 258 strikes in the local transport sector. See *CGSSE*, 2017, 91 and 109.
97. *Ibid.*, 98.
98. *Zoppoli*, 2017, 1145 et seq.
99. *CGSSE*, 2017, 93.

4.2.4 *The Contracting Out of Services by Public Agencies and Its Consequences on Strikes in Essential Services*

Economic strikes aim at increasing working condition, or at the safeguard of the workplace in occasion of redundancies. Strikes sometimes are called to claim wages from employers that have typically contracted with public administrations and receive late payments for the contracted service. Late payments by contractor also cause wildcat strikes that are unlawful in the essential services. The CGSSE has nevertheless decreed that a wildcat strike aimed at reacting to the employers' breach of contract in a case where the employer was ten months late in payment of wages was lawful.[100]

4.2.5 *The Duty to Bargain Fairly During the Cooling Off Period*

The CGSSE has the duty to assess acts of proclamation in order to prevent the possibility of unlawful strikes. Assessing the lawfulness of a strike has been one of the most important and effective CGSSE activities as confirmed by recent experience.[101] CGSSE preventive control is meant to ascertain if the strike has been called after unions have attempted to find an agreement with employers in order to avoid the strike. The law regulates two cooling off procedures: the first one just between unions and employers and the second one in front of the administrative authority. The air transport sector is another area of essential services where unions frequently call strikes: there were about 200 industrial actions in 2016.[102] The causes of strike are reorganization and redundancy processes, late payment of wages by contractors, the expiration of subcontracts and largely the violation of cooling off periods and arbitration procedures. The CGSSE has made it clear that arbitration procedures are compulsory and have to take place before the strike. Parties have to behave fairly, providing information and answering in due course to the other parties' request for a meeting[103] and give evidence to the CGSSE of an attentive approach to the duty to bargain fairly. Employers have a duty to inform the public on incoming strikes at least five days before the action takes place but the CGSSE has stated that employers have to repeat the information before the date of the strike if the first communication has been performed long before the date of the strike.[104] During a strike in the essential services companies and public agencies do not have to provide a full service to the public. The principle is that during strikes employers have to provide for a minimum service if the reduced service does not compromise constitutional rights. This rule has been applied since before the enactment of

100. *Ibid.*, 113.
101. *Ibid.*, 111.
102. *Ibid.*, Tab. 2.
103. *Ibid.*, 78.
104. *Ibid.*, 81.

Law no. 146/1990 on the basis of a decision taken by the Constitutional court.[105] The principle that only a contingent of workers has the duty to abandon the strike has been again stressed by the CGSSE reporting on the air transport sector where companies have organized in excess services to be performed during industrial actions so as to limit the right to strike beyond what was unavoidable. Companies therefore have to be transparent and declare in advance which flights and connections will operate during the industrial conflict, so that workers would understand if the workforce that will have to be in service is proportionate to the load of work.[106]

4.2.6 Strategies Meant at Overcoming the Limits for Strikes in the Essential Services

Sometimes employees try to overcome the limits for strikes in the essential services with strategies meant to mask the nature of their action. This was the case whereby local policemen on New Year's Eve 2014/2015 were absent en mass from services for illness and other lawful causes. The CGSSE had to operate a complex inquest and discovered that the actions had been organised by a trade union that was therefore condemned. The union claimed, during the Tribunal, that the decision by the CGSSE was unfair because the decision not to work due to illness was a decision taken by every single police officer.[107]

4.2.7 Spontaneous Protests as Opposed to Strikes Called by Unions

In 2017 one of the sectors mostly affected by industrial actions has been transport by taxi in conjunctions with new entrepreneurial initiatives aimed at competing with unlicensed taxi in the same sector. From the 15 February to the 21 February 2017 taxis stopped operating on all national territory causing great inconvenience to users of the service. The CGSSE had invited[108] taxi drivers' unions to suspend the strike which was unlawful under many profiles. Unions had in fact not given the notice required, unions had not communicated the length of the strike, and unions had not communicated the list of services that taxi divers were anyway required to perform during the industrial action. Taxi divers' unions had nevertheless replied that they were not responsible for the actions that would be considered spontaneous protests and had replied also that unions' representatives had already invited drivers to stop the strike. The CGSSE had therefore asked Prefects to send to the CGSSE any information useful in order to identify agents accountable for the interruption of the transport service

105. Corte costituzionale, 27 May, 1961, no. 26, Foro italiano, 1961, I, c. 888.
106. *CGSSE*, 2017, 82.
107. *Ibid.*, 125.
108. See Deliberation no. 17/148 of 11 May 2017, at www.cgsse.it/web/guest;jsessionid=Jeu-+JeBiXjKyWMrEQuHGw__.sgc8-prd-liferay, last visited on 20 November 2017.

by taxi. Only a few Prefects sent information and it soon came to light that the strike had been organised on social networks and chats on line. Eventually the Government opened a conference with drivers' unions in order to discuss issues at stake, eventually promising to enact a new regulation of transport by taxi in order to limit the competition by unlicensed drivers.

4.2.8 Lack of Collaboration by Elected Public Authorities

The CGSSE has the duty to sanction independent worker that take unlawful action. The CGSSE had then deliberated to ask the mayors of the towns where the industrial actions took place to communicate the names of the taxi drivers that had been on strike. Notwithstanding the request was sent at the beginning of 2017, few city mayors have since replied and no one has yet identified any participant in the unlawful strike. The CGSSE claims that the circumstances make evident a lack of collaboration between local authorities and the CGSSE, as city mayors supervise the organization of the taxi service in their municipality. This situation highlights areas of weak protection in the case of strikes in the essential services, especially when there is not an employer as in the case of taxi drivers, which in Italy are self-employed. As with any self-employed individual, taxi drivers are not subjected to an employer and therefore under the statute they are subjected to the power of CGSSE that has no power to directly access the administrative documentation held by local authorities. Local authorities, such as Mayors, are elected by residents, so they may have not a sufficient incentive to disclose the identity of protesters when protesters have the support of the mayor's electorate. In Autumn 2017 there was also an industrial action promoted for economic reasons by university professors and university researchers. Academic members of staff do not negotiate wages through collective bargaining nor are academics' strikes regulated by collective agreement. Statutes and secondary legislations regulate academic staff working conditions. Academic staff does not practice any sort of wage negotiation with Universities. Nevertheless Law no. 146/1990 lists the right to education among fundamental rights and contemplates course final examinations as essential services to be performed. The action taken by academic staff during 2017 resulted in the reduction of examination sessions to only one session from the 28 August to the 31 October. Here, regardless, academic staff also guaranteed students the possibility of completing their studies through the discussion of the written final essay. The CGSSE notwithstanding the lacking of specific regulation declared the modality of action taken by the academic staff compliant with Law no. 146/1990.[109] It seems nevertheless evident that this mild industrial action did not at least impact on to the Government that has not yet agreed on academic staff's requests.

109. See CGSS notice on http://www.cgsse.it/web/guest;jsessionid=Jeu-+JeBiXjKyWMr EQuHGw__.sgc8-prd-liferay, last visited on 20 November 2017.

5 RESTRICTION OF THE RIGHT TO STRIKE IN ESSENTIAL SERVICES

Limits to strike in the essential services are based on the complex system of rules aimed at setting a balance between the freedom to strike and other constitutional rights. Very few categories of employees are not allowed to strike. The Constitutional Court distinguishes between the freedom to strike and the right to strike. All workers (subordinated and independent) are entitled to the fundamental freedom to strike and therefore a limitation to this freedom by public powers must be an exception provided for by law exclusively where prevailing interests compete with labour's interests. It is therefore not surprising that members of judiciary bodies such as Courts' judges have the right to strike and in order to regulate strike, one among the associations of the members of the judiciary has actually adopted a regulation that has been submitted to and approved by the CGSSE.[110] In case of strike, as it happens also in situations where barristers take the industrial action, hearings are suspended[111] and postponed, unless the length of the trial may possibly impact on to the personal freedom of the defendant. Trials in matter of dismissal or redundancies or actions for interim injunctions would not be suspended.

5.1 Seamen

A situation where there is a limitation to strike is the maritime business. Seamen do not have the right to strike during navigation and an industrial action on the sea would be a criminal offence on the basis of Art. 1105 of the Navigation Code.[112] Other categories of worker that do not have the right to strike are staff in nuclear plants to the extent to which they are necessary to maintain the safe functioning of the nuclear plant.[113]

5.2 Members of the Military and Members of the State Corp of Police

Members of the military[114] and police constables and officers of the national corps of police do not have the right to strike.[115] The limitation is based on the special status of subordination to the Government[116] of the members of these corps, which may be ordered to act for protecting fundamental rights and public institutions in extreme situations. The conditions of work for members of these forces are regulated by secondary legislation. The content of the secondary

110. The regulation is available at http://www.cgsse.it/regolamentazioni/regolament_settore/magistrati%20ANM.pdf, last visited on 27 November 2017.
111. See Cass., 24 May 2016 no. 10715, www.iusexplorer.it, last visited on 27 November 2017.
112. Corte costituzionale, 28 December 1962, no. 124, quoted at nt. 31.
113. Art. 49, D.P.R. 13 February 1964, no. 185.
114. Art. 8 Law 27 July 1978, no. 382.
115. Art. 84 Law 1 April 1981, no. 121.
116. Tursi, 2004, 31, 38.

legislation is nevertheless aligned to agreements negotiated by representatives of the police and the military corps and ministers since 1978, when, as pointed out above[117], a body representative of the interests of the members of the military was regulated in order to allow the process of negotiation to operate. The limit for these categories should not cause any relevant issues. Recently, nevertheless, the limitation for members of the military has come to be problematic when the Italian State Forestry Corps, that was not considered a military body, was merged and incorporated into military corps, the "Carabinieri", and subsequently appeared to lose the right to strike. Unions of the Italian State Forestry Corps made an inquiry in 2016 to the CGSSE regarding whether they still could lawfully strike, but the CGSSE said that it is not up to the CGSSE to decide which bodies have the right to strike and instead it is in the power of Parliament to decide on the issue.

Local police officers fall under a different and less restrictive regulation, having the right to strike and the right to representation by trade unions so that they fully participate in the collective bargaining process. The difference between the situation of national police officers and local police officers is that collective agreements regulate immediately local police officers' condition of work, whereas negotiation for national police officers is only a part of the legislative process meant at regulating working conditions.

6 COMPENSATORY MEASURES FOR RESTRICTIONS

Cf. the previous two sections particularly regarding the CGSSE's mandate to mediate and arbitrate labour disputes.

7 SECURING ESSENTIAL SERVICES BY FURTHER MEANS

7.1 Alternative Methods of Protest in the Essential Services

Under the strict interpretation of the right to strike adopted by the Constitutional Court and the Court of Cassazione, only the suspension of work by employees and workers for the purpose of protesting is compliant with the law. Different behaviours that may typically take place during an industrial action do not therefore fall under any special protection and can be interpreted as a breach of contract, for example when an employee do not perform specific tasks during working hours,[118] or a crime as in the case of squatting[119] in an employer's plant. Among these behaviours one may include 'stonewalling', which is the practice of not performing preparatory activities in respect to the activity that has been

117. Law no. 382 of 1978, *supra* Section 5.2.
118. Corte costituzionale, 28 December 1962, no. 123, quoted nt. 25; Cass., 25 November 2003, no. 17995, Rivista Italiana di Diritto del Lavoro, 2004, II, 525.
119. Corte costituzionale, 17 July 1975, no. 220, quoted nt. 48.

agreed upon. A recurrent case of industrial action is overtime strike, which occurs when employees do not work overtime. The CGSSE has deliberated that in the case of overtime strikes in the essential services the industrial action falls under Law no. 146/1990.[120] It is nevertheless worth noting that overtime strikes are considered as lawful strike by Courts and not as an alternative action.[121] An alternative means of industrial action on which the CGSSE has taken a position is the use of the right to assembly in the workplace as a strategy for disrupting the service to clients of the essential services. The CGSSE has deliberated on the issue of assembly in the workplace as a way for overcoming limits to strikes in the essential services concluding that if the assembly is run in compliance with the legal regulation on the right to assembly and in compliance with the collective agreement applied by the employer the assembly does not fall under Law no. 146/1990. Whenever the assembly is run in a way that is not compliant with collective regulation, the assembly falls under Law no. 146/1990, so that unions have to apply the regulation on strikes in the essential services before the assembly. The CGSSE has nevertheless made it clear that in the latter case unions and employers have to perform essential services, so that the exercise of the right to assembly does not justify the suspension of essential services,[122] which a limited group of employees have to perform during the assembly.

7.2 The Virtual Strike

Among alternative forms of industrial action one might also include the virtual strike, which is the continuation of the activity by employees who nonetheless forfeit the right to pay, either completely or for half of their wage, in favour of a special fund. The employer has to pay into the fund a sum equivalent to forfeited wages.[123] The virtual strike is normally regulated by collective agreements because the imposition of the obligation to pay a fee without a legal basis is controversial. The CGSSE has regulated the virtual strike in an interim code to be applied in the helicopter emergency medical service.[124] However, during a recent Parliament hearing on strikes in the essential services, the former President of the CGSSE has clearly pointed out that the practice of virtual strikes is a difficult matter to regulate and most importantly that the decision on whether to regulate it should be left only to collective bargaining.[125]

120. *CGSSE*, 2003, 22.
121. 25 November 2003, no. 17995, Rivista italiana di diritto del lavoro, 2004, II, 525.
122. *CGSSE*, 2003a, 683 sub nt. 3.
123. Topo, 2004, 351 et seqq. Santini, 2011, 150.
124. *CGSSE*, 2012, 23.
125. http://www.cgsse.it/scioperi/avvisi/RelazioneAudizioneAlesse.pdf, last visited on 29 November 2017.

8 EVALUATION AND CONCLUSION

Strikes in the essential services are typically regulated through collective bargaining and self-regulation by the self-employed under the legal framework set by Law no. 146/1990. The CGSSE, which is the administrative authority in charge of monitoring strikes in the essential services, nevertheless plays an essential role as strikes regulator. The CGSSE gives advice to unions and employers on how to regulate the industrial action, regulates the modality of strikes when parties do not find any agreement on strikes, supervise industrial actions in order to prevent disruptions and damages to consumers. The CGSSE applies sanctions and monitors employers that have a duty to apply disciplinary sanctions on employees whenever employees violate a legal or contractual rule during a strike in the essential services. The intervention of the judiciary is therefore less relevant in the perspective of preventing disruptive actions whereas prevention is the key word for interpreting the Italian legal framework in the matter of strikes in the essential services. The Government through the prefects' power to issue orders to perform is also an important agent in the prevention of disruption caused by strikes in the essential services. The Government authority, at local level or at national level, has in fact the power of injunction and can impose a specific duty to work on workers and employees during a strike. The Government authority has also the power to issue and injunction against private and public managers in case of violation of collective agreements and legal rules on strikes, if the violations impact on the necessary performing of services. Notwithstanding the active role of many institutions that work with the aim of preventing wild strikes and interruptions of essential services, the CGSSE still points out emerging issues.

Among the most relevant problems one may find there is the contracting out of services by public administrations whose budget has shrunk over the last few years of recession. Local institutions have contracted out essential services or part of them to private contractors that do not pay or delay payments to employees, causing industrial actions in fundamental services such as waste disposal and local transport. The former president[126] of the CGSSE has nevertheless pointed out that issues caused by the reduction of public expenditure and reorganization of local public administrations exceed the competence of the CGSSE, which has not powers on the matter. A second relevant issue is the fragmentation of workers' representation. The problem arises from the right of every single union to call a strike independently from the consistency of its membership. This fact produces the consequence that in some sectors few employees on strike interrupt the service for all the clients, as it occurs in the

126. Audizione del Presidente della Commissione di garanzia dell'attuazione della legge sullo sciopero nei servizi pubblici essenziali, Roberto Alesse, presso le Commissioni Affari Costituzionali e Lavoro riunite del Senato della Repubblica (15 ottobre 2015), in www.cgsse.it/scioperi/avvisi/RelazioneAudizioneAlesse.pdf, last visited 30 November 2017.

education sector. In order to overcome the latter problem the regulation of a necessary ballot to be held before the strike could be a possible solution. On the basis of the report presented in 2015, it seems that it would be appropriate in the circumstances also the consolidation of the CGSSE's powers to arbitrate labour conflicts, which are the reason of the industrial conflict. The proposal could nevertheless be in contrast with the principle of freedom of association guaranteed to unions by Art. 39, par. 1. Constitution, which allows unions to freely regulate also arbitration procedures, through collective bargaining. The regulation of sanctions seems to be another issue for the good functioning of essential services. The report points out how inadequate the economic sanctions for private and public managers are in respect to the impact of their actions on the delivery of essential services, and also the inadequacy of the sanctions against self-employed that strike in the context of an unofficial strike promoted on social media without the support of a trade union.

The conclusion is that notwithstanding Law no. 146/1990 balances the right to strike with fundamental rights, having contributed to the reducing of the percentage of industrial actions in many sectors over the years (see Annex 1), it would be still necessary to reform the Law under different profiles. It would be also necessary to support Law no. 146/1990 effectiveness through the regulation of employees' representatives for the purpose of collective bargaining, in order to reduce the fragmentation of the industrial conflict. As the comparative experience demonstrates, it seems nevertheless problematic the option to extend only to the most representative unions the legitimation to strike[127], given also the peculiar by Courts acknowledged nature of fundamental right which gives also immediate "voice" to the people's political and not only professional instances.

Bibliography

Bellocchi, Paola, La libertà sindacale, in Proia (ed.), Organizzazione sindacale e contrattazione collettiva, Trattato di diritto del lavoro, vol. II, Padova, 2014, 3 et seqq.

Bellocchi, Paola, Organizzazione sindacale e contrattazione collettiva, in Proia Giampiero (ed.), Organizzazione sindacale e contrattazione collettiva, Trattato di diritto del lavoro, vol. II, Padova, 2014, 95 et seqq. (Bellocchi 2014a)

Branca, Giorgio (ed.) Commentario della Costituzione, Rapporti economici (Art. 35-40), 1979

127. *Laulome/Leclerc,* French report *supra,* where the Authors point out that 'the European Committee of Social Rights concluded that the regulation of the right to strike in France fell outside the provisions of European Social Charter. The Committee maintained that limiting the right to initiate a strike in the public sector to the most representative national trade unions restricts the right to strike and violates Article 6 of the ESC (*European Social Chart*) 1961'.

Canavesi, Guido, La precettazione, in Lunardon (ed.), Conflitto concertazione e partecipazione, Trattato di diritto del lavoro, vol. III, 2011, 542 et seqq.

Carinci Franco, Contrattazione e contratto collettivo, in Proia (ed.), Organizzazione sindacale e contrattazione collettiva, Trattato di diritto del lavoro, vol. II 2014, 981 et seqq.

Corso, Fulvio, I diritti sindacali, in Proia Giampiero (ed.), Organizzazione sindacale e contrattazione collettiva, Trattato di diritto del lavoro, vol. II, 2014, 341 et seqq.

CGSSE, Annual Report on 2016, 2017, http://www.cgsse.it/web/guest/visualizza-pdf?set = relazione-alle-camere&url = scioperi/relazioni/Relazione_annuale_2017.pdf, last visited on 30 November 2017

CGSSE, Deliberation no. 03/130, 11 September 2003, http://www.cgsse.it/static/discipline/Regolamentazioni/Trasporto_pubblico_locale.pdf, last visited 30 November 2017

CGSSE, Deliberation no. 04/212, 1 April 2004, http://www.cgsse.it/static/discipline/Regolamentazioni/Trasporto_aereo.pdf, last visited on 28 November 2017 (CGSSE, 2003a)

CGSSE, Deliberation no.12/461, 5 November 2012, http://www.cgsse.it/scioperi/relazioni/CgS_Rel_Annuale_2014.pdf, 23, last visited 30 November 2017

De Luca, Tamajo Raffaele, Accordo di Pomigliano e criticità del sistema di relazioni industriali italiane, Rivista Italiana di Diritto del Lavoro, no. 4, part. I, 2010, 797 et seqq.

Ferrari, Paola, Struttura e attività, Lunardon Fiorella (ed.), Conflitto concertazione e partecipazione, Trattato di diritto del lavoro, vol. III, 2011, 419 et seqq.

Gaeta, Lorenzo, Una storia giuridica dello sciopero nei servizi pubblici dall'Unità alla Costituzione, in Pino (ed.), Diritti fondamentali e regole del conflitto collettivo. Esperienze e prospettive, 2015, 161 et seqq.

Gernigon, Bernard/Alberto, Odero/Horacio, Guido, ILO Principles concerning the Right to Strike, 2nd ed., 2000

Ghezzi, Giorgio, La responsabilità contrattuale delle associazioni sindacali, 1963

Giugni, Gino, Commento all'art. 30, in Branca (ed.) Commentario della Costituzione, Rapporti economici (Art. 35-40), 1979, 257 et seqq.

Giugni, Gino, Diritto sindacale, 1968

Gragnoli, Enrico/Corti Matteo, La retribuzione, in Marazza (ed.), Contratto di lavoro e organizzazione, vol. IV, part 2, 2012, 1375 et seqq.

Hirschman, Albert Otto, Exit, Voice and Loyalty, Cambridge, MA, 1970

ILO, Reports of the Committee on Freedom of Association, Official Bulletin Vol. LXVII, Series B, No. 1, 233rd Report, Case No. 1255, 2013

Lassandari, Andrea, Il contratto collettivo aziendale, in Proia (ed.), Organizzazione sindacale e contrattazione collettiva, Trattato di diritto del lavoro, vol. II, 2014, 717 et seqq.

Luciani, Vincenzo, Le forme di conflitto diverse dallo sciopero, Lunardon (ed.), Conflitto concertazione e partecipazione, Trattato di diritto del lavoro, vol. III, 2011, 187 et seqq.
Lunardon, Fiorella, Conflitto concertazione e partecipazione, Trattato di diritto del lavoro, vol. III, 2011
Lyttelton, Adrian, The Seizure of Power: Fascism in Italy 1919-1929, Revised edition, 2004
Maio, Valerio, Struttura ed articolazione della contrattazione collettiva, in Proia (ed.), Organizzazione sindacale e contrattazione collettiva, Trattato di diritto del lavoro, vol. II, 2014, 446 et seqq.
Mancini, Giuseppe Federico, Commento all'articolo 4 della Costituzione, in Branca (ed.), Commentario alla Costituzione, 1975, 199 et seqq.
Marazza, Marco (ed.), Contratto di lavoro e organizzazione, vol. IV, part 2, 2012 et seqq.
Martone, Michel, La fase corporativa, in Persiani (ed.), Le fonti del diritto del lavoro, Trattato di diritto del lavoro, vol. I, 2010 et seqq.
Mengoni, Luigi, Fondata sul lavoro: la Repubblica tra diritti inviolabili dell'uomo e doveri inderogabili di solidarietà, in Napoli (ed.), Costituzione, lavoro, pluralismo sociale, 1998
Meny, Yves, La crisi politica, Rivista Trimestrale di Diritto Pubblico, fasc.3, 2016, 621 et seqq.
Pallini, Massimo, Le sanzioni nel sistema della legge n. 146/1990, in Lunardon (ed.), Conflitto concertazione e partecipazione, Trattato di diritto del lavoro, vol. III, 2011, 355 et seqq.
Pascucci, Paolo, Dalla giurisprudenza costituzionale alla legge sullo sciopero, in Lunardon (ed.), Conflitto concertazione e partecipazione, Trattato di diritto del lavoro, vol. III, 2011, 217 et seqq.
Persiani, Mattia (ed.), Le fonti del diritto del lavoro, Trattato di diritto del lavoro, vol. I, 2010 et seqq.
Pilati, Andrea, Il campo di applicazione della legge e i requisito di legittimità delle astensioni collettive, in Lunardon (ed.), Conflitto concertazione e partecipazione, Trattato di diritto del lavoro, vol. III, 2011, 277 et seqq.
Pino, Giovanni (ed.), Diritti fondamentali e regole del conflitto collettivo. Esperienze e prospettive, Milano, 2015
Proia, Giampiero (ed.), Organizzazione sindacale e contrattazione collettiva, Trattato di diritto del lavoro, vol. II, 2014 et seqq.
Proia, Giampiero/Gambacciani, Marco, Il contratto collettivo di diritto comune, in Proia (ed.), Organizzazione sindacale e contrattazione collettiva, Trattato di diritto del lavoro, vol. II, 2014, 595 et seqq.
Romagnoli, Umberto, La legge quadro sul pubblico impiego, 1986
Santini, Fabrizia, Le forme di sciopero, in Lunardon (ed.), Conflitto concertazione e partecipazione, Trattato di diritto del lavoro, vol. III, 2011, 83 et seqq.
Santoni, Francesco, La libertà e il diritto di sciopero, in Lunardon (ed.), Conflitto concertazione e partecipazione, Trattato di diritto del lavoro, vol. III, 2011, 3 et seqq.

Santoro, Passarelli Giuseppe, Questioni aperte dello sciopero nei servizi pubblici essenziali: Sciopero politico-economico, sciopero politico, sciopero generale e preavviso, Diritto delle relazioni industriali, no.1, 2008

*Sciarra, Silvana,*I diritti sociali e i dilemmi della giurisprudenza costituzionale, Rivista Italiana di Diritto del Lavoro, no. 3, 2017, 347 et seqq.

Scognamiglio, Renato, La Costituzione repubblicana, Persiani (ed.), Le fonti del diritto del lavoro, Trattato di diritto del lavoro, vol. I, 2010, 113 et seqq.

Suppiej, Giuseppe, Trent'anni di giurisprudenza costituzionale sullo sciopero e sulla serrata, Rivista Italiana di Diritto del Lavoro, 1989, no. 1, part. I, 25 et seqq.

Topo, Adriana, Raffreddamento e composizione del conflitto industriale nel settore dei servizi pubblici essenziali, Rivista Italiana di Diritto del lavoro, 2004, no. 3, 351 et seqq.

Topo, Adriana, Tutela e rappresentanza degli interessi collettivi nel lavoro autonomo, in Lavoro e Diritto, n. 2, 1997, 203 et seqq.

Tursi, L'ambito di applicazione della riforma: categorie e amministrazioni escluse dalla privatizzazione del rapporto di lavoro, in Carinci/Zoppoli (eds), Il lavoro alle dipendenze delle pubbliche amministrazioni, 2004, 31 et seqq.

Zoppoli, Antonello, Relazioni industriali e risorse umane, Diritto di sciopero e rappresentatività sindacale: il paradosso dei servizi essenziali tra sistema 'di fatto', istanze di moderna democrazia e bilanciamento dei diritti, Diritto delle relazioni industriali, no. 4, 2017, 1145 et seqq.

ANNEX

Anno	*Numero Proclamazioni*	*Iterventi Preventivi*	*Efficacia Interventi Preventivi*
2007	2017	620	66
2008	2195	567	70
2009	1899	528	74
2010	2093	632	81
2011	2229	653	90
2012	2330	514	87
2013	2338	368	92
2014	2084	379	88
2015	2261	324	99
2016	2352	466	99

Source: CGSSE, 2017, 53.

CHAPTER 11

Poland

Andrzej Marian Świątkowski

1 GENERAL BACKGROUND: COUNTRY PROFILE

The Constitution of the Republic of Poland of 2.4.1997 guarantees freedom of association in trade unions, socio-occupational organizations of farmers and in employers' organizations (Article 59 (1)). All entitled persons may benefit from the above-mentioned guarantee of association. Employees and other employed persons who are not employers may form and join trade unions. Also the unemployed and pensioners maintain the right to belong to trade union organisations. Individual farmers who are not in an employment relationship, who are engaged in self-employed business activity, who use the help of their family members, have the right to associate in socio-occupational organisations of individual farmers. Employers are guaranteed the right to form and join employers' organisations. Article 58 (1) of the Constitution of the Republic of Poland guarantees 'to everyone the freedom of association'. The above fundamental principle of freedom, considered one of the fundamental human rights, may only be subject to such statutory limitations as are permissible in accordance with international agreements to which the Republic of Poland is a party (Article 59 (4) of the Constitution). Law prohibits only such associations the purpose or activity of which is contrary to the Constitution of the Republic of Poland or to law enacted by the Parliament. Only courts may decide on the refusal to register an association, a trade union, an organisation of individual farmers or employers' organisation (Article 58 (2)). Trade unions, socio-occupational farmers' organisations and employers' organisations enjoy a specific status and are not subject to the act of 7.4.1989 – Law on Associations (OJ 2/89, item 104 as amended) or to the forms of administrative supervision of state prescribed by the Law. Constitution of the Republic of Poland guarantees to trade unions and employers and their organizations the right to bargain collectively and to conclude collective agreements and other normative arrangements regulating wage and working conditions (Article 59 (2)). Under Article 59 (3) of the Constitution, trade unions shall have the right to organize workers' strikes or other forms of protest. The limits of the above entitlement are laid down in the act on resolution of collective disputes of 23.5.1991 (consolidated act – OJ 255/15, item 295 as amended). The mentioned Article 59 (3) of the Constitution confirms the competences of legislative authority (both chambers of parliament – Sejm and Senate) do adopt an act which may restrict, in the interest of the 'public good' the organisation of strikes or establish a prohibition on the organisation of strikes by certain categories of employees in 'certain areas' which means spheres, sectors, scopes or domains of the activity. The act of 23.5.1991 on resolution of collective disputes restored the balance between the core relationship – the right to organize, the right to bargain, the right to strike, on which collective labour relations are based in a free and democratic state.

In the most current Third Polish Republic, after the change of the political and economic system, there were three separate acts adopted on 23.5.1991: the act on trade unions (consolidated act – OJ 167/2014, item 167 as amended), the act on employers' organisations (OJ 55/91, item 235 as amended) and the act on resolution of collective disputes (consolidated act – OJ 295/2015, item 295), which guaranteed to employees and employers the right to form and to join trade unions and employers' organisations, respectively. The purpose of the legally guaranteed freedom of association is to regulate the foundations and legal framework enabling representation of separate interests of social partners and protection of their rights in amicable manner and, ultimately, in a legal form of collective disputes.

2 COLLECTIVE LABOUR RELATIONS

The right to organize, the right to bargain collectively and in particular the right to strike derive from interpretation of the provisions of international law and labour law standards of the Council of Europe – the European Social Charter of 18.10.1961. The Charter requires Poland to recognize the right of workers and employers to collective action in cases of conflict of interests, including the right to strike.[1] The Committee of Freedom of Association of the Governing Body of ILO considered that the right to strike is an inherent consequence of employees' right to organise in trade unions protected under Article 3 of ILO Convention no. 87 on the Freedom of Association and Protection of the Right to Organise.[2] The right to strike is one of the essential legal instruments through which employees and trade unions may effectively pursue and protect their economic and social interests.[3] An identical standpoint was taken by the European Committee of Social Rights of the Council of Europe which interprets Article 5 of the Charter of Social Rights of the Council of Europe – the right to organise – in connection with Article 6 (4) of the above Charter which clearly stipulates that the Contracting Parties ratifying the provisions of the Charter shall 'recognize the right of workers (...) to collective action in conflicts of interest, including the right to strike (...)'. Poland ratified the ILO Convention no. 87 and the Charter.[4] Given the above, the state authorities, already during the previous political period, adopted provisions on trade unions which adapted the national system of collective labour law to the international standards.

3 THE RIGHT TO STRIKE

3.1 Formal and Legal Requirements

The freedom to strike is different from the right to strike in that the former is not limited by any formal and legal requirements established by applicable labour laws. The act of 23.5.1991 on resolution of collective disputes currently in force regulates in chapter 4, 'Strike' (Articles 17-27), the procedures of legal exercise by the workers of the right to strike and of organisation of strikes by trade unions. The Polish legislature differentiates between the right to strike, which is an individual right of every employee whose freedom to strike was not limited by

1. *Świątkowski*, 2016, 238.
2. *Id.*, 2008, 44.
3. *Ben-Israel*, 1988, 71.
4. *Świątkowski*, 2007, 189.

applicable laws, from the right to organise strikes. The latter is granted only to trade union organisations. The above monopoly of trade unions to organise strikes and other industrial actions was criticised by the Council of Europe as being not in compliance with Article 6 (4) of the European Social Charter. The Council of Europe revised the abovementioned critical view following determination of easy-to-meet conditions for entry of an established trade union organisation into a register stipulated in the act on trade unions of 23.5.1991. Chapter 4 of the act on resolution of collective disputes titled 'Strike' does not lay down any restrictions on the exercise of the right to strike but it sets out formal and legal requirements which should be met by a trade union – an organiser of a strike.[5] These include: (1) voluntary cessation of work by a group of employees (Article 17 (1) in connection with Article 18); (2) use of statutory procedures for amicable resolution of a collective dispute: bargaining and mediation. Strike is a last resort measure. Basically, with two exceptions laid down in the said provision, a strike cannot be legally organised if legal instruments for amicable resolution of a collective dispute have not been exhausted (Article 17 (2)); (3) consideration by the organiser of strike of proportionality of the demands put forward by a trade union and losses which will be caused as a result of interruption of work (Article 17 (3)); (4) prohibition on the participation in a strike by workers employed in the work positions, operating equipment or supervising installations where stoppage of work poses risk to human life and health or jeopardises the state security (Article 19 (1)); (5) prohibition on the organisation of strikes in public institutions listed in Article 19 (2) (army, police and other militarized and paramilitary organisations); (6) prohibition on strike action by employees who do not enjoy the right to strike, employees employed in the public authorities, central and local government administration, courts and prosecution service (Article 19(3)); (7) a statutory obligation of an organiser of a strike to obtain consent of a majority of voting employees employed at the establishment where the strike is to be organised. In the case of an undertaking which consists of two or more establishments, the consent for organisation of a strike must be given by a majority of voting workers employed at the establishments which are to be covered by the strike. The strike referendum should be attended by at least 50% of employees employed at the establishments where the strike is planned (Article 20 (1)-(2)); (8) an employer should be informed of declaration of a strike at least five days before its commencement (Article 20 (3)); (9) a strike cannot restrict a manager of the work establishment and other employees who do not participate in the strike in performing their duties relating to the protection of property of the establishment and uninterrupted work of facilities, equipment and installations the disruption of which might pose risk to human life or health or might prevent resumption of regular operations of the establishment after the strike ends (Article 21 (1)); (10) organisers of strike are obliged to cooperate with a manager of the work establishment in the fulfilment

5. *Id.*, 2009, 245.

of the obligations set out by the legislature in Article 21 (1) of the act on resolution of collective disputes. The jurisprudence has extended the legal restrictions on organisation of strikes not in compliance with law. The ban on strike applies to strikes which are legal but pose risk to life or health of persons who participate in such strike. Such strike is a hunger strike prohibited by the Supreme Court (a judgment of 27.11.1997, I PKN 393/97, OSNP 1998, no. 17, item 511) because of a disproportion between potential benefits and losses which may occur as specified in Article 17 (3) of the act on resolution of collective disputes.

3.2 Types of Strikes

The act of 23.5.1991 mentions two types of strikes organised in compliance with its provisions: 1) official ('real') strike and 2) sympathy (solidarity) strike. The former may be organised exclusively in the case of a collective dispute initiated by employees represented by a trade union (Article 2), concerning working conditions, social benefits, trade union rights and freedoms of workers or other groups of employed persons who are entitled to associate in trade unions (Article 1). The jurisprudence of collective labour law specifies the following types of strikes: (1) basic (classic) strike; (2) warning (preventive) strike; (3) sympathy (solidarity) strike.[6] The act in force does not provide for a prohibition on organisation of strikes aimed at achievement of political purposes. It was recognized that strikes accepted by the legislature, organised for the achievement of specific benefits in the categories of matters listed in Article 1 of the act of 23.5.1991 on resolution of collective disputes - working conditions, social benefits, trade union rights and freedoms, may be - and usually are - related to political issues. Economic, social and occupational interests cannot be separated from political issues. For that reason, the laws governing strikes currently in force do not include the prohibition on organisation of strikes for political purposes. The division of strikes in the Polish legislation and labour law jurisprudence into two types and several kinds of strikes distinguished in terms of their organisational form and methods does not allow distinguishing a strike to which all employees are entitled, regardless of the kind and place of work or type and profile of the employer. Identical right to strikes is granted to all employees whose freedom to strike was not restricted by the legislature. The above means that the legislature cannot divide the legal guarantees resulting from the freedom to strike, granted with no exceptions to all employees, into broader and narrower guarantees. The act of 23.5.1991 on resolution of collective disputes does not provide for the situations in which some employees could enjoy the freedom to strike to the full extent while others could enjoy it only to a limited extent. In practice, the following types of strikes, which are not regulated by the act on resolution of collective disputes, can occur: sporadic

6. *Żołyński*, 2013, 231.

strikes, competence strikes, rotating strikes, intermittent strikes, general strikes, absenteeism, demonstration strikes, temporary strikes, permanent, sit-down, work-to-rule strikes, 'wildcat' (illegal) strikes, hunger strikes, obstructionist strikes.

3.3 The Scope of Coverage of the Statutory Framework Act (23.5.1991) on Resolution of Collective Disputes

The act of 23.5.1991 is generally applicable. It regulates strikes and other industrial actions organised at public and private establishments. The above applies both to legal and 'wildcat' strikes. The legal guarantees of free exercise of trade union freedom apply in both sectors of employment, private and public. However, it should be noted that the public institutions mentioned in Article 19 (2)-(3) of the act of 23.5.1991 on resolution of collective disputes: the Internal Security Agency, the Intelligence Agency, the Military Counterintelligence Service, the Central Anti-Corruption Bureau, police units and unit of Armed Forces of the Republic of Poland, Prison Services, Border Guard, Customs Guard and fire protection organisational units, were considered by the legislature to be establishments at which all the employed persons, both public officers and civil staff performing work under contracts of employment, were deprived of the legal guarantees of the freedom to strike (Article 19 (2)). The right to strike was denied also to employees employed in the public authorities, central and local government administration, courts and prosecution service (Article 19 (3)). The same law – the act of 23.5.1991 – applies to strikes organised in the private and public sector, however the public sector employees listed in Article 19 (2)-(3) of the said act do not enjoy the legal guarantee granted to the private sector employees to organise and to participate in strikes. As regards initiators of strikes organised in state institutions listed in Article 19 (2)-(3) not in compliance with law (illegal) and other employees who fail to fulfil the obligations laid down in the act concerned, the provisions of chapter 5 'Liability for breach of provisions of the act' will apply (Articles 26 and 27). Employees participating in an illegal strike do not enjoy the immunity guaranteed under Article 23 (1) of the act of 23.5.1991 on resolution of collective disputes. The mentioned provision prohibits the employer from classifying participation of an employee in a legal strike as infringement of duties on the part of the employee. Therefore, participation of a state employee in illegal strike amounts to infringement of duties (misconduct). Depending on the assessment of gravity of the infringement, an employer may impose disciplinary penalties, including immediate dismissal of the insubordinate employee.

4 THE EXPERIENCE WITH STRIKES IN ESSENTIAL SERVICES

Cf. the remarks in the next section on strike activity and compliance with regulations concerning essential services.

5 RESTRICTIONS OF THE RIGHT TO STRIKE IN ESSENTIAL SERVICES

In the Polish traditional culture there exists a firmly grounded truth reflected by a saying 'while some must sleep, some must watch'. The legislature rightly considered the human life and health, state security and a material substance of the work establishment employing the workers on strike a 'common good'. Therefore, a disproportion between public services and essential services is not considered by the state employees concerned and by trade unions representing employees of the private sector to be in violation of the sense of social justice. The argumentation relating to the conviction that employees of public sector may accept or contest the legitimacy of a division of employees into two unequal categories one of which, employed in the private sector, has a guaranteed right to strike while the other, employed directly by the state, is deprived of this right, does not seem to be appropriate if it is based on arguments relating to democratic rules of distribution of funds by the state legislative bodies. In my opinion, the 'public services' *versus* 'essential services' dilemma cannot be resolved through such arguments. The state and public officers do not participate, even indirectly in substantive terms, in the legislative process. It can be observed that some employees employed in the state authorities make attempts to develop 'substitutes' of the right to strike of which they were deprived by the act of 23.5.1991 on resolution of collective disputes. The above applies to judges deprived of the right to strike under Article 19 (3) of the mentioned act. Courts and judges employed at the courts are responsible for administration of justice. Their work consists in resolving matters. Suspension of performance of this basic duties and replacing it with preparatory activities such as reading files or studying case-law on the days when court hearings usually take place can be treated as 'collective refraining from work in order to resolve an interest dispute'. This is how a strike was defined in Article 17 (1) of the act on resolution of collective disputes. Judges, prohibited by law from organising strikes, were raising claims against their employer - state justice authorities - demanding increase of their remuneration for work. Article 178 (2) of the Constitution of the Republic of Poland obligates the state employer to provide judges with appropriate working conditions and the remuneration consistent with the dignity of their office and the scope of their duties. Disputes initiated or supported by the social and professional organisations of judges met the conditions laid down in the act of 23.5.1991 to be considered collective disputes. This is because they related to wage and working conditions. The only obstacle to recognition of such disputes as collective disputes within the meaning of Article 1 of the mentioned act is a condition introduced by the legislature which refers to employees or other groups of employed persons having the right to associate in trade unions.

The prohibitions and restrictions laid down in Article 19 (1), (2) and (3) and Article 21 (1) of the act of 23.5.1991 on resolution of collective disputes take a legal form of: 1) the prohibition on cessation of work by the employees employed in the positions, on installations and equipment where stoppage of work poses risk to human life and health or jeopardises the state security (Article

19 (1)); 2) the prohibition on organisation of strikes by state employees mentioned in Article 19 (2); 3) the prohibition on strike by state employees mentioned in Article 19 (3); 4) the prohibition on refraining from work by the employees on strike who are obligated by the legislature to ensure protection of employer's property and uninterrupted operation of the facilities, equipment and installations, the disruption of which might pose risk to human life or health or prevent resumption of regular operations of the establishment (Article 21 (1)). According to the provisions of collective labour law mentioned above, the essential services are protected by the obligation of certain employees to continue work during a strike, the prohibition on organisation of strikes by all state employees mentioned by the legislature, depriving other employees mentioned by the legislature of the right to strike and an obligation to perform certain activities necessary to maintain in proper condition or resume the operations of the establishment where the strike is organised. The beneficiaries of the above-mentioned prohibitions and restrictions are employers. The prohibitions laid down in Article 19 (1) and Article 21 (1) serve to protect interests of all employers, both public and private. On the other hand, the prohibitions laid down in Article 21 (1), (2) and (3) apply only to public employers, primarily the institutions which protect public security and organisational units of judicial authorities. The addressees of the mentioned legal norms are employees and trade union organisations. The prohibitions laid down in Article 19 (1) and Article 21 (1) apply to employees who enjoy the right to fully exercise the freedom of strike and its guarantees which take a form of the right to strike and to organise strikes guaranteed by the provisions of the act of 23.5.1991. The prohibition laid down in Article 19 (2) of the act of 23.5.1991 does not apply to employees mentioned there but to trade union organisations which are exclusively authorised to organise strikes of certain category of employees they represent. The problem is that the state institutions listed in that provision employ public officers who enjoy a limited right of association in the trade unions listed by the legislature (for example, police officers may currently join only police trade unions) and other state employees who constitute a majority and who are deprived of the right of association in trade union organisations. Professional soldiers of Armed Forces of the Republic of Poland are not entitled to form or join trade unions. Article 19 (2) lays down a prohibition on organising strikes in state institutions in which trade unions cannot be formed and therefore a strike cannot be legally organised. A grammatical interpretation of the analysed provision may lead to a conclusion that public officers employed in state institutions listed in that provision might exercise the right to strike if there was a trade union organisation entitled to organise a strike. The above example is not impossible to imagine. The Armed Forces of the Republic of Poland as well as other state institutions mentioned in the analysed provision employ not only public officers, including professional soldiers, but also civil employees of the

army. The latter may be in an obligation relationships of employment with the army concluded under a contract of employment. Such persons may fully enjoy the freedom of association and the related rights, in particular the right to strike. Article 19 (2) of the act of 23.5.1991 is addressed to all persons employed in the public institutions listed in this provision. It applies both to persons who do not have the right of association in trade unions and are therefore deprived of the possibility to organise a strike and to employees who enjoy the legal guarantee of association and the right to strike which cannot be exercised by them because of the prohibition on organising strikes laid down in Article 19 (2).

5.1 Securing Essential Services by Exclusion from Collective Labour Relations Rights

5.1.1 Complete Exclusion Ex Ante Particular Group of Employees

Article 19 (1) of the act of 23.5.1991 imposed a prohibition to strike on all employees employed in work positions, on installations and equipment where stoppage of work poses risk to human life or health or jeopardises the state security. The above prohibition to strike is not of a general nature. It does not apply to all employees employed by a particular employer. It is not a personal prohibition since the legislature clearly indicates which employees are subject to this prohibition. It is a material exclusion. It applies only to the employees who during a strike appear to be necessary for the operations of the establishment in such sense that their absence from work caused by participation in a strike would threaten fundamental values protected by the legislature that is human life and health and state security. The prohibition laid down in this provision is specific. It was established in such a manner that it covers a situation before commencement of a strike however it may further be specified during the strike. An organiser of the strike is therefore obliged to assess the likelihood of risk to human life and health or to state security which may arise as a result of participation of particular employees in the strike. A problem arises when the assessment made by the employer and this made by the organiser of the strike differ. The discussed act of 23.5.1991 does not include any legal norms which might be used by the social partners concerned, the organiser of the strike – trade union and the employer, to resolve a dispute on the legal nature of the strike: whether the strike is legal or illegal. No judicial authority was authorised by the legislature to resolve such disputes. While interpreting the provisions of the act of 23.5.1991 establishing a total prohibition on strike as regards employees employed in the positions in which work cannot be stopped because of the need to protect human life and health or the state security, it is only possible to use a guideline adopted under the *in dubio pro libertate* principle (a judgment of the Supreme Court of 7.2.2007, I PK 209/06; a decision of a Court of Appeal in Katowice of 14.3.2016, III APz 8/16).

5.1.2 *Controlled Ad Hoc Right to Strike in Medical Services*

Deliberations on the prohibition to strike laid down in Article 19 (1) of the act of 23.5.1991 should be illustrated by an example concerning a specific strike of professional hospital employees - medical staff: doctors, nurses, laboratory assistants.[7] A factor which is essential for the assessment whether a strike organised in a hospital is legal or not is the number of persons on strike in each of the three abovementioned groups of medical personnel. Undoubtedly a general participation in the strike by all medical personnel of a hospital would pose risk to life or health of patients since there would not be any member of hospital staff who could undertake and perform the necessary specialist medical operations in the event of threat to life or health of patients. A common practice followed by trade unions organising strikes of medical staff in hospitals is refraining from work by the members of staff except the personnel on emergency duty who remain on standby, ready to undertake the necessary emergency operations in sudden and unexpected situations. The emergency duty is a common way of taking care of life and health of patients during days and hours which are days and hours off for the medical personnel. At that time no previously planned medical treatments are performed. A hospital is an institution which should guarantee fulfilment of the obligation to provide treatment to sick persons. Therefore, an organiser of a strike must decide how many members of operational staff should be excluded from the planned strike in each of the three abovementioned professional categories (doctors, nurses, laboratory assistants) so that the planned strike can be organised legally, without a risk of being accused of endangering life or health of patients. The assessment of the situation may change. An organiser of strike must be flexible which means that he should include into and exclude from the category of employees on strike a certain number of members of operational medical staff necessary to allow the management to perform both planned and emergency operations connected with protection of life and health of patients.[8] Most likely for these reasons the act of 5.12.1996 on the profession of doctor and dentist (OJ 27/2011, item 1634) does not contain provisions on the doctor's right to strike. Medical Code of Ethics adopted in 1993, a collection of ethical standards not considered applicable law (a decision of the Constitutional Tribunal of 7.10.1992, U 1/92), requires that a doctor on strike should provide professional help to a patient in a situation where non-fulfilment of the moral obligation might cause threat to life or health. Every doctor, both the one on strike and the one who performs work, has a moral obligation to secure the well-being of his patient. Doctors, nurses, laboratory assistants who are employed by the hospital, under a contract of employment or otherwise, and who participate in a legal strike must provide their employer with all the necessary information on the patient's situation in order to ensure continuance of treatment during their absence from work caused by the strike.

---

7. *Kurzynoga*, 2012, 18.
8. *Świątkowski*, 2017, 5.

Under labour law, participation of an employee in a strike constitutes a justified reason of employee's absence from work. Only some of the criminal lawyers share the above opinion of labour law specialists.[9] Other lawyers specialising in criminal law present other views concerning strike of medical personnel. According to some of them, a doctor on strike may be exempted from liability for ill health, serious damage to health or death of his patient if it is established that a manager of the hospital had a real possibility to ensure appropriate care to the patients.[10] It is therefore not clear whether the participation of medical personnel in a strike organised in compliance with law is treated as exercise of a right which guarantees to the persons on strike a leave from duties or it also plays a role of an immunity protecting a doctor from criminal liability.

5.1.3 Total Ban on Strikes

Employees which may not strike are those employed in: the President Office, the legislative offices (Sejm and Senate), the Prime Minister Office, particular ministries, national and central offices, such as for example: the Central Customs Office, the General Customs Inspectorate, the National Security Bureau, the Securities and Exchange Commission, the National Atomic Energy Agency, the State Election Commission, the Office of the Committee for European Integration, the Pension Fund Supervision Office, the Public Procurement Office, the Office for War Veterans and Victims of Oppression, the Office of Technical Inspection, the National Employment Office, mining authorities - State Mining Authority and Regional Mining Authority, the Patent Office, the Office of Competition and Consumer Protection, the Office of the Surveyor General of Poland, the Central Standardisation Inspectorate, the General Civil Aviation Inspectorate, the Central Office of Measures, the National Reserve Board, the Chief Inspectorate of Environmental Protection, the General Customs Inspectorate, the Office of the Inspector General for the Protection of Personal Data, the General Directorate of State Forests, the Central Flood Control Committee, the National Council of the Judiciary of Poland, the National Broadcasting Council, the National Rescue Coordination Center, the State Insurance Supervision Office, the Polish Committee for Standardisation; government administration offices (such as voivodeship offices); specialised administration offices (such as tax offices and tax chambers, customs offices and the bodies of the National Labour Inspectorate, the National Inspectorate of Environmental Protection, the National Trade Inspectorate, the National Veterinary Inspection, the Main Inspectorate of Plant Health, the National Telecommunications and Posts Inspectorate, the State Agency for the Protection of Monuments; local government administration offices, such as: commune offices, district, regional offices and

9. *Zatyka*, 2011, 124.
10. *Zoll*, 2008, 11.

marshals' offices; municipal guards; courts of general competence, administrative courts and the Supreme Court; the general and military prosecution units.

Employees that may join trade unions but have no right to bargain collectively are those who have the status of public officers – civil servants and employees of state offices employed under nomination or appointment, local government employees employed under election, nomination and appointment in marshal's offices, district offices, commune offices, offices of associations of local government units. Local government administration means a part of the public administration operating at all levels of the basic country's territorial division – commune, district, region, performing de-centralised portion of public tasks. Local government administration comprises bodies which constitute local government units, which include a commune council, district council, regional assembly, executive bodies of the local government units: heads of communes, mayors, management boards of district with their chairmen, and mayors, including the auxiliary offices – commune offices, district offices, regional offices.

5.2 Legal Strikes and the Contract of Employment

Employees who participate in a legal strike cannot bear any consequences. If a strike takes place, the contract of employment is not terminated. Therefore, the effect of a legal strike is not to terminate the employment contract, but to suspend it. On the other hand, participation in an illegal strike may be considered by the employer equal to infringement of duties (Article 23 (1) of the act of 23.5.1991). In such situation the employer may apply any and all penalties for breach of order in the workplace or disciplinary penalties governed by the provisions of the Labour Code or specific provisions applicable to employment relationships of a particular category of workers. Employers are entitled to withhold wages or male deductions from wages when faced with no performance or partial performance of work by employees engaged in strike.

Employees may be criminally liable to a fine or restriction of liberty if: 1) in connection with the position held or a function performed, they hinder initiation of a collective dispute or disturb lawful collective dispute (Article 26 (1)(1) of the act of 23.5.1991); 2) they fail to comply with the obligations laid down in this act (Article 26 (1) (2)); 3) they lead an illegal strike (Article 26 (2)). An organiser of an illegal strike – a trade union – is liable under civil law to compensation for damage caused (Article 26 (3)).

A liability for organising an illegal strike is governed by the act of 23.5.1991 on resolution of collective disputes. Article 26 (1) of that act applies to persons leading a strike organised contrary to the provisions of the act in question. Only an organiser of an illegal strike can be punished by a fine or restriction of liberty. An organiser of an illegal strike is also liable under Article 415 of the Civil Code for the damage caused by a tort which is the illegal strike. The organiser is liable solely for the consequences of results of actions which are in adequate causal link with the illegal strike. Employees participating in an illegal strike do not enjoy the immunity against liability for breach of duties.

6 COMPENSATORY MEASURES FOR RESTRICTIONS

The act of 23.5.1991 does not provide for alternative instruments which could be used by the employees who were not guaranteed the right of association in trade unions and/or the right to bargain collectively. The same applies in a situation where employees have the right to strike guaranteed but the applicable laws restrict the possibility to exercise such right because of the need to meet the essential public interests – protection of human life and health and state security. The prohibition on strike of employees employed in the positions which must be operated without interruption for the sake of protection of human life and health and state security are not deprived of the right to initiate collective disputes and to use the methods of amicable resolution of such disputes. Similarly to the employees who enjoy the freedom to strike guaranteed by the act of 23.5.1991, the employees employed in the positions listed in Article 19 (1) of the act concerned and trade unions representing their interests are entitled to bargain with the employer, submit the dispute to mediation and eventually take an attempt to resolve the dispute by submitting it for resolution by a social arbitration panel. Only a trade union may apply for submission of the dispute to the social arbitration panel. The social arbitration panel is presided over by a judge of a labour court and it consists of six members, three of them designated by one party and the other three by the other party to a collective dispute. The ruling of the arbitration panel is adopted by the majority of votes. It is binding upon the parties unless either of the parties decides otherwise. The act of 23.5.1991 does not provide for an obligatory submission of a collective dispute for resolution to a social arbitration panel.[11] If an agreement resolving a collective dispute is not reached in a mediation procedure, a trade union is entitled to commence a strike (Article 15). However, a trade union representing workers' interest in the dispute may, without exercising the right laid down in Article 15 of the act in question, attempt to resolve the dispute by submitting it for resolution to the social arbitration panel (Article 16 (1)).

Virtual strike as the quid pro quo for denying or limiting the right to strike is a legal notion not known in the Polish labour law system. According to a legal definition of strike laid down in Article 1 of the act of 23.5.1991, a strike means an actual and not virtual cessation of work by the employees.[12]

11. *Świątkowski*, 1994, 297.
12. *Id.*, 2011, 69.

7 SECURING ESSENTIAL SERVICES BY FURTHER MEANS

The jurisprudence, general courts, the Supreme Court and the Constitutional Tribunal do not resolve collective dispute matters except trade union rights and freedoms, since such disputes are not rights disputes but interest disputes. The social arbitration panels presided by judges are not considered judicial authorities. Criminal courts authorised to impose fines on natural persons, institutions and legal persons rule on imposition of a fine on persons who violate the provisions of the act of 23.5.1991 on resolution of collective disputes.

Social partners may introduce into collective agreements the provisions which prohibit or restrict the freedoms and rights to strike guaranteed under collective labour laws. It is a so called 'social peace' clause. According to it, bodies of a trade union which is a party to an applicable collective agreement may submit a declaration in which they undertake to refrain from exercising their right to organise strike actions during the term of the collective agreement and to prevent the represented employees from participating in such actions organised by another trade union organisation not bound by the 'social peace' clause.

There are no legal obstacles in place that would prevent trade unions from restricting, in the union's by-laws, their rights guaranteed by the generally applicable provisions of the act of 23.5.1991 and developing the strike procedures. The act of 23.5.1991 includes a list of maximum restrictions and prohibitions which may apply in the positions and to employees in such positions who are obliged to perform work during a legal strike in which they should not participate because of the need to protect human life and health and state security. The increased restrictions of the right to strike guaranteed under generally applicable laws may consist in extension of the period to notify the employer of the planned strike or strengthening the requirements necessary for a decision on organisation of a strike to be taken (a 100% quorum, which means that all persons employed at the establishment concerned must participate in the voting; qualified majority, two thirds or three quarters of votes cast for organisation of a strike). However, it must be emphasized that so far there has been no single case in which trade union organisations would impose 'self-restrictions' upon themselves as regards exercise of their right to organise strikes.

8 EVALUATION AND CONCLUSION

Nearly forty years ago, at the beginning of the 1980, strikes organised by persons who were not members of the 'official' trade unions were common in Poland. 'Solidarity' was a mass social movement which then transformed into nationwide confederation of trade unions. The movement was based not only on dissatisfaction with wage and working conditions. More than 10 million members sought to change the political and social system in the country. Most of the workers participated in strikes, also those who were obliged to protect the essential goods such as human life and health and state security. The assumption of the 'essential nature' of the services does not correspond with the developed catalogue of types of job, positions in which employees should not be guaranteed a natural right to exercise their freedom to strike and trade unions should not be guaranteed the freedom to organise strikes. The act of 23.5.1991 on resolution of collective disputes, still in force, strictly connected with two other acts adopted on the same date: (1) on trade unions and (2) on employers' organisations and the Labour Code which in 1974 guaranteed to the social partners the right to bargain collectively, meet the requirements laid down in the international law (ILO) and in the European labour law (Council of Europe) regarding the interdependence between the right to: (1) form and join trade unions granted to workers and other employed persons; (2) bargain collectively; (3) conduct collective disputes. In evaluating the legal mechanisms currently in force, regarding restriction of the right to strike justified by the need to perform work during a strike in the positions in which work cannot be ceased because of a possible risk to the goods of major importance for people: (1) human life and health and (2) state security, I think that the choice made more than a quarter of a century ago, in the act adopted in 1991 and concerning protection of the mentioned essential goods, was the right choice. The method of protection of such goods was also appropriate. It consisted in a general specification of prohibitions on strike in relation to the positions in which work cannot be temporarily ceased because of the possible risk to one or the other common goods, or two legally protected, most important values at the same time. The legislature defined in general terms, ex ante, the essential goods which were subject to legal protection laid down in the provisions establishing temporary prohibitions on strike. The laws indicated not the employees who should not exercise the freedom to strike but the positions in which participation in a legal strike was prohibited. The organisers of strike and employers affected by the strike action could take *ad hoc* decisions, depending on the situation and the level of risk for the fundamental, legally protected goods. The model of legal protection of, on one hand, the fundamental freedom of a worker to decide on participation in a strike action, and on the other hand, the obligation to protect human life and health and state security is unique as it combines the characteristics of selective and dynamic ex-ante and ad hoc models accepted in all systems of collective labour law as model conduct aimed at ensuring a balanced compromise between those who want to strike but for the protection of two important common goods should not stop their work even if they could do it.

However, the model adopted by the collective labour law system is not complete. The act of 23.5.1991 on resolution of collective disputes does not indicate an independent body to resolve disputes between organisers of strike and workers who intend to participate in a legal strike and the employer and his idea of how many positions necessary to guarantee protection of human life and health and state security should be subject to an *ad hoc* prohibition to strike. A divergence in this respect between the parties to a collective dispute is resolved only where a judicial authority specialising not in labour law but in criminal law, authorised to impose sanctions towards persons who violate the provisions of the act on resolution of collective disputes, finds that a strike posed risk to human life or health or to state security because a too large group of employees participated in it and some of these employees should not have stopped their work because by continuing their work they guaranteed security of goods protected by law.

The second critical argument relates to the lack of legal instruments which would guarantee balance to the parties in a collective dispute. In the event of diverging opinions between an organiser of a strike – trade union and an employer who believes that the employees on strike are employed in the positions in which they should not strike for the sake of protection of human life and health and state security, the employer has no possibility to exert pressure on the organiser of the strike to stop the strike. It seems that in such case the attitude of the persons on strike and organisers of strike could change if the employer declared a defensive lockout. In the Polish system of resolution of collective disputes lockout is a legal instrument not regulated in the collective labour laws. If employers were granted the right to organise lockout in certain situations, without a fear of criminal liability for breach of provisions of the act of 23.5.1991, this would contribute to restoration of balance in the collective labour relations. It would also facilitate agreement between the parties to a dispute regarding determination which employees employed in the positions, on installations and equipment covered by the prohibition to strike are needed by the employer to safeguard human life and health or state security and therefore cannot participate in a strike action. Article 19 (1) of the act of 23.5.1991 provides that work cannot be stopped as a result of strike action in certain, generally described, work positions. Therefore, it was left to the discretion of the parties in a collective dispute, acting as social partners in the collective labour relations, to resolve matters relating to determination how many workers employed in sensitive jobs in terms of protection of the goods mentioned in that provision should not participate in a strike concerned. If provisions of collective labour law guaranteed equal status to the parties by granting the employer threatened by a strike a right to organise a defensive lockout, it would contribute to restoration of imbalance in the last, non-irenic stage of resolution of a dispute, following the end of mediation or arbitration. If employees were aware that the employer affected by the strike may exercise his right to declare lockout against employees on strike, this should result in opening of negotiations. Such negotiations would be limited to selected issues regulated under Article 19 (1) of the act 23.5.1991, however they might contribute to implementation of a modern concept of social partnership also at the last stage of a collective dispute.[13]

13. *Id.*, 2013, 245.

Bibliography

Ben-Israel, Ruth, International Labour Standards: The Case of Freedom to Strike, 1988

Kurzynoga, Małgorzata, Kwestia prawa lekarzy do strajku *[Doctors' right to strike]*, Praca i Zabezpieczenie Społeczne 2015, no. 5

Świątkowski, Andrzej Marian, Ustawa o rozwiązywaniu sporów zbiorowych *[Act on resolution of collective disputes], in* Wratny/Walczak (eds)), Zbiorowe prawo pracy. Komentarz *[Collective labour law. Commentary]*, 2009

Id, Charter of Social Rights of the Council of Europe, Kluwer Law International, 2007

Id, Międzynarodowe prawo pracy, Tom I, Międzynarodowe publiczne prawo pracy – standary międzynarodowe, wolumen 2 *[International labour law, Volume I, International public labour law – international standards, volume 2]*, 2008

Id, Strajk – synteza zjawiska *[Strike – a synthesis]*, Monitor Prawa Pracy 2011, no. 2

Id, Gwarancje prawne pokoju społecznego w stosunkach pracy *[Legal guarantees of social peace in labour relations]*, 2013

Id, Labour Law: Council of Europe, 2 ed. Kluwer Law International, 2016

Id, Kontrolowany model prawa do strajku w służbie zdrowia [*Controlled Model of the Right to Strike in Medical Srvices*], Prawo i Medycyna [Law and Medicine] 2017, no. 2

Zatyka, Ewa, Lekarski obowiązek udzielenia pomocy *[Doctor's obligation to provide medical assistance]*, 2011

Zoll, Andrzej, Obowiązek udzielenia pomocy lekarskiej a prawo lekarza do strajku *[Obligation to provide medical assistance and doctor's right to strike]*, Prawo i Medycyna, 2008, no. 1

Żołyński, Janusz, Strajk i inne rodzaje akcji protestacyjnych jako metody rozwiązywania sporów zbiorowych *[Strike and other industrial actions as the methods of resolution of collective disputes]*, 2013

CHAPTER 12

Russia

*Nikita Lyutov**

* The author is very thankful to *Ilona Voitkovska*, Master Student of the MSAL and barrister at law, for invaluable help in work with the case law regarding the strikes.

1 GENERAL BACKGROUND: COUNTRY PROFILE

The Russian Federation is a federal state. Under Article 72 of the Constitution of the Russian Federation,[1] labour legislation is a joint sphere of competence of the Federation and the RF constituent entities (subjects of federation). Joint competence means that the RF constituent entities have the power to legislate in the field of law exclusively with regard to the issues that have not been regulated at the federal level. The matters of collective labour law are based on the Constitution, the Labour Code of the Russian Federation, the Federal Law 'On Trade Unions, their Rights and the Guarantees of their Activities', and other federal legislation (see Section 2). Therefore, although formally labour law, including freedom of association, collective bargaining and strikes, is within the joint competence of the federation and its constituent entities, the whole regulation is established at the federal level.

1.1 Economic, Political and Historical Background

Despite the collapse of the USSR more than a quarter of a century ago, the modern Russian system of collective labour law is heavily influenced by its Soviet past. Employees and trade unions in the Soviet Russia enjoyed a lot of labour rights except for the one which is considered to be a cornerstone in the market economies, namely, the right to strike.

According to the official Soviet labour law doctrine, workers in the socialist country didn't need the right to strike unlike their colleagues in capitalist countries. This statement was based on the argument that the socialist state formally belonged to proletariat, i.e., workers, all entities (employers) were state-owned. To this end, the entities were declared belonging to the workers themselves, which made any conflict of interests pointless.[2]

Socialist trade unions were quasi-governmental structures and, therefore, could not act in conformity with market-economy principles of freedom of association. Trade unions were not acting in the same way as real collective bargaining agents of the capitalist state and therefore were strongly criticized by

1. Konstitutsiya Rossiiskoi Federatsii [the Constitution of the Russian Federation], *Sobraniye Zakonodatelstva Rossiyskoy Federazii [SZ RF] [Russian Federation Collection of Legislation]*. January 26, 2009, No. 4, Item 445.
2. For more details of this doctrine see *Aleksandrov*, 1948, 129 et seqq.

the market economy countries and the International Labour Organization (ILO).[3]

This, however, doesn't mean that socialist trade unions were useless. They played *a different role.* Instead of being a representative of workers, which is traditional to the Western unions, socialist trade unions were rather an amalgam of an intermediate between the state and the employees, and a kind of social ministry – some explanation of this role will be given further in the Chapter.

Formally, there was collective bargaining in the socialist countries.[4] But as long as the right to bargain collectively was not accompanied with a right to strike, actually, it was an imitation of collective bargaining.

An idealistic part of the socialist labour law doctrine was that there was no inherent 'antagonist' conflict of interests between an employer and an employee, which is essential for privately owned business in market economies. Despite the now popular 'win-win' concepts concerning the market-economy collective bargaining, the main idea of the negotiation remains the same for the centuries: *bargaining*, i.e., the more the employee gets, the less will be left as the employer's profit. A socialist enterprise (employer) was not only remote from its formal 'owners' – the people, but in the same manner it wasn't controlled by anyone whose direct interest was to get the immediate profit from its economic activity. Being a part of a socialist economic machine, any entity's goal was twofold: (a) to fulfil the economic plan that was assigned to it by the governmental institution, and (b) to solve the social tasks – provide employment to the population of the region, to finance the social infrastructure, etc.

The managers of socialist entities were not motivated to economize the entity resources by spending less on the employees. On the contrary, they were interested in lowering the production plan to make their own life easier. In monetary terms workers were getting much lower wages than the employees in the richest capitalist countries, but this was in some way compensated by many goods and services in-kind: free or cheap housing, free medicine, free education of all levels, cheap transport services, cheap prices on basic foods, etc. From a social point of view, this system was in some way more humane than the capitalist one.[5]

In addition, to be a 'transmission gear' of the communist party to the 'masses' (i.e., workers) in Lenin's terms,[6] trade unions were significant social institutions. The first major function of trade unions was to control the social security, healthcare, leisure and tourism institutions – social security funds, funds, hospitals, sanatoriums, stadiums, etc. A huge property of this kind was assigned to trade unions by the socialist state. For instance, in the Soviet Union a People's Commissariat (Ministry) on Labour was liquidated in 1933, and all its

3. See *Hepple*, 2005, 33; *Gerasimova*, 2014, 259.
4. In the USSR collective agreements existed at the plant level only.
5. This corresponds more to the late period of socialism when there was no severe totalitarian rule and no economical-military mobilization.
6. *Lenin*, 1967, 349.

functions and property were assigned to the USSR Council of Trade Unions (VCSPS).[7] The members of trade unions could, for instance, travel on a 'trade union trip ticket' to an annual vacation at quite an affordable price. The principles of distribution of these trade union benefits were connected to the employee benefits in professional activities. Thus, trade unions in this field were a kind of employer's disciplinary body - a role unthinkable for the market economy system of industrial relations.

The other function of trade unions was negotiation with the employers on collective agreements at the plant level. The word 'bargaining' wouldn't be appropriate here - 'consultation' describes the situation better. The object of the bargaining was not the wage (as it was established at the centralized level by the state) but certain limited additional benefits. As there was no right to strike, there were no collective labour disputes or disputes of interest envisaged by the law. A totally different role of trade unions can be well illustrated by the fact that for a certain period they formed a pre-court instance for resolution of (individual) labour disputes, i.e., grievances. This means that 'workers' representative' was at the same time an arbiter between a worker and employer. In fact, the trade unions were mainly representing the employer's needs, but they were also supposed to be 'close to workers'. A good example of this situation may be found in the latest Soviet labour law history: the first collective labour dispute in mining sector in Kuzbass region of the USSR was settled by signing an agreement between the miners' *strike committee on the one side*, and the Joint Commission of the local Communist Party authority, the employer and the representative of the *Soviet Trade Union Committee on the other side*.[8]

The transition of former socialist trade unions into democratic organizations and the formation of new trade unions have been a difficult challenge in Russia. The soviet trade unions being former supporters of the socialist regime, the legitimacy and reliability of 'old' trade unions as real representatives of workers have been questioned for a long time. New trade unions founded after the transition face similar difficulties as their counterparts in other market economy countries, namely: the small number of members and, consequently, the problem of democratic representativity fading away. In modern Russia the most active and ready to perform the strike actions are the 'new' trade unions, mainly in the manufacturing companies with foreign investments.

1.2 Legal Framework

Russia is a civil law country with the legal system which is firmly rooted in the Soviet legal heritage. Long isolation of Russia by the Iron Curtain during the

7. *Sovetskoye trudovoye pravo*, 1972, 185.
8. Protocol on agreed measures between the Regional Strike Committee and ZK KPSS Commission, Council of Ministers of the USSR and VCSPS of 19 July 1989 (Quoted by *Lopatin*, 1995, 66).

Soviet period made the Russian legal system so specific that some academics say that it is distinct from both common and civil law systems.[9]

The basic law that regulates employment matters is the Labour Code of the Russian Federation[10] (the Labour Code). It includes chapters on an employment relationship and employment contract (including their respective definitions), collective labour law, the norms on wages, working time, labour discipline, mutual liability of the parties of the employment contract, occupational safety and health, resolution of individual and collective labour disputes, norms covering specific categories of employees, etc.

The legal status of trade unions is regulated by the special Federal Law 'On Trade Unions, their Rights and the Guarantees of their Activities' adopted in 1996.[11] This law provides for the list of rights of trade unions and the supporting mechanisms of their implementation. The status of employers' associations is regulated by the Federal Law 'On employers' associations' adopted in 2002.[12] The mechanisms of collective bargaining, resolution of collective labour disputes and performance of strikes are established by the Labour Code.

It is important that theoretically, there must be no 'judge made law' in the Russian legal system: formally, the courts only have the power to interpret the existing law and are not authorized to make a new law if they face a gap in regulation. However, the practice of interpretation is such that courts often have to interpret the law in quite an expansive manner in order to fill in the gap. The Supreme Court of the Russian Federation (the Supreme Court), which is the highest court instance,[13] issues statements with explanations to the lower courts on how they should apply and interpret law in different situations. Such statements do not have the formal legal power, but they usually are taken by lower courts as a firm instruction. There are no special labour courts in Russia,

9. See *David/Goré/Jauffret-Spinosi*, 2016, 127 et seqq. See also on the matter: *Przhilenskiy/ Zakharova*, 2016, 6 et seqq; *Sinyukov*, 1994, 3 et seqq.
10. Trudovoy Kodeks Rossiyskoy Federatsii [The Labour Code of the Russian Federation], adopted by Federal Law of 30 December 2001 No. 197-FZ. *Sobraniye Zakonodatelstva Rossiyskoy Federazii* [SZ RF] [Russian Federation Collection of Legislation] Jan. 7, 2002, No.1 (part 1), Item 3.
11. Federalnyi Zakon [Federal Law] Jan. 12, 1996 No. 10-FZ, *Sobraniye Zakonodatelstva Rossiyskoy Federazii* [SZ RF] [Russian Federation Collection of Legislation] Jan. 15, 1996, No.3, Item 148.
12. Federalnyi Zakon [Federal Law] Nov. 27, 2002, No. 156-FZ, *Sobraniye Zakonodatelstva Rossiyskoy Federazii* [SZ RF] [Russian Federation Collection of Legislation] Dec. 2, 2002, No.48, Item 4741.
13. Before 2014 there was a separate system of commercial jurisdiction headed by the Higher Arbitration Court of the Russian Federation. In 2014 the system of arbitration courts was subordinated to the Supreme Court of the Russian Federation and the Higher Arbitration Court was dismissed. There is also Constitutional Court of the Russian Federation which is not subordinated to the Supreme Court. However, the Constitutional Court does not resolve the disputes as such but gives the conclusions on the constitutionality of legal acts and practice.

but there is a specialization of certain judges in specific types of cases (including labour disputes). The higher courts have the special labour dispute chambers.

The courts generally try to avoid making statements that may be considered as creating a new legal rule. Therefore, they usually tend to ground their decisions on some written legal rules as much as possible. From the point of view of determining the legality of strikes, this means that courts usually give more trust to formalities than to proportionality of action or some factual circumstances of the case.

2 COLLECTIVE LABOUR RELATIONS

Collective bargaining in Russia is performed at a number of levels as established by Article 26 of the Labour Code:

- The federal level – the all-Russian level (the General Agreement between the Government of the Russian Federation and the unions of the most representative trade union confederations and the employers' associations).
- The interregional level – the level of two or more constituent entities of the Russian Federation (Interregional Agreements between respective representatives).
- The regional level – the level of constituent entities of the Russian Federation (Regional Agreements).
- The sectoral level – the level of a certain sector of economy (Sectoral Agreements).
- The territorial level – the level of municipality (Territorial Agreements).
- The local level – the level of the employer or a structural division of the employer (Collective accords between the employees and employer).

As it is stated in Article 26 of the Labour Code, at each respective level above the plant level 'the foundations for the regulation of relations in the field of labour' are established. For those levels that are above the plant level, the Labour Code uses a special term *soglasheniye* (agreement) as opposed to *kollekitvnyi dogovor* (collective accord) which is signed at the plant level. The phrase about 'foundations for the regulation' gives a good understanding about the usual contents of the higher-level agreements. They contain quite a few obligations of employers towards the employees. The wages almost never become a subject of regulation in the collective accords at the higher level. In many cases the obligations of employers are limited to empty phrases such as 'employers are recommended to undertake…', 'employers take measures aimed at…', etc.[14] In rare cases sectoral agreements contain provisions concerning the

14. See, for example, Sectoral agreement on the companies that are within the competence of Ministry of Education and Science of the Russian Federation for 2015-2017; Sectoral agreement for the mass media companies for 2015-2017; Sectoral tariff agreement on

amount of wages, but they establish just minimum, which is slightly above the statutory federal minimum wage. Taking into account that the statutory minimum wage is currently 11163 rubles per month (about 158.5 euro), this level usually does not reflect the actual situation in payment of wages.

Collective accords at the plant level in many cases just repeat the norms that have already been enshrined in the legislation. Only in the minority of cases they add something substantial to the statutory rights of employees.[15]

Therefore, although bargaining coverage in Russia seems to be quite high,[16] it would not be an exaggeration to state that collective bargaining at higher levels of negotiation acquires quite a modest added value in establishing the labour rights of workers.

2.1 Unions and the Rate of Unionization

In the Soviet time, trade union membership was not universal, but it was steadily increasing during the whole socialist period until trade unions united almost all workers in the late decades of the USSR existence.[17]

As it was said in *supra* Section 1.1, the trade union movement in Russia is divided significantly between the so-called 'old' and 'new' trade unions. This distinction is more important than division into private and public-sector unions. In Russia, the predecessor of the earlier union having monopoly is recently still the dominating union – the *Federation of Independent Trade Unions of Russia (Federatsiya nezavisimykh profsoyuzov Rossii, FNPR)*. According to the FNPR statement, it unites more than 95% of total union members in Russia.[18] The FNPR is frequently criticized for being more interested in having close relations with the state authorities rather than in defending the interests of the employees. After the change of the regime, some new trade union federations were formed (the main 'alternative' trade union federation is the Russian Labour Confederation (*Konfederatsiya Truda Rossii, KTR*).[19] But they are incomparably smaller and are much weaker at political level.

electric energy for 2013-2015 extended to 2018; Sectoral agreement on atomic energy companies for 2015-2017 et al. (Consultant Plus Database).

15. See *Pryazhennikov*, 2018, 215 et seqq.
16. Information on collective bargaining coverage is not considered in Russia. According to our calculations based on the information of the FNPR Executive Committee for 2011, 2012, 2013, 2014, 2015 and 2016 and Analytical information on development of social partnership in regions of Russia in 2011 and 2112 prepared for Rostrud and Mintrud, only coverage of FNPR organizations by collective agreements, which they negotiate, is accessible: around 91-92 per cent.
17. For the USSR see the dynamics of VCSPS membership in Bolshaya Sovetskaya Encyclopedia [Great Soviet Encyclopaedia], 1977 (available at http://bse.sci-lib.com/article 093699.html).
18. The Federation of Independent Trade Unions of Russia (FNPR) official site: http://fnpr.ru/n/252/4890.html.
19. The Confederation of Labour of Russia (KTR) official site: http://www.ktr.su/.

The level of trade union membership in the post-Soviet Russia is about 29 per cent of the total number of employees, but there is no reliable statistics on the issue.[20] While talking about the level of trade union membership, one must take into account that many unions can hardly be considered independent. There is a strict division between the dominant majority „old' trade unions and the „new' or „independent' trade unions in this respect. The former often act not as real collective bargaining agents but rather are affiliated to company management and in many cases are not in fact independent. Due to the system of collective bargaining that is established by the Russian Labour Code, they can effectively block the attempts of minority unions to perform real collective bargaining and organize the strikes. Therefore, the real number of active trade unionists that may seriously consider taking part in strikes, is much lower than the mentioned level of 29 per cent.

There is no statistics concerning the division of membership in private v. public sector unions. However, most state-owned companies have plant unions that have been established in these companies in the Soviet times and are currently affiliated to the FNPR. These unions have many members (often the majority of workers) on the inertial basis – just because workers don't bother themselves withdrawing from the union.

In private companies, the trade union membership is significantly lower except for the companies which were previously state owned and 'inherited' the plant-level unions from the Soviet past.

2.2 Employers' Associations and Rate of Organization

During the socialist period, the Soviet Union always had problems with representation of employers within the ILO structures. In the Soviet planned economy, all significant employers were belonging to the state and were directly controlled by the government. The Russian translations of ILO Conventions and Recommendations of that time called employers *predrinimateli* (lit. – entrepreneurs). Taking into account that the Penal Code of that time contained a crime of 'private entrepreneurship or commercial intermediary activity',[21] it is quite clear that there could be no real tripartite social dialogue in the USSR an that time.

20. There is no official statistics on trade union density. Our estimation is that union membership in Russia is about 29 per cent of total workforce, if the official statements of biggest trade-union associations is anything to go by. Officially the economically active population of Russia is 76,1 mln. for the beginning of 2017 (http://www.gks.ru/bgd/free/b04_03/isswww.exe/stg/d01/36.htm), with around 20 mln. members in the biggest TU Federation (FNPR) according to their latest official information of 2015 (http://www.fnpr.ru/n/252/4890.html), and around 2 mln. members in KTR.
21. Ugolovno-ispolnitelnyi Kodeks Rossiiskoi Federatsii [The Penal Code of the Russian Federation] Art. 153, *Vedomosti Verkhovnogo Soveta RSFSR [Bulletin of the RSFSR Supreme Council]*, 1960. No. 40, item 591.

Therefore, it is appropriate to talk about the employers' associations in the context of strikes only during the period after the collapse of the Soviet Union in 1991.

The most well-known employers' association in Russia is *Rossiyskiy soyuz promyshlennikov i predprinimateley* (Russian Union of Industrialists and Entrepreneurs, the RSPP)[22] which was founded in 1991 during the process of transition to the market economy. The main goal of the RSPP is to represent employers in *Rossiskaya tryokhstoronnyaa komissiya po regulirovaniyu sotsial'no-trudovykh otnosheniy (*the Russian Tripartite Commission on the Regulation of Social and Labour Relations, the *RTK*),[23] established for the consultation concerning the adoption of labour and social security legislation, other issues of social policy and bargaining concerning conclusion of the General Agreement between the Government and all-Russian federations of trade unions and employers' associations (i.e., the highest level collective agreement). There is no information concerning the dynamics of membership in the RSPP since the moment of its foundation. However, as it is clear from its data about member structures, it unites the majority of sector-level employers' associations and the biggest employers as separate members.[24] Another well-known employers' association is '*Opora Rossii*' (The Pillar of Russia) which unites employers of small and medium-size businesses. Although its main activity is concentrated in lobbying the interests of SMEs in relations with the state, they are also represented in the RTK.

Taking into account that strikes (irrespective of whether they are performed in essential services or not) in practice never happen at the levels above the single employer (see *infra* Subsection 2.3), employers' associations don't play a significant role in the situations of specific strikes. Their role regarding strikes seems to be limited to the conservation of current regulatory norms that make implementation of the right to strike close to impossible (see *infra* Subsections 2.3 and 3.3).

2.3 Data Regarding Strikes

There is no statistics regarding full v. partial strikes or strikes in public v. private sector. However, the official statistics for the recent years show that even the overall strike level is so low that it may be concluded that strikes almost never happen:[25]

22. See the RSPP official site: http://eng.rspp.ru/.
23. See the information about the RTK at http://government.ru/department/141/about/.
24. See http://рсПП.рФ/about/members.
25. See *Federalnaya Slujba Gosudarstvennoy Statistiki*, 2011; *id.*, 2016.

Year	*2000*	*2001*	*2002*	*2003*	*2004*	*2005*	*2006*	*2007*	*2008*	*2009*	*2010*	*2011*	*2012*	*2013*	*2014*	*2015*
Number of companies affected by strikes	817	291	80	67	5933	2575	8	7	4	1	0	2	6	3	2	5

Even a short glance at these data is sufficient to understand that official statistics does not represent any real picture. No dramatic events in 2004 and 2005 could be found to explain the rise of the strike record to four-digit numbers and then its immediate decrease to one-digits. The only explanation of this strange picture can be found in the method of calculation. Since 2006 official statistics includes only legal strikes.

For the country a population of with over 140 million, the strike statistics for the last ten years may only mean that only in the very exceptional cases the conflicts between workers and employers are settled within a framework of law. Only 10.2 thousand hours are officially reported to be lost due to strikes in 2015.[26] However, it's a big growth as compared to respective numbers of 0.4, 2.4, 0.2 and 5 thousand that were lost during the period from 2011 to 2014.[27] Although the number of strikes remains symbolic, in 2014 and 2015 they were declared at much bigger enterprises with more than 2 thousand employees on average.

Most conflict situations are resolved outside formal rules. The Russian Non-governmental Organization 'Centre for Social and Labour Rights' has been performing a monitoring of all actions of employees that have led to total or partial stoppage of enterprise activity (strikes, work stoppages provoked by non-payment of wages, hunger-strikes, take-overs of employer's facilities and any other actions either legal or illegal) since 2008.[28] The information was gathered through the Internet, mass media and internal communications with trade unions, non-governmental organizations and other available sources. The data are as follows:

Year	*2008*	*2009*	*2010*	*2011*	*2012*	*2013*	*2014*	*2015*	*2016*
Number of work stoppages	60	106	88	91	95	102	97	168	158

The first thing that comes clearly from the data is that illegal protests that fall outside the official statistics happen many times more frequently than the legitimate strikes. It is also obvious that contrary to the official data, the strike level has risen since the beginning of economic problems in Russia in 2008. Such a gap between official statistics and the real situation can be explained by the in-fact restrictive procedure of strikes announcement and performance established by the Russian Labour Code (see *infra*). Gaps in legislation are associated not only with strict procedural rules but also with discriminative procedures of collective bargaining relating to the minority trade unions, weak and further

26. *Id.*, 2016.
27. *Ibid.*
28. See *Bizyukov*, 2017.

weakening trade unionists' protection measures, and quite restrictive court attitude towards the legality of strikes.

During the last year sociologists note an increase in a number of stop-actions in the public sector (medicine, education, communal services). The share of state sector in stop actions in 2016 reached 24 per cent, which is the largest share in the last years.[29] Also, the year 2016 was notable by the first occurrence of protest actions among the state civil servants since 1990-ies.[30]

3 THE RIGHT TO STRIKE

3.1 Collective Labour Relations Rights

Article 37, paragraph 4 of the Constitution of the Russian Federation[31] provides for '*the right to individual and collective labour disputes with the use of methods of their resolution provided by the federal law including the right to strike*'. This means that:

- The constitutional right to strike is not absolute, but may only be realized in the manner established by the separate federal law. Such federal law regulation is mainly contained in Chapter 61 of the Labour Code.[32]
- Other limitations of the right to strike such as bans on strikes in essential services may be and actually are established by the federal legislation (see *infra*).

Article 409 of the Labour Code mentions the right to strike as the method of collective labour disputes' resolution with reference to Article 37 of the Constitution. The definition of strike is set forth in Article 398 of the Labour Code. '*Strike is a temporary voluntary refusal of employees to perform their labour duties (in whole or in part) with a goal to resolve the collective labour dispute*'. The same Article 409 of the Labour Code provides for the voluntary character of strikes and prohibition of any coercion in respect of strike performance, i.e., both positive and negative right to strike.

As long as the strike is understood only as means of resolving a 'collective labour dispute', its legal definition is also essential for the proper understanding of the meaning of the term 'strike'. The definition of a *collective labour dispute* is given in the same Article of the Labour Code. It is defined as '*non-resolved disagreements between employees (their representatives) and employers (their representatives) concerning the establishment and alteration of conditions of*

29. *Ibid.*
30. *Ibid.*
31. *Sobraniye Zakonodatelstva Rossiyskoy Federazii* [SZ RF] [Russian Federation Collection of Legislation] Jan. 26, 2009, No. 4, Item 445.
32. *Sobraniye Zakonodatelstva Rossiyskoy Federazii* [SZ RF] [Russian Federation Collection of Legislation] Jan. 7, 2002, No. 1, Item 3.

work (including wages), conclusion, alteration and execution of collective agreements and accords and also concerning the refusal of the employer to take into account the opinion of the employees' elected representative body during the process of adoption of local normative acts [of the employer – N.L.]'.

Limitation of the strike purpose to the resolution of collective labour disputes makes illegal performance of *solidarity actions* and *political strikes,* because in both cases the parties of the strike are not addressing their demands to *their* employer and, therefore, fall out of the definition of collective labour dispute.

The Russian Federation is a party to the *International Covenant on Social, Economic and Cultural Rights* establishing the right to strike[33]. Russia is also bound by Article 6, paragraph 4 of the *European Social Charter* which establishes the right to strike. Nevertheless, Russia has not ratified the Additional Protocol to the Charter setting up a collective complaints procedure and therefore is not subject to this control mechanism.

Russia is also a party to the ILO fundamental Conventions on freedom of association No. 87 and 98. These Conventions have no direct statements concerning the right to strike, but the ILO controlling bodies – the Committee of Experts on Application of Conventions and Recommendation (CEACR) and the Committee on Freedom of Association (CFA) – consider that the right to strike is an integral part of freedom of association established by these Conventions. Decisions of the CEACR and the CFA are not themselves sources of law that may be directly applied by Russian courts. Still, they may be used as a secondary source of interpretation of applicable norms.

Russia has received a significant amount of comments from the ILO monitoring bodies, as well as from the European Committee of Social Rights, responsible for exercising control over the application of the European Social Charter. Some of them relating to the strikes in essential services are commented further.

3.2 The Right to Strike

No official distinction between the *rights*' and *interests*'[34] disputes exists in the Russian labour legislation. Two different procedures on resolution of collective and individual labour disputes exist. Collective labour disputes are resolved in a manner usual for disputes of interest: conciliation, mediation, arbitration and strikes.[35] Individual labour disputes are always the disputes of rights and may be settled by courts and commissions on labour disputes (voluntary pre-court procedure)[36]. There is one type of disputes of rights that may be settled both as

33. International Covenant on Social, Economic and Cultural Rights. Art. 8, para. 1 (d).
34. See more about this division: *Gladstone*, 2010; *Goldman*, 2010, 721 et seqq.
35. See also *Lyutov*, 2014, 451.
36. Trudovoi Kodeks Rossiiskoi Federatsii [Labor Code of the Russian Federation]. Art. 381 and Art. 382.

an individual and a collective labour dispute, namely: the disputes about the execution of collective agreements. Consequently, two principally different procedures of resolution may be applied at the same time to practically the same dispute.

The demands on collective labour disputes must be addressed to the employer or its representative. If the demand itself would not be contradictory to the legislation and would be within the employer's control, there is no limitation on strikes arising out of disputes relating to issues that are not fit to be regulated by collective bargaining (management prerogatives).

Strikes arising out of inter-union disputes, political strikes or strikes to announce certain concerns to the public wouldn't be legal because demands of employees wouldn't be addressed to the employer or its representative (see *supra* Subection 3.1). By the same reason, all *political* or *quasi-political* strikes or *sympathy actions* would be considered illegal as long as they are not directly addressed at resolution of the dispute with the employer or the dispute between the trade union organization and employers' association, if collective dispute is resolved at a higher level than the level of single enterprise. The latter situation is purely theoretical: although it is envisaged by the Labour Code, in practice all strikes are performed at a plant level.

There is no direct mentioning regarding the regulation of *full or partial* strikes. However, the Labour Code mentions[37] that a strike committee must issue a strike notice at least five working days before the strike takes place, which, among other issues, should contain the information about the expected number of employees taking part in a strike. This may be interpreted as granting the right to the employees to decide, whether the strike will be full or partial.

Employees or their representatives have the right to call a strike if peaceful procedures have not lead to the resolution of the collective labour dispute, or the employer or its representative is evading to take part in peaceful procedures, or he does not execute the decision of labour arbitration which is binding to the parties[38], except for cases of prohibition of strikes established by the law.[39] Article 410, paragraph 2 of the Labour Code sets up an exception to this rule: if the strike has been announced by the trade union or trade unions' confederation, it may be performed upon the decision of workers of specific employer without exercising peaceful procedures.

The requirements for the approval of the strike by the workers' rank and file are set in Article 410 of the Labour Code. The decision to call a strike is taken by the meeting or a conference of employees of the employer.[40] The meeting quorum is no less than half of this employer's employees; the conference quorum is no less than two thirds of delegates. An initial quorum was two thirds

37. *Id.*, Art 410, para. 10.
38. *Id.*, Art. 409, para. 2.
39. *Id.*, Art. 413, see further details.
40. The term *conference* is used when the enterprise is too big to organize a meeting of all employees. In this case employees' delegates for the conference are elected.

for both conference and meeting, but after the criticism of the provision of the Labour Code on behalf of the ILO,[41] the quorum for the meeting was lowered in 2006. The decision to call a strike should be taken by no less than a half of the employees or delegates present at the meeting or conference. The period of notice that is required amounts to ten calendar days[42].

Conciliation is the only mandatory procedure among three peaceful collective labour dispute resolution procedures (conciliation, mediation and arbitration). The Conciliation Commission is to be set up within two calendar days since the day of beginning of the collective labour dispute or three days in hypothetic cases of disputes at the level higher than the enterprise level[43]. The day of the beginning of collective labour dispute is the day when the employer informs about declining of all or part of the employees' or their representatives' demands or the failure of the employer to inform about its decision[44]. The employer is obliged to provide such information within two days after receiving the demands or within three weeks - for disputes at the level higher than the enterprise level[45]. The Conciliation Commission has three calendar days to examine the collective labour disputes (five days - for higher-level disputes). Before the end of 2011 this term could be prolonged upon written consent of both parties of the dispute but now such provision is taken away from the Code[46]. This amendment was made in line with other changes of collective labour disputes regulation mainly associated with shortening of terms of different procedures. In general, such changes were declared as facilitation of the right to strike. But in this particular case such modification is leaving the parties without reasonable flexibility that could help them resolve the dispute by peaceful means.[47]

Conciliation may end in the decision on resolution of collective labour dispute. If the decision was approved by the parties, it is binding upon them. The dispute is considered to be resolved and no right to strike may be legally exercised in such a situation. Nevertheless, there is no prohibition in law for the employees to address to the employer demands similar to the demands that were

41. In August 2001 the Government of the Russian Federation made a request to the ILO to comment on the draft Labour Code adopted by the State Duma (the lower house of Parliament). In response to this request, the ILO experts prepared a Memorandum (hereinafter: Memorandum), addressed to the Government where certain proposals to amend the text were made. For further details see *Lyutov*, 2003, 173 et seqq.
42. Trudovoi Kodeks Rossiiskoi Federatsii [Labor Code of the Russian Federation]. Art. 410, para. 8.
43. *Ibid.* Art. 402.
44. *Ibid.* Art. 398.
45. *Ibid.* Art. 400.
46. Federalnyi Zakon 'O vnesenii izmenenii v Trudovoi Kodeks Rossiyskoi Federatsii v chasti sovershenstvovaniya v poryadke rassmotreniya i razresheniya kollektivnykh trudovykh sporov [Federal Law on Amendments to the Labour Code of the Russian Federation with Regard to Improvement of the Procedure of Considering and Resolving Labour Disputes] Nov. 22, 2011, No. 334-FZ.
47. See more on the issue: *Gerasimova*, 2012, 35-38.

raised in the course of the previous collective dispute – even the next day after the decision of the Conciliation Committee. However, I am not aware of such a practice.

According to Article 403 of the Labour Code, if collective labour dispute was not resolved by the Conciliation Commission, the parties to the dispute must sign the protocol on disagreement and start negotiations about the resolution of the dispute with the assistance of a *mediator*. Such negotiations must start the next day after signing the protocol. If the parties do not agree on the invitation of the mediator, they are under an obligation to negotiate the issue of resolution of the dispute through the *labour arbitration*. The mediator may only make recommendations to the parties concerning dispute resolution, while the condition for holding of arbitration is the agreement of the parties to abide by its decision.[48] In both cases the parties to the dispute are only obliged to discuss the possibility to use these two procedures (mediation and arbitration) but not to actually implement them. Exception to this rule is the case of compulsory arbitration in cases when the strikes are not permitted (see Subsection 6.2 further).[49]

A Collective Accord at the enterprise level[50] may contain an obligation not to strike '*in the event of fulfilment of a corresponding obligation by the employer*', i.e., the relative peace obligation[51]. Article 46 of the Labour Code concerning the contents of the multi-employer collective agreements[52] does not name such an obligation, although it doesn't prohibit parties to include it into the agreement. Nevertheless, the performance of strike that violates the peace obligation is not included in the exhaustive list of grounds to determine the strike illegal[53]. Arguably such a strike may be considered as being performed '*in breach of terms, procedures and requirements set up in the Code*'[54]. Still, the breach of peace obligation is the violation of a collective agreement and not of the Labour Code directly. No court decisions on the matter are known.

Moreover, it is up to the parties of a collective agreement to decide whether to include the '*peace duty*' into the collective agreement or not. Theoretically, the employer affected by the strike can claim rights which arise from the '*peace duty*', but no practice is known. Bound to the '*peace duty*' are the parties of collective agreement from the employees' side. These are all employees of the employer (at the enterprise-level) or of the employed being covered by the

48. Trudovoi Kodeks Rossiiskoi Federatsii [TK RF] [Labor Code of the Russian Federation]. Art. 404.
49. *Ibid.* Art. 404, para. 2.
50. *Kollektivniy dogovor* [Collective Accord] in terms of Russian legislation (see *supra* Section 2).
51. Trudovoi Kodeks Rossiiskoi Federatsii [TK RF] [Labor Code of the Russian Federation] Art. 41, para. 2.
52. *Soglasheniya* [Agreements] in Russian legislation (see *supra* Section 2).
53. Trudovoi Kodeks Rossiiskoi Federatsii [TK RF] [Labor Code of the Russian Federation] Art. 413.
54. *Ibid.*, Art. 413, para. 3.

multi-employer agreement. The union membership is irrelevant to collective bargaining purposes. The '*peace duty*' implies the prohibition of strike relating to the existing collective agreement.

The '*peace duty*' exists during the course of the validity of the collective agreement subject to limitations and the unclear character of the duty itself. In order for the '*peace duty*' to be fulfilled, only direct participation in a strike may be limited.

The strike rules are applied equally in *private and public* sector. The condition of the applicability of the strike rules established by the Labour Code, is the employee status of worker. Civil law contractors, public servants and other non-employee categories of workers don't have the right to strike (see further).

4 THE EXPERIENCE WITH STRIKES IN ESSENTIAL SERVICES

As it was mentioned above,[55] strikes in general are declared only in exceptional cases in Russia. The practice of legal strikes in essential services is even more exotic. However, this doesn't mean that the problem of strikes in essential services is not important for Russia. Illegal strikes or other forms of strike actions happen from time to time and, because of restrictive regulation, they often take quite tough forms, such as hunger-strikes, etc.

In the recent years the Russian economy has been facing stagnation,[56] the real (cleared from the inflation) incomes are declining starting from 2014 till the moment of writing (December 2017),[57] the incomes gap is quite big,[58] and therefore, there is no surprise that the level of discontent of workers in general is rising.

The essential services employees work mainly in the public sector, and this sector of economy is undergoing serious reforming aimed at enhancing its effectiveness and productivity. These reforms are also associated with increasing wages,[59] which at first glance may be considered as motivation to diminish dissatisfaction of essential service employees in public service. Nevertheless,

55. See *supra* Subsection 2.3.
56. See, for example, the World Bank Data at https://data.worldbank.org/indicator/NY.GDP.MKTP.PP.KD?locations = RU.
57. Federalnaya Slujba Gosudarstvennoy Statistiki, 2017. Available at http://www.gks.ru/free_doc/new_site/population/urov/urov_12kv.doc.
58. See the information about equality, e.g., using the Gini Index calculated by the US Central Intelligence Agency: The Central Intelligence Agency. World Factbook. Available at https://www.cia.gov/library/publications/the-world-factbook/rankorder/2172rank.html, or data calculated by the United Nations Development Agency (UNDP) in the Global 2016 Human Development Report. Available at http://hdr.undp.org/sites/default/files/2016_human_development_report.pdf.
59. There is a programme of alteration of wages to workers in medical and education sector with indicators compared to the average wages in respective regions established by the Presidential Decrees No. 597, 598 and 599 of May 7, 2012, *Sobraniye Zakonodatelstva Rossiyskoy Federazii* [SZ RF] [Russian Federation Collection of Legislation] May 7, 2012, No.19, item. 2335.

this increase is performed without big additional state funding. In practice, this means perspectives of massive collective dismissals because of sharing the same amount of work among the smaller number of workers. So, the essential services employees that are to be dismissed may start protesting against dismissals (although this will not constitute a valid subject of collective labour dispute and, therefore, there will be no right to strike in such a situation), and the employees that will retain their workplaces are already protesting against permanent growth of the workload.[60]

The essential service workers who are protesting against these reforms, are claiming that they are not just objecting to dismissals and intensification of the work process, but rather struggle against the threat to deteriorate the quality of service. These were the reasons of recent cases of protest picketing,[61] hunger-strikes[62] and work to rule actions[63] of the ambulance personnel.

Therefore, there are reasons to expect the further growing number of protest and strikes in the essential services, although most of them will be performed illegally.

There is no statutory definition of essential services in Russian labour law. Nevertheless, the Labour Code provides[64] that '*according to Art. 55 of the Constitution of the Russian Federation the strikes shall be declared illegal and shall not be allowed in the following cases:*

(a) during the period of military alert or the state of emergency, or specific measures taken in accordance with the legislation on the state of emergency; in structures of the Military Forces of the Russian Federation, other military, paramilitary bodies or organizations (or structural subdivisions) that are directly responsible for the issues of the country defence, security of the state, emergency rescuing, searching-rescuing, fire-fighting works, prevention or liquidation of natural disasters or emergency situations; in law enforcement bodies; in organizations (or structural divisions) that are directly servicing highly dangerous manufacturing and facilities, at ambulance stations;

(b) *in the organizations (or structural subdivisions) that are directly associated with securing life-sustaining of the population (energy provision, heating, water-supply, gas-supply, aviation, railroad and*

60. This is a subject of serious discontent among the public-sector employees already. For example, the Centre for Labour and Social Rights research has marked a significant growth of protests and stop actions of transport workers in the first half of 2017. See *Bizyukov*, 2017.
61. Kollektivnoye deystvie [Collective Action], 2015.
62. Profsoyuzi segodnya [Unions Today], 2015.
63. Meduza, 2015. Available at https://meduza.io/feature/2015/04/06/vrachi-na-iznose.
64. Trudovoi Kodeks Rossiiskoi Federatsii [TK RF] [Labour Code of the Russian Federation] Art. 413, para. 1.

water transport, communications, hospitals) in cases if the performance of strikes endangers the interests of state defence, security of the state, life and security of the people'.

First, it is clear from this list that the Labour Code provides for two different types of what may be called 'essential services'. In the first type of situations and structures (the ones that directly deal with the issues of state security and personal safety listed under letter 'a' in this article), the strikes are unconditionally prohibited. In the second list (letter 'b') the strikes may be prohibited if they endanger the interests of state and security of human beings.

Second, the prohibition of strikes in all listed situations is justified by the reference to Article 55 of the Constitution. Paragraph 3 of the Article speaks about the possibility to limit the rights and freedoms of a human and citizen by the federal law to the extent as it necessary to *protect the foundations of constitutional order, morality, health, rights and lawful interests of other persons and the needs of state defence and security*. Thus, in any case, the issues of security of state and people are named by the legislator as the legal ground for the statutory limitation of the right to strike.

Also, the Labour Code[65] contains a norm that provides for the power of the federal governmental body (the Ministry of Labour and Social Protection) to establish the list of minimum services performed during the strike, if the strike is performed against employers that are '*linked to the safety of people, the maintenance of their health, as well as vital interests of the society*'. Here more abstract motivation for the limitation of the right to strike (the 'vital interests of the society') is added.

Based on the provisions of Article 413 of the Labour Code, quite a substantial list of occupations and sectors where strikes are prohibited[66] has been set up by the legislation.

The *Constitutional Court of the Russian Federation* (the Constitutional Court) seems to widen the Labour Code approach towards the reasons of possible limitation of the right to strike. In the case where the Federation of Aviation Dispatchers of Russia has made a claim concerning non-constitutionality of the prohibition of strikes of the civil aviation personnel responsible for servicing and management of the air traffic,[67] the Constitutional Court dismissed the claim motivating its decision not only by Article 55 of the Constitution that is mentioned in this respect in the Labour Code, but also by Article 17, paragraph 3 of the Constitution. This Article of the Constitution provides for *inadmissibility to infringe rights and freedoms* of other people in the

65. *Ibid.* Art. 412, para. 3. See *infra* Subsection 5.2.
66. See *infra* Subsection 5.1.
67. Opredelenie Konstitutsionnogo Suda Rossiskoi Federatsii [The RF Constitutional Court Ruling] Oct. 16, 2003 No. 318-O, ConsultantPlus Database. Available at http://www.consultant.ru/cons/cgi/online.cgi?req=doc&base=LAW&n=45141&fld=134&dst=1000000001,0&rnd=0.14454863099112092#0.

process of exercising one's own rights.[68] In the case of strikes of the aviation personnel this clearly means the rights of passengers and (probably) the rights of the aviation personnel employers. It seems that this Constitutional Court Ruling may serve a good illustration of the official state position regarding reasoning of limitation of strikes in the essential services.

In another Constitutional Court case[69] that dealt with railroad transport, the Constitutional Court has made a very broad and vague interpretation of justification of limitation of the right to strike. In its Ruling of 2007 the Constitutional Court has mentioned that '... *any circumstances that may interrupt normal functioning of the railroad transport are affecting the interests of each human, as well as the interests of the state, which itself gives the ground for introduction of restrictions concerning the right to strike of certain specific categories of railroad transport employees, whose temporary stoppage of work may create the danger to the interests of state defense and security, life and health of people*'.[70] This quotation is a good example of intentional ambiguity of the wording in the court decision. The first half of the sentence seems to state that *any interests of the human and the state that may be affected*, can be considered a sufficient justification for limiting the right to strike. If that would be true, it would give a valid ground to declare *any* strike illegal, because it *always* affects at least the interests of employer. Such an interpretation would contradict at least the approach of the CFA towards the ground for possible limitation of the right to strike being a 'a clear and imminent threat to the life, personal safety or health of the whole or part of the population'.[71] However, further the Constitutional Court speaks about limitation of the right to strike of only those employees, whose stoppage of work may be dangerous from the point of view of safety and defence. If the Constitutional Court has meant the limitation of strikes for only these category of workers, why is it reasoned earlier by any limitation of any interests, not just by the issues of security? Being a Russian native speaker with legal education and significant experience in reading court decisions doesn't help understand what was meant in this passage of the Constitutional Court.

The *Supreme Court* usually makes decisions concerning the illegality of strikes in essential services interpreting Article 55 of the Constitution and Article 413, paragraph 1 of the Labour Code very expansively. For example, in one of the cases the Supreme Court ruled, that '...stoppage of technical service of the aircraft may endanger the life and health of people in cases if there will be a potential need to organize sanitary flights or emergency rescue works with the use of aviation, or works liquidate consequences of natural disasters, accidents,

68. Konstitutsiya Rossiiskoi Federatsii [The Constitution of the Russian Federation] Art. 17, para. 3.
69. Opredelenie Konstitutsionnogo Suda Rossiiskoi Federatsii [The RF Constitutional Court Ruling] Feb. 8, 2007, No. 275-O-P // Consultant Plus Database. Available at http://www.consultant.ru/cons/cgi/online.cgi?req=doc&base=LAW&n=68822&fld=134&dst=1000000001,0&rnd=0.007377757137777344#0.
70. *Ibid.* para. 4.
71. *ILO*, 2006, 119.

catastrophes, etc.'.[72] In this case the legality of one-hour stoppage of work of servicing departure flights in the airport of Omsk was under discussion. Among the sectors where the stoppage of work was interpreted as dangerous and, therefore, illegal, were the following: railroad service,[73] communal heating,[74] air-traffic control,[75] aviation personnel in general (the strike was declared illegal in general because it involved the stoppage of work of both workers who have no right to strike as well as the ordinary employees that were entitled to strike),[76] river ports.[77] At the same time, the same Supreme Court just few months after the decision concerning the illegality of strikes in river ports of Naberjnye Chelny[78] made directly opposite decision concerning port workers of Saint Petersburg.[79] This contrasting approach looks even more surprising taking into account that two of three judges including the chairman of the hearing were the same in both cases. This difference may be explained by the fact that an argument about essentiality of services was taken in the first case as quite a secondary one, while the main attention of the Court was paid to the procedure. Nevertheless, the arguments about (non-)essentiality of port works are clearly stated in both cases.

It seems that among listed cases only the air-traffic control falls within the notion of essential services in the strict sense according to the CFA approach,[80] others are specifically mentioned as not being the essential services in the strict sense.[81]

5 RESTRICTIONS ON THE RIGHT TO STRIKE IN ESSENTIAL SERVICES

5.1 Securing Essential Services by Exclusion from Collective Labour Relations Rights

Russian law uses a 'sweeping ban' ban approach towards the prohibition of strikes in the essential services. As it was already mentioned in Section 4, Article 413, paragraph 1 of the Labour Code contains the list of situations and sectors where the strikes are banned. Besides this, there is a number of laws that specify

72. Opredelenie Verkhovnogo Suda RF [The RF Supreme Court Ruling] Feb. 26, 2009, No. 3-47/08, SudAct Legal Database. Available at http://sudact.ru/vsrf/doc/qtleEvUSTSg0/.
73. *Id.*, July 29, 2002, No.3-268/02. Available at http://sudact.ru/vsrf/doc/FH0rV9FRj4Yt/.
74. *Id.*, Feb. 17, 2006, No. 3-25/05. Available at http://sudact.ru/vsrf/doc/I3iCBsnF9nLj/.
75. *Id.*, Nov. 19, 2002, No. 3-183/02. Available at http://sudact.ru/vsrf/doc/hFLvADA2Q5N5/.
76. *Id.*, Feb. 14, 2003, No. 3-200/02. Available at http://sudact.ru/vsrf/doc/6wYMoH6tDeZp/.
77. *Id.*, Oct. 14, 2005, No. 3П-1-56/05. Available at http://sudact.ru/vsrf/doc/MTRzq5MrjwUn/.
78. *Ibid.*
79. *Id.*, Dec. 16, 2005, No. 3-404/05. Available at http://sudact.ru/vsrf/doc/H4GZekKrVS6J/.
80. *ILC*, 2011, 120.
81. *Ibid.*, 121.

the prohibition of strikes in a specific sector (see *infra*). In the cases of disputes between the employer and strikers concerning the possibility to perform the strike, the decision is taken by the courts and usually it confirms the employer's claim for declaring the strike illegal (see also Section 4).

As for the regime of collective bargaining rights' limitations, there may be four legal situations:

(a) employee's work is not considered as an essential service - no limitations of freedom of association and collective bargaining rights, including the right to strike;

(b) the work is in the list of work where the strikes are prohibited - the right to form and join trade unions and to take part in collective bargaining is guaranteed except for the right to strike. Such a regime covers both essential services employees, and other categories of workers to whom the Labour Code is applied on the leftover principle, i.e., only for the matters that are not regulated by special norms (the norms regulating state or municipal service, including the police, procurators' office, security services etc.);

(c) the worker is not an employee (army service, civil contractors, etc.). The right to organize and join trade unions is still guaranteed by the Federal Law 'On Trade Unions, their Rights and the Guarantees of their Activities', 1996, that states that 'a trade union is a voluntary association of *citizens*[82] [*italicized by the author – NL*] that are joined by their production and professional interests which relate to their activity...'.[83] Such trade unions exist.[84] However, as such categories of workers are expressly excluded from the scope of the Labour Code,[85] unlike the second category, these workers are not entitled to collective bargaining and social dialogue rights that are established by Part II of the Labour Code.

(d) the worker is a convicted prisoner. Besides the direct prohibition on stoppage of work as a measure to resolve a labour conflict established by the Penal Execution Code of the Russian Federation,[86] the prisoners

82. The notion of 'citizens' is interpreted by the courts expansively as related to anyone who has legal residence in the territory of Russia.

83. Federalnyi Zakon RF 'O professionalnykh soyuzah, ikh pravah i garantiyah deyatelnosti' [The RF Federal Law 'On Trade Unions, their Rights and the Guarantees of their Activities'] Art. 26, 1996.

84. See, for example, the site of All-Russian Trade Union of Military Servicemen at http://www.npsv.ru/index.html.

85. Trudovoi Kodeks Rossiiskoi Federatsii [TK RF] [Labor Code of the Russian Federation] Art. 11, para. 8.

86. Ugolovno-ispolnitelnyi Kodeks Rossiiskoi Federatsii [The Penal Code of the Russian Federation] Art. 103, para. 6, Jan. 8, 1997, No. 1-FZ. *Sobraniye Zakonodatelstva Rossiyskoy Federazii [SZ RF] [Russian Federation Collection of Legislation]* Jan. 13, 1997, No. 2, Item 198.

are not entitled to be among founding members of social organizations[87] (that include trade unions). This doesn't mean that a prisoner cannot stay in the trade union where he or she was a member before the conviction, but he or she cannot form the union of prisoners as such. There was an attempt to form such a union in practice, but it was winded up upon the court decision.[88]

For the sake of clarity this variety of regimes may be shown as follows:

	'Non-essential Employees'	*Essential Employees and Civil Servants*	*Military Servicemen and Others Excluded from the LC Scope*	*Convicted Workers*
Right to strike	Yes	No	No	No
Right to collective bargaining	Yes	Yes	No	No
Right to form and join the union	Yes	Yes	Yes	No

The norms on prohibition of strikes are included in the legislation concerning *'state civil service'*[89] and *'municipal service'*[90]. Regulations of law on state civil service and on municipal service cover only government and municipal officials. Any employees performing secondary functions in the government institutions are covered by the provisions of the Labour Code and have the right to strike. These two laws also do not cover employees of state-owned companies and institutions. Policemen, procurator's office servants, military servants and people serving an alternative civil service, state messengers, and state security services officials have no right to strike according to separate legislation establishing their status.

87. Federalnyi Zakon 'Ob obshchestvennyh ob'edineniyah' [Federal Law 'On Social Organizations'] Art. 19, May 19, 1995, No.82-FZ. *Sobraniye Zakonodatelstva Rossiyskoy Federazii [SZ RF] [Russian Federation Collection of Legislation]* May 22, 1995, No. 21, Item 1930.
88. Sud likvidiroval profsoyuz, zashchischchavshiy interesy zaklyuchyonnykh [The Court winded-up trade union that was protecting prisoners' interests], Pravo.ru, May 14, 2012. Available at https://pravo.ru/news/view/72219/.
89. Federalnyi zakon 'O gosudarsvennoi grazhdanskoi sluzhbe' [Federal Law 'On State Civil Service] Art. 17, para. 15, Jul. 27, 2004. *Sobraniye Zakonodatelstva Rossiyskoy Federazii [FZ RF] [Russian Federation Collection of Legislation] Aug.* 2, 2004, No. 31, Item 3215.
90. Fedearlnyi zakon 'O munitsipalnoi sluzhbe' [Federal Law 'On Municipal Service] Art. 14, para. 14, Mar. 2, 2007. *Sobraniye Zakonodatelstva Rossiyskoy Federazii* [SZ RF] [Russian Federation Collection of Legislation] Mar. 5, 2007, No. 10, Item 1152.

Employees of state-owned companies in general have the right to strike. Chief executive officers of state unitary enterprises have no right to take part in strikes.[91] Such a regulation was established as a response to the practice of state-owned enterprises directors in 1990s to organize strikes as method of putting pressure on the Government to get funding. Nevertheless, there is no prohibition for company directors of other organizational forms (e.g., joint-stock companies) to take part in a strike, even if such companies are totally state-owned.

Apart from general mentioning in Article 413 of the Labour Code, there is a special legislation concerning the prohibition of strikes during the state of military alert,[92] state of emergency[93] or special measures taken in accordance with the legislation on state of emergency; in the military forces of the Russian Federation, other military, paramilitary and other organizations or their divisions that are directly involved into the issues of state defence, state security, emergency and rescue services, fire-fighting services, services of prevention and liquidation of consequences of natural disasters and emergency situations; the police and other state security services; organizations (or their divisions) directly servicing dangerous production or equipment, at ambulance stations.

The *Federal Law on the 'Use of Nuclear Energy'* prohibits strikes, meetings, demonstrations and picketing, transport blocking and other social actions near nuclear industry enterprises and strikes that may endanger the work of such enterprises.[94]

Article 52 of the *Air Code of Russia*[95] prohibits strikes for the aviation personnel of civil aviation responsible for servicing and directing the air transport. Because of these restrictions flight dispatchers are known to perform hunger-strikes.[96] Without the official declaration of the strike in such situations they are taken away from their work by doctors for medical reasons, and have

91. Federalnyi zakon 'O gosudarstvennyh I munitsipalnyh unitarnyh predpriyatiyah' [Federal Law 'On the State and Municipal Unitary Enterprises'] Art. 21, para. 2, Nov. 14, 2002, No. 161-FZ. *Sobraniye Zakonodatelstva Rossiyskoy Federazii [SZ RF] [Russian Federation Collection of Legislation] Dec. 2*, 2002, No. 48, Item 4746.
92. The state of military alert is being announced according to the Federal Constitutional Law 'On the State of Military Alert' of January 30th, 2002, No. 1-FKZ. *Sobraniye Zakonodatelstva Rossiyskoy Federazii* [SZ RF] [Russian Federation Collection of Legislation] Art. 375, Feb. 4, 2002, No. 5.
93. The state of emergency is announced according to the Federal Constitutional Law 'On the State of Emergency' of May 30, 2001, No. 3-FKZ. *Sobraniye Zakonodatelstva Rossiyskoy Federazii* [SZ RF] [Russian Federation Collection of Legislation] Jun. 4, 2001, No. 23, Item 2277.
94. Federalnyi zakon 'Ob ispolzovanii yadernoi energii' [Federal Law 'On the Use of Nucl*ear Energy']* Nov. 21, 1995, No. 180-FZ, *Sobraniye Zakonodatelstva Rossiyskoy Federazii* [SZ RG] {Russian Federation Collection of Legislation] Jan. 27, 1995, No. 48, Item 4552.
95. Vozdushnyi Kodeks Rossiiskoy Federatsii [The Air Code of Russian Federation], Federalnyi Zakon [Federal Law] Mar. 19, 1997, No. 60-FZ. *Sobraniye Zakonodatelstva Rossiyskoy Federatsii* [SZ RF] [Russian Federation Collection of Legislation] Mar. 24, 1997, No. 12, Item 1383.
96. See, for example, Gubski, 2013.

the possibility to put a pressure on their employer at the cost of their own health. Strikes are prohibited[97] for the employees of the *railroad transport* whose work is connected with trains' operations, manoeuvring operations, passengers', senders and recipients of cargo shipment service according to the list established by the Federal Law. This list is so wide that almost any railroad employee has no right to participate in strikes.

The norms concerning aviation and railroads were challenged as unconstitutional. In 2007 the Constitutional Court refused to consider that right to strike was excessively limited in respect of railroad workers.[98] Therefore, the law has been left unchanged.

In a slightly more radical situation concerning civil aviation, the Constitutional Court considered[99] the law as unconstitutional in 1995. The then existing law on 'Collective Labour Disputes'[100] prohibited strikes in civil aviation enterprises *in whole*. Such prohibition being based only on the fact of an enterprise belonging to a certain economic sector was found unconstitutional and was abrogated by the Constitutional Court. However, more recent and less restrictive norms of the Air Code were considered not to be in the contradiction with the Constitution in 2003.[101]

There are no *special sanctions* for the illegal participation in the strike in essential services. Such a strike would be considered illegal by the court, and the next day after the receiving the court decision, strikers are obliged to return to work.[102] The very fact of workers' participation in such a strike[103] will not constitute a separate misconduct. The employee may be disciplined for the refusal to stop the strike after receiving the decision of the court. However, there are situations in practice, when courts refuse to consider the stoppage of work aimed at resolving the dispute with an employer, as a strike case because it does

97. Federalnyi zakon 'O zheleznodorozhnom transporte' [Federal Law 'On Railroad Transport'] Jan. 10, 2003, No. 17-FZ. *Sobraniye Zakonodatelstva Rossiyskoy Federazii* [SZ RF] [Russian Federation Collection of Legislation] Jan. 13, 2003, No. 2, Item 169.
98. Opredelenie Konstitutsionnogo Suda RF [The RF Constitutional Court Ruling] Feb. 8, 2007 No. 275-O-P. *Sobraniye Zakonodatelstva Rossiyskoy Federazii* [SZ RF] [Russian Federation Collection of Legislation] May 22, 1995, No. 21, Art. 1976. For more details see *supra* Section 2.
99. Postanovlenie Konstitutsionnogo Suda RF [Resolution of the Constitutional Court of the RF] May 17, 1995, No. 5-P. *Sobraniye Zakonodatelstva Rossiyskoy Federazii* [SZ RF] [Russian Federation Collection of Legislation] May 22, 1995, No. 21, Art. 1976.
100. Zakon SSSR 'O rassmotrenii kollektivnykh trudovykh sporov' [Law of the USSR 'On Resolution of Collective Labour Disputes (conflicts)] May 20, 1991 No. 2179-1. *Vedomosti SND and VS of USSR [Bulletin of the CPD of the RF and SC of the RF]* Jun. 1991, No. 23, Art. 654.
101. See *supra* Section 2.
102. See more details in *infra* Section 7.
103. Except for the prisoners. Their strike is considered as major breach of the rules of imprisonment according to Art. 116, para. 1 of the Penal Code. This may lead to the quite severe sanctions depending on the grade of penal regime they are subject to (the list of sanctions is established in Art. 115 of the Penal Code of the RF).

not fall within the legal definition of a strike.[104] In such cases the employees may be disciplined for the strike action which took place before the court decision. In the worst case for them, they may be dismissed for '*progul*', i.e., absence at work without a just cause for four consecutive hours or more or during the whole working day.[105] In such cases the workers may be punished for the breach of labour discipline, while in the ordinary cases they may only be disciplined for refusal to get back to work after the court ruling concerning illegality of the strike.

Under the Labour Code, the employees' representative body that is responsible for the organization of an illegal strike, and that did not stop it after receiving the court decision, may be liable for damages incurred by the employer as a result of the strike in the amount that shall be determined by the court.[106] The courts tend to interpret this power as the only possibility to oblige the trade union to pay litigation expenses.[107]

Instead of direct and open incompliance with the ban on strikes in essential services, the employees tend to use 'alternative' practices which are not established by the labour legislation: work to rule actions, hunger strikes, etc. There was even a discussion in the State Duma concerning the need to prohibit hunger-strikes for the essential service workers, but it did not lead to the adoption of any legislation up to the moment of writing.[108]

5.2 Securing Essential Services by Imposing Limitations on the Right to Strike (Controlled Strike Model)

The obligation of employees to perform the *minimum works (services)* to be performed during any strike is directly associated with the issue of essential services. The employer, the state bodies of executive power, municipal authorities as well as an employees' body that is in charge of the strike performance are under an obligation to take measures for '*...keeping the social order, ensuring the preservation of employer's and employees' property, as well as functioning of machinery and facilities, if their stoppage may constitute a direct danger to life*

104. Opredelenie Verkhovnogo Suda RF [The RF Supreme Court Ruling] Feb. 26, 2009, No. 3-47/08. SudAct Legal Database. Available at http://sudact.ru/vsrf/doc/qtleEvUSTSg0/. See also *ibid.*, para. 7.
105. Trudovoi Kodeks Rossiiskoi Federatsii [TK RF] [Labor Code of the Russian Federation]. Art. 81, part 1, para. 6(a).
106. Trudovoi Kodeks Rossiiskoi Federatsii [TK RF] [Labor Code of the Russian Federation]. Art. 471, para. 2.
107. See Leningrad Regional Court Decision of November 22, 2013, on case No. 3-64/2013, Leningrad Regional Court Decision of 25 January 2013, on case No. 3-5/2013, Primorsky Regional Court Decision of 29 April 2011, on case No. 3-36/11, Sverdlovsk Regional Court Decision of 24 February 2011, (case number anonymized), SudAct Legal Database.
108. See Smirnova, 2015.

and health of people'.[109] It is clear that performance of minimum works (services) is based on generally the same grounds as the ban on strikes in essential services (see Section 4).

The sector level lists of minimum services have to be adopted by the federal executive power body responsible for the governance in the respective sector of economy according to the methodology approved by the Government.[110] Currently 22 such lists are adopted by the responsible ministries.[111] One of the most problematic sectors from the point of view of essential services strikes sectors, i.e., the railroads, had its list of minimum works successfully challenged in the court. One of two all-Russian railroad unions, being more militant[112] and the only one taking part in strikes in this sector, has appealed the fact of adoption of the list by the Ministry of Transportation without involving this union into the process of coordination of its contents.[113]

The specific list of minimum works (services) to be performed during a particular strike has to be defined by the agreement between the parties to the collective labour dispute together with a local government authority within three days since the announcement of the strike[114]. It is not permitted to include into such a list the works (services) which are not included into the lists of minimum works (services) adopted in respect of the sector of the economy or territory.

In case of disagreement between the parties concerning the list, it has to be approved by the government authority of the constituent entity of the Russian Federation. The latter issue has been a matter of examination of the ILO monitoring bodies. The CFA has noted that any disagreement concerning specific contents of minimum services must be resolved by the independent body that has the credibility of all the parties. The government authority in charge of resolution of such disputes is the *State Service on Labour and Employment* (*Rostrud*) which is subordinated to the Ministry of Labour and Social Protection. It is clear, that in many cases, especially when the dispute

109. Trudovoi Kodeks Rossiiskoi Federatsii [TK RF] [Labor Code of the Russian Federation]. Art. 412, para. 2.
110. Postanovlenie Pravitelstva Rossiiskoi Federatsii [The Resolution of the Government of the Russian Federation] Dec. 17, 2002, No. 901. Garant Database. Available at http://base.garant.ru/185339/.
111. See the Ministry of Transport of the Russian Federation Order of October 7, 2003 No. 197 (for the transport sector in general); the Ministry of Communications of Russia Order of December 28, 2016 No. 719 (for the communications sector); the Ministry of Agriculture of the Russian Federation Order of January 19, 2006 No. 3 (for agriculture) et al. ConsultantPlus Database.
112. See about the relations between majority and minority unions *supra* Subsection 2.1.
113. Opredelenie Verkhovnogo Suda Rossiiskoi Federatsii [The Supreme Court Ruling] Jul. 6, 2006, No. KAC 06-221. ConsultantPlus Database.
114. Trudovoi Kodeks Rossiiskoi Federatsii [TK RF] [Labor Code of the Russian Federation]. Art. 412, para. 4.

relates to the state-owned employer, a governmental agency cannot be considered neutral. The CFA has addressed the Government of Russia in 2003 with the request to amend Article 412 of the Labour Code in order to meet this requirement.[115] Later (in 2011) the request was repeated by the CEACR,[116] and later (in 2014) the European Committee of Social Rights also asked for clarification of that regulation.[117] Nevertheless, the legislation was not changed.

Another tool that may be used by the employer to minimize the damage caused by the strike, is the court injunction to stop it. In cases of danger that the strike would cause disproportionally big damage to the employer, the courts take decisions on immediate execution of their orders to stop the illegal strikes.[118]

Sanctions for not performing minimum works (services) or not stopping the strikes according to the court order are the same as for the non-compliance with the court decision on illegality of strike and following back to work order (see *supra* Subsection 5.1).

6 COMPENSATORY MEASURES FOR RESTRICTIONS

6.1 The Alternative Means to Advance and Protect Employees' Interests for Those Who Are Not Allowed to Unionize and Bargain Collectively

The amount of benefits that are assigned to the workers in essential services depends greatly on peculiarities of the category of workers. First of all, it should be noted that taking into account negligibly low strike activity in general, which may mainly be explained by quite restrictive legislation on the right to strike (see *supra* Subsections 2.3 and 3.2), the essential services workers don't lose much compared to other categories of workers. That is well understood by the Government, and any measures that are aimed at giving some privileges or benefits to the specific category of workers is not understood by the Government, by employers, or by workers themselves as the compensation for the lack of the right to strike.

115. Committee on Freedom of Association cases. Case No. 2199 (Russian Federation) – Complaint date: 18 Aril 2002. The Russian Labour Confederation (KTR). Paras. 991, 995. ILO Normlex Database http://www.ilo.org/dyn/normlex/en/f?p=1000:50001:0::NO:50001:P50001_COMPLAINT_FILE_ID:2897348.
116. *ILC*, 2011. 149.
117. *Council of Europe*, 2014, 42.
118. Reshenie Leningradskogo raionnogo suda [Leningrad Regional Court Decision] Jan. 25, 2013, on case No.3-5/2013; Opredelenie Verhovnogo Suda Rossiskoi Federatsii [The RF Supreme Court Ruling] Mar. 21, 2008, on case No.78-G08-5, Opredelenie Verhovnogo Suda Rossiskoi Federatsii [The RF Supreme Court Ruling] Jan. 25, 2008, on case No.5-G07-113. SudAct Legal Database.

Probably, the main incentive for different categories of workers to stay in the profession or to keep industrial peace is the payment of wages. According to the official statistics, the average wage in Russia in September 2017 was 38,083 roubles per month.[119] One of the most militant categories of essential services employees work in the sector of aviation and space. The average wages for this category of workers is 130,933 roubles[120] – almost three times more than average age. However, this may be explained not by the compensation for the lacking right to strike, but rather by the fact that it is a highly qualified work with international competition between employers for the employees. Aeroflot, the biggest air-carrier in Russia, was recently complaining that many pilots are leaving the company despite wages that look astronomic to the majority of Russian population: about 650,000 roubles per month for the first pilot and about 350,000 roubles for the second. Still, many pilots are leaving, especially to China, where they can expect few times larger wages for the same job.[121]

Contrastingly, other highly skilled category of workers, the medical personnel, many of whom are also essential service workers, receive incomparably lower wages. Their amount is even lower than the country average – 30,345 roubles.[122] Despite the attempts to increase their wages in the course of budgetary sector reform (see *supra* Section 4), there seems to be no much success in this issue up to now. Both categories: well-paid aviation personnel and badly paid medical personnel are mainly contesting too intensive workload that leads to the burning out, reduction of quality of work and danger to other people. There seems to be not much attention on their behalf to the issue of non-sufficient collective bargaining rights.

Workers in the area of state governance, security and army forces receive wages that are slightly higher than average – 43,085 roubles.[123] This does not tell much about the real situation for many of these workers whose salaries are highly unequal depending on their rank. While higher officials' wages in these sectors are scandalously high and accompanied with the social security rights that are unheard of by the majority of the population, most of lower-rank civil and military servants receive quite a modest amount of wages. A big income gap in this sector reflects unhealthy social situation and much influence of the highest officials to the amount of their own benefits without enough control on behalf of the civil society. It can't be seriously considered as compensation for lack of the right to strike which is much more relevant for the lower officials who are underpaid.

119. *Federalnaya Slujba Gosudarstvennoy Statistiki*, 2017a.
120. *Ibid.*
121. See *Vedomosti*, 2017.
122. *Federalnaya Slujba Gosudarstvennoy Statistiki*, 2017a.
123. *Ibid.*

6.2 Measures Provided by Law for Assuring Basic Tenets of Free Collective Bargaining and/or to Settle Labour Disputes for Employees Who Are Denied the Right to Strike

Compulsory arbitration is a substitution mechanism for the ban of the right to strike provided by law.[124] According to Article 404, paragraph 8 of the Labour Code, if the parties of the collective labour dispute, in which employees are not entitled to the right to strike, cannot agree on creation of ad-hoc voluntary labour arbitration or referral of their dispute to the permanent labour arbitration, the governmental body responsible for the settlement of collective labour disputes shall establish compulsory arbitration to resolve such a dispute, being Rostrud.[125] As it was already said, Rostrud is a governmental structure. Therefore, it cannot be considered fully neutral and independent from the state and employer as it is required by the CFA, especially when it comes to the disputes with the state-owned employers that constitute the majority of the cases in essential services.

There is no much open information about the practical outcome of compulsory labour arbitration as it is considered to be a confidential information. However, there is case law[126] concerning illegality of strikes when essential services employees were trying to organize the strike without taking part in compulsory arbitration. This may be considered as a sign of not enough trust to this institution.

7 SECURING ESSENTIAL SERVICES BY FURTHER MEANS

Russian legislation that regulates the general procedure of collective labour disputes resolution (see *supra* Subsection 3.2) as well as many specific legal limitations of strikes in the essential services (see Sections 5 and 6) do not leave much space for any other limitations: these legal means are already enough to turn the practice of even non-essential services strikes into something quite exceptional (see *supra* Subsection 2.3).

Nevertheless, the other frequently used method of limitation of the right to strike (both in essential and non-essential services) is the *employers' recourse to courts* with claims on declaring the strikes illegal. According to the Labour

124. Trudovoi Kodeks Rossiiskoi Federatsii [Labor Code of the Russian Federation]. Art. 404, para. 8.
125. The power to settle a collective labour dispute is established in para. 5.5.10 of the Rostrud Statute approved by the Decree of the Government of the Russian Federation of June 30, 2004 No. 324. *Sobraniye Zakonodatelstva Rossiyskoy Federazii* of 17 July 2004, No. 28, Item. 2901.
126. Opredelenie Verkhovnogo Suda RF [Supreme Court Ruling] Feb. 10, 2006, No.74-G06-4, Opredelenie Verkhovnogo Suda RF [Supreme Court Ruling] Oct. 14, 2005, No. 11-G05-21 // SudAct Legal Database.

Code,[127] the decision on declaring the strike illegal is taken by the high courts of the constituent entity of the Russian Federation. Besides the situations of ensuring the state and human beings security as well as the rights and lawful interests of other people and cases directly established by the federal laws,[128] the strike may be declared illegal by the court if it is called on in breach of terms and procedures established by the Labour Code.[129] If the court has declared the strike illegal, the employees are obliged to get back to work no later than the next day after the strike committee receives the court decision.[130] The court has also the power to suspend the strike which has been declared but has not been started for up to fifteen days when such a strike may cause danger to the health and life of people.[131]

The examination of case law shows that in the vast majority of cases[132] the employers' claims to declare the illegality of strikes were satisfied by the courts. This approach of courts may be explained not by especially cautious attention to the need to provide essential services, but rather by the restrictive attitude to strikes in general. The proportion of cases when the courts approved the claims of illegality of strikes when the essentiality was not under discussion, is approximately the same.[133] In many cases of discussion of illegality of strikes in essential services, the argument of breach of procedure of strike performance was also used by the courts.

It is important that the court practice seems to be changing in a time, and the approach to application of the same norms by the same Supreme Court seems to become more restrictive in the later years.[134]

There are court decisions when provisions of trade unions by-laws were declared contradictory to law on the ground that they provided the right to strike to workers who were considered to be involved in essential services.[135] Nevertheless, the main argument in such cases was not essentiality of service, but again, the procedure: the courts mentioned the right to declare the strike as belonging directly to workers and not to trade unions.

127. Trudovoi Kodeks Rossiiskoi Federatsii [TK RF] [Labor Code of the Russian Federation]. Art. 413, para. 4.
128. See *supra* Section 4.
129. Trudovoi Kodeks Rossiiskoi Federatsii [TK RF] [Labor Code of the Russian Federation]. Art. 413, para. 3.
130. *Ibid.*, para. 6.
131. *Ibid.*, para. 7.
132. Thirteen among sixteen under examination which is close to covering all case law on the issue.
133. Among 23 disputes the claims of employers were satisfied in 17 cases of non-essential services strikes.
134. *Gerasimova*, 2017, 26 et seqq.
135. Reshenie Moskovskogo Gorodskogo Suda [Moscow City Court Ruling] Jan. 14, 2011, No. 33-307. ConsultantPlus Database; Reshenie Tomskogo Raionnogo Suda [Tomsk Regional Court Decision] Jul. 27, 2010, No. 2-821/10. SudAct Legal Database. Available at http://sudact.ru/regular/doc/NFu0XLf9Wjx1/.

8 EVALUATION AND CONCLUSION

8.1 Performance Evaluation

The general assessment of legal regulation of the right to strike in essential services in Russia is that it is greatly unbalanced in favour of the state and employers. The aim of the legal limitation of the right to strike in essential services is theoretically grounded mainly with regard to the issues of safety of people and state security (see *supra* Section 5). Nevertheless, the practical interpretation of these limitations is so expansive, that in practice the right to strike as it is regulated now presents no serious obstacle to the proper level of functioning of the employers.

On the other hand, such regulation obviously cannot serve as an example of effective collective bargaining. Even a negligibly low level of strikes in general, not only in essential services (see *supra* Subsection 2.3) in the great majority of cases is declared illegal when contested in courts by employers (see *supra* Section 7).

In quite significant number of issues (quorum concerning calling the strike in general, the determination of what is understood by essential services, insufficient impartiality of a state institution that has the power to resolve disputes over the minimum services and compulsory arbitration, etc.) Russian legislation that regulates strikes in essential services cannot be considered as complying with the international labour standards imposed by the ILO and the CE.[136]

The experience of discussions of personal preferences in collective bargaining and strikes with active trade unionists that are practically involved in strikes activities, shows that they prefer the actions that fall outside of the legal framework. Usually, it is the choice for them either to follow official procedures established in the Labour Code or to be actually involved in the industrial action. From employers' standpoint, the preference for autonomous and informal or official legal regulation in the situations of disputes is not that clear and depends on personal preferences and policy of the management.

It may be stated that current Russian regulative policy in the area of strikes in essential services is quite consistent in its generally restrictive approach towards the possibility to legally organize the strikes. This consistency, however, cannot be considered optimal and acceptable because the protests of highly discontented workers happen despite formal legal prohibition, and the legislation on strikes does not serve its goal as a safety valve for the society.

136. See also *Gerasimova*, 2017, 17 et seqq.

8.2 Summary and Conclusions

Historically, the Russian regulation of strikes, including strikes in essential services, has been very restrictive. There were few short periods in the history when the whole country has been almost paralyzed by the strike activity. This happened during the first Russian Revolution of 1905-1907, during the revolutionary events of 1917, and in the course of the Soviet system decay in the early 1990s. Each time the explosion of a wide protesting movement was preceded by the highly restrictive anti-strike state policy and legal regulation. Since the late 19th century up to the fall of the USSR the strike activity was taken by government as a threat to state security and social stability. Current regulation is based on the early 2000s social consensus between the society and the state, when the majority of workers were tolerating the low level of industrial and political democracy in exchange for the constant growth of economy and their living standards.

However, this consensus is not operating smoothly since the interruption of economic and income growth. There is a clear trend of rise of labour protests with the majority of them happening outside the scope of legal framework. Essential services are not the exception in this trend. More than that, taking into account that chances of performing the strike legally for quite a significant group of employees are close to zero, they don't even try to recourse to the official collective labour dispute resolution procedure.

The essential services strikes are the part of a bigger problem for Russia: the restrictive attitude towards the strikes in general. Therefore, the issue of essentiality of strikes is discussed usually within the framework of restriction of strikes as such, as one of many other mechanisms of such restriction.

The current regulation of strikes is very unbalanced and gives quite a good protection for employers' and consumers' interest leaving almost no space for the lawful protection of the workers' rights.

Whether or not this regulation will change in the near future, the answer to this question greatly depends on the political future of the country, which is quite difficult to predict.

Bibliography

-----, Aeroflot pytaetsya uderzhat' pilotov den'gami [Aeroflot tries to hold the pilots by money], Vedomosti, 13 June 2017, Available at https://www.vedomosti.ru/business/articles/2017/06/13/694163-aeroflot-defitsi tom-pilotov

-----, Sankt-Peterburg. Mediki vyshli k ZAKSu [Saint-Petersburg. Medicals came to the State Assembly] Kollektivnoye deystvie [Collective Action]. Available at http://www.ikd.ru/node/19473.

-----, Sud likvidiroval profsoyuz, zashchischchavshiy interesy zaklyuchyonnykh [The Court winded-up trade union that was protecting prisoners' interests], Pravo.ru, May 14, 2012. Available at https://pravo.ru/news/view/72219/

-----, Vrachi na iznosye: pochemu v Ufe golodayut doktora 'skoroy pomoshchi' [Doctors' burning-out: why ambulance doctors go on hunger-strike in Ufa] // Meduza. Available at https://meduza.io/feature/2015/04/06/vrachi-na-iznose

Aleksandrov, Nikolay A., Labour Legal Relation [Trudovoe pravootnoshenie]., 1948, 129 et seqq

Aleksandrov, Nikolay A., Sovetskoye trudovoye pravo [Soviet Labour Law], 1972

Bizyukov, Petr, Trudovye protesty v pervoy polovine 2017 gg. Analiticheskiy otchet [Labour Protests in the first half of 2017: An Analytical Research], Tsentr sotsialno-trudovykh prav [Centre for Social and Labour Rights] 2017. Available at http://trudprava.ru/expert/analytics/protestanalyt/1900

Bizyukov, Petr. Trudovye protesty v Rossii v 2008-2016 gg. Analiticheskiy otchet [Labour Protests in Russia in 2008-2011: An Analytical Research], Tsentr sotsialno-trudovykh prav [Centre for Social and Labour Rights], 2017. Available at http://trudprava.ru/expert/analytics/protestanalyt/1807

Central Intelligence Agency. World Factbook. Available at https://www.cia.gov/library/publications/the-world-factbook/rankorder/2172rank.html,

Council of Europe, Conclusions of the European Committee of Social Rights (Russian Federation), 2014

David, René/ Goré, Marie/ Jauffret-Spinosi, Camille, Les grandes systémes de droit contemporains, 12-e ed., 2016. 127 et seqq.

Federalnaya Slujba Gosudarstvennoy Statistiki (Rosstat Rossii) [Federal Service on State Statics (Rosstat of Russia)], Real'nye raspologaemye denezhnye dokhody naseleniya [Real incomes of the population], 2017. Available at http://www.gks.ru/free_doc/new_site/population/urov/urov_12kv.doc

Federalnaya Slujba Gosudarstvennoy Statistiki (Rosstat Rossii) [Federal Service on State Statics (Rosstat of Russia)], Rossiysky Statisticheskiy Ejegodnik [Russian Statistical Annual], 2011. Available at http://www.gks.ru/bgd/regl/b11_13/IssWWW.exe/Stg/d1/05-26.htm

Federalnaya Slujba Gosudarstvennoy Statistiki (Rosstat Rossii) [Federal Service on State Statics (Rosstat of Russia)], Rossiysky Statisticheskiy Ejegodnik [Russian Statistical Annual], 2016. Available at http://www.gks.ru/free_doc/doc_2016/year/year16.pdf

Federalnaya Slujba Gosudarstvennoy Statistiki (Rosstat Rossii) [Federal Service on State Statics (Rosstat of Russia)], Uroven' zhizni i dokhody naseleniya v oktyabre 2017 [The level of life and incomes of the population in October 2017], 2017. Available at http://www.gks.ru/bgd/free/B17_00/IssWWW.exe/Stg/dk10/6-0.doc (Federalnaya Slujba Gosudarstvennoy Statistiki, 2017a)

Gerasimova, Elena S, Collective Labour Disputes and Strikes in Russia: The Impact of Judicial Precedents and Enforcement, Russian Law Journal, No 5(2), 2017, 26 et seqq. Available at http://www.russianlawjournal.org/jour/article/view/271/161

Gerasimova, Elena S, Izmenyon poryadok razresheniya kollektivnykh trudovykh spoov i organizatsii zabastovok. Dostignuta li tsel'? [The Oder of Resolving Labour Disputes and Organizing Strikes Has Changed. Did It Reach the Goal?], Trudovoye parvo [Labour Law] 2012, 51 et seqq.

Gerasimova, Elena S, The Resolution of Collective Labour Disputes and the Realization of the Right to Strike in Russia, in Tiraboschi et al. (eds), Labour Law in Russia: Recent Developments and New Challenges, Iss. 6 2014, 259 et seqq.

Gerasimova, Elena S, Zakonodatel'stvo Rossii o kollektivnykh trudovykh sporakh i zabastovkakh: problemy i napravleniya sovershenstvovaniya [Russian Legislation on Labour Disputes and Strikes: Problems and Ways to Improve], Trudovoye pravo v Rossii i za rubezhom [Labour Law in Russia and Abroad], 2012

Gladstone, A, Settlement of Disputes over Rights, in Blanpain (ed.), Comparative Labour Law and Industrial Relations in Industrialized Market Economies, 10th ed. 2010, 721 et seqq.

Goldman, A, Settlement of Disputes over Interests, in Blanpain (ed.), Comparative Labour Law and Industrial Relations in Industrialized Market Economies, 10th ed. 2010, 751 et seqq.

Gubski, P, Golodovka aviadispetcherov [Flight dispatchers' hunger-strike], 161.ru News 2010. Available at http://161.ru/text/news/277784.html

Hepple, Bob, Labour Laws and Global Trade, 2005

International Labour Organisation, International Labour Conference, 100th Session, 2011. Report of the Committee of Experts on the Application of Conventions and Recommendations (CEACR). Report III (Part 1A), 2011. Available at http://www.ilo.org/wcmsp5/groups/public/---ed_norm/---relconf/documents/meetingdocument/wcms_151556.pdf

International Labour Organisation, Freedom of Association: Digest of decisions and principles of the Freedom of Association Committee of the Governing Body of the ILO. 5th edition, 2006. Available at http://www.ilo.org/wcmsp5/groups/public/---ed_norm/---normes/documents/publication/wcms_090632.pdf

Lenin, Vladimir I., Complete works [Polnoe sobranie sochineniy], 5th ed., Izdatelstvo politicheskoy literatury [Political Literature Publishing], 1967

Lopatin, L.N., Istoriya rabochego dvijeniya Kuzbassa [The History of Kuzbass Labour Movement], 1995

Lyutov, Nikita. The Role of the ILO in the Adoption of the New Russian Labour Code, The International Journal of Comparative Labour Law and Industrial Relations 2003, Vol. 19(2), 173 et seqq.

Lyutov, Nikita, The Right to Strike: Russian Federation, in Waas (ed.), The Right to Strike: A Comparative Overview, 2014, 451 et seqq.

Perviy den' 'italyanki v Moskve: 'vbrosy' chinovnikov i vpechatleniya medikov [The first day of 'Italian Strike' in Moscow: leaks carried out by officials and impressions of medical workers], Profsoyuzi segodnya [Unions Today] 2015. Available at http://www.unionstoday.ru/news/ktr/2015/03/25/20373

Pryazhennikov, Maksim, Lokalnoe regulirovanie v sfere truda: teoretiko-pravovoy aspect [Local regulation in the area of labour: theoretical and legal aspects], Ph.D. Thesis in Law, 2018. 215 et seqq.

Przhilenskiy, Vladimir/ Zakharova, Mariya, Which Way is The Russian Double-headed Eagle Looking?, Russian Law Journal 2016 Vol. 4(2), 6 et seqq.

Sinyukov, Vladimir, Rossiyskaya pravovaya Sistema: vvedenie v obshchuyu teoriyu [The Russian Legal System: An Introduction to the General Theory], 1994

Smirnova A., Deputaty khotyat zapretit' golodovki [The deputies wish to prohibit the hunger-strikes], Utro.ru, 29 April 2015. Available at https://utro.ru/articles/2015/04/29/1242553.shtml

United Nations Development Agency (UNDP), Global 2016 Human Development Report, 2016. Available at http://hdr.undp.org/sites/default/files/2016_human_development_report.pdf

CHAPTER 13

South Africa

Darcy du Toit, Mario Jacobs & Roger Ronnie

1 GENERAL BACKGROUND: COUNTRY PROFILE

1.1 Economic, Political and Historical Background

The Republic of South Africa was established on 31 May 1961, superseding the Union of South Africa which had been formed in 1910. The Union, like its colonial predecessors, had been premised on racial segregation and white minority rule. In 1948 an Afrikaner Nationalist government was elected which imposed a systematic form of white domination and racial segregation by police-state methods, known as apartheid. This led to growing resistance within South Africa from the 1970s onwards, resulting in deepening instability and prompting international pressure for change. In 1990 the government was compelled to commence a process of reform, including the lifting of political restrictions and the abolition of racial segregation. This paved the way for multi-party negotiations that culminated in the adoption of a democratic interim

Constitution.[1] The first non-racial elections on 27 April 1994 resulted in Nelson Mandela, leader of the previously banned African National Congress, being elected as the first President of the new democratic state.

In 2017 the population of the country was estimated at 56.52 million, of whom 51 per cent were female.[2] Racial classification by the State has been abolished but, for reasons of employment equity and social redress, demographic statistics based mainly on self-classification are maintained. By this measure, 80.8 per cent of the population is identified as Black African, 8.8 per cent as coloured, 8 per cent as white and 2.5 per cent as Indian or Asian. Of the 37 million people of working age, 18.9 million are female. The official unemployment rate in November 2017 stood at 27.7 per cent but, if discouraged work-seekers are included, unemployment increases to 36.4 per cent.[3]

The political economy of South Africa is characterised by extreme inequality. The country is rich in mineral resources, with the largest economy in Africa, a well-developed financial sector and the largest number of dollar billionaires on the continent.[4] Yet it has been unable to rid itself of increasing unemployment, widening inequality and growing poverty affecting the majority of the population. In 2015 income inequality stood at 0.68,[5] while 55.5 per cent of South Africans were poor in terms of the upper-bound poverty levels.[6] Stubborn degrees of unemployment have been a feature of South Africa both before and after the advent of democracy, never dropping below 20 per cent between 1994 and 2017. The global economic crisis that started in the United States of America in 2007 led to well over one million further jobs being lost in South Africa.[7]

The prospect of significantly improved economic growth in the short to medium term looks slim. A technical recession in the first two quarters of 2017, and the country's downgrade to 'junk' status by two of the three major international rating agencies, will negatively impact on South Africa's

1. Constitution of the Republic of South Africa, Act 200 of 1993.
2. *Statistics South Africa*, 2017, Table 8.
3. *Id.*, 2017a. The official rate is limited to persons between the ages of 15 and 64 who actively look for work over a reference period and excludes those who are not looking for employment. Youth unemployment stood at 52.2 per cent. A total of 16.19 million people found themselves in some form of employment.
4. *Nsehe*, 2017.
5. Measured by using the Lorenz curve (Gini index) where 0 represents full equality and 100 full inequality.
6. *Statistics South Africa*, 2017a. The South African statistical agency uses three measures to define poverty: the upper-bound poverty line (ZAR992 or $70.27per person per month), the lower-bound poverty line (ZAR647 or $45.83 per person per month); and the food poverty line (ZAR441 per person per month or $31.24). The lower-bound poverty headcount stood at 40 per cent and the food poverty line stood at 25.2 per cent of the population.
7. *The Presidency*, 2014).

international borrowing capacity.[8] This, in turn, will impact on state spending on basic services such as healthcare, education and housing in a climate where growing public discontent at inadequate service provision has already led to high levels of community protest action.[9]

Social volatility has been deepened by ineffective political and governmental leadership, epitomised by the unpopular administration of former President Jacob Zuma. Numerous instances of corrupt and unethical conduct were exposed on the part of the ex-President and his supporters, resulting in deep divisions within the ruling African National Congress (ANC) and a ruptured relationship with its liberation alliance partners, the Congress of South African Trade Unions (COSATU) and South African Communist Party (SACP). This has aggravated uncertainty in an economy where commodity prices are highly vulnerable to market volatility. However, it has also regenerated civil society activism, which contributed to Zuma's resignation and his replacement by Cyril Ramaphosa in February 2018. This, and events leading up to it, demonstrated the vigour of South Africa's constitutional democracy, manifested also in repeated judicial interventions to strike down irregular acts by government or state officials.[10]

This combination of economic, social and political pressures has affected all workers, including essential service workers, creating significant strain in the labour relations system and a rising level of strike action. Notably, a growing proportion of strikes have been unprocedural and hence legally unprotected, with the result that striking workers face dismissal.[11] This trend became manifest with strike waves in the (highly organised) mining sector and (largely unorganised) agricultural sectors in 2012. Despite the fact that the strikes were unprotected, the workers in both cases achieved significant wage increases without losing their employment, thus setting a precedent for others.

8. *Fin24*, 2018. Uncertainty about the government's policy direction following a cabinet reshuffle by former President Zuma and poorly performing state-owned enterprises were among the causes, which the new administration of President Ramaphosa has set out to address. At the time of writing it is too early to assess the impact of the reforms.
9. Over the period 2007–2015 the number of service delivery protest never dropped below 100 per year. More worryingly, from 2010 onwards violence during protest action has been a common feature. *People's Assembly*, 2016.
10. On 26 March 2018 summons was served on Zuma to stand trial on numerous charges of corruption.
11. See discussion *infra* Section 2. Government's response in the form of amendments to the LRA imposing stricter regulation of the right to strike, including compulsory secret ballots and advisory interest arbitration in where strikes are deemed to be 'no longer functional to collective bargaining', provoked major opposition on the part of trade unions and added to the tensions: see Labour Relations Amendment Bill B-2017, clause 16. The amendments have since been accepted by Parliament.

1.2 Legal Framework

The Constitution[12] is the supreme law of South Africa. It creates three interrelated spheres of government at the national, provincial and local levels and establishes a separation of powers between the legislative, executive and judicial branches of government. Crucially, the Constitution also contains a justiciable Bill of Rights,[13] including labour rights, with which all laws must comply. Numerous laws have been declared invalid to the extent that they were found to be in conflict with the Bill of Rights.

The principal labour statutes - the Labour Relations Act,[14] the Basic Conditions of Employment Act[15] and the Employment Equity Act[16] - were enacted to bring South Africa's labour law in line with the Constitution and international law. The LRA established a specialist labour dispute resolution system, with the Commission for Conciliation, Mediation and Arbitration (CCMA) as the first port of call to conciliate all disputes and arbitrate most disputes, a Labour Court with jurisdiction to hear more serious disputes as well to review arbitration awards and a Labour Appeal Court to hear appeals from the Labour Court.[17] The highest court is the Constitutional Court, with final jurisdiction over the validity of laws and all other constitutional questions.

2 THE STATUS AND ROLE OF COLLECTIVE LABOUR RELATIONS

2.1 Unions and Rate of Unionisation

In the private sector, the degree of unionisation and the influence of the trade union movement have declined, while alternative forms of organisation and new collective bargaining models have not developed sufficiently to fill the regulatory gap. Table 13.1 shows that between 1997 and 2013 trade union membership in the private sector declined from 36 per cent to 24 per cent whereas, in the public sector, it increased from 55 per cent to 69 per cent. The high level of unionisation in the public sector can be ascribed to what amounts to compulsory collective bargaining in the public service, as outlined in more detail below.[18]

12. Constitution of the Republic of South Africa, 1996 (the 'final Constitution').
13. Chapter II of the Constitution. Labour rights are discussed below.
14. Act 66 of 1995 ('the LRA').
15. Act 75 of 1997.
16. Act 55 of 1998.
17. The Labour Court has a status equivalent to that of a division of the High Court, and the Labour Appeal Court has a status equivalent to that of the Supreme Court of Appeal.
18. See *infra* Section 2.2.

Table 13.1 Trade Union Density 1997–2013[19]

Year	*Private Sector*	*Percentage*	*Public Sector*	*Percentage*
1997	1 813,217	35.6%	835,795	55.2%
2001	1 748,807	30.6%	1 070,248	70.1%
2005	1 925,248	30.1%	1 087,772	68.4%
2010	1 888,293	26.3%	1 324,964	74.6%
2013	1 868,711	24.4%	1 393,189	69.2%

2.2 Employers' Associations and Rate of Organisation

The Department of Labour's data on employers' associations give no indication of the number of individual employers or the total number of employees that they employ, nor does it give details of the sectors covered. While a decrease in the number of employers' associations is reflected in Table 13.2, it is difficult to discern whether this indicates a decline in coverage or a consolidation of employers' associations. However, it mainly reflects employers' associations in the private sector, since the state is the principal employer in the public sector except at the level of local government, where municipalities are separate employers organised in the South African Local Government Association.

Table 13.2 Employers' Associations, 2008–2015[20]

Year	*Number of Employers' Associations*
2008	180
2009	167
2010	164
2011	166
2012	164
2013	163
2014	159
2015	157

2.3 Data Regarding Strikes

The years following the introduction of the LRA saw a consistent decrease in the number of strikes. That lasted for about nine years, followed by a sharp increase

19. *Bhorat/Naidoo/Yu*, 2014, Table 1.
20. *Department of Labour*, 2016.

in strike activity between 2004 and 2005. Since then strike action has fluctuated, with periodic decreases and increases, but at a generally high level. Of particular note is the upward trajectory in recent years, resulting in the highest level of strikes since the enactment of the new labour laws being recorded in 2016[21] and, especially, the high and growing number of unprocedural ('wildcat') strikes.[22] As noted elsewhere, a significant factor contributing to the increase in strike action is the worsening triple crisis of unemployment, inequality and poverty.

Table 13.3 Number of Strikes over the Period 1999–2016 [23]

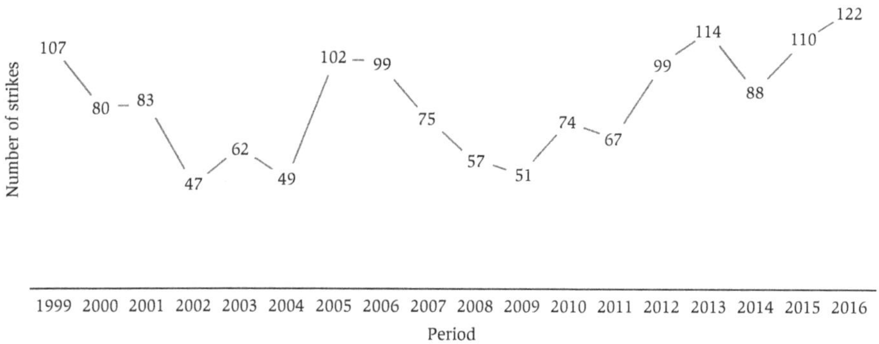

3 THE RIGHT TO STRIKE

3.1 Collective Bargaining Rights

3.1.1 Background

Collective bargaining in SA, like most aspects of labour policy, has its roots in racial segregation. The first national labour statute, the Industrial Conciliation Act of 1924, was introduced to appease White miners after more than a decade of violent conflict arising from mine-owners' efforts to replace unionised white workers with low-paid African workers.[24] The Act granted trade union and voluntary collective bargaining rights at sectoral level to white, coloured and

21. 946 323 working days were lost in 2016 as a result of 122 work stoppages, compared with 903 921 working days lost in 2015: *Department of Labour*, 2017, 2.
22. In 2016, 59 per cent of strikes were unprotected: *Ibid.*, 5. This is despite the fact that the LRA provides a relatively simple procedure for protected strike action: see *infra* Section 3.
23. *Department of Labour*, 2016.
24. The conflict culminated in the 'Rand revolt' of 1922, an armed uprising of White miners which left 153 dead (including 72 soldiers and policemen, 39 strikers and 24 Africans) and 534 wounded. Four strike leaders were executed: *Du Toit*, 1981, 92.

Indian workers, but expressly excluded pass-bearing (male) African workers. By 1956 all African workers, female as well as male, were excluded.[25]

Despite this, steep rises in consumer prices after World War I led to strikes by African miners, dockers and other workers during 1918–1920 and the emergence of African worker organisation.[26] This was part of the prelude to the 1924 Act: it became important for the state to secure the backing of White workers, both to prevent the emergence of cross-racial worker unity and to broaden the support base for its policies of racial segregation.[27] At the same time, the enforced racial divide among workers created a skills hierarchy, with white workers occupying the higher levels and African workers largely confined to unskilled and semi-skilled jobs.

Rapid economic growth from the 1940s onwards, however, meant a growing African working class and made rigid segregation in the workplace less and less sustainable. The first cracks in the system appeared after a wave of illegal wage strikes by African workers in 1973 which the state was unable to suppress. This was followed by uprisings of black youth and growing political unrest, compelling the government to introduce extensive labour law reforms from 1979 onwards.[28] The most important of these were the inclusion of African workers in the collective bargaining system and the creation of an Industrial Court to settle labour disputes as an alternative to industrial action.

As a result, the 1980s saw the emergence of a predominantly African but expressly non-racial labour movement which became the major force in the overthrow of apartheid. At the same time, the Industrial Court developed a body of labour jurisprudence which, contrary to the government's intentions, was essentially based on international labour standards.

3.1.2 The Current Dispensation

Following the first democratic elections in 1994, the Government of National Unity led by the ANC introduced a new labour relations system based on the labour rights entrenched in the Constitution and international law.[29] The new LRA refined the existing system of sectoral bargaining by providing for the establishment of bargaining councils,[30] while also permitting voluntary

25. I.e., in terms of the Industrial Conciliation Act 28 of 1956, which remained in force until its replacement, after many amendments, by the current Labour Relations Act of 1995.
26. *Davies*, 1977.
27. *Ibid.* See also *Godfrey/Maree/Du Toit/Theron*, 2010, chapter 2; *Du Toit/Godfrey/Cooper/Giles/Cohen/Conradie/Steenkamp*, 2015, chapter 1.
28. *Wiehahn*, 1979.
29. Constitution of the Republic of South Africa, 1993, superseded by the Constitution of the Republic of South Africa, 1996. Labour rights are comprehensively set out in s. 23 of the Constitution. Collective labour rights derive, amongst others, from ILO Conventions 87 and 98.
30. Bargaining councils in the private sector are voluntarily established by registered trade unions and employers' organisations: LRA, chapter III part C. The LRA provides for the

collective bargaining at other levels. Collective agreements were made legally binding, and considerable scope was created for varying statutory rights and minimum standards by means of collective agreement. Furthermore, collective agreements entered into by majority trade unions can be extended to all workers both at sectoral and workplace levels.[31] In addition, trade unions were afforded organisational rights depending on their level of representivity at the 'workplace'.[32] Both at sectoral and workplace levels, however, various organisational and other rights are reserved for majority unions.[33] This has contributed to union rivalry, manifested most acutely in violent confrontations in the mining sector.[34]

The drafters of the LRA sought to balance adversarial bargaining with the establishment of participatory structures at workplace level known as workplace forums.[35] Trade unions, however, saw this as a danger that would lead to 'co-option by management and the blunting of class struggle'.[36] An attempt to appease union suspicions by giving majority unions effective control over the establishment and operation of workplace forums was unsuccessful. The result has been a practical absence of functioning workplace forums in South Africa.[37]

A second shortcoming of the LRA was its failure to respond to the growth of non-standard work.[38] Despite an increasingly diverse workforce spanning both 'formal' and 'informal' work, the Act applies only to 'employees' and is premised on standard employment. Trade unions have acknowledged the need to organise non-standard workers but, in practice, have concentrated mainly on workers in standard employment.[39] Amendments introduced in 2014 extended protection to temporary, part-time and agency workers at an individual level but did not change the underlying model.[40] As a result, non-standard workers have no collective voice and remain highly vulnerable to structural change as well as contractual manipulation.

---

mandatory establishment of bargaining councils in the public service (ss 35–38) and local government sector (s 27). This creates an effective duty to bargain in most of the public sector.

31. Sections 23 and 32, LRA.
32. Since the enactment of the LRA, the definition of 'workplace' has been controversial: see *Association of Mineworkers and Construction Union v Chamber of Mines of South Africa* [2017] ZACC 3; 2017 (6) BCLR 700 (CC) where the 'workplace' was defined as the employer's entire operation and a union was held to be a minority union despite having majority membership at five mines.
33. In particular, the right to have collective agreements extended to non-members.
34. *Theron/Godfrey/Fergus*, 2015; *Hartford*, 2012. For an account of the conditions faced by workers in Marikana, see *Benya*, 2015.
35. Chapter V, LRA.
36. *Hepple*, 2012, 265.
37. *Du Toit/Godfrey/Cooper/Giles/Cohen/Conradie/Steenkamp*, 2015, 393; *Steadman* 2004, 1170.
38. *Godfrey/Maree/Du Toit/Theron*, 2010; *Theron*, 2016. 'Non-standard' work, referring mainly to part-time, temporary, agency and contract work, is not the same as 'informal' work, but there is an overlap between the two.
39. *Du Toit/Ronnie*, 2012. See also *LEP/SLP*, 2017.
40. Labour Relations Amendment Act 6 of 2014.

Effective worker organisation is essential to any policy for regulating industrial action. Given that the vast majority of essential services are located in the public sector, the powerful union presence could be conducive to orderly dispute resolution in essential services. However, it also creates a climate where strikes can be highly effective and unions can negotiate a high level of protection against dismissal or loss of wages as a consequence of unprotected strikes. This is discussed further in *infra* Section 4.

3.2 The Right to Strike

3.2.1 Restrictions and Limitations on the Right to Strike

Section 23(2) of the Constitution states that '[e]very worker has the right ... to strike', thus avoiding the uncertainties of inferring an implied right to strike.[41] Together with the extensive protection of labour rights in legislation, this is a legacy of the key role played by organised labour in bringing South Africa's first democratic government to power in 1994. In contrast, employers' statutory right to lock out is not entrenched in the Constitution.[42]

The right to strike is regulated by Chapter IV of the LRA and can be exercised by following a relatively simple procedure. If this is done, the strike is 'protected' and employees taking part in it are protected against disciplinary measures or civil law claims based on their participation in the strike. However, this protection does not apply if the statutory procedure is not followed. In addition, the right to strike is excluded in certain exceptional instances (outlined below). Most importantly for present purposes, strikes and lock-outs in essential services are prohibited.[43]

3.2.2 Definition of 'Strike' and the Distinctions Between Different Forms of Industrial Action

Not every work stoppage is a 'strike'. To be capable of acquiring protected status, industrial action must fall within the definition of a 'strike'.[44] The

41. As in the case of ILO Convention No. 87 of 1948 and certain other constitutions: see *Bellace*, 2014; *Saskatchewan Federation of Labour v. Saskatchewan* 2015 SCC 4, 2015 CSC 4, 2015 CarswellSask 32 (2015).
42. Section 76, LRA allows employers to use replacement labour during a protected strike as well as during a protected lock-out in response to a strike. This is in conflict with the ILO position that 'replacement workers at legal strikes in non-essential services [are] infringing upon freedom of association principles': *International Labour Organisation*, 2009, para. 637. See *In re: Certification of the Constitution of the Republic of South Africa, 1996* 1996 (10) BCLR 1253 (CC) paras 664–68.
43. LRA Sec 65(1)(d)(i); see *infra* Section 5.
44. Section 213 of the LRA defines a strike as 'the partial or complete concerted refusal to work, or the retardation or obstruction of work, by persons who are or have been

Constitutional Court has summed up the four essential elements of the definition as

> '(a) a partial or complete concerted refusal to work or retardation or obstruction of work, (b) by persons who are or have been employed by the same employer or by different employers, (c) for the purpose of remedying a grievance or resolving a dispute, (d) in respect of a matter of mutual interest between employer and employee.'[45]

'Work' refers to work that employees are contractually obliged to perform as well as voluntary overtime work. The term 'concerted' has been interpreted as meaning that a single employee cannot take strike action.[46] The definition extends to virtually every form of industrial action, such as an overtime ban, provided it is aimed at 'remedying a grievance or resolving a dispute'.[47]

Thus, a work stoppage in an essential service will not be a 'strike' if it does not fall within the definition and will therefore not be affected by the prohibition on strikes in essential services. However, it would amount to breach of contract and could well be in breach of various legislative requirements.

Scope of the right to strike

In terms of the definition, a strike must concern 'a matter of mutual interest between employer and employee'. 'Mutual interest' refers to 'the industrial or economic relationship between employer and employee'[48] in the widest sense.[49] 'Between employer and employee' allows strikes against multiple employers but excludes stoppages of a purely political nature. Separate provision is made for

---

employed by the same employer or by different employers, for the purpose of remedying a grievance or resolving a dispute in respect of any matter of mutual interest between employer and employee...'.

45. *TAWUSA obo Ngedle and Others v Unitrans Fuel and Chemical (Pty) Ltd* 2016 (11) BCLR 1440 (CC) para. 105.
46. *Schoeman and Another v Samsung Electronics SA (Pty) Ltd* [1997] 10 BLLR 1364 (LC) 1367; see also minority judgment in *SATAWU and Others v Moloto NO and Another* 2012 (11) BCLR 1177 (CC). However, the Constitution vests the right to strike in 'every worker', and in *Co-operative Worker Association and Another v Petroleum Oil & Gas Co-operative of SA and Others* [2007] 1 BLLR 55 (LC) the Labour Court accepted that a single worker may strike.
47. Thus, refusal to work in protest against new rules or on a religious holiday does not constitute a 'strike': *Simba (Pty) Ltd v FAWU and Others* [1998] 9 BLLR 971 (LC); *FAWU and Others v Rainbow Chicken Farms* [2000] 1 BLLR 70 (LC). Similarly, a refusal by employees to continue working because their employer had not paid them was not a strike but an exercise of the employees' common-law right to refuse to perform until the employer rectified its non-performance: *NUM and Others v Via Doro Manufacturing Ltd* [2000] 7 BLLR 827 (LC) paras 17–19.
48. *Brassey/Cameron/Cheadle/Olivier MP*, 1987, 246.
49. Including, for example, questions of economic policy such as outsourcing: *Vanachem Vanadium Products (Pty) Ltd v NUMSA and Others* [2014] 9 BLLR 923 (LC).

'protest action to promote or defend socio-economic interests of workers', typically to make policy demands on government.[50]

Strikes and lock-outs may also be excluded by a peace clause in a collective agreement or by agreement that an issue must be referred to arbitration.[51] Furthermore, industrial action is prohibited where the issue in dispute is one that can be referred either to arbitration or to the Labour Court[52] or where it is regulated by a collective agreement, arbitration award or ministerial determination.[53] Finally, strikes and lock-outs are prohibited where the workers are engaged in an 'essential service' or a 'maintenance service'.[54]

Requirements for Protected Strikes

The procedural requirements for a strike to be protected are intended to be as simple as possible, while still ensuring that industrial action remains a measure of last resort. The requirements are identical in the public and private sectors, but for the provisions dealing with notice periods. Only two steps are involved. First, the issue in dispute must be referred to conciliation,[55] and a certificate must be issued stating that the dispute remains unresolved or a period of 30 days must elapse.[56] Secondly, the employer must be given at least 48 hours' written notice of the commencement of a strike[57] or, where the state is the employer, seven days' notice.[58] All employees of the affected employer(s), not only members of the trade union which referred the dispute, are then entitled to take part in the strike.[59]

There are certain exceptions to the general requirements. If the dispute is about an employer's refusal to bargain, an advisory award must be obtained from the bargaining council or the CCMA before notice of the strike can be given.[60] Secondly, the LRA's procedural requirements can be dispensed with where a procedure laid down in a bargaining council's constitution or in a collective agreement is followed, or if the strike is called in response to an

50. Section 77, LRA.
51. Section 65(1)(a), (b).
52. Subject to limited exceptions, where trade unions can elect whether to take legal action or take strike action: see s 65(2)(a) and s 189A(8)(b)(ii), LRA.
53. In terms of s 44 of the LRA or chapter 8 of the Basic Conditions of Employment Act 75 of 1997. However, the prohibition may be varied by collective agreement.
54. Section 65(1)(d), LRA.
55. I.e., to a bargaining council with jurisdiction or, if there is none, to the CCMA. In terms of the LRA, accredited bargaining councils have dispute resolution powers (conciliation and arbitration) within their sectors equivalent to those of the CCMA within its national jurisdiction.
56. Section 64(1)(a), LRA.
57. Section 64(1)(*b*). If the dispute is within a bargaining council, notice must be given to the council: *Ibid.*
58. Section 64(1)(*d*).
59. *SATAWU and Others v Moloto NO and Another* [2012] 12 BLLR 1193 (CC) paras 83 and 88–92.
60. Section 64(2), LRA. 'Refusal to bargain' is defined in s 64(2)(a)-(d).

unprotected lock-out.[61] Thirdly, if the dispute is about a unilateral change by an employer to terms and conditions of employment, the workers can include a so-called '*status quo* notice' in the referral of the dispute, requiring the employer not to implement the change or, if it has done so, to restore the *status quo ante* for the duration of the conciliation proceedings.[62] If the employer fails to comply within 48 hours, the employees may strike without following the statutory procedure.[63]

Consequences of Protected and Unprotected Strikes

Employees who take part in a strike in compliance with the requirements of the LRA are protected against the consequences that would normally follow from a refusal to work. Thus, an employer may not dismiss an employee for taking part in a protected strike[64] and any dismissal for this reason is 'automatically unfair'.[65] Participation in a protected strike also does not constitute breach of contract and cannot give rise to claims in delict (tort)[66] or any other civil liability.[67] However, employees are not entitled to payment of remuneration for the duration of a strike,[68] and may be dismissed for a fair reason based on their conduct during the strike or on the employer's operational requirements.[69]

A registered trade union may authorise a picket by its members and supporters for 'peacefully demonstrating' in support of a protected strike or in opposition to a lock-out. Picketing may take place in any public place outside the employer's premises or, with the employer's permission, on its premises.[70] The conduct of a picket and the drafting and enforcement of picketing rules are extensively regulated.[71]

None of these rights apply in the case of an unprotected strike. Participation in an unprotected strike, or conduct in contemplation or furtherance thereof, 'may constitute a fair reason for dismissal'.[72] The Labour Court is also given

61. Section 64(3), LRA.
62. Section 64(4), LRA.
63. Section 64(3)(*e*), LRA.
64. Section 67(4), LRA. Protection extends also to any lawful conduct 'in contemplation or in furtherance of a protected strike or a protected lock-out': s 67(2)(b), LRA.
65. Section 187(1)(a), LRA. The maximum compensation payable for an automatically unfair dismissal is double that which can be ordered for other categories of unfair dismissal: s 194(3), LRA.
66. Section 67(2) LRA.
67. Section 67(6), LRA.
68. Section 67(3), LRA, subject to certain qualifications in the case of remuneration paid in kind.
69. Section 67(5), LRA. This applies also in respect of operational requirements arising as a consequence of the strike, provided that the strike as such is not the main cause of the dismissals: see *SACWU and Others v Afrox Ltd* [1999] 10 BLLR 1005 (LAC).
70. Section 69, LRA. Section 69(3) provides that such permission may not be withheld unreasonably.
71. Section 69, LRA, read with *Code of Good Practice on Picketing.*
72. Section 68(5), LRA.

special powers to prohibit any person from participating in an unprotected strike and to order the payment of compensation for any loss that is caused by such a strike.[73] Clearly, all these sanctions are applicable to strikes in essential services.

4 THE EXPERIENCE WITH STRIKES IN ESSENTIAL SERVICES

4.1 The Prevalence of Strikes in Essential Services

Strikes in essential services had also been prohibited by the legislation that preceded the LRA. However, the prohibition was very broad and often included services that were not essential in terms of the narrow definition adopted by the ILO and confirmed by its Freedom of Association Committee.[74] Section 213 of the LRA now defines an essential service in accordance with the ILO's approach as 'a service, the interruption of which endangers the life, personal safety or health of the whole or part of the population.' In addition, it includes the Parliamentary service and the South African Police Service.[75]

But, notwithstanding the prohibition, strikes in essential services remain a feature of South African labour relations. A major reason for this lies in the broad designation of essential services by the Essential Service Committee (ESC) notwithstanding the narrow definition in the LRA. As a result, the 'flexibility necessary to regulate successfully the complex issue of dispute resolution in essential services'[76] that had been envisaged with the introduction of the 1995 LRA was not achieved. This was acknowledged by government when it introduced far-reaching amendments to the relevant sections of the LRA in 2014,[77] which are discussed in the next part of this chapter.

The precise extent of strikes in essential services is not known. Employers are required to submit returns in respect of strikes or other forms of industrial action. But, while employers must indicate whether strike action was protected, the prescribed form does not specifically require them to state whether essential service workers were involved.[78] Anecdotal evidence, however, makes it clear that workers engaged in designated essential services have repeatedly engaged in industrial action in support of wage and other demands, often of lengthy duration and accompanied by violence. But, in the absence of a reporting duty, the extent to which this is happening is less clear.

---

73. Section 68(1), LRA. Again, the sanctions extend to 'conduct in contemplation or in furtherance' of an unprotected strike. Interdicts or urgent interdicts may also be granted in terms of s 158(1)(a), LRA.
74. *ILO*, 2006, Chapter 10. See *Le Roux/Cohen*, 2016, 7.
75. Section 71(10), LRA.
76. *Ministerial Legal Task Team*, 1995, 304.
77. Labour Relations Amendment Act 6 of 2014; see also the Explanatory Memorandum to the Labour Relations Amendment Bill, 2013.
78. LRA Form 9.2 as required by s 205(3)(a) of the LRA.

In the period 2007–2013, for example, 28 245 974 working days were lost due to strikes in the public sector where most essential services are located.[79] Although industrial action often extended to designated essential services such as electricity, health services, water, sanitation and other local government services, no data is available on the number of essential service workers involved.[80]

Similarly, members of the three trade unions organising the majority of essential service worker – the National Education Health and Allied Workers Union (NEHAWU), South African Municipal Workers Union (SAMWU) and the Independent Municipal and Allied Workers Union (IMATU) – were involved in strike action accounting for 205 488 work days in 2015 and 156 480 work days in 2016.[81] Again, no details are available of how many workers in essential services were involved.

4.2 The Prevalence of Strikes in Essential Services in the Future

The partial privatisation of the state-owned electricity corporation Eskom, through the introduction of Independent Power Producers (IPPs), has emerged as an issue that could see trade unions in the sector embark on strike action.[82] The absence of ratified MSAs,[83] combined with a tradition of workers showing scant regard for legal restrictions, point towards the likely continuation of industrial action in essential services for the foreseeable future.

4.3 Finding the Balance Between the Right to Strike and the Right to Essential Services

South African policy regarding essential services is framed by the Bill of Rights in the Constitution which obliges the state to provide services such as health-care, food, water and social security. The Bill of Rights also provides that every worker has the right to strike. Contrary to earlier legislation, the current LRA draws no distinction between public and private providers for purposes of determining if a service is essential. Its starting point is the need to find a balance

79. Fn 3 at 6. See also *Brand*, 2013. In 2010 and 2011 strikes in the public and municipal sectors lasted 21 and 16 days respectively.
80. *Brand*, 2010.
81. *Department of Labour*, 2017, Table 7.
82. The Congress of South African Trade Unions (COSATU) and the new trade union federation the South African Federation of Trade Unions (SAFTU), while supporting a change to alternative energy sources in principle, have both come out strongly against the introduction of IPPs in the absence of further consultation and policies to avoid job losses. The National Union of Metalworkers of South Africa (NUMSA), the largest union in the country and a SAFTU affiliate, organizes workers in Eskom.
83. Discussed in *infra* Section 5.2.

between workers' right to strike and rights of the broader public to enjoy access to essential services.

5 RESTRICTION OF THE RIGHT TO STRIKE IN ESSENTIAL SERVICES

5.1 Securing Essential Services by Exclusion from Collective Labour Relations Rights

The LRA excludes two groups of workers from its application, including the right to strike: members of the South African National Defence Force (SANDF) and the State Security Agency. Despite this, the Constitutional Court as far back as 1999 held that members of the national defence force may join military trade unions and engage with the state about working conditions in terms of defence force regulations.[84] The judgment extended to permitting defence force members to participate in protest action. Members of the SANDF are, however, precluded from striking.

5.2 Securing Essential Services by Imposing Limitations on the Right to Strike

5.2.1 The LRA and the Prohibition of Strikes in Essential Services

The LRA prohibits strikes by workers covered by the LRA if they are engaged in essential services.[85] Strikes in 'maintenance services' are also prohibited.[86] A maintenance service is defined as a service, the interruption of which has the effect of material physical destruction to any working area, plant or machinery.[87] When determining a maintenance service upon application by an employer, the Essential Service Committee (ESC, discussed immediately below) may direct that disputes involving employees performing that service must be resolved by arbitration.[88] Conversely, where the whole or part of the employer's service has been designated a maintenance service, employers are prohibited from engaging replacement labour in the event of a strike outside the maintenance service.[89]

84. *SA National Defence Union v Minister of Defence & another* (1999) 20 *ILJ* 2265 (CC). The right was derived from the constitutional right of 'every worker' to engage in collective bargaining.
85. Section 65(1)(d)(i) and (ii), LRA.
86. Section 65(1)(d)(ii), LRA.
87. Section 75(1), LRA.
88. Section 75(5) and (6), LRA. This applies only (i) in respect of employees who would ordinarily enjoy the right to strike, (ii) where the number of employees within the maintenance service are a minority of the employer's workforce and (iii) no collective agreement regulates the terms and conditions of employment of the maintenance service employees.
89. Section 76(1)(a), LRA.

As noted already, the South African Parliamentary Service and the South African Police Service (SAPS) are expressly incorporated in the definition of an essential service. The Constitutional Court subsequently held that only members of the South African Police Services employed in terms of the South African Police Service Act - i.e., who are engaged in law enforcement - constitute an essential service. All other persons employed by SAPS in terms of the Public Service Act are not *per se* essential and may strike.[90]

5.2.2 The Essential Service Committee

The LRA requires the establishment of a specialised committee, the ESC, for designating essential and maintenance services.[91] This committee is charged with conducting investigations as to whether the whole or part of a service is 'essential' and deciding whether to designate the whole or only a part of the service as essential.[92] It is also empowered to deal with disputes as to whether a service is essential and whether employees are engaged in an essential service.[93] Furthermore, it must ratify minimum service level agreements and determine minimum service levels if parties are unable to conclude an agreement, as discussed below.

Organised business, labour and government as constituents of the National Economic and Labour Development Council (NEDLAC) must nominate the members of the ESC.[94] However, the chairperson must be independent of NEDLAC and the deputy chairperson must be a senior commissioner of the CCMA.

5.2.3 The Designation of Essential Services

Historically, two approaches have been used in South Africa for designating essential services. The previous LRA had adopted what was called the 'enumeration' approach, in which essential services were identified mainly in terms of employers that were considered to be providing essential services. Their employees were prohibited from embarking on industrial action and the law provided for a system of compulsory arbitration to resolve disputes. An ILO Fact-Finding and Conciliation Committee in 1991 criticised these provisions on the grounds of their excessive breadth.[95]

The second approach refers to the potential consequences of industrial action within services to determine whether they are 'essential'. No distinction is drawn between the private and public sectors in applying this approach. As

90. *SAPS v POPCRU and Another* (2011) 32 *ILJ* 1603 (CC).
91. Section 70, LRA.
92. Section 70D(1), LRA.
93. Section 73, LRA.
94. Section 70A, LRA. NEDLAC is the apex tripartite institution in South Africa.
95. *ILO*, 1992, para. 330 - 337 992) paras 330–337, See also *Roskam*, 2009, 26.

noted already, the 1995 LRA combined the two approaches, defining 'essential services' with reference to the consequences of their interruption in accordance with the ILO approach, while specifically listing the parliamentary and police services.[96]

The determination of essential services in accordance with the LRA's definition has, however, proven to be problematic. Shortly after the enactment of the LRA, the ESC designated a number of services in the public and local government sectors as 'essential'.[97] This was done by convening public hearings and thereafter publishing the determinations in Government Gazettes, whereby they assumed the status of legislation.[98] But, as noted already, the determinations did not adhere to the narrow definition of essential services in the LRA but, instead, tended to identify sectors or subsectors within which essential services are performed rather than the essential services themselves.[99]

This was not accidental. It had been anticipated that trade unions and employers would contribute to the narrowing or 'fine-tuning' of these designations by concluding minimum service agreements (MSAs) within designated sectors,[100] thereby removing any unreasonable limitations of the right to strike.[101] To this end, the LRA provides for parties in an essential service to reach agreement on the minimum services that would be maintained in the event of a strike. If ratified by the ESC, this minimum service level would for practical purposes be designated as the essential service, thereby leaving all workers not included in the minimum service free to participate in strike action.

Until very recently, however, only two such agreements were concluded and ratified by the ESC, both of which have since lapsed.[102] And, though both the South African Local Government Bargaining Council and the Public Service Co-ordinating Bargaining Council concluded framework agreements several years ago to guide the conclusion of MSAs at workplace level, few agreements have emerged in the municipal sector and none in the public service.

Prior to the 2014 amendments to the LRA, trade unions laid the blame for this state of affairs at the door of the employers. They claimed that it was a strategy of employers to deny as many workers as possible the right to strike by preserving the status quo where workers in truly essential services as well as those performing related but non-essential functions were all lumped together under 'essential service' determinations. But, at the same time, many workers

96. See part 4 para. 1 of this chapter. The listing of the Parliamentary service is clearly questionable in the context of the ILO definition.
97. See the Notices published by the ESC in 1997 and 1998: GNR 784 of 6 June 1997; GNR 1216 of 12 September 1997; GNR 1542 of 21 November 1997 and GNR 436 of 27 March 1998. The services proclaimed as 'essential' are listed in Annexure A.
98. Section 71, LRA.
99. *Le Roux/Cohen*, 2016, 7.
100. In terms of s 72, LRA; and see part 7 of this chapter.
101. *Pillay*, 2012, 809.
102. *Le Roux/Cohen*, 2016, 8.

engaged in genuinely essential services have shown scant regard for the prohibition of strike action.[103]

The 2014 amendments were aimed at addressing weaknesses in the ESC relating to its composition, powers, functions and resources. The amendments allow it to impose minimum services levels on parties that fail to conclude MSAs within a specified time.[104] However, a recent report to Parliament by the Department of Labour showed that progress has been slow in arriving at minimum service determinations either by way of ratified agreements or by way of determination by the ESC itself.[105] According to the ESC, it has set itself targets as a means of giving effect to the 2014 amendments and to promote compliance with the essential service determinations.[106] These include 60 MSAs for each of the municipal and public service sectors and 25 for other institutions falling with the ambit of essential services. Most progress has been made in the municipal sector where six MSAs have been concluded, 16 minimum service determinations have been made and 58 other MSAs are under negotiation. However, no progress has been made in the public service.

There had in the past been conflicting court decisions as to where a dispute about whether a service is essential, whether a worker falls within an essential service, or the interpretation of an MSA, must be referred for determination. The LRA, as amended, now provides that all disputes of this nature must be decided by the ESC.[107]

5.2.4 Limitations on the Right to Strike in Essential Services

As discussed in part 3 of this chapter, the right to strike enjoys a high degree of protection in South Africa.[108] However, no right is absolute. The Constitution permits a right in the Bill of Rights to be limited by a law of general application to the extent that the limitation is reasonable and justifiable in an open and democratic society based on human dignity.[109] The prohibition of the right to strike in essential services may be seen as a limitation of this nature; alternatively, it may be construed as regulating rather than limiting the right to strike by

103. *Roskam*, 2009, 5.
104. Section 72(1) and (2), LRA.
105. *Department of Labour*, 2017B.
106. *Gildenhuys*, 2018.
107. Section 73(1), LRA. This follows the judgment of the Supreme Court of Appeal in *Eskom Holdings Ltd v NUM* (2012) 3 BLLR 254 (SCA) that only the ESC, and not the CCMA, can determine disputes relating to the terms of a MSA. Compulsory arbitration in terms of s 74, in other words, is reserved for disputes arising *within* essential services or minimum services, and not about the extent of such services.
108. The Constitutional Court has ruled that an employer's right to lock out is not equivalent to the right to strike, given that employers enjoy greater social and economic power than individual workers and may exercise this power in various ways: *In re: Certification of the Constitution of the Republic of South Africa, 1996* 1996 (10) *BCLR* 1253 (CC) para. 66.
109. Section 36, Constitution.

'[balancing it] with other fundamental rights such as those to health, care, food, water and social security which are also enshrined in our Bill of Rights'.[110]

The constitutionality of the prohibition has not been challenged; and, given the position of the ILO supervisory bodies that the prohibition of strikes by essential services workers does not infringe the right to freedom of association, the LRA's prohibition would be difficult to challenge, at least to the extent that it conforms to the ILO definition of essential services in the strict sense.[111]

As indicated above, the procedural requirements for strikes in essential services where minimum services have been designated are identical to those for strikes in non-essential services. The major substantive requirement is the existence of a ratified MSA or a designated minimum service.

5.2.5 Sanctions Against Essential Service Workers and Their Unions That Engage in Strike Action

Workers who engage in unprotected strike action face the sanction of dismissal. In practice, however, employers have not resorted to dismissing strikers in essential services and have restricted their actions to applying, at most, the no work, no pay principle. One obvious explanation for this is the practical difficulty, if not impossibility, of replacing large numbers of workers, often with special skills (e.g., fire-fighters), at short notice and thus causing further disruption to the service.

The Labour Court has the power to interdict unprotected strikes and also to grant an order of compensation and/or damages in any circumstances contemplated in the LRA. The court has issued many interdicts to halt unprocedural strike action, including strikes in essential services. It has also, on occasion, handed down costs and damages orders against unions held responsible for such action. Unions or workers who knowingly disregard interdicts can be held liable for contempt of court and fined or imprisoned.[112]

In general, however, employers have been constrained in bringing to bear the full force of the law against striking essential service workers. This may have emboldened workers and their unions to disregard the prohibition on strike action or, at most, to use their own discretion in limiting the impact of industrial action. It also indicates an imbalance between the present regulatory framework and the processes which it seeks to regulate.

110. *Brand*, 2010, 2.
111. In *National Union of Metalworkers of South Africa and Others v Bader Bop (Pty) Ltd and Another* (2003) 24 *ILJ* 305 (CC) the Constitutional Court referred approvingly to the decisions of the ILO supervisory committees in this regard: at para. 32.
112. In terms of s 157(2), LRA. Contempt orders have been made in various cases, although orders of imprisonment are in most if not all cases suspended.

6 COMPENSATORY MEASURES FOR RESTRICTIONS

6.1 Compulsory Binding Arbitration

Concessions and compromises underpin the process of orderly collective bargaining, depending on the strength of the parties' bargaining positions. If either party can inflict a serious cost of disagreement on the other, the likelihood of a settlement is advanced. In contrast, it has famously been stated, collective bargaining without a right to strike amounts to collective begging.[113] In other words, without a right to strike the inducement for employers to reach agreement will decline and the process of orderly collective bargaining will fall into disrepute, creating a climate conducive to unprocedural strike action.

To avoid this, the ILO's Committee on Freedom of Association has held that workers who are denied the right to strike should be provided with 'adequate, impartial and speedy conciliation and arbitration proceedings in which the parties concerned can take part at every stage and in which the awards, once made, are fully and promptly implemented'.[114] In line with the ILO's position, the LRA provides that any dispute in an essential service may be referred to the CCMA, or to a bargaining council with jurisdiction, for conciliation and, if it remains unresolved, for final and binding arbitration.[115]

There is only one exception to this rule: in the case of certain arbitration awards against the state, Parliament has the power to decide whether the award will be binding. This, and other problems associated with compulsory interest arbitration, are discussed below.

6.2 Arbitration Awards Against the State

Since most essential services are in the public sector, the question of how and when an award becomes binding on the state is important. On the one hand, Parliament has an exclusive constitutional power to appropriate monies.[116] Similarly, local government must take into account municipal budgets, the fiscal efficiency of municipalities and national economic policies in concluding any collective agreement.[117] On the other hand, the ILO's Committee on Freedom of Association has ruled that the reservation of budgetary powers to legislative authorities should not affect compliance with the terms of awards by a compulsory arbitration tribunal.[118]

The LRA seeks to resolve the tension between these contrasting imperatives by stipulating that any arbitration award against the state which has

113. *Jacobs*, 2010, 659 et seq.
114. *ILO*, 1992, para. 333.
115. Section 74, LRA; and see Gernigon/Odero/Guido, 1998, 26 et seqq.
116. Section 213, Constitution.
117. Section 72(2), Local Government: Municipal Systems Act 32 of 2000.
118. *Servais*, 2009, 9.

financial implications will become binding 14 days after the award is issued, unless the Minister of Labour has tabled the award in Parliament within that period, in which case Parliament has 14 days to decide whether the award is binding.[119] If it decides that the award is not binding, the dispute must be referred back for further conciliation and arbitration.[120] The LRA does not say whether a second award will be final or, if Parliament again rejects the award, whether the process recommences. The ILO's position suggests the former, but the courts have yet to clarify the question.[121]

Furthermore, arbitration is intended to be a speedy process. However, the process outlined above as well as the limited number of interest disputes that have been referred to arbitration suggest the opposite. The only major interest arbitration in the public service thus far, which took place in 1999, continued for seven months and led to an inconclusive result.[122]

6.3 Problems with Interest Arbitration

6.3.1 The Absence of Specific Criteria

The first problem is the lack of criteria for making awards in interest arbitration. Unlike in court proceedings and rights arbitrations, where judges and arbitrators are bound to give decisions in accordance with law and precedent, arbitrators in interest arbitrations are not bound by any specific rules. Approaches range from so-called 'final offer' arbitration to 'pendulum' arbitration and 'fairness'. For instance, settling a wage dispute may involve consideration of criteria varying from the cost of living to the living wage and other factors, such as the weight to be attached to the workers' loss of bargaining power through their loss of the right to strike. An arbitrator must decide which criteria are relevant and how much weight to attach to each. Thus, two arbitrators trained in interest arbitration may examine the wage dispute from different perspectives and deliver entirely different awards.[123]

119. Section 74(5), LRA.
120. Section 74(6), LRA.
121. In *Public Servants Association obo its members v National Prosecuting Authority and Another* (2012) 8 *BLLR* 765 (LAC) the Labour Appeal Court upheld an arbitration award ordering the payment of salary increases which had not been budgeted for, on the basis that the responsible Minister could approach Parliament for additional funding. The court accepted that the award was 'equivalent' to a strike, but also that the outcome was 'subject to the final oversight of parliament': paras 16, 32.
122. *PSA and Others and The Government of the RSA* (case no. PSBC 1 1999–2000).
123. Carman/O'Byrne/Searle, 2015. On the cost of interest arbitration as well as its 'chilling' and 'narcotic' effects, see *ILO*, 1999, para. 158.

6.3.2 The Complexity of Sector-Wide Arbitrations

The complexity of sector-wide disputes does not encourage parties to follow the arbitration route. With 257 municipalities in South Africa, for example, compulsory arbitration to resolve a wage dispute affecting essential service workers in the municipal sector would involve as many mini-arbitrations within the main process. In this sector as in others, furthermore, essential and non-essential workers are part of the same bargaining unit. Since no MSA is in place, it means that separate referrals must be made for essential and non-essential workers if an interest dispute arises.[124]

6.3.3 The Effect of a MSA on Dispute Resolution

Further problems have arisen from the wording of the provision for MSAs.[125] Once ratified, it has been noted, the effect of such an agreement is that the minimum service becomes the essential service and all workers not included within it retain the right to strike. In this event, section 72(b) of the LRA originally provided that the compulsory arbitration provisions contained in section 74 'do not apply'.

There were, however, different interpretations of what this meant. One view was that compulsory arbitration fell away for the entire service that was originally designated, including the minimum service. A second view was that workers outside the minimum service could no longer invoke compulsory arbitration but that those within the minimum service could do so. A third view was that the workers outside and inside the minimum service could exercise a collective option of resorting either to compulsory arbitration or to strike action to resolve a common dispute, in which case the workers outside the minimum service could strike on behalf of those within it.

The 2014 amendments sought to clarify matters by providing that 'the agreed or determined minimum services are to be regarded as an essential service' and that 'the provisions of section 74 [i.e., compulsory arbitration] do not apply'.[126] However, it was still not explained what section 74 does not apply to. It was also added that, where a minimum service level *has been determined by the ESC* within a designated essential service (as opposed to being agreed upon), workers within the designated essential service as a whole retain the right to refer a dispute to arbitration, provided the majority of workers in the designated service vote in favour of doing so.[127]

The intention was probably to encourage workers in essential services to conclude MSAs without having to give up the option of referring a dispute to arbitration. If so, it had obviously escaped the notice of the parties at NEDLAC

124. *City of Cape Town v SALGBC and Another* (2011) 5 *BLLR* 490 (LC).
125. Section 72, LRA; discussed in *supra* Subsection 5.2.3.
126. Section 72(3), LRA. However, it was still not explained *to what* s 74 does not apply.
127. Section 72(5), LRA.

and in the parliamentary process that the amendment only referred to essential services where the ESC had determined minimum services, but made no mention of essential services determined by MSAs. To address the problem, the Labour Relations Amendment Bill of 2017[128] has extended the arbitration option from cases where the ESC has determined a minimum service to cases where it has ratified a MSA.[129] The effect of this change remains to be seen.

7 SECURING ESSENTIAL SERVICES BY FURTHER MEANS

7.1 Legal Enforcement Measures

Clearly, the prohibition of strikes in essential and minimum services under South African conditions has had limited effect.[130] Court action to interdict such strikes has done little to prevent them, perhaps because it is reactive rather than proactive. Other than this, the social partners have developed no measures either collectively or individually to deal with strikes in essential services.

This suggests that further means for securing essential services may need to be considered. Within the present constitutional framework, there is little scope for adopting a more draconian approach. For example, ad hoc legislative measures to compel striking essential service workers to return to work are practically excluded by the participatory and consensus-seeking process for the enactment of labour legislation.[131] The constitutional protection of labour rights also means that any legislation that is ultimately adopted would have to remain within the existing paradigm of rights and freedoms.

The LRAB has introduced an exercise of this nature. It has created a complex process whereby advisory arbitration can be initiated by the Director of the CCMA where a strike or lock-out is 'no longer functional to collective bargaining' or poses a serious threat to constitutional rights or to the 'normal social and economic functioning of the community'.[132] In terms of this scheme, an advisory award can ultimately become binding by default if the affected trade union is 'deemed' to have accepted it through failing to meet the procedural and

128. R 1273, *Government Gazette* No 41257, 17 November 2017 (hereafter 'LRAB'). At the time of writing it has been approved by Parliament but has not yet been promulgated.
129. Clause 6(a), LRAB. A 'ratified minimum service' or 'determined minimum service' is defined to mean 'the minimum number of employees in a designated essential service who may not strike in order to ensure that the life, personal safety or health of the whole or part of the population is not endangered': clause 6(b).
130. See *supra* Section 4.
131. For example, NEDLAC must 'consider all proposed labour legislation relating to labour market policy before it is introduced in Parliament': s 5(1)(c), National Economic, Development and Labour Council Act 35 of 1994.
132. Clause 16 LRAB: proposed new s 150A(4).

substantive requirements for opposing it.[133] However, the LRAB has encountered strong opposition from organised labour and, at the time of writing, it remains to be seen what it will mean in practice.

Beyond this, the President has the power to declare a state of emergency 'if the life of the nation is threatened by war, invasion, general insurrection, disorder, natural disaster or other public emergency' and 'the declaration is necessary to restore peace and order'.[134] It is conceivable that a protracted strike by essential service workers could lead to an emergency of this magnitude. However, no regulations have been issued under the Act and there is no precedent for its implementation. Hypothetically, it could make it possible to call on the defence force to provide support, as has been done in many countries under emergency conditions. Since the military disposes over an array of skilled personnel, it is capable of rendering certain essential services.[135] However, such interventions would only be sustainable for limited periods and would hardly be appropriate in the typical situation of localised or short-term disputes in essential services. At the same time, it may easily compromise or undermine labour rights. The focus should remain on measures that find a balance between the right of citizens to uninterrupted essential services and workers' right to the fair resolution of disputes.

7.2 Improving the Arbitration Process

It has been noted that the experience of compulsory arbitration by employers as well as workers provides little incentive for following this route. The process could be assisted if criteria were provided for assessing the submissions made by parties, possibly in the form of regulations or a Code of Good Practice. In particular, greater use of 'final offer' arbitration could encourage parties to adopt realistic stances earlier in the process.[136] At the point of dispute, parties are often far apart in their demands although, in some cases, parties resort to the use of power even when differences are small. A speedy final offer arbitration process, where the criteria for determining the outcome are common knowledge, is an option that deserves more attention.

The extent of Parliament's power to interfere with arbitration awards against the state should also be clarified and, if necessary, curtailed. Linked to this, the establishment of a panel of arbitrators who are familiar with the public sector and could ensure predictable outcomes may give the arbitration route greater credibility. Similarly, a panel of suitably skilled facilitators could assist parties to reach MSAs more easily.

133. Clause 16, LRAB: proposed new s 150C.
134. Section 1, State of Emergency Act 64 of 1997 read with s 37 of the Constitution.
135. *Donnelly/Mendick*, 2015.
136. See *Thompson*, 2010, 60 and 'Ohio Revised Code, title [41] xli labor and industry, chapter 4117: public employees' collective bargaining': *Ibid.*, 76 et seq.

7.3 A Premium for Essential Service Workers

A more controversial option is the possibility of paying essential service workers a premium as a quid pro quo for the loss of their right to strike. It is uncertain how this will be perceived by other workers who may have to take strike action in support of their wage demands, with the consequent loss of earnings. The existing provisions of the LRA encouraging workers engaged in minimum services and their co-workers not performing minimum services to engage in joint arbitration[137] form a possible starting point for designing an arrangement whereby wages or wage increases could be equitably distributed among workers who are entitled to strike and those who are not.

7.4 Voluntary Provision of Essential Services

A further option, where MSAs or determinations are not in place, is for the trade unions and workers concerned to determine voluntarily what minimum services should be rendered in the event of strike action. Such arrangements could go some way to resolving the tension between each worker's right to strike and the social need to provide essential services without interruption, but compromise the duty of the state to provide essential services.

7.5 Rethinking Bargaining Units

Public sector bargaining councils are extensive. Different categories of workers, from highly skilled to less skilled, may be found in the same bargaining units. This may dissipate common interests among them, creating a climate which is not conducive to orderly collective bargaining and could foster the level of frustration among certain groups, and the risk of violence, that have come to characterise industrial action in the public sector. A review of the public-sector bargaining councils and the delineation of more discreet bargaining units could promote more orderly collective bargaining, speedier dispute resolution and less propensity for industrial action. Such a review would affect essential services also.

It has furthermore been suggested that a more explicit duty to bargain within essential services could contribute to more orderly dispute resolution and avoidance of disruptions.[138]

137. See section 4.3 of this chapter.
138. *Brand*, 2010, 15.

8 EVALUATION AND CONCLUSION

Major amendments to the relevant sections of the LRA in 2014 have brought no significant change in the regulation of disputes in essential services as yet.[139] The question has also been raised whether compulsory arbitration is an effective quid pro quo for the denial of the right to strike. The ILO has noted that experts are divided as to its viability.

There are, however, more general problems affecting the regulatory framework as a whole. The labour relations environment remains characterised by a highly adversarial climate in which dispute resolution mechanisms aimed at fostering legal compliance have limited effect. The shift in the concentration of unionisation from the private to the public sector, where most essential services are located, has been accompanied by a rising level of militancy and strike action, also in essential services.

This demonstrates the limits of the law. Workers in essential services who take strike action run the risk of being dismissed or held in contempt of court if they disregard a court order interdicting a strike. Yet strikes take place regularly, and interdicts are breached, with little or no consequence for the workers. This is partly because employers are faced with a dilemma: dismissing the strikers would be self-defeating from the perspective of ensuring the uninterrupted delivery of essential services, and 'bringing in the army' as an emergency measure is likely to aggravate the existing levels of mistrust.

The obvious answer is that, unless the degree of adversarialism in the public sector is reduced, means of safeguarding essential services against strikes will remain elusive. The law can only do so much. In any event, it could be argued that the LRA (as amended) already provides an adequate framework for regulating disputes in essential services and that it is up to the parties to make it work. All roads lead back to the problem of adversarialism and the need for a sea change at a policy level to address its causes.

That inquiry falls beyond the scope of the present discussion.[140] Within the framework of the law, the paucity of minimum services agreements and the limited success of the ESC thus far to proactively nudge employers and unions towards concluding such agreements allow little scope for evaluating what does or does not work. However, while it is too early to dismiss the efficacy of the ESC, all parties may be well advised to consider additional means for securing essential services.

A step forward may be for the ESC, as a matter of urgency, to review existing determinations and identify discreet operations within 'essential services' which, if interrupted, would in fact 'endanger the life, personal safety and health of the whole or part of the population'. This may provide greater impetus for directing parties towards concluding MSAs and if they fail to do so, for the

139. *Department of Labour*, 2017B.
140. For an analysis from this perspective, see *Cheadle et al.*, 2017, Chapter 2*a*.

ESC to determine the appropriate minimum services in terms of the 2014 amendments to the LRA.[141]

Given past experience, however, the question remains to what extent parties would adhere to minimum service determinations made against their will and whether, or why, enforcement mechanisms would be any more effective than they are at present. This underlines the fact that successful remedial measures would have to be based on a shared vision of fairness; that is, an appropriate balance between workers' right to strike and the public right of access to essential services. Negotiations involving employers, unions and other organisations that are genuinely representative of all relevant stakeholders, including the users of essential services, would be crucial in achieving this outcome.

Bibliography

Books and Chapters in Books

-----, Moody's keeps SA at investment grade, Fin24 23 March 2018. Available at https://www.fin24.com/Economy/just-in-moodys-keeps-sa-at-investment-grade-20180323 (accessed 27 March 2018)

Brassey, Martin/Cameron, Edwin/Cheadle, Halton/Olivier, Marius, The New Labour Law, 1987

Cheadle, Halton/Cohen, Tamara/Conradie, Bradley/Du Toit, Darcy/Fergus, Emma/Jacobs, Mario/Steenkamp, Anton, Strikes and the law, 2017

Du Toit, Darcy/Godfrey, Shane/Cooper, Carole/Giles, Graham/Cohen, Tamara/Conradie, Bradley/Steenkamp, Anton, Labour Relations Law: A Comprehensive Guide, 6th ed., 2015

Du Toit, Darcy, Capital and labour in South Africa, 1981

Du Toit, Darcy/Ronnie, Roger, The Necessary Evolution of Strike Law, in *Le Roux, Rochelle/Rycroft, Alan* (eds), Reinventing Labour Law: Reflecting on the First 15 years of the Labour relations Act and future Challenges, 2012

Godfrey, Shane/Maree, Johann/Du Toit, Darcy/Theron, Jan, Collective Bargaining in South Africa: past, present and future?, 2010

141. The major labour federation proposed, at the time that the amendments were being considered, that the ESC, when considering whether a whole or part of a service was essential, should make the designation in a way that least restricts the right to strike and the recourse to lock-out. It also called for the LRA to provide for ratified MSAs and designations to be reviewed every three years and existing designations to be reviewed within 12 months of the amendments coming into effect. See COSATU submission on the Labour Relations Amendment Bill [b16-2012] and the Basic Conditions of Employment Amendment Bill [b15-2012], presented to the Portfolio Committee on Labour on 31 July 2012: available at http://www.cosatu.org.za/show.php?ID=6379 (accessed on 15 December 2017).

Jacobs, Antoine, The law of strikes and lockouts, in *Blanpain* (ed.), Comparative Labour law and Industrial Relations in Industrialized Market Economies, 10th ed., 2010

Theron, Jan, An argument for a right to decent work in South Africa, in *Busby, Nicole/Brodie, Douglas/Zahn, Rebecca* (eds) The Future Regulation of Work: New Concepts, New Paradigms, 2016

Journal Articles, Monographs, Reports and Working Papers

Bellace, Janice, The ILO and the right to strike, International Labour Review 2014, 29 et seqq.

Benya, Asanda, The invisible hands: women in Marikana, Review of African Political Economy 2015, 545 et seqq.

Bhorat Haroon/Naidoo Karmen/Yu Derek, Trade Unions in an Emerging Economy. Development Policy Research Unit Working Paper, 2014

Carman, Nigel/O'Byrne Brian/Searle, Neil, Collective bargaining and beyond: The role of interest arbitration in developing economies. Paper presented at 21st World Congress of the ISLSSL, 2015

Brand John, Essential Services and the Implications of MSAs within the Public Service. Presentation to the 3rd Biennial Public Service Conference, 2013

Brand, John, Strikes in essential services. Paper presented to SASLAW Seminar, 2010

Congress of South African Trade Unions, Submission on the Labour Relations Amendment Bill [b16-2012] and the Basic Conditions of Employment Amendment Bill [b15-2012], Portfolio Committee on Labour, 2012

Davies, Rob, Capital, The State, and White Wage Earners: An Historical Materialist Analysis of Class Formation and Class Relations in South Africa 1900–1960, Doctoral dissertation, University of Sussex 1977

Department of Labour, Explanatory Memorandum to the Labour Relations Amendment Bill, 2013

Department of Labour, Industrial Action Report, 2016

Department of Labour, Briefing by the Department of Labour on all the overall performance and plans of the Essential Services Committee of the CCMA, 2017. Available at https://pmg.org.za/committee-meeting/25441 (accessed on 15 December 2017)

Donnelly, Laura/Mendick, Robert, Army poised to cover for striking NHS doctors, The Telegraph 28 November 2015

Gernigon, Bernard/Odero, Alberto/Guido, Horacio, ILO Principles Concerning the Right to Strike, 1998

Gildenhuys, Annelie, Presentation to the 2nd ESC Stakeholder Conference, 8–9 March 2018

Hartford, Gavin, The mining industry strike wave: What are the causes and what are the solutions. Polity.org.za, 2012

Hepple, Bob, Negotiating Social Change in the Shadow of the Law, South African Law Journal 2012, 248 et seqq.

International Labour Organisation, 353rd Report of the Committee on Freedom of Association, 2009

International Labour Organisation, Digest of decisions and principles of the Freedom of Association Committee of the governing body of the ILO, 2006

International Labour Organisation, Prelude to Change: Industrial Relations Reform in South Africa, Industrial Law Journal 1992, 739 et seqq.

International Labour Organisation, Report of the Fact Finding and Conciliation Commission on Freedom of Association concerning the Republic of South Africa, 1992

International Labour Organisation, New Trends in Prevention and Resolution of Labour Disputes, 1999

Labour and Enterprise Policy Research Group (LEP)/Social Law Project (SLP), ILO Future of Work Initiative: South Africa, 2017

Le Roux, Rochelle/Cohen, Tamara, Understanding the limitations to the right to strike in essential and public services in the SADC Region, Potchefstroom Electronic Law Journal 2016

Ministerial Legal Task Team, Explanatory Memorandum, Draft Labour Relations Bill of 1995, Industrial Law Journal 1995, 278 et seqq.

Nsehe, Mfonobong, The African Billionaires, 2017

People's Assembly, Infographic: Service Delivery Protests, 2016, https://www.pa.org.za/blog/service-delivery-protests (Accessed on 6 November 2017)

The Presidency RSA, Twenty Year Review South Africa: 1994–2014, 2014

Theron, Jan/Godfrey, Shane/Fergus, Emma, Organisational and collective bargaining rights through the lens of Marikana, Industrial Law Journal 2015, 849 et seqq.

Thompson, Clive, Dispute prevention and resolution in public services labour relations: Good policy and practice. International Labour Organisation Working Paper, 2010

Pillay, Dhaya, Essential Services: Developing tools for MSAs, Industrial Law Journal 2012, 801 et seqq.

Roskam, Anton, Draft – Essential and minimum services and the right to strike, Development Policy Research Unit, 2009

Servais, Jean-Michel, The ILO law and the freedom to strike. Paper presented to the University of Toronto Symposium, 2009

Statistics South Africa, Mid-Year Population Estimate, 2017

Statistics South Africa, Poverty Trends in South Africa, 2017 (Statistics South Africa, 2017a)

Steadman, Felicity, Workplace Forums in South Africa: A Critical Analysis, Industrial Law Journal 2004, 1170 et seqq.

Wiehahn, Nicholas, Report of the Commission of Inquiry into Labour Legislation, 1979

Legislation, Regulations and Codes

South Africa

Code of Good Practice on Picketing (GN 765 in *Government Gazette* 18887 of 15 May 1998)
Constitution of the Republic of South Africa Act 200 of 1993
Basic Conditions of Employment Act 75 of 1997
Industrial Conciliation Act 28 of 1956
Labour Relations Act 66 of 1995
Labour Relations Amendment Act 6 of 2014
Labour Relations Amendment Bill B-2017, *Government Gazette* No 41257 (17 November 2017)
Local Government: Municipal Systems Act 32 of 2000
State of Emergency Act 64 of 1997
Notice published by the essential services committee, GNR 784, 6 June 1997
Notice published by the essential services committee, GNR 1216, 12 September 1997
Notice published by the essential services committee, GNR 1542, 21 November 1997
Notice published by the essential services committee, GNR 436, 27 March 1998

Other

Ohio Revised Code, Title [41] xli labor and industry, chapter 4117: public employees' collective bargaining

Case Law

South Africa

City of Cape Town v SALGBC and Another (2011) 5 BLLR 490 (LC)
Co-operative Worker Association and Another v Petroleum Oil & Gas Co-operative of SA and Others [2007] 1 BLLR 55 (LC)
Eskom Holdings Ltd v NUM (2012) 3 BLLR 254 (SCA)
FAWU and Others v Rainbow Chicken Farms [2000] 1 BLLR 70 (LC)
In re: Certification of the Constitution of the Republic of South Africa, 1996 1996 (10) BCLR 1253 (CC)
National Union of Metalworkers of South Africa and Others v Bader Bop (Pty) Ltd and Another (2003) 24 ILJ 305 (CC)
NUM and Others v Via Doro Manufacturing Ltd [2000] 7 BLLR 827 (LC)
Public Servants Association obo its members v National Prosecuting Authority and Another (2012) 8 BLLR 765 (LAC)
PSA and Others and The Government of the RSA (Case no. PSBC 1 1999–2000)
SACWU and Others v Afrox Ltd [1999] 10 BLLR 1005 (LAC)

SA National Defence Union v Minister of Defence & another (1999) 20 ILJ 2265 (CC)

SAPS v POPCRU and Another (2011) 32 *ILJ* 1603 (CC)

SATAWU and Others v Moloto NO and Another [2012] 12 BLLR 1193 (CC)

Schoeman and Another v Samsung Electronics SA (Pty) Ltd [1997] 10 BLLR 1364 (LC) 1367

Simba (Pty) Ltd v FAWU and Others [1998] 9 BLLR 971 (LC)

TAWUSA obo Ngedle and Others v Unitrans Fuel and Chemical (Pty) Ltd 2016 (11) BCLR 1440 (CC)

Vanachem Vanadium Products (Pty) Ltd v NUMSA and Others [2014] 9 BLLR 923 (LC)

Other

Saskatchewan Federation of Labour v. Saskatchewan 2015 SCC 4, 2015 CSC 4, 2015 CarswellSask 32 (2015)

Annex

The following services have been listed as essential services by the Notices set out below.

1. Notice published by the essential services committee, GNR 784, 6 June 1997:
    - The regulation and control of air traffic;
    - the Weather Bureau of the Department of Environmental Affairs and Tourism, being a service which supports the regulation and control of air traffic.
2. Notice published by the essential services committee, GNR 1216, 12 September 1997:

    2.1 Services:

    (a) Municipal traffic services and policing;
    (b) municipal health;
    (c) municipal security;
    (d) the supply and distribution of water;
    (e) the security services of the Department of Water Affairs and Forestry;
    (f) the generation, transmission and distribution of power;
    (g) fire fighting;
    (h) the payment of social pensions one month after they fall due;
    (i) the services required for the functioning of courts;
    (j) correctional services; and
    (k) blood transfusion services provided by the South African Blood Transfusion Service.

2.2 Parts of sanitation services:
  (a) The maintenance and operation of water-borne sewerage systems, including pumping stations and the control of discharge of industrial effluent into the system;
  (b) the maintenance and operation of sewage purification works;
  (c) the collection of refuse of an organic nature;
  (d) the collection of infectious refuse from medical and veterinary hospitals or practices;
  (e) the collection and disposal of refuse at a disposal site; and
  (f) the collection of refuse left uncollected for 14 (fourteen) days or longer, including domestic refuse and refuse on public roads and open spaces.

2.3 Services provided by the public sector until 31 March 1998:
  (a) Emergency health services and the provision of emergency health facilities to the community or part thereof.
  (b) nursing; and
  (c) medical and paramedical services.

2.4 Services in support of the services referred to in paragraph 2.3 until 31 March 1998:
  (a) Catering;
  (b) medical records;
  (c) security;
  (d) porter and reception;
  (e) pharmaceutical and dispensary;
  (f) medicine quality control laboratory;
  (g) forensics;
  (h) laundry;
  (i) clinical engineering;
  (j) hospital engineering;
  (k) waste removal;
  (l) mortuary; and
  (m) pest control.

2.5. Services provided by the private sector which are funded by the public sector:
  (a) Emergency health services and the provision of emergency health facilities to the community or part thereof;
  (b) nursing; and
  (c) medical and paramedical services.

2.6. Services in support of the services referred to in paragraph 2.5:
  (a) Boiler; and
  (b) water purification.

2.7. Services provided by nursing homes which are registered as welfare organisations to patients in need of moderate and maximum) care:
   (a) Emergency health services and the provision of emergency health facilities;
   (b) nursing; and
   (c) medical and paramedical services.

2.8. Services in support of the services referred to in paragraph 2.7:
   (a) Physiotherapy;
   (b) dispensary;
   (c) catering;
   (d) laundry;
   (e) boiler;
   (f) transport; and
   (g) security.

2.9. Services provided by civilian personnel in the Department of Defence to support the South African National Defence Force:
   (a) The Secretariat for Defence;
   (b) the Intelligence Division;
   (c) the Finance Division;
   (d) the parachute seamstresses of the South African Army;
   (e) the parachute packing operators of the South African Army;
   (f) the military intelligence functionaries of the South African Army;
   (g) the storemen in the South African Navy;
   (h) the provisioning officers and clerks in the South African Navy;
   (i) the technical personnel in the South African Navy;
   (j) the tugboat personnel in the South African Navy;
   (k) the surveyors in the South African Navy;
   (l) the South African Medical Service;
   (m) those serving in military posts in the South African National Defence Force;
   (n) the cryptographers in the South African National Defence Force; and
   (o) the maintenance services in the South African National Defence Force.

3. Notice published by the essential services committee, GNR 1542, 21 November 1997:
   Computer services provided or supported by the Central Computer Service of the Department of State Expenditure:
   (a) The Persal system;
   (b) the social pension system;
   (c) the hospital systems; and
   (d) the flood control system.

4. Notice published by the essential services committee, GNR 436, 27 March 1998
   4.1 Services in the public sector:
      (a) Emergency health services and the provision of emergency health facilities to the community or part thereof;
      (b) nursing; and
      (c) medical and paramedical services;
   4.2 Services which support the services referred to in 4.1:
      (a) Catering;
      (b) medical records;
      (c) security;
      (d) porter and reception;
      (e) pharmaceutical and dispensary;
      (f) medicine quality and control laboratory;
      (g) forensics;
      (h) laundry work;
      (i) clinical engineering;
      (j) hospital engineering;
      (k) waste removal;
      (l) mortuary services; and
      (m) pest control.
   4.3 Blood transfusion services:
      (a) Eastern Province Blood Transfusion Service;
      (b) Western Province Blood Transfusion Service;
      (c) Natal Blood Transfusion Service;
      (d) Northern Blood Transfusion Service; and
      (e) Border Blood Transfusion Service.

CHAPTER 14

Sweden

Birgitta Nyström

1 GENERAL BACKGROUND: COUNTRY PROFILE

1.1 The Country

Sweden is situated in the north of Europe and is one of the Scandinavian countries. It is a large country, the third largest in Europe. Over 10 million people, mainly located in the southern and central parts, populate Sweden. The capital Stockholm is approaching 1 million inhabitants. Sweden is divided into 20 county councils/regions, particularly for the administration of the public health service, and 290 municipalities for local government.

Sweden has had a long and continuous development as an independent state. According to the Constitution, all public power emanates from the people. The Swedish monarch merely performs representative and symbolic functions. The Parliament (*Riksdag*) has 349 members, elected for four-year terms and based on proportional representation. The largest political party is the Social Democratic Party[1] that was in power from 1932 until 1976, sometimes in coalition with other parties. Non-social governments have been in power 1976–1982, 1991–1994, 2006–2014. Since 2014, the Social Democrats are in power in coalition with the Green Party.

For a long time, the Swedish population has been very homogenous; 75 years ago, about 1 per cent of the Swedish population was born outside Sweden, today the same figure amounts to more than 15 per cent. Following the Second World War Sweden experienced large-scale immigration. Up to the beginning of the 1970s, this consisted mainly of immigrant labour, but since the mid-1980s, the immigration has mainly been confined to refugees. As in many countries, the increasing number of elderly is considered problematic. In 2012, 19 per cent of the Swedish population was 65 years of age or older. In 2050, it is estimated that the corresponding figure will be between 21 and 26 per cent.

Sweden has a high overall rate of labour participation, as well as a high rate of women's labour force participation, almost 50 per cent. Nevertheless, there is an uneven distribution of men and women between various sectors of the labour market, and a significant number of women work part-time. The pay-level structure is comparatively narrow, and income taxes comparatively high. Women earn between 87 and 95 per cent of men's wages (depending on how the difference is calculated), but there is at least a 5 per cent gender differential that cannot be explained. Unemployment rates are relatively low; between 6 and 8 per cent. Unemployment is especially frequent among young people and immigrants. Recently, efforts to reduce unemployment among young people have met

1. In the period after 2006, the Conservative Party's strength has occasionally been larger than the Social Democratic Party's.

with some success, but the very high unemployment rates among non-European immigrants are considered a serious problem.

The Swedish' economy is dependent on export. Labour costs have been comparatively high in Sweden, but do not seem to be so any longer. At least wages are not particularly high, but in addition, employers for social insurance as well as fringe benefits in accordance with collective agreements (pension schemes etc.) pay high percentages.

In 2015, almost 29 per cent of the work force was occupied in the public sector. Total public expenditure, which includes consumption, investment and transfers to individuals and enterprises as part of social and economic policy, amounts to over 50 per cent of the gross national product. Public services are highly developed. An active labour market policy has gained general support.

Sweden is since 1995 a member of the European Union (EU), but is not a part of the Euro-zone.

1.2 Legal Framework

Sweden is a civil law country. It has a Code dating from 1734, but most of it has been replaced by new enactments. New legislation is partly inserted into the Code, but mostly, as with labour legislation, issued as separate statutes.

Legislation is the main legal source. Legislative power is according to the Constitution vested in the Parliament. The Government issues the laws, which are passed by the Parliament, generally based on a Government Bill (*proposition*). The Government is authorised to issue, on its own behalf, decrees and directives on certain topics. The Government can also be authorised to delegate to subordinate authorities the power to issue directives. In the labour law area, the Swedish Work Environment Authority (*Arbetsmiljöverket*) issue many directives concerning the work environment and health and safety at work issues.[2]

The legislative process generally starts with a report from a Commission or an Inquiry (*utredning*) appointed by the Government.[3] The report is based on terms of reference issued by the Government, often in accordance with wishes expressed by the Parliament.[4] This report, which often contains a complete draft law with detailed explanations, is referred to authorities and organisations that have a special interest in and knowledge of the matter concerned, for their deliberations and opinions. Then, the Government ministry concerned prepares a Bill based on the Inquiry's report and the material received during the reference procedure.[5] The Government may as a final stage in the preparation refer the Bill to the Law Council, composed of judges from the Supreme Court

2. Available at www.arbetsmiljoverket.se.
3. The report is published in the SOU series (*Sveriges Offentliga Utredningar*, the Swedish Government's Official Reports), and usually contains a summary in English.
4. Such instructions are published as Dir. (*utredningsdirektiv*, directives).
5. The report could also be abandoned or the matter referred to a new inquiry for further investigation.

and the Supreme Administrative Court. Based on the Bill the Parliament makes the final decision. The Act is issued by the Government and published in an official publication.[6]

The system of general courts is based on three instances, with the Supreme Court at the apex. The administrative courts are also based on three instances. There are a few additional courts; the Labour Court established from 1929 is one of these.

There were no provisions in the Swedish Constitution concerning labour rights until a new Constitution was passed in the 1970s (see further *infra* Subsections 3.1 and 3.3). The provisions in the Constitution protecting labour rights are regarded more as codification of existing law than an expression intending to establish new legal principles.[7]

2 COLLECTIVE LABOUR RELATIONS

The Swedish state has always avoided involving itself in dealings between the social partners whenever possible. The state has sought to remain neutral and tried not to introduce unnecessary measures. The system is based on the fundamental principle of the social partners' responsibility for bargaining and collective agreements. The traditional Swedish model for regulating employment relationships are through collective agreements. An important principle is the social partners' possibility to use industrial action in order to exercise pressure on the other party in collective bargaining.[8]

The Swedish labour market began to assume a well-defined structural pattern at a relatively early date. By the turn of the 19th century, a system of organisations on both sides had been established, and working conditions was to an increasing degree regulated in collective agreements. The Government and Parliament encouraged collective bargaining and collective agreements, and avoided legislation and state control on the labour market. The first nationwide collective agreement was concluded in 1905 between the Metal Workers' Union and the Swedish Engineering Industries. In 1906 a very important step was taken when the Trade Union Confederation (LO) and the Employers' Federation (SAF) agreed that the employers should accept trade unionism, and in turn the employee side accepted that it was the employer who directed and distributed the work as well as to hire and fire workers (the 'December compromise', see

6. *Svensk författningssamling* (SFS), the Swedish Code of Statutes.
7. The right to organise, the right to take industrial action, prohibition of discrimination, freedom of expression and the right to anonymity (a ban to inquire into the identity of a person to have communicated information (whistle blowing) are rights with labour law relevance that are protected in the Swedish Constitution.
8. Generally about Swedish labour and employment legislation in English, *Adlercreutz/Nyström*, 2015; *Fahlbeck/Sigeman*, 2001; *Fahlbeck/Mulder*, 2009; *Eklund/Sigeman/Carlson*, 2008; *Edlund/Nyström*, 1988; *Carlson/Edström/Nyström*, 2016; *Wahlgren*, 2002. A summary in English of the State Mediation Office's annual reports, which deals with the annual wage rounds, the labour market parties, industrial action etc., is found on www.mi.se.

infra Subsection 3.1). In 1906 an Act on Conciliation[9] was issued, which placed mediators at the parties' disposal for the peaceful settlement of disputes between them. Collective agreements came to govern more and more aspects of working conditions.

In 1928 legislation regarding collective agreements and the Labour Court was introduced, and in 1936 an Act on freedom of association and collective bargaining. In 1938 LO and SAF (see *infra* Subsections 2.1 and 2.2), under the threat that the state should regulate the right to industrial action, concluded the Basic Agreement or the so-called *Saltsjöbaden* agreement (named after the location where the agreement was signed). The agreement contains rules about bargaining procedures prior to industrial action and restrictions in industrial action, for example rules to protect neutral third parties, see further *infra* Subsection 3.3.1. Parts of the agreement are still in force. The *Saltsjöbaden* agreement was a starting point for a series of agreements between LO and SAF concerning cooperation on important issues, for example rationalisation and consultation.

Public-sector employees received, in principle, full rights of collective bargaining and collective action in 1966 and since then, all legislation has been enacted under the principle that there should be no difference as to whether the employee is white-collar, blue-collar, and private or public employee. The few rules especially applying to public sector employees prescribes minor restrictions for those that exercise public authority with the aim to secure their impartiality.

Although, the principle of self-regulation is still the point of departure, legislation in the labour market area has grown rapidly since the 1970s. In the 1970s, several new laws were enacted in order to increase the rights of employees and trade unions and for example; legislation on security of employment was introduced. Pre-existing legislation was revised and a long succession of completely new enactments were introduced. The 1976 Co-determination (in the Workplace) Act[10] replaces the Act concerning freedom of association and collective bargaining from 1936 and the Act on collective agreements from 1928, and adds new rules about participation rights for trade unions. Still, collective agreements are probably the most important source of labour and employment regulation. It is to some extent also possible to deviate from labour law by means of collective agreements.

Since 1995, when Sweden became a member of the European Union (EU), legislative measures to implement EU labour law has extended the area of labour law even further. After 1995, EU law has influenced practically all changes that have been made in Swedish labour legislation.

9. There is no difference between conciliation and mediation in legislation and in practice in Sweden.
10. SFS 1976:580.

The 1980s was a time of unrest on the Swedish labour market, with the largest industrial conflict ever in 1980,[11] wage drift and high inflation. The early 1990s were characterised by a deep depression and for Swedish standards extremely high unemployment figures. Several measures were taken in order to impose stabilisation agreements on the labour market parties. Also the rules concerning industrial conflict, especially in the public sector, were under debate and the Government appointed several inquiries to investigate questions concerning wage negotiations and industrial action. In 1997, the negotiation parties in Swedish industry reached a bargaining agreement on Industrial Development and Wage Formation, the 'Industry Agreement'. In 2011 it was replaced by a new Industry Agreement, and from June 2016 a new revised Industry Agreement is in force. An aim for the Industry Agreement is that negotiations should be concluded in such a way as to ensure that they are completed before the previous agreement expires. The Swedish labour market has been peaceful after the conclusion of the Industry Agreement. The agreement has served as a pattern for similar bargaining agreements in other sectors of the labour market (see *infra* Subsection 3.3.3). The old mediation system, practically unchanged since 1906, was in 2000 replaced by the National Mediation Office that is equipped with more resources.

The social partners have a strong position in the field of industrial conflict and the resolution of industrial disputes. The trade unions are responsible for the control of compliance with legislation. It is only concerning the work environment that there is a public agency for control: the Swedish Work Environment Authority.

Sweden does not have any legislation on minimum wages. It is not considered to be in harmony with the Swedish system where it is left to the labour market parties to negotiate wages. To combat wage dumping the normal way is for the trade union to ask the employer to negotiate for a collective agreement, and to use industrial action if the employer does not want to negotiate, or if the employer does not sign a collective agreement.

Today, EU law and internationalisation constitutes a challenge to the traditional Swedish labour market model and its principles of self-regulation and self-control.

2.1 Trade Unions

Characteristic for Sweden is the role the trade unions play as almost exclusive representatives of workers' interests. Unionism is divided into three main central organisations, one for blue-collar employees, one for white-collar employees and one for professionals. LO (the Swedish Trade Union Confederation)[12] is

11. There has only been two General Strikes in Sweden, in 1909 and in 1980. In both General Strikes, there were more employees on lockout than on strike.
12. *Landsorganisationen i Sverige.*

mainly for trade unions organising manual (blue-collar) workers. The oldest national blue-collar unions still in existence date from the latter half of the 1880s.[13] The national blue-collar unions founded LO in 1898. Salaried employees' organisations are of a later date. The first central organisations in this area were founded in the 1930s. Gradually two central organisations emerged; the Central Organisation of Salaried Employees (TCO),[14] and the Swedish Federation of Professional Associations (SACO).[15] All three central organisations contain trade unions representing employees in the private and in the public sector.

The organisational structure of the trade union side has three levels, the central level with the central organisations, and the national branch level with nation-wide trade unions for different branches, which then in turn are divided into local unions. The trend has been to amalgamate into fewer and larger unions.

The rate of unionisation is traditionally very high in Sweden, but as in other European countries, it has been declining during the last 20 years. Today, the average rate of unionisation is about 70 per cent.[16] Employees in the public sector are now unionised to a larger extent compared to private sector employees. LO has seen its membership rates in their field decrease from about 90 per cent to almost 60 per cent. The decrease in union membership is especially obvious in the service sector. Among salaried employees, the rate of unionisation is slowly increasing.

Established trade union is not a concept used in Swedish legal texts, but the legislation introduced in the 1970s assigns special privileges to trade unions that have a collective agreement with the employer.

2.2 Employers' Organisations

In reaction to attempts from the workers to gain bargaining power through unionism and strikes employers in the private sector started to form organisations in the late 19th century. The Swedish Employers' Federation (SAF) was founded in 1902. SAF became the dominant organisation on the employers' side for the private sector, and for many decades it was SAF and its counterpart LO that formed the main parts of Swedish labour market regulation. In 2001, SAF merged with the Federation of Swedish Industries to form the Confederation of Swedish Enterprise (SN).[17]

---

13. A typographers' society founded in 1846 is usually considered to be the first trade union in Sweden.
14. *Tjänstemännens Centralorganisation.*
15. *Sveriges Akademikers Centralorganisation.*
16. In 1993, the average rate of unionisation was 85 per cent.
17. *Svenskt Näringsliv.*

In the local government and regional sector, there is the Swedish Association of Local Authorities and Regions,[18] a federation for all local authorities and provincial councils in Sweden. In the state sector, there is the Swedish Agency for Government Employers.[19] Compared to the private sector, it was later that the public employers were represented by organisations.

On the employers' side, the rate of organisation is also very high: nearly 90 per cent.[20]

2.3 Industrial Action in Practice

Developments in industrial action after the *Saltsjöbaden* agreement 1938 were mainly peaceful up until the 1970s. The great illegal strike in the state-owned mining company LKAB in 1969/79 marked a turning point. A more militant attitude could be observed in the labour market and illegal strikes were not uncommon. In 1980 there was a general industrial conflict involving all sectors of the labour market with extensive strikes, lockouts were even more extensive. Almost all parts of society came to a standstill. More than one million workers were involved and almost 800,000 working days lost. Peace was restored when the social democratic Government persuaded the private employers in SAF to accept a proposal by the state mediators. The 1980s was a time of unrest in the labour market, with high pay increases and even higher inflation. There were industrial actions in almost every wage round, especially in the public sector (*see infra* Subsection 4.1). Illegal strikes was earlier rather frequent in Sweden, but after 1990, almost none have occurred. They are often of a short duration in time, usually a couple of hours.[21]

Overall, figures regarding strikes and lockouts as well as working days lost are very low after the difficulties in the 1980s and the 1990s that ended with the Industry Agreement 1997. Here follows some examples from the last years' more extensive bargaining rounds: In 2012, about 500 nation-wide collective agreements on pay and general terms of employment were negotiated and signed. Notice of industrial action was served in 23 cases. There were strikes in five cases; almost 40,000 working days were lost. The largest dispute in 2012 took place in the construction sector. In the 2013 bargaining round more than 500 nation-wide agreements expired and over 2,7 million employees were affected by collective bargaining. In 19 cases there were notice of industrial action and in

18. *Sveriges Kommuner och Landsting.*
19. *Arbetsgivarverket.*
20. This figure is calculated by counting the share of employees that has an employer who belongs to an employers' organisation. The Mediation Office's annual report 2017 (*Avtalsrörelsen och lönebildningen 2017*) 224.
21. General Swedish statistics do not divide between different forms of industrial action, or if action is taken in the private or the public sector. The only general division is between strikes and lockouts, and legal and illegal strikes. However, the figures concerning illegal strikes are uncertain, because of difficulties to find reliable information.

seven cases action was taken. 7,000 working days were lost; the most of them concerned local bus transportation. In addition, 2016 round of bargaining was wide-ranging, about 500 nation-wide agreements were negotiated, and there were notice of industrial action in 25 cases. In seven cases action was taken, six of them were strikes, and in six of the seven cases the employers answered by notice of lockout. Lockout was taken in two cases. In the 2017 wage rounds 497 nation-wide collective agreements were concluded without any industrial action taken. The working days lost this year (2,570) were mainly due to the local conflict in the Gothenburg Harbour (see *infra* Section 7). Most of the working days lost in Sweden since 2000 are due to strikes in the municipal and the regional sector (see also *infra* Subsection 4.1).

3 THE RIGHT TO STRIKE

3.1 The Right to Organise

In 1906, an important step was taken when LO and SAF agreed that the employers should accept employee unionism, and in turn, the employees' side accepted that it was the employer that directed and distributed the work as well as to hire and fire workers (the December compromise). The Labour Court recognised the right to organise as being connected with the nature of the collective agreement and as a legal effect of it in 1933.[22] It was more difficult for salaried employees to obtain the employers' recognition of their unions, and in 1936, an act on the rights of association and negotiation was passed. It was applicable to all employees, but the purpose of the act was to secure the salaried employees' right to organise. The rules in the 1936 Act on the Right to Organise and the Right to Collective Bargaining were transferred to the 1976 Co-determination Act.

The right to organise is also protected in the Swedish Constitution. In the Instrument of Government, under the subtitle 'Fundamental rights and freedoms' every citizen is in relation to the community secured freedom of opinion, freedom of expression, freedom of assembly, of association and of demonstration (Section 2, Article 1). This includes the right to organise in trade unions and employers' organisations.

In the Co-determination Act Section 7 the right of association is defined as the right of employers and employees to belong to an employer's organisation or a trade union, to make use of such a membership and work for the organisation or for its formation. It should be noted that the right to organise is safeguarded not only for employees but also for employers.[23] The right of association is conferred only in relation to the other party, and only to individuals, not to organisations. The refuse of an employer to employ members of a trade union is

22. AD (the Labour Court) 1933 No. 94.
23. This was so already in the December compromise.

not a violation of the right to organise, because only an employee, not a job seeker is protected. A violation is defined in Section 8 of the Act as a measure taken by employers or employees against someone on the other side as a consequence of the utilisation of the right to organise, or with a view to making him/her refrain from exercising the right to organise. In order to make it easier to satisfy the claims of evidence, the Labour Court has deemed it appropriate to divide the burden of proof. It is sufficient to prove the probability that the motive for a measure was of an impermissible nature, the burden of proof is transferred to the other side, which then must prove that the measure was taken for other reasons.

No groups of employees are excluded from the right to organise. Forepersons and supervisors have formed a union of their own (today *Ledarna*), which is independent, not affiliated to any of the three central employee organisations and today tries to organise all kinds of employees in managerial positions. In collective agreements, there are examples of rules according to which an employer has the right to demand that an employee who holds a managerial position should not be a member of a certain trade union. For example, according to collective agreements for salaried employees in the private sector, an employer has the right to demand that an employee who holds a management position should not be a member of the organisation of salaried employees. Employees falling within this 'free circle' are executive mangers and their private secretaries, and employees representing the enterprise vis-á-vis salaried employees in matters concerning their terms of employment.

3.2 The Right to Bargain Collectively

The right to negotiate is fundamental for trade union activity. The right to bargaining was confirmed in legislation by the 1936 Act on the Right to Organise and the Right to Collective Bargaining. The blue-collar workers had already by the December Compromise from 1906 achieved the right to organise and in practice the right to bargain.

The rules regarding the right to bargaining are nowadays found in the 1976 Co-determination Act, which applies to all kinds of employees, and to all sectors of the economy. The Co-determination Act regulates three different kinds of bargaining; collective bargaining aiming at concluding a collective agreement, grievance negotiations aiming at solving disputes of rights, and co-determination ('cooperative') negotiations aiming at giving the employees, through their organisations, the right to information and consultation in questions under the employers' prerogative.

The general right to negotiate according to the Co-determination Act Section 10 is the right for an employee organisation to negotiate with an employer on any matter relating to the relationship between the employer and any member of the organisation who is, or has been, an employee of that employer. An employer has the equivalent right to negotiate with an employee organisation. In addition, the organisations have a right to negotiate vis-á-vis each other. This general right to negotiate applies both to disputes of interest and disputes of rights.

The duty to negotiate involves the duty to attend the meeting for negotiations, and, when necessary, make proposals, supported by reasons, for the settlement of the issue. The duty to negotiate does not imply any obligation to conclude an agreement.

During the last decades, the earlier much centralised collective bargaining system has been decentralised. Still, from an international perspective the Swedish collective bargaining system is centralised. Collective bargaining takes in principle place at two levels; nation-wide and then – within the limits that the nationwide agreement allows – on enterprise level.[24]

The coverage of collective agreements is very high, about 90 per cent, due to the high rate of organisation on the Swedish employers' side. In the public sector, collective agreement coverage is 100 per cent. It is not possible to extend a collective agreement by some kind of decree or legislation in order to cover all employees (*erga omnes effect*), but the employer is obliged to apply the main rules in the collective agreement also to non-unionised employees and employers that belong to other unions than the signatory.

When collective bargaining results in a collective agreement, as soon as the agreement is reached, the right of the parties and their members to take industrial action in principle ceases according to the Co-determination Act, see further *infra*.

3.3 The Right to Take Industrial Action[25]

3.3.1 Development

In the 1800s attempts were made to get workers to refrain from strike by criminalising industrial action, The use of strike breakers was abolished in the early 1900s. The right to strike was essential in order for the blue-collar workers to be able to force the employers to bargain and conclude collective agreements. The right to lockout was by the employers considered to be essential in order to meet strikes. Already in the late 19th century, there were discussions in Parliament regarding possible methods to regulate or restrict the right to take industrial action.[26]

By a judgment from the Swedish High Court in 1915, it was established that a collective agreement was a binding instrument (like other agreements). This meant that it was not possible to resort to collective action during the lifetime of

24. So-called basic agreements, like the *Saltsjöbaden* agreement, pension scheme agreements etc. are often negotiated between the central organisations, like LO and SN (see *supra* Subsections 2.1 and 2.2) and then accepted by their member organisations.
25. Generally, see *Malmberg/Johansson*, 2014, 525 et seqq.
26. Different kinds of arbitration arrangements were discussed.

a collective agreement (*pacta sunt servanda*). This principle is still an underlying principle on the Swedish labour market.

The discussions in Parliament concerning industrial action started again around 1930 because of frequent strikes and lockouts due to the economic crisis at that time. Under the threat that the state should legislate in the area of industrial conflict LO and SAF in 1938 concluded the *Saltsjöbaden* agreement. The Agreement contains provisions intended, *inter alia*, to prevent labour conflict that would threaten essential services, see *infra* Subsection 7.2.

Before 1966, public employees were denied the right to strike. The reason for this was that they in their work had to be loyal to the state. From 1966 (by legislation from 1965), public employees were allowed to use strikes as a means of exercising pressure on the employer in disputes over collective agreements (see *infra* Subsection 3.3.3).

As already mentioned the 1980s was a time of unrest on the Swedish labour market, with the largest industrial conflict ever in 1980, and several industrial conflicts, especially in the public sector, during the 1980s and the beginning of the 1990s. The extensive possibility for the parties in the public sector to use industrial action began to be questioned, and the Parliament and Government again started to show interest in questions concerning industrial action. In 1997, the negotiating parties in Swedish industry reached a bargaining agreement on Industrial Development and Wage Formation, the 'Industry Agreement'. An explicit objective for the Agreement is that negotiations should be conducted in such a way as to ensure that they are completed before the previous agreement expires (see *infra* Subsection 3.3.3). The Industry Agreement, which has even been called 'the second *Saltsjöbaden* agreement', has become a pattern for similar bargaining agreements in other sectors of the labour market. In 2001 a National Mediation Office equipped with more resources and more power replaced the old conciliation system for labour disputes of interests with roots from 1906 (see *infra* Subsection 3.3.3).

Since the 1970s, industrial action has been protected in the Swedish Constitution. According to Section 2 Article 14 of the Instrument of Government, a trade union or an employer or an employers' organisation shall have the right to take industrial action unless otherwise provided for in an act of law or under an agreement. (This exclusively refers to a collective agreement.) This means that the constitutional right to take industrial action is equal for both sides on the labour market. It is worth mentioning that the right to industrial action is a right for those subjects that can be parties to a collective agreement: trade unions, employers and employers' organisations. Individual employees have no right of collective bargaining, cannot be parties to a collective agreement, and cannot legally take industrial action on their own initiative. The right in Section 2 Article 14 is an exception from the main rule that a constitutional right only is applicable towards the community; Section 2 Article 14 is applicable also towards private subjects. The Labour Court has accepted industrial action according to Section 2

Article 14 because there were no grounds neither in legislation nor in collective agreements to limit this right.[27]

According to the Constitution, the right to take industrial action can be restricted 'in an act of law or under an agreement'. Restrictions in legislation can be found in the 1976 Co-determination Act (that applies to the entire labour market) and a few further limitations in the 1994 Act on Public Employment.[28] These legal restrictions are few. The most important limitation in the Co-determination Act is that there is as a main rule a peace obligation for the duration of a collective agreement. The main rule in the public sector is that industrial action is permitted to the same extent as in the private sector.

According to the Co-determination Act Section 41, industrial action is prohibited in certain situations. This prohibition is directed to employers and employees as well as their organisations as far as they are bound by a collective agreement. Industrial action which not has been decided by an organisation in due form is illegal. Thus, all unauthorised strikes (wildcat strikes) are considered as contrary to the peace obligation. An illicit aim or purpose may make any industrial action illegal. Such disputes are for example disputes of rights (see *infra* Subsection 3.3.4). The most important instance of permissible industrial action during the life of a collective agreement is sympathy actions in support of a party that takes a permissible primary action. The sympathy action should not have an independent purpose, it is has to be only in sympathy for others. Both parties in the labour market have been anxious to retain this freedom to support other parties, but in view of developments in the modern labour market, employers now want to restrict the right of sympathy actions. The trade union side still considers sympathy actions as important means to make trade union claims effective.

A trade union or an employers' organisation is not allowed to initiate, facilitate or in any other way act to promote unlawful industrial action (Section 42 of the Co-determination Act). An organisation bound by a collective agreement is obliged to attempt to prevent and endeavour to achieve a cessation of unlawful industrial action.

It is possible to conclude a collective agreement which differs from Section 41 of the Co-determination Act, but only in the sense that it establishes a stricter peace obligation. There are a number of restrictions to industrial action in collective agreements. These restrictions could concern the aim of the conflict, the form of the conflict, or an obligation to follow certain procedures before taking action. There are, for example, for different sectors of the labour market collective agreements regarding industrial action endangering vital services (see *infra* Subsection 7.2). There are also examples of collective agreements where the parties have agreed on a certain order to follow regarding collective bargaining and have private mediation arrangements with private mediators

27. See AD 2003 No. 46, AD 2006 No. 58. See also AD 2003 No. 25, AD 2001 No. 89, 2008 No. 34 (concerning political strikes).
28. SFS 1994:260.

that have a more active role than the state mediators – all with the aim to conclude collective agreements without industrial action (see further *infra* Subsection 3.3.3). Earlier, there were even examples of total peace agreements in the daily newspaper industry.

A lawful industrial action does not terminate the employment contract it merely suspends it. The employment contract continues, but main duties on either side (perform work, pay wages) are suspended. The liability for the employee is limited in case of a breach of the peace obligation without a decision from the union (a wildcat strike). Liability for other illegal industrial action is in the first place designated to the organisations.

3.3.2 Relation to International Law

The European Convention on the Protection of Human Rights and Fundamental Freedoms (ECHR) was ratified by Sweden in 1950 and implemented into Swedish law in an Act in 1994, hereby having a stronger position than other international law instruments in Sweden. The right of industrial action has been acknowledges in the freedom of association according to Article 11. Sweden ratified the 1961 European Social Charter in 1962 and the Revised Charter in 1998. Articles 5 and 6 of the Social Charter, which are of special interest when it comes to industrial action, are accepted by Sweden. Sweden also has ratified ILO Convention No. 87 and ILO Convention No. 98.

Ratifying these international instruments have more or less been seen as a confirmation of already existing situations in Sweden, and any new national legislative steps have been deemed unnecessary.

3.3.3 Restrictions

Generally, negotiations according to rules in collective agreements shall be exercised before it is permitted to take industrial action.

During the lifetime of a collective agreement the main rule is that all forms of industrial action, including strikes, are forbidden. The parties to the collective agreement, as well as their members, are bound by the peace obligation. The peace obligation prohibits industrial action relating to a concluded collective agreement. Further, it is not permitted to take industrial action to bring about an amendment of an existing collective agreement. In practice, there are limited possibilities for claiming that there are questions not covered by a collective agreement.[29] Nevertheless, there are some situations when industrial action may be taken if a collective agreement is in force. The most important is the possibility of taking sympathy action (see *supra* Subsection 3.3.1).[30] In addition,

29. According to case law, there are a number of 'invisible clauses' or 'implied terms' that are considered to fall within the general frame of a collective agreement.
30. Co-determination Act Section 41 paragraph 1 1–4.

a trade union may call industrial action for the purpose of exacting unpaid wages during the time that the collective agreement is in force (Section 41 paragraph 2 of the Co-determination Act).[31] Political strikes could also be called under very limited circumstances (see *infra* Subsection 3.3.4).[32] The CJEU's decision in the *Laval*-case[33] has resulted in restrictions to take industrial action against employers posting workers to Sweden (Section 41 c of the Co-determination Act).

If the employer (employers' organisation) and the trade union are not bound by a collective agreement, there are only a few limitations to the right to take industrial action. According to the Co-determination Act there is a prohibition of industrial action against a sole trader and against family businesses (Section 41 b). In addition, an employer is not allowed to withhold already earned salary (Section 41 a). The Labour Court has been cautious when it comes to restricting the possibility for social partners to take industrial action in situations where they are not bound by a collective agreement.

There has been a state system for mediation/conciliation in Sweden since 1906. Since 2000, the Swedish National Mediation Office is responsible for this (Sections 46–53 of the Co-determination Act). The Mediation Office may appoint, with the consent of the parties, one or more mediators.[34] If there is a risk of industrial action, the Office may appoint a mediator without the consent of the parties'. (A collective agreement including a private mediation arrangement also restricts the Office's possibility to appoint a mediator without the consent of both parties, see *infra*.) The mediator shall seek agreement between the parties and may submit own proposals for agreement, which is common in practice. The mediator shall also seek to ensure that the parties postpone or cancel industrial action. The mediators usually adhere to this and the parties often accept it. If not so, the mediator may request the National Mediation Office to postpone a collective action for up to 14 days. This is a new instrument for mediators since 2000, and it has hitherto been used only in a handful of cases. According to legislation there is no duty for the parties to exhaust mediation, or any other dispute resolution process, before taking industrial action, but examples of such rules are found in collective agreements.

31. This possibility is of minor importance nowadays, since there is a system of wage guarantee in case of an employers' insolvency.
32. There is also a possibility to take industrial action in order to bring about a co-determination agreement, although there is a collective agreement concerning wages and working conditions in force, i.e. an agreement concerning the employees' influence on the employers' prerogative. This has not been used in practice.
33. *CJEU*, 18 Dec. 2007, C-341/05 *Laval un Partneri Ltd v. Svenska Byggnadsarbetareförbundet et.al.*
34. The Swedish National Mediation Office has not any professional mediators employed. Mediators are appointed on an ad hoc basis. It is considered important that both parties agree upon the person(s) appointed. Nowadays, usually two mediators are appointed in a dispute involving national social partners, and the mediators often are retired trade union or employers' organisation officials.

An important agreement limiting the parties' freedom of industrial action is the above mentioned Industry Agreement. The parties agree upon their own mediation process setting aside the general legislated provisions about mediation in the Co-determination Act. There is a strict timetable for negotiations with the intention of concluding industry-wide collective agreements before the current agreement has expired. One month before the expiry date one of the mediators that have been appointed according to the Agreement shall support the parties. The mediators has a wide range of possible measures to use, including putting forward own proposals or delay industrial action at most 14 calendar days. The Industry Agreement has become a pattern for similar agreements (collaboration agreements) in other sectors. Parties who have agreed that they are bound by a collective agreement that contain the schedules for negotiations, time framework and rules for the appointment of mediators and the powers of mediators and rules concerning notice of termination of the agreement, may give notice of the agreement to the Mediation Office for registration. After registration, a mediator may not be appointed by the Mediation Office without the consent of the parties (Section 47 b of the Co-determination Act). Fifteen collective agreements of this kind were registered in 2016, comprising over 30 per cent of Swedish employees.[35]

According to the Co-determination Act, the party who intends to implement industrial action or to extend industrial action must give a written notice to the other party and the National Mediation Office seven working days in advance (Section 45 of the Co-determination Act). This is only a rule of order. If a party doesn't give notice, this could be ground for damages, but the industrial action will not be unlawful. The requirement of a notice was introduced in legislation in the 1930s and is very important, not only because the other party and the Mediation Office have some days for preparations, the notice is often the point of departure for discussions between the parties concerning limitations from the notice (for example, in the interest of third parties).

A few trade unions have internal rules about ballots before decisions concerning strikes, but ballots have never been popular on the Swedish labour market and have rarely been used. Today, ballots in principle do not occur.

It has been mentioned above that a legal industrial action in Sweden must be decided/sanctioned by an employers' organisation or by a trade union. This restriction has not been considered to be an extensive restriction; it is relatively easy to constitute an organisation for employers or a trade union in Sweden. A labour market organisation (including both trade unions and employers' organisations) is, according to the Co-determination Act, an association of employees or employers respectively, which according to its own rules has as its objective to protect and care for its members' interests in the employer – employee relation.

35. The Mediation Office's annual report for 2016 (*Avtalsrörelsen och lönebildningen 2016*) 61.

The right to take industrial action lies, according to the trade unions' and the employers' organisations' own rules, within the nationwide organisations. The organisations on national level are also in charge of the economic means to support their members during a conflict.

There is no definition of the concept 'threatening public interest' or 'essential services', either in legislation or in case law (about collective agreements, see *infra* Subsection 7.2).

There is no proportionality principle in Sweden regarding industrial action, neither in legislation, in case law nor in collective agreements. Such a rule (with intended application in only three defined situations) was suggested in a state Inquiry 1998, but has not led to any legislative proposal.[36]

3.3.4 Objective or Goal

Swedish law makes a distinction between disputes of interests and disputes of rights. Industrial action should have the aim to put pressure on the other party in a dispute concerning interests. However, there is no general rule in Swedish legislation that prohibits industrial action in disputes of rights.

A secondary action, a sympathy action, must be of pure sympathy. It is unlawful if there is an aim to put pressure on and influence the own employer or the own collective agreement. (About sympathy actions, see *supra* Subsection 3.3.1.)

Industrial action in support of workers or trade unions abroad, and political strikes are not regulated in legislation. Political strikes are very rare in Sweden. There are few decisions from the Labour Court, and there is no clear demarcation line between legal and illegal. If it is a short protest and demonstration action and it does not intervene with the employers' right to conduct business, the action is not considered illegal.[37] (About political strikes in the public sector, see *infra* Section 5.)

It is possible that industrial action could be illegal even where there is no valid collective agreement between the parties. It is, according to case law,[38] illegal to take industrial action to push out of the way or make changes in another collective agreement. This principle means that all trade unions, although they are not bound by a collective agreement, shall respect a collective agreement that another trade union already have concluded with an employer. If the union using industrial action does not intend to push away or make changes in the collective agreement that the employer already has concluded with another trade union, the striking union's intent is only to conclude a parallel collective agreement, then the action is legal. The Labour Court has explicitly stated that the point of departure is that a trade union can use

36. SOU 1998:41 *Medling och lönebildning* (Mediation and wage formation).
37. AD 1984 No. 91.
38. AD 1989 No. 120, and Section 42 para. 1 of the Co-determination Act. See also AD 2005 No. 110, 2012 No. 13, 2017 No. 32.

industrial action with the aim to conclude a collective agreement ('collective agreement 2') with an employer who already has a collective agreement for the same kind of work with another trade union ('collective agreement 1'), although 'collective agreement 2' may be incompatible with 'collective agreement 1'. If the agreements are incompatible, this problem should be solved by legal principles governing competing agreements, not by limiting the right to industrial action. (About the ongoing conflict in Gothenburg Harbour, see *infra* Section 8).

It is considered that collective action aiming at concluding a collective agreement that would not be legally valid is illegal.[39]

According to the *Saltsjöbaden* agreement industrial action with certain undue aims are illegal. This includes industrial action aiming at harass someone because of his/her religious or political opinions. Neutral third parties are also protected according to the agreement. See further *infra* Subsection 7.2.

3.3.5 Means

Swedish law has no explicit definition of industrial action. According to the Co-determination Act, industrial action may be of various kinds but must be adopted for exercising pressure on the opposite party. Already a threat put forward as a pressure, and even a mere notice of industrial action could be considered an offensive action.[40] The Co-determination Act Section 41 lists as industrial action work stoppages (strike and lockout), blockades, boycotts or other comparable hostile measures. Other comparable hostile measures could be bans on overtime working, going slow, or working to rule, and many other types of industrial action may be used. According to the preparatory works of the Co-determination Act, general statements, propaganda, wishes, requests to negotiate and other comparable initiatives are not considered to fall within the notion 'action'.[41]

Actions that are or could be considered criminal, for example, violent picketing, occupation or blockades, in the sense that it is impossible to enter the workplace, are not permitted. Refusal of an employer to pay out wages due in the course of a strike, and earned before the strike, is – as has been mentioned above – illegal according to the Co-determination Act.

A ban on overtime or a blockade is a very effective weapon, often used as a first step before a strike. A blockade put on new employment contracts or an overtime ban has developed to be the normal way to start industrial action nowadays. It is also regularly used when the main aim of the industrial action is to allow for following sympathy actions that could be more effective than the primary action.

---

39. *Schmidt*, 1977, 234 et seq. *Tore Sigeman* is responsible for the revised chapter.
40. AD 1975 No. 85.
41. SOU 1975:1 353.

Partial strikes (or lockouts, or other partial industrial actions) are not treated in any other manner than full strikes, with the exception that public employees exercising public authority are not allowed to use partial strikes, see *infra* Section 5.

4 THE EXPERIENCE WITH STRIKES IN ESSENTIAL SERVICES

4.1 Frequency

The overall picture is that the Swedish labour market is peaceful. This is even truer when it comes to essential services, but naturally, such actions sometimes occur.

During the General Conflict in 1980, strikes and lockouts affected key sectors such as public communications, transport, medical care, radio and television. Large sectors of the community were paralysed. About 750,000 private sector employees were locked out and 100,000 were on strike. In the public sector 26,000 employees were involved, half of them were locked out. The dispute was solved after six weeks' mediation and extensive industrial action that lasted a little more than one week.

A Government Inquiry 'the Industrial Conflict Inquiry' stated in its reports 1984[42] that the model for industrial action overall was well functioning, and that the minor changes needed was a task for the labour market parties to solve in agreements. Another Inquiry[43] stated in 1988 in a short report that legislation in this area should be avoided but the trade unions in the public sector had not fully taken their anticipated responsibility when they received full rights of collective bargaining and industrial action in 1966. A third Inquiry[44] presented in a short report in 1991 some suggestions concerning, among other things, legislation about essential services. One of the reasons for the Inquiry's proposal was the far-reaching integration between public and private sector and the increasing vulnerability of society. The Inquiry recognised criticism, especially from employers, that the councils or boards created by the social partners in collective agreements (see *infra* Subsection 7.2) had been unable, because of their composition, to make any decisions. The Inquiry therefore suggested that legislation should establish one council/board for the whole labour market that should assess if industrial action threatens essential services. This board should consist of three members from each employer and employee side, and an impartial chairperson. If the parties did not follow the board's decision, the board should notify the Government. This proposal has not resulted in any legislative proposals.

---

42. SOU 1984:18, 19 *Arbetsmarknadsstriden* I, II (Industrial Conflict I, II). This Inquiry's task was to map industrial conflict on the modern Swedish labour market; it was not supposed to make suggestions about new legislation.
43. Ds 1988:2 *Fack & samhälle* (Trade unions and society).
44. SOU 1991:13 *Spelreglerna på arbetsmarknaden* (The rules of play in the labour market).

In 1985 white-collar state employees were on strike; 20,000 national government employees, mainly in railway and air transportations, education, police, and customs service. The state as employer locked out 80,000 employees, mainly teachers. The parties made far-reaching exemptions from noticed and current actions, in order to avoid damaging essential services. The Board established according to the Basic Agreement in the state sector examined if the customs strike endangered essential services, but was unable to agree on a decision. (About this Board, see *infra* Subsection 7.2.) After two and a half weeks, the dispute was resolved by the parties' adopting a proposal put forth by the mediators.

In 1986 dentists, doctors and social welfare officers were on strike. The state as employer gave notice of a lockout of 45,000 employees, mainly teachers about to begin their summer holidays. Upon request by the mediators the social partners suspended all industrial action during the summer, but strikes followed in the autumn. This time mainly in public transportation, national government service, postal service and nursing sectors. The unions gave several exemptions from the actions in order to secure essential services. Finally, the parties accepted the mediators' proposal.

In 1990, there was an extensive conflict in the banking sector. 700,000 working days were lost, 675,000 because of lockouts. 1,500 employees were on strike, and the employer answered with a lockout of 45,000 employees. Practically all banking activities came to a standstill. After almost three weeks of mediation the dispute was settled. (There were no arrangements in collective agreements for this sector concerning restrictions in industrial action for the benefit of essential services and third parties.)

In the 1995 bargaining rounds, industrial unrest was extensive with 125,000 employees on strike and 627,000 working days lost. The majority of the working days were lost in the public sector, mainly concerning nurses that were on strike for seven weeks. There was also a strike by the Swedish Municipal Workers' Union (*Kommunal*) which lasted for almost four weeks. This strike caused a lot of attention because sports facilities were closed which had major repercussion on series games in various sports.

In 2003, there was an extensive conflict in the municipal sector. The Swedish Municipal Workers' Union (*Kommunal*) gave notice of strikes etc. generally in all municipalities and regions concerning certain groups of employees and partial actions in a couple of regions and municipalities. This was later extended to strikes in the health care sector and in certain hospitals. Industrial action was then further extended to other hospitals, childcare etc. Finally, *Kommunal* gave notice of very extensive actions, but avoided strikes that would affect the most vulnerable, for example homes for the disabled. Sympathy actions very noticed. Being in danger extensive actions in health care, childcare, transport etc. the parties again started to negotiate and finally accepted the mediators' suggestion. 600,000 working days were lost.

In 2008, the Swedish Association of Health Professionals (*Vårdförbundet*[45]) rejected the mediators' proposal and gave notice of strike in 9 regions (hospitals) and 12 municipalities (mainly caretaking of elderly and disabled). There were several changes in the noticed actions as well as postponements of actions. The conflict lasted for 38 days, more than 10,000 employees were on strike some time during this period and 95,000 working days were lost. The National Mediation Office's wrote in its yearly report that this conflict had visible negative effects on third parties who, for example, had their treatment or operation postponed.[46]

4.2 The Normative Dilemma

It is difficult to know beforehand what would constitute a disruption of essential services. That an activity takes place in the public sector does not in itself constitute it as an essential service.[47] One normative possibility is to decide that certain activities are so important that no strikes are permitted; the other possibility is to measure the disturbance in each industrial conflict when it occurs. If the trash is not collected in the city for a week, that is probably not a disturbance of essential service, but it may be after two weeks. If the engine drivers are on strike that is probably not a disturbance of essential services if there are busses instead, but if both engine drivers and bus drivers go on strike at the same time it may be a disturbance. If 10 per cent of the medical doctors in one hospital in one town go on strike for three days, and this is followed by 10 per cent of the medical doctors in one hospital in another town for four days the next week, this is probably not threatening essential services. The situation could be considered otherwise if the medical doctors continue with these partial and 'rotating' strikes from town to town for months, or if one single hospital is the object of more extensive strikes.

Due to changes in production and services and to the fact that there are a growing number of specialists with unique knowledge, the labour market has been more vulnerable for disturbances. This means that smaller actions can have considerable effects. This is true both for traditional public activities (health care) as well as for traditionally private activities (power plants). Transport is found in both sectors. Therefore, the increasing privatisation has not caused any considerable changes when it comes to essential services.

The protection of vital needs in essential services is in Sweden based only on voluntary methods. It is common that when there is notice of industrial action

45. *Vårdförbundet* organises nurses, midwives, biomedical scientists and radiographers.
46. The Mediation Office's annual report for 2008 163. According to the Swedish Association of Local Authorities and Regions 40,000 medical or other examinations and 15,000 operations were cancelled or postponed.
47. SOU 1960:10 *Statstjänstemäns förhandlingsrätt* (The right for state employees to bargain collectively).

the parties voluntarily grant exemptions from the noticed action before the action is intended to enter into force with the aim not to disturb essential services.[48] This could be done on the noticing party's own initiative, or after suggestions from the opposite party. There are also arrangements in collective agreements with the aim to avoid disturbances of essential services, see *infra* Subsection 7.2.

Legislation to prevent or prohibit industrial disputes in essential services has been mooted on several occasions, but the outcome has been a consensus that it is primarily the labour market parties' responsibility to respect the interests of society and third parties.

5 RESTRICTIONS OF THE RIGHT TO STRIKE IN ESSENTIAL SERVICES

By the end of the 19th century when trade unions began to use strikes in order to put pressure on employers to conclude collective agreements, it was not questioned that professions such as police officers, postal workers, engine drivers, etc. were not allowed to take any part in this. These professions were employed by the state and thus, by that time, forbidden to bargain and to strike. By legislation 1965, public employees were allowed to use strikes in collective bargaining concerning wages and working conditions.[49] By the Public Employment Act in 1976, public employees were in principle put in the same situation as private employees, and the new Public Employment Act 1994 did not alter this. Strike and lockouts can be used in, for example, the defence forces, the police forces and the judicial system.

This means that in Sweden industrial action in essential services is judged in the same way independent of the sector in question. Although privatisation of traditionally state or public activities during the last decades, there are still parts of the public sector that is especially vulnerable for disturbances, like hospitals, the police force, the courts etc.

The point of departure in the 1994 Public Employment Act[50] is that also employees in work that comprise the exercise of public authority, or which is unavoidably necessary in order to ensure the exercise of public authority, has the right to use industrial action even if this should have the result that a public authority is paralysed. Partial industrial action (with the exception of a refusal of overtime and blockade of new employment) is not permitted for those public employees exercising public authority. Sympathy action is for those exercising public authority only permissible in favour of other public employees. The

48. SOU 1984:18 Chapter 8, and SOU 1984:19 Chapter 4.
49. Basic agreements, like the *Saltsjöbaden* agreement, was a prerequisite for this legislation, *see infra* Section 6.2.
50. Sections 23–26 of the Act deals with industrial conflicts.

reason behind these restrictions is that a refusal to do certain tasks or to work with certain cases, or the possibility to use sympathy action towards a private employer could constitute a contradiction to the constitutional right for everybody to be treated equal from public authorities.[51] The exercise of public authority could be considered to be inconsistent and even contradicting constitutional principles of objectivity and legality.

In the public sector, there is according to the 1994 Public Employment Act a general ban on political strikes aiming at influencing domestic political affairs. In addition, according to the Act, public employees administrating public authority are not allowed to participate in any industrial action with a political purpose.[52]

It should also be mentioned that in the public sector there are specific rules concerning the protection of political democracy. The state and the regions/ municipalities are not in their role as employers to conclude agreements concerning public sector aims, directions, volume and quality. In addition, the exercise of public authority is included. When the 1976 Co-determination Act and the 1976 Public Employment Act were accepted by the Parliament the social partners in the public sector concluded a Special Basic Agreement where they agreed to strive for peaceful bargaining and avoiding industrial conflict in such questions. According to the agreement, a Special Board is founded with 13 members; seven parliamentarians and three from each party side. Industrial action is not permitted when the Board deals with the question. The Board's decision is a recommendation.[53]

6 COMPENSATORY MEASURES FOR RESTRICTIONS

Restrictions in the constitutional right to take industrial action are few in Sweden. There is no legislation in Sweden concerning industrial action in essential services, and no definition of this concept in law, see *supra* Subsection 3.3.3. The few and minor restrictions concerning industrial action that follows from the Public Employment Act aim at securing the constitutional rights of equality, objectivity and legality in public administration, see Section 5.

To summarise, there are no special restrictions in the right to take industrial action in essential services in Swedish legislation. Since there are no restrictions, there is no need for any compensatory measures.

51. Prop. (Government Bill) 1975/76:105 bil. 2 97 et seqq., 192 et seqq.; prop. 1993/94:63 56 et seqq.
52. AD 1986 No. 108, AD 1987 No. 157.
53. The Board has dealt with a question concerning working time for prison employees, and decided that the trade union demands concerning working time was an infringement of the political decision to reorganise prison work.

7 SECURING ESSENTIAL SERVICES BY FURTHER MEANS

7.1 The Legislature

There are no statutory restrictions concerning essential services in Swedish legislation, neither by exclusion from collective labour rights nor by imposing or limiting the right to take industrial action with the aim to secure essential services. The minor restrictions in the 1994 Public Employment Act concerning employees exercising public authority are not primarily aimed at securing these services see *supra* Section 5.

There is partial legislation concerning 'protective' work, which means work necessary to avert risks of harm to people or property. The 1994 State Employment Order,[54] which applies to central-government employees, prescribes that employees in event of an industrial dispute is required to phase out operations in a technically satisfactory manner or to prevent danger to people or damage to property. The 1973 Seafarers Act[55] has similar rules, and similar rules are found in several basic collective agreements (see *infra*). According to such agreements, those who perform protective work during at dispute do not lose their neutral status in relation to the disputing parties.

It is commonly recognised that the state may intervene with legislation when in an individual case industrial conflict threatens vital societal needs.[56] There are no general rules concerning this. Such an intervention has only occurred once. It was in 1971 when about 50,000 graduate level state employees (railway transports, pilots, teachers, judges, medical doctors, dentists, military personal, social security officials) were on strike and lockout. The Government argued that this threatened essential services.[57] Legislation brought into operation again the previous collective agreements, and thus the peace obligation. Ad hoc legislation has been prepared on a few other occasions in order to settle conflicts, but the conflicts have been settled before legislation was passed.[58] There are also some examples where the parties following political pressure have called off industrial action.

In 1990, a social democratic Government proposed a general wage stop. The proposal included a non-strike clause. The Government Bill was rejected by the Parliament and the Government had to leave Office.

54. SFS 1994:373.
55. SFS 1973:282.
56. According to the Constitution, this has to be in form of legislation.
57. During the conflict, the Board in the state sector (see Subsection 7.2) in seven different cases had to consider if essential services were threatened. In one case the Board found that essential services were threatened, it concerned veterinaries, The Board in the municipal area had two conflicts to consider and in both cases it found that the actions that concerned veterinaries and social security officers threatened essential services.
58. Policemen in 1947, nurses in 1951, naval officers in 1955, see SOU 1984:19 36–37, 44–47.

7.2 The Social Partners

The only way of regulating strikes in essential services in Sweden is through collective agreements. Here we find rules about so-called free circles (employees in certain positions not belonging to (certain) unions, see *supra* Subsection 3.1[59]), protective work, neutrality for those not taking part in a conflict, and the establishment of boards/councils for the assessment of when a conflict dangers essential services.

The *Saltsjöbaden* Agreement from 1938 prohibits industrial action during negotiations according to the agreement, certain types of industrial action are forbidden, and restrictions in the use of pressure directed against outsiders neutral third parties and directed against family businesses with no employees. There are also rules concerning protective work; such work that must in the course of a work stoppage be performed for the discontinuation of the production in a technically reasonable way, or for preventing danger to people or damage to buildings, machinery, goods etc. Chapter V of the agreement concerns the Handling of Conflicts Threatening Essential Public Services. The Labour Market Board, also set up by the *Saltsjöbaden* Agreement, shall consider questions of preventing, limiting or settling labour conflicts in essential services. The Labour Market Board is in questions concerning essential services composed of three representatives from each of the two central organisations (SN and LO). In order to prevent labour conflicts from disturbing essential public services, SN and LO shall jointly take up for prompt consideration any conflict situation where protection of any public interest is called for by either of the two organisations or by a public authority or by any other similar body representing the public interest in question. The Labour Market Board acts here without a neutral chairperson. Only if a majority is won in favour of preventing or settling the dispute wholly or partly, are the parties, SN and LO, obliged to take immediate measures, each for its part, to bring about a settlement between the parties concerned. The Board has no power to impose a settlement on the parties. The Board has been used only in a handful of cases. Only once, in 1953 concerning private power plants, has the Board made a joint recommendation to the parties to stop industrial action because of a threat to essential services.[60] In the General Conflict 1980, the Board dealt with two cases, one concerning oil refineries and one concerning petrol distribution, but the Board was unable to make decisions in both cases.[61]

The solutions in the *Saltsjöbaden* Agreement have served as a pattern for similar procedures in basic agreements covering other areas of the labour market.

59. After the conflict in 1971 (see *supra*) the collective agreements on the public sector were supplemented with rules on a 'free circle'.
60. SOU 1984:19 37.
61. SOU 1984:19 59.

When almost equal freedom to take industrial action as in the private sector was introduced in the public sector in the 1960s, agreements similar to the *Saltsjöbaden* agreement was concluded between the state and the relevant trade unions in that sector, and the same happened on the local government side (regions and municipalities). Such agreements were a prerequisite for the new legislation. The 1980s and 1990s industrial unrest in the public sector led to discussions about more firm rules especially regarding essential services. The Boards in the public sector, which – just like the Labour Market Board – consisted of an equal number of representatives from both sides, where then, added with impartial members.

The Basic Agreement for the state sector provides rules on mediation, cooling-off periods and notification. It gives some examples of areas and functions where the right to use industrial action should be used with particular caution: national security, enforcement of law and order, health care etc. The parties also agree to avoid industrial action that may have severe social and economic effects or be objectionable on humanitarian grounds. The Board constituted to consider essential services consists of three members form the employers' side, three from the trade union side, and two impartial members who the parties appoint jointly. One of the impartial members is appointed chair, and has the casting vote. If a party considers that a noticed action could disturb essential services, the party should ask for negotiations. If the parties are unable to agree during negotiations, the Council could judge the noticed action. In principle the parties are forbidden to resort to industrial action for two weeks, but the Council can decide to postpone industrial action for a third week if they need the time. There is no legal obligation for the parties to follow the Council's decision, but it is presupposed that they do so. The Basic agreement for the state sector also entails rules regarding neutrality and protective work.

The Basic agreement for the regional/municipal sector, establishes the 'Central Council' for the assessment of essential services. It is composed of three members from each party and three impartial members.[62] The term 'Essential services' is in this agreement defined as danger to a person's life or the risk for permanent ill health. It also entails rules about protective work and neutrality. Protective work is defined as work needed to complete work in a technically satisfactory manner, avoid danger to people or property damage. The employer decides what should be considered as protective work.

Outside the three large main labour market areas (private, state, municipal/regional) there are a few other examples of collective agreements establishing joint councils for limiting labour conflicts in essential services.

The board in the municipal and regional area, the Central Council, have been most called for, because of industrial action in the health care sector. During the conflict 1995 when nurses were on strike for seven weeks, a Board was set up according to the Basic agreement. The Central Council had one case

62. SOU 1984:18 147 et seqq, SOU 1984:19 44, 59, 62, Ds 1988:2 68 et seqq.

to consider but did find the action to be a danger to essential services. In 2008, there was a very large conflict in the health care area and a Central Council was constituted, but after the exhortation from the Council that the parties should continue to bargaining, the parties succeeded to conclude a collective agreement (see *supra* Subsection 4.1).

The latest example when a board/councils established by collective agreements was set up occurred during the wage rounds in 2016. The main question in a dispute between Swedish IT & Telecom Industries, on the one side, and *Unionen*[63] and The Swedish Association of Graduate Engineers, on the other, concerned flexible retirement (i.e., the possibility to work part time and receive part time pension benefits during the last years of active working life). On 6 April, after bargaining without any results, the trade unions gave notice of strikes and blockade. The notice concerned around ten large companies and sixty workplaces. The next day two mediators were appointed. There were also notices of sympathy actions from other trade unions. Before the noticed action was supposed to enter into force, the Swedish Post and Telecom Authority (PTS)[64] on 13 April requested certain limitations concerning the announced actions because of public interest. The Board that was established according to the basic agreement for the sector in question met on 18 April, but were unable to agree if the notice of industrial action threatened public interests.[65] On 14 April the employer turned to the Labour Court claiming that the noticed action was illegal on the ground that it concerned a dispute of rights, not a dispute of interests, because the disputed question was already regulated in a collective agreement regarding pension rights. On 15 April, the trade unions brought action before the Labour Court claiming for an interim decision that that the noticed actions were legal. The trade unions also postponed the noticed actions. On 21 April, the Labour Court decided to reject the union's claim,[66] stating that the collective agreement referred to regulated the pension questions and therefore the noticed industrial action was illegal. The trade unions withdrew their notice of industrial action and mediation was closed the same day. Later, a collective agreement concerning wages and working conditions between the parties was concluded. This agreement did not regulate flexible pensions. No industrial action entered into force during this dispute.

63. *Unionen* is affiliated to the central organisation TCO. With its over 640 000 members, *Unionen* is the largest Swedish trade union, and the largest white-collar union in the world, www.unionen.se.
64. PTS is a State Authority directly under the Government, which monitors the electronic and postal sectors in Sweden.
65. The Basic Agreement for the public companies' sector was concluded in 1982, and according to the agreement, there are an equal number of members from both parties in the established board.
66. AD 2016 No. 31.

8 EVALUATION AND CONCLUSION

The wide legal possibility to take industrial action in Sweden is dependent upon the fact that the Swedish way to combat social dumping and secure good working conditions for employees is through collective agreements. In order to put pressure on the opposite party in collective bargaining industrial action is used. The labour market parties usually handle this possibility with responsibility. In the absolute majority of cases, the knowledge of the other party's possibility to take industrial action is enough. The councils/boards established by collective agreements to discuss and/or make decisions concerning if noticed industrial action could threaten vital interests in society work in the same way: The councils work best when they are not used – to know that they exist are in most cases enough.

The Swedish scholar Reinhold Fahlbeck writes: 'Industrial action activity and collective agreement bargaining are closely interwoven. Though the level of industrial strife is low in Sweden, collective agreement bargaining is conducted in an environment where resort to industrial action is always present as a possibility. Both sides know that. Both sides also know that they can inflict serious damage at each other, thus strongly influencing each other. Both sides also know, however, that such gains come at a price. Relations between the parties can be pestered for years to come, for example.'[67]

It is generally considered that solutions in collective agreements, not only concerning wages and working conditions, but also concerning the important basic principles on the labour market, such as how to bargain and how to solve conflicts and avoid industrial strife, are preferable. Agreements is more legitimate than legislation, they are more flexible and can be easily adapted to different sectors or workplaces. However, in times of declining union membership and international competition, the Swedish system is under strain. A self-regulating system needs to be legitimate. Still, in an international perspective there is a very high rate of organisation on both sides of the labour market.

There are in collective agreements different kinds of negotiation orders with the aim of concluding a new collective agreement before the old one expires. About 30 per cent of Swedish employees are covered by special collaboration agreements (patterned after the Industry Agreement) that contain certain time schedules for negotiation, rules for appointment of a private mediator and the powers of the mediators. For the rest of the labour market, without collaboration agreements, the National Mediation Office will appoint mediators. The parties often by their own initiative make exemptions from noticed action, and very often, they follow the mediators' advice to make exemptions or to postpone noticed action. Only in very rare situations, industrial action that could threaten essential services will be pursued. In these rare cases there are, according to the basic agreements for different sectors councils/boards

67. *Fahlbeck*, 2008 50.

set up by the parties with the task to decide if an action threatens essential services. These boards have been used only in a few situations and their efficiency in decision-making is not persuasive. Nevertheless, the fact that the parties have elaborated this self-regulating model, where the boards are only one of several instruments, has resulted in a situation where there at the moment are no calls for any restrictions or amendments concerning industrial action in essential services.

Industrial action has been considered a general problem for the Swedish society only a few times, and the labour market parties have been responsive to when the state authorities have considered that the parties are not sufficiently responsible (see *supra* Section 2). In the late 19th century there were discussions in the Swedish Parliament that industrial action should be solved by compulsory arbitration. In 1906 the December compromise was concluded and the 1906 legislation on mediation was issued. During the 1930s several government inquiries that concerned industrial action were appointed. In 1938 the *Saltsjöbaden* agreement was concluded. When the state, regional and local government employees received full rights of collective bargaining and industrial action by legislation in 1965 it was a requirement that the labour market parties in these sectors should conclude collective agreements where parts of the *Saltsjöbaden* agreement was seen as a pattern. After the 1980s and increasing industrial unrest, again several government inquiries were appointed. The result was the Industrial Agreement in 1998 and the new legislation on mediation 2000. Also, the Basic Agreement for the state sector and the Basic Agreement for the regional/municipal sectors were revised and the boards that assess threats of essential service were reinforced by impartial members (see *supra* Section 7.2).

In Sweden it is the labour market parties who decide how to define essential services and if any restrictions in the right to take industrial action is needed. The possibility for public employees and employees working in essential services to use the strike weapon is probably the widest in the world. Why is it that this old and traditional model for regulating the labour market still works in a satisfactory way? There are, of course, many explanations for why a system like this can function. Part of the answer is that, although the social partners are aware of their divergent interests there is an underlying trust between them. Another part is the responsibility taken by the labour the labour market parties, and that the state has hesitated to intervene. Further, an important condition is that there are a limited number of actors that have been able to guarantee that the system is used with balance and responsibility. The social partners usually try to avoid the disturbance of essential services. Often they agree to give exemptions from noticed action in order to avoid such disturbance. It is important to have the support of the general society in an industrial conflict. The parties realise that they, so to speak, are in the same boat and if they move too much they know that they everyone will get wet.

However, what happens if there is one player on the market that do not accept the common rules on the market? Since 2016 there has been a conflict in Gothenburg harbour (the largest harbour in Scandinavia). The employer's organisation has concluded a collective agreement on national level with the Transport Workers' Union that belongs to the central organisation LO. Most of the employees in the Gothenburg harbour are not members of the Transport Workers' Union; they belong to the independent union (not affiliated to any central organisation, *see* Subsection 2.1) the Harbour Workers' Union.[68] The Harbour Workers' Union is not bound by any collective agreement. There have been several strikes and blockades from the Harbour Workers' Union and the employer has responded with lockouts. A lengthy mediation process has been unsuccessful. It is not quite clear what the Harbour Workers' Union exactly want, but it is clear that they do not intend to push aside the collective agreement with the Transport Workers' Union (which would have been unlawful, see *supra* Subsection 3.3.4). The conflict has caused considerable economic loss and damage to the employer. The whole region is affected; the harbour normally handles about 60 per cent of Sweden's international container traffic, and 30 per cent of Sweden's export goods. In 2017 497 nationwide collective agreements were signed concerning 2.3 million employees. Only 2,570 working days were lost, most of them in the local conflict in Gothenburg harbour (about 164 days due to strikes, and about 2241 days due to lockouts).[69] It is clear that the Harbour Workers' Union and their employer can lawfully take industrial action since they are not bound by any collective agreement between them.[70] A Government Inquiry was appointed in June 2017 with the aim of investigating if there should be any restrictions in legislation concerning strikes in a situation where an employer already is bound by a Swedish collective agreement for the same work.[71] The Inquiry presented its report in May 2018. Just before the report was published the main head organisations: LO, TCO, Saco from the trade unions' side and SN from the private employers' side together presented a paper where they had agreed on suggestions on changes in the Co-determination Act restricting industrial action in situations where an employer is already bound by a collective agreement for the work in question. In addition, the Inquiry's report suggests some new restrictions in the Co-determination Act in this situation.[72] According to the Minister of Labour Market Affairs, it is obvious in a system where the social partners have such an important role that it will be their suggestion that the Government will use for preparing a Bill.[73]

---

68. There are a few independent trade unions not affiliated to any of the central organisations, for example the Swedish Firefighters Union, the Swedish Air Line Pilots Association, the Swedish Train Drivers Association, and the Harbour Workers' Union.
69. The National Mediation Office's yearly report 2017, 81–87.
70. The Labour Court, AD 2018 No. 9, 2018 No. 10, has recently decided other disputes between the two parties concerning questions of rights.
71. Dir. 2017:70.
72. SOU 2018:40 *Vissa fredspliktsfrågor* (Some questions concerning the peace obligation).
73. Usually, in situations like this there are conflict resolution mechanisms in place. If two trade unions belonging to the same central organisation, both want to conclude a collective agreement for the same work, the central organisation would decide which trade union should bargain and conclude the collective agreement. Another possibility is that

Bibliography

Adlercreutz, Axel/Nyström, Birgitta, Labour Law in Sweden, 2nd ed. 2015

Carlson, Laura/Edström, Örjan/Nyström, Birgitta (eds), Globalisation, Fragmentation, Labour and Employment Law. A Swedish Perspective, 2016

Edlund, Sten/Nyström, Birgitta, Developments in Swedish Labour Law, 1988

Eklund, Ronnie/Sigeman, Tore/Carlson, Laura, Swedish Labour and Employment Law: Cases and Materials, 2008

Fahlbeck, Reinhold, Employee Participation in Sweden Union Paradise and Employer Hell or ...?, 2008

Fahlbeck, Reinhold/Mulder, Johann, Labour and Employment Law in Sweden, 3rd ed. 2009

Fahlbeck, Reinhold/Sigeman, Tore, European Employment and Industrial Relations Glossary: Sweden, 2001

Malmberg, Jonas /Johansson, Caroline, The Right to Strike: Sweden, in Waas (ed.), The Right to Strike. A Comparative View, 2014, 525 et seqq.

Nyström, Birgitta, Developments in Swedish Labour Law 2012–2016, Europäische Zeitschrift für Arbeitsrecht 2/2017, 282 et seqq.

Schmidt, Folke, Kollektiv arbetsrätt, 1977

Wahlgren, Peter (ed.), Stability and Change in Nordic Labour Law, Scandinavian Studies in Law, Vol. 43 2002

there is an agreement between two nation-wide trade unions stipulating which of them should have the right to conclude a collective agreement in situations where they foresee that there could be problems. (For example, the demarcation line between blue-collar work and white-collar work could sometimes be difficult to draw.)

CHAPTER 15

United Kingdom

Tonia Novitz

1 GENERAL BACKGROUND: COUNTRY PROFILE

1.1 The Political Unit to Be Covered

This report offers what is primarily an English legal analysis of the law relating to industrial action and the right to strike. England makes up just one part of a multi-faceted United Kingdom (UK) consisting also of the semi-autonomous devolved governments of Northern Ireland, Scotland and Wales. The legislative enactments relating to these constitutionally distinct entities indicate the significance of each domestic jurisdiction

Northern Ireland has the general power to legislate independently in the employment field (with the exception of binding EU law and the UK national minimum/living wage, the former being potentially relevant for purposes of regulation of the right to strike, but the latter not).[1] Northern Ireland has not, so far, enacted any law implementing the Trade Union Act 2016 adopted by the Parliament for Great Britain (encompassing England, Scotland and Wales). This

1. See Northern Ireland Act 1998, ss 4 and 6; see also Schedule 2.

is significant because this piece of legislation places systematic restrictions on so-called 'important public services', which arguably do not necessarily fall within International Labour Organisation (ILO) definitions of either 'essential' or truly 'public' services.[2] The importance of this statute for English law is discussed further below.

Arguably, Scottish law is the most distinctive, having civil and common law elements as well as a partially independent devolved legislature. However, industrial relations and employment law currently lie outside the scope of the Scottish Parliament's powers, including implementation of EU law in those fields.[3] So, we might expect the Trade Union Act 2016 to apply in that jurisdiction unchallenged. Nevertheless, the Scottish government led by the Scottish National Party, while understanding that the legislation is binding, has used its constitutional fundraising powers to create a £250,000 fund to promote trade union modernization and assist trade unions in overcoming the additional burdens which the 2016 Act would impose on them.[4] Law in action is such that the 2016 legislation has not been fully implemented in fact in Scotland.

Again, in Wales there has been as much rejection of the Trade Union Act 2016 as is constitutionally permissible. The powers of the Welsh Government are set out under the Government of Wales Act 1998 and a later Government of Wales Act 2006. These were the subject of recent litigation in *Agricultural Sector (Wales) Bill – Reference by the Attorney General for England and Wales* [2014] UKSC 43. The judgment of the UK Supreme Court recognized that Wales has certain devolved powers in eighteen fields including, for example, education and training, health and health services, as well as highways and transport and public administration. Schedule 7 to the 2006 Act sets out in detail twenty 'headings' and the subjects that come within the legislative competence of the Welsh Assembly. Although employment and industrial relations are not one of the devolved powers, the provision of various services (such as educational, health and transport services) is so devolved. On this basis, the Welsh Assembly has adopted the Trade Union (Wales) Act 2017 which indicates, among other matters, under section 1(4) that as regards requirement of ballot before action by trade unions, the regulations to be adopted in respect of 'important public services' will not cover 'services provided by a devolved Welsh authority'. This keeps many spheres that might be subject to greater restrictions on strike action immune from such controls. Similarly, under section 2, the Trade Union (Wales) Act 2017 makes it clear that 'a devolved Welsh authority' may not use temporary workers to cover strike action. The 2017 Welsh legislation may now however be subjected to challenge. Since these provisions were adopted, there has been a further Wales Act 2017 which adopts the Scottish 'conferred powers' model,

2. See for analysis *Ford/Novitz* 2016, 277.
3. Scotland Act 1998, ss 29 – 30; and Schedule 5.
4. Details of the 'trade union modernization fund' are available on the Scottish government website at: https://beta.gov.scot/news/250-000-for-trade-unions/, last checked 24 March 2018.

offering a more longstanding basis for devolution of Welsh government, but as in Scotland expressly excludes industrial relations and employment law from their ambit. The UK Government is now insisting that the Trade Union Act 2016 (and its treatment of 'important public services') should apply throughout Great Britain (namely, England, Scotland and Wales), so that the legislative rebellion in Wales may soon be at an end.[5]

In this state of uncertainty regarding the law applicable to the UK as a whole, this chapter focuses on English law as the central case study of strikes in essential services, as this is the only jurisdiction in the UK where the Trade Union Act 2016 is applied systematically and straightforwardly. It may also be of interest that trade union membership levels are falling more in England than in other parts of the UK. 'Trade union membership levels in England decreased by around 755,000 between 1995 and 2016, compared with a 109,000 decrease in Scotland and a 12,000 reduction in Wales. Trade union membership decreased in Northern Ireland by 19,000 between 1995 and 2016.'[6]

1.2 Economic, Political and Historical Background

There has long been de facto recognition in England that an individual worker has little capacity to influence the terms on which they are hired, which tend to be dictated by the employer. Otto Kahn Freund identified the innate subordination inherent in the contract of employment.[7] While collective bargaining and collective action could overcome this imbalance of bargaining power, it took some considerable period of time for there to be English legal recognition of this entitlement with respect to workers or their organizations. Instead, collective bargaining was viewed as anti-competitive behaviour, with trade unions considered to be operating as an illegal restraint of trade. Their operations were only legalized by the Trade Union Act 1871. Judges then seemed determined to find trade unions liable in tort (if not under criminal law), so that workers could be found to be engaged in civil conspiracy[8] and trade unions liable for economic torts.[9] The result was the adoption of a Trade Disputes Act 1906 by a Liberal Government to offer protection from liability for certain torts 'in contemplation of furtherance of a trade dispute'. This has come to be known as the 'golden formula', which over time has been expanded and retracted in its scope in response to the creativity of the judges[10] and political exigencies.[11]

For the majority of the twentieth century, English trade unions were reluctant to engage with the courts. Their ideal scenario was to bargain with

5. *Davies*, 2018, 135 et seqq.
6. *DEIS*, 2017, 19.
7. *Davies/Freedland* 1983, 18.
8. *Quinn v Leathem* [1901] AC 495, HL.
9. *Taff Vale v Amalgamated Society of Railway Servants* [1901] AC 426.
10. See *Rookes v Barnard* [1964] AC 1129.
11. Discussed in *Ewing*, 2006.

employers to set norms that governed the employment relationship unhindered by the judiciary (or indeed the legislature, which was only significant in that it continued to allow the bargaining parties the immunity from statutory liability to do so). This state of affairs was described by Kahn-Freund in the period post the Second World War as '*collective laissez-faire*'. He made the hopeful claim that: 'What the State has not given, the State cannot take away'.[12] However, autonomy of collective bargaining was premised on fairly generous statutory provision for union immunity from civil liability in tort when calling industrial action. That statutory immunity was considerably eroded from 1979 onwards, when Margaret Thatcher's Conservative Government first took power, such that employers sought to rely increasingly on legal measures, such as injunctions, so as to prevent strikes from taking place.[13] For the first time, balloting requirements imposed by statute became a precondition for immunity from civil liability for trade unions. This immunity then became linked to protection from dismissal, first indirectly through the introduction of protection for dismissal only in respect of 'official' industrial action authorized or endorsed by the trade union, which was only likely to occur when a trade union would not be exposing itself to civil liability in this way. (Currently, under the Trade Union and Labour Relations (Consolidation) Act (TULRCA) 1992, section 237, which sets 'official industrial action' as a precondition for protection from selective dismissal under section 238.) This link was made more explicit by a 'New Labour' Government in 1999, which provided for additional protection for dismissal where the strike was not only 'official' but 'protected' because its aims and the manner in which was called (balloting and notice) complied with the statutory requirements for immunity from tort (TULRCA 1992, section 238A as amended). The scope of the statutory immunity for strikes has been eroded further by the Trade Union Act 2016, which was introduced by a Conservative Government. This more recent legislation places further constraints on the remit of lawful strike action by for example changing balloting requirements, in particular as regards what are to be regarded as 'important public services' (see further *infra*).

1.3 Legal Framework

There is no constitutional protection of the right to strike in England. There is also no national legislation which proclaims that workers have a positive right to strike. This is due to the refusal of English courts to contemplate such a development at the common law and the reluctance of the legislature to ensure its introduction via statute, which provides instead strictly circumscribed protections from dismissal for striking workers and limited immunity for trade unions from liability in tort.

12. *Kahn-Freund*, 1954, 44; cf. Dukes, 2009.
13. *Fredman* 1992; *Simpson* 1987; and *Davies/Freedland* 1993.

The English common law provides the foundation for regulation. The contract of employment is not suspended during a strike, but is regarded as having been breached by a failure to perform contractual obligations to work. This is so, even in respect of what could be called a 'defensive' strike, itself a response to a repudiatory breach of contract by the employer.[14] Action short of a strike, such as an over-time ban, which is not apparently in breach of the express terms of the contract of employment, may still be regarded as a breach of implied terms, such as fidelity and mutual trust and confidence.[15] The result is that, at common law, the employer has entirely free discretion to dismiss an employee who has taken industrial action by reason of breach of a fundamental term of the contract of employment; although an employer may elect not to do so. Employees in England are therefore dependent on statutory intervention to provide for protection from dismissal (TULRCA 1992, ss 237, 238 and 238A). Contractual deductions from pay for time spent taking industrial action can also be imposed by an employer.[16]

Additionally, courts have found that to call a strike can be regarded as actionable under certain economic torts. Primarily, calling industrial action is regarded as an inducement of breach of contract, giving rise to civil liability in tort.[17] Further liability may arise in tort for the way in which collective action has led indirectly to breach of a contract of supply of goods or services.[18] On this basis, and in reliance on other economic torts, such as interference with trade or business by unlawful means, courts have imposed civil liability on an organizer of industrial action, whether the organizer is an individual or a union. The impetus for imposing liability in this way seems to have slowed,[19] but there remains a residual potential for liability in tort without statutory immunity for calling lawful trade disputes. In this respect the potential for liability for the tort of statutory duty can have a chilling effect on industrial action in public and essential services (as discussed below).

The primary legislative source which regulates collective action in the UK is the Trade Union and Labour Relations (Consolidation) Act (TULRCA) 1992. This statute does not make any express provision for a right to strike; nor does

14. *Wilkins v Cantrell and Cochrane* (GB) Ltd [1978] IRLR 483; *Solihull Metropolitan Borough v NUT* [1985] IRLR 211.
15. *Secretary of State v ASLEF* (No. 2) [1972] 2 QB 455. The same issue may arise in respect of a refusal to work overtime (*Express & Star v Bunday* [1987] IRLR 423.
16. But note *Hartley & others v King Edward VI College* [2017] UKSC 39, indicating that the amount deducted can be the subject of judicial scrutiny and is not to be punitive.
17. Dating from the original case of *Taff Vale Railway v Amalgamated Society of Railway Servants* [1901] AC 426.
18. *DC Thomson & Co v Deakin* [1952] Ch. 646; and *Torquay Hotel Ltd v Cousins* [1969] 2 Ch. 106.
19. After *OBG Ltd v Allan* [2008] 1 AC 1174 (HL) discussed in *Deakin/Randall* 2009.

the Human Rights Act (HRA) 1998, which gives qualified domestic legal effect to the European Convention on Human Rights (ECHR) 1950. Rather, TULRCA 1992 allows 'employees'[20] to protection from unfair dismissal under UK labour law. Further, TULRCA 1992, section 219 allows organizers of industrial action to claim immunity from civil liability in tort, which would otherwise arise under common law. Notably, the scope of these entitlements to protection and immunity are extremely limited, as shall be demonstrated below.

2 COLLECTIVE LABOUR RELATIONS

2.1 Unions and Rate of Unionization

The rate of unionization is in decline. Union membership has fallen from a peak of 65% (approximately 13 million employees) in 1980 to 23.5% in 2016 (approximately 6.2 million employees). This is a decrease of 8.9% even since 1995.[21]

Membership is eroding in both the private and public sectors. In the private sector, membership declined in 2015-16 for the first time in 6 years and stands only at 13.4%, while in the public sector it is now 52.7%. In 2015-16 both declined in a way which has been described as 'statistically significant'.[22] This can be contrasted with previous growth in public sector trade union membership from 1995 - 2005 and stability until 2010.[23]

Recent Government statistics indicate that: 'Employees in industries with higher proportions of public sector workers are more likely to belong to trade unions, including the "public administration and defence" and "education" industries.'[24]

2.2 Employers' Associations and Rate of Organization

There is little sectoral bargaining at national level in England (or even across the UK); instead the focus is on enterprise level bargaining. Arguably, the absence of sectoral bargaining can be linked to the prohibition of secondary action, which does not fall under the statutory immunity for strikes by virtue of section 224 of TULRCA 1992. This decline in sectoral bargaining has been the subject of trenchant criticism.[25]

20. As defined under the Employment Rights Act 1996 (ERA), s. 230.
21. See *Cully et al.*, 1999, 235 et seqq.; *DEIS* 2017, 3.
22. *DEIS* 2017, 3, 6.
23. *Ibid.*, 12.
24. *Ibid.*, 13.
25. For example, by *Ewing/Hendy*, 2017, who advocate legal and policy measures to reinstate effective negotiation and enforcement of sectoral collective agreements.

There is scope to register employers' associations with the Certification Officer under section 123 of TULRCA 1992, but given the prevalence of enterprise bargaining, there are relatively few listed currently as being in operation. The details and annual returns of those registered are available online.[26] In 1983 there were 375 employers' associations; today there are 91 registered, with a further 39 of which the Certification Officer has knowledge but are unregistered.[27] There is no clear division between private and public sector employers' associations as, being oriented around industrial and service sector divisions, they tend to span this divide in a country given to public-private partnerships and forms of public to private 'contracting out'.

2.3 Data Regarding Strikes

There has been a decline in the incidence of strike action, namely the days not worked by reason of an industrial dispute. The Office of National Statistics (ONS) reports on the UK as a whole and states that 'the number of working days lost due to labour disputes in 2016 was 322,000, which was more than in 2015 (170,000) and the eighth lowest annual total since records began in 1891' (ONS 2017). These statistics must be set in the context of the peak of industrial action in the UK, which occurred in 1984 (during Margaret Thatcher's Conservative Government), when 27,135,000 working days were lost in work stoppages. In other words, the incidence of industrial action is today just over 1% of what it was then.

More days were lost to strike action in England than elsewhere. This was due to the dispute involving junior doctors in the English National Health Service (NHS) 'which accounted for 129,000 working days lost (around 40% of the total working days lost for 2016)'.[28] The ONS 2017 also reports that: 'Looking at the figures for 2016, there were more working days lost in the public sector (243,000) than the private sector (79,000) but there were more strikes in the private sector (60) than in the public sector (41).' The greater rate of days lost due to strikes in the public sector may be due to at least two factors. The first being the higher rate of unionization in the public section; the second being the intensive restructuring and reduction of the size of the public sector leading to a greater incidence of industrial disputes. In this respect, the strikes in the NHS are a case in point. Notably, health services are deemed 'important public services' under the new Trade Union Act 2016 (and accompanying Important Public Services (Health) Regulations 2017), which seems to be aimed at reducing the incidence of strikes in that sector.

26. *Certification Officer*, 2017a.
27. *Certification Officer*, 2017, 3 et seqq.
28. *ONS*, 2017.

3 THE RIGHT TO STRIKE

3.1 Recognition of the Right to Organize, the Right to Bargain Collectively and the Right to Strike

There is no explicit recognition of a right to organize, right to bargain collectively or a right to strike in any constitutional or legislative instrument in the UK. Instead, legislation (TULRCA 1992) provides for:

- apparatus for trade unions to be registered,
- procedures enabling independent trade unions to seek statutory recognition (subject to various restrictions),
- the potential enforcement of collective agreements (but only in exceptionally rare circumstances in which the parties both agree an agreement should be legally binding and the relevant clause of the collective agreements are deemed suitable for such a purpose) and
- narrowly circumscribed protections from dismissal for striking workers and restricted immunity for trade unions from liability in tort.

In relation to the last of these, the Donovan Commission Report (1968) observed at paragraph 935: 'The right to strike is, basically, a right to withdraw labour in combination without being subject to the legal consequences which would, in the past, have followed. This situation is now well recognised and we do not think it can be improved by granting the right in express terms.' This is not a view that holds much sway amongst contemporary academics. As Davies[29] has noted, 'the concept of an 'immunity' does not have the same rhetorical force as the term 'right'' and, as Syrett[30] also explained, an immunity may even have negative connotations. For example, Hayek, Shenfield[31] and others at the Institute of Economic Affairs used the language of 'immunities' to make trade unions sound like an indefensibly privileged group. Immunities are also more vulnerable to redefinition and retraction, as we have seen regarding the new balloting and notice requirements in the Trade Union Act 2016.

Instead, it has been the courts who have made the strongest statements in support of recognizing a right to strike; the most recent of which relies on case law emerging under the European Convention on Human Rights 1950 (ECHR) which has particular influence in England by virtue of the Human Rights Act (HRA) 1998. However, when traced over time, judicial support for the right to strike has been variable.

For example, Lord Wright stated in *Crofter Hand Woven Tweed v Harris*: 'Where the rights of labour are concerned, the rights of the employer are conditioned by the rights of the men to give or withhold their services. The right

29. *Davies*, 2009, 229.
30. *Syrett*, 1998.
31. *Hayek*, 1984; *Shenfield*, 1986.

of workmen to strike is an essential element in the principle of collective bargaining.'[32] By way of contrast, in the Court of Appeal, Lord Justice Maurice Kay LJ asserted: 'In this country, the right to strike has never been much more than a slogan or a legal metaphor. Such a right has not been bestowed by statute.'[33] On this basis, he proceeded to downplay the impact of the recent findings of the European Court of Human Rights that the right to strike could be protected under the more general guarantee of freedom of association provided under Article 11 of the ECHR.

A view more sympathetic to trade unions was taken, again in the Court of Appeal, by Elias LJ.[34] He began by explaining the basic English legal position regarding a right to strike (at paragraph 2): 'The common law confers no right to strike in this country.' However, he went on to make a bolder claim for protection of trade unions which call industrial action (and their members too) (at paragraph 8): 'Although the common law recognises no right to strike, there are various international instruments that do: see for example Article 6 of the Council of Europe's Social Charter and ILO Conventions 98 and 151. Furthermore, ... the right to strike is conferred as an element of the right to freedom of association conferred by Article 11(1) of the European Convention on Human Rights which in turn is given effect by the Human Rights Act.' He concluded at paragraph 9 that, if there were merely an immunity for taking industrial action, TULRCA 1992 should be construed strictly to restrict its scope, but as there is a right to strike protected under international law, 'the starting point [is] that it should be given a "likely and workable construction"...'

3.2 Relation to International Law

There are various significant sources of the UK's international obligations regarding the right to strike, which should be respected under English law. These include:

- the ILO Constitution and ILO Conventions Nos. 87 and 98,
- the United Nations' International Covenant on Economic, Social and Cultural Rights, Article 8(i)(d),
- the Council of Europe's European Social Charter, Article 6(4), and
- the Council of Europe's European Convention on Human Rights and Fundamental Freedoms, Article 11.

UK law on industrial action has been held to be in breach of these international treaties in decisions issued over many years by international and European supervisory bodies. This is due to the inadequate protection of the right to strike offered under UK legislation and by UK courts.

32. *Crofter Hand Woven Tweed v Harris* [1942] AC 435 at 463.
33. See *Metrobus v UNITE* [2010] ICR 173 (CA) at para 118.
34. See *RMT v Serco* [2011] ICR 848.

For example, (as discussed by Lorber and Novitz[35]) the UN Committee on Economic, Social and Cultural Rights held in 1997 and reiterated in 2002, in its regular reviews of the UK that 'failure to incorporate the right to strike into domestic law constitutes a breach of Article 8 of the Covenant . . . . The Committee recommends that the right to strike be established in legislation, and that strike action does not entail any more the loss of employment, and it expresses the view that the current notion of freedom to strike, which simply recognises the illegality of being submitted to an involuntary servitude, is insufficient to satisfy the requirements of Article 8 of the Covenant . . .'.[36]

The difficulty is that the UK operates under a 'dualist' rather than a 'monist' system of law, such that actual legislation needs to be adopted to give international treaty obligations effect in domestic law. For this reason, the UN Committee on Economic, Social and Cultural Rights has also asked that further legislative action be taken to ensure that the Covenant be incorporated in the domestic legal order, but no UK Government has taken action to do so. This explains the significance of the Human Rights Act 1998, which gives legal effect to 'Convention rights' derived from the ECHR and obliges English courts to have due regard to the judgments of the European Court of Human Rights. Further, through this 'backdoor', the tendency of the European Court of Human Rights to offer an 'integrated approach'[37] to the interpretation of Convention rights, such as freedom of association under Article 11 of the ECHR, enables European Social Charter, ILO and UN standards to remain relevant to the interpretation of UK law. Nevertheless, English law has an anomalous approach to protection of the right to strike (and collective bargaining more generally), which has led Ewing and Hendy[38] to conclude that the European Court of Human Rights utilizes a very broad proportionality test and a wide margin of appreciation when approaching UK compliance with Article 11.

3.3 General Restrictions of the Right to Strike

There have long been general restrictions on the right to strike for *all* employees, regardless of whether they are placed in the public or private sector. As explained above, there is no positive entitlement to strike under UK common law. This legal position is only ameliorated by various statutory protections for employees and trade unions. The key statutory reference point is the TULRCA 1992, as amended by various pieces of legislation including the Trade Union Act (TUA) 2016.[39]

35. *Lorber/Novitz* 2012, 107.
36. See Concluding Observations of the UN Committee on Economic, Social and Cultural Rights 1997 (UK), para. 11 and 2002 (UK), para. 16.
37. As outlined by *Mantouvalou*, 2013.
38. *Ewing/Hendy*, 2016.
39. See the general discussion in *Novitz*, 2016, from which this summary is derived.

A lawful trade dispute, where the trade union has followed correct procedures regarding balloting and notice, will be regarded as exempt from the economic torts of inducement of breach of contract, interference with contract, conspiracy and intimidation under section 219 TULRCA 1992. Any failure to comply with notice provisions and balloting requirements can lead to an action by the employer for injunctive relief.[40] The dispute must also be within the substantive remit of section 244 discussed below. These provisions also have implications for protection from dismissal.

3.3.1 *Links Between Liability for Calling the Strike and Protection from Dismissal*

Sections 20–22 of TULRCA 1992 provide for a trade union to be subjected to liability in tort where its officials have 'authorized' or 'endorsed' the action in question, or at least has not repudiated the actions of its members, subject to a 'cap' on liability and statutory immunity for some torts. Provision is also made under sections 237 and 238 of TULRCA 1992 for protection from selective dismissal of strikers, but this is limited to the situation where the trade union has authorized or endorsed the action and so is contingent on the willingness of the trade union to be exposed to civil liability. There is also potential for an automatic period of twelve weeks protection from dismissal under section 238A of TULRCA 1992 for industrial action called by a trade union which is protected from civil liability under the statutory immunity. That twelve week period can be extended to take account of conduct by the parties to the dispute. For example, a lockout by the employer and even the unreasonable refusal of an employer to take procedural steps to resolve the dispute can lead to an extension.

3.3.2 *The Procedural Scope of the Statutory Immunity: The Significance of Balloting*

There are also detailed balloting and notice provisions set out in sections 226–234A of TULRCA 1992, which are elaborated upon in the Code of Practice on Industrial Action Ballots and Notice to Employers. These place procedural restrictions on access to statutory immunity.

An industrial action ballot must be 'secret' and take place by post (TULRCA 1992, section 230). An independent review commissioned regarding introduction of electronic balloting under section 4 of the TUA 2016 reported back in December 2017 recommending a trial of e-balloting.[41] However, the Secretary of State is not obliged to accept the results of any such review. No action has been taken at the time of writing.

---

40. See *Countouris/Freedland*, 2010; and *Simpson*, 2013.
41. *UK Department for Business, Energy & Industrial Strategy*, 2017.

Previously a bare majority of those voting had to endorse their union's industrial action in a ballot, but since the adoption of the TUA 2016 there is now a further requirement regarding turnout. At least '50% of those who were entitled to vote in the ballot' have to actually do so for the ballot to be valid (TUA, section 2 amending TULRCA, section 226). From 2016, in respect of ballots in 'important public services', the TUA (section 3 also amending TULRCA 1992, section 226) introduced a further balloting requirement whereby at least 40% of those entitled to vote in the ballot must have given their approval (in addition to the 50% turnout threshold and the requirement of a majority of those voting supporting the action). Regulations (discussed further below) specify to which 'important public services' this rule applies covering: (a) health services; (b) education of those aged under 17; (c) fire services; (d) transport services; and (e) border security.

In 1999, a 'New Labour' government introduced a key qualification to these procedural requirements, namely section 232B, which states that certain 'small accidental failures' that do not affect the result of the ballot can be disregarded. This provision still stands. It is limited in that it concerns ostensibly only balloting and not notice provisions, although these may be subject to a '*de minimis*' rule, which allows for minor errors (see *infra*).

Following the TUA 2016 (section 9 amending TULRCA 1992, section 234), the mandate given by a ballot to industrial action will expire six months after the date of the ballot (or up to nine months if the parties so agree). After that time, a 'fresh ballot' has to take place to authorize industrial action (with the attendant costs this may incur).

3.3.3 Provisions in a Collective Agreement Regarding Mediation or Conciliation

There is no requirement that either mediation or conciliation takes place unless this is written into an enforceable collective agreement. See *Royal Mail Ltd v Communication Workers Union*,[42] where the ballot followed all the necessary procedural requirements including a 74% turnout and 89% in favour of a walkout, but the strike call was found to be in breach of a provision in the relevant Agreement. It was necessary to honour the statement that any disagreement between the employer and trade union to be referred first to 'external mediation' for a period not exceeding one month. This was an unusual case, which indicates that even when trade unions can overcome the more stringent provisions of the TUA 2016, they can still be vulnerable to findings from a court that there is a legally enforceable mediation or conciliation clause; this is despite findings in other cases that collective agreements will not usually have such stringent legally binding effects.[43]

42. *Royal Mail Ltd v Communication Workers Union* [2017] EWHC 2585 (QB).
43. See, e.g., *Malone v British Airways* [2010] EWCA 1225.

3.3.4 *Notice of the Ballot to the Employer*

In terms of notice of the ballot, this must be given to the employer at least seven days before it is held and a sample voting paper is sent to the employer more than three days beforehand (TULRCA, section 226A). The costs of the ballot must be met by the union. Where the number of those to be balloted exceeds 50 the ballot has to be overseen by an independent suitably qualified scrutineer and this process of managing and reporting on the ballot can be costly (see TULRCA, section 226B).

There must be sufficient information on the notice of ballot to tell the employer the categories of employee and potential workplaces affected as well as the numbers involved. This information 'must be as accurate as is reasonably practicable in the light of the information in the possession of the union at the time…' (TULRCA, section 226A(2D)). There are also detailed provisions setting out what is to be placed on the voting paper itself (which must include a 'health warning' regarding the potential for dismissal) as well as the option for the action to be a strike or 'short of a strike' (TULRCA, section 229). Since the reforms introduced by the TUA 2016, the voting paper must specify further 'the type or types of industrial action… either in the question itself or elsewhere on the ballot paper' as well as 'the period or periods within which the industrial action or, as the case may be, each type of industrial action is expected to take place' (TUA 2016, section 5 amending TULRCA, section 229 by inserting (2C) and (2D)). It is unclear to what extent, if at all, the union may depart from what is set out subsequently, for example, in the context of negotiations aimed at averting action. The first case on the new requirements for the ballot paper was *Thomas Cook Airlines Ltd v British Airline Pilots Association*[44] where the employer, Thomas Cook, sought an injunction to prevent a strike being called on the basis that the voting paper was required to state more than a mere proposal 'to take discontinuous action in the form of strike action on dates to be announced over the period from 8th September 2017 to 18th February 2018'. The Court took the view that the point of the TUA 2016 amendment was 'that a trade union member should know what he is being asked to vote for' (paragraph 13). Applying this to the facts at hand, the level of detail on the voting paper was treated as sufficient: 'difficult and potentially insoluble conundrums could arise if the relevant expectation for the purpose of the subsection is taken to be the trade union's best guess as to how the trade dispute will end…' (paragraph 18).

Additionally, since 2016, the ballot paper 'must include a reasonably detailed indication of the matter or matters in issue in the trade dispute to which the proposed industrial action relates' (TUA, section 5 amending TULRCA, section 229 by inserting (2B)). This can be linked to the substantive constraints on the lawful subject matter of strikes. It suggests that sufficient information must be given to those voting to enable them and the employer to ascertain

44. *Thomas Cook Airlines Ltd v British Airline Pilots Association* [2017] EWHC 2253 (QB).

whether this is a lawful trade dispute. If there are doubts, the employer may again wish to seek injunctive relief to prevent the action from taking place; indeed the vague words 'reasonably detailed' almost invites litigation to avert a strike.

Further requirements are imposed regarding notice of the result to all those entitled to vote and to the employer (under TULRCA 1992, ss 231 and 231A). Since 2016, that notice must not only state the number of votes cast, votes in favour, votes against and spoilt ballot papers, but also whether or not the number of votes cast is at least 50% of the number of individuals who were entitled to vote in the ballot and, where important public services are concerned, whether the requisite 40% threshold is met (TUA 2016, section 6 amending TULRCA 1992, section 231). Then notice must be given to the employer of the industrial action itself, which (due to TUA 2016, section 8) is to be given two weeks prior to its commencement, having been just one week previously. Action has to be taken normally within four weeks of the date of the ballot, although this may be extended by agreement up to eight weeks or in the event of legal proceedings up to twelve weeks (TULRCA 1992, ss 233, 234(1)-(6)). Also, there is now an obligation for a trade union to notify the Certification Officer in the 'annual return' regarding any industrial action taken (TUA 2016, section 7 inserting TULRCA 1992, section 32ZA).

Although there is no statutory provision governing minor errors in the context of notice of a ballot or industrial action, it has been established by case law that a *de minimis* rule applies, such that a minor error or omission should not be taken to invalidate the notice when trade unions have done what is reasonable to comply with the statutory requirements (which comes out of the approach taken by Elias LJ to interpretation of TULRCA 1992, i.e., in accordance with international recognition of the right to strike).[45] Notably, in a case decided in 2012,[46] it was acknowledged at paragraph 32 that: 'Very sensitive issues of policy arise in this context as to where the balance should be struck between striving for democratic legitimacy and imposing unrealistic burdens on unions and their officers'. It is not sufficient to be 'doing one's incompetent best or ...being lax about taking proper steps to obtain the most up to date information available', (paragraph 34) but neither should unreasonably stringent standards be demanded. The response of the Coalition Conservative-Liberal Democrat government to this judgment was to introduce a legislative requirement for trade unions to conduct a stringent 'membership audit' which would inform the ballot notice and its conduct.[47]

45. In *RMT v SERCO; ASLEF v London Birmingham Railway Ltd* [2011] IRLR 399 at para. 87.
46. *Balfour Beatty Engineering Services v Unite* [2012] ICR 822, IRLR 452.
47. Under The Transparency of Lobbying, Non-Party Campaigning and Trade Union Administration Act 2014, ss 40 and 32.

3.3.5 Injunctive Relief

In the UK, the ready availability of injunctive relief has become notorious. Where employers consider they have a *prima facie* case that the substantive or (more commonly) procedural requirements for statutory immunity were not met, then they can seek an injunction on the balance of convenience.[48] Given the costs to an employer liable to arise when any industrial action takes place, this 'balance' almost invariably would lie in the employer's favour. Although section 221 of TULRCA 1992 says that injunctive relief should be issued on the basis of the likelihood of the defence succeeding at trial, this approach has been neglected in much of the case law which has permitted injunctive relief on the basis of very minor delays or inaccuracies in notice.[49] The approach advocated by Elias LJ in *RMT v SERCO* signals a move away from the courts' proclivity to issue injunctions. However, it should still be acknowledged that his recognition of a right to strike did not lead to the creation of a presumption in favour of legality of the workers' and unions' collective action. Rather, the legislation regarding balloting and notice requirements has to be 'construed in the normal way, without presumptions one way or the other' as to the superiority of union or employer interests.[50]

3.4 Restrictions Depending on a Strike's Underlying Objective

3.4.1 The Content of a Lawful Trade Dispute

Distinctions are made between strikes on the basis of their underlying objective or goal. A lawful trade dispute must be 'a dispute between workers and their employer which relates wholly or mainly to one or more' of a list of matters set out in section 244(1) of TULRCA 1992. These concern various work-related subjects, such as terms and conditions of employment and termination.

This formulation (alongside a second explicit statutory exclusion under section 224) precludes any secondary action in support of a dispute between other workers and their employer. An attempt to challenge this exception before the European Court of Human Rights[51] was unsuccessful, on the rather

48. Under principles established in *American Cyanamid Ltd v Ethicon* Ltd [1975] AC 396 at 407.
49. See, e.g., *British Airways v Unite* [2009] EWHC 3541, at para 82; *EDF Energy Powerlink Ltd v National Union of Rail Maritime and Transport Workers* [2010] IRLR 114; and *Milford Haven Port Authority v Unite the Union* [2010] EWCA Civ 400.
50. RMT v SERCO; *ASLEF v London Birmingham Railway* Ltd [2011] IRLR 399 at para. 9; as discussed by *Dukes* 2011).
51. In *RMT v UK*, Application No. 31045/10 (Judgment of 8 April 2014).

questionable basis that 'secondary industrial action constitutes an accessory rather than a core aspect of trade union freedom' (paragraph 77).[52]

The wording of section 244 also places 'political disputes' outside the scope of statutory immunity from tort. This exclusion was the subject of litigation in *Mercury Communications Ltd v Scott-Garner*[53] where the Post Office Engineers Union (POEU) called on its members to refuse to connect Mercury, a private company, to the British Telecommunications (BT) network. Mercury claimed this was unlawful industrial action on the basis that its aims were political, namely to avoid privatization, while the POEU argued that its primary aim was to avoid job losses which would follow from privatization. The Court of Appeal sided with Mercury on the basis that had job security been the union's chief concern, the union could have sought to have the matter dealt with under the Job Security Agreement. The union had therefore failed to satisfy the 'wholly or mainly' test and could not establish a 'trade dispute' under section 244. Ironically, following this action, the privatized British Telecom engaged in employment restructuring, deciding to remove an entire layer of management confirming the union's fears.

Moreover, section 244 has been interpreted such that industrial action must not relate to the terms and conditions that will apply to future employees or indeed future employers, having implications for action taken regarding the sale of businesses or restructuring of public or corporate enterprises. This also has particular implications for privatization. In a transfer of undertaking situation, workers (and their representatives) can take industrial action to defend their own terms and conditions of employment in relation to their present employer, but cannot strike to protect their interests vis-à-vis the commercial entity that might be their employer after a transfer or sale, or ensure parity of terms and conditions within the workforce.[54]

3.4.2 *Where EU Law Is Engaged: Proportionate Action for the Protection of Workers*

To these substantive restrictions is also currently added those which emerged under European Union (EU) law from December 2007. The EU is distinct from the Council of Europe, having a market orientation with its own legal order framed around freedom of movement (of goods, services, establishment and

52. For critical comment and an analysis of the potential political motivations for this finding, given that the UK was at that time threatening to end its acceptance of the European Convention on Human Rights 1950, see *Bogg/Ewing*, 2014.
53. *Mercury Communications Ltd v Scott-Garner* [1983] IRLR 494.
54. *University College London Hospital NHS Trust v Unison* [1999] IRLR 31 (Court of Appeal); found not to be in violation of Article 11 of the European Convention on Human Rights (ECHR) by the European Court of Human Rights (ECtHR) in *Unison v UK* [2002] IRLR 497. Again, for critical comment, see *Novitz* 2015, 254 et seq.

persons) as well as competition law.[55] Respect for fundamental rights, including social rights, is recognized by the EU especially under the EU Charter of Fundamental Rights (EUCFR). Notably, Article 28 of the EUCFR recognizes the entitlement of workers to 'take collective action to defend their interests, including strike action'. However, industrial action is treated as a constraint on the implementation of the market freedoms of EU law. The right to strike cannot operate as a basis for independent EU regulation. Article 153(5) of the Treaty on the Functioning of the European Union (TFEU) provides that the legislative powers of the EU concerning social policy 'shall not apply to pay, the right of association, the right to strike or the right to impose lock-outs'.

The judgment of the European Court of Justice in *Viking*[56] established that where the exercise of a right to strike under national legislation obstructs the free movement of establishment by an employer, this can only be defensible if it is for the 'protection of workers' and proportionate. This indicates that only a strike aimed at protecting the immediate terms and conditions of those taking action is legitimate; and that a strike with cross-border EU aspects has to be taken in a way that is the least restrictive on an employer's free movement rights. The absurdity of such a restriction for industrial action was highlighted by various commentators.[57]

Further, the judgment in *Laval*[58] indicated that if collective action affects free movement of services and, in particular, collective bargaining over the minimum terms on which posted workers are hired, this interference can only be justified by demonstrating that there has been 'social dumping', presenting an even higher and uncertain threshold. If such defences cannot be established, the trade union calling the action can be found liable for potentially unlimited damages claimed by the employer.[59]

In an English dispute,[60] it was argued by the employer that EU free movement rights could provide a basis for injunctive relief to stop the strike being called by ASLEF. It was claimed that industrial action called to challenge the use of driver only operated (passenger) trains (DOOP) could impinge on the right of establishment under Article 49 TFEU (as Govia was 35% owned by a French company). In the alternative, passengers' entitlement to delivery of free movement of services was claimed to be affected under Article 56 TFEU. The Court of Appeal rejected these arguments. Elias LJ found (at paragraph 39) that: 'in our judgment it is inconceivable that a rule which did not discriminate on

55. *Novitz/Syrpis*, 2010.
56. Case C-438/05 *International Transport Workers' Federation (ITF) and Finnish Seamen's Union (FSU) v Viking Line* [2007] ECR I-10779.
57. Such as *Bercusson*, 2007, 304; and *Davies*, 2008.
58. Case C-341/05 *Laval un Partneri v Svenska Byggnadsarbetareförbundet* [2007] ECR I-11767 i.
59. See *Apps*, 2009.
60. *Govia Gtr Railway Ltd v The Associated Society of Locomotive Engineers And Firemen (ASLEF)* [2016] EWCA Civ 1309.

grounds of nationality and which required a driver and a guard on all trains to ensure the safe closing of doors rather than just a driver, could be said to constitute a deterrent to freedom of establishment or to make it less attractive.' Further, (at paragraph 44) Elias LJ observed that: 'It seems to us that every strike by workers in a particular EU state may be said at some level to make it less attractive for a company in another EU state to continue to operate in that state, and certainly it might discourage it from expanding its operations. The logic of this argument... is that every such action will prima facie involve a breach of Article 49 and in every case the issue will be whether the union - the onus being on it - can justify its actions. ... But it would hardly be compatible with the freedom of association or the protection of the right to strike as a fundamental right effectively to put the legality of industrial action in every strike with cross-border impact into the hands of the courts, with the onus on the union to persuade them that the action was not disproportionate.'

We may find litigious challenges based on EU law more prominent given the elaboration on the causes of the trade dispute now required to be set out in the ballot paper (from 2016 onwards) by virtue of the TUA 2016, section 5. However, if British exit of the European Union (Brexit) does take place as is planned for March 2019, it is highly unlikely that these constraints on industrial action stemming from the EU free movement rights of employers, will remain a feature of UK law.[61]

3.5 Full Versus Partial Strike

Under section 246 of TULRCA 1992 a strike means 'any concerted stoppage of work'. There are few distinctions made in law between a partial strike and a complete withdrawal of labour. Protection for 'industrial action' under section 219 of TULRCA 1992 encompasses any act done in pursuit of a trade dispute, which might be itemized on a ballot paper as a 'strike' or action 'short of a strike' (TULRCA 1992, section 229). In terms of protection from dismissal, the provisions relate to strikes and other forms of industrial action (see TULRCA 1992, ss 237 - 238A).

It has recently been established by the Supreme Court that the usual appropriate daily rate of deductions from pay will be 1/365, at least where there is a complete withdrawal of labour due to a strike on that day.[62] At common law, partial industrial action can lead to a partial deduction of pay.[63] In the case of *Sim*, the local authority which was the employer deducted a percentage of the salary of teachers who refused to cover the teaching of absent colleagues. Their breach of the implied contractual duty of trust and co-operation caused damage to the employer, the cost of which could be deducted from their wages under the

61. See *UK Department for Exiting the European Union*, 2017; and clause 7 of the European Union Withdrawal Bill.
62. See *Hartley and others v King Edward VI College* [2017] UKSC 39.
63. As in *Sim v Rotherham Metropolitan Borough Council* [1987] Ch 216.

doctrine of equitable set-off. There is also the possibility that partial action (such as refusing to answer certain queries) can lead to an employer withholding all pay,[64] but only where the employer does not direct any other work to be done. If instructions are issued that other tasks be performed, then the employer must compensate the worker for these.[65] Unions such as the University and College Union (UCU) sought to name and shame employers which deducted a day's pay for a two hour strike,[66] but were unsuccessful in practice.

3.6 Private Versus Public Sector

There is no obvious differentiation in the treatment of industrial action on the grounds of a straightforward public/private distinction. It does not matter whether the action is taken with respect to a private or public sector employer. Political strikes aimed at changing government policy would normally not be acceptable by virtue of the restriction on the substance of a lawful trade dispute under section 244(1), but it is worth knowing that industrial action can seek lawfully to influence decisions by Ministers of the Crown where they will be directly responsible for the terms and conditions of the workers involved. Under section 244(2) of TULRCA, this is possible if the dispute relates to matters which have been referred for consideration by a joint body on which the Minister is represented by virtue of any enactment or which cannot be settled without the Minister exercising a power conferred on the Minister by or under any enactment. It would seem that the application of this provision is confined to circumstances where the employer has to rely on the government to authorize the grant of the workers' demands, and industrial action is not otherwise rendered inappropriate by legislation governing that sector of employment (such as that concerning the police or armed forces – for which, see *infra*.)

4 THE EXPERIENCE WITH STRIKES IN ESSENTIAL SERVICES

4.1 The Prevalence of Strikes in Essential Services

There is not a major problem with the incidence of strikes or industrial action in the UK, which is at historically low levels (see *supra*). However, after the financial crisis of 2007/8 there have been significant cuts in government spending to address the UK sovereign debt crisis inherited from the New Labour Government's 'bailout' of the banks. The desire to initiate such cuts has been the subject of protests by trade unions in the public sector and by 2010 employers were urging new balloting rules for 'essential services' to be implemented by an

64. As in *Wiluszynski v London Borough of Tower Hamlets* [1989] IRLR 259 and *Spackman v London Metropolitan University* [2007] IRLR 744.
65. See Fox LJ and Nicholls LJ in *Wiluszynski*, last note.
66. See *UCU*, 2014.

incoming coalition Government.[67] Where public sector restructuring has taken place, for example regarding shift work and weekend working in the NHS, intensive industrial action has followed.[68]

4.2 The Role of Privatization and Outsourcing

Privatization and outsourcing of what were public sector services occurred in the 1980s, relating to (for example) water, gas and electricity.[69] This has led to imposition of statutory duties in those sectors, which is significant because the tort of breach of statutory duty is not covered by the immunity provided otherwise for a lawful trade dispute under section 219 of TULRCA 1992 (as discussed below). Privatization of the railways occurred in the 1990s, so that transport is strictly speaking a private sector matter in the UK.[70] It has been argued that even sectors like health, which seem apparently to be under state control, have shifted to forms of contracting out under public-private partnerships that also amount to a form of privatization (see Pownall 2013). The new restrictions of strikes in 'important public services' introduced by the Trade Union Act 2016 encompass both the private sector (e.g., transport and thereby the trains), and services which are currently (ostensibly) publicly provided by the state (such as the NHS). As the latter are currently subject to budgetary cuts and restructuring, additional restrictions on strikes in those services operate as a deterrent to trade union action resisting such changes.

4.3 Reactions in Policy Discourse

There are continuing proposals for further reform of strikes in essential services. For example, in September 2017 the Centre for Policy Studies published a paper by Sir Nicholas Finney arguing for more extensive restrictions on strikes in essential services, akin to those available elsewhere in Europe.[71] This is ostensibly on the basis of the hardship that strikes in such sectors cause to consumers and ordinary citizens in the UK. He makes a case for a total ban on strikes in essential services, as well as greater alignment of new restrictions on strikes in 'important public services' in the Trade Union Act 2016 with treatment of 'essential services' internationally. There is, however, for the time being in the UK no overarching principle that public sector workers are unable to strike or prohibition of strikes in essential services. The legal regime is more nuanced, as is shown below.

---

67. See *BBC*, 2014.
68. See *ONS*, 2017, which reports that the dispute involving junior doctors in the English National Health Service (NHS) 'accounted for 129,000 working days lost (around 40% of the total working days lost for 2016)'.
69. See *Kay/Thompson*, 1986.
70. *Gibb et al.*, 1996.
71. See *Finney*, 2017.

5 RESTRICTIONS OF THE RIGHT TO STRIKE IN ESSENTIAL SERVICES

In England (and indeed in the UK in general) there is no blanket ban on unionization or industrial action in 'essential services', except as regards the police and armed forces to whom criminal sanctions can apply. For other workers, the law relating to the contract of employment, economic torts and statutory requirements for immunity and protection from dismissal interact in more complex ways.

5.1 Exclusion from Collective Labour Relations Rights

Under the Police Act 1996, section 91 anyone who seeks to induce a police officer not to perform his or her duties commits a criminal offence with a potential penalty of two years' imprisonment and/or an unlimited fine, but no one has ever been so charged. Similar provision is made in respect of members of the armed forces by virtue of the Incitement to Disaffection Act 1934. In this way the UK legal system *excludes completely and ex ante* these particular groups of employees due to the presumed essential nature of their service from the right to strike. These restrictions would seem to be compliant with the view that such workers are 'members... of the administration of the state' under the ECHR.[72] This also coheres with exceptions set out in ILO Conventions Nos. 87 and 98. There is no record of any challenge to these exclusions from the right to strike.

5.2 Limitations on the Right to Strike (Controlled Strike Model)

Notwithstanding the excluded groups, prevention of strikes in essential services is achieved through two means grafted onto the peculiarities of the English legal treatment of industrial action (combining liability in tort with the conditions for statutory immunity from liability). One is the deliberate legislative extension of the tort of breach of statutory duty which does not come within the immunity otherwise given to industrial action under section 219 of TULRCA 1992. The other consists of the new balloting requirements for 'important public services' imposed by the Trade Union Act 2016 and associated secondary legislation.

5.2.1 The Relevance of the Tort of Breach of Statutory Duty

From a common law perspective, a particular concern is the tort of breach of statutory duty, which would seem to place particular constraints on employees delivering essential services. This tort is not expressly covered by the statutory immunity otherwise available under section 219 of TULRCA 1992, which refers to instead to such torts as:

72. As applied to government communication workers under *CCSU v UK*, Application No. 11603/85 (1987) 10 EHRR 269.

- Inducement of breach of contract
- Interference with contract
- Intimidation and
- Conspiracy.

In *Meade v Haringey*,[73] organization of strike action was considered to have arguably induced the local authority to breach its statutory duty to provide full time education to school students; although the case did not itself concern the liability of the union and the tort has not subsequently been used to restrict industrial action. The tort of inducement to breach a statutory duty is now explicitly set out in respect of sectors that have since been privatized. For example, under section 104 of the Communications Act 2003 regarding provision of telecommunication services[74] and would also seem to apply in respect of disruption to gas (by virtue of the Gas Act 1986, section 30), electricity (under section 22 of the Water Industry Act 1991) and water (according to section 27 of the Electricity Act 1989). So, there does remain a possibility that calls for action in these sectors cannot claim statutory immunity under section 219 of TULRCA, with consequent effects on protection from dismissal under section 238A. There is no case law on the scope of these statutory torts; instead they have had a profound chilling effect, such that industrial action has not been called in these sectors.

In respect of prison officers, the obligation not to induce breach of statutory duty is even more extensive. Anyone who seeks to induce a prison officer to strike or take industrial action commits a breach of statutory duty by virtue of the Criminal Justice and Public Order Act 1994, section 127 as amended by the Criminal Justice and Immigration Act 2008, section 138.[75] In such a situation, the Secretary of State to whom the duty is owed can bring an action (for example, for injunctive relief) and more generally there is a statutory right to apply for an injunction by any other person to whom the duty is owed. It is generally accepted therefore that, even when the corresponding findings of a Pay Review Body are not honoured, that the Prison Officers Association (POA) has no entitlement to call lawful industrial action.[76] Also, an instruction from the POA to its members to work according to the specific terms of their contract in a 'circular' has been regarded as a 'call' to take industrial action, which is grounds for injunctive relief due to the statutory restrictions on such action.[77]

By way of contrast, the older offences of interference with the Royal Mail (see the Post Office Act 1953, ss 58 and 68) no longer apply in respect of industrial action in contemplation or furtherance of a lawful trade dispute

73. *Meade v Haringey* [1979] ICR 494.
74. See *Deakin/Morris*, 2012, 1045.
75. As discussed by *Davies*, 2015, 464 et seq.; and *Deakin/Morris*, 2012, 1045.
76. See below for more detailed discussion of The *Ministry of Justice v POA* [2008] ICR 702; [2008] IRLR 380 (QB).
77. See *Ministry of Justice v POA* [2017] RWHC 1839 (QB).

(Postal Services Act 2000, section 83[78]). Industrial action has recently been called by Royal Mail workers with respect to pensions and the injunction issued was not due to any statutory tort, but rather the content of a collective agreement between the union and Royal Mail requiring conciliation before action was taken.[79]

5.2.2 The Restrictions on 'Important Public Services' under the Trade Union Act 2016

The Trade Union Act 2016 does not ban outright those employed in 'important public services' from taking industrial action. Instead, the legislation seeks to deter them from doing so by imposing different balloting requirements on the call for action in such services.

From 2016, section 3 of the TUA 2016 (amending TULRCA 1992, section 226) introduced additional requirements in respect of industrial action ballots in 'important public services', namely approval from 40% of those eligible to vote (as well as the new standard 50% turnout). Those 'important public services' covered are elaborated in the following statutory instruments: Important Public Services (Health) Regulations 2017; Important Public Services (Fire) Regulations 2017; Important Public Services (Border Security) Regulations 2017; Important Public Services (Transport) Regulations 2017; Important Public Services (Education) Regulations 2017. The definition of 'important public services' and corresponding lists in the Regulations are notorious for the legislature's complete refusal to take account of the case law of the ILO Committee on Freedom of Association regarding 'essential services'.

The high threshold of support for ballots in 'important public services' can be linked to an attempt to ensure that trade union action would not interfere with wage cuts, restructuring and redundancies entailed in bringing public finances under control in response to budgetary measures planned by the Conservative Government of the time. On election to government in May 2015, the Chancellor, George Osborne, announced £12 billion of spending cuts. In this way, the ability of trade unions to challenge forms of privatization of public services, such as new forms of contracting in the NHS would diminish.[80] The initial Impact Assessment (IA) of 2015 estimated (at paragraph 80) that the reduction of the number of strikes in the transport, education, health and social work and border force sectors would be 'in scope of the £2 billion deregulatory target'.[81]

In this respect, the slippage from 'essential public services' to 'important public services' in the TUA was interesting. This was done not, as the ILO supervisory bodies would allow, to prevent danger to 'the life, personal safety or

78. As discussed by *Deakin/Morris*, 2012, 1117.
79. *Royal Mail Group v Communication Workers Union* [2017] EWHC 2585 (QB).
80. See *House of Commons*, 2016.
81. Discussed in *Novitz*, 2016.

health of the whole or part of the population'.[82] At the time that the legislation was proposed, Ford and Novitz[83] observed that neither 'education' nor 'transport' are regarded as an 'essential service' by the ILO CFA. Firstly, temporary interruption of schooling does not endanger 'life, personal safety or health'. Teachers therefore retain the right to strike without interference, despite some inconvenience and financial burdens for parents and their employers. Nor, more generally, does the broader economic impact of industrial action render a service 'essential'. The CFA states clearly that: 'The possible long-term consequences of strikes in the teaching sector do not justify their prohibition.'[84] Similarly, transport is not usually regarded as an 'essential service' for, although 'it is recognized that a stoppage in services or undertakings such as transport companies, railways... [etc.] might disturb the normal life of the community, it can hardly be admitted that the stoppage of such services could cause an acute national emergency.'[85] The key exception would be air traffic control, in respect of which a minimum service or 'compensatory guarantee' of compulsory arbitration could be appropriate. It is therefore not surprising that in 2016 on reviewing the content of the Trade Union Act 2016, the ILO Committee of Experts on the Application of Conventions and Recommendations (CEACR) requested that 'the Government to review this matter with the social partners concerned ... so as to ensure that the heightened requirement of support of 40 per cent of all workers does not apply to education and transport services.'[86]

5.2.2.1 *The Special Provision Made for Balloting Requirements*

As noted above, the new requirement for important public services requires that at least 40% of those entitled to vote in the ballot must have given their approval of the action (in addition to the 50% turnout threshold and the requirement of a majority of those voting supporting the action).

A consultation paper titled *Ballot Thresholds in Important Public Services*[87] issued prior to enactment of the Trade Union Act 2016 considered the rationale for this measure. It said (at 1) that disruptive action on the basis of low ballot turnouts was 'undemocratic' and that the Government's key objectives were 'to ensure that industrial action is only used as a measure of last resort', as well as to avoid the far-reaching effects of strikes in public services. What was needed for a legitimate ballot in these sectors was 'clear and ongoing support'.

This phraseology and the notion of the need in 'important public services' for 40% approval of those eligible to vote had a precedent. It was set, not by a past Conservative government, but by legislation introduced by New Labour in

82. *ILO*, 2006, para. 585.
83. *Ford/Novitz*, 2015, 531 et seq.
84. *ILO*, 2006, para. 590.
85. *Ibid.*, para. 637.
86. *Ewing/Hendy*, 2016, 405.
87. *Department for Business, Energy & Industrial Strategy*, 2015.

1999 in respect of balloting thresholds for statutory recognition of a union so as to enable collective bargaining on pay, hours and holidays. Statutory recognition must be supported 'by a majority of the workers voting' *and* 'at least 40 per cent of the workers constituting the bargaining unit' (TULRCA, Schedule A1, paragraph 29, inserted by the Employment Relations Act 1999). The then Labour Government articulated the issue as follows: 'First, without real and substantial support amongst employees, collective bargaining simply will not work. Second, since collective bargaining has an impact on all employees, not just those claiming union representation, it is right that it should be granted only in circumstances where substantial support is demonstrated'.[88]

That iteration of 'substantial' or 'clear' or 'clear and on-going' support was repeated by the UK Conservative government in 2016 due to the 'far-reaching effects on significant numbers of ordinary people who have no association with the dispute'. The 40% requirement is apparently designed to 'get the balance right between the interests of union members and the interests of the majority of people who rely on the services they provide'.[89]

5.2.2.2 The Legal Consequences of These Restrictions

The legal consequence of these restrictions on balloting in 'important public services' where the threshold of approval of 40% of those eligible to vote is not met (in addition to the 50% turnout and the requirement of a majority in favour of the action) is that they prevent the industrial action called having the protection of the statutory immunity. This means that an employer can seek injunctive relief to prevent the strike taking place and, if it does take place, can seek damages from the union in tort (subject to the restrictions under sections 20–22 of TULRCA 1992). This will also have flow on effects for protection for strikers (in important public services) from dismissal. If these special balloting thresholds are not met, then they will not be able to claim protection under the automatic twelve week period by virtue of section 238A of TULRCA 1992.

Ironically, the de facto effects of the specific restrictions on 'important public services' may have relatively little impact in practice. Darlington and Dobson[90] have observed that it is the 50% turnout rule which would have the most devastating effects due to a history of apathetic turnout in industrial action ballots in the UK. Their study demonstrates that between 2002 and 2014 only 85 out of 158 strike ballots would have met the 50% threshold, and that it is much more difficult to secure the threshold in larger strikes reaching across a sector. Only 440,000 workers achieved a turnout rate over 50%, while 3.3 million workers would have been debarred from taking lawful action. The effect of the 40% approval threshold in important public services, however, 'would have

88. *Board of Trade by Command of her Majesty*, 1998, para. 4.16.
89. *UK Department for Business Innovation & Skills*, 2015, 3 et seq.
90. *Ibid.*, 24 et seqq.

very little *further effect*',[91] particularly in fire service and transport where the relevant unions tend to obtain large turn-outs and overwhelming majorities. Nevertheless, it is possible that the 50% turnout is having unintended consequences, leading to more engagement with strike ballots. One example is the Royal Mail ballot (discussed above) entailed a 73.7% turnout and 89% in favour of a strike.[92] A second illustration is the recent industrial dispute (also involving pension provision) taken by university staff nationally, in which only six universities (out of 68 potentially in dispute) were unable to reach the threshold in the first ballot. The turnout at the University of Bristol was 64.1% turnout and 90.1% in favour of taking strike action.[93] In neither the case of the Royal Mail nor the University of Bristol did the further 40% threshold apply, as these do not constitute 'important public services', but it would have been satisfied in both cases.

6 COMPENSATORY MEASURES FOR RESTRICTIONS

There is generally no quid pro quo for the more subtle forms of restriction (relating to the tort of breach of statutory duty or the additional balloting requirements for 'important public services'). There is no compensatory system for those in the telecommunications, gas, electricity or water sectors - nor generally for those deemed to be in 'important public services'. There are special measures taken in relation to the police, armed services and prison officers to provide pay review. However, it seems that these are not regarded by the government as binding.

In a case concerning industrial action taken by prison officers in 2007,[94] interim injunctive relief was ordered by Mr Justice Ramsey to stop their union acting in support of the strike. In 2008, the merits of the union's case were argued in full when determining whether an injunction should be maintained in respect of any future industrial action.

It was alleged by the Ministry of Justice that the strike was in breach of a Joint Industrial Relations Procedural Agreement (JIRPA), under which prison officers forego industrial action and agree instead that their pay be determined in response to recommendations made by an independent Pay Review Body (PRB). In 2007, the Government agreed to the pay increase recommended by the PRB, but only implemented it over a two year process. Counsel for the POA argued that the Government was not adequately implementing the recommendations of the PRB and were not, therefore, seeking an equitable remedy 'with clean hands' and were not entitled to injunctive relief. The submissions focussed also on the extent to which UK procedures, and the ability to depart from the recommendations of an independent pay review body, constituted a departure from ILO

91. *Ibid.*, 31.
92. *BBC*, 2017.
93. See *UCU*, 2018.
94. *The Ministry of Justice v POA* [2008] ICR 702; [2008] IRLR 380 (QBD).

Conventions and the recommendations of ILO supervisory bodies, as well as the jurisprudence of the ECHR.

Nonetheless, an injunction was issued with reference to the effects of any industrial action in this sector, namely those identified by per Mr Justice Wyn Williams (at paragraph 63) as an inability 'to provide decent and safe prison regimes' and the generation of 'incidents of prisoner unrest'. His view (at paragraph 64) was that 'very significant inequitable conduct on the part of the Claimant would be necessary before there would be a proper justification for withholding the injunction'.

7 SECURING ESSENTIAL SERVICES BY FURTHER MEANS

Delivery of essential services can be ensured by other means under the emergency powers reserved to government in the UK under currently the Civil Contingencies Act (CCA) 2004 (the successor to the Emergency Powers Act 1920). This enables the government to act by proclaiming a state of emergency or to coordinate responses regarding emergencies.

7.1 The Legislature, Executive and Local Authorities

Part 2 of the CCA 2004 updates the 1920 Emergency Powers Act, which was previously operationalized on various occasions including the Miners' Strike of 1972.[95] This legislation allows for the making of temporary special legislation (emergency regulations) to help deal with the most serious of emergencies. These powers are however best regarded as being under the control of the executive branch of government as opposed to the legislature *per se*. Emergency regulations issued cannot entail forced labour; they can neither impose compulsory military service nor (under section 23(3)) 'prohibit... participation in, or any activity in connection with a strike or other industrial action'.

The Emergency Powers Act 1920 was used twelve times in Britain and used to mobilize to address strikes, but military can be drafted in to carry out certain vital tasks under both the CCA 2004 and the Emergency Powers Act 1964 without proclamation of an emergency, as were 18,000 troops for the Olympic Games of 2012 in London.[96] Notably, however, this was not done to avert strikes. Instead, the rail, tube and bus unions managed to negotiate 'bonuses' for their members to take account of the additional work that the Olympic Games demanded.[97]

Part 1 of the Civil Contingencies Act 2004 (and supporting Regulations) on 'emergency preparedness' establish who is required to respond to an emergency, including those responsible at the local level who are divided into two

95. *Deakin/Morris* 2012, 1118.
96. As discussed in *Brooke-Holland* 2017, 2.
97. See *BBC*, 2011; *Evening Standard*, 2012; *The Telegraph*, 2011.

categories. The first category consists of organizations core to the response to most emergencies (the emergency services, local authorities, NHS bodies). They are subject to the full set of civil protection duties, including:

- Assessment of the risk of emergencies occurring and contingency planning
- Emergency plans
- Business continuity management arrangements
- Arrangements for public information
- Sharing of information with other local responders to enhance co-ordination
- Cooperation and coordination with other local responders
- Advice and assistance to businesses and voluntary organizations (anticipated to be given by local authorities only)

The second category of organizations are termed 'cooperating bodies' and include the Health and Safety Executive, transport and utility companies. They are more likely to be engaged in assisting with incidents that affect their own sectors and their duties are less onerous. Local resilience 'forums' are formed by both category 1 and 2 organizations.

It has been observed that the CCA 2004 does however offer 'more defined geographical bounds' rather than requiring the whole of Great Britain or Northern Ireland to be affected. There was also a need to take account of the arrangements for devolution in Scotland, Wales and, to a lesser extent, Northern Ireland'.[98]

7.2 The Judiciary (Courts and Tribunals)

The courts and tribunals do not *per se* invoke special rules when injunctions are sought against strikes in essential services. Rather, they merely evaluate the case for injunctive relief on the standard *American Cyanamid* principles, namely whether there is a prima facie case and where the balance of convenience lies. They should also, of course, consider whether a party has an arguable case that could succeed at trial (section 221 of TULRCA 1992).

However, in cases regarding injunctions, the courts have had regard to the consequences of not granting the relief sought in terms of its effects. In a case involving prison officers,[99] a circular distributed by the union stated that members had no obligation to volunteer for additional work and should cease to do so. This would include, for example, offering first aid and working additional hours to cover staffing shortages. While the judge accepted that the Ministry of Justice was relying on the goodwill of prison officers such that there was no obvious breach of contract, there was an obligation to comply with additional

98. *Walker*, 2014, 212.
99. *Ministry of Justice v Prison Officers' Association* [2017] EWHC 1839.

reasonable lawful orders and the judge was 'not oblivious to the force of the contention that the concerted withdrawal of services might have on prison safety generally' (paragraph 50). This is arguably reminiscent of consideration of these effects in an earlier case.[100] Courts do not however act as arbiters regarding minimum pay or as mediators and conciliators regarding resolution of the underlying conflict.

7.3 The Social Partners

It is possible for the social partners to conclude 'no strike' agreements. An example can be found in the collective agreement (discussed above) concluded between Royal Mail and the Communication Workers Union (CWU), which is no doubt a legacy of old legislative requirements that industrial action would not disrupt the post. While easily meeting the new statutory balloting requirements for both normal strikes and 'important public services' under the Trade Union Act 2016, the requirement under the collective agreement to pursue mediation was binding.[101]

It is strange that the new balloting requirements for 'important public services' were introduced in respect of the fire service, where the social partners have already made provision for a minimum service.[102] Given that the union in the fire service is capable of generating large turnouts and large majorities, these minimum service arrangements makes more sense in ensuring that the public service continues to be delivered, and is in accordance with the mechanism endorsed by the ILO.

It is always possible for trade unions to implement further balloting restrictions via their rules, but in the light of extensive restrictions imposed by legislation, this option has not been utilized.

8 EVALUATION AND CONCLUSION

8.1 Performance Evaluation

In terms of a performance evaluation, there are no serious allegations in an English (or UK) context that the strikes in essential services jeopardize a proper level of service. In part, this seems to be due to self-monitoring by unions in these sectors. For example, even in relation to the English junior doctors' strike, considerable care was taken by those organizing and conducting the action to find minimum replacement labour which would not lead to lives being endangered or further negative health effects. While day long stoppages were staged,

100. *The Ministry of Justice v POA* [2008] ICR 702; [2008] IRLR 380 (QBD).
101. See *Royal Mail Group v Communication Workers Union* [2017] EWHC 2585 (QB).
102. As was even acknowledged in the relevant consultation paper (*UK Department for Business Innovation & Skills*, 2015, 6).

week long action was abandoned due to the effects this would have.[103] This however did lead to a capitulation, by and large, to Government demands regarding the content of new junior doctor contracts. To this extent, the inability to strike (alongside the unreliability of enforcement of Pay Review Body findings) means that there is little effective bargaining in such sectors. The current Conservative Government seems unconcerned by clear non-compliance with international standards, having deliberately ignored the findings of international supervisory bodies in relation to the Trade Union Act 2016.[104] Any autonomous, self-imposed regulation by trade unions has to be understood in terms of the shadow of the law under which it is adopted. The complex matrix of treatment of complete bans on some public sector strikes, operation of the tort of breach of statutory duty (which seems to lie outside the statutory immunity otherwise application to calls for strikes under TULRCA 1992) and new balloting rules for 'important public services' all have a significant chilling effect. It is arguable in the UK that neither the process nor the outcomes are acceptable.

8.2 Summary and Conclusions

The law relating to treatment of strikes in essential services in the UK is remarkably complex. Further, the UK is composed of (differently demarcated) devolved legislatures which depart from (or seek to detract from) labour legislation otherwise adopted by the UK Parliament in various respects. This state of affairs is exemplified by the treatment of the TUA 2016, which is arguably only fully implemented in England, being treated in different ways in Wales, Scotland and Northern Ireland. The English legal and industrial relations systems were therefore the focus of this case study.

There is no constitutional or legislative right to strike in England, but instead certain acts in the context of a 'trade dispute' fall within the scope of statutory immunity provided by TULRCA 1992 (as amended by the TUA 2016). Understanding the operation of this immunity and consequent protections from dismissal therefore turns on an understanding of:

(a) the economic torts which are (and are not) covered by the statutory immunity;
(b) the extensive procedural requirements concerning balloting and notice; and
(c) the limitations on the substance of a lawful trade dispute, which has had significant implications for the privatization of essential services.

103. See *Campbell*, 2018.
104. *Ewing/Hendy*, 2016.

There is no distinctive regulatory overarching regime for public (as compared to private) employers nor for essential services (in comparison with other services and sectors of the economy).

Some workers engaged in delivering essential services (such as the police and armed forces) are barred from taking industrial action through the imposition of criminal liability, although there have been no recent prosecutions (as there has been no industrial action). Other sectors, such as water, gas, electricity and telecommunications, are limited through the tort of breach of statutory duty made explicit in statutes governing the delivery of former public services now wholly or partially privatized. Notably, this is an economic tort that is not covered by immunity under TULRCA 1992. There has also been a recent regulatory innovation made in respect of 'important public services' (covering a mixture of public and private and essential and non-essential services) under the TUA 2016, which imposes a higher balloting threshold (40% of those eligible to vote being in favour in addition to the now standard 50% turnout and bare majority vote). Additionally, there is scope for exercise of emergency powers to assist in civil contingencies, although there is little evidence that these have recently been used to avert industrial action. Together, all these measures have a substantial chilling effect on access to industrial action in essential and other services. In this regard, the English situation appears irrational and inconsistent and in no way compliant with established international labour standards.

Bibliography

-----, UCU tells universities to pay unlawfully docked money back to striking staff, UCU 15/5/2014. Available at https://www.ucu.org.uk/article/7061/UCU-tells-universities-to-pay-unlawfully-docked-money-back-to-striking-staff (last checked 24 March 2018)

-----, Essential services strike ban 'may need to be option', BBC 6/8/2014. Available at http://www.bbc.co.uk/news/uk-10888785 (last checked 24 March 2018)

-----, *Olympics: RMT union says rail pay deal 'groundbreaking', BBC 10/5/2011. Available at https://www.bbc.com/news/uk-england-london-13343578*

-----, *No bus strikes during the olympics as drivers accept 577 bonus cash offer, Evening Standard 18/7/2012. Available at https://www.standard.co.uk/news/transport/no-bus-strikes-during-the-olympics-as-drivers-accept-577-bonus-cash-offer-7956627.html*

-----, *Tube drivers to get £1,800 bonus not to strike during the Olympics, The Telegraph 14/9/2011. Available at http://www.telegraph.co.uk/sport/olympics/news/8761441/Tube-drivers-to-get-1800-bonus-not-to-strike-during-the-Olympics.html*

-----, Royal Mail staff vote to strike over pensions, BBC 3/11/2017. Available at https://www.bbc.com/news/business-41484024

Apps, Katherine, Damages Claims Against Trade Unions after Viking and Laval, European Law Review 34/2009, 141 et seqq.
Bercusson, Brian, The Trade Union Movement and the European Union: Judgment Day, European Law Journal 13/2007, 279 et seqq.
Board of Trade by Command of her Majesty, White Paper Fairness at Work. Cm3968, 1998
Bogg, Alan and Ewing, Keith, The Implications of the RMT Case, Industrial Law Journal 43(3)2014, 221 et seqq.
Brooke-Holland, Louisa, Military Aid to the Civil Authorities, Parliamentary Briefing Paper, 2017
Campbell, Denis, BMA calls off September junior doctors' strike after 'scores' of protests, The Guardian 5/9/2016. Available at https://www.theguardian.com/society/2016/sep/05/bma-calls-off-september-junior-doctors-strike-after-scores-of-protests
Certification Officer, Annual Report 2016-17, 2017
Certification Officer, Corporate report. Employers' associations: current list and schedule, 2017. Available at https://www.gov.uk/government/publications/public-list-of-employers-associations-listed-and-unlisted/employers-associations-current-list-and-schedule#about-the-list/, last checked 24 March 2018 (c)
Countouris, Nicola/Freedland, Mark, Injunctions, Cyanamid and the Corrosion of the Right to Strike in the UK, UCL Working Paper, LRI WP 1/2010, 2010
Cully, Mark et al., Britain at Work: As Depicted by the 1998 Workplace Employee Relations Survey, 1999
Darlington, Ralph/Dobson, John, The Conservative Government's Proposed Strike Ballot Thresholds: The Challenge to Trade Unions, 2015
Davies, ACL, Employment Law, 2015
Davies, One Step Forward, Two Steps Back? The Viking and Laval Cases in the CJEU Industrial Law Journal 37/2008, 126 et seqq.
Davies, Perspectives on Labour Law, 2nd ed, 2009
Davies, The Trade Union (Wales) Act 2017/Y Ddeddf Yr Undebau Llafur (Cymru) 2017, Industrial Law Journal 2018, 47, 135 et seqq.
Davies, Paul/Freedland, Mark, Kahn-Freund's Labour and the Law, 3rd ed. 1983
Davies, Paul/Freedland, Mark, Labour Legislation and Public Policy, 1993
Deakin, Simon/Morris, Gillian, Labour Law, 6th ed., 2012
Deakin, Simon/Randall, John, Rethinking the Economic Torts, Modern Law Review 72/2009, 519 et seqq.
Department for Business, Energy and Industrial Strategy (BEIS), Trade Union Membership 2016: Statistical Bulletin, 2017
Donovan Royal Commission, Report on Trade Union and Employers' Associations 1965 - 1968 Cmnd 3623, 1968
Dukes, Ruth, Otto Kahn-Freund and Collective Laissez-Faire: An Edifice without a Keystone?, Modern Law Review 72/2009, 220 et seqq.
Dukes, Ruth, The Right to Strike under UK Law: Something more than a slogan? Industrial Law Journal 40/2011, 302 et seqq.

Ewing, Keith (ed.), The Right to Strike: From the Trade Disputes Act 1906 to a Trade Union Freedom Bill 2006, 2006

Ewing, Keith/Hendy, John, The Trade Union Act 2016 and the Failure of Human Rights, Industrial Law Journal 45(3)2016, 391 et seqq.

Ewing, Keith/Hendy, John, New Perspectives on Collective Labour Law: Trade Union Recognition and Collective Bargaining, Industrial Law Journal 46(1)2017, 23 et seqq.

Finney, Nicholas, Strikes in the Essential Services: time for further protection for the public? Centre for Policy Studies paper, 2017. Available at https://www.cps.org.uk/publications/strikes-in-essential-services-time-for-further-protection-for-the-public, last accessed 24 March 2018

Ford, Michael/Novitz, Tonia, An Absence of Fairness... Restrictions on Industrial Action and Protest in the Trade Union Bill 2015, Industrial Law Journal, 44(4)2015, 522 et seqq.

Ford, Michael/Novitz, Tonia, Legislating For Control: The Trade Union Act 2016, Industrial Law Journal 45(3)2016, 277 et seqq.

Fredman, Sandra, The New Rights: Labour Law and Ideology in the Thatcher Years (1992) Oxford Journal of Legal Studies 12/1992, 24 et seqq.

Gibb, Richard, Lowndes, Theresa and Charlton, Clive, The Privatization of British Rail, Applied Geography 16(1)1996, 35 et seqq.

Hayek, F.A., 1980s Unemployment and the Unions: Essays on the Impotent Price Structure of Britain and Monopoly in the Labour Market, 2nd ed., 1984

Head, Michael, Calling out the troops and the Civil Contingencies Act: Some Questions of Concern, Public Law 2010, 340 et seqq.

House of Commons, Trade Union Bill, 2016. Available at https://hansard.parliament.uk/Commons/2016-04-27/debates/16042764000002/TradeUnionBill, last accessed 24 March 2018

ILO, Committee on Freedom of Association (CFA) Digest of Decisions, 5th ed., 2006

Kahn-Freund, Otto, Legal Framework, in Flanders, in Allan and Clegg, Hugh (eds)), The System of Industrial Relations in Great Britain, 1954

Kay, John Alexander/Thompson, David J., Privatisation: A policy in search of a rationale. The Economic Journal 96(381)1986, 18 et seqq.

Lorber, Pascale/Novitz, Tonia, Industrial Relations Law in the UK, 2012

Mantouvalou, Virginia, Labour Rights in the European Convention on Human Rights: An Intellectual Justification for an Integrated Approach to Interpretation, Human Rights Law Review 13/2013, 529

Novitz, Tonia, The Paradigm of Sustainability in a European Social Context: Collective Participation in Protection of Future Interests? The International Journal of Comparative Labour Law and Industrial Relations 31/2015, 243 et seqq.

Novitz, Tonia, UK Regulation of Strike Ballots and Notices – Moving Beyond 'Democracy'? Australian Journal of Labour Law 29/2016, 226 et seqq.

Novitz, Tonia/Syrpis, Phil, Giving with One Hand and Taking with the Other: Protection of Workers' Human Rights in the European Union in Fenwick/Novitz (eds), Human Rights at Work, 2010

Office for National Statistics (ONS), Labour disputes in the UK: 2016, 2017. Available at https://www.ons.gov.uk/employmentandlabourmarket/peopleinwork/workplacedisputesandworkingconditions/articles/labourdisputes/latest#review-of-1997-to-2016

Pownall, Holly, Neoliberalism, Austerity and the Health and Social Care Act 2012: The Coalition Government's programme for the NHS and its implications for the public sector workforce, Industrial Law Journal 42(4)2013, 422 et seqq.

Shenfield, Arthur, What Right to Strike? With Commentaries by Cyril Grunfeld and Sir Leonard Neal, 1986

Simpson, Bob, The Labour Injunction, Unlawful Means and the Right to Strike, The Modern Law Review 50/1987, 506 et seqq.

Simpson, Bob, The Labour Injunction and Industrial Action Ballots, Industrial Law Journal 42/2013, 54

Syrett, Keith, 'Immunity', 'Privilege' and 'Right': British Trade Unions and the Language of Labour Law Reform, Journal of Law and Society 25/1998, 388 et seqq.

University and College Union (UCU), USS ballot results: January 2018. Available at https://www.ucu.org.uk/ussballotresult_jan18

UK Department for Business, Energy & Industrial Strategy, Electronic balloting for industrial action: Knight review, 2017

UK Department for Business, Energy & Industrial Strategy, Trade union Act, BIS/15/418, 2015

UK Department for Business Innovation & Skills, Ballot Thresholds in Important Public Services. Impact Assessment, BIS/15/418, 2015

UK Department for Exiting the European Union, White Paper, Legislating for the United Kingdom's withdrawal from the European Union. Cm9446, 2017

Walker, Clive, The governance of emergency arrangements, The International Journal of Human Rights 18(2)2014, 211 et seqq.

CHAPTER 16

United States

Joseph Slater

1 GENERAL BACKGROUND: COUNTRY PROFILE

1.1 Introduction

To understand the strike rights of employees in essential services in the United States of America ('the US'), two points must be stressed at the outset. First, labor laws in the US do not define 'essential services' for the purpose of strike rights or otherwise, and generally such laws do not follow the rules the International Labour Organization (ILO) has set out in this area. Second, strike rights and other rights relating to collective bargaining are typically quite different for public employees and private employees. Private employees have broad strike rights at least on paper under federal statutes: the Railway Labor Act (RLA, covering the railway and airline industries), and, more relevant here, the National Labor Relations Act (NLRA) (governing employees in most other occupations).[1] Examining the law 'in action', however, shows that strike rights for private employees are often significantly limited in practice. Public employees, in contrast, are typically covered by the laws of the states in which they work, and sometimes by the laws of counties or cities within those states. The clear majority of public-sector labor laws in the US bar strikes by *all* public employees.[2]

In the absence of a formal definition of 'essential employees', this chapter will consider the strike rights of the following types of employees: police, firefighters, prison guards, and hospital, and utility workers. Police and fire employees are exclusively public employees (and thus covered by state and local government laws); prison guards are mostly, but not exclusively, public employees; and hospital and utility employees can be either public or private employees. The rights to strike (or lack thereof) of all these employees are determined primarily by whether they are public or private workers, not by the type of work that they do.

1. National Labor Relations Act, 29 USC. §§ 151-169.
2. See generally *Harris/Slater/Lofaso/Garden*, 2016, chapter 11.

No single book chapter could discuss the laws governing public employees in each of the fifty states in the US However, US public-sector labor laws have many important things in common regarding the strike rights of the relevant employees; further, where they differ, they tend to use one of several discrete types of models. For example, no public-sector labor law in the US permits police, fire service, or prison guards to strike. A minority of states do not even authorize collective bargaining for these (or other) public employees. Thus, in a majority of states, public employees have a legal right to bargain collectively, but no legal right to strike. Instead, US public-sector labor law has developed various, but at least somewhat standardized, alternative methods for resolving bargaining impasses, using combinations of mediation, 'fact-finding' and various types of interest arbitration.[3]

This chapter first describes the political and historical background that led to modern US labor laws. It then describes strike rights and related rules for essential employees in the private sector. It then turns to the more complex issue of bargaining and strike rights for employees in the public sector, among other things describing the different types of models of bargaining and strike rights that exist among the states. This includes, but is not limited to, sanctions for illegal strikes and alternatives to strikes. The chapter also discusses policy debates and actual experience with strikes. It ends with this author's evaluation of US labor law rules in this area.

1.2 Political and Historical Background

The first question to ask about US law is why such a sharp distinction exists between labor law rules for the private and public sectors. In addition to the differences noted above, while most private-sector workers won the right to bargain collectively and strike in 1935 when the NLRA was enacted, public workers did not begin to win collective bargaining rights until decades later, with most states passing laws authorizing at least some form of collective bargaining for at least some public employees in the 1960s and 1970s. Even today, eight US states do not permit any public employees to bargain collectively, much less strike, around a dozen more only let one-to-four categories of public employees bargain collectively, and fewer than a dozen permit any public employees at all to strike.[4] As other chapters of this book demonstrate, this is somewhat unusual: in most of the other countries discussed, the rights of public and private sector workers are much more similar.

These distinctions arose for several reason. First is the legacy of a strike by essential employees: the Boston police strike of 1919. While public workers in the US had no collective bargaining rights at that time, some had organized unions as early as the 1830s. By the second decade of the twentieth century,

3. *Ibid.*
4. *Kearney/Mareschal*, 2014, 65 et seq., 245 et seq., 269 et seq.

public-sector unionization began a small but significant uptick, with several major public-sector unions (including but not limited to the American Federation of Teachers and the International Association of Firefighters) forming and affiliating with the American Federation of Labor (AFL, the main umbrella group for labor unions in the US). In 1919, the AFL reversed its previous policy against chartering police unions, and in less than a year, the AFL had chartered thirty-seven police locals. Public employers and private business interests strongly opposed police unionization. This came to a head in Boston, where police officers, dissatisfied with their 'independent' worker organization, decided to form an AFL-affiliated local. Boston's police commissioner barred such affiliation. After leaders of the police union refused to leave the AFL, the commissioner suspended several of them. In response, essentially all of Boston's police officers went on strike in September 1919. The strike was illegal, and for a few days, Boston suffered significant lawlessness and some deaths related to the strike. The governor of the state, Calvin Coolidge, sent in troops to break to the strike. None of the strikers was ever rehired, and the aftermath of the strike significantly restrained the movement for public-sector unions. All police unions affiliated with the AFL were soon destroyed or disbanded. Various local governments barred police (and often all other public employees) from affiliating with the AFL. Courts upheld such bans until the late 1960s. After years of increases, the union density rate in the public sector fell in the 1920s. More broadly, for many decades to come, union opponents used the memory of this strike to combat not just the idea of police strikes and police unions, but also to oppose suggestions that any type of public employee should have the right to bargain collectively.[5]

The Boston strike was not the only reason public-sector labor law developed so differently than private-sector labor law. Constitutional and political concerns regarding states' rights and federalism made any notion of a federal law granting collective bargaining rights to state and local government employees a non-starter. Specifically, the 10th Amendment of the US Constitution, which reserves powers not granted to the federal government to the states, would have been a significant obstacle to a federal law regulating the labor relations of states and their subdivisions.

The highly subdivided nature of government in the US also played a crucial role. Cities, and even political subdivisions of cities such as school boards, had significant political independence, and political leaders of such entities, *e.g.* mayors of cities, were not keen on giving their employees collective bargaining rights. In the absence of legislation, state courts made the 'common law' of public-sector labor law, and these courts were quite deferential to the judgments of public officials that unionization of public workers was inappropriate and

5. *Slater*, 2004, chapter 1.

harmful. In the middle of the 20th century, some courts added the otherwise obscure 'non-delegation' doctrine of an older era of constitutional law to hold that even *voluntary* collective bargaining by a public employer was an unconstitutional delegation of public power (*e.g.*, power to set wages of public employees) to a private party (a union). By the late 20th century, most jurisdictions in the US had rejected that approach, but, as discussed further below, non-delegation objections still block some public-sector union rights in some jurisdictions. Further, even though after the Boston police strike through at least the mid-1960s, public-sector unions essentially all renounced the strike weapon, judges still routinely upheld bars on public-sector workers merely belonging to unions, on the ground that this would inevitably lead to strikes. Judges in this era simply were incapable of conceiving of a system of labor relations that did not involve traditional strikes.[6]

The structure of the state in the US continues to play a role. Because public-sector labor law is set by state and sometimes local governments, states controlled by more conservative, anti-union forces have been able to deny not just the right to strike for essential public employees, but the right even to bargain collectively for most or all public employees. The US has always had a strain of anti-union politics more virulent than that of, say, Western Europe or Canada, and to the extent such forces are concentrated in certain states and regions (*e.g.*, the southern states), they have effectively blocked labor rights.

Meanwhile, for private employees, the NLRA was enacted into law in 1935. It provided the right to strike to the private-sector employees that it covered. Relevant here, the NLRA has always covered private utilities and their employees. It was not until the 1974, however, that the NLRA was amended to cover employees in private hospitals.[7] Utility workers, workers in private prisons, and hospital employees all have strike rights under the NLRA, but there are a few more limits on the hospital employees, discussed further below.

Currently in the US generally, strike rights, limits, and prohibitions are a matter of statutory law, but in a few instances (noted below) common law rules on strikes are still relevant.

2 COLLECTIVE LABOR RELATIONS

Public-sector unionism, in the past half-century, has become an increasingly large part of US unionism as a whole. In 1955, all the public-sector unions put together in the US had a combined membership of around 400,000. By the 1970s, the total was over 4 million.[8] In 2016, unions represented 7,834,000 public employees, compared with 8,437 million workers in the (much larger) private sector. In 2016, unions represented 37.9% of public workers, substantially

6. See *Slater*, 2000.
7. 29 USC § 152 (1974).
8. *Slater*, 2000, 193.

higher than the 7.3% rate for private-sector workers.[9] These figures represent trends of public-sector union density rates around 35-40% since the later 1970s, and private-sector union density figures steadily declining into single digits from a high of around 35% in the mid-1950s.

Unions in the US are mostly under the umbrella of the AFL-CIO. The old AFL merged with the Congress of Industrial Organizations (formed in the 1930s) in the mid-1950s. A few of the most significant public-sector unions, however, are not affiliated with the AFL-CIO: notably here, the Fraternal Order of Police (the largest police union in the U.S.) is not affiliated. This too is in significant part due to the Boston police strike and the resulting long history (through the later 1960s) of public employers forbidding their employees to join unions affiliated with the AFL, and later AFL-CIO.

Employers also have organizations. In the private sector, the Chamber of Commerce and National Association of Manufacturers have long been active in labor relations. In the public sector, organizations of government actors such as the National League of Cities and the National League of Counties have also regularly participated in labor relations policy. More recently, right-wing legislative organizations, notably the American Legislative Exchange Council, have taken the lead in facilitating legislation limiting or eliminating union rights in the public sector.

3 THE RIGHT TO STRIKE

3.1 Sources of Rights to Organize, Bargain Collectively, and Strike

In the private sector, federal statutes (the RLA and NLRA) set the rights to organize, bargain collectively and to strike. In the public sector, since the late 1960s, the US Supreme Court has recognized a right under the First Amendment of the US Constitution for at least most public-sector employees to join or support unions. However, this constitutional right does not extend to the right to bargain collectively or the right to strike.[10] A few states (Florida, Hawaii, and Missouri) include a right to bargain collectively that applies to public employees in their state constitutions. But usually, if public employees have rights to bargain or, less commonly, to strike, such rights come from state or local statutes.

In earlier periods, in the absence of any relevant legislation, state courts applying the common law found no right for public workers to organize unions, much less bargain collectively or strike. While the overwhelming weight of state court authority has been that, in the absence of legislation, public-sector strikes

9. *US Department of Labor*, 2017b.
10. *Harris/Slater/Lofaso/Garden*, 2016, 65 et seqq.

are illegal under common law,[11] a few state cases have held otherwise, notably in California.[12]

The US does not follow international law regarding strike rights or collective bargaining rights. Indeed, in 2007, in response to a complaint by a union, the ILO called on North Carolina to repeal its statutory ban on all collective bargaining in the public sector in that state.[13]

Thus, in sum, strike rights in the US, for 'essential' employees and others are set by statutes: federal statutes in the case of private-sector employees, and (in almost all cases) state and local government statutes for public employees. Since most states bar all public employees from striking, and all states bar police, fire service, and prison guards from striking, alternative impasse dispute processes, discussed in detail below, are very important in US law, as are penalties for illegal strikes.

3.2 The Right to Strike in the Private Sector

For relevant private-sector employees, the NLRA sets strike rights. This section describes what strike activities are and are not 'protected' by the NLRA, procedural requirements for strikes, some general potential limits on strikes, and practical limitations based on (often very limited) rights to reinstatement after a strike.

The NLRA does not exempt any category of employees because those employees are in essential services. While the NLRA has a number of important exclusions—supervisors, managers, employees who deal with confidential personnel information, agricultural employees, public employees, and independent contractors—none of these exemptions, with the possible, partial exception of public employees, is premised on the 'essential' nature of the employee's work.[14]

3.3 Right to Strike for Covered Employees

Section 7 of the NLRA protects workers engaging in 'concerted activities for mutual aid or protection', which includes strikes. Further, Section 13 of the

11. *See Anchorage Educational Ass'n v. Anchorage School District*, 648 P.2d 993, 695-96 (Alaska 1982) (citing cases from fourteen states as authority for the proposition that '[b]y 1972, not one of the jurisdictions which had considered the question had found such strikes to be legal' under common law, and following this precedent.
12. *County Sanitation Dist. No. 2 of Los Angeles County v. Los Angeles County Employees Ass'n Local 660, SEIU*, 38 Cal.3d 564 (Cal. 1985).
13. *Malin/Hodges/Slater/Hirsch*, 2016, 418; see http://southernworker.org/wp-content/uploads/downloads/2013/08/ILO-Decision-on-US-and-North-Carolina.pdf containing the decision in Case No. 2460, Complaint against the Government of the United States by the United Electrical, Radio, and Machine Workers.
14. *Secunda/Lofaso/Slater/Hirsch*, 2014, 42 et seqq.

NLRA states that the NLRA should not be interpreted 'either to interfere with or impede or diminish in any way the right to strike, or to affect limitations or qualifications on that right.' On a day-to-day basis, the most common restriction on striking are the 'no strike/no lockout' clauses routinely contained in collective bargaining agreements between unions and employers. And even such clauses may not bar strikes in response to serious employer 'unfair labor practices' ('ULPs, meaning violations of NLRA Section 8(a)).[15] Still, the NLRA contains some general restrictions regarding strikes.

First, the NLRA contains some mandatory notice and 'cooling off' procedures that must be observed for a strike to be legal. Section 8(d)(1) of the NLRA requires that a party wishing to terminate or modify a labor contract must give the other party written notice of that fact sixty days prior to the contract's expiration date. Section 8(d)(2) requires the party to meet with the other party for the purpose of negotiating a new or modified contract. Section 8(d)(3) then requires that, thirty days after the initial notice, the parties must notify a federal agency, the Federal Mediation and Conciliation Service (FMCS), of this issue. The FMCS may offer mediations services, but, crucially and in contrast with common practice in the public-sector, under the NLRA, mediation is not required. Section 8(d)(4) bars strikes until after sixty days from the original notification.

Notice requirements are the only instance in private-sector law in which any type of 'essential' employee is treated any differently than any other type of employee in terms of strike rights, and this difference is relatively minor. NLRA Section 8(g) has a procedural requirement for striking that applies only to unions in the health care industry. Such unions, and such unions only, must give notice to the employer and the FMCS ten days before any strike or picketing.

Second, the NLRA, via Sections 206-210 of the Taft-Hartley Act (a 1947 Amendment to the NLRA)[16] provides for special limitations in cases of strikes that that are deemed to constitute a national emergency. Notably, these provisions have only been invoked twice in the history of the NLRA, most recently in 2002 when the George W. Bush administration used them to enjoin a lockout of longshoreman. In short, in a national emergency, the President is empowered to create a Board of Inquiry to determine whether the strike would threaten national health or safety. If such a finding is made, the Attorney General may petition a federal court for a sixty-day injunction. Even in such cases, the injunction must be dissolved after eighty days.[17] Similarly Section 10 of the RLA[18] authorizes the president to create a special emergency board to investigate and make recommendations when a railroad or airline strike threatens to provide any section of the country of essential transportation services. The

15. The leading case on no-strike clauses and employer ULPs is *Mastro Plastics Corp. v. National Labor Relations Board*, 350 US 270 (1956).
16. 29 USC §§ 176-80.
17. *Secunda/Lofaso/Slater/Hirsch*, 2014, 200 et seq.
18. 45 USC § 160.

emergency board has thirty days to make its report, after which the parties must maintain the status quo for an additional thirty days. This provision also has rarely been invoked.

More commonly, issues arise over whether the NLRA actually protects certain strikes or strike-like activities. If the NLRA does not protect the strike, then the employer generally has the legal right to discharge employees for taking part in the strike. First, 'sit-down' strikes, in which employees occupy the employer's property for any significant amount of time, are not protected (especially if strikers damage the employer's property).[19] Second, the NLRA does not protect strikes which feature significant amounts of unlawful conduct (*e.g.*, extensive violence and/or destruction of property).[20] Third, 'partial' strikes in which employees refuse to do some, but not all, of their work are unprotected.[21] In general, as the US Supreme Court has stated, the NLRA does not protect 'employees who engage in violence, mass picketing, unfair labor practices, contract violations, or other improper conduct, or who force the employer to violate the law.'[22]

Notably, unlike the law in many other countries, the NLRA bars 'secondary' strikes. With only a few, relatively minor exceptions, it violates NLRA Section 8(b)(4) for a union at one employer to strike in support of union at a separate employer. This is generally true even if one employer is a customer or supplier of the other employer, and even if one employer is a general contractor and the other a subcontractor hired by the general contractor.[23]

Striking workers have different types of reinstatement rights depending on the purpose of the strike. Specifically, 'economic' strikers and 'ULP strikers' have different reinstatement rights. First, under *NLRB v. MacKay Radio*, 304 US 333 (1938) and its progeny, employers may legally 'permanently replace' 'economic strikers.' Economic strikers are those motivated to strike over wages, hours, or working conditions. 'Permanently replace' means that an economic striker only has a legal right to be reinstated after the strike if there is a job opening. But an employer does not violate the NLRA if it keeps employing replacement workers after the strike, meaning there often is no job opening. Being 'permanently replaced' is not literally the equivalent to being 'fired.' An employer cannot legally fire economic strikers, *NLRB v. Browning-Ferris Industries*, 700 F.2d 385 (7th Cir. 1983). The difference is that economic strikers must be reinstated if a job vacancy becomes available later, *Laidlaw Corp.*, 171 N.L.R.B. 1366 (1968), *enforced* 414 F.2d 99 (7th Cir. 1969). There is no time limit on an employer's obligation to reinstate economic strikers, *Brooks Research &*

19. The leading case on 'sit down' strikes is *National Labor Relations Board v. Fansteel Metallurgical Corp.*, 306 US 240 (1939).
20. A colorful example of this is *Southern S.S. Corp v. NLRB*, 316 US 31 (1942), which found a work stoppage about a ship at sea unprotected because it violated federal laws against mutiny. See generally Harris/Slater/Lofaso/Garden, 2016, 815 et seq.
21. *Harris/Slater/Lofaso/Garden*, 2016, 816 et seq.
22. *Complete Auto Transit, Inc. v. Reis*, 451 US 401, 415 n. 16 (1981).
23. *Secunda/Lofaso/Slater/Hirsch*, 2014, 244 et seqq.

Mfg., Inc., 202 N.L.R.B. 634 (1973).[24] This is often a distinction without a practical difference, however. Because an economic striker has no reinstatement rights unless and until a job occupied by a replacement becomes vacant, being 'permanently replaced' is often effectively identical to being fired.

Employers who strike over at least in significant part over an employer's violations of the NLRA — 'ULP strikers' — have superior reinstatement rights. ULP strikers have a legal right to reinstatement if and when they make an 'unconditional offer to return to work.' *NLRB v. International Van Lines,* 409 US 48 (1972); *Pennant Foods Co.*, 347 N.L.R.B. 460 (2006). The rules governing reinstatement rights of different types of strikers are not contained in the text of the statute (the NLRA), but rather evolved through judicial interpretation of the statute.

3.4 Sanctions for Illegal Strikes

In the private sector, the most important sanctions for illegal strikes are (i) the employer may legally fire individual strikers; and (ii) the union, if it authorized or encouraged the illegal strike, may be liable for economic damages the strike caused. NLRA § 10(l) provides for injunctions against illegal secondary strikes. There are, however, few if any significant cases in recent memory involving private-sector workers in essential services striking illegally.

3.5 Strike Rights in the Public Sector

Rules on strikes by public employees are, again, set by state statutes. The vast majority of states (thirty-eight out of fifty) do not allow *any* public employees to strike under any circumstances. Indeed, even today, about a dozen states still do not permit any public employees to bargain collectively. While some larger, more densely populated states permit some public employees to strike (*e.g.*, California, Illinois, and Ohio), other such states bar all such strikes (*e.g.*, New York, Texas, Florida, and Michigan). Crucially here, no state permits public safety or other public employees involved in similarly 'essential' services to strike. And even those states which permit some public employees to strike will make any such strike illegal if and when the strike creates a threat to public health, safety, and/or welfare.[25] Thus in broad brush, states use one of three models for public employees: (a) such employees have no legal right to bargain or strike (a minority approach); (b) such employees have a right to bargain, and some have a legal right to strike (another minority approach); and (c) such

24. See also *NLRB v. Fleetwood Trailer Co.*, 389 US 375 (1967), in which the US Supreme Court held that if and when a relevant job becomes available for a former economic striker, the striker is entitled to reinstatement unless the employer has a legitimate and substantial business justifications for denying reinstatement.
25. *Harris/Slater/Lofaso/Garden*, 2016, 941; *Kearney/Mareschal*, 2014, 244-46.

employees have a right to bargain collectively but no right to strike (the plurality approach).

3.6 A Policy Debates

As to strike and other union rights, the normative policy debate in the US has been framed around the distinction between public and private employees. To a limited extent, this could be considered a proxy for 'essential services', as, again, most essential services are provided by the public sector. Still, the major divide is between public and private workers: private-sector hospital and utility workers have the right to strike, workers in public-sector hospitals and in public utilities in the clear majority of states do not. Thus, this section examines policy debates concerning the public sector.

In a plurality of states, public-sector unions are permitted to bargain collectively but not strike. Policy objections to unions striking sometimes overlap with policy objections to public-sector unions bargaining collectively. In their influential book *Unions and the Cities*, Harry Wellington and Ralph Winter argued that public officials would, for political reasons, capitulate quickly to public sector strikes, hurting the public. Wellington and Winter departed from the older objections to public sector strikes: that they would interrupt essential public services and undermine governmental sovereignty. Wellington and Winter found that argument inadequate because many public workers do not, in fact, perform 'essential' services. Instead, they stressed that public employees, through bargaining and strikes, would get 'two bites of the apple' in the competition for public resources: like all groups, they could lobby and act politically, but unlike other groups, they could also use bargaining and strikes to pressure government officials. This was especially true, they argued, because politicians would be more concerned with being reelected than with the public fisc., and market forces were no constraint in the public sector. Thus, they continued, politicians would quickly give in to strikes, and unions would be able to win extravagant demands. Further, they argued, even as to issues that did not involve direct expenditures of money, policy decisions about how government operates should be made by elected government officials, with no special power given to unions over such decisions.[26]

Others responded to these claims. First, it had become increasingly clear that public officials generally did *not* simply cave to union demands; indeed, there was often significant political advantage to be seen as 'standing up' to union demands. President Reagan's aggressive and successful opposition to the 1981 PATCO strike was the most famous example of this, but it was hardly atypical.[27] As to the 'two bites of the apple' argument, scholars such as Clyde

26. *Wellington/Winter*, 1971. For descriptions of older objections, see *Hanslowe/Acierno*, 1982, 1060-66 (1982).
27. *Olson*, 1988.

Summers, Kurt Hanslowe, and John Acierno made powerful rebuttals along the following lines. First, the general public prefers both high levels of public service and low costs for those services; at the voting booth, the general public vastly outnumbers public employees; and groups dedicated to, say, reducing taxes are well-organized and funded. Meanwhile, public employees have legitimate interests *as employees* that deserve protection through collective bargaining just as in the private sector. To the extent certain issues involve fundamental policy choices by elected officials that should not be constrained by obligations to bargain, that can be dealt with by removing certain issues from the scope of mandatory bargaining. For example, whether or not to create a civilian review board to investigate charges of police abuse should not be a mandatory topic of bargaining. But issues which primarily affect employees as employees (*e.g.*, just cause discipline procedures) are proper topics for union negotiations.[28]

In 1970, Hawaii and Pennsylvania became the first states granting some public employees limited rights to strike. The Governor's Commission to Revise the Public Employee Law of Pennsylvania explained the rationale. While the distinction being debated is public vs. private, rather than essential vs. non-essential, the 'essential' point is implicit in the distinction between public gardeners and police. Note also the idea that allowing some public-sector workers to strike in limited circumstances could actually reduce the incidence of strikes.

Twenty years of experience [under a law barring strikes] has taught us that such a policy is unreasonable and unenforceable. ... It is based upon a philosophy that one may not strike against the sovereign. But today's sovereign is engaged not only in government but in a great variety of other activities. The consequences of a strike by a policeman are very different from those of a gardener in a public park. ... The collective bargaining process will be strengthened if this qualified right to strike is recognized. It will be some curb on the possible intransigence of an employer; and the limitations on the right to strike will serve notice on the employee that there are limits to the hardships that he can impose. ... We can look upon the limited and carefully defined right to strike as a safety valve that will in fact prevent strikes.[29]

This remains, however, is a minority approach; again, today, most states flatly bar strikes by any and all public employees.

4 THE EXPERIENCE WITH STRIKES IN ESSENTIAL SERVICES

While statistics are incomplete, it is clear that in both the private and public sectors, strike rates in the US have significantly diminished in recent decades. In the private sector, from 1976 to 2016, the number of major work stoppages (defined as those affecting 1,000 or more employees) per decade declined

28. *Summers*, 1987; *Hanslowe/Acierno*, 1982.
29. Quoted in *Harris/Slater/Lofaso/Garden*, 2016, 941.

approximately 90 percent. The decade from 2007 to 2016 was the lowest yet, with an average of around fourteen major work stoppages per year.[30]

The US Department of Labor stopped compiling strike statistics in the public sector in the 1980s. It is clear that there were very few public-sector strikes of any consequence after the Boston police strike of 1919 through the early 1960s.[31] The later 1960s and 1970s was a period of relative militancy among many public-sector unions; this era featured short strikes and related job actions by, among others, police and firefighters (although still nothing like the rate of strikes in the private sector in that era). The 1980s and beyond has seen a steep decline in public-sector strike rates.[32] In the absence of national figures, state-level data confirms these trends. For example, there were many more strikes in the public sector in the state of Ohio in the period of 1974-79 (282 strikes) than in the longer period of 1984–1992 (110 strikes); the even longer period of 2000-10 saw even fewer strikes (43).[33] Significantly, the low strike rates in the public sector *even in states where strikes by most public employees are legal*, such as Ohio. This is due in large part to the alternative impasse resolution mechanisms discussed further below.

The last truly significant strike by essential workers in the public sector was done by a union of federal air traffic controllers (PATCO, the Professional Air Traffic Controllers Union) in 1981, and that strike was soundly defeated.[34]

While most arguably 'essential' employees are in the public sector, there also have been few if any significant strikes of arguably essential employees in the private sector in decades. This is likely due to a steep decline in rates of strikes generally in the US in the past several decades.[35] Given these trends, it seems unlikely that there will be a significant increase in strikes in essential services in the future.

5 RESTRICTIONS OF THE RIGHT TO STRIKE IN ESSENTIAL SERVICES

5.1 Exclusions from Labor Statutes

Because there are many different public-sector labor laws in the US, there are a wide variety of types of exclusions. Further, there are many different purposes of these exclusions. Some are to avoid strikes in 'essential' services, but many other

30. US Department of Labor, 2017a.
31. *Slater*, 2000, 82.
32. *Malin/Hodges/Slater/Hirsch*, 2016, 367.
33. *Slater*, 2012, 480 et seq. Notably, while Ohio is one of the states that permit some public employees to strike, that rule was not enacted until 1983, so the public-sector strike rate in that state was highest when all such strikes were illegal.
34. For a detailed description of this strike, see *McCartin*, 2011.
35. See *US Department of Labor*, 2017. This document shows the number of such private-sector strikes dramatically decreasing. For example, in 1970, there were 381 such strikes; in 1980, 187; in 1990, 44; in 2000, 37; and in 2010, 11.

exclusions are for other purposes (typically, a part of a general antipathy toward public-sector collective bargaining). While this chapter cannot provide a complete listing of the exclusions under all public-sector laws, it will provide a general guide to US law in this area.

First, the main federal statute governing federal employees (which permits most employees of the Executive branch to bargain collectively while barring strikes)[36] specifically excludes from even collective bargaining rights certain employees: the army, intelligence agencies, and other federal employees engaged in national security work.[37]

States vary considerably as to which public employees they permit to bargain. As noted above, while the most prevalent model is to allow most public employees to bargain collectively, a significant minority allows only a few types of public employees to bargain collectively, and a smaller minority does not allow any public employees to bargain collectively. Notably, in states that only allow a few types of public employees to bargain collectively, police and firefighters (along with teachers) are the most common examples of employees authorized to bargain.[38] While this is likely a result of the relatively stronger political clout of such unions compared to other public-sector unions, perhaps ironically, fears of strikes in modern years have sometimes been used to justify *superior* bargaining rights for 'public safety employees.' For example, when Wisconsin amended its public-sector labor statute in 2011, it essentially gutted existing collective bargaining rights for all public employees *except* public-safety workers. One rationale proponents of this change gave for this distinction was fear that public safety workers would be more likely to strike in the absence of collective bargaining rights.[39]

As to *strike* rights, in most states, public workers in essential services may not strike under general rules that bar all public employees from striking. Further, even in states that permit most public employees to strike, none extend that right to public safety and related essential employees. This means, again, that police, firefighters, and public-sector prison guards may not legally strike in any state in the US.

Beyond those categories, states that permit most public employees to strike vary somewhat as to which other types of employees may not strike. For

36. Federal Service Labor Management Relations Act, USC §§ 7101-7135. This statute was passed as part of the Civil Service Reform Act of 1978.
37. Multiple provisions of this statute provide exclusions for national security reasons, including sections 7103(a)(3); 7103(b)(1); and 7112(b)(6). For a full discussion of this topic, see *Slater*, 2004.
38. See *Kearney/Mareschal*, 2014, 65 et seq.
39. See the discussion of this issue in *Wisconsin Education Assn Council v. Walker*, 705 F.3d 640 (7th Cir. 2013) (upholding the Wisconsin law, Act 10, against a Constitutional challenge, in part because it was rational to distinguish public safety workers for this reason). This case also found another motivation: public-safety unions, unlike almost all the unions who lost rights under this amendment, tended to support the Republican Party, and the Republican Party was essentially the exclusive source of support for Act 10.

example, Ohio, which allows most types of public employees to strike after completing various forms of impasse resolution procedures, bars strikes by not just by police, firefighters, and prison guards, but also by 'employees of the state school for the deaf or the state school for the blind' and 'employees of any public employee retirement system.'[40] In short, in states that allow most, but not all, public employees to strike, the distinction is likely drawn on the grounds of trying to avoid interruptions in essential services.

5.2 Remedies for Illegal Strikes

This is a bigger issue in the public sector than in the private sector. First, there have traditionally been more illegal strikes in the public sector. This is likely because most public employees in the US are not allowed to strike under any circumstances, and even those who are allowed to strike are obliged to fulfill many more procedural requirements before they may strike legally (an issue discussed in detail below). Second, relevant here, most employees in 'essential services' in the US are in the public sector.

Because this is a matter of state law, sanctions for illegal strikes vary somewhat from state-to-state. Also, most of the rules involving penalties for illegal strikes do not distinguish between illegal strikes by essential employees and other types of public employees. They are simply the sanctions for illegal strikes.

This section provides an overview of four types of remedies for illegal strikes. First, penalties against individual strikers. Second, penalties against unions. Third, whether private parties or the employer can recover money damages as a result of losses for an illegal strike. Fourth, whether any penalties could be mitigated if the employer's bad acts (typically the ULP of failing to bargain in good faith) contributed to the strike. This section also discusses injunctions ordering unions to stop striking, and what penalties are available if unions violate such injunctions. In some cases, public-sector labor statutes themselves provide specific answers to these questions. In other cases, though, labor boards and courts have significant discretion.

5.2.1 Remedies Against Individual Strikers

The law governing federal employees makes it a *crime* for federal employees to strike, and a number of the PATCO strikers in 1981 were later prosecuted criminally. Given that this was the most prominent strike by employees in 'essential' services in at least the past half-century in the US, it is also worth noting here that all the PATCO strikers were fired (a penalty the relevant statute permitted by did not require). Also, President Ronald Reagan issued a directive

40. Ohio Revised Code § 4117.14(D)(1) and (2).

barring all PATCO strikers from employment with the Federal Aviation Administration (FAA). The FAA, in turn, adopted a policy barring private employers with whom it had contracts from employing any former PATCO striker. These policies remained in place until 1993 when

President Clinton repealed them. And the union PATCO was decertified.[41]

With the exception of the discharges, though, most of these penalties are unusual. While some states use some other sanctions, the main penalties against individual employees who strike illegally are usually fines, discipline (up to and including discharge), and limits on future public employment.

The Ohio public-sector labor statute (which bars strikes by public safety workers) provides a fairly typical menu of possible penalties against strikers. The Ohio law provides that, in cases where a public employee has been found to have struck illegally, the public employer:

(1) May remove or suspend those employees who one day after notification by the public employer of the board decision that a strike is not authorized continue to engage in the nonauthorized strike; and
(2) If the employee is appointed or reappointed, employed, or reemployed, as a public employee, within the same appointing authority, may impose the following conditions:
    (a) The employee's compensation shall in no event exceed that received by him immediately prior to the time of the violation.
    (b) The employee's compensation is not increased until after the expiration of one year from the appointment or reappointment, employment, or reemployment.
(3) Shall deduct from each striking employee's wages, if the board also determines that the public employer did not provoke the strike, the equivalent of two days' wages for each day the employee remains on strike commencing one day after receiving the notice called for in division (B)(1) of this section . . . .[42]

Note that subsection (3) contains a mitigating provision, under which the two-day pay penalty can be avoided if the public employer provoked the strike.

Other state laws provide similar penalties, with a few variations. Some states penalize one day's wages instead of two, while New York's law requires fines equal to twice the strikers' daily rate of pay for each day on strike in all cases.[43]

Employers do not always exercise their authority to fire illegal strikers. One can imagine the practical and political difficulties involved in, for example, replacing most or all teachers in a school district, or police officers in a town. For example, in early 2018, nearly all the public-school teachers in the state of West

41. *Harris/Slater/Lofaso/Garden*, 2016, 885.
42. OH. REV. CODE §4117.17.23(B)
43. N.Y MCKINNEY'S CIV. SERV. L. §210.

Virginia went on a (clearly illegal) strike, and were not fired (indeed, they won a raise).[44] Still, employers have exercised this power, and courts have given them wide discretion in so doing. In *Hortonville Joint School District v. Hortonville Education Association*, 426 US 482 (1976), the US Supreme Court upheld the discharge of a large number of teachers who struck. It rejected a challenge under the Due Process clause of the US Constitution that was based on the fact that the school board members who had run the discharge hearings had themselves provoked the strike.

5.2.2 Remedies Against Unions

As in the private sector, unions in the public sector may be held responsible for illegal strikes that the union supported, but not unauthorized 'wildcat' strikes the union did not sanction. *Ann Arbor Public Schools and Teamsters State, County, and Municipal Workers Local 214*, 15 MPER ¶33037 (Mich. PER 2002). But usually if there is a strike, the union did support it, and in such cases, unions are subject to a variety of sanctions.

Injunctions and Contempt Sanctions

Injunctions are a traditional equitable remedy permitting courts to order a party to take an action or cease taking certain actions before a full hearing on the merits of the dispute may be had. While generally in US law, injunctions are 'extraordinary' remedies that are not available in most cases, they are fairly routine in cases of illegal public-sector strikes. Public-sector labor statutes in the US generally make injunctions available to public employers faced with an illegal strike. Public employers frequently seek such injunctions, because they are the quickest way to end a strike; the union can be ordered to stop striking immediately, long before all the normal procedures of civil litigation are exhausted.

Unions engaged in illegal strikes have tried various legal strategies to avoid injunctions with relatively little success. For example, *Feaster v. Vance*, 832 A.2d 1277 (D.C.App. 2003) upheld an injunction issued after school employees struck illegally. The court first rejected the union's argument that, because an illegal strike was a ULP, the employer had to go to the D.C. Labor Board before going to court. The court explained that while ULP proceedings normally must first go to the Labor Board, a separate part of the D.C. Code made strikes illegal, and allegations of violations of that Code section could be taken directly to court.[45] The court also rejected the union's claim that the Norris–LaGuardia Act barred this injunction. That Act prohibits many types of injunctions in private-sector labor relations, but, as the court explained, it does not apply to the public sector.

44. See *Goldberg*, 2018; *Allen/Sacks*, 2018.
45. In some jurisdictions, employers do need authorization from a labor board before seeking injunctions against illegal strikes in court. See, e.g., *San Jose v. Operating Engineers Local 3*, 49 Cal.4th 597 (Cal. 2010).

Finally, *Feaster* upheld the lower court's ruling that the traditional equitable factors required to grant an injunction were met. These equitable factors are as follows. Plaintiff (here the employer) must demonstrate that (1) there is a substantial likelihood plaintiff will prevail on the merits; (2) plaintiff is in danger of suffering irreparable harm during the pendency of the action; (3) more harm will result to plaintiff from the denial of the injunction than will result to the defendant [union] from its grant; and, where applicable; and (4) that the public interest will not be disserved by the issuance of the injunction.

Especially important here, *Feaster* rejected the union's equitable defense of 'unclean hands', which was based on the union's allegation that the employer prompted the strike by bargaining in bad faith. In equity generally, courts may refuse to grant injunctions based on the bad behavior ('unclean hands') of the requesting party. A few courts had used the 'unclean hands' doctrine in refusing to issue injunctions against illegal public-sector strikes if the employer had provoked the strike by failing to bargain in good faith.[46] But few if any jurisdictions follow that approach today.[47] Even Ohio's statute, which (as shown above) provides that if employer ULPs provoked a strike, strikers are not subject to the usual fines, also specifically states that the role of employer ULPs in provoking a strike is not a defense to an injunction for strikes by public safety and other personnel not permitted to strike in Ohio.[48]

If a union continues to strike after a court issues an injunction ordering the strike to cease, the union is subject to contempt sanctions. Contempt can be civil, with penalties of fines, and in some cases it may be criminal, resulting in additional fines and possible jail sentences for at least union officials.

Criminal cases raise additional legal issues. *New York City Transit Authority v. Transport Workers Union of America* (N.Y. Sup. Court, App. Div. 2006), involved criminal contempt charges arising out of a union's failure to obey an injunction against an illegal strike by transit workers in New York City in 2005. This case held that in this instance, the Sixth Amendment to the US Constitution did not grant a right to a jury trial as a condition of imposing criminal sanctions. Civil contempt never requires a jury trial, but in criminal contempt cases a jury trial is required if the offense was 'serious' (as opposed to 'petty'). In *New York City Transit Authority*, the penalty was an initial fine of $1,000,000, with the fine then doubling each additional day the union continued to strike in violation of the injunction. The court explained that the possible doubling was prospective, avoidable, and therefore civil, so the question was whether the initial $1,000,000 was 'serious' enough to trigger Sixth Amendment protections. The court held it was not, given this union's significant assets and large membership.

---

46. See, e.g., *School Dist. No. 351 Oneida County v. Oneida Educ. Ass'n*, 98 Idaho 486 (1977); *School Dist. For City of Holland v. Holland Educ. Ass'n*, 380 Mich. 314 (1968).
47. In Michigan, a 1994 amendment to the relevant state statute essentially overruled the *Holland* case. Mich. Comp. Laws §423.202a(10).
48. Oh. Rev. Code §4117.23.

Individual union officers who lead illegal strikes that continue after an injunction may also be held in civil and criminal contempt. In a case arising out of the same illegal transit workers strike, *New York City Transit Authority v. Transport Workers Union of America*, 39 NYPER ¶7510 (N.Y. Sup. Ct., 2006), ordered a fine of $1,000 for the union president and ten days' incarceration, and $500 fines for two other union officers.

Forfeiture of Rights under Dues Check-Off Clauses

In some states, for example New York, unions who strike illegally can be denied any rights to 'dues check-off' they have under a collective bargaining contract, at least for a certain amount of time. 'Dues check-off' means that the employer will automatically deduct whatever amount of dues individual members of union bargaining units owe to the union that represents them, and forward those amounts to the union. While the amount of dues employees owe unions is independent of whether dues check-off exists, unions obviously derive a benefit from this form of automatic deduction (as opposed to having to bill members individually).

The typical issues in a case involving forfeiture of dues check-off rights are whether this penalty is justified, and if it is justified, how long the forfeiture should last. *MTA Bus Company v. Transport Workers Union of America* 820 N.Y.S.2d 479 (N.Y. Supreme Ct., 2006), arising from the same transit workers' strike, involved this penalty. The court first found that the sanction was appropriate because the union engaged in a serious, illegal strike. As to duration, the court explained that it must consider the extent of the union's willful defiance of the law, the impact of the strike on public health, safety, and welfare, the financial resources of the union, and, if relevant, any 'acts of extreme provocation' by the employer. The court stressed the inconveniences the 2005 strike caused, and the fact that the same union had struck illegally three times previously. On the other hand, the court noted that the union had tried to mitigate the effect of the strike by, among other things, safeguarding facilities. The court rejected the union's claim that the employer had engaged in 'extreme provocation', even though it had bargained in bad faith by trying to bargain over pension benefits, an illegal topic of bargaining for these employees. In the end, the court ordered an 'indefinite' forfeiture of dues check-off. The union would be allowed, no earlier than three months from the date of the order, to ask for the forfeiture to end based on representations that it would comply with the law.

In determining the duration of the forfeiture, the behavior of both the union and the employer is relevant. The union's (relatively) good behavior surrounding an illegal strike prompted a shorter than normal period of forfeiture in *City of New Rochelle and Uniformed Fire Fighters Ass'n, Inc., Local 273, IAFF*, 35 NYPER ¶3005 (N.Y. PERB, 2002) (six months instead of eighteen). Public inconvenience was limited to the cost of extra overtime to non-striking workers, the union had not struck previously, and the parties were working together in good faith to repair their damaged relationship. The employer's especially bad behavior led to similar penalty in *Buffalo Teachers Federation*, 16 NYPER ¶3018 (N.Y. PERB,

1983). There, the Labor Board found that the employer engaged in acts of 'extreme provocation' during negotiations preceding the strike by violating its duty to bargain in good faith in various ways.

Decertification

Some public-sector laws permit decertification of unions that strike illegally. As noted above, PATCO was decertified after its 1981 strike. Florida's statute also specifies that decertification is a potential penalty for an illegal strike.[49]

Suits for Damages Caused by the Illegal Strike

In some cases, private parties who suffered damages because of an illegal public-sector strike have sued the striking union to recover those damages. While states are divided over whether such damages are available, the majority of jurisdictions that have faced the question have held that they are not. For example, *Burns, Jackson, Miller, Summit & Spitzer v. Lindner*, 451 N.E.2d 459 (NY 1983) rejected such a claim. This case involved an illegal strike by transit workers in New York City in 1980. Plaintiff, the Burns, Jackson firm, sought millions of dollars in damages, ostensibly for loss of business and related costs. Plaintiff alleged various causes of action, including '*prima facie* tort', public nuisance, intentional interference with business relations, and breach of plaintiff's rights as a third-party beneficiary of the labor contract. The court rejected all of these theories. Most notably here, the court held that the state labor statute did not create a private cause of action, in part because such an action would upset the balance the legislature struck in setting statutory penalties for illegal strikes. Private remedies such as those requested here could destroy unions, the court reasoned, and might even be used against individual strikers. The intentional interference with business theory failed because the effects on business were only an 'incidental result' of the strike, and again because the legislature had balanced the penalties in the labor statute. Similarly, *White v. International Association of Firefighters, Local 42*, 738 S.W.2d 933 (Mo. App. 1987) rejected a claim by private parties who had suffered property damage from a fire during an illegal strike by firefighters. This court also reasoned that allowing private suits would disturb the balance of penalties in the labor statute, and that the potential liability of individual firefighters would discourage people from joining the profession thus inhibiting effective firefighting.[50]

A few jurisdictions have allowed private suits. For example, *Boyle v. Anderson Firefighters Association Local 1262*, 497 N.E.2d 1073 (Ind.App. 1986), held that because a firefighters' strike was illegal, the strikers owed a legal duty to property owners either not to strike or to fight fires. Thus, strikers could be held individually liable for damages their breach of that duty caused.

---

49. *Malin/Hodges/Slater/Hirsch*, 2016, 774, citing *Professional Traffic Controllers Organization v. FLRA*, 685 F.2d 547 (D.C. Cir. 1982) and FLA.STAT.ANN. § 447.507(6)(a).
50. An Illinois court reached a similar result for similar reasons in *Jackson v. Chicago Firefighters Union, Local No. 2*, 160 Ill.App.3d 975 (1987).

Some cases have considered the separate issue of whether the struck *employer* could bring an action for the economic damages the employer suffered due to an illegal strike. Courts have been more sympathetic to this type of suit than to suits by private parties. Notably, *White* which, as noted above, rejected a suit by a private party, specifically distinguished suits by employers and allowed them. *White* explained that the employer, unlike private parties, was a member of the class for whose specific benefit the public-sector law was passed. Similarly, *Koons by Koons v. Kaiser,* 567 N.E.2d 851 (Ind.App. 1991) held that a struck public employer could sue teachers for illegally striking, but an individual student could not. *Franklin Township Board of Education v. Quakertown Education Association,* 643 A.2d 34 (N.J. App. 1994) also allowed a struck employer to sue striking teachers. Florida's public-sector labor statue authorizes public employers to sue unions who strike illegally for damages, and the statute provides that the employer may attach the union's dues check-off receipts in order to satisfy the judgment. That statute does also state that a court contemplating this remedy must consider any actions of the employer that may have provoked the strike.[51]

Some jurisdictions hold that struck employers cannot sue for damages in illegal strike cases. These cases generally rely on the argument that the legislature struck the proper balance of penalties in the labor statute to bar these suits as well as suits by private parties. For an example of such holding, see *City and County of San Francisco v. United Ass'n of Journeyman & Apprentices of the Plumbing & Pipefitting Industry of the United States & Canada, Local 38,* 42 Cal.3d 810 (1986).

5.3 Effectiveness of Sanctions

The evidence on the effectiveness of sanctions, such as it is, is mixed. On one hand, some evidence suggests that relatively severe strike sanctions do inhibit strikes. The state of Michigan, for example, experienced fewer teacher strikes after the state amended its public-sector statute in the 1990s to enhance penalties for such strikes.[52] More generally, studies show that consistently enforced penalties tend to reduce illegal strikes.[53]

On the other hand, studies have also shown that the best way to avoid public-sector strikes is to provide robust collective-bargaining rights with effective and fair alternative mechanisms for resolving bargaining impasses. In both Ohio and Illinois, the number of public-sector strikes decreased dramatically *after* each state passed a law making strikes (and in the case of Ohio, collective

51. Fla.Stat.Ann. § 447.507(4).
52. *Lawler,* 2016 ('In 1994, [Michigan] Public Act 112 placed stricter prohibitions on public school employee strikes specifically. Since that time, strikes have become a rarity in the state').
53. *Kearney/Mareschal,* 2014, 247 et seq.

bargaining generally) legal for most public employees.[54] It may seem counter-intuitive that legalizing an activity would decrease the rate of participation in that activity. But strikes may be more likely when unions have no other option, whereas robust collective bargaining rights and other viable options to resolve bargaining impasses can make them less likely. In general, strikes are least likely to occur in jurisdictions that provide for compulsory, binding interest arbitration to resolve bargaining disputes.[55] That process is discussed in detail below.

Also, legal rules are not the only determinative factor in the outcome of strikes. While the PATCO strike was a disaster for the union and the employees, under the very same federal law, eleven years earlier (in 1970), US postal workers engaged in a major work stoppage with fairly positive results. Around 200,000 workers struck, and ultimately the strike was settled with the union receiving increased collective bargaining rights (full rights under the NLRA except the right to strike) and a significant pay hike that was greater than that other federal employees received at the time.[56]

5.4 Challenges to Sanctions

Beyond the case listed above, challenges to entire categories of sanctions have been rare and unsuccessful. For example, courts have upheld the constitutionality of revoking dues checkoff rights. *See, e.g., Buffalo Teachers Federation v. Helsby*, 676 F.2d 28 (2d Cir. 1982). More broadly, *United Federation of Postal Clerks v. Blount*, 325 F.Supp. 879 (D.D.C.) *aff'd w/o opinion*, 404 US 802 (1971) rejected a constitutional challenge to the bar on strikes by federal employees. The court explained, 'At common law, no employee, whether public or private, had a constitutional right to strike . . . . When the right of private employees to strike finally received full protection, it was by statute . . . . It seems clear that public employees stand on no stronger footing in this regard than private employees . . . .'

5.5 Limitations on the Right to Strike

In US law, employees typically either have the right to strike or they do not have the right to strike: there is no middle ground. Unlike some other countries this book discusses, US law does provide for a 'controlled strike' alternative. Nor does US law attempt to follow the model which the ILO Committee on Freedom of Association developed distinguishing between levels of essential employees (the Alaska statute described below is the only arguable exception). Still, US law does contain a few rules relevant here.

54. *Malin*, 1993.
55. *Kearney/Mareschal*, 2014, 247-48.
56. *Ibid.*, 243.

In the public sector, in a few jurisdictions, employees who are arguably essential have greater restrictions on their right to strike than other employees, but still may strike. For example, Alaska bars police, firefighters, and prison guards from striking altogether; it has a comparatively robust right for most other public employees to strike; but it has a more limited right to strike for employees involved in sanitation and snow removal.[57] Illinois, which provides most public employees (but not public safety employees) the right to strike recently amended its Educational Labor Relations Act to make it more difficult for employees of the Chicago public schools to strike than other public employees who are allowed to strike. Specifically, bill SB7 amended the relevant law to require a vote of at least 75% of the union bargaining unit to authorize a strike (no such requirement exists for other employees permitted to strike).

More significantly, public-sector labor statutes routinely provide that strikes which begin as legal strikes (*i.e.*, the employees were allowed to strike at the time they went out on strike) may nonetheless be enjoined if, at some point during the strike, the strike threatens the health, safety, and/or welfare of the public. For example, the Ohio statute provides that if 'the public employer believes that a lawful strike creates clear and present danger to the health or safety of the public', it may seek to have the strike enjoined. If the labor board and court agree to the injunction, the parties will also be ordered to resume bargaining with a mediator.[58]

While these rules apply to all public employees who have the right to strike, in practice, they are applied to employees whose work involves a middle category in the 'essential' scale: often, workers in public transportation and public school teachers.

These cases are often difficult for labor boards and courts because of the obvious tension: strikes are meant to cause *some* dislocations and inconveniences, so at what point does an otherwise legal strike create the types of problems that threaten the health, safety, or welfare of the public? For example, *Masloff v. Port Authority of Allegheny County*, 613 A.2d 1186 (Pa. 1992) wrestled with a 'health, safety, and welfare' exception in a strike (legal at its inception) by mass transit workers. *Masloff* upheld an injunction over a dissent. The majority opinion explained that 'ordinary inconveniences resulting from a strike will not suffice to establish a clear and present danger', but distinguished situations 'when such matters accumulate to such an extent, have continued for so long, or are aggravated by unexpected developments.' The majority opinion stressed that the city had introduced thirty witnesses who testified about the negative impact of the strike, including blind, epileptic, professionals, 'blue-collar' and

57. Alaska Stat. § 23.40.200(a)-(c). In short, while most public employees in Alaska may strike after a secret ballot vote, employees involved in sanitation and snow removal may only strike after a secret ballot vote and a mandatory mediation process, and even then the strike is permitted only 'for a limited time. The limit is determined by the interests of the health, safety, or welfare of the public.'

58. Ohio Revised Code § 4117.16.

student citizens. It added that the strike had delayed medical and police and fire services because of traffic congestion, that citizens were endangered because they had to walk along public roads, and that some had to find alternative living arrangements because of the inaccessibility of work, school, or day care. The majority rejected the union's argument that this is what one would normally expect in a strike by transit workers. The dissent in *Masloff* argued that all these effects were the normal, foreseeable consequences of a transit workers strike, and that the state legislature must have anticipated these effects when it permitted such workers to strike. If the normal inconveniences of a transit workers strike were sufficient to allow an injunction, the dissent concluded, how could these employees ever have an effective strike? As in Ohio and other states that use this rule, the consequence of this injunction was an order to negotiate, in this case under court supervision.

Other cases have created similar disagreements on this issue. In *Jersey Shore Educ. Association v Jersey Shore Area School District*, 548 A.2d 1202 (N.J. 1988) the New Jersey Supreme Court upheld an injunction of an initially legal strike by public school teachers. It stressed that the strike threatened a loss of state subsidies to schools because the strike could cause a failure to comply with a sate statutory requirement of providing 180 days of instruction. This, the majority held, threatened the public health, safety, or welfare. Again showing that these cases are not easy, this decision prompted two separate dissents.

These cases are difficult in large part because the statutes provide essentially no guidance to courts and labor boards. The language from the Ohio statue, quoted above, is typical in that it lists no particular services or types of employees most likely to fall under this restriction, nor does it list any criteria to use in determining whether a strike has reached the point that it has created a threat to the public health, safety, or welfare.

6 COMPENSATORY MEASURES FOR RESTRICTIONS

As shown above, most employees in the US who would be deemed 'essential' do not have the right to strike. Private-sector employees covered by the NLRA or RLA have a right to strike. But most 'essential' employees are in the public sector, most states do not permit any public employees (essential or not) to strike, and those that permit some public employees to strike do not permit public safety workers to strike. Further, some states do not permit most or all of their public employees to bargain collectively, much less strike.

6.1 Public Employees Without the Right to Bargain Collectively or Strike

Employees not permitted to bargain collectively still have some protections, although nothing resembling strike rights. Most public employees, including those in essential services, have a Constitutional right to join unions. In jurisdictions where unions are not permitted to bargain, unions typically try to use political action: lobbying, supporting relatively sympathetic candidates in local elections, and related activity. Such activity sometimes brings some successes, but it is generally not a powerful tool.[59]

In these jurisdictions, compensation and other terms of employment are typically set by statute, mainly through civil service laws. Civil service rules often, but not always, provide covered public employees, including those in essential services, with 'just cause' protections in discipline and discharge. These laws generally create commissions to hear, at least in the first instance, charges by employees that the employer has violated civil service rules.[60] Unions in these jurisdictions can help represent individual employees in civil service commission hearings. They may also help in claims brought under the many employment laws (*e.g.*, anti-discrimination and wage and hour laws) that cover employees generally.[61]

6.2 Public Employees With the Right to Bargain Collectively, But No Right to Strike

In contrast, in most states that permit most public employees to bargain collectively, a fairly robust set of alternative impasse dispute mechanisms have developed. These typically include some form of mediation, fact-finding, and/or interest arbitration. In some states, these processes are used for all public employees; in others, where strikes are allowed for some employees, they are used for public safety and other employees who cannot strike (the most 'essential' services). While some standardization across states exists, there are also significant variations. This sections summarizes the major approaches states use.[62]

6.2.1 Mediation

Mediation involves a neutral party who has no power to impose any terms of a collective bargaining agreement working with the union and employer to try to facilitate an agreement over whatever bargaining issues are at impasse. Most commonly, the state public-sector labor agency selects the mediator. Almost all states that permit public employees to bargain provide for some type of

59. See *Hodges*, 2009 (comparing union activities in Virginia, which bars public-sector collective bargaining, with union activities in Illinois, which authorizes such bargaining).
60. For a description of civil service rules and practices, see *Malin/Hodges/Slater/Hirsch*, 2016, 227 et seqq.
61. See *Hodges*, 2009. For a detailed description of laws protecting public employees that do not involve collective bargaining rights or unions *per se*, see *Malin/Hodges/Slater/Hirsch*, 2016, 61 et seq.
62. For more detailed descriptions of these procedures, see *Harris/Slater/Lofaso/Garden*, 2016, 891 et seqq.; and *Malin/Hodges/Slater/Hirsch*, 2016, 799 et seqq. Most of the material in this section is drawn from these sources.

mediation. In some states mediation is required if one party requests it; in others, both parties must request it; and in some, the state labor board can require mediation on its own initiative. Mediation is non-binding, and is typically most effective when there are other, binding procedures that follow if mediation is not successful.

6.2.2 Fact-Finding

Most states that provide for public-sector collective bargaining also use fact-finding in resolving impasses. Either a neutral party or a panel of neutrals is tasked with finding facts relevant to the impasse and making non-binding recommendations, based on the facts and statutory criteria. The process is designed to give the parties more information and a more realistic view of their chances at the potential interest arbitration proceeding that usually could follow fact-finding. Also, many public-sector statutes provide that the fact-finder's recommendations become public if the parties do not accept them[63]; this is designed to bring political pressure on the parties to agree.

The statutory criteria fact-finders are obliged to use are typically the same as those interest arbitrators must use. As discussed below, these vary somewhat state-to-state, but the most common and usually most important factors are analyzing comparable employees, the employer's ability to pay, the interest of the public, and past labor contracts. These factors dictate the evidence that fact-finders consider. So, for example, the fact-finder will hold hearings to determine what similar employees in similar cities or towns are paid, and examine the relevant public employer's budget. Unions and employers present evidence on such issues.

The fact-finder's recommendations are not binding, but they can be very influential. First, if the process moves beyond fact-finding to interest arbitration, the fact-finder's report and recommendations can be used as evidence in the arbitration hearing. Second, some statutes make it relatively difficult for parties to reject a fact-finders' recommendations. For example, in Ohio, the recommendations are rejected if either side rejects it, but it requires a two-thirds vote by either side to reject—and in the case of unions, that means a vote by two-thirds of *the entire bargaining unit*, not just two-thirds of those who actually vote on the issue. If neither side rejects the recommendations, the recommendations become the terms of the labor contract.[64]

63. For example, Ohio Revised Code §4117.14(C)(6)(a).

64. Ohio Revised Code §4117.14(C)(6)(a). Suppose, for example, a bargaining unit has 210 members; in a vote on whether to accept the fact-finder's recommendation, 150 of those members vote; and of those 150, 135 vote not to accept it. In this situation, the union is deemed to have accepted the fact-finder's recommendation, because it would require a vote of 140 members of the bargaining unit (two-thirds of 210) to reject it.

6.2.3 Interest Arbitration

Interest arbitration is the most common mechanism to settle bargaining impasses in public-sector law. It is especially common for police and firefighters, a significant subset of 'essential' employees. For example, in Ohio, while most public-sector employees have the right to strike, public-safety employees cannot legally strike and must use binding interest arbitration as final step of impasse resolution.

Interest arbitration involves a neutral arbitrator, or sometimes a panel of arbitrators, holding hearings, evaluating relevant evidence, and making decisions that are usually, but not always binding, based on the evidence and the criteria the public-sector statute describes. The arbitration only applies to whatever issues remain at impasse after negotiations and previous steps of the impasse resolution process have ended.

There are three main variations of interest arbitration: (a) 'conventional'; (2) 'final offer, issue-by-issue'; and (3) 'final offer, total package.' In conventional arbitration, the arbitrator may, for any issue involved in the hearing, select the union's final offer, the employer's final offer, or craft a compromise. For example, suppose the parties were at impasse over the percentage of wage increase in a contract's third year: the union's final offer was a 3% increase and the employer's final offer was a 1% increase. In a conventional arbitration, the arbitrator could impose a 3% increase, a 1% increase, or any percentage increase between those numbers (in theory, the arbitrator could choose a number outside the 1-3% range, but that rarely happens).

In final offer, issue-by-issue arbitration, the arbitrator is not allowed to compromise between the final offers of the parties. For each issue in the arbitration, the arbitrator must select either the union's proposal or the employer's proposal. Suppose in the previous example there was also an impasse over how many days of paid vacation employees would receive in a year: the union's final proposal was fifteen, the employer's final proposal was five. The arbitrator could select either a 3% increase or a 1% increase in the third year (but not any other number) and either fifteen days or five days' paid vacation (but not any other number).

In final offer, total package arbitration, the arbitrator is limited to selecting either all the final offers on all issues at impasse from the employer, or all the final offers on all the issues at impasse from the union. Thus, in the example from the previous paragraph, the arbitrator could only choose (a) the employer's final offers of a 1% increase in the third year and five vacation days, or (b) the union's final offers of a 3% increase in the third year and fifteen vacation days.

There are further variations on this. For example, the Michigan law governing police and firefighters provides that for economic issues, the arbitrator must use the final offer, issue-by-issue model, but for other issues, the arbitrator should use the conventional arbitration model.[65] In Ohio, the provisions that cover interest arbitration for police, fire, and prison guards state that the default is final-offer, issue-by-issue, but if the parties both agree, they may choose other models, including conventional arbitration or final offer, total package arbitration.[66]

State public-sector labor statutes also set out the criteria the interest arbitrators must consider in making their awards. Again, these laws typically provide that fact-finders must consider the same factors. Typically, the most important factors are the terms and conditions of employment of 'comparable' employees, the ability of the employer to pay, the interests of the public, and past labor contracts.

State statutes vary in how detailed and specific the criteria are. For example, some statutes give some rules to determine what types of employees are 'comparable'; refer to particular cost-of-living measures; and/or instruct arbitrators to weigh some factors more heavily than others. Thus, for example, while the Ohio statute states that arbitrators should compare the employees at issue to 'other public and private employees doing comparable work',[67] the Oregon statute specifically states that 'comparable' employees 'is limited to communities of the same or nearest population ranges within Oregon.' The Oregon statute further provides the following specific rules: arbitrators can consider comparable employees 'out of state', but only in interest arbitrations involving employees of cities with a population of more than 325,000, counties with a population of more than 400,000, or state employees.[68]

Perhaps because 'comparable employees' is such an important criterion, other issues and variations arise. For example, different arbitrators and different jurisdictions give different emphasis to two distinct types of comparable employees: external and internal. External comparables are those who do similar work for a similar but different employer than the employer the union is bargaining with. For example, in a case involving firefighters in a small town in a given state, external comparables would typically be firefighters in other small towns in the same state. Internal comparables involve different employees of the same public employer. So, in this example, internal comparables would include police officers employed by the small town and employees of the same fire department who are not firefighters.

Determining who the appropriate 'comparables' are is a frequent litigation point in interest arbitrations. This is both because this determination can often be at least mostly determinative in resolving certain issues, and because public-sector labor statutes usually give little guidance to arbitrators (at least in reasonably close cases) about which plausible groups of employees to include or

65. For this and other examples, see *Anderson/Krause*, 1987.
66. Ohio Revised Code §§ 4177.14(C)(1), (D)(1), and (G)(7).
67. Ohio Revised Code §§ 4177.14(G)(7)(b).
68. Oregon Revised Statutes, § 243.746.

exclude. In deciding what employees are appropriate to use as external comparables, arbitrators will typically consider the job duties of the allegedly comparable employees, and the size, budget, and location of the allegedly comparable city.

The other most important factor in these cases is the employer's ability to pay. This is not an exact science. But arbitrators typically consider evidence regarding projected tax revenue, expected expenditures (on employee compensation and otherwise), and the anticipated impact on other city or state departments beyond the agency or division involved in the arbitration. The common but rather amorphous criteria of 'the public interest' may be combined with the 'ability to pay' factor as well.

Also, most statutes require the arbitrator to consider past labor contracts between the parties. In practice, this often creates a bias in favor of preserving the status quo, at least on most issues, unless one party offers a significant *quid pro quo* for altering the status quo.[69]

Most interest arbitration systems provide that the decision of the arbitrator will be binding, but in a few states, the decisions of interest arbitrators are merely advisory. Relevant here, in Michigan, decisions involving certain public-safety workers are subject to binding interest arbitration, whereas other types of workers (who also cannot strike) do not have a right to binding interest arbitration.[70] In some states, this is a policy decision by legislatures. But also, courts in five states have held that binding interest arbitration violates state constitutional provisions barring delegation of inherently governmental powers to private parties.[71]

Also, some states end their impasse dispute procedures without any arbitration or binding decision. For example, Florida, Kansas, and Kentucky use only mediation and fact-finding. Georgia uses only mediation. [72]

Decisions of interest arbitrators may be appealed to court. Courts generally are fairly deferential to interest arbitrators.[73] Still, courts do reverse some decisions of interest arbitrators, most commonly on the grounds that the arbitrator did not properly consider all the criteria set out in the relevant statute. Also, courts will reverse the decisions of interest arbitrators if they consider issues that are not properly at impasse, or if they use a different model of arbitration than that which the statute requires.[74]

69. For a critique of this, *see* Bloom, 1988.
70. Compare Michigan Complied Laws §§ 423-231-33 and 423.271-87 with Michigan Compiled Laws § 423.207-207(a).
71. *Kearney/Mareschal*, 2014, 287.
72. *Ibid.*, 65, 269.
73. See, e.g., *Hillsdale PBA Local 207 v. Borough of Hillsdale*, 137 N.J. 71 (NJ 1994) (stating a deferential standard of review).
74. For an example of the latter, see *UAW Region 2*, 719 N.E.2d 632 (Oh.App. 1998) (arbitrator improperly ordered a compromise position when the default statutory requirement, which the parties had not agreed to change, was final offer, issue-by issue).

6.2.4 *Comparison to the ILO Model*

As the above demonstrates, US law in this area does not even attempt to comply with the ILO 'protocol' on strike substitutes. Beyond that, again, the major relevant distinction in US law is generally not 'essential' versus 'non-essential' services, it is 'private vs. public sector.'

The alternatives to strikes available to public employees often do not meet the ILO criteria, for several reasons. First, a significant number of public employees, including those in essential services, are in states that do not permit any public employees to bargain collectively, much less have the right to strike or the right to an alternative procedure to resolve impasses.

Second, in states that do permit public employees in essential services to bargain collectively, not all have mandatory, binding arbitration as the final step. And even where they do, courts may review the decisions of interest arbitrators (albeit under a deferential standard).

Where mandatory, binding interest arbitration is in place, US practices do seem to conform to other aspects of the ILO protocol. Both sides have the right invoke arbitration and keep the process going, even over the opposition of the other side. Both sides have equal opportunity for input into choosing neutral arbitrators. And interest arbitrators have authority to decide on every issue at impasse between the parties.

6.2.5 *Workability and Effectiveness of Alternatives to Strikes*

For employees who lack both the right to strike and the right to bargain collectively, there are essentially no alternatives to strikes. For example, in states where public employees in essential services cannot bargain collectively, while civil service, teacher tenure, and other employment laws provide individual employees various rights (*e.g.*, 'just cause' discharge protection), they do not provide rights for collective action regarding wages, hours, and working conditions. Not surprisingly, employees in states who lack collective bargaining rights generally do worse, *e.g.*, in terms of compensation, than similarly-situated employees in states with collective bargaining rights.[75]

For employees who have the right to bargain collectively but not the right to strike (police and firefighters in the majority of states are in this category)[76], it is best to consider two broad categories of impasse dispute processes that are used as alternatives to strikes. First, procedures that end in mandatory, binding

75. See, e.g., *Hodges*, 2009, comparing employees in Illinois (robust collective bargaining rights for public employees) and Virginia (no collective bargaining rights for public employees).
76. *Kearney/Mareschal*, 2014 (police and/or firefighters have collective bargaining rights in approximately thirty-five states).

arbitration. Second, procedures that end with something less, either no arbitration at all (the process ends with either mediation or fact-finding) or arbitration that is not binding. The former is more common than the latter.[77]

For states that permit collective bargaining but have only mediation or fact-finding as the final step in impasse resolution, the disadvantage from the union perspective is obvious. Mediation will likely be much less useful when there is no prospect of a strike or arbitrator's award potentially forcing the employer to accept something it does not wish to accept. This is also true of fact-finding, a process that ends in non-binding recommendations. Indeed, giving the employer increased discretion to simply reject union proposals is the main point of such systems. Fact-finding can produce some positive results, for example by giving information to the parties they did not previously have, making expectations more realistic, and in some cases bringing public pressure to bear. This can lead to issues being settled that were not settled at the mediation stage. But in practice, the public is often indifferent to the details of labor disputes, and the record of achieving salutary compromises is mixed at best, mainly because the employer can often simply choose not to compromise with no adverse consequences.[78]

The most common model for public employees generally and especially for 'essential' public employees is to permit collective bargaining, bar strikes, and use binding interest arbitration as the final step in the impasse resolution process. There are several advantages to this model. First, it has been the most successful system in preventing strikes (more so than strike bans with no union rights).[79] It also gives unions realistic power to make the employer accept certain terms even if the employer doesn't wish to, which not only may be viewed in a good in and of itself, but also, for reasons noted above, is likely to make mediation and fact-finding more effective and fair.

Still, interest arbitration has its critics, flaws, and limitations. Interest arbitration can interfere with collective bargaining by allowing unions and employers to avoid accountability and instead shift responsibility to the arbitrator. Further, there can be a 'chilling effect' on negotiations if a party thinks it has a chance at a better outcome in an arbitration.[80]

Also, each 'model' of arbitration has drawbacks. Conventional arbitration, which allows arbitrators to award 'compromise' terms, may create disincentives for the parties to compromise during the bargaining process, especially if they assume the arbitrator will 'split the baby.' Final offer arbitration can avoid that problem, but in its 'total package' form, the arbitrator sometimes must adopt individual unreasonable proposals by one side simply because that side's proposals were better overall as a group. 'Issue by issue' final offer avoids that

77. *Ibid.*, 269 et seq., 281 (twenty-seven states use interest arbitration, the great majority of those use binding interest arbitration).
78. *Ibid.*, 277 et seqq.
79. *Ibid.*, 285 (citing sources).
80. *Ibid.*, 288 et seqq; *Malin*, 2013.

problem, but, the proposals of both sides on one or more issues may be too extreme. It also creates an incentive to leave more issues unresolved at bargaining, on the theory that the arbitrator will want to rule on some issues for both sides. It even has spurred litigation over whether a position on two closely related issues is really one issue or two.[81]

Still, for many 'essential' public employees, there is no realistic alternative of striking. Again, no state in the US permits police, firefighters, or prison guards to strike, and there is no plausible prospect that any state will in the foreseeable future. Thus, binding interest arbitration, even with its flaws, is the best-case scenario for such employees.

For arguably essential employees who have the right to strike in some states (*e.g.*, public school teachers), the question is more difficult. Professor Martin Malin has argued in favor of the right to strike, as opposed to binding arbitration. He notes that the fear that unions would benefit inordinately from a too-powerful strike weapon have not been borne out by experience; that arbitrators are too wedded to the status quo in fixing contract terms; and that interest arbitration awards do not necessarily reflect the importance of various issue to the parties.[82]

It is worth noting here that thus far, for legal strikes, public employers have not engaged in the widespread use of permanent replacements that has so undermined the practical effectiveness of strikes in the private sector in the US Indeed, there is literally no reported case in the US of a public employer using permanent replacements in a legal strike.[83] One could reasonably wonder if strikes were permitted more broadly in the public sector, whether this practice would spread.

7 SECURING ESSENTIAL SERVICES BY FURTHER MEANS

The primary ways strikes by essential employees are regulated in the US are discussed above. There is, for example, no practice of 'back to work' legislation in the US Courts are empowered to issue injunctions as described above. The rarely-used power of the executive to declare an emergency is also mentioned above.

In older times, the executive (President) claimed the power to 'seize' a plant or business to ensure continued flow of essential services. However, the US Supreme Court struck down the last attempt at this many decades ago, in the 'steel seizure' case, *Youngstown Sheet & Tube Co. v. Sawyer*, 343 US 579 (1952). In that case, the Court held that President Harry Truman's attempt via Executive Order to seize certain steel mills (ostensibly to prevent a labor stoppage during the Korean War) was not a valid use of presidential powers.

81. *Harris/Slater/Lofaso/Garden*, 2016, 913 et seq.
82. *Malin*, 1993.
83. *Harris/Slater/Lofaso/Garden*, 2016, 959 et seq.

On the other hand, 'no strike/no lockout' provisions in contracts are ubiquitous in US labor law where strikes are legal. Thus, while essential employees in the private sector have broad rights to strike under statutory law, if there is a collective bargaining agreement in place, that agreement almost certainly will bar strikes during its duration, especially strikes over wages, hours, or working conditions. The same is true for public employees who have strike rights.

8 EVALUATION AND CONCLUSION

The US does not abide by ILO or other international guidelines regarding the rights to collective bargaining or the right to strike, for essential employees or others. Further, US labor law does not use ILO rules or other criteria to carve out specific categories of 'essential' employees. Rights to bargain and strike are mainly determined by whether the employee is in the private or public sector and, if the latter, what state the employee is in.

Further, again, in all sectors of employment, the rate of strikes in the US has plummeted, even adjusting for declining rates of union membership. In 1990, about 16.7 million US workers were union members, and there were 793 strikes. In 2015, 14.8 million workers in the US were union members, and there were only 102 strikes.[84]

Essential employees in the private sector have, at least on paper, broad rights to strike. In practice, however, that right has been severely limited by, among other things, the widespread use of permanent replacements in economic strikes and the bar on secondary strikes and pickets.[85] Notably, the Committee on Freedom of Association of the ILO has held that these two practices (which again are not limited to essential employees) violate international standards.[86]

Thus, while employees in private hospitals, private utilities, and other arguably essential services do have the formal right to strike, the absence of a robust, *effective* right to strike naturally inhibits collective bargaining for these (and other private-sector) employees, because strikes are the only tool available to private sector unions to resolve bargaining impasses.

Most 'essential' workers in the US are in the public sector, and the rules and problems are significantly different there. While policy-makers must balance the goal of providing essential services with the goal of providing effective rights for workers to bargain collectively and resolve bargaining impasses fairly, the latter goal, especially in actual practice, seems unfulfilled for many essential employees employed by governments.

Again, in some states, such employees (along with other public employees) have no right to collectively bargain. This violates ILO norms. In a model used by

84. *Lee*, 2017.
85. *Pope et al.*, 2017, 3.
86. *Ibid.*

more states, at least many public workers (including 'essential' employees) have the right to bargain collectively, but have no right to strike. This too may run afoul of ILO practices. For example, the Committee on Freedom of Association of the ILO determined that the anti-strike provisions of the New York public-sector labor law used against striking transit workers in cases described above violate international norms.[87] Providing essential employees with access to binding interest arbitration is more defensible.

It is useful to think of two categories of 'essential' public employees in the US. First are public safety workers such as police officers and firefighters, for whom strike rights are both unrealistic and arguably undesirable even for advocates of union rights. Second are employees whose work stoppages are likely to have a significant effect on the public, but who have, in some jurisdictions, some strike rights: for example, public school teachers, public transportation employees, and employees of public hospitals.

As to the first category, police and fire, this author believes that an impasse dispute resolution process that includes mediation, fact-finding, and binding, mandatory interest arbitration is likely the best system that could realistically be created in the US. Interest arbitration has its drawbacks. But there is no plausible prospect that such employees will be granted strike rights in any US state. And in comparison to systems in the US that lack this final step (and instead rely only on mediation and fact-finding), it makes collective bargaining significantly more robust and effective. In this analysis, the major flaw in US law is that some states do not permit such public employees to bargain collectively and some that do permit them to bargain collectively do not provide for mandatory, binding interest arbitration.

For employees in the second category, the question is more difficult. While barely a dozen states permit any public employees to strike, in some large and influential states (including California, Illinois, and Ohio), teachers, public transportation workers, and employees of public hospitals have a right to strike. This strike right is typically limited in a variety of ways. For example, as described above, in Ohio, a union can only reject the recommendations of a fact-finder and thus be permitted to strike by a two-thirds vote of the *entire bargaining unit*. And all jurisdictions that permit public employee strikes have rules permitting enjoining such strikes if and when they threaten the public health, safety, and welfare. Thus, in reality, strikes by such employees are few and far between.

One could imagine three broad types of alternative. First, one could call for all states to provide the type of limited strike rights for the second category of employees that exist in the minority of states that currently permit such employees to strike. Second, one could call for more robust strike rights for these

87. *Ibid.*, 7; *Committee on Freedom of Association* of the International Labor Organization, 2011.

employees: allowing strikes without having to complete mediation or fact-finding, for example. Third, one could decide that interest arbitration was in fact a better alternative than striking for such employees.

The traditional argument of labor advocates, and an argument still made today, is to maximize strike rights along the lines of the second option. Reasons for this range from the idea that the right to strike is (or should be considered) a fundamental right to the idea that strikes are the most effective way to maximize the power of worker collective action.[88] This author is sympathetic to these arguments and, if forced to choose, would likely choose this option.

It is, however, worth considering political realities, and it is this author's view that this option of maximizing strike rights has essentially no chance of being adopted in any significant number of states. Further, if it were, given current political realities in the US, one could easily see the types of practices that have vitiated the practical power of strikes in the private sector used in the public sector: specifically, the use of permanent replacements. On the other hand, in this author's view, interest arbitration does have sufficient downsides that the third option seems unattractive. Thus, as a 'Plan B' for the second group of employees, this author would choose the option of using rules that permit strikes, but under more limited circumstances than in the private sector. In other words, adopt the rules used in states that permit some public employees to strike for all states. At the time of this writing, even that seems fairly unrealistic. But as always, the future is unwritten.

Bibliography

Allen, Ron/Sacks, Ethan, West Virginia Teachers Strike Ends After Governor Approves Raises, NBC News, 6 March 2018. Available at https://www.nbcnews.com/news/us-news/west-virginia-teachers-strike-state-lawmakers-reach-deal-pay-raise-n854021

Anderson, Arvid/Krause, Loren, Interest Arbitration: The Alternative to the Strike, Fordham Law Review 56/1987, 153 et seqq.

Bloom, David, Arbitrator Behavior in Public Sector Wage Disputes, in Freeman/Ichniowski (eds.), When Public Sector Workers Unionize, 1988

Committee on Freedom of Association of the International Labour Organization, Report on Complaint against United States by Transport Workers Union (Case no. 2741), 2011

Goldberg, Michelle, The Teacher's Revolt in West Virginia, New York Times, 5/3/2018. Available at https://www.nytimes.com/2018/03/05/opinion/west-virginia-teachers-strike.html

Hanslowe, Kurt/Acierno, John, The Law and Theory of Strikes by Government Employees, Cornell Law Review 67/1982, 1055 et seqq.

88. For a recent reiteration of these and other arguments, see *Pope/Bruno/Kellman*, 2017.

Harris, Seth/Slater, Joseph/Lofaso/Anne Marie/Garden, Charlotte, Modern Labor Law in the Private and Public Sectors, 2nd ed., 2016

Hodges, Ann, Lessons from the Laboratory: The Polar Opposites on the Public Sector Labor Law Spectrum, Cornell Journal of Law and Public Policy, 18/2009, 735 et seqq.

Kearney, Richard/Mareschal, Patrice, Labor Relations in the Public Sector, 5th ed., 2014

Lawler, Emily, Illegal Teacher Strikes Common in Michigan Long Before Detroit Public Schools Sick-Outs, Michigan News, 25 January 2016. Available at http://www.mlive.com/news/index.ssf/2016/01/illegal_teacher_strikes_common.html

Lee, Jacqueline, Union Membership Decline Doesn't Explain Drastic Drop in Strikes, Daily Labor Reporter (BNA) 27 November 2017, 3

Malin, Martin, Two Models of Interest Arbitration, Ohio State Journal on Dispute Resolution, 28/2013, 145 et seqq.

Malin, Martin, Public Employees' Right to Strike: Law and Experience, University of Michigan Journal of Law Reform, 26/1993, 313 et seqq.

Malin, Martin/Hodges, Anne/Slater, Joseph/Hirsch, Jeffrey, Public Sector Employment: Cases and Materials, 3rd ed., 2016

McCartin, Joseph, Collision Course: Ronald Reagan, the Air Traffic Controllers, and the Strike that Changed America, 2011

Olson, Craig, Dispute Resolution in the Public Sector, in *Aaron/Najita/Stern* (eds.), Public Sector Bargaining, 2nd ed., 1988

Pope, James/Bruno, Ed/Kellman, Peter, The Right to Strike, Boston Review Forum 2/2017, 107 et seqq. Available at https://papers.ssrn.com/sol3/papers.cfm?abstract_id = 3074092

Secunda, Paul/Lofaso, Anne/Slater, Joseph/Hirsch, Jeffrey, Mastering Labor Law, 2014

Slater, Joseph, Homeland Security vs. Workers' Rights? What the Federal Government Should Learn from History and Experience, and Why, University of Pennsylvania Journal of Labor and Employment Law 6/2004, 295 et seqq.

Slater, Joseph, Public Workers: Government Employee Unions, the Law, and the State 1900-62, 2004 (Slater, 2004a)

Slater, Joseph, The Court Does Not Know 'What a Labor Union is': How State Structures and Judicial (Mis)Constructions Deformed Public-Sector Labor Law, Oregon Law Review 79/2000, 981

Slater, Joseph, The Rise and Fall of SB-5: The Rejection of an Anti-Union Law in Historical and Political Context, University of Toledo Law Review, 43/2012, 473 et seqq.

Summers, Clyde Bargaining in the Government's Business: Principles and Politics, University of Toledo Law Review, 18/1987, 265 et seqq.

US Department of Labor, Bureau of Labor Statistics, Work Stoppages Involving 1,000 or More Workers, 1947-2016, 2017. Available at https://www.bls.gov/news.release/wkstp.t01.htm

US Department of Labor, Work Stoppages Summary, 2017. Available at https://www.bls.gov/news.release/wkstp.nr0.htm (US Department of Labor, 2017a)

US Department of Labor, Union Members Summary, 2017. Available at https://www.bls.gov/news.release/union2.nr0.htm (US Department of Labor, 2017b)

Wellington, Harry/Winter, Ralph, The Unions and the Cities, 1971

PART IV Conclusion

CHAPTER 17

Comparative Analysis

Christina Hießl & Monika Schlachter

1 INTRODUCTION

As Otto Kahn-Freund put it back in 1972 when writing about *Laws against Strikes*, '[n]othing is more difficult than to gauge the influence which the law has in various countries on the organisation and on the functioning of industrial relations [....] Even among countries with comparable states of economic development and similar cultural and legal traditions, even among countries belonging to the EEC[1], comparison may be most difficult.'[2] When embarking on our ambitious undertaking of cross-country comparison, we were well aware of this difficulty. Anyone who has ever attempted to fully grasp any country's approach to industrial action has probably observed that the law - even when including case law and executive acts - is but a part of a much larger picture, shaped by extra-legal factors and power relations like hardly any other area of law. Aiming to research these issues for a sizable set of highly diverse countries and coming up with conclusions of true comparative value was thus a challenge, to say the least.

At the same time, the issue of how to reconcile a commitment to protect the right to strike while avoiding disruptions to 'essential' services is a problem common to virtually all legal orders, and one that is continuously gaining importance across countries. In today's economy characterized by the mounting interrelatedness of economic activity, more and more services play a role in enabling the continuance of what is perceived as 'essential' for the normal functioning of a state and the daily life of its population. Concurrently, the protection of the right to strike as a fundamental freedom is increasingly being

1. European Economic Community.
2. *Kahn-Freund/Hepple*, 1972, 10.

embraced – albeit to different degrees – by legal orders around the globe. Given the exceptional controversy that tends to surround rules aimed at regulating industrial relations, there is a justified interest in the different approaches taken to this common problem internationally, and their merit in resolving the underlying conflict in an appropriate way.

With this in mind, the following paragraphs will seek to provide an insight into common features and differences as they have appeared from the country reports, without claiming at any point that regulation appearing to 'work well' for one or even a majority of countries would therefore likely work in another country. To emphasize the necessity of such an approach, it suffices to stress that even the most basic question of whether sophisticated regulation to limit strike in essential services is needed or desirable in the first place depends fundamentally on attitudes of governments and the population at large towards collective action. This is well reflected in the country reports included in this study. To illustrate, one may consider the traditionally hostile approach described for countries such as Russia and the US – which has triggered restrictive regulation notwithstanding the absence of a large-scale incidence of strike in essential services – in comparison to the development described for Sweden, where even a 'paralysation of large sectors of the community' during the General Conflict of 1980 did not lead to a political call for introducing significant legal restrictions. Also intriguingly, only few contributions (notably the German and American one) refer to major debates on whether the use and possible abuse of a union's power to launch effective strike action because its members happen to perform key functions for the economy at large raises concerns of fairness in industrial relations.

While being thus cautious about generalizations based on any individual country's experience, the following sections will be interspersed with references to the one common benchmark that can claim authority on the international level, which is the International Labour Organization's (ILO) approach as set out in Conventions C 87 and 98 and the case law of its supervisory bodies and summed up in *supra* Part II. Although not all the countries included in this book have committed themselves to these conventions by means of ratification (see *infra*), this set of rules which doubtlessly comes closest to a universally accepted minimum standard seems the natural point of reference for providing an orientation about where a country 'stands' with respect to the protection of core labour rights.

One point worth noting before zooming in on various aspects of regulation that have been dealt with in the preceding chapters is that the majority of the countries included in this study does not report to experience at present a critically high level of strike in essential services which would be viewed as a major social problem by the general public. With the possible exception of Israel, South Africa and Brazil, none of these countries is described as having recently experienced significant interior disturbance by numerous and/or large-scale strikes. To the contrary, many contributors explicitly describe the incidence of strikes as a minor or largely unproblematic issue in current practice (cf.

particularly the reports on Canada, Japan, Russia, Sweden, UK and US). Strike incidents are, however, increasingly concentrated in the public sector (UK, Italy and France) where essential services still dominantly belong. Arguably, in itself, this finding is of little explanatory value due to the crucial influence of extra-legal factors determining the propensity of workers to go on strike – be it in a 'positive' (workers see no need to strike) or 'negative' way (workers are deterred or see no hope that strike would help). At any rate, the fact that few if any of the regulatory systems portrayed in the book appear as overall 'too permissive' and therefore incapable of keeping unwarranted strike action under control indicates that specific attention may have to be paid whether some of these regulations are rather likely to overshoot the target and restrict a fundamental right beyond what is necessary to protect other interests of equal value. Already from an international law perspective, strikes posing a threat to life, health and the security of the population, which legitimately may be restricted or banned, must be differentiated from conflicts representing primarily an inconvenience for the normal functioning of societies.

In what follows, a summary of the types of regulation dealing with strike in essential services as described by the country reports should shed some light on the diverse forms of regulatory intervention and the way in which they function in practice.

2 THE RIGHT TO STRIKE IN GENERAL

Obviously, there is no common grounds internationally as to the question of the scope of legal strike entitlements in general. And although a detailed comparison would clearly be beyond the intended scope of this study, a brief appraisal of the legal point of departure of strike regulation in the countries represented in this book appears necessary to put the following examination in context.

To begin with, as of today, all legislations at issue do protect the right to take collective action in one way or another. Most countries have ratified both the most relevant conventions of the ILO in this respect, No 87 and 98, and those who have not (the US failed to ratify both, Brazil and Canada one each) are nevertheless subject to scrutiny by the ILO's supervisory bodies on the basis of the Declaration on Fundamental Principles and Rights at Work. The degree to which international norms such as ILO Conventions No 87 and 98 and the supervisory bodies' case law have actually influenced national lawmakers and courts seems difficult to assess: on the one hand, reforms and reappraisal in case law that were inspired by international standards do not necessarily refer to them explicitly; and vice versa, an explicit reference to the standard may be made more 'out of convenience' to justify a decision already made for other reasons.

On the national level, the protection of the right to strike actually has a constitutional basis (either explicitly or via its interpretation by the courts) in a majority of countries. Prominent counter-examples are Australia, the UK and the

US. Combined with the fact that there seems to be striking unanimity among the 'common law countries' that the right to strike is not granted as such by common law, this means for the three countries mentioned that the legal protection of striking workers and unions does not go beyond what is explicitly granted by statutes. This is well reflected in some of the very far-reaching restrictions of strike rights in Australia, the UK and the US that will be set out below, which are rare among countries that consider the freedom to take collective action a constitutional right. Canada, however, has recently moved away from such uniform common-law approach as the Canadian Supreme Court developed a constitutional basis for strikes under the influence of international law.

Generally speaking, the trend of the past decades has been for national law to become somewhat 'strike-friendlier'. Australia in 1993 became the last country to abolish an approach that made it effectively impossible for any group of employees to take collective action without facing serious sanctions. Constitutional protection of the right to strike was declared by last-instance jurisprudence successively in a number of countries, including Canada in 2015. Clearly, these developments increase the relevance of the question whether strike can and should be restricted in certain areas identified as 'essential services'.

Yet, needless to say, important differences remain, with some jurisdictions such as France or Sweden granting trade unions wide discretion to initiate strike action, whereas other countries' laws set out a range of preconditions for a strike to be lawful or 'protected'. Among the most common restrictions applicable also in 'non-essential services' are the requirement that strikes be peaceful, organized by a recognized union, initiated for 'valid' reasons (i.e., usually with the aim of improving the striking workers' own working conditions) and only after genuine attempts to settle the conflict with the employer by other means (ultima ratio requirement). Self-evidently, these trends do not hold true for all countries and in all instances (cf. e.g., the permissibility of wildcat strikes in Italy or of political strikes and secondary action in Canada and Sweden).

Beyond that, there is a variety of procedural prescriptions even for 'ordinary' strikes across countries. Reference could be had to the requirement to conduct strike ballots and communicate their outcomes (in Canada, Poland, the UK and Australia, where even prior approval by a Committee is required) and to give prior notice to the employer (two days before a strike in South Africa, three days in Australia, five days in Poland and Russia and even two weeks in the UK and Israel). In some cases (Canada, Poland, Russia, South Africa), even conciliation or mediation procedures are compulsory before a strike can be called. Finally, also the scope of protection of striking workers – which regularly includes freedom from civil or criminal liability or disciplinary sanctions – is not uniform, as illustrated most vividly by the permissibility to 'permanently replace' striking workers in the US – which is tantamount to a dismissal.

Whereas one might expect that where the general approach to protected strikes is comparably restrictive, the need for additional measures regarding employees in essential services will be less pronounced, the country reports show rather the opposite: countries with generally strict conditions for protected strikes are also more likely to have broadly framed additional restrictions for 'essential services', such as, e.g., a sweeping exclusion of public sector employees.

3 THE STATUS QUO OF INDUSTRIAL RELATIONS AND STRIKE ACTIVITY IN PRACTICE

Self-evidently, the degree to which strike in essential services is perceived as a societal issue that merits or requires regulatory attention depends on the degree to which the workers in question are organized and appear likely to initiate strike action. In this regard, similar constitutional principles about collective labour rights in many countries are opposed to a highly different situation on the ground in view of the dominant 'culture' of industrial relations and industrial conflict. In the absence of internationally comparable data on strike in 'essential services', a natural starting point is to refer to comparative data about general strike rates in the countries included in this book.

Table 17.1 Days Not Worked per 1000 Workers due to Strikes and Lockouts

Country	*2004*	*2005*	*2006*	*2007*	*2008*	*2009*	*2010*	*2011*	*2012*	*2013*	*2014*	*2015*	*2016*
AU (OS/AR)	45.4/–	26.4/–	14.9/–	5.4/–	20.8/–	–	–	–	–/12.8	–	–/7.9	–/11.6	–
CA (AR)	236.7	304.8	57.1	125	61	154.1	84.2	92.8	61.3	100.2	113.5	119	32.6
FR (ES)	–	151	116	–	107	136.3	318.5	77	60	–	81	–	–
DE (AR)	1.3	0.5	12.4	8.1	1.7/3.7	2.1	6.2	3.9	2.2	2.7	4.8	1	–
IL (OE)	497.2	95.5	50.9	907.3	–	84.3	65.9	209.2	157.9	17.3	33.3	52.6	–
IT (OS)	43.3	54.9	32.8	52.6	–	–	–	–	–	–	–	–	–
PL (ES/AR)	–/1	–/0	–/0	–/2	–/28	0.9/–	1.5/–	2.7/–	1.3/–	–	0/–	11.1/–	1/–
RU (OE/AR)	–/4.3	–/1.8	–/0	–/0	–/0	–	–	–	–	–	10.9/–	12.2/–	–
ZA (AR)	107	221	334	753	–	–	–	–		28.5	–	–	–
SE (OS/AR)	–	–	–	–	–	0.4/–	7/0	–/8.9	–/1.7	–/0.8	–/0.1	–/2.1	–
UK (AR)	34.4	6	28	38	28	17	14	52	9	17	27	6	–
US (AR)	–	–	–	–	1	1	0	0	1	1	1	–	–

Source: ILO, ILOSTAT Multi Country Report.

AR – Administrative records, EM – Estimate of ministry, ES – Establishment survey, OE – Official estimate, OS – Official source.

Despite various issues of comparability – data incompleteness, differences in definition, compilation methods etc. – Table 17.1 indicates that there is a wide variety between (very) low levels of strike activity in countries such as the US, Germany, Russia and Sweden, compared to (partly) very high numbers for Israel, South Africa, Canada and France. Whereas Brazil is not represented in the ILO's data, South American countries (not shown in the extract above) generally have the highest strike rates in the total sample. Arguably, the absence of a common definition of 'essential services' compromises comparability even more than for strikes in general, and several country reports (especially the Russian and South African one) point to the general absence of reliable data about the incidence of strike in essential services. Yet, the trends that flow from the ILO's data are highly compatible with indications or estimates about the frequency of strike in 'essential services' by the national contributors to this study. This indicates that strike activity in 'essential services' follows the general trend and does not usually deviate from a country's general 'strike culture'.

At any rate, the country reports confirm that both unionization rates and the frequency of collective action appear to be in decline in most developed countries, both those with a long-standing corporatist tradition and those where the union movement has never constituted a powerful political and economic actor. This is different in countries such as Brazil and South Africa, where, in the context of adverse economic development, industrial action has risen in frequency in recent years. Yet, many reports note that public sector employees (which are as a rule responsible for a major share of essential services) tend to be both more unionized and – as far as they are legally allowed to bargain collectively – covered by collective agreements.

in this context, it deserves mentioning that the Canadian, German, Italian, Japanese and UK reports refer to the privatization of services as a factor that increases the likelihood of strike in essential services – either by actually putting these employees in a more vulnerable or disadvantaged position, or by bringing them under a different legal regime that allows strikes more readily, or a combination of both. In Italy, this has prompted a practice of obliging private contractors and subcontractors to abide by rules that were originally developed for the public sector. Quite to the contrary, the Polish report expressly notes that privatization does not have the effect of a rise in strike activity, and for Israel (with its rather extensive 'strike culture' in the public sector) it is noted that privatization and the accompanying de-monopolization have in fact led to a significant *reduction* in strike activity in the sectors concerned. Finally, in France, essential services continue to be located overwhelmingly in the public sector, which comprises 20% of the workforce, so that until today the legal approach to strike in essential services is restricted to provisions for employees of the public sector.

4 DEFINITION OF ESSENTIAL SERVICES

Which are the work activities that are perceived as so 'essential' for the general public that specific measures are taken against their withdrawal by means of industrial action?

As obvious from the examples mentioned in the country reports, the range of activities that are perceived as essential services (whether or not they fall under any specific legal definition) is impressive. The areas mentioned include public administration (Germany, South Africa, Sweden), the police (Sweden, US), fire-fighters and prison guards (France, US), border control (Australia), customs services (Sweden), judges (Poland); health services in general (Italy, South Africa, Sweden, UK) and specifically hospital staff (Brazil, Germany, Poland, US), nurses (Australia, Italy, Sweden), midwives (France) and dentists (Sweden); childcare and educational institutions (France, Germany, Italy, Sweden; even university staff in Australia), social welfare officers (Sweden) and employees of the Bureau of Meteorology (Australia); transport workers in general (Brazil, France, Italy, Sweden, UK) and specifically staff of local traffic providers (Canada, Germany, Sweden), railway (Germany, Italy, Russia, Sweden, UK) and airway staff such as pilots and flight attendants (Australia, France, Germany, Russia, Sweden) as well as related services such as air traffic controllers (US, Russia), technical aircraft services (Russia), port or dockworkers (Australia, Russia); utility workers (US), municipal cleaning (Germany), garbage collection and storage (Italy), electricity (Australia, Brazil, South Africa), heating (Russia), water and sanitation (South Africa), banks (Sweden), power plant staff (Brazil, France, Germany, Sweden), postal services (Germany, Sweden), communication, radio and television (France, Sweden), data processing (Brazil) and even museums and places of cultural interests (Italy).

All these areas are thus seen as 'essential' in the sense that they affect rights and interests of the public. At the same time, the variety of activities enlisted here also shows that the degree to which they may be considered genuinely indispensable may vary substantially. In line with this, also the legal approach of the ILO's supervisory bodies as described *supra* in Part II uses a combination of abstract and rather concrete ('public servants exercising authority in the name of the State') definitions, and differentiates between 'essential services in the strict sense' for which serious restrictions up to a prohibition of strikes are possible, and a broader array of activities where minor restrictions such as the imposition of a minimum service requirement are permitted. By the same token, almost all countries included in this study have a multi-layered approach to limiting strike in essential services, which rests on a mix of abstract definitions by reference to the rights and interests endangered by the strike, concrete enumerations of groups of employees and general interest-balancing approaches without any underlying definition.

4.1 Definition by Protected Rights and Interests

Whether or not motivated by the wish to comply with international standards, several countries follow the ILO's approach to 'essential services in the strict sense' very closely. South Africa is noteworthy for reproducing the ILO's definition literally by referring to 'a service, the interruption of which endangers the life, personal safety or health of the whole or part of the population.' In a similar fashion, Polish law refers explicitly to the protection of human life and health as well as state security; Canadian law to services 'necessary for the safety or security of the public or a segment of the public' or 'necessary to prevent an immediate and serious danger to the safety or health of the public'; Russian law to 'securing of life-sustaining of the population' and strikes 'endangering the interests of state defence, security of the state, life and security of the people'. However, specifically in Russia, already the legislative exemplary enumeration of sectors shows that the definition is actually conceptualized broader than by the ILO (including also rail and air transportation), and case law has enhanced this discrepancy by a very extensive interpretation of the concept.

Other countries explicitly adopt a broader definition of the protected interests that justify restrictions of the strike right. This is the case for Australian law, whose definition encompasses not only strikes that endanger life, personal safety, health, or welfare, but also those threatening to damage the national economy. The report notes that the country has been repeatedly adjudged by ILO bodies as being in breach of international standards, particularly with a view to the broad interpretation of 'damage to economy'. Reference is made for instance to a case concerning a labour dispute between an airline and its employees which was subjected to arbitration based on the economic interest in the continuity of services.[3] Another case decided very recently in 2018 (concerning rail traffic in Sydney) illustrates that also the criterion of 'welfare' is being given a very extensive interpretation to the detriment of the remaining scope for permitted strike action. An even broader approach can be found in Italy, where restrictions apply in case of a threat to any of the following constitutional rights: the right to life, health, personal freedom and security, freedom to travel, right to assistance and social security, education and freedom of communication.

The determination whether a concrete type of service falls under such an abstract definition is usually left to the courts or labour boards, which are called to rule on disputes whether consequences such as the duty to ensure minimum services apply. A specific ex-ante determination procedure is described for South Africa, where a specialized independent committee is in charge of designating essential services after conducting public hearings. A more problematic approach exists in the Canadian public sector, where the decision is made by the government as an employer, and unions' rights to be consulted in this process

3. The case is also noteworthy for pointing out the moral hazard of an employer to exacerbate the economic consequences of an industrial dispute (by means of a lockout) to achieve a prohibition of all industrial action in respect of its activity.

and opt for an arbiter's decision have been subject to frequent change in recent legislation. A further legislative reform is to be expected after the Supreme Court found the current version of the law to violate the constitution, but has not moved beyond the first reading back in November 2016.

4.2 Concrete Reference to Sectors, Activities or Groups of Employees

In addition to or instead of an abstractly defined category of essential services, most countries have in place regulation for groups of employees which are – explicitly or implicitly – motivated by the assumption of 'essentiality' of the services provided by those employees. As emphasized particularly by the Canadian report, the identification of such services is a highly political question and depends on the historical context, as illustrated by the past designation as 'essential' of areas such as mining (in 1907) and later war production industries. The enumerative approach may be used in an isolated fashion to supplement an abstract definition (as in South Africa, where the law refers to police and parliamentary services), or to add special rules for areas with a history of controversies over strikes (as in France, where three laws contain rules for land and air transportation and public primary schools), or also for establishing extensive lists of essential service sectors.

The latter is the case in Brazil, where the list comprises water treatment and supply, electric energy, gas and oil production and distribution, medical and hospital assistance, food and medicine distribution and commercialization, funerary, public transportation, sewage and waste collection and treatment, telecommunications, guarding, use and control of radioactive substances, nuclear equipment and materials, air traffic control, bank clearing, and data processing related to essential services. The report emphasizes, though, that this broad approach has been mitigated by a restrictive interpretation by the courts. Similarly broadly conceived lists have been enacted in Israel (including the civil service, all statutory bodies, municipalities and local governments, healthcare services, the whole education system including higher education, air transportation and cargo, and production and supply of fuel, electricity, water and telephone services), Australia (e.g., in New South Wales energy services, transport of persons or freight, fire-fighting, health, ambulance and pharmaceutical services, sanitation, water supply conduct of welfare institutions and prisons) and Italy, where the mentioned already extensive abstract definition is supplemented by a list of sectors (health, cleaning of public spaces, waste management, energy and primary goods supply, justice, environmental protection, transport, pension and wage payment by banks, education, post, telecommunication, public radio and television and – due to a much-contested reform in 2015 – the surveillance of museums and cultural and artistic sites) for which special rules apply. Also Japan combines, as far as the private sector is concerned, a general clause (undertakings which provide services essential to the daily life of the general public) with an exemplary enumeration (transportation, post and telecommunications, water supply, electricity, gas, medical treatment and public health) and the Prime Minister's competence to designate 'undertakings of importance for the national economy' for a period of maximum one year. The last country to adopt this enumerative approach was the UK, where the concept 'important public services' was introduced only in 2016/2017 and includes the sectors health, fire-fighting, border control, transport and education in a comprehensive manner.

The broadest type of regulation which implicitly aims at ensuring essential service continuity can be seen in the imposition of general restrictions for employees in the public sector. Provisions of this type exist in Canada, France, Germany, Israel, Japan, Poland and the US. Their scope ranges from rules only for civil servants appointed under public law to a very broad definition in France which includes privately employed workers in public or even private companies 'in charge of a public service'. It should be emphasized, though, that in the case of public sector employees the rationale of preserving essential services is usually combined with other – including budgetary – motivations. Especially in Germany, (now contested) case law has found collective bargaining and strike incompatible with civil servants' status as *Beamte* irrespective of the nature of the work performed, so that the protection of the continuance of essential services is more a side effect of this prohibition. The same holds true for the exclusion from the strike right of a large share of employees of German religious organizations, which is motivated by the constitutional protection of these organizations' right to autonomous regulation of their labour relations, but in practice has the effect of avoiding strikes in sectors such as health care and education. Similarly, the Japanese exclusion of the entire public sector from the strike right is essentially based on the consideration that for workers paid from tax funds working conditions need to be stipulated by law, and the US report refers to mixed purposes including a 'general antipathy toward public-sector collective bargaining'.

4.3 Case-by-Case Restrictions Without an Ex-Ante Definition

In several countries the applicability of restrictions to a basically recognized right to strike has been deduced from general principles (especially constitutional ones) by the courts. This is done by balancing the fundamental rights of different stakeholders to conclude whether and to what degree the exercise of the right to strike might disproportionately compromise other rights of the same rank. This plays a particularly important role in the case of Germany, which lacks any conceptual definition of essential services. Proportionality tests and the balancing of rights are also described as key approaches of case law in countries such as France, Israel and Russia, and are frequently an issue of much controversy. Especially the Russian report points out that constitutional and other last-instance jurisprudence tends to attach much weight to the rights of users such as passengers to justify very far-reaching restrictions of the right to strike. As for France, constitutional jurisprudence has been criticized for allowing restrictions beyond the ones enacted by legislation to be defined by ministerial decrees - which have been put in place in various sectors such as radio broadcasting, weather forecast, postal, rail and air transportation services, and even by directives of the head of an entity in charge of providing the service at issue.

By contrast, for Swedish law, it is expressly noted that the proportionality test approach is not used in relation to strikes, which makes the legislative approach to strike astonishingly minimalistic, with narrowly defined restriction applying only for central government employees and seafarers. For all other employees, regulation is left to agreements between the social partners, who, starting in 1938, have set up an autonomous system of dealing with the issue of strike compromising third party interests (see *infra*).

5 RESTRICTIONS FOR 'ESSENTIAL' CATEGORIES OF EMPLOYEES

There is a striking diversity of approaches to the restriction of the freedom to take collective action for the sake of preventing too sudden or too far-reaching interruption of essential services. In the following subsections, an overview will be given of the types of regulation that apply to the groups identified by the mentioned abstract-definitional, enumerative or individual-determinative approaches. After setting out the content of such regulation, also the envisaged sanctions and practical compliance as indicated in the country reports will be depicted.

5.1 Content of Regulation

5.1.1 Ex-Ante Exclusion of Employees from the Right to Strike

Exclusion from collective labour rights in a wider sense

Needless to say, the harshest form of restrictive regulation is the complete exemption of certain categories from the strike right. With the exception of Sweden with its remarkably complete coverage of the entire workforce by the full array of collective labour rights, all countries still have legislation in place that rules out collective action for some groups of workers. Most notably, there is relative unanimity among countries that strike cannot be tolerated among employees performing key security functions. When it comes to the armed forces (and military police, where such exists), the majority of countries actually excludes them not only from the right to strike, but also from collective bargaining, sometimes even from the right to unionize. Understandably, provisions of that kind are much under fire nowadays as being clearly at odds with international labour standards. This is illustrated by the European Court of

Human Rights' condemnation of France for violating the European Convention of Human Rights by its legislation on military personnel, which led to the introduction of unionization rights for this group in 2015. Contrary to this trend of increasingly recognizing at least the right to form and join trade unions even for the most 'essential' employees, the Israeli report notes that government has attempted at several instances in recent years to deprive an additional category (fire-fighters) of unionization rights (in addition to police, intelligence and prison guards).

Whereas the complete denial of the right to organize is thus applicable only in exceptional cases, legislation which denies the right to collective bargaining on top of the prohibition of strikes is still common across the country sample for activities related to public security. Apart from the armed forces, Canada and Israel exclude also intelligence service employees; Israel, Japan, the UK and US states, such as, Ohio police force members; Israel and Ohio prison guards; Japan and Ohio also fire-fighters. Also here, one may identify a tentative trend of decreasing the scope of this severe restriction of collective labour rights. Most recently, the exclusion of the Royal Canadian Mounted Police was found unconstitutional by the Canadian Supreme Court, leading to a legislative recognition of bargaining, but not strike rights for this category of workers in 2017. In general, the report notes that the newer case law of the Court, which recognizes also the right to strike as a constitutional principle, may challenge many of the restrictions in place for workers in essential services.

Even beyond immediately security-related activities, Polish law generally excludes appointed public officers from collective bargaining rights, and the same is true for a minority of states of the US, whereby the report refers also to the criticism issued at North Carolina in this regard by the ILO. In Germany, the constitutional court has upheld a sweeping exclusion of civil servants from collective bargaining as well as the right to strike in a recent ruling of 2018, and also the equally broad exclusion usually envisaged by churches and religious organizations for their employees seems to be here to stay for the time being.

Exclusion from the strike right while allowing for collective bargaining

A wider group of employees is denied the right to strike while being entitled to collective bargaining and usually also the conclusion of collective agreements (although France, Italy, Japan and South Africa know intermediate forms of regulation that permit collective bargaining but not the conclusion of collective agreements).

As far as employees whose tasks relate to state security and law enforcement are not subject to the even more far-reaching restrictions described in the last subsection, they are likely to fall under this category – military personnel in Italy and South Africa, (parts of) the police force in Canadian Ontario, France, Italy, Poland, and South Africa, prison staff in France, judges in France and Poland and fire-fighters in Brazil and Ontario. The same is true for security- and/or health-relevant activities in the private sector, so that employees of nuclear industry enterprises are excluded in Russia, power plant security staff and seamen during navigation in Italy, air navigation workers France and hospital staff in Ontario. Restrictions for these groups might arguably be permitted under the ILO's approach to 'services the interruption of which would endanger the life, personal safety or health' of the population, whereby the complete ex-ante exclusion still raises questions in terms of compliance with that standard. By contrast, the denial of the right to strike quite clearly contravenes international labour standards in cases such as Russian aircraft and railroad personnel, employees of the Toronto Transit Commission and parliamentary service employees in South Africa.

Obviously, the same holds true for provisions containing a sweeping exclusion of civil servants or public employees in general, as is the case in Japan, Poland, Russia (where even chief executives of public enterprises are included) and the US (where only a minority of 12 states envisages strike rights for public employees). Finally, employees of religious organizations in Germany tend to fall into this category as far as they are not also denied collective bargaining rights.

5.1.2 Ex-Ante Restriction of the Possible Type or Scope of Strikes

Regarding specific restrictions of the possible type of industrial action, one may note that legislations with a comparatively generous concept of permitted strike action tend to be somewhat less permissive when it comes to essential services. For instance, Italian essential service employees may not participate in wildcat strikes; public employees are prohibited from staging rotational strikes in France, or partial or political strikes in Sweden. South African public employees may organize sympathy strikes only in respect of other public employees.

Much more practically relevant than these restrictions of permitted types of strikes are ex-ante limitations of their possible scope by predefined requirements about the provision of minimum services. In general, the requirement of installing minimum services to ensure the most important needs and interests of the public can be seen as the internationally preferred model for restricting strike in essential services in a proportionate way, which is also endorsed by the ILO's bodies. And while the main emphasis of this requirement is usually on the ad hoc assessment of the services that need to be continued to attenuate adverse consequences for public needs and interests (see *infra*), several countries have put in place regulation that defines in advance the necessary scope of such minimum services for specific types of work.

First of all, country reports such as the German one note that unions tend to voluntarily include provisions about minimum services in case of strike in their by-laws. A legal requirement of an advance designation of minimum services exists in Italy since 1990, where the parties to a potential labour dispute in the sectors identified as 'essential' as described above are requested to conclude agreements about the core services that must be ensured also during such a dispute. Some directions for these agreements, which are concluded at national, regional and company/institution level, are contained in the law. They need to be submitted to a commission, which is in charge of facilitating the conclusion of an agreement but can also reject its contents and eventually enact a temporary regulation replacing the agreement in case of continued disagreement. The education sector is named as an example where until today no agreement could be reached between the Ministry for Education and teachers' unions. Similarly, France stipulates a requirement to conclude preliminary agreements about the extent of minimum services in the three sectors subject to specific laws (primary schools, land and air transport). They need to contain detailed identification, e.g., of train stations that will be served at specific times during a railway strike. In case of a failure to reach agreement, the employer has to enact a minimum service scheme unilaterally, and is liable vis-à-vis the users of the service to ensure that it covers the essential needs protected by law. This relatively recent legislation adds to older regulation aimed at the public sector, prescribing minimum services for public broadcasting and aviation safety services, the details of which are equally determined by advance agreements between the parties to a potential conflict.

The only country that departs from an ex-ante imposition of minimum service regulation by administrative authorities is Russia, where the ministries are in charge of developing sector level lists of minimum services in their area of competence. To date, 22 such lists have been adopted by the responsible ministries, whereby the list on railroad services as one of the practically most relevant strike areas was successfully challenged in court for a failure to involve unions in its establishment.

5.1.3 Additional Procedural Requirements

For various groups of occupations considered essential, states have put in place regulation that, while not limiting employees' possibility to go on strike, is meant to prevent strikes from being called too 'light-heartedly' and/or allow stakeholders to prepare for a planned interruption of essential services. This can be done by introducing various procedural requirements.

First, as for requirements to hold a strike ballot, they tend to be no more demanding in essential services than elsewhere. In general, ballot requirements exist only in four countries: Australia, Poland and the UK require employees in all sectors to meet a double 50%-threshold (a majority of eligible employees must cast a vote, a majority of which must be in favour of the strike), whereas Russia used to prescribe even a double two-thirds threshold, of which at least the turnout threshold was lowered to 50% in 2006 after criticism by the ILO. The only jurisdiction that contains additional ballot requirements for 'important public services' is the UK, where since 2016 the total number of strike-approving votes must constitute 40% of those entitled to vote. It is noteworthy that not only union members are entitled to vote, as would be the case if balloting requirements were enshrined in union by-laws (Germany), but all members of the relevant bargaining unit. This poses specific difficulties to the union to motivate a high enough number of workers to participate in the vote, especially if electronic voting procedures are not accepted. The report notes that the ballot requirement was criticized by the ILO's Committee of Experts on the Application of Conventions and Recommendations (CEACR) in 2016, considering that as described above the concept of 'important public services' includes also the transport and education sector, which are not essential services in the strict sense. Yet, in practice, the 50% turnout rule equally introduced in 2016, which concerns all sectors, is expected to be more difficult to secure in most cases. Generally, the detailed prescription on notice to be given in advance of a ballot, its conduct, notice on its result and finally on industrial action itself add up to a complex procedural burden for unions, each step of which may be challenged in court, that serves as a deterrent. The ensuing likelihood of procedural mistakes leads to employers obtaining injunctions rather easily. Court injunctions deprive not only unions but also individual employees from all immunities for a lawful trade dispute.

Much more frequent than this focus on balloting procedures is the stipulation of additional notice and cooling-off requirements in essential services. This is intended first to give the parties additional time to go back to the bargaining table once the definite intention to go on strike has been declared, launch one more attempt at finding a solution and else prepare for the responsibilities that usually rest upon the parties in case of a strike in essential services (see *infra*). In South Africa, the mentioned general duty to give notice to the employer two days in advance of a strike is extended to seven days in essential services. What is more, several jurisdictions without a stipulation of notice periods for general employees prescribe notice periods only for strike in essential services: three days in Brazil, five days in France (for public employees), and ten days in Italy, Japan and the US (for healthcare workers). In Italy, this notice needs to include the reasons, length and operating methods of the strike and must not overlap with another strike announcement by the union. Also Israel, while not extending the general 15-day notice period, enhances the qualitative requirements for proper notice in essential services by requiring it to be supplemented with a statement about the involvement of essential services and 2-3 days in advance about the exact type of strike action and its duration. Finally, German judges have found prior notice to be a potential requirement for a strike to be proportionate on a case-by-case basis, depending on the individual circumstances.

Notably the French report stresses that notice requirements are not necessarily effective at ensuring reliable strike warnings, referring to union practices of giving notice in numerous instances while actually launching a strike only in very few of them. Similar practices are described as common in Italy, particularly in the education and transport sector. Thereby, the strike announcement itself is causing losses to the service provider as customers might decide to use alternative services, even if the envisaged action will be cancelled before it started. In France, this has led to the introduction in 2012 of a preliminary negotiation duty for maximum eight days before calling a strike in passenger transport or schools, and an individual duty of each worker to announce their own participation in the strike 48 hours and their return to work 24 hours in advance. Under Italian law, since 2000 it is considered unfair practice to call a strike and then to cancel it without a reason. Italy is also the only country to require an agreement between the parties to stipulate in advance the cooling off and arbitration procedures that need to be completed before calling a strike. As long as there is no such agreement, a commission adopts a preliminary scheme unilaterally.

Italy and Japan require notice to be given not only to the employer but also to a public authority. A notice to the general public is prescribed one day before the strike in France (by the employer, where passenger transportation is affected), three days in advance in Brazil (by the union), five days in Italy (by the union), and without temporal specification in Japan (by the minister).

Interestingly, none of the countries included here prescribes a particular form of alternative dispute resolution mechanism (such as arbitration or mediation) to be completed specifically in essential services sectors before a strike can be called. However, as the fact that essential services are concerned by the strike may be taken into consideration in the context of the ultima ratio principle, the parties may more likely be expected to exhaust all possible procedures that stand any reasonable chance of resolving the conflict without recourse to collective action.

5.1.4 Stricter Sanctions

Israel is the only country where the legislator attempted to curb strike in essential services by imposing harsher (employment and tort law based) sanctions in order to secure compliance with the procedural restrictions in the sectors concerned – with very limited success, as described in the report.

5.1.5 Ad-Hoc Full or Partial Prohibition / Requirement of Minimum Services

By the union or an agreement of the parties

Once a strike has been called, it needs to be established whether the workers concerned can walk off the job unrestrictedly, whether this is fully prohibited or subject to the condition of putting in place a minimum service of a certain extent. In the first place, this is typically a responsibility of the union calling the strike. In Sweden, this duty of unions is actually the only area where the law contains any stipulation about safeguarding 'essential services': central-government employees and seafarers are legally required to phase out operations in a technically satisfactory manner and perform 'protective work' to prevent danger to people or damage to property. But also in other sectors without such legal prescriptions, unions are described as proactive in avoiding undue harm to third parties, to the point of granting exceptions from a strike to avoid disturbances. Similarly, the Israeli report stresses the importance of 'exceptions committees' installed by unions to grant services to seriously affected users on a case-by-case basis, which is taken into account by courts when assessing the legality of a strike.

If the union does not on its own initiative limit the strike to a degree that leaves key services in place to the degree required by law, many legislations charge (also) the employer with the liability to ensure them, either by agreement with the union or ultimately by demanding a court's or labour board's decision. A minimum service should primarily be determined by an agreement of the conflicting parties in countries such as Brazil, the Canadian private sector, Germany, South Africa and Russia (as a concretization of the mentioned lists enacted by the ministries, whereby also the local government authority is party to the agreement). Yet, particularly the Brazilian report points out that in most cases up to now such agreement could not be reached, so that the extent of the required minimum service needed to be determined by the courts.

In the Canadian public sector, the procedure for determining the services that must not be abandoned during a strike involves unilateral decision-making by the government, consultation of the concerned unions and the possibility of arbitration, and is, as mentioned above, currently in the middle of a reform process.

By a court

In most countries, in case of dispute, a court decision can be requested to determine the legality or illegality of a strike or stipulate conditions such as a minimum service. For many countries, the practical importance of injunctions for arriving at a speedy decision and potentially stopping illegal strikes before they cause substantial damage is noted. Yet, particularly for Russia, the UK and the US, the reports indicate that the system makes it very easy for employers to obtain injunctive relief, nipping a significant share of strikes in the bud.

Before the court, the withdrawal of essential services by the strike in violation of explicit legal provisions or more general (constitutional) considerations of proportionality can frequently be invoked by the employer as a fact that makes a strike illegal. Thereby, the courts are entrusted with the crucial task of concretizing abstract legislative principles concerning strike in essential services, producing a substantial body of case law in countries such as France and Germany. Alternatively, the law may explicitly grant actions against basically lawful strikes, as is the case in US states such as Ohio if 'a lawful strike creates clear and present danger to the health or safety of the public'. Apart from employers, some jurisdictions also entitle public authorities or other third parties to bring an action against strikes in essential services. For instance, the UK report refers to the entitlement of the Secretary of State or even 'any other person to whom the duty is owed' in case of a strike by prison officers in defiance of the statutory prohibition. in the US, a complex procedure that has been used only twice in history involves the creation of a Board of Inquiry by the President, which can determine that industrial action would threaten national health or safety, which then enables the Attorney General to petition a federal court for an injunction.

Quite to the contrary, the Polish report notes that the legislator has failed to identify a competent authority to resolve disputes about the legality of a strike with a view to the minimum services offered by the union. In general, in the absence of legislative indications or substantial case law, there is a broad diversity of opinions as to which services fall under the mentioned broad legal reference to risks to human life, health and state security, and which concrete positions must be exempted from a strike to avoid such risks. Similarly, the US report emphasizes the lack of any legislative guidance for resolving the conflict of interests between legitimate industrial action and continuity of essential services, which makes case law highly unpredictable.

The Brazilian report provides insights into the concrete degree of service maintenance that courts have required in terms of minimum service – e.g., 40% in data processing, 50% in electric energy facilities, 70% in hospitals and 20-80% in transportation depending on whether rush hours are concerned. At the same time, this case law reportedly fails to follow a clear pattern. Inconsistencies in case law are found also in Germany, where most cases end after an injunction procedure that is not subject to appeal in higher instance. Whereas there is broad agreement about the general necessity of some degree of minimum service in sectors such as health care, fire-fighting, water- and electricity supply, the maintenance of public order and security or the delivery of social security payments, much controversy persists about services such as public transport or education.

By administrative authorities

Eventually, many jurisdictions provide for administrative bodies to intervene into strikes where the public interest is at stake.

Procedures of little practical relevance

First, some countries envisage executive termination or suspension of a strike in exceptional cases of national emergency. Examples include a Polish provision referring to cases of the imposition of martial law, natural disaster or state of emergency relating to the constitutional order or safety of citizens, a Russian provision applicable during a period of military alert, or the South African President's power to declare a state of emergency 'if the life of the nation is threatened by war, invasion, general insurrection, disorder, natural disaster or other public emergency'.

Other countries' concepts of administrative intervention are framed somewhat more broadly in theory (involving economic considerations) but have hardly been applied in practice. This is particularly the case for a Japanese rule vesting the Prime Minister with the power to issue an 'emergency adjustment' if collective action threatens to gravely imperil the normal operation of the national economy or the daily lives of people. The report notes that this possibility has been utilized only once in 1952 to end a large-scale coal mine strike. But also Australian regulation which permits administrative prohibitions on industrial action in a widely framed area of essential services in many states has been little relied on in practice, and the federal government's power to proclaim a 'serious industrial disturbance prejudicing or threatening interstate or overseas trade' has never been used. The report estimates that if used such orders would be more likely to exacerbate than resolve any ongoing industrial dispute. Despite this lack of practical relevance, the power to terminate industrial action for economic reasons has been repeatedly adjudged as violating international law standards.

Another procedure rarely invoked is the US-American presidential power to create a special emergency board to investigate and make recommendations within 30 days when a railroad or airline strike threatens to deprive any section of the country of essential transportation services, thereby suspending industrial action for another 30 days. Finally, in 2014 South African law entrusted the committee which is also in charge of designating essential service sectors with the additional competence of defining appropriate minimum services for these sectors in the event of a strike call – a procedure found to have made little practical progress as of 2017.

Procedures of practical importance

Basically, again, the Russian regulation is the only one which provides for the imposition of a minimum service regulation by an authority subordinated to the labour ministry in case of disagreement between the parties as a regular procedure and alternative to a court order. The report emphasizes that this has been criticized repeatedly on the international level by the ILO's CFA and the European Committee of Social Rights. But also administrative disperse orders intended for situations of urgency have come to play a significant role in practice in some countries with a high incidence of strikes. One example of that is France, where the law allows for the requisitioning of striking workers by local prefect 'when required by a real or foreseeable breach of the peace, public health, public order and public safety'. Equivalent injunctions by the prefect, but also the Prime Minister or other ministers, are envisaged under Italian law. Such orders may contain a suspension, imposition of minimum services or complete termination of the strike. They are subject to judicial review by administrative tribunals, which have, e.g., found a 100% requisition of striking midwives illegal in France. In Australia, the Fair Work Commission is given the power and duty to suspend or terminate protected industrial action on its own initiative or upon application by one of the conflicting parties, the competent minister or any 'organization or other person directly affected'.

5.2 Sanctions

The sanctions envisaged across countries for striking in contravention of a prohibition share a number of common features.

For employees, all countries envisage disciplinary sanctions ranging from reprimand to dismissal, whereby particularly the range and detail of measures envisaged in US state Ohio (regarding current and future employment status, wages, promotion etc.) are impressive. Italian law stands out by actually obliging employers to disciplinarily sanction employees for non-compliance with an administrative injunction to terminate the strike as described above, and to communicate the applied sanction to the competent commission. Notably, dismissal is explicitly not envisaged under Italian law as a sanction for a violation of the rules on strike in essential services. In the South African context, the practically very rare use of dismissal for strike action due to the impossibility to replace workers at short notice is pointed out. In striking contrast, the Australian report shows that the sanction of removal from the job can be harshly enforced even in the case of workers with rare and precious skills – as in that case, pilots, after the government had sided with the employers and facilitated the issuance of visas for foreign pilots to replace them (see *infra* Section 7).

Employees might also face administrative fines, and the same is usually true for unions, whereby particularly the Brazilian and Canadian report point out that these may be very severe. Also for France, the imposition of very severe fines is noted specifically with reference to a prison staff strike in 1989. Additionally, some jurisdictions provide for specific union sanctions such as the forfeiture of rights to dues check-off (Italy, US), the suspension of trade union officials' right to working leaves for union activities (Italy), a ban from collective bargaining for two months after a strike (Italy) or even deregistration of the union (parts of Australia and the US).

In several cases also prosecution under criminal law is provided for, including the threat of prison sentences in countries such as Australia, Canada, France and the US. Whereas in general prison sentences do not appear to be applied in a practically significant way in any country, Canada and the US mention cases in which imprisonment has actually been ordered by a court where workers struck in violation of a statutory prohibition. The UK report mentions that the threat of criminal prosecution is limited to the police and the army.

A very delicate question relates to unions' potential tort liability vis-à-vis those relying on essential services. Granting such actions arguably has the potential of triggering huge waves of litigation and exorbitant amounts of damage claims against unions, which would make strikes in certain areas an act of financial self-destruction. Accordingly, for Australia, unions' full tort liability is invoked as a major reason for the factual suppression of strikes to continue even after their legalization in principle in the late 1920s. Also for today, the Australian, and in a similar fashion the British report describe impressively how under common law full tort liability for inducement to breach a statutory duty ensures that unions must seek to comply with all preconditions for the tort immunity of 'protected' strikes. Uncertainties about the scope of tort liability are liable to deter strike action before it is even called.

Also with a view to these consequences, courts in many countries have been cautious to award such damages to service users. German case law has stated that third parties can in principle rely on a violation of their own fundamental rights by an illegal strike withdrawing essential services, but for giving rise to a claim to damages the claimant must prove a serious and targeted obstruction by the union. Also case law in the majority of states of the US does not grant claims for damages brought by third parties against unions after a strike. Several reports also indicate that such tort claims have not been brought in practice. To the contrary, the Israeli report mentions two instances of successful third-party tort damage claims against unions, one of which even concerning a legal strike against which an injunction had been denied by the Labour Court earlier.

5.3 Compliance

Whereas there is obviously wide variation both among countries and in historical development concerning compliance, the majority of reports does not see widespread violations of ex-ante restrictions or ad-hoc limitations imposed on strike in essential services at present. Where the reports refer to the degree of compliance with ex-ante prohibitions to strike, they tend to note that non-compliance is uncommon in practice (as for Canada, France, or Israel). However, in the event that strikes do occur in the prohibited areas, their consequences are more likely to be genuinely devastating. Reference can be made to the Boston police strike of 1919, which involved lawlessness on the streets for days and several violent deaths and left a lasting mark on the discourse about public sector strikes in the US, or the even more fatal military police strike that took place in Brazil 2017, which left 199 people dead, ended without any gain and the indictment of more than 700 participants. Whereas these incidents could be seen as a confirmation of the necessity of a strict prohibition of strikes for these groups of employees, the US report emphasizes that 'studies have also shown that the best way to avoid public-sector strikes is to provide robust collective-bargaining rights with effective and fair alternative mechanisms for resolving bargaining impasses'. This view seems to be confirmed not only by the fact that the Boston strikers were actually fighting against an uncompromising prohibition for their union to affiliate with a labour union confederation, but also very illustratively by the South African report, which refers to a wave of strikes by African workers in the 1970s when they were severely repressed and excluded from collective labour rights.

Also where ad-hoc restrictions (back-to-work orders, imposition of minimum service requirement etc.) are pronounced against announced or ongoing strikes, unions are reported to comply as a rule in most countries. Major issues of non-compliance are, however, pointed out in the Israeli and South African report. A notable remark in the Israeli case points to a connection between unyieldingly confrontational approaches by governments and unions, observing that in the peak period of governmental emergency back-to-work-orders being routinely issued against major strikes, compliance by the unions plummeted to under 70%.

Also the imposition of sanctions for non-compliance is highly diverse, with reports such as Israeli one stating a reluctance to apply the legally envisaged sanctions in the first place, and Brazil noting that unions were first heavily fined but eventually granted an amnesty (just as the worker subject to disciplinary sanctions). Whereas such amnesties may have been primarily motivated by the unions' sheer financial incapacity of paying the fines, the non-imposition of sanctions may as well reflect the government's (or the employer's, in case of disciplinary sanctions) preference for a peaceful settlement of the dispute. This is indicated in the French report, which notes that sanctions are actually 'rarely implemented', referring to a very recent example of a successfully negotiated collective agreement for prison guards, after those had staged a strike in defiance of the strict prohibition to demand safer working conditions and pay rises.

Additionally, complying with the rules is not, as such, equivalent to reducing the number of strikes in essential services. Playing by the rules may still leave opportunities to put pressure on employers; much rather, some countries providing rather elaborated, detailed intervention mechanisms (France, Italy) are still complaining about insufficient levels of effects. Succeeding in reducing the number of strikes, on the other hand, is not necessarily equivalent to securing consumers' interest. Legal systems putting in place strong deterrent effects against conducting a legally accepted strike can face the outcome of workers turning to extra-legal measures instead (Brazil, Russia).

Generally, it needs to be stressed that particularly regarding actual compliance, comparability between countries is inherently limited. As pointed out most illustratively in the Russian report, the level of compliance is effectively dependent not only on the content of restrictions, the envisaged sanctions and their practical application, but also fundamentally on the general strength and leverage of unions and other structural issues outside the scope of the present study.

6 COMPENSATORY MEASURES FOR RESTRICTIONS

6.1 The Need to Compensate Employees for Restrictions

While strikes are being prohibited or restricted (more or less substantially) at least in some services considered essential in almost any country represented in this study, the question whether and to what extent it seems necessary to compensate for such measures receives quite different answers. Principally, the existence of compensatory means appears determined by the respective predominant degree of acceptance of a right to strike in general. Where collective action is principally considered a threat to political and social stability, the state by intervening in such action is acting as the guarantor of internal peace and security. It therefore does not need either justification for intervention measures, nor to provide any compensation. A vivid example of the continuing effect of a predominant anti-strike culture is reported for Australia: employees easily accept the many measures of restricting and avoiding collective action for it having been prohibited by law for decades, even after the prohibition was repealed. Where collective action is, however, principally considered a human right of workers and their organizations, states consider restrictions as needing both objective justification and adequate compensation.

What constitutes adequate compensation is, again, determined by the predominant culture: states creating specific categories of public servants by providing them a distinct civil service-status with specific duties and privileges (Poland, Japan, Germany) tend to regulate their wages and working conditions by legal provisions. In that case, the loss of a right to collective action is understood as quid pro quo for obtaining the privileged status, and no further compensation is deemed necessary. In some reports, the category of public service as such is deemed to be obliged to operate under specific limitations without compensation (Australia, US, Japan). The same is in fact frequently the case for the specific categories of public employees facing the severest restrictions, as it is stressed, e.g., for the police force, prison guards and secret service employees in Israel. Where, however, compensation is provided, the most common means implies some dispute resolution mechanisms with different levels of obligations for the government as an employer. Finally, in situations where regulations for essential services include mere procedural restrictions to collective action, such measures are usually considered inherent conditions of working in such sector, which employees must simply accept without specific compensation.

6.2 Compensating the Exclusion from the Right to Strike by Alternative Dispute Resolution Mechanisms

The instrument of alternative dispute resolution, which is ultimately present in all countries included in this study, may have a fundamentally different role to play depending on the national legal setup. In the present context, a central question is whether and under which conditions this instrument is meant to compensate employees for an exclusion of the free exercise of the strike right. The category of 'compensation' is built on the ILO's approach much rather than on an explicit domestic legal mechanism developed as a 'quid-pro-quo' for workers having lost a specific right. As described earlier (*supra* Part II), the ILO's monitoring bodies argue that when employees are legitimately excluded from exercising a right to strike, states must develop sufficient guarantees to protect their interests, including 'appropriate, impartial and prompt conciliation and arbitration procedures'. Thereby the ILO committees demand that the right to strike as 'the most fundamental means for workers and their representatives to promote their economic interests' may not be taken away without providing an adequate replacement, capable of effectively protecting the interests that otherwise would have been pursued by collective action. Even though the countries surveyed in this study do provide some forms of alternative dispute resolution measures, they do not necessarily share the theoretical idea of such mechanisms representing a compensation for a workers' rights lost, or a compensatory measure necessarily being equally effective as collective action.

During the last century, the most far reaching regulation was implemented in Australia, where the right to strike was replaced completely and for everyone by a system of dispute resolution. The approach undertaken was based on the notion that 'reason should replace force', thereby relegating collective action to the category of unreasonable force to be avoided at all costs. Dispute resolution measures, on the other hand, are understood as peaceful means achieving more reasonable results to all potential industrial conflicts. This attitude remains influential even after the total prohibition was repealed, so that strike actions are permitted yet strictly controlled by law. In essential services, specifically, industrial action is still easily barred by Ministerial declaration or a state authority once it is considered to have adverse effects on (parts of) the population or the economy. In this case, the Fair Work Commission (a state authority) is competent to make an arbitrated determination of wages and working conditions once the parties have failed to find an agreement for 21 days,

Also in other countries a functional replacement of strikes by other means is common. In sectors, professions or specific categories of personnel where strikes are prohibited ex-ante, some forms of authoritative determination may be established, such as pay legislation (Germany, Poland), imposed wage settlements or compulsory binding interest arbitration (Canada). Where legal strikes may be terminated or suspended ex-post due to their actual or perceived threat to public goods, they will also usually be functionally replaced by alternative dispute resolution for adapting pay levels and working conditions to changing economic circumstances, as described, e.g., for the US. An interesting variation to this approach is pursued by Canada for such essential services in which administration has determined the level of services to be maintained during a strike at a very high level: where 80% of a bargaining unit's workers are barred from undertaking collective action, the remaining part of the workforce not forbidden to strike is regularly lacking the power for conducting a successful strike and can therefore opt for binding arbitration instead.

Such relationship between a lost or substantially weakened power to strike and alternative dispute resolution methods is a widely shared approach but not exclusively so. In Sweden, the right to strike is provided to everyone, including the whole public sector and all parts of the economy, but anyhow an extended mediation and conciliation system is applied. In this setting, the mechanism is obviously not understood as a 'compensation' to any restriction of workers' rights but as an ancillary part of the regular bargaining process. While in principle offered by a state-run Mediation Office, this procedure may be, and indeed mostly is, replaced by the labour market parties through a dispute resolution process created by collective agreements.

Alternative dispute resolution measures, however different in their concrete application under different legal systems, involve a third party making recommendations or taking decisions on the content of an agreement, thereby bringing a labour dispute to its end. The varying degree of self-determination left to the conflicting parties represents the most obvious difference in approaches reported here. Whether or not a specific legal system is effectively replacing strikes by alternative means can be judged by different standards, e.g., whether the political goal pursued was reducing strikes in essential services as much as possible, saving tax money by securing that unions would not interfere with wage cuts or restructuring, preserving social peace or establishing an efficient replacement tool for furthering workers' interests. The ILO standards described above do not prescribe details for such procedure, leaving states a substantial margin of discretion, but are clear in the goal pursued: any alternative to the right to strike must represent a comparably powerful tool for workers and their unions to further their social and economic interests. In other words, if the right to strike is taken away – which may be permissible in the cases set out above – workers must have access to alternative means for furthering their interests. Dispute resolution must be provided by a competent, neutral body or person that is not only independent from state authority in fact but is also perceived as being independent by the conflicting parties. The procedure must not be unnecessarily delayed, and it must provide binding results which are speedily implemented.

Concerning access to dispute resolution systems, the decision to submit industrial disputes varies in the degree of compulsoriness: it can be left to the conflicting parties themselves, to be determined either in advance by collective agreement, or on an ad-hoc basis once a dispute is deemed unresolvable (Brazil). The decision to submit a conflict to dispute resolution may be taken by both parties on a completely voluntary basis (Sweden), by one party unilaterally as for Japanese 'industrial public employees' (employed by a state-run industrial undertaking) and for Polish essential services employees in the private sector. It may rest in the competency of the disputes resolution institution, which generally could be set up as a privately organized panel, a state authority (Japan), a state-appointed individual (Canada) or committee of experts (Italy) or a court (Brazil), to initiate the procedure. The most far reaching option includes automatic compulsory submission to a dispute resolution procedure once other procedures fail (Israel, US, Australia, Russia, and the Canadian province of Ontario for the hospital sector). While such option would generally be available also in France, the procedure is rarely used in practice because it is taken into consideration that conflicting parties prefer submitting the dispute to courts.

Concerning the neutral and impartial arbitrator, different solutions are provided. Where the conflicting parties are competent to select arbitrators / panel members themselves (Germany) or replace state-run institutions by other instruments (Sweden), no problems of independence will arise. State-appointed bodies of experts (Italy) may statutorily receive a degree of independence securing an image of neutrality. If the dispute resolution is provided by a regular court (Brazil), their professional independence may be guaranteed by rules of procedure. If arbitrators are state-run institutions or appointed by the state (Australia, Canada), specific procedures will be necessary to safeguard independence, as the state establishing the arbitrator represents in parallel the employer for many essential services employees (Russia). The state may also influence the neutrality of the determination process by prescribing by law the criteria that must be considered. Where relevant criteria include the obligation to orient the decision towards conditions of comparable employees in other sectors or the general society (Canada, Japan, US), this may not hamper an independent decision. If, however, arbitrators are legally bound to respect the states' fiscal and general economic policy, the states' 'ability to pay' (Australia, Canada, US), the neutrality of the determination process may be questioned by unions.

Concerning the binding effect of the final decisions, two separate aspects must be taken into consideration. First, replacement measures may only be comparably effective as collective action if their results are respected by the state as employer. By way of example, South Africa provides unilaterally to the public employer a 14-day time laps before the arbitration decision becomes binding, followed by a specific procedure in parliament allowing for rejecting the decision. Where an arbitrated award may be reviewed or replaced by a political decision, the dispute resolution does not represent an effective replacement mechanism.

Distinct from such implementation problem, the binding or non-binding effect of dispute resolution mechanisms influences the level of self-determination still resting with the conflicting parties. If the procedure is compulsory, both parties are bound by a decision on the content of a future collective agreement; they are disallowed from deviating from it subsequently. Alternatively, parties may remain competent to bargain a different solution if they both agree to depart from the arbitrated decision. Finally, the dispute resolution system may produce a non-binding recommendation the parties may or may not accept, i.e., provide ancillary functions for the bargaining process leaving party autonomy comparably intact (Germany). By implication, however, this would allow the parties to resort to collective action in case the recommendation is not accepted by one or both parties. Legal systems pursuing the political goal of avoiding strikes in essential services as far as possible therefore combine the recommendation procedure with a binding mechanism if no agreement is reached (US, Poland, South Africa), so that no effective chance of rejecting even a non-binding recommendation is provided.

6.3 Compensating the Prohibition by 'Privileged' Employment Conditions

Occasionally, reports refer to legislation as a means of regulating wages and working conditions for employees deprived of a right to collective action. This wage determination model is sometimes as such considered a compensation for restricting collective measures, because an act of parliament represents as such the highest available standard of legality. Some legal systems combine the determination modus with the state's obligation to regularly review the adequacy of existing pay levels: salaries of the public service may be regulated by law, and legislation is obliged to review and adapt the existing pay level annually for securing compensation for inflation losses. For Brazil it is reported, however that the government is deemed reluctant to provide the full level of adaptation. Also in the UK, the level of pay for the military, police and prison guards determined by regulation must be regularly reviewed, but the results of the reviewing process are not considered binding on the government. The compensatory effect of the review mechanism therefore seems doubtful in practice as it leaves the decision de facto to the state's policy as employer.

Another means of compensating for the loss of bargaining power is represented by some form of wage indexation (Brazil), a determination of working conditions following suggestions of a state authority aiming at mirroring developments in general society (Japan), or orientation towards the conditions of comparable employees not exempted from the right to strike (Israeli police, prison guards or secret service members). In Italy, for some public service members excluded (not from the right to strike but) from having their working conditions regulated by collective agreements, the determination by legislation replacing collective bargaining must be based on collective agreements concluded in other sectors. The loss of the bargaining procedure is then compensated by making the determination of working conditions by regulation conditional on taking over the outcome of a collective bargaining procedure in a different sector. This used to be the practice for civil service employees excluded from the right to strike also in Germany, which has however been cancelled by public employers eager to save on public expenditure. The compensatory effect of the mechanism therefore appears to be dependent in practice on whether it is respected also by the state. Measures intended to solve conflicts in essential services depend to a large extent on the willingness of the state to play by the rules; where this is not guaranteed, measures will likewise seem no longer acceptable for unions.

An alternative approach offers public sector unions monetary incentives for their reduced rights: they may be entitled to financial compensation for any breach of a collective agreement by a public employer without having to prove an actual damage occurred (Israel). As this regulation was never applied in practice, however, there is no experience concerning its potential effectiveness.

7 SECURING ESSENTIAL SERVICES BY FURTHER MEANS

Beyond a description of the legally envisaged restrictions and sanctions for non-compliance as they have been set out above, the 'law in action' approach of this book has shed some light on the way in which threats to the delivery of essential services are effectively dealt with in the countries studied. This last section of our comparative overview will be dedicated to measures taken with the aim of securing essential services beyond a mere regular implementation of these regulations. This may either take the form of repressive approaches stifling collective action when it emerges and/or deterring it preventively, but also, quite to the contrary, proactive measures aiming at securing essential services without curtailing the right to strike.

7.1 Restrictive / Deterrent Approaches

7.1.1 Ad-Hoc Measures Terminating Collective Action

In sectors where strikes have neither been prohibited ex-ante nor declared illegal through a regularly envisaged procedure (yet), other measures to limit strike action are likely initiated once essential services are delivered at a non-satisfactorily level. Indeed, authorities at different levels and in various capacities have reacted to essential services sector strikes by adopting diverse ad-hoc measures beyond those basically envisaged by the legal system. States differ in their approaches as to which section of the state is adopting the respective measures, as both the legislative and the administrative branch might take the lead in this process.

Incidents of *ad-hoc legislation* terminating strikes in essential services seem to happen relatively rarely. It is, however, common practice in Canada to use back-to-work legislation in sectors such as education, health care, transportation and communication for terminating lawful strikes by ad-hoc statutes; in the case of a teachers' strike, a law was to create child care services in schools. Legislation for ending a strike was accepted as a means of 'ultima ratio' for preventing on-going disputes from threatening vital social needs also in Sweden; a specifically cautious approach is then underlined by using the measures extremely rarely. For Israel however, preventive legislation on strikes in essential services was tabled in parliament times and again but never was enacted. Essentially, it was not legislation as such that induced labour market parties to settle their disputes by other means than continuing the industrial conflict. Much rather, the act of regularly tabling draft bills on restrictive measures against strikes in essential services in parliament works as a deterrence against continuation of collective action.

As for *administrative ad-hoc measures* to terminate or limit strikes, it should first be recalled that those might simply be a part of a state's general regulatory approach to strike in essential services, in which administrative authorities are called to implement the legally envisaged limits to the strike right in the individual case. As such, these measures have been described above (Section 5). However, beyond this, some reports indicate that authorities are in practice relying on competences which are basically by no means intended to constitute an instrument of collective labour dispute management in reaction to disruptions to essential services. This effect is illustrated impressively by the Israeli report, which describes how emergency orders came to play a key role in the government's approach to strike in essential services. Whereas the sanctions for 'unprotected' strikes envisaged by statutory law have hardly been used in practice, emergency disperse orders have been issued on a current basis over the past decades. By relying on an instrument meant to provide the government with exceptional powers in armed conflict, authorities could act free from judicial review, prompting the Attorney General, whose approval is required in this process, to act as the only regulatory instance against all too improvident use of these orders by the government. This has contributed to the decline of this practice since the early 2000s when they were still a regular form of intervention against strike in essential services. Similar practices of an abundant use of declarations of emergency as a basis for terminating strike in essential services are reported for Brazil, and the UK report notes that such has occurred twelve times under the current legislative framework passed in 1920.

Where workers engage in further-going collective action such as picketing, demonstrations and plant occupation, administrations may forcefully terminate this by sending in police or even the armed forces. Incidences of the latter kind are reported, e.g., for the US in relation to the notorious Boston police strike of 1919, and more recently for Brazil with reference to collective action in oil plants.

7.1.2 Ad-Hoc Measures to Replace Striking Workers

Alternatively or additionally, a strike may effectively be broken where authorities take measures to enable the provision of essential services by others while workers are on strike.

First, this may be done by directly ordering public employees without a right to strike to perform essential tasks previously undertaken by strikers. Most notably, recourse is had to the military or state security services, which are typically excluded from the strike right as described above. The use of soldiers in this regard is reported, e.g., for Israel and for the UK, where this is exemplified by the 18,000 troops brought in for the Olympic Games of 2012 in London. Similarly, the Australian government ordered the air force to provide aircraft for securing domestic travel despite ongoing collective action by pilots. Most recently, in France, striking prison guards were replaced by police in 2018. Beyond this recourse to security forces, in states where broader categories of public servants are deprived of the right to strike, also those may be susceptible to be used as 'striker replacements'. This is reported, e.g., for Germany with specific reference to postal service strikes.

Second, authorities may to different degrees facilitate the recruitment of replacement staff by (private) employers affected by collective action. Here, of course, already the general regulatory approach diverges widely between states, ranging from a strict prohibition of replacement hiring (in general or at least through temporary work agencies as in Germany) as an inherent part of protecting the right to strike to the mentioned US approach of permitting even 'permanent replacements', which are tantamount to dismissals. Beyond this, particularly the Australian report refers to cases in which the administration has actively supported such replacement efforts by employers – most notably in the case of the 1991 pilot strike, in which the government changed regulations to make it easier for foreign pilots to obtain visas and work permits to be hired by Australian airlines.

7.1.3 Deterrent Use of Sanctions

In sectors where strikes are prohibited, any other means for securing adequate delivery of essential services will only be deemed necessary if such prohibition is not sufficiently complied with. In such cases, several country reports describe a deliberately harsh application of sanctions aimed at deterring workers and unions from violating the prohibitions.

Whereas the highly diverse approaches to sanctions and their implementation has been set out *supra* (Section 5), it should be pointed out in the present context that several country reports refer to incidences in which authorities were perceived to consciously set a warning example by applying particularly severe sanctions in highly publicized cases. Most illustratively, this is described by the US report, starting from the crackdown on public sector union activity after the Boston police strike. The example of the US also shows impressively that this 'strategic' use of sanctions is not necessarily conditional upon the legal provision of far-reaching competences to act against strikes. Notably, also after the most far-reaching option for the President to 'seize' a plant for ensuring continuation of essential services had been struck down by the Supreme Court, this apparently did not confront authorities with a shortage of options for deterrent sanctions – as exemplified by one incidence of collective action in the aviation sector, in response to which a presidential directive effectively barring strikers from all future employment with the Federal Aviation Administration. For the UK, it is noted that courts frequently 'seemed determined to find trade unions liable in tort (if not under criminal law)' to achieve such deterrent effect, and a similar 'determination' appears from descriptions of the response to strike in various cases in Australia, Canada and other countries where the tradition has met strike action with strong reservations.

7.2 'Soft' Approaches Avoiding Restrictions of the Right to Strike

In clear contrast to what has just been described, country reports point to various measures taken by different stakeholders that appear to enable rather than hamper the maintenance of a meaningful right to take collective action also in essential service sectors. This seems to be the case particularly where such measures promote and facilitate without compulsorily imposing the peaceful resolution of industrial disputes and/or limit the impact of strikes on essential services provision without depriving employees of their leverage on the employer.

An interesting example of the latter type is provided by French legislation that creates a framework for child care service in schools in case of a teachers' strike. As a result, teachers' unions retain their power to exercise pressure by withdrawing their (educational) labour, but the essential task of supervising children while their parents are working is not interrupted. Apart from the legislator, also executive and administrative authorities may play a role in preventing intractable conflicts between essential service provision and the exercise of the strike right, by assuming a role in the prevention and management of industrial conflicts. Instances of such 'non-restrictive' involvement of the government are reported, e.g., in the Italian context, where governments have sought dialogue with unions determined to strike, whereas the Israeli report stresses that various public actors including courts have repeatedly taken the lead in mediating between the parties to the dispute.

Apart from such 'non-hostile' approaches of public authorities, some reports invoke primarily *measures taken by the labour market parties* themselves to secure essential services. Here, the boundaries between what the parties are obliged to do based on legal proportionality or good faith requirements (cf. *supra* Section 5) and what they add in their own interest of preserving industrial peace and/or avoiding public resentment due to essential services interruptions are frequently blurred.

One means in this perspective is the setting up of autonomous rules about procedural requirements such as cooling-off periods and particularly minimum services, either by previous collective agreements or by unilateral decisions taken by unions (Canada, UK, Japan, Israel, Italy, Sweden, Germany). Another form of securing minimum services is the determination of undertakings or services being exempted from strike actions by 'exception committees' (Israel, Sweden). This way, conflicting parties will not have to decide under the impression of an ongoing conflict how to reduce potential damages to third parties. It may, however, also induce strategic decisions to announce collective action in overly broad terms which will later be renounced upon application to the exception committee, but may nevertheless have caused financial loss by the early announcement in itself.

Alternatively, parties may agree to integrate no-strike-clauses in collective agreements (US, Israel, Poland, Japan, UK), effectively barring strikes in the undertakings or sectors concerned. In other countries, a similar effect may be provided by legal doctrine, under which any collective agreement is held to automatically include a peace obligation disallowing strikes concerning the topics already regulated therein during the lifetime of such agreement (e.g., Japan, Sweden and Germany). Such obligation ceases to exist once the agreement is terminated, so that services cannot be secured for a period following the agreements' end. Another comparably effective prevention mechanism is provided by collective agreements obliging parties to attempt to resolve their conflict through dispute resolution before they may take collective action (France, Germany). Once such procedure is not compulsory but represents genuine self-determination it is reported to induce high compliance. In Israel, however, a no-strike agreement was combined with binding arbitration as a compensation.

Finally, one interesting concept of a 'virtual strike' was introduced in Italy and Israel, whereby the professional activity as such is fully or partially continued during the conflict but wages are (partially) paid to a specific fund while employers are obliged to contribute an equivalent amount. Such measure is conditional on there being a specific legal basis which can only be created via collective agreement, i.e., with the explicit consent of both parties.

8 EVALUATION AND CONCLUSION

8.1 Evaluation

In most countries participating in this study, the incidence of collective action has not significantly increased in absolute terms during recent times. Reports, however, state that for several countries strike incidents tended to concern the public sector – or services that happened to be privatized only recently – more frequently than in earlier decades. This observation did certainly not happen by coincidence; it much rather represents a logical consequence of a low union density in the private sector: Sectors where unions used to be strong, such as production, tend to turn from signature sectors into a shrinking part of the economy, whereas the services sector is gaining in numbers. As public sector employees represent one group where trade unions are still strong enough for organizing support for collective action, most strikes meanwhile are targeting the public sector. Therefore, from a consumers' perspective, strike action literally seems ever more frequent, as it now tends to materialize in workplaces interacting with consumers. Whereas the 'classical' industrial conflict in the post–World War II period taking place in the metal, automotive, mining or chemical industry would not immediately impact consumers' everyday lives, a strike in metropolitan transport, at airports, in child care or in refuse collection probably will. So even if in absolute numbers strike action may not have increased in most countries, the sectors concerned by such conflicts will be more directly engaged with consumers.

How governments react to secure consumers' interests in a continuous flow of essential services seems closely related to the predominant traditional approach to collective action in the respective country. It is much easier for a government to effectively restrict strikes in essential services by prohibiting them altogether where collective action is generally considered to endanger social peace and political stability. Compliance with such strict measures may then be secured by heavy sanctions, and unions will be aware that sanctions will be applied literally in case of non-compliance (US, Australia, Japan, Poland, Russia). Consequentially, strikes in essential services are effectively reduced to very low numbers of incidents so that consumers' interests may be perfectly ensured. However, the Russian report also mentions that a low incidence of industrial disputes is still not able to guarantee social peace: while a majority tolerates a low level of industrial democracy in exchange for a growing standard of living, discontent workers tend to protest outside the legal system.

On the other hand, some reports refer to labour relations as being characterized by a highly adversarial climate (Brazil, South Africa), and governments as aiming to reduce conflicts by prohibitions combined with heavy fines. Such measures proved much less effective though, as seemingly the huge gap between strict regulations and deviating practice is persistent. Occasionally, even a complete ban of strikes in specific public services can be regularly disrespected (Brazil), and the general attitude towards strikes nevertheless be less negative in society. The Brazilian report states that conflicting parties meanwhile expect parliament to legislate amnesties for fines imposed by courts on illegal strikers as their implementation might further unrest and social instability. South Africa's attempts to replace strike measures by dispute resolution procedures also had limited effects in furthering compliance. In Israel, administrative mechanisms minimizing union power were apparently successful in reducing numbers of strike incidents, but not in achieving social peace in parallel.

Furthermore, alternative measures such as spontaneous protests (Italy, France) or boycotts and plant occupations (France) may be undertaken for putting pressure on public institutions. Such approach may be the consequence of labour disputes representing some forms of industrial democracy, i.e., giving workers a voice in social policy through 'political economic strikes' (Italy) which may be accepted in society as main function of collective action. Consequently, many more employees than the (comparably low) number of unionized workers are taking part in collective action the aim of which is not immediate improvement of working conditions but influencing social policy decisions such as pension reforms or the privatization of publicly owned undertakings (France). However, a rather high number of strikes in essential services leads to the implementation of preventive measures aimed at reducing those numbers (Italy) but were not sufficiently effective in so doing.

Sweden and Germany in turn are characterized by a comparably peaceful labour market. In Sweden, high union density provides some equilibrium of power between the labour market parties who are united in their desire to regulate collective labour relations among themselves while reducing state influence as much as possible. Restrictions to the right to strike in all parts of the economy are almost non-existent, but disputes are anyhow frequently resolved by alternative means. In Germany, labour market parties traditionally accepted the lack of statutory and administrative regulation of industrial disputes, securing minimum services by collectively agreed procedures while leaving unresolved conflicts for the courts to decide. This attitude partially changed when upcoming specialized unions questioned the consensus model; the same difficulties are reported for Italy. German employers' associations, on the other hand, took the relocation of strike actions to the services sector as a chance for winning public support for suggesting statutory limitations to the right to strike. However, legal systems mostly or principally abstaining from interference in industrial disputes are not necessarily less successful than others in providing essential services at an acceptable level even during industrial disputes; social peace is also mostly achieved this way.

The most commonly used means for replacing collective action, i.e., measures of dispute resolution, merits a closer look, too. While several reports state that compulsory arbitration may be very effective in reducing the number of strike incidents (if compliance can be secured), also a considerable downside is reported. In Canada, under the no-strike model compulsory arbitration had chilling effects on collective bargaining, producing less effective, lower results. Likewise, for the US it is mentioned that negotiating parties under an arbitration system systematically avoid accountability. The positive effects of a negotiated outcome, i.e., the willingness to potentially accept even lower than expected levels of compromise, cannot be obtained once results are not based on self-determination. Positive results are, however, reported once arbitration is based on collective agreements (France, Germany, Sweden), or labour market parties remain competent to reject an arbitrated award.

8.2 Conclusion

The comparative analysis of the reports provided in this study shows a huge variety of solutions developed for dealing with a common problem, strikes in essential services. Such strikes are mostly considered specifically dangerous for the general population even if they are not increasing in numbers. So, most states share the approach of solving the underlying problem by restricting or prohibiting industrial action for protecting the expectations of consumers. But beyond this wish for solving the problem, similarities between approaches almost end. The strong dependency of the different regulatory measures on the social fabric and the political system in which they operate, on the historic experiences made, and on the distribution of power in the respective communities essentially lead to stating that, in comparison, all legal systems are different. Differences include their specific approaches as well as the means applied, their effects, and the degree of compliance achieved.

The aspiration of a comparative study to present potential solutions to a problem readily available for being adopted by policy makers elsewhere gets more challenging given such results. Much rather, one might recall the insights provided by Otto Kahn-Freund, one of the founding fathers of comparative labour law in Europe, who understood collective labour relations to be among those areas of law least suitable for 'legal transplants'.[4] His estimation was that 'substantive rules wrenched out of their [...] constitutional, political and industrial context could (not) successfully be made to fit the needs of a country with [different] institutions and traditions'.[5] This estimation may, however, be overly pessimistic given that countries, despite their profoundly different institutions and traditions, have in their great majority accepted one common legal approach to strikes, the one developed by ILO Conventions No. 87 and 98 in their interpretation by the supervisory bodies. While standards developed at ILO level are by no means universally accepted or followed, they represent a common frame of reference which can be used for comparative purposes. A state considering taking over means applied elsewhere is thereby in the position to evaluate both systems, the domestic and the foreign, against international law and use their respective compliance level as a proxy for sufficient similarity to try importing a solution. It may, however, also consider that industrial conflicts increasing in a specific sector or getting replaced by other forms of spontaneous protests represent an indicator for the necessity of change. Severe enough global influences may create the necessity of eventually changing established traditional customs even if this may take a long and at times painful adaptation process. In such case, international experiences may provide some orientation to a political process.

All in all, this study hopefully provides fresh insights in the broad variety of legal approaches undertaken, occasionally later rejected or never properly implemented, for solving the conflict between the regulatory competence and responsibility of states and the balancing of a right to take collective action with a right to receive essential services.

Bibliography

Kahn-Freund, Otto/Hepple, Bob, Laws against Strikes, 1972.

Kahn-Freund, Otto, On Uses and Misuses of Comparative Law, The Modern Law Review 37/1974, 22 et seqq.

4. Kahn-Freund, Otto, On Uses and Misuses of Comparative Law. In: The Modern Law Review 1974(37), 22 et seqq.
5. *Ibid.*, 26 et seqq.

Index

F

S

STUDIES IN EMPLOYMENT AND SOCIAL POLICY

1. W. Beck, L. van der Maesen & A. Walker (eds), *The Social Quality of Europe*, 1997 (ISBN 90-411-0456-9).
2. R. Blanpain, M. Colucci, C. Engels, F. Hendrickx, L. Salas & E. De Smyter, *Institutional Changes and European Social Policies after the Treaty of Amsterdam*, 1998 (ISBN 90-411-1018-6).
3. V. Lo, *Law and Industrial Relations: China and Japan after World War II*, 1998 (ISBN 90-411-1075-5).
4. A. Den Exter & H. Hermans (eds), *The Right to Health Care in Several European Countries*, 1998 (ISBN 90-411-1087-9).
5. M. Biagi (ed.), *Job Creation and Labour Law from Protection towards Pro-Action*, 2000 (ISBN 90-411-1432-7).
6. W. Beck, L. van der Maesen, F. Thomése & A. Walker (eds), *Social Quality: A Vision for Europe*, 2000 (ISBN 90-411-1523-4).
7. F. Pennings, *Introduction to European Social Law*, 3rd ed., 2001 (ISBN 90-411-1628-1).
8. J. Murray, *Transnational Labour Regulation: The ILO and EC Compared*, 2001 (ISBN 90-411-1583-8).
9. R. Blanpain & C. Engels (eds), *The ILO and Social Challenges of the 21st Century*, 2001 (ISBN 90-411-1572-2).
10. M. Biagi (ed.), *Towards a European Model of Industrial Relations? Building on the First Report of the European Commission*, 2001 (ISBN 90-411-1653-2).
11. J. Clasen (ed.), *What Future for Social Security? Debates and Reforms in National and Cross-National Perspective*, 2001 (ISBN 90-411-1671-0).
12. A. Numhauser-Henning (ed.), *Legal Perspectives on Equal Treatment and Non-Discrimination*, 2001 (ISBN 90-411-1665-6).
13. R. Blanpain (ed.), *Labour Law, Human Rights and Social Justice* 2001 (ISBN 90-411-1697-4).
14. M.-C. Kuo, H.F. Zacher & H.-S. Chan (eds), *Reform and Perspectives on Social Insurance: Lessons from the East and West*, 2002 (ISBN 90-411-1819-5).
15. P. Foubert, *The Legal Protection of the Pregnant Worker in the European Community*, 2002 (ISBN 90-411-1842-X).
16. M. Biagi (ed.), *Quality of Work and Employee Involvement in Europe*, 2002 (ISBN 90-411-1885-3).
17. F. Pennings, *Dutch Social Security Law in an International Context*, 2002 (ISBN 90-411-1887-X).

18. T. Carney & G. Ramia, *From Rights to Management: Contract, New Public Management and Employment Services*, 2002 (ISBN 90-411-1889-6).
19. R. Blanpain & M. Colucci, *European Labour and Social Security Law, Glossary*, 2002 (ISBN 90-411-1905-1).
20. I.U. Zeytinoglu (ed.), *Flexible Work Arrangements: Conceptualizations and International Experiences*, 2002 (ISBN 90-411-1947-7).
21. J. Berghman, A. Nagelkerke, M. Boos, R. Doeschot & G. Vonk (eds), *Social Security in Transition*, 2002 (ISBN 90-411-1969-8).
22. R. Blanpain, *The Legal Status of Sportsmen and Sportswomen under International, European and Belgian National and Regional Law*, 2003 (ISBN 90-411-1980-9).
23. R. Blanpain & M. Weiss (eds), *Changing Industrial Relations & Modernisation of Labour Law, Liber Amicorum in Honour of Professor Marco Biagi*, 2003 (ISBN 90-411-2008-4).
24. J. Malmberg (ed.), *Effective Enforcement of EC Labour Law*, 2003 (ISBN 90-411-2160-9).
25. M. De Vos (ed.), *A Decade Beyond Maastricht: The European Social Dialogue Revisited*, 2003 (ISBN 90-411-2163-3).
26. M. Sewerynski (ed.), *Collective Agreements and Individual Contracts of Employment*, 2003 (ISBN 90-411-2190-0).
27. R. Blanpain & M. Van Gestel, *Use and Monitoring of E-Mail, Intranet and Internet Facilities at Work: Law and Practice*, 2004 (ISBN 90-411-22-66-4).
28. A. C. Neal (ed.), *The Changing Face of European Labour Law and Social Policy*, 2004 (ISBN 90-411-2312-1).
29. E. Sol & M. Westerveld (eds), *Contractualism in Employment Services: A New Form of Welfare State Governance*, 2005 (ISBN 90-411-2405-5).
30. F. Pennings (ed.), *Between Soft and Hard Law – The Impact of International Social Security Standards on National Social Security Law*, 2006 (ISBN 978-90-411-2491-3).
31. L. Dickens & A. C. Neal (eds), *The Changing Institutional Face of British Employment Relations*, 2006 (ISBN 978-90-411-2541-5).
32. G. Sebardt, *Redundancy and the Swedish Model in an International Context*, 2006 (ISBN 978-90-411-2503-3).
33. A.M. witkowski, *Charter of Social Rights of the Council of Europe*, 2007 (ISBN 978-90-411-2608-5).
34. M. Sargeant (ed.), *The Law on Age Discrimination in the EU*, 2008 (ISBN 978-90-411-2522-4).
35. G. Di Domenico & S. Spattini (eds), *New European Approaches to Long-Term Unemployment: What Role for Public Employment Services and What Market for Private Stakeholders?*, 2008 (ISBN 978-90-411-2614-6.)
36. C. Welz, *The European Social Dialogue under Articles 138 and 139 of the EC Treaty: Actors, Processes, Outcomes*, 2008 (ISBN 978-90-411-2744-0).
37. M. Rönnmar (ed.), *EU Industrial Relations v. National Industrial Relations: Comparative and Interdisciplinary Perspectives*, 2008 (ISBN 978-90-411-2770-9).

38. F. Pennings, Y. Konijn & A. Veldman (eds), *Social Responsibility in Labour Relations: European and Comparative Perspectives*, 2008 (ISBN 978-90-411-2783-9).
39. F. Pennings & C. Bosse (eds), *The Protection of Working Relationships: A Comparative Study*, 2011 (ISBN 978-90-411-3289-5).
40. S. Devetzi & S. Stendahl (eds), *Too Sick to Work?: Social Security Reference in Europe for Persons with Reduced Earnings Capacity*, 2011 (ISBN 978-90-411-3426-4).
41. U. Becker, F. Pennings & T. Dijkhoff (eds), *International Standard-Setting and Innovations in Social Security*, 2013 (ISBN 978-90-411-3233-8).
42. E. Ales (ed.), *Health and Safety at Work: European and Comparative Perspective*, 2013 (ISBN 978-90-411-4661-8).
43. F. Pennings, T. Erhag & S. Stendahl (eds), *Non-public Actors in Social Security Administration: A Comparative Study*, 2013 (ISBN 978-90-411-4917-6).
44. A. Neal (ed.), *Cross-Currents in Modern Chinese Labour Law*, 2014 (ISBN 978-90-411-4763-9).
45. B. Waas (ed.), *The Right to Strike: A Comparative View*, 2014 (ISBN 978-90-411-5007-3).
46. A. Ojeda-Avilés, *Transnational Labour Law*, 2015 (ISBN 978-90-411-5858-1).
47. A. Numhauser-Henning & M. Rönnmar, *Age Discrimination and Labour-Law: Comparative and Conceptual Perspectives in the EU and Beyond*, 2015 (ISBN 978-90-411-4979-4).
48. A. Perulli & T. Treu (eds), *Enterprise and Social Rights*, 2017 (ISBN 978-90-411-8234-0).
49. Dr F.C.A. van Haasteren, *Decent Flexibility: The Impact of ILO Convention 181 and the Regulation on Temporary Agency Work*, 2017 (ISBN 978-90-411-9236-3).
50. T. Dijkhoff & L.G. Mpedi (eds), *Recommendation on Social Protection Floors: Basic Principles for Innovative Solutions*, 2018 (ISBN 978-90-411-8623-2).
51. A. Perulli & T. Treu (eds), *Sustainable Development, Global Trade and Social Rights*, 2018 (ISBN 978-90-411-9235-6).
52. M. Mironi & M. Schlachter (eds), *Regulating Strikes in Essential Services: A Comparative 'Law in Action' Perspective*, 2019 (ISBN 978-90-411-8997-4).

www.ingramcontent.com/pod-product-compliance
Ingram Content Group UK Ltd.
Pitfield, Milton Keynes, MK11 3LW, UK
UKHW020224290926
15470UKWH00001B/371

9 789041 189974